MOON HANDBOOKS®
UTAH

© SALT LAKE CITY CONVENTION AND VISITORS BUREAU

City and County Building, Salt Lake City

butte near Goblin Valley

© SALT LAKE CITY CONVENTION AND VISITORS BUREAU / JASON MATHIS

MOON HANDBOOKS®

UTAH

SEVENTH EDITION

W. C. McRAE & JUDY JEWELL

AVALON
TRAVEL

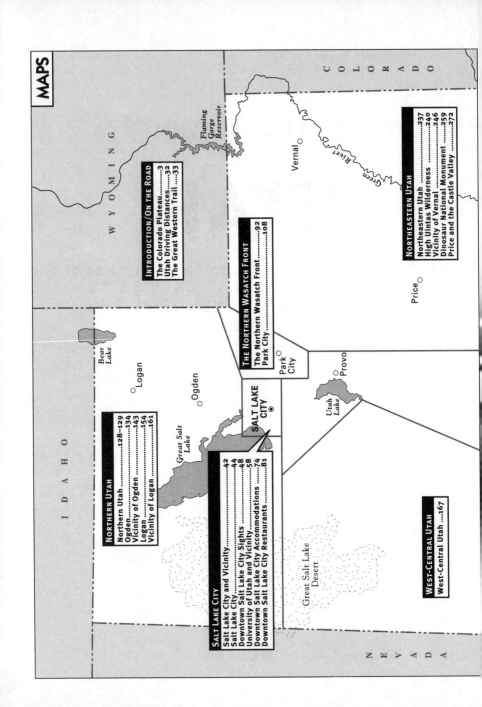

MAPS

IDAHO

WYOMING

COLORADO

NEVADA

Bear Lake

Logan

Ogden

Great Salt Lake

SALT LAKE CITY

Park City

Utah Lake

Provo

Great Salt Lake Desert

Price

Vernal

Green River

Flaming Gorge Reservoir

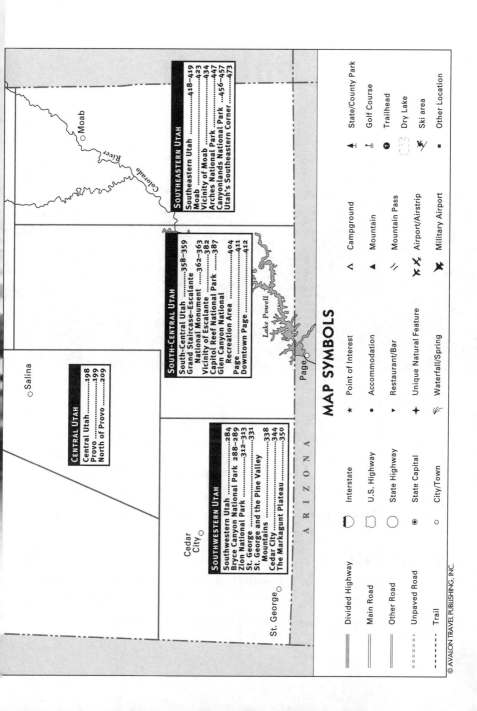

○ Salina

○ Moab

Colorado River

CENTRAL UTAH
Central Utah 198
Provo 199
North of Provo 209

Cedar
City ○

SOUTHWESTERN UTAH
Southwestern Utah 284
Bryce Canyon National Park 288–289
Zion National Park 312–313
St. George 331
St. George and the Pine Valley
Mountains 338
Cedar City 344
The Markagunt Plateau 350

St. George ○

SOUTH-CENTRAL UTAH
South-Central Utah 358–359
Grand Staircase–Escalante
National Monument 362–363
Vicinity of Escalante 382
Capitol Reef National Park 387
Glen Canyon National
Recreation Area 404
Page 411
Downtown Page 412

Lake Powell

Page ○

SOUTHEASTERN UTAH
Southeastern Utah 418–419
Moab 423
Vicinity of Moab 434
Arches National Park 447
Canyonlands National Park ..456–457
Utah's Southeastern Corner ...473

A R I Z O N A

MAP SYMBOLS

═══ Divided Highway

═══ Main Road

─── Other Road

===== Unpaved Road

------- Trail

◗ Interstate

⬭ U.S. Highway

◯ State Highway

◉ State Capital

○ City/Town

★ Point of Interest

• Accommodation

▸ Restaurant/Bar

✦ Unique Natural Feature

🐾 Waterfall/Spring

⋀ Campground

▲ Mountain

⫽ Mountain Pass

✈ Airport/Airstrip

✈ Military Airport

⛴ State/County Park

⛳ Golf Course

⬤ Trailhead

▦ Dry Lake

⛷ Ski area

▪ Other Location

© AVALON TRAVEL PUBLISHING, INC.

Contents

Salt Lake City

Booming Salt Lake City boasts some of the best-preserved historic architecture in the West, including ornate storefronts, Victorian mansions, and the sacred sights of Temple Square. Edged by mountains, the city also enjoys backdoor access to winter skiing and summer hiking—just minutes from downtown.

The Northern Wasatch Front

With its spectacular mountains and canyons, it's no surprise that the Wasatch Range offers the world's best powder skiing. Former mining town Park City has become a winter playground not only for skiers, but also New York and Hollywood glitterati, who crowd the streets and the slopes during January's Sundance Film Festival.

Northern Utah

A rich railroad history winds through northern Utah. Once a thriving rail hub, handsome Ogden retains its early-20th-century charm. In a scenic alpine valley to the north, lively Logan draws crowds with its summer art and music festivals.

West-Central Utah 166

This is Utah's Wild West, where ghost towns like Ophir and Gold Hill still haunt the landscape. Follow in the hoofprints of the Pony Express through unfenced wilderness. Or strike out on your own for rockhounding in the desert or hiking on little-traveled mountain trails.

Central Utah 197

With a striking setting beneath majestic peaks on the edge of Utah Lake, Provo is home to Brigham Young University, which serves up a busy calendar of cultural and sporting events. From here, you can head up or down: Wind your way along the Alpine Scenic Loop or explore quiet villages and pioneer-era architecture in the low country.

Northeastern Utah **236**

*This is dinosaur country—bone excavations near Vernal
and Price give a glimpse of the giants that once
wandered this region, while ancient petroglyphs reveal a
human past lost to memory. Create some memories of
your own, rafting down the Green River or trout fishing
in the crystal streams of the lofty Uintas.*

Southwestern Utah

Many visitors first experience Utah's extreme landscape at these two national parks: Zion, with its sheer cliffs and towering monoliths, and Bryce Canyon, with its intricate maze of hoodoos, their color shifting with the light. The diversity of recreation available makes this area popular with everyone from family vacationers to serious outdoor enthusiasts.

South-Central Utah

Here there's endless backcountry to explore, whether following Highway 12 through untamed desert; wandering Escalante's eye-popping slickrock country; or discovering Capitol Reef's rainbow of sculptured rock layers. Nearby, watersports mecca Lake Powell will parch your thirst.

Southeastern Utah 417

Arches National Park offers delicate rock bridges and petrified sand dunes, while remote and otherworldly Canyonlands National Park is abundant with rock art and vertical desert landscapes—perfect for a multiday backpacking trip. Gateway city Moab has become a destination in its own right as a launchpad for slickrock mountain biking and Colorado River rafting.

National Monument; Bluff; Arch Canyon; Natural Bridges National Monument;
Dark Canyon; Grand Gulch Primitive Area; Mexican Hat; Monument Valley;
Four Corners Monument; Kayenta

Resources

ABOUT THE AUTHOR
W. C. McRae

Born and raised on a traditional cattle and sheep ranch in Montana, Bill was brought up with one foot in the saddle. From an early age his real passion was for the culture of Europe, a taste that he evolved from stories of his grandparents' native Scotland. He made his first trip to the United Kingdom at 18, which awakened a serious urge to travel. This was the 1970s and much of the world seemed like a well-meaning and courteous place to have a party. And so he did. He used his college years as an excuse to travel, attending universities in England, Scotland, France, Canada, and the United States. He finished his education at the University of Kent, with an M.A. in Modern Literature. All of this traipsing about didn't make for much of an academic career, but it was a great education in life.

After university, Bill moved to Portland, Oregon, which is still his home. Since moving to Portland, Bill has supported his writing habit by working at a number of *real* jobs, including university teacher, caterer, journalist, and tile-setter. With his name on various travel guides, including *Moon Handbooks Montana* and *Moon Handbooks Zion & Bryce,* Bill has also worked as an editor and contributor for Expedia.com, GORP.com, *National Geographic,* and the Mobil Guide series. Between travel writing junkets, Bill makes his money writing about technology. You can always interest him in a hand of bridge, a camping trip, or cooking up something French and full of calories.

Bill McRae has been traveling to Utah for a couple of decades, each time getting further off the road and digging deeper into the landscape. Every trip has a different focus, whether it's hiking into a new and more remote canyon, fixating on ancient rock art, or going deluxe at guest ranches. For Bill, Utah is the kind of place that gets under your skin, where you find yourself already planning your next adventure before you've finished up the current one.

ABOUT THE AUTHOR
Judy Jewell

© PAUL LEVY

Judy Jewell was born and raised in Baltimore, Maryland, where crossing a busy street was a typical outdoor adventure. She became a Western woman after she broke her right leg falling from a tree house at a camp where she worked; a small cash settlement prompted her to pack up her stuff and move to Portland, Oregon.

Salt Lake City was on the Greyhound route between Baltimore and Portland, and during a particularly long bus layover there, Judy began to explore the West. She was initially struck by the Salt Lake Temple, just a block from the bus station, brightly lit and gleaming white against the night sky. When the bus finally rolled out of town, the sun was rising and the Wasatch Range came into view, indicating that perhaps Salt Lake's call was not only to the religious.

Over the next 20-some years, Judy's visits to Utah were part of long, rambling Southwestern roadtrips to the national parks. She harbored a desire to ski Alta, but feared that, as a strikingly average skier, she was not worthy.

When the call came from her friend and colleague W. C. McRae to help update *Moon Handbooks Utah,* Judy saw this as an excuse to take her battered skis off to explore every blue run in the Wasatch Range. (She also tumbled down a few black runs, and found that Utah skiers are very nice about helping you round up your skis and poles after a spectacular fall.)

Judy is also the author of several other guidebooks, including *Moon Handbooks Montana* (also with W. C. McRae). When she is not writing about the outdoors and travel, she is the lead technical writer at Camp Dusty Technical Services. She lives with her husband and dog in Portland, where they enjoy swimming, yoga, skiing, gardening, cooking, and chasing the quacky duck.

Introduction

Few places on earth combine such spectacular terrain and unusual history as does Utah. The state hosts the majestic splendor of the Rocky Mountains, the colorful canyonlands of the Colorado Plateau, and the remote desert mountain ranges of the Great Basin. This region beckoned as the "Promised Land" to members of the struggling Church of Jesus Christ of Latter-day Saints in the 1800s—a place where those faithful to the Book of Mormon could survive and prosper. Today you can comfortably enjoy the scenic splendor of Utah, much of it little changed since the first pioneers arrived in 1847.

Salt Lake City in the north and the five national parks in the south rank at the top of most visitors' lists, but many other beautiful and intriguing places remain undiscovered. Utah's superb ski conditions and resorts are recognized as some of the best in North America, as shown during the 2002 Winter Olympics. Incredibly varied canyon country, rugged mountain ranges, glistening salt flats, Native American reservations, old mining towns—this handbook will help you discover these and many more attractions.

Joshua trees grow in the remote desert near St. George.

The Land

GEOGRAPHY

Utah's 84,990 square miles place it 11th in size among the 50 states. You could fit Maine, Vermont, New Hampshire, Connecticut, Massachusetts, New Jersey, and Maryland within its borders and still have room to squeeze in Rhode Island. The varied landscape is divided into three major physiographic provinces: the **Basin and Range Province** to the west; the **Middle Rocky Mountains Province** of the soaring Uinta, Wasatch, and Bear River Ranges to the north and northeast; and the **Colorado Plateau Province** of canyons, mountains, and plateaus in the southeast. Some physiographers argue for a fourth province, the **Basin and Range–Colorado Plateau Transition.** This area, also known as the High Plateaus, stretches from the Wasatch Range south into Arizona. Mountains and plateaus in this area share structural features with both neighboring provinces.

Basin and Range Province

Rows of fault-block mountain ranges follow a north-south alignment in this province in the Great Basin west of the Wasatch Range and the High Plateaus. Most of the land lies at elevations between 4,000 and 5,000 feet. Peaks in the Stansbury and Deep Creek Mountains rise more than 11,000 feet above sea level, creating "biological islands" inhabited by cool-climate plants and animals.

Erosion has worn down many of the ranges, forming large alluvial fans in adjacent basins. Many of these broad valleys lack effective drainage, and none have outlets to the ocean. Terraces mark the hills along the shore of prehistoric Lake Bonneville, which once covered most of this province. Few perennial streams originate in these rocky mountains, but rivers from eastern ranges end their voyages in the Great Salt Lake, Sevier Lake, or barren silt-filled valleys.

Middle Rocky Mountains Province

The Wasatch Range and the Uinta Mountains, which form this province, provide some of the most dramatic alpine scenery in the state. In both mountainous areas, you'll find cirques, arêtes, horns, and glacial troughs carved by massive rivers of ice during periods of glaciation. Structurally, however, the ranges have little in common. The narrow Wasatch, one of the most rugged ranges in the country, runs north-south for about 200 miles between the Idaho border and central Utah. Slippage along the still-active Wasatch Fault has resulted in a towering western face with few foothills. Most of Utah's ski resorts lie in this area. The Uinta Mountains in the northeast corner of the state present a broad rise about 150 miles west to east and 30 miles across. Twenty-four peaks exceed 13,000 feet, with Kings Peak (elev. 13,528 feet) the highest mountain in Utah. An estimated 1,400 tiny lakes dot the glacial moraines of the Uintas.

Colorado Plateau Province

World-famous for its scenery and geology, the Colorado Plateau covers nearly half of Utah. Elevations lie mostly between 3,000 and 6,000 feet, but some mountain peaks reach nearly 13,000 feet. The Uinta Basin forms the northern part of this vast complex of plateaus; it's bordered on the north by the Uinta Mountains and on the south by the Roan Cliffs. Although most of the basin terrain is gently rolling, the Green River and its tributaries have carved some spectacular canyons into the Roan and Book Cliffs. Farther south, the Green and Colorado Rivers have sculpted remarkable canyons, buttes, mesas, arches, and badlands. Uplifts and foldings have formed such features as the San Rafael Swell, Waterpocket Fold, and Circle Cliffs. The rounded Abajo, Henry, La Sal, and Navajo Mountains are examples of intrusive rock—an igneous layer that is formed below the earth's surface and later exposed by erosion. The High Plateaus in south-central Utah drop in a series of steps known as the Grand Staircase. Exposed layers range from the relatively young rocks of the Black Cliffs (lava flows) in the north to the increasingly older Pink

THE
COLORADO
PLATEAU

© AVALON TRAVEL PUBLISHING, INC.

Cliffs (Wasatch Formation), Gray Cliffs (Mancos Shale), White Cliffs (Navajo Sandstone), and Vermilion Cliffs (Chinle and Wingate Formations) toward the south.

GEOLOGIC HISTORY

The land now contained in Utah began as undersea deposits when the North American continental plate sat near the equator, about 500 million years ago. The spectacular canyon country, now known as the Colorado Plateau, began as a basin of silt and sand deposits at the verge of a shallow sea. This basin sat on a continental plate that rose and fell; it was sometimes below the waters of ancient seas—at which time fossils of early marinelife were encased in the deposits—and sometimes, during more arid periods, above sea level, with vast sand dunes covering the landscape.

Beginning about 200 million years ago, in the Mesozoic era, the North American continental plate broke away from Europe and Africa and began its westward movement over the top of the Pacific Ocean seafloor. This massive collision of tectonic plates resulted in the buckling of rock formations—which formed mountains, including the Rockies and the Uintas—and in thrust faulting, where older formations were pushed up and onto younger rocks; one such range is the Oquirrh Mountains.

All of this activity happened at the verges of the Colorado Plateau, which by the Cretaceous period—the age of the dinosaurs, about 65 million years ago—had again sunk back to sea level, resulting in thick formations of sand, mud, and ancient vegetation. These formations would later be revealed in the region's mighty canyons and in the coal fields of northeastern Utah. In some places, fossilized mud footprints of dinosaurs provide unmistakable evidence of the era's far damper climate!

Basin and Range

In the Tertiary era, the new formations west of the old Colorado Plateau were shot through with volcanoes. Then, as the North American continental plate pivoted to the southwest, the earth's crust under this region—which would become the Basin and Range Province—stretched thinner and thinner. In fact, the Great Basin of Utah and Nevada is about twice as wide as it was about 18 million years ago. This stretching has resulted in a much thinner layer of underlying basement rock here than in other parts of the continent, and the entire area is riven by faults where parts of the crust have pulled apart. Given the differential forces at work in the earth's mantle, sometimes half of a fault would be pushed up to mountain heights while the other half would sink, causing a basin. The spectacular fault-block mountains of the Great Basin result from such parallel rising and falling along fault lines. The most famous instance of this type of formation is the rugged Wasatch Mountains, which rise directly above the basin of the Great Salt Lake.

To the east of this momentous fault-block mountain building, the old Colorado Plateau remained relatively undisturbed. However, within the last 10 million years the entire intermountain region bowed up in a broad arch, elevating the old sandstones of the Colorado Plateau; this corner of Utah has risen 5,000 feet during this time! The rivers that once wound across the surface of eastern Utah were forced to cut ever deeper canyons as the formations rose. The erosive power of the Green, Colorado, San Juan, and other rivers and streams have cut down through hundreds of millions of years of rock.

Ice Age Utah

During the geologically recent Pleistocene era, ice-age mountain glaciers and climatic changes brought an abundance of moisture to Utah. The runoff and meltwater flooded the basins of fault-block mountain ranges, forming enormous lakes. The largest of these was Lake Bonneville, the name given to the ice-age predecessor of the Great Salt Lake. At its greatest extent, Lake Bonneville covered nearly all of northern and west-central Utah and was nearly 900 feet deeper than the current Great Salt Lake. Even at that depth, finding an outlet to the sea was not simple. It was only after the lake waters breached Red Rock Pass in Idaho that the lake found an outlet into the Snake and Columbia River systems, about 16,000 years ago.

After the ice ages ended, about 10,000 years ago, Lake Bonneville diminished in size and dropped below the level necessary to cut through Red Rock Pass, resulting in the saline Great Salt Lake. You can easily see the old lake shorelines along the Wasatch Front, and cities like Logan, Provo, and Salt Lake City sprawl along these stairsteplike ledges. Much of the old lake bottom west of Salt Lake City is salt desert and extremely flat. In the Bonneville Salt Flats, the valley is so flat and unbroken that the curvature of the earth can be seen; a person of ordinary height can see for three miles simply by standing up.

Spring tends to be unpredictable—wet and windy one day, sunny and calm the next—but it's then you'll find the deserts at their greenest.

CLIMATE

The hot summer sun awakens wildflowers in the mountains and turns desert areas brown. Autumn brings pleasant weather to all elevations until the snow line begins to creep down the mountain slopes. Winter snowfalls provide excellent skiing and add beauty to the landscape but cause many mountain roads to close. On those roads that don't close, you'll need chains or snow tires. Spring tends to be unpredictable—wet and windy one day, sunny and calm the next—but it's then you'll find the deserts at their greenest.

Utah's mid-continent location brings wide temperature variations between the seasons. Only a small part of the south experiences winter temperatures that average above freezing. State records include a high of 116°F at St. George in 1892 and a low of -50°F at Woodruff in 1899 and at Strawberry East Portal in 1913.

Precipitation

Most of Utah is dry—evaporation exceeds precipitation. In fact, of the 50 states only Nevada receives less average moisture annually than Utah's 13 inches. Precipitation varies greatly from place to place due to local topography and

the irregularities of storm patterns. Deserts cover about 33 percent of the state; the driest areas are in the Great Basin, the Uinta Basin, and on the Colorado Plateau, where annual precipitation is around 5–10 inches. At the other extreme, the highest peaks of the Wasatch Range receive more than 50 inches of annual precipitation, most of it as snow; approximately 24 percent of Utah has a highland climate. About 40 percent of the state, classified as steppe, receives 8–14 inches of annual precipitation and supports grasslands suitable for ranching. Three percent of the state's land is humid continental—ideal for agriculture. This heavily populated strip lies along the Wasatch Front. Utah enjoys lots of sunshine, but storm systems can briefly darken the skies at any time.

Winter and Spring Weather Patterns (October–April)

Periods of high-pressure systems broken by Pacific storm fronts shape most of Utah's winter weather. The high-pressure systems cause inversions when dense cold air flows down the snow-covered mountain slopes into the valleys, where it traps moisture and smoke. The blanket of fog or smog maintains even temperatures but is the bane of the Salt Lake City area. Skiers, however, enjoy bright, sunny days and cold nights in the clear air of the mountain peaks. The blankets of stagnant air in the valleys are cleaned out when cold fronts roll in from the Pacific. When skies clear, the daily temperature range is much greater until the inversion process sets in again.

Most winter precipitation arrives as snow, which all regions of the state expect. Fronts originating over the Gulf of Alaska typically arrive every 6–7 days and trigger most of Utah's snowfall.

Summer and Autumn Weather Patterns (May–September)

During summer, the valleys still experience inversions of cold air on clear, dry nights, but with a much less pronounced effect than in winter.

The canyon country in the south has higher daytime temperatures than do equivalent mountain elevations because there's no source of cold air in the canyons to replace the rising heated air. Also, canyon walls act as an oven, reflecting and trapping heat. Thunderstorms are most common in summer, when moist warm air rises in billowing clouds. The storms, though they can produce heavy rains and hail, tend to be erratic and concentrated in small areas less than three miles across. Southeastern Utah sees the first thunderstorms of the season, often in mid-June; by mid-July, these storms have spread across the entire state. They lose energy as autumn approaches, and by October they're supplanted by "lows aloft" (low-pressure systems at high altitudes) and Pacific storm fronts. Lows aloft move in erratic patterns but can cause long periods of heavy precipitation. They're often the main source of weather disturbances during October, late April, and May. Surprisingly, most of Utah's moisture originates in the Gulf of California or the Gulf of Mexico. The Pacific fronts often lose most of their moisture by the time they reach Utah, yet their cold air can produce heavy precipitation when it meets moist warm air from the south. Hikers need to be aware that the highest mountain peaks can receive snow even in midsummer.

Storm Hazards

Rainwater runs quickly off the rocky desert surfaces and into gullies and canyons. Flash floods can sweep away anything in their path, including boulders, cars, and campsites. Do not camp or park in potential flash-flood areas. If you come to a section of flooded roadway—a common occurrence on desert roads after storms—wait until the water goes down before crossing (it shouldn't take long). Summer lightning causes forest and brush fires, posing a danger to hikers foolish enough to climb mountains when storms threaten.

Flora and Fauna

A wide variety of plants and animals find homes within Utah's great range of elevations (more than 11,000 feet). Regardless of the precipitation, the environment is harsh, and most plants and animals have had to adapt to endure the challenging climate. To help simplify and understand the different environments, some scientists use the Merriam system of life zones, which offers a concise way to get an overview of Utah's vegetation and animal life. Because plants subsist on rainfall, which is determined largely by elevation, each life zone can be identified with an elevation range. These ranges are not exact, however, due to the different rainfall patterns and evaporation rates.

Utah's lowest elevations lie in the Lower Sonoran Life Zone (below 3,500 feet). This zone is found in the Mojave Desert, which extends into the southwest corner of the state. Most of Utah's northern deserts and canyonlands are considered part of the Upper Sonoran Life Zone (3,500–5,500 feet). As rainfall increases near mountain ranges, the Transition Life Zone (5,500–8,000 feet) begins. The Transition Zone is best developed on the High Plateaus and the Uinta Mountains and less so in the Great Basin and the Wasatch Range. At successively higher elevations are the Canadian Life Zone (8,000–10,000 feet), the Hudsonian Life Zone (10,000–11,000 feet), and the Alpine Tundra Life Zone (above 11,000 feet).

DESERT FLORA

In the southern Lower Sonoran deserts near St. George, less than eight inches of rain falls yearly. Creosote bush dominates the plantlife, though you're also likely to see rabbitbrush, snakeweed, blackbrush, saltbush, yucca, and cacti. Joshua trees grow on some of the higher gravel benches. Flowering plants tend to bloom after either the winter rains (the Sonoran or Mexican species) or the summer rains (the Mojave or Californian species).

In the more temperate Upper Sonoran Zone, shadscale—a plant resistant to both salt

wildflowers in Albion Basin, Little Cottonwood Canyon

and drought—grows on the valley floors and the lower slopes of the Great Basin, Uinta Basin, and canyonlands. Commonly growing with shadscale are grasses, annuals, Mormon tea, budsage, gray molley, and winterfat. In salty soils, more likely companions are greasewood, salt grass, and iodine bush. Nonalkaline soils, on the other hand, may have blackbrush as the dominant plant. Sagebrush, the most common shrub in Utah, thrives on higher terraces and in alluvial fans of nonalkaline soil. Grasses are commonly found mixed with sagebrush and may even dominate the landscape. Piñon pine and juniper, small trees often found together, can grow only where at least 12 inches of rain falls annually; the lower limit of their growth is sometimes called the "arid timberline." In the Wasatch Range, scrub oaks often grow near junipers.

MOUNTAIN FLORA

As elevation rises and rainfall increases, you'll see growing numbers of ponderosa pine and chaparral in the forest. The chaparral association includes oak, maple, mountain mahogany, and sagebrush. Gambel oak, juniper, and Douglas fir commonly grow among the ponderosa in the Uintas and the High Plateaus.

Douglas fir is the most common tree within the Canadian Zone in the Wasatch Range, the High Plateaus, and the northern slopes of the Great Basin Ranges. In the Uintas, however, lodgepole pine dominates. Other trees of the Canadian Zone include ponderosa pine, limber pine, white fir, blue spruce (Utah's state tree), and aspen.

Strong winds and a growing season of less than 120 days prevent trees from reaching their full size at higher elevations. The Hudsonian Zone receives twice as much snow as the Canadian Zone just below. Often gnarled and twisted, Engelmann spruce and subalpine fir grow in the cold heights over large areas of the Uintas and Wasatches. Limber and bristlecone pines live in the zone, too. Lakes and lush subalpine meadows are common.

Only grasses, mosses, sedges, and annuals can withstand the rugged conditions atop Utah's highest ranges. Freezing temperatures and snow can blast the mountain slopes even in midsummer.

INTRODUCTION

UTAH VEGETATION ZONES

PRECIPITATION

DRY   MOIST   WET

ELEV. IN METERS

4,000

3,000

2,000

1,000

500

GRASS AND SHRUB

SPRUCE

FIR

ASPEN

DOUGLAS FIR

PONDEROSA PINE

MOUNTAIN BRUSH

PINYON PINE

JUNIPER

SAGEBRUSH

SHADSCALE

YUCCA

JOSHUA TREE

CREOSOTE BUSH

TREELINE

ALPINE TUNDRA LIFE ZONE

HUDSONIAN LIFE ZONE

CANADIAN LIFE ZONE

TRANSITION LIFE ZONE

SONORAN LIFE ZONES

ELEV. IN FEET

14,000
13,000
12,000
11,000
10,000
9,000
8,000
7,000
6,000
5,000
4,000
3,000
2,000
1,000

COLD   WARM   HOT

TEMPERATURE

HIGHEST POINT IN UTAH 13,528 FEET AT KINGS PEAK

LOWEST POINT IN UTAH 2,350 FEET AT BEAVER DAM WASH

© AVALON TRAVEL PUBLISHING, INC.

DESERT FAUNA

Most desert animals retreat to a den or burrow during the heat of the day, when ground temperatures can reach 130°F! Look for wildlife in early morning, during late afternoon, or at night. You may see kangaroo rat, desert cottontail, black-tailed jackrabbit, striped and spotted skunks, kit fox, ringtail cat, coyote, bobcat, mountain lion, and several species of squirrels and mice. Birds include the native Gambel's quail, roadrunner, red-tailed hawk, great horned owl, cactus wren, black-chinned and broad-tailed hummingbirds, and rufous-sided towhee. The endangered desert tortoise lives here, too, but faces extinction in a losing battle with livestock, which trample and graze on the tortoise's precious environment.

The rare Gila monster, identified by its bead-like skin with black and yellow patterns, is the only poisonous lizard in the United States. In Utah, it's found only in the state's southwest corner. Although slow and unaggressive, it has powerful jaws and excretes a potentially lethal venom from a gland in its lower jaw. Once the reptile gets a grip, it doesn't let go and the jaws must be pried loose—even if the head has been cut off. Sidewinder, Great Basin, and other western rattlesnakes are occasionally seen. Also watch for other poisonous creatures; scorpions, spiders, and centipedes can inflict painful stings or bites. It's a good idea when camping to check for these unwanted guests in shoes and other items left outside. Be careful, too, not to reach under rocks or into places you can't see.

In the more temperate Upper Sonoran Zone, you'll see plenty of desert wildlife, though you might also see Utah prairie dog, beaver, muskrat, black bear, desert bighorn sheep, desert mule deer, and the antelope-like pronghorn. Marshes of the Great Basin have an abundance of food and cover that attract waterfowl; species include whistling swan, Great Basin Canada goose, lesser snow goose, great blue heron, seagull (Utah's state bird), common mallard, gadwall, and American common merganser. Chukar (from similar desert lands in Asia) and Hungarian partridge (from eastern Europe and western Asia) thrive under the cover of sagebrush in dry-farm areas. Sage and sharp-tailed grouse also prefer the open country. Rattlesnakes and other reptiles like the Upper Sonoran Zone best.

Not surprisingly, few fish live in the desert. The Great Salt Lake is too salty to support fish life; the only creatures that can live in its extremely saline water are bacteria, a few insect species, and brine shrimp, which are commercially harvested. The Colorado River, which cuts through southeastern Utah, supports a number of fish species, several of which are endemic to the river and are now considered endangered. (See the sidebar "Endangered Fish of the Colorado River Basin" in the Canyonlands National Park section.)

MOUNTAIN FAUNA

In the thin forests of the Transition Zone, squirrels and chipmunks rely on pinecones for food; other animals living here include Nuttall's cottontail, black-tailed jackrabbit, spotted and striped skunks, red fox, coyote, mule deer, Rocky Mountain elk (Utah's state mammal), moose, black bear, and mountain lion. Moose did not arrive until the 1940s, when they crossed over from Wyoming; now they live in northern and central Utah. Merriam's wild turkey, originally from Colorado, is found in oak and ponderosa pine forests of central and southern Utah. Other birds of the Transition Zone include Steller's jay, blue and ruffed grouse, common poorwill, great horned owl, black-chinned and broad-tailed hummingbirds, gray-headed and Oregon juncos, white-throated swift, and the common raven. Most snakes, such as the gopher, hognosed, and garter, are harmless, but you may also come across western rattlers.

Utah has over 1,000 fishable lakes and numerous fishing streams. Species range from rainbow and cutthroat trout to large mackinaw and brown trout to striped bass, walleye, bluegill, and whitefish. Bear Lake in extreme northern Utah is home to the Bear Lake whitefish, Bonneville whitefish, Bonneville cisco, and Bear Lake sculpin—all are unique to Bear Lake and its tributaries. Because of their restricted range, they are vulnerable to extinction from habitat alteration due to water management of Bear Lake and its tributaries.

Deer and Rocky Mountain elk graze in the Canadian Zone but rarely higher. Smaller animals of the high mountains include northern flying squirrel, snowshoe rabbit, pocket gopher, yellow belly marmot, pika, chipmunk, and mice.

Even higher, in the Hudsonian Zone, on a bright summer day the trees, grasses, and tiny flowering alpine plants are abuzz with insects, rodents, and visiting birds. Come winter, though, most animals will have moved to lower, more protected areas. Few animals live in the true alpine regions. White-tailed ptarmigan, recently introduced to Utah, live in the tundra of the Uinta Mountains.

Environmental Issues

Like many other western states, Utah is deeply conflicted about environmental issues. One of the most conservative states in the nation, Utah has always been very business oriented, especially toward the historic extractive industries such as mining, logging, and agriculture. Utah has also proved to be very friendly to the military; large portions of northeastern Utah are under Pentagon control as bases, weapons research areas, and munitions dumps.

On the other hand, tourism and high-tech industries are breathing life into Utah's economy. Tourism brings in 18 million visitors a year, making it the single largest employer in Utah. Wasatch Front cities are experiencing a phenomenal boom in population growth and new, low-environmental-impact industry. A large part of the reason for this modern migration is Utah's quality of life—pristine wilderness and world-class outdoor recreation are available right out the back door. The interests of the tourist industry and new residents are often at odds with the interests of the state's traditional power base. With supporters of resource extraction industries ensconced both in Washington and in Utah, the state finds itself in the crosshairs of the battle to save or level the West.

This issue came to a head in 2003 when some leaders in the outdoor gear industry, including several Utah companies, threatened to move the twice-yearly Outdoor Retailer show from Salt Lake City to protest an agreement Governor Mike Leavitt signed with Interior Secretary Gale Norton. That agreement essentially ended interim protection that the BLM, under the Clinton administration, had granted to about 2.6 million acres of lands in addition to the 3.2 million acres already protected as official "wilderness study areas."

The outfitters trade show brings in enough revenue to the Salt Lake City economy—roughly $24 million—that Leavitt felt the need to meet with Outdoor Retailer representatives. He stated that he wanted to meet with them to enlist their aid in salvaging wilderness protection for the remaining 3.2 million acres of Utah land protected since 1979 as wilderness—an odd case of a Republican governor seeming to appeal to environment-friendly industry to help stop the onslaught of Leavitt's fellow Republicans. According to the old saw, all politics is local, and apparently this duck and cover plays in Utah.

NUCLEAR WASTE DISPOSAL ON THE GOSHUTE INDIAN RESERVATION

The disposal of nuclear waste from atomic energy generation plants has long been a problem, as the waste has typically been stored at the plants themselves, which don't have adequate or safe storage facilities. However, it's not exactly easy to get someone to open up land to build a nuclear waste dump: it's the ultimate Not In My Back Yard (NIMBY) situation.

Scientists have isolated a number of sites in the Nevada Desert that they claim could be used to create a safe and stable storage facility—areas with little ground water to contaminate, few faults that could be triggered by an earthquake, and almost no population centers around to irradiate if something did go wrong.

Although the siting of a long-term nuclear waste dump is being fought by many in Nevada, the Goshute tribe and the federal government arrived at an interim solution for the storage of nuclear waste. The Goshute invited the federal government and a consortium of eight power generation companies to build a temporary storage facility at Skull Valley on their arid, west-central Utah reservation about 45 minutes west of Salt Lake City. In return, the Goshute tribe, one of the poorest in the United States, would receive a windfall of money and infrastructure development.

In 2003, the Atomic Safety and Licensing Board ruled that a private nuclear waste storage facility in Skull Valley could not be built because of proximity to a nearby U.S. Air Force training range. Although the waste facility would meet other safety standards, including earthquake resistance, the board said the danger of an F-16 crashing into the storage site was too great.

The utility consortium has asked the board to reassess the aircraft analysis and has submitted a scaled-back waste storage plan that would decrease the chances of a jet fighter crashing into the facility. The Atomic Safety and Licensing Board has agreed that the resubmitted proposal will be expedited upon appeal.

WATER USE

The early Mormon pioneers came from well-watered New York and New England and the rich Midwestern prairies. When they arrived in Utah, they set about transforming the desert, following the scripture that says the desert will blossom as a rose. Brigham Young encouraged this endeavor, saying that God would change the climate, giving more water if the settlers worked to establish agriculture.

So the settlers planted fruit orchards, shade trees, and grass, turning the desert into an oasis. They built dams and created reservoirs. They dug canals, piping water from farther and farther away, turning the desert green.

Utah now has the second highest per-capita water use in the nation, despite having experienced its fifth year of drought in 2003 and being the second driest state in the United States.

Water conservationists maintain that Utahns, including state officials in charge of water-use policy, have not let go of 19th-century ideals about water development and conservation. The state's current goal is to cut water use by 25 percent over the next 50 years, which environmentalists see as incredibly wishy-washy.

Meanwhile, many individuals view the drought as a wake-up call, and see water conservation and native-plant landscaping as the way of the new Utah pioneer.

History

PRE-SETTLEMENT UTAH

Utah in Prehistory

Archaeologists have evidence that Paleo-Indians began to wander across the region that would become Utah about 15,000 years ago—hunting big game and gathering plant foods. The climate was probably cooler and wetter when the first Native Americans arrived; food plants and game animals would have been more abundant than today. The early tribes continued their primitive hunting and gathering despite climate changes and the extinction of many big-game species about 10,000 years ago.

The first tentative attempts at agriculture were introduced from the south about 2,000 years ago and brought about a slow transition to a settled village life. The Fremont culture emerged in the northern part of the Colorado Plateau, the Anasazi in the southern part. Although both groups developed crafts such as basketry, pottery, and jewelry, only the Anasazi progressed to the construction of masonry buildings in their villages. Their corn, beans, and squash enabled them to be less reliant on migration and to construct year-round village sites. Thousands of stone dwellings, ceremonial kivas, and towers built by the Anasazi still stand. Both groups also left behind intriguing rock art, either pecked into the surfaces (petroglyphs) or painted on (pictographs). The Anasazi and the Fremont departed from this region about 800 years ago, perhaps because of drought, warfare, or disease. Some of the Anasazi moved south and joined the Pueblo tribes of present-day Arizona and New Mexico. The fate of the Fremont people remains a mystery.

About the same time, perhaps by coincidence, the nomadic Shoshoni in the north and the Utes and Paiutes in the south moved through Utah; none of these groups seemed to have knowledge of their more sophisticated predecessors. Relatives of the Athapascans of western Canada, the seminomadic Navajo, wandered into New Mexico and Arizona between A.D. 1300 and 1500. This adaptable tribe learned agriculture, weaving, pottery, and other skills from their Pueblo neighbors and became expert horsepeople and sheepherders with livestock obtained from the Spanish.

The size of prehistoric populations has varied greatly in Utah. There were probably few inhabitants during the Archaic period (before A.D. 500), but many more during the time of the Anasazi and Fremont cultures (A.D. 500–1250), rising to a peak of perhaps 500,000. Except for the Athapascan-speaking Navajo, all of Utah's historic tribes spoke Shoshonian languages and had similar cultures.

Explorers and Colonizers

In 1776, Spanish explorers of the Dominguez-Escalante Expedition were the first Europeans to visit and describe the region during their unsuccessful attempt to find a route west to California. Utes guided the Spanish expedition through the Uinta Basin.

Retreating to New Mexico, the explorers encountered great difficulties in the canyons of southern Utah before finding a safe ford across the Colorado River. This spot, known as the "Crossing of the Fathers," now lies under Lake Powell. Later explorers established the Old Span-

ANASAZI OR ANCESTRAL PUEBLOAN?

As you travel through the Southwest, you may hear reference to the "ancestral Puebloans." In this book, we've chosen to use the more familiar name for these people—the Anasazi. The word *Anasazi* is actually a Navajo term that archaeologists chose, thinking it meant "old people." A more literal translation is "enemy ancestors." For this reason, some consider the name inaccurate. The terminology is in flux, and which name you hear depends on whom you're talking to or where you are. The National Park Service now uses the more descriptive term ancestral Puebloan. These prehistoric people who built masonry villages eventually moved south to Arizona and New Mexico, where their descendants, such as the Acoma, Cochiti, Santa Clara, Taos, and the Hopi Mesas, live in modern-day pueblos.

ish Trail through this area of Utah to connect New Mexico with California.

Adventurous mountain men seeking beaver pelts and other furs entered northern Utah in the mid-1820s. They explored the mountain ranges, the rivers, and the Great Salt Lake and blazed most of the trails later used by wagon trains, the Pony Express, telegraph lines, and the railroads. By 1830, most of the mountain men had moved on to better trapping areas and left the land to the Native Americans; some, however, returned to guide government explorers and groups of pioneer settlers. The names of several mountain men are remembered on maps today: Peter Skene Ogden (Ogden), Etienne Provost (Provo), Jim Bridger (Bridgerland is the nickname of Cache and Rich Counties), John H. Weber (Weber River and County), and William Ashley (Ashley National Forest).

Joseph Walker, who served under Captain Benjamin Bonneville, crossed the northwest corner of Utah in 1833 on a trip to California. He reported such difficult conditions that no one else attempted the route for the rest of the decade. California-bound wagon trains took heed and followed a more northerly path through Idaho on the Oregon Trail. An exception was the Bartleson-Bidwell wagon train, which turned south into Utah in 1841 and skirted the northern edges of the Great Salt Lake and the Great Salt Lake Desert. Though members suffered immense hardships and later had to abandon their wagons, they eventually made it across. The group was the first to take wagons across Utah and included the first European women known to have crossed Utah and Nevada to California.

In 1843, John C. Frémont led one of his several government-sponsored scientific expeditions into Utah. Frémont determined the salinity of the Great Salt Lake and laid to rest speculation that a river drained the lake into the Pacific Ocean. Two years later, he led a well-prepared group across the heart of the dreaded Great Salt Lake Desert despite warnings from the local Native Americans that no one had crossed it and survived. His accounts of the region described not only the salty lake and barren deserts but also the fertile valleys near the Wasatch Range. Mormon leaders planning a westward migration from Nauvoo, Illinois, carefully studied Frémont's reports.

Langsford Hastings, an ambitious politician, seized the opportunity to promote Frémont's desert route as a shortcut to California. Hastings had made the trip on horseback but failed to anticipate the problems of a wagon train. On this route in 1846, the Donner-Reed wagon train became so bogged down in the salt mud that many wagons were abandoned. Moreover, an 80-mile stretch between water holes proved too far for many of the oxen, which died from dehydration. Today, motorists can cruise in comfort along I-80 on a similar route between Salt Lake City and Wendover.

Native Americans vs. Settlers

The Paiutes and Utes befriended and guided the early explorers and settlers, but troubles soon began for these and other groups when they saw their lands taken over by farmers and ranchers. None of the tribes proved a match for the white population, which eventually drove the Native Americans from the most desirable lands and settled them on the state's five reservations.

The Navajo's habit of raiding neighboring tribes and white settlements brought about their downfall. In 1863–1864 the U.S. Army rounded up all the Navajo they could find and forced the survivors on "The Long Walk" from Fort Defiance in northeastern Arizona to a bleak camp in eastern New Mexico. This internment was a dismal failure, and the Navajo were released four years later.

In 1868, the federal government "awarded" to the Navajo land that has since grown to a giant reservation spreading from northeastern Arizona into adjacent Utah and New Mexico.

THE MORMON MIGRATION
The Early LDS Church

At the time of his revelations, the founder of the Church of Jesus Christ of Latter-day Saints, Joseph Smith, worked as a farmer in the state of New York. In 1830, he and his followers founded the new religion and published the first edition of the Book of Mormon. But Smith's revelations evoked fear and anger in many of his neighbors, and in 1831 he and his new church moved to Kirtland, Ohio. They set to work building a temple for sacred ordinances, developing a missionary program, and recruiting new followers. Mormons also settled farther west in Missouri, where they made plans for a temple and a community of Zion.

Persecution by non-Mormons continued to mount in both Ohio and Missouri, fueled largely by the church's polygamist practices, the prosperity of its members, and the Latter-day Saint claim that it was the "true" church. Many perceived the Mormons as a dire threat to existing political, economic, and religious systems; Missourians disliked the Mormons' anti-slavery views. Violence by gangs of armed men eventually forced church members to flee for their lives.

The dark winter of 1838–1839 found Joseph Smith in jail on treason charges and many church members without homes or legal protection. The Missouri Mormons made their way east to Illinois, not knowing where else to go. Brigham Young, a member of the Council of the Twelve

Apostles, directed this exodus, foreshadowing the much longer migration he would lead eight years later.

Nauvoo the Beautiful

The Mormons purchased a large tract of swampy land along the Mississippi River in Illinois and set to work draining swamps and building a city. Joseph Smith, allowed to escape from the Missouri jail, named the Mormons' new home Nauvoo—a Hebrew word for "the beautiful location." Despite extreme poverty and the inability to secure reparations for the losses they had suffered in Missouri, the Mormons succeeded in building an attractive city that would one day rival any in the United States. A magnificent temple, begun in 1841, rose above Nauvoo. Despite their success, the Mormons continued to face virulent opposition from those who objected to their religion.

Smith, who had withstood tarring and feathering, among other punishments, met his death in 1844 at Carthage, Illinois. He had voluntarily surrendered to authorities to stand trial for treason, but a mob stormed the jail and killed Smith and his brother Hyrum in a hail of bullets. Opponents thought that the Mormons would disband on the death of their leader. When they did not, their crops and houses were destroyed and their livestock was driven off. Brigham Young, who succeeded Smith, realized the Mormons would never find peace in Illinois. He and other leaders began looking toward the vastness of the West. They hoped the remote Rocky Mountains would provide a sanctuary from mobs and politicians. Plans for departure from Nauvoo began in the autumn of 1845.

The Exodus

Attacks against Nauvoo's citizens made life so difficult that they had to evacuate the following February despite severe winter weather. Homes, businesses, the temple, and most personal possessions were left behind as the Saints crossed the Mississippi into Iowa. (Mobs later took over the town and desecrated the temple; not a single stone of the structure is in its original position today.) The group slowly pushed westward through the snow and mud. Faith, a spirit of sharing, and competent leadership enabled them to survive.

Brigham Young thought it best not to press on all the way to the Rocky Mountains that first year, so the group spent a second winter on the plains. Dugouts and log cabins housed more than 3,500 people at Winter Quarters, near present-day Omaha. By the early spring of 1847, the leaders had worked out plans for the rest of the journey. The Salt Lake Valley, an uninhabited and isolated region, would be their goal. Mountain men encountered on the journey gave discouraging descriptions of this place as a site for a major settlement. Samuel Brannan, a Mormon who had settled on the West Coast, rode east to meet Brigham Young and present glowing reports of California. But Young wouldn't be swayed from his original goal. On July 24, 1847, Young arrived at the edge of the Salt Lake Valley and announced, "This is the right place."

The City of Zion

The pioneers immediately set to work digging irrigation canals, planting crops, constructing a small fort, and laying out a city. Nearly 2,000 more immigrants arrived that same summer of 1847.

By necessity, these early citizens had to be self-sufficient; the nearest outposts of civilization lay 1,000 miles away. Through trial and error, farmers learned techniques of irrigating and farming the desert land. The city continued to grow—immigrants poured in; tanneries, flour mills, blacksmith shops, stores, and other enterprises developed under church direction; residential neighborhoods sprang up; and workers commenced raising the religious structures that still dominate the area around Temple Square.

The Colonization of Utah

Soon other areas in Utah were colonized: In 1849–1850, Mormon leaders in Salt Lake City took the first steps in exploring the rest of the state when they sent an advance party led by Parley P. Pratt to southern Utah. Encouraging reports of rich iron ore west of Cedar Valley and of fertile land along the Virgin River convinced the Mormons to expand southward.

Calls went out for members to establish missions and to mine the iron ore and supply iron products needed for the expanding Mormon empire. In 1855, a successful experiment in growing cotton along Santa Clara Creek, near present-day St. George, aroused considerable interest among the Mormons. New settlements soon arose in the Virgin River Valley. However, poor roads hindered development of the cotton and iron industries, which mostly ended when cheaper products began arriving on the transcontinental railroad.

In the 1870s and early 1880s, the LDS Church sent out calls for members to colonize lands east of the Wasatch Plateau. Though at first the land looked harsh and barren, crops and orchards eventually prospered with irrigation.

An Agrarian Paradise

By the end of the 19th century, the small agricultural settlements in Utah—mostly free of gentile influence—had by and large become the utopian religious communities envisioned by the religion's founders. Various tenets of the faith dictated nearly all aspects of life, from the width of the streets to social customs. Cultural homogeneity was greatly stressed; farmers and ranchers were discouraged from living on their land and encouraged instead to live in towns within range of the church. For a period, the church encouraged full-fledged communal and cooperative farm towns as the ideal social structure.

The Mormons were hardworking farmers and managed to convert an unyielding desert into a land of abundance. Streams were diverted into irrigation canals, and acres of orchards and fields blossomed. Little farm towns, all laid out with uniform street grids, were planted with trees and flowers; substantial homes of stone announced the prosperity of the LDS way of life.

The internal structure of the church—the ward (the parish) and stake (the diocese)—became the organizing principle of all religious and social life. Nearly all the social events of a

small community were sponsored by the church, including dances, sports events, hay rides, swimming parties, and picnics. The overlap between church and civic authority was nearly complete.

The Road to Statehood

After many years of persecution, the early Latter-day Saints realized the importance of self-government. However, when the Mormon pioneers arrived in their new homeland of Zion, the land actually belonged to Mexico. However, after victory in the Mexican War in 1848, the United States took possession of a vast territory in the American West, including the land that would become Utah.

The LDS Church quickly assessed the positive benefits that statehood would bring the new territory, and in 1849 a convention was called "to consider the political needs of the community." The convention created the proposed state of Deseret, which encompassed a great swath of the West, including all or parts of the current states of Utah, Nevada, Arizona, Wyoming, Colorado, New Mexico, Oregon, Idaho, and parts of southern California (San Diego was to be the state's port city). The convention wrote a constitution, elected officials (Brigham Young was elected governor), and sent a delegate to the U.S. Congress. However, the House of Representatives declined to admit the delegate from Deseret, and the statehood was effectively quashed. In fact, LDS-dominated Utah would find it exceedingly difficult to attain statehood. Nearly 50 years would pass before Utah would finally become a state.

The federal Senate did pass legislation naming Utah as a territory in 1850; however, a number of factors—especially the thorny cultural and moral issues surrounding polygamy—worked to exacerbate tensions between the new territory and the federal government.

In 1857–1858, the U.S. government sent a 2,500-man army to occupy Salt Lake City and remove Brigham Young from the governorship (accompanying the army was Alfred Cummings, whom President Buchanan had selected as territorial governor). The army reached Salt Lake

City to find it newly deserted, and Cummings assumed the governorship, ending at least in theory Utah's flirtation with theocracy. Cummings soon made peace with the Mormons, and residents returned to Salt Lake City.

Second and third attempts at statehood for Deseret were met in Washington with defeat and actually seemed to stir up anti-Mormon sentiment: Congress quickly passed legislation prohibiting polygamy in the territories. The same legislation also sought to unincorporate the LDS Church.

The building of the transcontinental railroad through Utah in the 1860s decreased Utah's isolation from the rest of the United States; however, greater contact with the outside world also meant increased Mormon-gentile hostility. In 1874, Congress passed a bill effectively disenfranchising LDS-controlled district courts. In 1879, the U.S. Supreme Court upheld legislation that made the practice of plural marriage a criminal offense. Subsequent federal legislation made it illegal for polygamists to vote, hold public office, or serve on juries. The result was persecution and pursuit of avowed polygamists, many of whom were forced into hiding or exile in Mexico. The federal government's anti-Mormon campaigns also had the effect of empowering the territory's non-Mormon minority far beyond its small power base.

In 1890, LDS president Wilford Woodruff issued the startling proclamation that henceforward he advised his brethren "to refrain from contracting any marriage forbidden by the law of the land." The new doctrine was published across the country, and while many doubted the proclamation's sincerity, it signaled a major shift in direction for the statehood movement. Finally, in 1894 Congress passed the Enabling Act, which set forth the steps Utah had to follow to achieve statehood (the act stipulated that the state constitution declare polygamy be banned forever). In 1896, President Cleveland proclaimed Utah the 45th state.

It's helpful to remember the long and rancorous disputes between Utah's LDS population and the federal government in the 19th century when trying to understand the state's fervid, ongoing anti-government tendencies. In some ways, the state's current anger over the establishment of the Grand Staircase–Escalante National Monument is just an example of Utah's long memory of perceived past injustice.

MODERN TIMES

Utah's close-knit Mormon farm towns thrived from the late 19th century until the Depression years. The dust bowl years were particularly hard in Utah, as most farms were entirely dependent on irrigation and the decade-long drought greatly reduced the flow of already scarce water. Communities quickly rebounded during World War II, especially as federal money poured into military camps like Wendover Air Base in the deserts west of Salt Lake City.

The designation of five national parks (beginning with Zion in 1919), two huge national recreation areas, and the new and vast Grand Staircase–Escalante National Monument has brought an ever-increasing stream of tourists to the state. Today, tourism is the state's largest industry, dwarfing such stalwarts as mining and lumber. Eighteen million people visit Utah annually (a full million of them from overseas). In 2002, the Winter Olympics were held in the Salt Lake City area, and the world spotlight shone on the state as never before.

This surge of secular interest in the sacred homeland of the LDS Church has led to concerns about the effect of the tourist boom on both the environment and traditional Mormon communities. Clashes between pro-growth business interests, environmentalists, and Mormon conservatives over the future of the state often make for some odd bedfellows.

GOVERNMENT AND ECONOMY

Utah became a territory in 1850 and a state in 1896. Utah is represented in Washington, D.C., by two senators and three representatives. Utah's two senators, Orrin Hatch and Bob Bennett, are both Republicans, as are all members of the house delegation.

The state legislature consists of 75 house members and 30 senators. Utah is generally considered to be one of America's most politically conservative states; it has the largest percentage of registered Republican voters of any state in the Union.

Agriculture and mining have historically been considered the twin pillars of the Utah economy. Copper, tin, silver, lead, oil, and coal are among the primary minerals found in the state.

Almost all agriculture is irrigated and includes a significant dairy industry, fruit orchards, grain, and hay production. Cattle and sheep graze the uplands and the mountain meadows.

Recently, tourism has overtaken these more traditional economic powerhouses to become the state's largest employer. Utah is also a center for the aerospace and military-related industries and has a number of military bases in the western deserts.

The People

One of the oddest statistics about Utah is that it's the most urban of America's western states. Eighty-five percent of the state's population of 2,316,000 citizens live in urban areas, and a full 80 percent reside in the Wasatch Front area.

A relatively young population, combined with the Mormons' emphasis on family life and clean living, has resulted in Utah's having one of the highest birth rates and lowest death rates in the country. Racially, the state largely reflects the northern European origins of Mormon pioneers; in 2000 the state was 89 percent white. The state's population includes Hispanics (9 percent), Native Americans (1.3 percent), Asians (1.7 percent), and African Americans (0.8 percent).

UTAH'S NATIVE AMERICANS
Shoshoni
Nomadic bands of Shoshoni occupied much of northern Utah, southern Idaho, and western Wyoming for thousands of years. Horses obtained from the Plains tribes—who had obtained them from the Spanish—allowed hunting parties to cover a large range. The great Chief Washakie led his people for 50 years and negotiated the tribe's treaties with the federal government. The Washakie Indian Reservation, near Plymouth in far northern Utah, belongs to the Northwestern band of Shoshoni, though few live there now. Tribal headquarters are in Rock Springs, Wyoming, south of the large Wind River Indian Reservation.

Goshute (or Gosiute)
This branch of the Western Shoshoni, more isolated than other Utah tribes, lived in the harsh Great Basin. They survived through intricate knowledge of the land and use of temporary shelters. These peaceful hunters and gatherers ate almost everything that they found—plants, birds, rodents, crickets, and other insects. Because the Goshute had to dig for much of their food, early explorers called the tribe Digger Indians. White men couldn't believe these people survived in such a barren land of alkaline flats and sagebrush. Also known as the Newe, the tribe now lives on the Skull Valley Indian Reservation in Tooele County and on the Goshute Indian Reservation along the Utah-Nevada border.

Ute
Several bands of Utes, or Núuci, ranged over large areas of central and eastern Utah and adjacent Colorado. Originally hunter-gatherers, they acquired horses in about 1800 and became skilled raiders. Customs adopted from Plains tribes included the use of rawhide, tepees, and the *travois* (a sled used to carry goods). The discovery of gold in southern Colorado and the pressures of farmers there and in Utah forced the Utes to move and renegotiate treaties many times. They now have the large Uintah and Ouray Indian Reservation in northeast Utah, the small White Mesa Indian Reservation in southeast Utah, and the Ute Mountain Indian Reservation in southwest Colorado and northwest New Mexico.

RELIGION IN UTAH

Quick, a little free-association test. When I say "Utah," what do you think? Most people, unsurprisingly, respond "Mormon." And Mormonism is inescapable for anyone traveling around Utah with eyes even half-open. Just as sensitive travelers would not denigrate Catholicism in Ireland or Buddhism in Thailand, travelers in Utah would do well to keep an open mind about Utah's predominant religion.

Remember that the church's proper title is the Church of Jesus Christ of Latter-day Saints, and that members prefer to be called "Latter-day Saints," "Saints" (usually this term is just used among church members), or "LDS." While calling someone a Mormon isn't *wrong*, it's not quite as respectful.

The religion is based in part on the Book of Mormon, the name given to a text derived from a set of "golden plates" found by Joseph Smith in 1827 in western New York. Smith claimed to have been led by an angel to the plates, which were covered with a text written in "reformed Egyptian." A farmer by upbringing, Smith translated the plates and published an English-language version of the Book of Mormon in 1830.

The Book of Mormon tells the story of the lost tribes of Israel, which, according to Mormon teachings, migrated to North America and became the ancestors of today's Native Americans. According to the Book of Mormon, Jesus also journeyed to North America, and the book includes teachings and prophecies that Christ supposedly gave to the ancient Native Americans.

The most stirring and unifying aspect of Mormon history is the incredible westward migration made by the small, fiercely dedicated band of Mormon pioneers in the 1840s. Smith and his followers were persecuted in New York and then in their newly founded utopian communities in Ohio, Missouri, and Illinois. After Smith was murdered near Carthage, Illinois, in 1844, the group decided to press even farther westward toward the frontier, led by church president Brigham Young. The journey across the then very Wild West to the Great Salt Lake basin was made by horseback, wagon, or handcart—hundreds of Mormon pioneers pulled their belongings across the Great Plains in four-by-four-foot carts. The first group reached the Salt Lake City area in 1847. The bravery and tenacity of the group's two-year migration forms the basis of many Utah residents' fierce pride in their state and religion.

Most people know that LDS members are clean-living, family people who eschew alcohol, tobacco, and stimulants, including caffeine. This can make it a little tough for visitors to feed their own vices (and indeed, it may make what formerly seemed like a benign habit feel a little more sinister). But Utah has loosened up a lot in the past few years, largely thanks to hosting the 2002 Winter Olympics, and it's really not too hard to find a place to have a beer with dinner, though you may have to make a special request. Towns near the national parks are particularly used to hosting non-Saints and attach virtually no stigma to waking up with a cup of coffee or settling down with a glass of wine.

Southern Paiute

Six of the 19 major bands of the Southern Paiutes, or Nuwuvi, lived along the Santa Clara, Beaver, and Virgin Rivers and in other parts of southwest Utah. Extended families hunted and gathered food together. Fishing and the cultivation of corn, beans, squash, and sunflowers supplemented the diet of most of the bands. Today, Utah's Paiutes have a tribal headquarters in Cedar City and scattered small parcels of reservation land. Southern Paiutes also live in southern Nevada and northern Arizona.

Navajo

Calling themselves Diné, the Navajo moved into the San Juan River area about 1600. The tribe has proved exceptionally adaptable in learning new skills from other cultures: many

Navajo crafts, clothing, and religious practices have come from Native American, Spanish, and Anglo neighbors. The Navajo tribe was the first in the area to move away from a hunting and gathering lifestyle, relying instead on the farming and shepherding techniques they had learned from the Spanish. The Navajo have become one of the largest Native American groups in the country, occupying 16 million acres of exceptionally scenic land in southeast Utah and adjacent Arizona and New Mexico. Tribal headquarters is at Window Rock in Arizona.

THE MORMONS

If you're new to the "Beehive State," you'll find plenty of opportunities to learn about Mormon history and religion. At least half of Utah's population actively participates in the Church of Jesus Christ of Latter-day Saints; three-quarters of the population were born into the faith. Temple Square in Salt Lake City offers excellent tours and exhibits about the church. You'll also find many other visitors centers and historic sites scattered around the state.

The Church of Jesus Christ of Latter-day Saints, which is headquartered in Salt Lake City, has a worldwide membership of nearly 11 million, due largely to a vigorous missionary program. Members usually call themselves "Latter-day Saints" or LDS. Nonmembers commonly use the nickname "Mormon" because of the emphasis the church puts on the Book of Mormon—members of the church prefer to be referred to simply as LDS, not Mormon.

Members believe that God's prophets have restored teachings of the true Christian church to the world "in these latter days." Although the LDS Church considers itself a Christian denomination, Mormons don't classify themselves as either Catholic or Protestant. They believe their church presidents, starting with Joseph Smith, to be prophets of God, and they hold both the Bible and the Book of Mormon as the sacred word of God. The latter, they believe, was revealed to Joseph Smith from 1823 to 1830. The text tells of three migrations from the Eastern Hemisphere to the New World and the history of the people who lived in the Americas from about 600 B.C. to about A.D. 400. The book contains 239 chapters, which include teachings Christ supposedly gave in the Americas, prophecy, doctrines, and epic tales of the rise and fall of nations. It's regarded by the church as a valuable addition to the Bible—but not a replacement.

Membership in the LDS Church requires faith, a willingness to serve, tithing, and obedience to church authorities. The church emphasizes healthful living, moral conduct, secure family relationships, and a thoughtful approach to social services.

RELIGION

The Church of Jesus Christ of Latter-day Saints is by far the dominant religion in Utah; about 65 percent of the population belongs to the church. Most major Christian denominations are represented in mid-sized towns, and in Salt Lake City there are small Jewish and Islamic congregations as well.

INTRODUCTION

Conduct and Customs

If you've never traveled in Utah before, you may find that Utahns don't initially seem as welcoming and outgoing as people in other western states. In many smaller towns, visitors from outside the community are a relatively new phenomenon, and not everyone in the state is anxious to have their towns turned into tourist or recreational meccas. The Mormons are very family- and community-oriented, and if certain individuals initially seem insular and uninterested in travelers, don't take it as unfriendliness.

Mormons are also very orderly and socially conservative people. Brash displays of rudeness or use of foul language in public will not make you popular.

Alcohol and Nightlife

Observant Mormons don't drink alcoholic beverages, and state laws have been drafted to make purchasing alcohol relatively awkward. If going out for drinks and nightclubbing is part of your idea of entertainment, you'll find that only Salt Lake City, Park City, and Moab offer much in the way of clubs and nightspots. Most towns have a liquor store; outside of the Wasatch Front and Moab, don't expect restaurants to have liquor licenses.

Private Clubs

Most drinking establishments—and certainly the ones that will seem most normal to outsiders—are private clubs. Clubs that serve hard liquor without

SAY IT RIGHT!

The following place-names are easy to mispronounce. Say it like a local!

Duchesne	du-SHANE
Ephraim	E-from
Escalante	es-kuh-LAN-tay
Hurricane	HUR-uh-kun
Kanab	kuh-NAB
Lehi	LEE-high
Manti	MAN-tie
Monticello	mon-tuh-SELL-o
Nephi	NEE-fi
Panguitch	PAN-gwich
Salina	suh-LINE-uh
Tooele	too-WILL-uh
Uinta	yoo-IN-tuh
Weber	WEE-ber

food and feature live music or other entertainment are almost all private clubs, which means you need to be a member to get in. Thankfully, it's not an overwhelming obstacle. You can buy a two-week membership, usually for $5.

Smoking

Smoking is taboo for observant Mormons, and in almost all public places smoking is prohibited. You're also not allowed to smoke on church grounds.

On the Road

Salt Lake City

Salt Lake City is home to the Church of Jesus Christ of Latter-day Saints, the Mormons. Temple Square preserves historic religious architecture, while the city booms with new businesses, restaurants, and the arts.

Every tourist should visit the sacred sights of Temple Square. Although the gleaming white temple is not open to non-Mormons, the tabernacle is. Plan to attend a free musical event (the 320-voice Mormon Tabernacle Choir has free concerts twice a week) to witness the structure's famed acoustics. Visitors centers and museums explain the Mormon faith and display religious art. You can also visit Brigham Young's home, built in 1854.

The Utah State Capitol Building dominates the skyline just north of downtown. The building is modeled after the U.S. Capitol and sits amid 40 acres of lawns and gardens. Nearby is the Pioneer Memorial Museum, which tells the story of the 2,000-mile journey of the original Mormon pioneers in 1847.

The Northern Wasatch Front

Some of North America's finest skiing and best resorts are within an easy hour's drive from downtown Salt Lake City. Head up either Big or Little Cottonwood canyons, or out I-80 to Park City

© JUDY JEWELL

Highway 21 runs through the San Francisco Mountains.

for deep, dry powder. Each resort has its own distinct character, from folksy yet ski-crazy Alta to plush Deer Valley. Park City is also famed as a getaway for the rich and famous; this small town at the crest of the Wasatch Range, with a population of 6,500, has more art galleries than Salt Lake City and has one restaurant for every 60 inhabitants.

Northern Utah

Ogden, just north of Salt Lake City, was once a thriving rail hub. Today it's practically subsumed as a suburb of Salt Lake City. The city's old downtown area, centered on 25th Street, retains early-20th-century storefronts, which are now home to good cafés and restaurants, plus antique stores and boutiques. Ogden's huge and handsome rail station at the head of 25th Street no longer receives rail passengers, but it does house four museums, a restaurant, and an art gallery.

Logan is one of the most attractive small cities in Utah; located in a green fertile valley and hedged round by towering peaks, its small downtown area has charming Victorian storefronts facing onto a park. Summer festivals make Logan a lively place: The nationally acclaimed Utah Festival Opera brings big voices to town for a three-opera season, Festival of the American West brings in buckskin-clad mountain men and cowboy poets, and the Old Lyric Theater hosts a season of musicals and comedies. Bear Lake, on the Idaho border, is a large, high-altitude lake with good fishing and cool summer temperatures; it's popular with the motorboat set.

West-Central Utah

This is the part of Utah to visit if you want to get away from it all. The Great Basin desert alternates with arid mountain ranges, and only a few paved roads even cross this forlorn landscape. This is the best place in the state for rockhounding, and there's lots of history in the old mining ghost towns of Ophir, Gold Hill, and others. The Pony Express crossed this lonely stretch of desert, and remnants of old stations and inns can still be seen. If you're looking for solitude, backpacking trails lead into the little-visited Deep Creek and House Mountain Ranges. Just across the Utah border in Nevada is

Great Basin National Park, with Lehman Caves (tours daily year-round), archaeological sites, and alpine hiking.

Central Utah

Provo is Utah's second largest city and home to Brigham Young University. Provo is a good base for exploring the dramatic Wasatch peaks that rise directly behind the city. An especially nice back road is the Alpine Scenic Loop, which climbs up to 7,500 feet through dramatic mountain scenery. Along the way you'll pass Sundance Resort, owned by Robert Redford and noted for its skiing and good restaurants. Timpanogos Cave National Monument is on the north flank of Mount Timpanogos and is open in summer for tours (it's an hour-long strenuous hike to the cave's entrance).

South of Provo are small sleepy towns that serve the needs of local ranchers and farmers. Fillmore was once the territorial capital of Utah, and the 1855 statehouse is preserved as a museum. The town of Beaver has more than 200 historic homes and buildings, most from the 1870s.

To the east, U.S. 89 follows the Sanpete River, which lies in a lovely agricultural valley flanked by mountains. The little towns along the route are showcases of historic Mormon architecture.

Northeastern Utah

Dinosaur country! Vernal and Price each have dinosaur museums and easy access to dinosaur digs and paleontology labs. Dinosaur National Monument preserves a quarry with semi-excavated bones, plus a museum and research center; the Cleveland-Lloyd Dinosaur Quarry is less developed and features trails to dig sites.

The Green River cuts a mighty canyon through the Uinta Mountains, exposing cliffs of deep red and ochre. Called the Flaming Gorge, the canyon now contains a reservoir that's the center of a national recreation area and the focus of lots of boat-centric recreation. Rafting the Green River below the Flaming Gorge Dam is a popular summer adventure for families.

This region has excellent ancient Native American rock art and petroglyph areas, particularly along the Nine Mile Canyon Backcountry Byway (east of Price) and at Dry Fork, northeast of Vernal. The lofty but rounded Uinta Mountains are noted for their high-country, trout-rich streams and lakes.

Southwestern Utah

St. George, at the northern tip of the Sonoran Desert, makes the most of the year-round sun as a retirement and golf center. Just to the north, Cedar City is a pleasant town known for its summer Utah Shakespearean Festival, with eight plays each season. Kanab has a long history as a film-making center—you can tour the sets where *Gunsmoke* and *My Friend Flicka,* plus nearly 150 other films and TV shows, were shot.

Zion National Park is one of the most popular in the park system; hiking trails lead up narrow canyons cut into massive stone cliffs, passing along quiet pools of water and groves of willows. Zion is so breathtaking and awe-inspiring that the early Mormons named these canyons for their vision of heaven.

© JUDY JEWELL

Bryce Canyon National Park

Bryce Canyon National Park has famous vistas across an eroded amphitheater of pink sandstone hoodoos. Easy hikes lead down into a wonderland of fanciful formations and outcrops.

Other areas of southwestern Utah are not quite so busy. The Cedar Breaks National Monument preserves an area with formations similar to Bryce Canyon, but without the rampaging tour bus crowds. Red Canyon is adjacent to Bryce Canyon and shares its geology, but since it's not a national park you can mountain bike and ride horses amid the red-rock formations.

South-Central Utah

The Grand Staircase–Escalante National Monument preserves some of the Southwest's best canyon hiking. Numerous long-distance hiking trails follow the slot canyons of the Escalante River system. Off-road driving enthusiasts follow the Hole-in-the-Rock Road or the Burr Trail to visit some of the same landscape; just following scenic Highway 12 across Escalante country in a car is an eye-popping experience to most travelers.

Even though Highway 24 runs along the northern edge of Capitol Reef National Park and gives access to a historic Mormon orcharding town, much of this park remains remote and unvisited. The long Waterpocket Fold formation that forms the southern two-thirds of the park is an excellent destination for long-distance hikers seeking solitude in the often busy Utah national parks.

Southeastern Utah

Moab is the center of the vast recreational area known as the canyonlands. Mountain biking is spectacular here; rafting down the Colorado and Green Rivers is nearly mandatory. The canyonlands are an exciting and vibrant destination filled with outdoor recreation, brewpubs, and large youthful crowds.

Vast chunks of the land here are preserved as national parks or monuments. Just up the road from Moab is Arches National Park, with its famous rock bridges. Canyonlands National Park is remote and otherworldly, and a visit that involves more than just a drive to a vista point

ON THE ROAD

requires a little planning and forethought. This area offers a wealth of rock art, Anasazi ruins, and vertical desert landscapes—a perfect place for a multiday backpacking trip.

The far southeastern corner of Utah is home to the famed red-rock towers at Monument Valley, plus the charming town of Bluff. From here explore side trips to rock-art sites, or take a rafting trip down the San Juan River. If all this desert has you hankering for water, go to Lake Powell, a massive reservoir on the Colorado River and a houseboating paradise.

Recreation

OUTDOOR ACTIVITIES

By far the best place to begin looking for information on recreational opportunities in Utah is the comprehensive www.utah.com website. The site contains information on most sports and activities and provides lots of links to yet more outfitters and sites.

Mountain Biking

More than any other single recreational activity, mountain biking has put Utah on the map. Trails in the slickrock canyon country near Moab attract more than 150,000 biking enthusiasts a year, and now nearly all corners of the state promote their old Forest Service or mining roads as a biking paradise. There's good info for planning bike trips at www.utah.com/bike, and excellent biking guidebooks are available from bookstores. See Suggested Reading in the Resources section for suggestions.

In general, Utah summers are too hot for mountain biking. The peak season in Moab runs March–May and again September–November.

River-Running

Rafting or canoeing Utah's rivers is another favorite activity for tourists and adventurers. The most notable float trip is down the Colorado River between Moab and the backwaters of Lake Powell. This multiday trip passes through Cataract Canyon, and for spectacular adventure it's second only to trips through the Grand Canyon. The Green and San Juan Rivers are also popular. For these trips, plan well in advance, as spaces are limited and demand more than outstrips availability. In towns like Moab, Green River, Vernal, and Bluff, numerous outfitters provide exciting day trips that can usually take people with only a day's notice. Ask state tourist offices for their *Utah Rivers* magazine or check out the official website at www.utah.com/raft.

Hiking, Backpacking, and Camping

Utah offers lots of backcountry for those interested in exploring the scenery on foot. One increasingly popular activity is canyoneering— exploring mazelike slot canyons. Hundreds of feet deep but sometimes only wide enough for a hiker to squeeze through, these canyons are found in the southern part of the state, particularly near Escalante and in the Paria River area. You'll need to be fit to explore these regions—and watch the weather carefully for flash floods.

Hikers will find great trails in almost all parts of the state. The rugged Wasatch Range near Salt Lake City is a popular day-hiking destination for urban residents of the Wasatch Front, while the lofty, lake-filled Uintas in northeastern Utah are perfect for long-distance trips. The remote and little-explored deserts of western Utah make for great wilderness adventures. Much of the canyonlands of southern and southeastern Utah are accessible only by foot; visits to remote Anasazi ruins and petroglyphs reward the long-distance hiker.

Campers are in luck in Utah. The state has a highly developed network of campgrounds, both public and private. During peak tourist season, make reservations or arrive at your destination early.

Skiing and Snowboarding

You may have noticed the legend on the license plates: "Ski Utah!" It is almost a command dur-

HOW TO SELECT AN OUTFITTER

Utah has a number of outfitters, guides, trail-drive operators, and guest ranches, all of whom promise to get you outdoors and into an Old West adventure. However, all outfitting and recreational services are not created equal. The most important consideration in choosing an outfitter is safety; the second is your comfort. Make sure you feel confident on both counts before signing on.

Here are some points to ponder while you plan your adventure vacation.

All outfitters should be licensed or accredited by the state and be happy to provide you with proof. This means that they are bonded, carry the necessary insurance, and have the money and organizational wherewithal to register with the province. This rules out fly-by-night operations and college students who've decided to set up business for the summer. If you're just starting to plan an excursion, contact the Utah Travel Council at Capitol Hill, Salt Lake City, 801/538-1030 or 800/200-1160. The council's website, www.utah.com, contains an extensive network of outfitters and guides.

Often a number of outfitters offer similar trips. When you've narrowed down your choice, call and talk to the outfitters on your short list. Ask lots of questions, and try to get a sense of who these people are; you'll be spending a lot of time with them, so make sure you feel comfortable. If you have special interests, like bird- or wildlife-watching, be sure to mention them to your potential outfitter. A good outfitter will also take your interests into account when planning a trip.

If there's a wide disparity in prices between outfitters for the same trip, find out what makes up for the difference. The cheapest trip may not be the best choice for you. Food is one of the most common areas to economize in. If you don't mind having cold cuts each meal for your five-day pack trip, then maybe the cheapest outfitter is okay. If you prefer a cooked meal, or alcoholic beverages, or a choice of entrées, then be prepared to pay more. On a long trip, it might be worth it to you. Also be sure you know what kind of accommodations are included in multiday trips. You may pay more to have a tent or cabin to yourself; again, it may be worth it to you.

Ask how many years an outfitter has been in business and how long your particular escort has guided this trip. While a start-up outfitting service can be perfectly fine, you should know what level of experience you are buying. If you have questions, especially for longer or more dangerous trips, ask for referrals.

Most outfitters will demand that you pay a portion (usually half) of your fee well in advance to secure your place, so be sure to ask about your outfitter's cancellation policy. Some lengthy float trips can cost thousands of dollars; if cancellation means the forfeiture of the deposit, then you need to know that. Also, find out what the tipping or gratuity policy is for your outfitter. Sometimes 15 or 20 percent extra is added to your bill as a tip for the "hands." While this is undoubtedly nice for the help, you should be aware that your gratuities for a week's stay can run into the hundreds of dollars.

ing the winter months. Skiing has always been excellent in the Wasatch Front ski areas near Salt Lake City and Park City, and since the 2002 Winter Olympics, the world knows about Utah's uncrowded slopes, which provide some of the best powder skiing in North America. If you've always wanted to ski or board Olympic-quality slopes, plan a trip to Utah: All the runs and facilities developed for the Olympics are still in place. For a good overview of Utah's ski areas and information on special package deals, check www.skiutah.com.

Fishing

The Wasatch and Uinta Ranges are dotted with lakes and drained by streams that are rich in rainbow and cutthroat trout. Fly-fishing is a major sport in many mountain communities, and most towns have at least one fly shop and an outfitter anxious to take you out to a stream. Favorite fishing spots include Bear Lake, with good fishing for lake and cutthroat trout; Flaming Gorge Reservoir on the Green River, offering good fishing for lake trout, smallmouth bass, and kokanee salmon; and Lake Powell, with good fishing for catfish, striper, and bass.

Horseback Riding

While guest ranches are the best places to experience a Western-style vacation on horseback (see Accommodations later in this chapter), the ski areas at Park City also offer riding in summer. In winter, sleigh rides are featured.

Rockhounding

Utah is rich in curious stones, fossils, and gems. The lack of vegetation and the high level of erosion make rockhounding a relatively simple matter. One of the best places to plan a rock-hunting expedition is the Delta area, where you can explore for geodes, agates, garnets, and other treasures.

Golfing

There are dozens and dozens of golf courses across Utah. Notable courses dot the Salt Lake City area and also lie near Ogden, Logan, Provo, and Park City. The state's greatest concentration of courses, though, is in St. George, in the southern part of the state. Perhaps it's rhetorical to wonder which comes first, retirees or golf courses, but St. George's excellent courses amid magnificent red-rock formations certainly have contributed mightily to the town's reputation as a retirement haven.

NATIONAL PARKS AND MONUMENTS

Utah is home to five major national parks, seven national monuments, two national recreation areas, and one national historic site. Three of the crown jewels of the national park system—Zion, Arches, and Bryce Canyon—are here, as well as the less traveled Capitol Reef and Canyonlands parks. Just across the border in Nevada is Great Basin National Park, and just south in Arizona is the Grand Canyon. In 1996, the Grand Staircase–Escalante National

© SALT LAKE CITY CONVENTION AND VISITORS BUREAU/RICK MCCLAIN

Salt Lake City has greens in remarkable settings.

Monument added protection to 1.9 million acres of public land to Utah's inventory of scenic wild lands. These national park areas and national monuments are the state's largest tourist attractions, bringing in nearly 18 million people yearly.

The parks are all open year-round, though spring and fall are the best times to visit—you'll avoid the heat and crowds of high summer. The entry fee for the national parks has gone up greatly in the past few years; admission to Zion is now $20 per vehicle. If you're planning on making the rounds of the Utah national parks, it's an excellent idea to purchase the park system's Golden Eagle Passport ($65) or the National Parks Pass ($50), both of which cover admission costs at national parks.

STATE PARKS

Utah boasts 41 state parks, ranging from golf courses to fishing holes, from historic forts to Anasazi ruins. Entry fees to state parks vary, though in general there's a $5–7 per-vehicle charge at the recreational parks. Many of these have campgrounds; you can make reservations by calling 800/322-3770. For general information on Utah's state parks, contact Utah State Parks, 1636 W. North Temple, Ste. 116, Salt Lake City, UT 84116-3456, 801/538-7220. Or visit http://parks.state.ut.us.

WILDERNESS TRAVEL

As more people seek relief from the stress of urban life, wilderness areas are becoming increasingly popular. Fortunately, Utah has an abundance of this fragile and precious resource. The many designated wilderness areas have been closed to mechanized vehicles (including mountain bikes) to protect both the environment and the experience of solitude. Most designated areas lie within national forests or Bureau of Land Management lands, and many are free to visit without a permit; others require permits, and some have entrance fees. The national parks and monuments require backcountry permits for overnight stays.

Some of the most spectacular and memorable hiking and camping await the prepared outdoorsperson. If you are new to hiking, start with easy trips, then work up gradually. The following are suggestions for backcountry travel and camping:

• Before heading into the backcountry, check with a ranger about weather, water sources, fire danger, trail conditions, and regulations. Backpacking stores are also good sources of information.

• Tell rangers or other reliable people where you are going and when you expect to return; they'll alert rescuers if you go missing.

• Travel in small groups for the best experience (group size may also be regulated).

• Try not to camp on meadows, as the grass is easily damaged.

• Use a portable stove in order to avoid leaving fire scars.

• Resist the temptation to shortcut switchbacks; this causes erosion and can be dangerous.

• Avoid digging tent trenches or cutting vegetation.

• Help preserve Native American and historic ruins.

• Camp at least 300 feet away from springs, creeks, and trails. Camp at least a quarter-mile from a *sole* water source to avoid scaring away wildlife and livestock.

• Avoid camping in washes at any time; hikers need to be alert to thunderstorms.

• Take care not to throw or kick rocks off trails—someone might be underneath you.

• Don't drink water directly from streams or lakes, no matter how clean the water appears; it may contain the parasitic protozoan *Giardia lamblia,* which causes giardiasis. Boiling water for several minutes will kill giardia as well as most other bacterial or viral pathogens. Chemical treatments and water filters usually work, too, although they're not as reliable as boiling (giardia spends part of its life in a hard shell that protects it from most chemicals).

• Bathe away from lakes, streams, and springs.

• Bring a trowel for personal sanitation; dig four to six inches deep.

• Bring along plenty of feed for your horses and mules.

• Leave dogs at home if possible; they may disturb wildlife and other hikers and foul campsites. If you do bring a dog, please keep it under control at all times.

• Take home all your trash.

• If you realize you're lost, find shelter. If you're sure of a way to civilization and plan to walk out, leave a note with your departure time and planned route.

ARTS AND ENTERTAINMENT

Music

Generally speaking, Salt Lake City is the center of the state's arts scene. The state's Mormon heritage is reflected in the city's love of and support for fine music. The glittering Abravanel Concert Hall is home to the noted Utah Symphony, and the tabernacle at Temple Square is often filled with concerts and recitals. The famed Mormon Tabernacle Choir performs here, as do various other church-related music groups. Best of all, all performances at Temple Square are free, making this a great opportunity for travelers to soak up culture at a good price.

Salt Lake City is also the state's major venue for rock and alternative music. A number of lively clubs host both local bands and traveling acts from both coasts. In most cases, music clubs are private clubs and you'll need to either buy a temporary membership or get sponsored by a member. Despite the rigmarole, the music's usually good and the crowds are interesting.

Come summer, there's fine music at more out-of-the-way places. Venues at Park City offer a full summer schedule ranging from rock concerts at The Canyons Ski Area to the Utah Symphony at classy Deer Valley Resort. In Logan's sparkling Capitol Theatre, the Utah Festival Opera company puts on a summer season of grand opera.

Theater

Again, Salt Lake City is the center of things theatrical in Utah. Several year-round theatrical troupes dish up everything from Broadway musicals to serious plays like Tony Kushner's *Angels in America*.

In the summer, Cedar City's Utah Shakespearean Festival (visit www.bard.org for more information) offers eight different plays performed by a professional repertory company. Both Shakespearean and contemporary plays are featured; the Bard's works are presented under the stars in an outdoor theater.

Dance

Salt Lake City supports a number of dance troupes, all with excellent reputations. Ballet West performs a mix of classical and contemporary pieces, while the Ririe-Woodbury Dance Company has a more eclectic approach to dance.

Cinema

While you'll be able to see most first-run films and some art-house fare in Salt Lake City and, to a lesser extent, in smaller cities in Utah, the real cinematic event in Utah is the Sundance Film Festival, held every January in Park City. Founded by actor Robert Redford as a forum for little-seen documentary and independent films, the festival has grown into a major showcase of new, high-quality cinema. Make lodging and ticket reservations well in advance if you want to attend. For more information and to get on the mailing list, call 801/328-FILM.

Museums

Utahns are very proud of their pioneer past, and nearly every community in the state has a Daughters of Utah Pioneers (DUP) museum, which recounts the story of local Mormon settlement. In fact, church history and state history are so closely interconnected that the primary state history museums are the various Temple Square institutions and the LDS-dominated Pioneer Memorial Museum. The museum at the Utah Historical Society isn't even in the same league.

Utah has a number of good museums dedicated to the dinosaurs and other forms of ancient life. The area around Price and Vernal is rich in fossils, and both towns have good dinosaur museums; additionally, there are fossil digs with visitors centers at Dinosaur National Monument and at the Cleveland-Lloyd Dinosaur

Quarry. The Museum of Ancient Life at Lehi has one of the largest collections of complete dinosaur skeletons in the country.

Ogden has converted its large and handsome railroad depot into a multi-museum complex with collections of minerals, fine art, firearms, and historic automobiles and train cars.

Art Galleries

Utah isn't exactly known for its fine-art collections, but the Salt Lake Art Center has a changing lineup of traveling shows that focus on regional artists. The universities in Salt Lake City, Provo, and Logan each have art galleries, and Ogden boasts the Myra Powell Art Gallery in the historic train depot. If you're looking for commercial art galleries, the state's richest pay dirt is in Park City. This small resort community has more fine art galleries than Salt Lake City.

Accommodations

Utah is a major tourist destination, and you can plan on finding high-quality, reasonably priced motels and hotels in most cities and towns. Reservations are a good idea in major centers like Salt Lake City, Park City, and Moab—especially on weekends. Along the national parks loop, off-season rooms are limited (some establishments are seasonal), so call ahead to make sure there's a room at the inn.

Hostels

Hostels aren't available everywhere in Utah. Salt Lake City has a couple, as do Moab, Hurricane, and Kanab. Hostels are open to travelers of all ages, and most Utah hostels don't require membership cards. You may need to provide your own sleeping cloth. For locations of hostels in Utah and elsewhere in the United States, order a free hostelling map of the United States from Hostelling International (HI-AYH) Map Brochure, 8401 Coalsville Rd., Ste. 600, Silver Spring, MD 20910, 301/495-1240, www.hiayh.org.

Bed-and-Breakfasts

With its wealth of pioneer-era homes and mansions, Utah also offers travelers some comfortable bed-and-breakfast accommodations. If you're only familiar with British-style B&Bs, you'll discover that in American B&Bs are more like small, well-appointed inns—usually in historically or architecturally significant homes. Smoking and pets are restricted, some inns have rules against young children, and others are reserved for couples only. Most require advance booking.

In Utah's B&Bs you'll find a friendly welcome, personalized advice on sites and recreation, a chance to meet fellow travelers, and, of course, a fine breakfast.

For more information on bed-and-breakfasts, contact the visitors centers in the regions you plan to visit; contact B&B Inns of Utah Incorporated, P.O. Box 3066, Park City, UT 84060-3066, 435/645-8068, www.bbiu.org, a membership organization representing bed-and-breakfasts across the state; or contact the Utah Travel Council, 801/538-1030, for a more general list.

Guest Ranches

Utah has fewer guest ranches than other western states, but some have sprung up here and there. Most are family ranches that take in guests during the summer. These tend to be authentic, horse-powered operations where you'll work alongside the family and stay in no-frills cabins or bunkhouses. Others are more upscale and offer a dude-ranch atmosphere with a number of recreational options.

Most guest ranches ask for minimum stays, and prices include all meals and lodging. Advance reservations are usually required. If you're contemplating staying at a guest ranch, be sure to ask specific questions about lodgings and work requirements. Expectations of the guest and host can vary widely. The Utah Travel Council can provide a full listing of Utah guest ranches; it's also available from the www.utah.com website.

Food and Drink

Utah is not one of the culinary capitals of the world. Outside of Salt Lake City, Park City, and Moab, restaurants in Utah generally serve standard American fare, with family restaurants and grills setting the standards even in midsize towns. Even the steak house, omnipresent elsewhere in the West, is curiously absent here. Most towns have a vintage American-Chinese restaurant, which is usually the best bet for a vegetarian. After a couple of days on the road, you may be glad to note that Pizza Hut usually offers a salad bar and that you can get a fresh salad at McDonalds.

The good news is that in the three towns noted above, you can eat quite well. Park City has some excellent high-end restaurants. Moab offers a varied selection of restaurants, including two excellent brewpubs with complete dining facilities. Salt Lake City has restaurants to satisfy most every taste, including some excellent ethnic options.

Having a drink with your meal is easier in the above three cities than elsewhere in the state. Access to alcohol in restaurants varies quite a bit from community to community, and some towns are practically "dry"—alcohol-free.

Drinking Laws

The state's liquor laws are rather confusing and peculiar. Several different kinds of establishments are licensed to sell alcoholic beverages.

Taverns, which include brewpubs, can sell only 3.2 percent beer (not wine, which is classed as hard liquor in Utah). You don't need to purchase food or be a member of a private club to have a beer in a tavern. With the exception of brewpubs, taverns are usually fairly derelict and not especially cheery places to hang out.

UTAH BREWPUBS

Utah is catching up with the rest of the West and the brewpub craze. Each of the following pubs brews its own beer and serves full meals. Brewpubs by and large escape the restrictions that apply to other bars (though all beer is 3.2 percent alcohol), and travelers will find them good places to meet the locals and eat light meals.

MOAB

Eddie McStiff's, 57 S. Main in Western Plaza, 435/259-BEER (435/259-2337), is popular with young mountain bikers; there's a garden patio in back.

Moab Brewery, 686 S. Main St., 801/259-6333, serves good food in a classy atmosphere.

OGDEN

Rooster's 25th Street Brewing Company, 253 25th St., 801/627-6171, is a high-design pub in the historic district.

PARK CITY

Wasatch Brew Pub, 250 Main St., 435/649-0900, is where you stop to sip a Polygamy Porter, marketed with the motto, "Why have just one?"

PRICE

Grogg's Pinnacle Brewing Co., 1653 N. Carbonville Rd., 435/637-2924, offers handcrafted beer in an unlikely location on the outskirts of Price.

SALT LAKE CITY

Squatters Pub Brewery, 147 W. Broadway, 801/363-2739, was Utah's first brewpub; it offers outdoor seating.

Red Rock Brewing Company, 254 South 200 West, 801/521-7446, is very popular and serves great food.

Desert Edge Brewery, Trolley Square, 700 East 500 South, 801/521-8917, provides inexpensive food in a post-industrial ambience.

Licensed restaurants sell beer, wine, and hard liquor but only with food orders. However, it's not always easy to tell if drinks are served, because a long-time—but now defunct—law forbade servers from asking customers if they cared for a drink. In many parts of the state, you still need to specifically ask for a drink or the drink menu to begin the process. In Salt Lake City, Moab, and Park City, most restaurants have liquor licenses. In other cities and towns, very few eating establishments offer alcohol.

Private clubs are essentially the same as bars in other parts of the United States. You can have drinks with or without food during opening hours. However, you must be a member to eat or drink in a private club. For the traveler, this doesn't present an insurmountable hurdle, as you can buy temporary memberships (a two-week membership usually costs around $5). If you're fond of a drink and nightlife, it might well be worth it. Most live music clubs are private clubs, for instance. Also, members of a club are able to sign in up to five friends on a nightly basis. You can ask a friendly-looking stranger to sign you in, or, if you're part of a group, one of you can become a member and sign the others in.

Nearly all towns have a state-owned liquor store, and 3.2 percent beer is available in most grocery stores. Carrying a bottle of your favorite beverage to your room may be the easiest way to enjoy an evening drink.

The state drinking age is 21.

Transportation

GETTING THERE

By Air

More than a dozen major airlines serve Salt Lake City, which has the only major airport in the state. Salt Lake City is the western hub for Delta Air Lines, which provides the most international and regional links (www.delta.com). You'll have the best chance of getting low fares by planning at least two weeks ahead.

By Train

Amtrak now runs only one passenger train across Utah. The California Zephyr runs daily between Oakland and Chicago via Salt Lake City.

Amtrak charges more than Greyhound for one-way tickets but has far roomier seating, lounge cars, and sleepers. Special fares and round-trip discounts often make train travel a good value. For information and reservations, see a travel agent or contact Amtrak at 800/872-7245, www.amtrak.com. A USA Railpass is sold by travel agents outside the United States.

By Bus

The Greyhound bus line offers frequent service to Utah on its transcontinental routes along I-15 and to Denver along U.S. 40. Greyhound often features special deals on bus passes and one-way "anywhere" tickets. Outside the United States, residents may purchase a Greyhound Ameripass at additional discounts.

By RV

Many foreign travelers enter Utah in RVs, which they rent to drive on a tour of the western national parks. It takes more planning to line up a rental RV than a car, but there are plenty of agencies in Los Angeles, Phoenix, Las Vegas, and Salt Lake City able to do the job. Most travel agents can help, or you can contact the local travel office in the city of your departure.

GETTING AROUND

By Air

Regional airlines connect Salt Lake City with other communities in the state. Regular scheduled flights link to Vernal, St. George, and Cedar City. The cost per mile of these short hops is high, but you'll often have excellent views!

By Train

Amtrak can get you to Price, Helper, Provo, and Salt Lake City, but that's about all. Public transportation to other points of interest, such as the national parks, is notably absent.

By Bus

There's frequent Greyhound bus service up and down I-15 and along U.S. 40 to Vernal, but these routes really don't get you close to the sorts of sights that most people come to Utah to see. The Wasatch Front area (from Provo to Ogden and from Salt Lake City out to Tooele) is served by Utah Transit Authority (UTA), a regional bus company with excellent service. Park City and other Salt Lake City ski areas are accessible via a number of ski-bus operations, some of which pick up at the airport.

The only form of public ground transport to Moab and other towns in southeastern Utah is a once-daily van that provides transport to and from the Salt Lake City Airport.

By Car

Public transportation serves cities and some towns but very few of the scenic, historic, and recreational areas. Unless you're on a tour, you really need your own transportation. Cars are easily rented in any large town, though Salt Lake City offers by far the greatest selection. Four-wheel-drive vehicles can be rented, too, and will be very handy if you plan extensive travel on back roads.

Most tourist offices carry the Utah road map published by the Utah Department of Transportation; it's one of the best available and is free. Most regular-grade unleaded gasoline in Utah is only 85 octane. If your automobile owner's manual calls for a higher grade of octane you might need a higher grade of gasoline.

By Bicycle

Touring on a bicycle is to be fully alive to the land, skies, sounds, plants, and birds of Utah.

UTAH DRIVING DISTANCES

© AVALON TRAVEL PUBLISHING, INC.

The experience of gliding across the desert or topping out on a mountain pass goes beyond words. Some effort, a lightweight touring or mountain bike, touring gear, and awareness of what's going on around you are all that's needed. Start with short rides if you're new to bicycle touring, then work up to longer cross-country trips. By learning to maintain and repair your steed, you'll seldom have trouble on the road. An extra-low gear of 30 inches or less takes the strain out of long mountain grades. Utah has almost every kind of terrain and road condition imaginable; mountain bicyclists find the Moab area in the southeast especially challenging and scenic. Note that designated wilderness areas are closed to cycling.

Most bookstores and bicycle shops have good publications on bicycle touring. *Bicycle Touring*

THE GREAT WESTERN TRAIL

As its name implies, the Great Western Trail, when completed, will traverse some of the West's most spectacular country. The Utah stretch, approximately 350 miles long, will link trails in Arizona and Idaho with others in New Mexico, Wyoming, and Montana (the Utah section is now 90 percent complete). Planners envision a trail network stretching all the way from Mexico to Canada, providing travel possibilities for bicycles, horses, and motorized vehicles, as well as hikers. About 90 percent of the finished network will employ existing roads and trails.

The southernmost Utah section follows washes and canyons across land administered by the Bureau of Land Management; elevations drop as low as 4,800 feet. The Dixie National Forest section skirts the western edge of Bryce Canyon National Park and continues across high plateaus to Boulder Top, where it reaches elevations topping 11,000 feet. Fishlake National Forest has more fine alpine country and expansive views from Thousand Lake Mountain, Windstorm Peak, and the UM Plateau areas. In the Manti–La Sal National Forest, the trail ascends the lofty Wasatch Plateau and extends for 75 miles through rolling meadows and forest country. Uinta National Forest features lush forests beneath the jagged summits of the Wasatch Range's Mount Timpanogos and Lone Peak. The ups and downs of the Wasatch Range continue as the trail winds through the Wasatch-Cache National Forest high above Salt Lake City and the Great Salt Lake. The northernmost trail section in Utah climbs into the Bear River Range and meets the Idaho border near Beaver Mountain.

Note that some trail sections are open to off-road vehicles and pets and some aren't. You can obtain the latest trail information from the agencies below. The **Great Western Trail Association** needs volunteers for trail construction and maintenance. If you'd like to help, contact the association at P.O. Box 1428, Provo, UT 84602. The group has a fledgling website at www.gwt.org.

**Cedar City District Office—
Bureau of Land Management**
176 E. DL Sargent Dr., Cedar City, UT 84720
801/586-2401

Dixie National Forest
P.O. Box 580, 82 North 100 East
Cedar City, UT 84720
801/865-3700

Fishlake National Forest
115 East 900 North, Richfield, UT 84701
801/896-9233

Manti–La Sal National Forest
599 W. Price River Dr., Price, UT 84501
801/637-2817

Uinta National Forest
88 West 100 North, Provo, UT 84601
801/377-5780

Wasatch-Cache National Forest
8230 Federal Bldg., 125 S. State St.
Salt Lake City, UT 84138
801/524-5030

ON THE ROAD

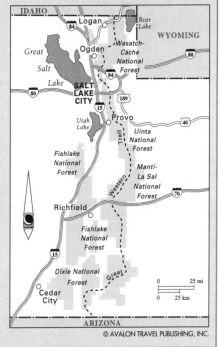

© AVALON TRAVEL PUBLISHING, INC.

in *Utah* and *The Mountain Bike Manual,* both by Dennis Coello, contain general information and details on various rides within the state. As when hiking, always have rain and wind gear and carry plenty of water. Cyclists with a competitive spirit can test themselves in a series of U.S. Cycling Federation–sanctioned races in the northern part of the state; local bicycle shops have schedules of races and training events. Even though Utah has no helmet law for cyclists, don't forget to wear a bicycling helmet.

Information and Services

INFORMATION

General tourist literature and maps are available from the **Utah Travel Council,** Council Hall/Capitol Hill, Salt Lake City, UT 84114-7420, 801/538-1030, fax 801/538-1399, www.utah.com. Utah's many chambers of commerce also have free material and are happy to help with travel suggestions in their areas (see Information in the specific sections of this book). Also listed are national forest offices and other government agencies that have information on outdoor recreation in their areas.

Bureau of Land Management

The state Bureau of Land Management office, on the fourth floor at 324 S. State St., Salt Lake City, UT 84111-2303, 801/539-4001, has general information on BLM areas in Utah and sells recreation and land-status maps of the state.

Utah State Parks and Recreation

Obtain literature and the latest information on all of Utah's state parks from the Utah State Parks and Recreation office, 1594 W. North Temple, Salt Lake City, UT 84114, 801/538-7220, or check http://parks.state.ut.us. If you're planning a lot of state park visits, ask about the $65 annual park pass or the $45–55 annual pass for a specific park (these cover only day-use fees). Reservations for campgrounds and some other services can be made by calling 801/322-3770 or 800/322-3770; a reservation fee of $5 per family or $10 per group applies.

Utah Division of Wildlife Resources

The Utah Division of Wildlife Resources, 1594 W. North Temple, Salt Lake City, UT 84114, 801/538-4700, www.wildlife.utah.gov, issues fishing and hunting licenses and information.

GAY AND LESBIAN TRAVELERS

Gay travelers will find Utah even less welcoming to openly gay people than many of the surrounding western states. There's a gay scene of sorts in Salt Lake City, but very little sign of support elsewhere in the state. In 1996, a bookstore owned by two gay men was burned in southern Utah and the owners were forced to leave town. Not surprisingly, Utah gays and lesbians tend to be extremely discreet.

Unfortunately, there aren't a lot of community resources for gay and lesbian travelers. Salt Lake City's *Pillar* newspaper carries gay news and is a good place to get a flavor for the Utah gay scene. Many of the support groups that do exist in the state are concerned with supporting gay and lesbian Mormons.

TRAVELERS WITH DISABILITIES

Travelers with disabilities will find Utah quite progressive when it comes to accessibility issues, especially in Salt Lake City and the heavily traveled national parks in southern Utah. Most parks offer all-abilities trails, and many hotels advertise their fully accessible facilities. The National Ability Center, based in Park City, provides recreational opportunities for people of all ages and abilities, including a skiing program at nearby Park City Mountain Resort. Check the center's website, www.nationalabilitycenter.org, or call 435/649-3991.

HEALTH AND SAFETY

Utah has one of the lowest crime rates in the United States. Although parts of Salt Lake City look pretty scruffy, there's little reason to fear random violence unless you put yourself in unwise situations.

In emergencies, you can dial 911 in most communities in Utah; otherwise, use the emergency number listed on most telephones or dial a zero for an operator. Hospital emergency rooms offer the quickest help but cost more than a visit to a doctor's office or clinic. Hospital care is very expensive—medical insurance is recommended.

Animal Threats

Probably a greater threat to health are poisonous rattlesnakes and scorpions. When hiking or climbing in desert areas, never put your hand onto a ledge or into a hole that you can't see. Both are perfect lairs for snakes and scorpions. While snakebites are rarely fatal anymore, they're no fun, either. If you are bitten, immobilize the affected area and seek immediate medical attention.

If you do much hiking and biking in the spring, there's a good chance you'll encounter ticks. While ticks in this part of the United States don't usually carry Lyme disease, there is a remote threat of Rocky Mountain spotted fever, spread by the wood tick. If a tick has bitten you, pull it off immediately. Grasp the tick's head parts (as close to your skin as possible) with tweezers and pull slowly and steadily. Do not attempt to remove ticks by burning them or coating them with anything. Removing a tick as quickly as possible greatly reduces your chance of infection.

Utah is home to black bears, which aren't as menacing as their cousins the grizzly bear. However, black bears weigh more than most humans and have far sharper claws and teeth. An encounter with a black bear is rarely fatal, but it's something to be avoided.

If you encounter a bear, give it plenty of room and try not to surprise it. Wearing a fragrance while in bear country isn't a good idea because it attracts bears, as do strong-smelling foods. *Always store food items outside the tent,* and if you're in bear territory, sleep well away from the cooking area. Waking up with a bear clawing at your tent is to be avoided. Hanging

GIARDIA

It can be tough to resist: Picture yourself hiking in a beautiful area by the banks of a crystal-clear stream. The water in your canteen tastes stale, hot, and plastic; the nearby stream looks so inviting that you can't resist a cautious sip. It tastes delicious, clean, and cold, and for the rest of your hike you refresh youself with water straight from the stream.

Days pass and you forget about drinking untreated water. Suddenly one evening after your meal you are terribly sick to your stomach. You develop an awful case of cramps and feel diarrhea beginning to set in. Food poisoning?

Nope—it's the effects of giardia, a protozoan that has become common in even the remotest mountain streams. Giardia is carried in animal or human waste that is deposited or washed into natural waters. When ingested, it begins reproducing, causing a sickness in the host that can become very serious and may not be cured without medical attention.

You can take precautions against giardia with a variety of chemicals and filtering methods or by boiling water before drinking it. The various chemical solutions on the market work in some applications, but because they need to be safe for human consumption they are weak and ineffective against the protozoan in its cyst stage of life (when it encases itself in a hard shell). Filtering may eliminate giardia, but there are other water pests too small to be caught by most filters. The most effective way to eliminate such threats is to boil all suspect water. A few minutes at a rolling boil will kill giardia even in the cyst stage.

food in a bag from a tree is a long-standing and wise precaution. If a bear becomes aggressive, try to drop something that will divert its attention while you flee. If that isn't possible, the next best bet is to curl up into a ball, clasp your hands behind your neck, and play dead, even if the bear begins to bat you around. Taking precautions and having respect for bears will ensure not only your continued existence, but theirs as well.

In recent years, as humans have increasingly moved into the mountain lions' habitat (and as their numbers have increased), they have become a threat to humans, especially small children. Never leave children unattended in forests and never allow them to lag far behind on a family hike. Nearly every summer newspapers in the western states carry tragic stories of children stalked and killed by mountain lions. Safety is in numbers.

Hypothermia

The greatest danger outdoors is one that can sneak up and kill with very little warning. Hypothermia—a lowering of the body's temperature below 95°F—causes disorientation, uncontrollable shivering, slurred speech, and drowsiness. The victim may not even realize what's wrong. Unless corrective action is taken immediately, hypothermia can lead to death. This is why hikers should travel with companions and always carry wind and rain protection. Space blankets are lightweight and cheap and offer protection against the cold in emergencies. Remember that temperatures can plummet rapidly in Utah's dry climate—a drop of 40°F between day and night is common. Be especially careful at high elevations, where summer sunshine can quickly change into freezing rain or a blizzard. Simply falling into a mountain stream while fishing can also lead to hypothermia and death unless proper action is taken. If you're cold and tired, don't waste time! Seek shelter and build a fire, change into dry clothes, and drink warm liquids. If a victim isn't fully conscious, warm him or her by skin-to-skin contact in a sleeping bag. Try to keep the victim awake and offer plenty of warm liquids.

Hantavirus

Hantavirus is an infectious disease agent first isolated during the Korean War and then discovered in the Americas in 1993 by a task force of scientists in New Mexico. This disease agent occurs naturally throughout most of North and South America, especially in dry desert conditions. The infectious agent is airborne, and in the absence of prompt medical attention, its infections are usually fatal. This disease is called hantavirus pulmonary syndrome (HPS). It can affect anyone, but given some fundamental knowledge, it can also be very easy to prevent.

The natural host of the hantavirus appears to be rodents, especially mice and rats. The virus is not usually transmitted directly from rodents to humans; rather, the rodents shed hantavirus particles in their saliva, urine, and droppings. Humans usually contract HPS by inhaling particles that are infected with the hantavirus. The virus becomes airborne when the particles dry out and get stirred into the air (especially from sweeping a floor or shaking a rug). Humans then inhale these particles, which leads to the infection.

Since transmission usually occurs through inhalation, it is easiest for a human being to contract hantavirus within a contained environment, where the virus-infected particles are not thoroughly dispersed. Being in a small building, a crawl space, or a barn where rodents can be found poses elevated risks for contracting the infection. Also be wary of dusty caves where there is an accumulation of rat droppings. Rodents can thrive in such places, especially in cold weather. The gathering dust only increases the infectiousness of the disease.

Simply traveling to a place where the hantavirus is known to occur is not considered a risk factor. Camping, hiking, and other outdoor activities also pose low risks, especially if steps are taken to reduce rodent contact.

The very first symptoms can occur anywhere between five days and three weeks after infection. They almost always include fever, fatigue, and aching muscles (usually in the back, shoulders, and/or thighs) and other flu-like conditions. Other early symptoms may include headaches, dizziness, chills, and abdominal discomfort (such as vomiting, nausea, and/or diarrhea). These are shortly followed by intense coughing and shortness of breath. If you have these symptoms, seek medical help immediately. Untreated infections of hantavirus are almost always fatal.

The Sun and Heat

Utah in summer is a very hot place. Be sure to use sunscreen, or else you risk having a very uncomfortable vacation. Heat exhaustion can also be a problem if you're hiking in the hot sun. Drink plenty of water; in midsummer, try to get an early start if you're hiking in full sun.

Getting Lost

Part of the attraction of Utah's vast wilderness backcountry is its remoteness. And if you're hiking in the canyon country in the southern part of the state, you'll spend most of your time hiking at the bottom of narrow and twisting canyons. It's easy to get lost, or at least disoriented! Always carry adequate and up-to-date maps and a compass—and you need know how to use them if you're heading off into the backcountry. Always plan a route. Planning usually saves time and effort. Tell someone (like a family member or a ranger) where you are going and when you'll be back, so they know where and when to start looking for you in case you get into trouble. Always take at least one other person with you: *Do not* venture into the desert alone. Parties of four people (or two vehicles) are ideal, because one person can stay with the person in trouble, while the other two escort each other to get help. It's a good idea to carry your cell phone in case you need to make an emergency call or send an email.

Flash Floods

Thunderstorms can wash hikers away and bury them in the canyons and washes of the Southwest. Flash floods can happen almost any time of year but are most prevalent in the summer months. Before entering slot canyon areas like Paria or the Escalante Canyons, check with rangers or local authorities for weather reports. And while you're hiking read and heed the clouds. Many washes and canyons drain large areas, with their headwaters many miles away. The dangerous part is that sometimes you just can't tell what's coming down the wash or canyon because of the vast number of acres that these canyons drain, and because the cliff walls are too high to see out to any storms that may be creating flood potential upstream. At any sign of a threat, get out of the canyon bottom—at least 60 vertical feet up—to avoid water and debris. Since many of these canyons are narrow, there are places where it's not possible to get out of the canyon on short notice. Never drive a vehicle into a flooded wash. Stop and wait for the water to recede, as it usually will within an hour.

MONEY

Prices of all services mentioned in this book were current at press time. You're sure to find seasonal and long-term price changes, so *please,* don't use what's listed here to argue with the staff at a motel, campground, museum, airline, or other office!

Banking

Cash machines or ATMs are available throughout Utah, even in the smallest towns. It's hard to exchange foreign currency or traveler's checks outside of central Salt Lake City, so foreign travelers should exchange all they'll need before setting out for rural parts of the state. Credit cards are generally accepted at most businesses.

Taxes

A 6.25 percent sales tax is added to most transactions on goods, food, and services. Additional room taxes are added and vary by community.

Tipping

It's customary to tip 15–20 percent to food and drink servers; tips are almost never automatically added to the bill. Taxi drivers receive a 10–15 percent gratuity; bellhops get at least $1 a bag.

TIME ZONES

The state is in the mountain time zone and goes on daylight saving time (advanced one hour) May–October. Nevada is in the Pacific time zone (one hour earlier); all other bordering states are in the mountain time zone. An odd exception is Arizona, which stays on mountain standard time all year (except for the Navajo Reservation, which goes on daylight saving time to keep up with its Utah and New Mexico sections).

The biggest surprise to many travelers will be that nearly all businesses close on Sunday in Utah.

COMMUNICATIONS

Normal post office hours are 8:30 A.M.–5 P.M. Monday–Friday and sometimes 8:30 A.M.– noon Saturday. U.S. post offices sell stamps and postal money orders. Overnight express service is also available.

Utah has two area codes: 801 is the code for the greater Salt Lake City area, which includes suburbs as far south as Provo and as far north as Ogden. The rest of the state has the area code 435.

Toll-free numbers in the United States have an 800, 888, 877, or 866 area code. To obtain directory assistance, dial 411. In rural areas, you may need to dial the state area code, then 555-1212. Many airlines and motel chains offer toll-free numbers; dial 800/555-1212 for toll-free information.

The cost of a call from a pay phone is usually $.50. Phones that accept prepaid phone cards are only dependably available in the Salt Lake/Park City area.

BUSINESS HOURS

In Utah, most commercial businesses are open 9 A.M.–6 P.M. Monday–Saturday. The biggest surprise to many travelers will be that nearly all businesses—and almost certainly those away from Salt Lake City, big recreational hubs, and the national parks—close on Sunday in Utah. *Again, almost all businesses in Utah, including*

restaurants, are closed on Sunday. This includes local public transportation. Even in Salt Lake City it can be difficult to find a place to eat on Sunday; even fast-food restaurants are closed. Imagine how difficult it might be to find a bite to eat in— say—Monticello. If you're traveling outside the Wasatch Front on Sunday, ask your motel clerk if you'll be able to find a meal at your intended destination. Usually some gas stations along the interstates are open on Sunday, but in out-of-the-way places it's not guaranteed, so be sure to fill up on Saturday. Plan well ahead; it's easy to get stranded, hungry, and disappointed.

Note that many museums, recreation areas, and other tourist attractions close on Thanksgiving, Christmas, New Year's, and other holidays. These closings are not always mentioned in the text, so call ahead to check.

DRIVING HAZARDS

Summer heat in the desert puts an extra strain on both cars and drivers. It's worth double-checking your vehicle's cooling system, engine oil, transmission fluid, fan belts, and tires to make sure they are in top condition. Carry several gallons of water in case of a breakdown or radiator trouble. Never leave children or pets in a parked car during warm weather—temperatures inside can cause fatal heatstroke in minutes.

At times the desert has *too much* water, when late-summer storms frequently flood low spots in the road. Wait for the water level to subside before crossing.

Dust storms can completely block visibility but tend to be short-lived. During such storms, pull completely off the road, stop, and turn off your lights so as not to confuse other drivers.

Radio stations carry frequent weather updates when weather hazards exist. Continuous weather forecasts can be received on a VHF radio (162.4 or 162.55 MHz) in the Salt Lake City area (Wasatch Front), Logan (Cache Valley), Vernal (Uinta Basin), Cedar City, Glen

FESTIVALS AND EVENTS

Utah has a full schedule of rodeos, parades, art festivals, historical celebrations, gem and mineral shows, and sporting events. Stop at a tourist office or chamber of commerce to see what's coming up. The offices should also have the annual *Utah! Travel Guide,* which lists major events.

Utah's biggest summer event is **Pioneer Day,** July 24, with parades and fireworks in almost every Utah community.

JANUARY
Park City, Sundance Film Festival

FEBRUARY
Park City, Snow Sculpture Winterfest

MARCH
Brian Head, Spring Carnival
Park City, National Freestyle Ski Jumping Championships

APRIL
Ogden, Mountain Man Rendezvous

MAY
Green Valley, Green Valley–Moab Friendship Cruise
Kanab, Greyhound Gathering
Moab, Moab Arts Festival
Ogden, Taste of Ogden
Promontory, Golden Spike National Historic Site Re-enactment Event

JUNE
Cedar City, Utah Shakespearean Festival (through September)
Manti, Mormon Miracle Pageant
Price, Black Diamond Stampede PRCA Rodeo
Salt Lake City, Utah Art Festival

JULY
Deer Valley, Utah Symphony Summer Concert Series
Logan, Utah Festival Opera
Ogden, Street Festival
Vernal, Dinosaur Days

AUGUST
Bonneville Salt Flats, Speed Week
Park City, Park City Arts Festival
Wellsville, Festival of the American West

SEPTEMBER
Brigham City, Peach Days Festival
Salt Lake City, Utah State Fair
Springdale, Southern Utah Folklife Festival

OCTOBER
Moab, Canyonlands Fat Tire Mountain Bike Festival
St. George, Huntsman World Senior Games

NOVEMBER
Cedar City, Iron Mission Days

DECEMBER
Logan/Hardware Ranch, Elk Feeding

Canyon National Recreation Area, and Las Vegas, Nevada, areas.

If stranded, either on the desert or in the mountains, stay with your vehicle unless you're *positive* of where to go for help, then leave a note explaining your route and departure time. Airplanes can easily spot a stranded car (tie a piece of cloth to your antenna), but a person walking is more difficult to see. It's best to carry emergency supplies: blankets or sleeping bags, first-aid kit, tools, jumper cables, shovel, traction

mats or chains, flashlight, rain gear, water, food, and a can opener.

MAPS

The Utah Department of Transportation prints and distributes a free, regularly updated map of Utah. Ask for it when you call for information or when you stop at a visitors' information office. If you're planning on extensive backcountry exploration, be sure to ask locally about conditions.

Backcountry enthusiasts or back-road explorers should also pick up Benchmark Maps' *Utah Road and Recreation Atlas*.

ELECTRICITY

In the United States, the electrical current functions on 110 volts, 60 cycles of alternating current (AC). Plugs have either two flat or two-flat-plus-one-round prongs. Older homes and hotels may only have two-prong outlets, and you may well be traveling with computers or appliances that have three-prong plugs. Ask your hotel manager for an adapter; you may need to buy a three-prong adapter, but the cost is small.

Salt Lake City

In 1847 the Mormon prophet Brigham Young proclaimed this site the "right place" for a new settlement. Today, many residents and visitors would still agree. Modern Salt Lake City offers an appealing mix of cultural activities, historic sites, varied architecture, shopping, sophisticated hotels, and elegant restaurants. About 180,000 citizens live in the city, making it by far the largest and most important urban center in Utah, while over one million people reside close by in sprawling suburbs.

By far the most popular tourist site in Salt Lake City is Temple Square, the spiritual center of the Mormon Church. You could easily spend a day just visiting the church's museums, religious and historical sites, and administrative buildings. Utah's political life centers on the imposing capitol, which overlooks the city from a hill just north of downtown. The University of Utah serves a major role in education and research from its 1,500-acre campus in the foothills east of the city. Another high point of any visit to Salt Lake City should be a tour of the city's historic architecture. The early Mormons' pride in their City of Zion is clearly seen in the old residential districts, with their beautiful Victorian mansions, and the downtown's ornate storefronts and civic structures. Few cities in the West retain such a wealth of period architecture.

Once a prosperous though inward-looking trade center for local farmers and ranchers—and a virtual theocracy—Salt Lake City in the last 50 years has emerged from its isolation to join the ranks of the leading cities of the American

Salt Lake City skyline

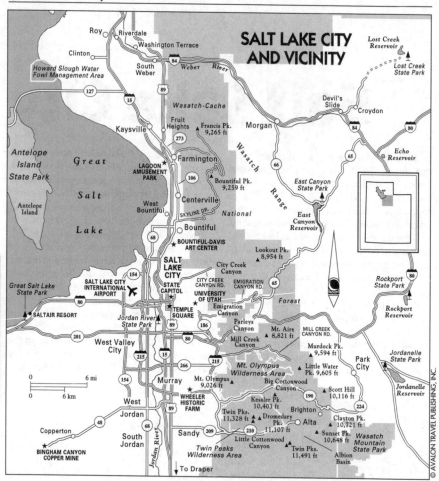

SALT LAKE CITY

West. A measure of the city's new prestige is the fact that Salt Lake City hosted the 2002 Winter Olympics, the largest city ever to have hosted the winter games. The city spared no expense or trouble to ready itself—construction cranes dominated the skyline, and entire freeways were rebuilt to accommodate the crowds. Post-Olympics, the infrastructure now seems over-built, with vacant storefronts and closed restaurants attesting to the boom-and-bust economics of Olympic fever. However, Salt Lake and its surrounding ski and winter recreation centers now seem a relatively good value for Olympic-level snow sports, while its hotels and restaurants frequently offer exceptional deals on quality lodging and food.

THE SETTING

Salt Lake City lies on the broad valley floor and terraces once occupied by prehistoric Lake Bonneville. The Great Salt Lake, the largest remnant of that ancient inland sea, lies just northwest of the city. The Wasatch Range rises immediately to

SALT LAKE CITY HIGHLIGHTS

Temple Square historic sites
Historic Mormon architecture
State Capitol tours
Red Butte Garden and Arboretum
Free summer concerts
Hiking City Creek Canyon
Salt Lake Farmers Market at Pioneer Park
Fine dining that explores regional Rocky
   Mountain cuisine
Local brewpubs

the east; these rugged mountains, with many peaks exceeding 11,000 feet, are cut by steep canyons whose streams provide the area's drinking and irrigation water. In minutes from downtown you can be skiing on some of the world's best powder in winter, or hiking among wildflowers in summer. On the other side of the valley, to the west, Lewiston Peak (elev. 10,626 feet) crowns the Oquirrh Mountains.

ORIENTATION

The indisputable center of Salt Lake City is Temple Square, which sits at the north end of downtown. The Salt Palace Convention Center is south and west one block, and three blocks to the west is Delta Center, home of the National Basketball Association's Utah Jazz. The principle downtown retail core extends south of Temple Square along South Temple, Main, and State Streets. The handsome late-19th-century business precinct, called the Exchange District, sits at the corner of Main and 400 South Streets.

Dominating the skyline north of downtown is the Utah State Capitol; to the east, between downtown and the Wasatch Front, is the University of Utah. Most of the city's residential areas spread to the south in the wide valley of the Jordan River. West of the city lie the airport and the southern shores of the Great Salt Lake.

Getting Around

Although Salt Lake City's street system is the

same as many other towns founded by Mormon settlers, it can be confusing to first-time visitors—mostly due to the scale of the city. Temple Square is the center of the city's address numbering grid. North, South, and West Temple are the streets that run along respective sides of the square, and Main Street flows along the east side; these streets effectively divide the city into quadrants. All further streets are numbered. For instance, West Temple is 100 West, then comes 200 West, and so on. One block south of South Temple is 100 South, 200 South, and so on (300 South is also called Broadway, by the way). In conversation many people use the shorthand "4th South," "3rd West," and so on to indicate 400 South or 300 West.

While this street numbering system is a picture of precision, it's also confusing at first. For instance, all addresses have four parts. When you see the address 436 North 100 West, for instance, the system tells you that the address will be found four blocks north of North Temple, on 100 West. One rule of thumb is to remember that the last two segments of an address (300 South, 500 East, 2300 West) are the street's actual name—the equivalent of a single street signifier such as Oak Street or Front Street.

To add more confusion, there are several exceptions to the general rule. The one most likely to affect travelers involves the area just east of the capitol and north of South Temple, called The Avenues. This area was plotted by the city's non-Mormon population and is an island of addresses that follow their own numbering system. If you see an address for a numbered avenue (Fourth Avenue, for instance) or on a letter street (J Street), then you know you are talking about The Avenues.

Blocks are very large in Salt Lake City: Brigham Young laid them out to resemble the heavenly City of Zion, which had been revealed to him in visions. At a full 10 acres each, each side of a block is 780 feet long! Streets are also Zion-sized: there's 132 feet between blocks—usually enough for four lanes of traffic and two parking strips. When making appointments or hotel reservations, remember that just six blocks make up a mile in Salt Lake City. It will take longer than you

Great

Salt

Lake

Wasatch-

Cache

National

Forest

BOUNTIFUL-DAVIS
ART CENTER

WOOD
CROSS

BOUNTIFUL

NORTH
SALT LAKE

ORCHARD DR.

SALT LAKE CITY

0   2 mi

0   2 km

SEE DOWNTOWN
SALT LAKE CITY
MAPS

Wasatch-

Cache

15

SEE
"UNIVERSITY OF UTAH
AND VICINITY" MAP

National

SALT LAKE CITY
INTERNATIONAL
AIRPORT

STATE
CAPITOL

S. TEMPLE ST.

UNIVERSITY
OF UTAH

Forest

N. TEMPLE ST.

TEMPLE
SQUARE

S.   ST.

"This is the Place"
State Park

400

172

154

Jordan River
State Park

LIBERTY
PARK

INTERNATIONAL
PEACE GARDENS

1300   S.   ST.

HOGLE
ZOO

186

2100   S.   ST.

BANGERTER HWY.

215

89   71

W.   ST.

WESTMINSTER
COLLEGE

80

SOUTH
SALT
LAKE

15

80

3500   S.   ST.

3200   ST.

1700

171

3300   S.   ST.

195

WEST
VALLEY

3900   S.   ST.

E.   ST.

700

181

4500   S.   ST.

2300   ST.

4700   S.   ST.

266

266

215

5400   S.   ST.

Mount

TAYLORSVILLE

173

STATE   ST.

MURRAY

VAN WINKLE EXPWY.

Olympus

Wilderness

Area

SALT LAKE CITY
MUNICIPAL
AIRPORT

68

WHEELER
HISTORIC FARM

215

7000   S.   ST.

7800   S.   ST.

48

anticipate to get around on foot. Travelers from outside of Utah will also marvel at the audacity with which local drivers make U-turns in the middle of streets. It's a freedom you have if streets are all a divinely inspired eight rods across!

CLIMATE

The city experiences a full range of seasons at its 4,300-foot elevation. Rapidly moving storms can bring rain or snow one day and sunshine the next. Average temperatures range from highs in the upper 30s in January to the lower 100s in July. Total precipitation averages 15.3 inches for the year. Most of the winter moisture arrives as snow; average annual snowfall is 54 inches in town and considerably more in the mountains.

HISTORY

The Vision

Salt Lake City began as a dream—a utopia in which the persecuted Latter-day Saints would have the freedom to create a Kingdom of God on earth. Their prophet, Brigham Young, led the first group of 143 men, three women, and two children to the valley of the Great Salt Lake in July 1847. The bleak valley, covered with sagebrush and inhabited mainly by lizards, could best be described as "the land nobody wanted." Many Mormon settlers wanted to continue under Young's leadership to the rich lands of California. But Young saw the value in staying: He had declared that the Kingdom of God should be independent of gentiles, and this land's remoteness would protect them from enemies.

Settlement

The pioneers put their doubts aside and set to work digging irrigation canals, planting crops, constructing a small fort, and laying out a city as nearly 2,000 more immigrants arrived that first summer.

Through trial and error, farmers learned techniques of irrigating and farming the desert land. Then, in 1848, disaster struck. A plague of "crickets" (actually a flightless grasshopper, *Anabrus simplex*) descended from the hills to the east and began devouring the crops, nearly ending chances for the community's survival. But flocks of California seagulls appeared out of the west to feed on the insects. Considered a miracle by the Mormons, the seagull intervention saved part of the crops and gave the pioneers hope that life in the Great Salt Lake Valley would eventually be fruitful.

Meanwhile, the city continued to grow. Immigrants from Europe and the eastern United States poured in, many under the sponsorship of the Perpetual Emigrating Fund Company. Tanneries, flour mills, blacksmith shops, stores, and other enterprises developed under church direction. Beautiful residential neighborhoods sprang up, reflecting both the pride of craftsmanship and the sense of stability encouraged by the church. Workers commenced to raise the temple, the tabernacle, and the other religious structures that still dominate the area around Temple Square. Colonization of the surrounding country proceeded at a rapid pace.

As the Mormons' earthly City of Zion, Salt Lake City came close to its goal of being a community devoted to God. Nearly all aspects of political, economic, and family life came under the influence of the church during the first 20 years. Of all the utopian social experiments ever tried in the United States, the Mormon settlements at Salt Lake have had the greatest and most lasting success.

The "Mormon War"

Even in distant Utah, the Mormons continued to have antagonistic relations with the U.S. government. Utah became a territory in 1850, but instead of incorporating American democratic institutions as envisioned by Congress, the Mormon leadership arranged to hand the civil territorial titles to the LDS priesthood; church president Brigham Young was named territorial governor. The U.S. government, already chafing at the Utah Territory's refusal to outlaw polygamy, dismissed the territorial government as a theocracy. President James Buchanan, considering these acts rebellion, in 1857 dispatched the largest peacetime army ever assembled in the United States to settle the score.

The "Mormon War" never really materialized. Mormon "guerrillas" managed to delay the troops by driving off livestock and cutting supply lines. Meanwhile, nearly the entire population of Salt Lake City staged an orderly evacuation southward. When columns of soldiers marched down the deserted streets in June 1858, they found only a handful of men remaining, standing ready to torch the houses and buildings in case the U.S. Army chose to occupy the city. Level heads prevailed, and residents soon returned.

Coming of the Gentiles

The isolation that had shielded Salt Lake City from outside influence began to fade around 1870. The "Mormon War" had brought U.S. forts to the Salt Lake Valley; off-duty soldiers prospected for gold and found enough of it to encourage a mini-gold rush. Completion of the transcontinental railroad through Utah in 1869 encouraged non-Mormons to seek opportunity in the territory.

Even in this new social climate, Mormons and gentiles remained largely segregated. Each group developed its own social and political organizations and its own schools. Political life had been very dull during the first decades, when only a single set of church-appointed candidates appeared on the ballots. Voters had the option of voting "no," but they knew that their numbered ballots could be traced. The church discouraged political parties, believing they would lead to corruption and disharmony, and that civil government should be an arm of the church.

With the rising power of the gentile population in the 1870s, the church founded the People's Party to counter the anti-church Liberal Party. Salt Lake City's two major newspapers date from this time, with the *Deseret News* stating Mormon views and the *Salt Lake Tribune* representing the gentiles. Such fine shades of the political spectrum as the Republican or Democratic Party rarely entered the picture. The Mormons steadily lost control of their city; from a 93 percent majority population in 1867, they slipped to only 50 percent by 1891. In 1889 the first non-Mormons were elected to city offices.

The church leadership lost its grasp on Salt Lake City during the legal battles over polygamy in the 1880s. Embarking on a new course, the church ended the practice of multiple marriages, dissolved its People's Party, and sold off most of its businesses. Even the famed ZCMI—a Mormon co-op that is thought to be the first department store in America—became a private, profit-making concern. The end of the 19th century saw Salt Lake making the transition from a Mormon village to an American city.

Modern Times

Wealth from successful mining operations fueled much of the development in Salt Lake City's business district, located in the blocks south of Temple Square. As a rule, the blocks nearest the temple had affiliations with the church, while those farther south belonged to non-Mormons. In the early 1900s, skyscrapers began sprouting high above East Temple Street—which was rechristened Main Street. Exchange Place became the non-Mormon financial center.

The Depression was hard on all of rural Utah, as the dust bowl droughts sapped an already precarious water supply. The local economies picked up during World War II, as federal spending began to pour in and military installations took shape in the deserts west of Salt Lake City. Suburban growth began, providing the first exodus from the city's older neighborhoods. By the 1970s, the LDS Church began to spend money on revitalization of the city's downtown core, and the church's renewed focus worked: The city center is graced by a profusion of towering office blocks, busy shoppers, and legions of tourists.

Like any major metropolitan area, Salt Lake City suffers its share of air pollution and traffic congestion. The amount of homelessness and vagrancy will surprise travelers who have overblown expectations of the City of the Saints. (However, SLC is on the whole a very safe city.)

On the brighter side, a new interest in historical conservation has preserved many graceful mansions, ornate churches, and stately early-20th-century office towers. New downtown parks provide open spaces for concerts, lunchtime picnics, and opportunities for getting out into the open air.

The 2002 Olympic Winter Games

In February 2002, Salt Lake City hosted the Winter Olympics. Although many of the signature events took place at the ski resorts of the Wasatch Front, others, such as figure skating and the opening and closing ceremonies, happened in Salt Lake City itself. The Olympic Village was on the University of Utah grounds.

Hosting the Olympic games was an incredibly big deal to the leaders of Salt Lake City, and the city had a lot of pride and self-image invested in the games' success. Of course, Salt Lake wanted to throw a good party to showcase the athletes and the games themselves, but the drive to succeed drew at least part of its vigor from other motivations. After years of struggling with the reputation of being the insular capital city of Mormonism—a provincial and backward city run as a wholly owned fiefdom of the church elders—Salt Lake City was anxious to reestablish itself as a sparkling, thriving urban center of the New West—a "world-class city," to borrow an oft-quoted phrase used by many of Salt Lake's boosters.

However, the city may have wanted the games just a little too much. In late 1998, a Swiss member of the International Olympic Committee (IOC) alleged that the selection of Salt Lake City as the venue for the 2002 Winter Games was accompanied by pervasive bribery and vote-buying on the part of the Salt Lake Olympic Bid Committee (the SLOC). Internal investigations by the IOC, the U.S. Olympic Committee, and the SLOC ensued. These inquiries and media investigations revealed a wide assortment of payoff schemes that funneled money, scholarships, real estate, and other perquisites from the SLOC to influential members of the IOC. While members of the IOC denied that the payments and gifts—reportedly totaling more than $1 million—influenced their vote, and members of the SLOC stated that the payments were not meant to buy the votes of the committee, no one denies that the payments were made.

In July 2000, two members of the SLOC were indicted on federal conspiracy, racketeering, and fraud charges, but in the end, the games were highly successful and will be remembered as much for French ice-skating judges and post–September 11 security concerns as for the slippery payoffs to Olympic officials by Utah politicians. In fact, high-ranking officials in the SLOC avoided indictments and lived to play another day: SLOC president Mitt Romney was elected governor of Massachusetts in 2002.

Sights

TEMPLE SQUARE AND MORMON HISTORIC SITES

Easily Salt Lake City's most famous attraction, this complex has a special meaning for Mormons: this is the Mecca or the Vatican of the Church of Jesus Christ of Latter-day Saints. Brigham Young chose this site for Temple Square in July 1847, just four days after arriving in the valley. Nearby, Young built his private residences; the tabernacle, museums, and a host of other buildings that play a role in LDS Church administration also line the streets around Temple Square. You're welcome to visit most of these buildings, the Assembly Hall, exhibits in the North and South Visitors Centers, and historic monuments—all of which provide an excellent introduction to the LDS religion and Utah's early history.

Enthusiastic guides offer several tours of Temple Square, which covers an entire block in the heart of the city. A 15-foot wall surrounds the square's 10 acres; you can enter through wrought-iron gates on the south, west, and north sides. Temple Square is open daily 9 A.M.–9 P.M. All tours, exhibits, and concerts are free. Foreign-language tours are available, too—ask at the North Visitor Center. Smoking is prohibited on the grounds.

Musical Concerts: Temple Square is the site for an ongoing series of free musical concerts. Organists demonstrate the sounds and versatility

SALT LAKE CITY

DOWNTOWN SALT LAKE CITY SIGHTS

0   0.2 mi
0   0.2 km

CHILDRENS MUSEUM OF UTAH

VICTORY RD.
WALL ST.
CENTER ST.
CAPITOL ST.
COLUMBUS ST.
DESOTO ST.
CORTEZ ST.
EAST CAPITOL BLVD.

City Canyon (Memory Grove Park)

600 N. ST.
500 N. ST.
400 N. ST.
300 N. ST.
200 N. ST.
N. TEMPLE ST.

13TH AVE.
12TH AVE.
11TH AVE.
10TH AVE.
9TH AVE.
8TH AVE.
7TH AVE.
6TH AVE.
5TH AVE.
4TH AVE.
3RD AVE.
2ND AVE.
1ST AVE.

THE AVENUES DISTRICT

MARMALADE HISTORIC DISTRICT

STATE CAPITOL BUILDING

UTAH HERITAGE FOUNDATION

PIONEER MEMORIAL MUSEUM

UTAH TRAVEL COUNCIL (COUNCIL HALL)

CONFERENCE CENTER

MUSEUM OF CHURCH HISTORY AND ART

LDS OFFICE BUILDING

BRIGHAM YOUNG CEMETERY

TRIAD CENTER

FAMILY HISTORY LIBRARY

TEMPLE SQUARE

JOSEPH SMITH MEMORIAL BUILDING

BEEHIVE HOUSE TEMPLE

FIRST PRESBYTERIAN CHURCH

KEARNS MANSION

UNION PACIFIC DEPOT

GREYHOUND BUS STATION

TRAX LIGHT RAIL LINE

ABRAVANEL SYMPHONY HALL

BRIGHAM YOUNG MONUMENT

CATHEDRAL OF THE MADELEINE

THE GATEWAY

DELTA CENTER

SALT LAKE ART CENTER/ VISITORS CENTER

CROSSROADS PLAZA SHOPPING CENTER

SOCIAL HALL

CLARK PLANETARIUM

SALT PALACE CONVENTION CENTER

ZCMI SHOPPING CENTER

PROMISED VALLEY PLAYHOUSE

CAPITOL THEATER

UTAH STATE HISTORY MUSEUM (DENVER AND RIO GRANDE DEPOT)

WAGNER PERFORMING ARTS CENTER

PERRY HALL COMPLEX

Pioneer Park

EXCHANGE PLACE HISTORIC DISTRICT

To the University of Utah

CITY AND COUNTY BUILDING

CITY LIBRARY

TROLLEY CORNERS

TROLLEY SQUARE

TRAX LIGHT RAIL LINE

© AVALON TRAVEL PUBLISHING, INC.

of the tabernacle's famous instrument in half-hour recitals. These are held Monday–Saturday at noon and 2 P.M. and on Sunday at 2 P.M. in the summer months. The rest of the year, the recitals are at noon only Monday–Saturday.

The renowned Tabernacle Choir sings on Sunday mornings at 9:30 A.M. (you must be in your seat by 9:15 A.M. and remain seated during the entire performance). You can also hear the choir during rehearsals 8–9:30 P.M. on Thursday evenings; you can come and go during the rehearsals. Occasionally, when the choir is on tour, a youth choir, youth symphony, or other group replaces it. A concert series presents programs featuring soloists, small ensembles, or full orchestras on Friday and Saturday evenings throughout the year in Assembly Hall or in the tabernacle. Except for a few special events, you won't need tickets to attend Temple Square performances. For additional activities check the bulletin boards as you enter Temple Square, ask any of the guides, or call 801/240-2534 or 800/537-9703 for programs and times.

Temple Square Historical Tour: Guides greet you at the gates of the square and offer an introduction to Salt Lake City's pioneers, the temple, tabernacle, Assembly Hall, and historic monuments. The free 40-minute tours begin every 10 minutes during the summer season and every 15 minutes the rest of the year; hours are usually 9 A.M.–9 P.M. Custom group tours can be scheduled in advance. Points of interest, which you may also visit on your own, include the Seagull Monument (commemorating the seagulls that devoured the plague of "crickets" in 1848); a bell from the abandoned Nauvoo Temple; sculptures of Christ, church leaders, and handcart pioneers; an astronomy observation site; and a meridian marker (outside the walls at Main and South Temple Streets) from which surveyors mapped out Utah. Although the tour leaders don't normally proselytize, the tours do give the guides a chance to witness their faith.

The Salt Lake Temple

Mormons believe that they must have temples within which to hold sacred rites and fulfill God's commandments. According to the LDS faith, baptisms, marriages, and family-sealing ceremonies that take place inside a temple will last beyond death and into eternity (prior to entering a temple, members prepare for a spiritual experience

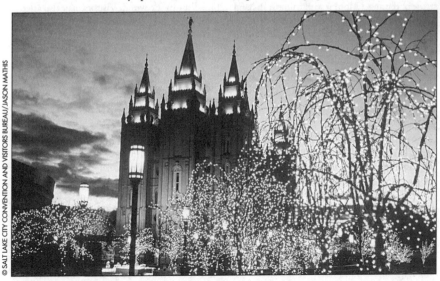

© SALT LAKE CITY CONVENTION AND VISITORS BUREAU/JASON MATHIS

the Salt Lake City Temple

by dressing in white clothing, which represents purity). The temple is used only for these special functions; normal Sunday services take place in local stake or ward buildings—in fact, the temple is closed on Sunday.

Only LDS members who meet church requirements of good standing may enter the sacred temple itself; others can learn about temple activities and see photos of interior rooms at the South Visitor Center. Non-Mormons are not allowed to enter the temple or the grounds. However, you can get a good look at the temple's east facade from the Main Street gates.

The plan for Salt Lake City's temple came first as a vision to Brigham Young when he still lived in Illinois. Later, Young's concept became a reality with help from church architect Truman O. Angell; construction began in 1853. Workers chiseled granite blocks from Little Cottonwood Canyon, 20 miles southeast of the city, then hauled them by oxen and later by railroad for final shaping at the temple site. The foundation alone required 7,478 tons of stone. Walls measure nine feet thick at the base and taper to six feet on the second story. The tallest of the six slender spires stands 210 feet and is topped by a glittering statue of the angel Moroni with trumpet in hand. The 12.5-foot statue is made of hammered copper covered with gold leaf. As with all Mormon temples, the interior was open to the public for a short time after completion. Dedication took place on April 6, 1893—40 years to the day after work began.

The Tabernacle

Pioneers labored from 1863 to 1867 to construct this unique, dome-shaped building. Brigham Young envisioned a meeting hall capable of holding thousands of people in an interior free of obstructing structural supports. His design, drawn by bridge-builder Henry Grow, took shape in massive latticed wooden beams resting on 44 supports of red sandstone. Because Utah lacked many common building supplies, the workers often had to make substitutions. Wooden pegs and rawhide strips hold the structure together. The large organ pipes resemble metal, balcony pillars appear to be marble, and the benches look

like oak, yet all are pine wood painted to simulate these materials.

The tabernacle has become known for its phenomenal acoustics, due to its smooth arched ceiling, and its massive pipe organ is regarded as one of the finest ever built. From 700 pipes when constructed in 1867, the organ has grown to about 12,000 pipes, five manuals, and one pedal keyboard. Daily recitals at noon and 2 P.M. Monday–Saturday and at 2 P.M. Sunday in summer (the rest of the year Monday –Saturday at noon only) demonstrate the instrument's capabilities. Temple Square tours include a stop in the tabernacle for a short presentation on the history of the building; an acoustic demonstration shows that a dropped pin can be heard even in the back rows—170 feet away!

Important church conferences take place in the tabernacle every spring and autumn, but the seating capacity of about 6,500—considered huge when it was built—is now far too small, despite the addition of a balcony. The renowned Mormon Tabernacle Choir, 320 voices strong, sings on Sunday mornings over national radio (CBS) and regional TV networks. The choir's radio broadcast, which dates back to 1929, is the longest-running broadcast in the world. Visitors may also attend choir rehearsals Thursday evenings at 8 P.M. or the broadcast performance on Sunday at 9:30 A.M. (be seated by 9:15 A.M.); both are free. Families with infants can sit in a glassed-in room at the rear without fear of disturbing other listeners. For information on performances in the tabernacle, call 800/537-9703.

Assembly Hall

Thrifty craftspeople built this smaller, Gothic Revival structure in 1877–1882 using granite left over from the temple construction. The truncated spires, reaching as high as 130 feet, once functioned as chimneys. Inside the hall, there's seating for 1,500 people and a choir of 100. The baroque-style organ, installed in 1983, has 3,500 pipes and three manuals; of particular note are the organ's horizontal pipes, called trumpets. Initially, the Salt Lake Stake Congregation met here; now the building serves as a concert hall and hosts church functions.

SALT LAKE CITY FOR KIDS

Children's Museum of Utah

None of the exhibits at this children's favorite display Do Not Touch signs; in fact, many of the displays are hands-on. Kids get to explore by "excavating" a saber-toothed tiger skeleton, piloting a 727 jet trainer, implanting an artificial heart in a dummy, creating art projects, and using computer exhibits. Handicap-awareness simulations allow youngsters to experience firsthand what it might feel like to be blind or to use a wheelchair. The museum, north of downtown at 840 North 300 West (U.S. 89), 801/328-3383, is open 10 A.M.–5 P.M. Monday–Saturday (until 8 P.M. on Friday). Admission is $4, free for children under 3. The adjacent city park offers picnic tables, a playground, and tennis courts.

Lagoon Amusement Park and Pioneer Village

History, recreation, and thrilling rides come together at this attractively landscaped park 16 miles north of Salt Lake City, 801/451-8000 or 800/748-5246. Lagoon traces its own history back to 1887, when bathers came to Lake Park on the shores of the Great Salt Lake, two miles west of its present location. The vast Lagoon Amusement Park area includes roller coaster rides, a giant Ferris wheel, and other midway favorites. There are also musical performances. Other things to do include picnicking and playing miniature golf (extra charge). Lagoon A Beach provides thrilling water slides and landscaped pools.

Pioneer Village brings the past to life with authentic 19th-century buildings, stagecoach and steam-train rides, a Ute museum, a carriage museum, a gun collection, and many other exhibits. Wild West shoot-outs take place several times daily. Food booths are scattered throughout the park, or you can dine at the Gaslight Restaurant near the Opera House. Lagoon Amusement Park, Lagoon A Beach, and Pioneer Village open at 11 A.M. Sunday–Friday and 10 A.M. Saturday and close at 11 P.M. or midnight (depending on weather and day of week). The complex is open Saturday and Sunday early April–Memorial Day weekend, daily between Memorial Day and Labor Day weekends, then Saturday and Sunday through September. An all-day ride pass (the best deal, as individual rides cost $3–4) is $30 adults, $25 for children over age 3 and up to 50 inches in height, $16 for children 3 and under, and $18 for seniors. The all-day pass includes Lagoon A Beach privileges. An additional $6 is charged for parking. Take I-15 to the Lagoon exit and follow signs.

Wheeler Historic Farm

Kids enjoy a visit to this working farm to experience the rural life of milking cows, gathering eggs, churning butter, and feeding animals. Hay rides (sleigh rides in winter) take visitors around the farm. Henry and Sariah Wheeler started the farm in 1887 and developed it into a prosperous dairy and ice-making operation. Tour guides take you through the Wheelers' restored Victorian house, built 1896–1898, the first in the county to have an indoor bathroom. Signs on other farm buildings recount their history and use. The "Ice House" now sells crafts and snacks. The Salt Lake County Recreation Department operates the farm and offers special programs for both youngsters and adults; call or write for a schedule: 6351 South 900 East, Salt Lake City, UT 84121, 801/264-2241. There's no admission charge to the farm, but you'll pay for individual activities. A tour costs $2 adults, $1.50 children 3–11 and seniors 65 and up; milking the cow costs just $.50. Though it was once on the outskirts of town, suburbs now surround Wheeler Historic Farm. Open daily 9:30 A.M.–5:30 P.M. in spring and fall, 9:30 A.M.–8 P.M. in summer, and 1–5 P.M. in winter.

North Visitor Center

Wander around on your own or ask the ever-present tour guides for help. Murals on the lower floor depict Old Testament prophets; head upstairs to see paintings of the life of Christ. A spiraling ramp leads to the upper level where *Cristus*, an 11-foot replica of a sculpture by Bertel Thorvaldsen, stands in a circular room whose wall mural depicts the universe. The Resource Center, near the bottom of the ramp, offers touch-screen video programs. Downstairs display areas and theaters have other offerings, including *Legacy*, an hour-long film that tells the story of the Mormon pioneers' westward trek.

South Visitor Center

Two new exhibits cover the building of the Salt Lake Temple and "Strengthening the Family." Exhibits on the main level include paintings of prophets and church history, a baptismal font supported by 12 life-size oxen (representing the 12 tribes of Israel) as used in temples, photos of the Salt Lake Temple interior, and a scale model of Solomon's Temple. Head downstairs to see replicas of the metal plates inscribed with the Book of Mormon, which Mormons believe were revealed to Joseph Smith in 1823. Ancient plates of Old World civilizations and stone boxes from the Americas are exhibited to support the claim that the plates are genuine. LDS literature can be obtained at a desk near the entrance.

Museum of Church History and Art

Brigham Young encouraged the preservation of church history, especially when he saw that Salt Lake City's pioneering era was drawing to a close. The collection of church artifacts, begun by the Deseret Museum in 1869, includes the plow that cut the first furrows in the Salt Lake Valley. Exhibits document each of the past church presidents and religious paintings and sculpture. Perhaps the most striking piece is the gilded 11.5-foot statue of Moroni, which crowned a Washington, D.C., chapel from 1933 to 1976. Temporary exhibits also display Mormon artistry and themes in photography, abstract art, textiles, furniture, and woodworking.

Step outside to see the 1847 log cabin, one of only two surviving from Salt Lake City's beginnings. The interior has been furnished as it might have been during the first winter here. The free Museum of Church History and Art, just west of Temple Square at 45 N. West Temple, 801/240-4615, is open 9 A.M.–9 P.M. Monday–Friday and 10 A.M.–7 P.M. Saturday, Sunday, and holidays April–December and daily 10 A.M.–7 P.M. (until 9 P.M. Monday and Wednesday) January–March.

Family History Library

This building houses the largest collection of genealogical information in the world. Library workers have made extensive travels to many countries to microfilm documents and books. More than 500 employees are assisted by over 400 volunteers to keep track of the records. The LDS Church has gone to this effort to enable members to trace their ancestors, who can then be baptized by proxy. In this way, according to Mormon belief, the ancestors will be sealed in the family and the church for eternity. However, the spirits for whom these baptisms are performed have a choice of accepting or rejecting the baptism.

The library is open to the public. If you'd like to research your family tree, bring what information you have and get the library's *A Guide to Research* booklet. A brief slide presentation explains what types of records are kept and how to get started. Staff will answer questions. In most cases the files won't have information about living persons because of rights to privacy. The church leaves nothing to chance in preserving its genealogical records and history—master copies on microfilm rest in vaults deep within the mountains southeast of Salt Lake City. The Family History Library, just west of Temple Square at 35 N. West Temple, 801/240-2331, opens at 7:30 A.M. Monday–Saturday and closes at 5 P.M. Monday, 10 P.M. Tuesday–Saturday; it's closed Sunday and federal holidays.

Conference Center

Completed in 2000, this block-square, 10-acre building is used both as a performance space and a place of worship. The main auditorium, which seats 21,000, serves as a meeting hall for large LDS assemblies. The building is fronted by white granite. The many-tiered design incorporates four acres of landscaping, with trees, flowers, fountains, and waterfalls. From a distance the building looks like the Hanging Gardens of Babylon. Free tours are offered 9 A.M.–9 P.M.

Brigham Young Monument

This monument stands in the middle of Main between North and South Temple Streets. Brigham Young, in bronze, stands atop a granite pedestal with figures below representing a Native American, a fur trapper, and a pioneer family. Unveiled on July 24, 1897, it celebrates the first 50 years of settlement in Salt Lake City. A plaque lists the names of the first group of 148 Mormon pioneers. The statue is also the originating point for the city's street-numbering system.

© BILL WEIR

The Brigham Young statue welcomes visitors to Temple Square.

Joseph Smith Memorial Building/Hotel Utah

Built of white terra-cotta brick in modern Italian Renaissance style, this building, at 15 E. South Temple, opened in 1911 as a first-class hotel for church and business leaders. However, in 1987 the LDS Church, which owned the hotel, converted it into an office building and a memorial to LDS founding father Joseph Smith. The opulent lobby, with its massive marble columns, chandeliers, and stained-glass ceiling, remains intact; you definitely should walk through the lobby and admire the grand architecture.

On the ground floor the **Family Search Center,** 801/240-4085, has computers available to trace family ancestry; open 8 A.M.–10 P.M. Also on the ground floor is a large-screen theater showing the hour-long film *The Testaments of One Fold and One Shepherd,* which entwines the life of Jesus with contemporary events in ancient America as related in the book of Mormon. Admission is free, but you'll need a ticket for entry (one can be obtained at the information desk at the building's Main Street entrance); call 801/240-0080 for reservations. The 10th floor offers observation areas, the formal **Roof Restaurant,** 801/539-1911, and the less formal **Garden Restaurant** (same phone). The building is open Monday–Saturday but is closed on Sunday except to those attending worship services.

LDS Office Building

Day-to-day running of the massive church organization is centered in the 28-story tower east of Temple Square, at 50 E. North Temple, 801/240-2190. Such a volume of correspondence takes place that the building has its own zip code. Free tours begin in the main lobby and explain a bit about the work here, but the big attraction is a visit to the 26th-floor observation deck. You'll see Temple Square and the whole city spread out below like a map. Weather permitting, the valley, the Great Salt Lake, and the surrounding mountains stand out clearly. Tours last about 30 minutes, depending on how long you want to take in the panorama. The main lobby has some noteworthy artwork, including a giant 66- by 16-foot mural of Christ appearing to his apostles just prior to his ascension. Gardens and fountains grace a small park behind the building. You can take guided tours 9 A.M.–5 P.M. Monday–Friday; the building is closed Sunday and holidays.

Beehive House

This former house of Brigham Young was built in 1854 and occupied by him until his death in 1877. The adobe and brick structure stood out as one of the most ornate houses in early Salt Lake City. Free tours lasting 30–40 minutes take visitors through the house and tell of family life within the walls. The interior has been meticulously restored with many original furnishings. A beehive symbol, representing industry, caps the house and appears in decorative motifs inside. Brigham Young had about 27 wives, but only one stayed in this house at a time; other wives and children lived next door in the Lion House. Downstairs in the main house, Young's children gathered in the sitting room for evenings of prayer, talks, and music. Upstairs, he entertained guests and dignitaries in a lavish reception room called the Long Hall. Other rooms to see include the kitchen, family store, bedrooms, playroom, and the "fairy castle," where small children could peer through a window at grown-ups in the hallway below.

The Beehive House is in the shadow of the LDS Church office building, at 67 E. South Temple, 801/240-2671. Tours leave 9:30 A.M.–4:30 P.M. Monday–Saturday (until 6:30 P.M. Monday–Friday in summer) and 10 A.M.–1 P.M. Sunday; closed on Thanksgiving, Christmas, and New Year's Day; open other holidays but usually only until 1 P.M.

The **Lion House,** next door at 63 E. South Temple, was built in 1855–1856 of stuccoed adobe; a stone lion guards the entrance. Brigham Young used it as a supplementary dwelling for his many wives and their children. Today, the pantry and basement of the building are open to the public as the **Lion House Restaurant.**

Brigham Young Cemetery

Church president, founder of Utah, colonizer, and territorial governor, Brigham Young rests here with five of his wives and his eldest son. Several monuments on the grounds honor the pioneers and Young's family. From State Street

© SALT LAKE CITY CONVENTION AND VISITORS BUREAU/JASON MATHIS

Beehive House

near Beehive House, travel a half-block east on First Avenue.

Eagle Gate

This modern replacement of the original 1859 gate spans State Street just north of South Temple Street. It once marked the entrance to Brigham Young's property, which included City Creek Canyon. The bronze eagle has a 20-foot wingspan and weighs two tons. The present gate, designed by Brigham Young's grandson, architect George Cannon Young, was dedicated in 1963.

OTHER DOWNTOWN SIGHTS

Abravanel Concert Hall

Easily the most striking modern building in Salt Lake City, Abravanel Hall, 123 W. South Temple (next to the Salt Palace), glitters with gold leaf, crystal chandeliers, and more than a mile of brass railing. Careful attention to acoustic design has paid off: the concert hall is one of the best in the world. The Utah Symphony Orchestra inaugurated its new home in 1979 after $12 million and three years of construction. An illuminated fountain flows outside on the plaza during concerts. Call the box office, 801/355-2787, for concert dates.

Salt Lake Art Center

This civic gallery hosts a changing lineup of traveling and thematic exhibits, including displays of painting, photography, sculpture, ceramics, and conceptual art. Diverse art classes and workshops are scheduled along with films, lectures, poetry readings, musical concerts, and theater. A gift shop offers art books, posters, crafts, and artwork. The center, 20 S. West Temple (between Abravanel Concert Hall and the Salt Palace Convention Center), 801/328-4201, is open 10 A.M.–5 P.M. Monday–Saturday (till 9 P.M. Friday) and 1–5 P.M. Sunday; admission is free, but a donation is requested.

Salt Palace Convention Center

This enormous structure, between 200 South and South Temple along West Temple, 801/534-

4777, just keeps getting larger. After its expansion in 2000, the Salt Palace encompasses 370,000 square feet of exhibit space, a 45,000-square-foot ballroom, and 53 individual meeting rooms. Even in the sprawling scale of downtown Salt Lake City, this is a big building. The center also houses the Salt Lake Convention and Visitors Bureau and the **Visitor Information Center,** 90 S. West Temple, 801/521-2822.

Clark Planetarium

This planetarium and science center, in the new Gateway shopping center, 110 South 400 West, 801/456-7827, combines a 3D IMAX theater with a five-story screen plus popular family-oriented science and space exhibits. A highlight is the Hansen Star Theatre, which employs state-of-the-art technology to project a star show on a 360-degree 55-foot dome. Also in the star theater are *Cosmic Light Shows,* which combine computer animation, special effects, and a 12,000-watt digital surround-sound system. The museum exhibit halls are open 9 A.M.–5:15 P.M. and 7–9 P.M. Monday–Saturday and 1–4 P.M. Sunday; free.

Social Hall Heritage Museum

Early settlers built Utah's (and the West's) first theater 1852–1853 under the direction of Brigham Young. Recent excavations have unearthed the foundation and sandstone walls of the venerable building, which was torn down and buried in 1921. The ruins and historic exhibits lie within a glass enclosure south of the old Hansen Planetarium at 39 S. State Street, 801/321-8745. An underground passage connects Social Hall with ZCMI Shopping Center; both are open daily. Free admission.

Utah State Historical Society Museum

The Denver and Rio Grande Railroad built this grand terminal in 1910 while in keen competition with Union Pacific, which kept a depot two blocks away. A series of displays called "Utah at the Crossroads" outlines state history in the museum's spacious lobby. The museum, at the west end of 300 South at 400 West, 801/533-3500, is open 8 A.M.–5 P.M. Monday–Friday; free. The Utah State Historical Society operates a bookstore just off the lobby with an excellent selection of Utah history and travel books. Upstairs, the society offers a research library containing thousands of books and photos about Utah's past.

UTAH STATE CAPITOL AND VICINITY

The State Capitol

Utah's granite capitol occupies a prominent spot on a hill just north of downtown. The architectural style may look familiar; the building was patterned after the national capitol. The interior, with its Ionic columns, is made of polished marble from Georgia. Murals depict early explorers and pioneers; smaller paintings and statues show all of the territorial and state governors and prominent Utah figures of the past. The Gold Room, used for receiving dignitaries, provides a formal setting graced by chandeliers, wall tapestries, elegant furniture, and cherubs on the ceiling. Enter the chambers of the House of Representatives, Senate, and Supreme Court from the mezzanine. Photo exhibits of the state's scenic and historic spots, beehive memorabilia, mining, and agriculture line hallways on the ground floor.

Forty acres of manicured parks and monuments surround the capitol. From the steps leading to the building, you can look out over Salt Lake City and straight down State Street, which runs south about 28 miles without a curve. From near the Mormon Battalion Monument, east of the capitol, steps lead down into a small canyon and **Memory Grove,** another war memorial, and a series of streamside parks.

The Utah State Capitol, 300 North and State Street, 801/538-3000, is open 8 A.M.–8 P.M. daily. Free tours in summer depart every half hour 9 A.M.–4 P.M. Monday–Friday. Meet in front of the large map on the first floor; call 801/538-1563 for tour details. Visitors are welcome to dine at the circular cafeteria (open 7 A.M.–4 P.M. Monday–Friday) behind the capitol. Annual legislative sessions begin in January and last about 45 days.

Pioneer Memorial Museum

Descendants of Utah's Mormon pioneers have packed all four levels of this museum with a huge collection of pioneer artifacts, portraits, and memorabilia that tell the story of the 2,000-mile exodus from Nauvoo, Illinois, to Salt Lake City. A video shown on request introduces the collection.

While some exhibits here are of interest mostly to Mormons (for example, the personal effects of Brigham Young), other displays in the museum's four floors provide insights into the daily life of frontier Utah. The two-story **Carriage House,** connected to the museum by a short tunnel, displays pioneer-era conveyances, including a mule-drawn streetcar, stagecoaches, and the wagon in which Brigham Young is believed to have arrived in the Salt Lake Valley. The Pioneer Memorial Museum, 300 N. Main St. (near the State Capitol), 801/538-1050, is open 9 A.M.–5 P.M. Monday–Saturday and 1–5 P.M. Sunday on Sundays in June, July, and August; closed on major holi-

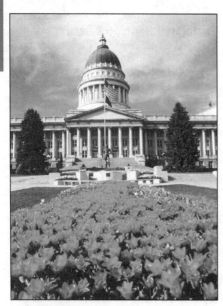

Utah State Capitol

SALT LAKE CITY'S HISTORIC ARCHITECTURE

S alt Lake City contains some of the best-preserved historic architecture in the American West. From the magnificent public buildings to the craftsmanship of humble workers' cottages, the city's structures say a lot about the early citizens' pride in their earthly City of Zion.

The **Utah Heritage Foundation,** located at 355 Quince Street, has information and self-guided tour brochures on Salt Lake City's historic districts. In addition to Temple Square and the State Capitol, any tour of the city's historic architecture should include the following:

South Temple Street was probably the most prestigious street address in all of early Utah. Many religious and business leaders owned stately mansions along South Temple, once known as Brigham Street. (A number of these homes are now B&Bs.) Twin towers and gargoyles embellish the imposing Catholic **Cathedral of the Madeleine,** 331 E. South Temple, 801/328-8941; open daily year-round and for concerts Sunday evenings in spring and summer. Adjacent is the equally impressive **First Presbyterian Church,** 347 E. South Temple. The palatial **Kearns Mansion,** 603 E. South Temple, now serves as the official governor's residence. Thomas Kearns, noted for his silver-mining wealth, became a U.S. senator and publisher of the *Salt Lake Tribune.* The Kearns Mansion is open for free tours Monday–Saturday in summer and on a limited schedule the rest of the year; 801/538-1005.

Just north of South Temple Street is the district known as **The Avenues,** where the majority of Salt Lake City's (SLC's) early Catholics lived. While most of these homes aren't grand mansions, they are excellent examples of Victorian workers' homes. Streets in the **Marmalade District** on the hillside west of the capitol bear the names of fruit trees—hence the term "marmalade." Many residences date from the 19th century. The **McCune Mansion** at 200 N. Main, is one of the city's most eye-catching old houses. The turn-of-the-20th-century turreted structure features a tiled roof and exceptional interior woodwork.

Downtown's grandest building is undoubtedly the **City and County Building,** at 400 South and State Street. This confection of a building resembles a fanciful Scottish castle right out of *Brigadoon* and once served as the Utah State Capitol; it's now the seat of SLC's local government. Across the street at Main and 400 South is the **Exchange District,** a clutch of grandly handsome office towers that served as the banking center for turn-of-the-20th-century Salt Lake City.

days; free. Free parking is available at a lot between the museum and the State Capitol.

Council Hall

The venerable Council Hall lies across the street from the capitol. Dedicated in 1866, the brick building served as the city hall and a meeting place for the territorial and early state legislatures. Council Hall used to stand downtown before being moved here in 1963.

It is now the home of the **Utah Travel Council.** Drop in to see the staff of the **Utah Tourism and Recreation Information Center** on the main floor for information on sights, services, and events in the state. Council Hall and the information center, 801/538-1030 or 800/200-1160, are open 8 A.M.–6 P.M. Monday–Friday, 9 A.M.–5 P.M. Saturday. The 1883 Gothic Revival building just to the east was also moved here. Formerly the 18th Ward Chapel of the LDS Church, it's now **White Memorial Chapel** and is used for community events.

UNIVERSITY OF UTAH AND VICINITY

University of Utah

Mormon pioneers established a university in their short-lived town of Nauvoo, Illinois, and they brought its books with them to Utah. The University of Deseret opened in 1850, just 2.5 years after the first colonizers reached the Salt

UNIVERSITY OF UTAH
AND VICINITY

Lake Valley. It was renamed the University of Utah in 1892 and moved to its present site on a terrace east of town in 1900. The state-assisted institution now sprawls across a 1,500-acre campus. A giant "U" on the hillside lights up during sporting events, and if the university team wins, the lights flash.

About 28,000 students study a wide range of fields including the liberal arts, business, medicine, science, engineering, and architecture—some 16 colleges and schools in all. The adjacent Research Park is a partnership of the university and private enterprise involving many students and faculty. A center of culture, the University of Utah is home to the Utah Museum of Natural History, the Utah Museum of Fine Arts, musical concerts, and theater groups. Visitors are wel-

come at cultural and sporting events, libraries, bookstore, movie theater, and Olpin Union food services. Most recreational facilities are reserved for students. For a campus map, a list of scheduled events, and other information, drop by the Park Building at the top of President's Circle, 801/581-6515, or the Olpin Union, 801/581-5888. On-campus parking is available at metered spaces around the grounds and in pay lots next to the Olpin Union and the Marriott Library; free parking can be found off campus on residential streets. The general information number for the university is 801/581-7200.

Utah Museum of Natural History
This large and varied collection of geology, biology, and anthropology exhibits tells the natural

and early Native American history of Utah. Impressive natural history models include dinosaurs, early mammals, and the varied wildlife of the present day. Look for the exhibit of California gulls *(Larus californicus)* devouring the plague of grasshoppers. Exhibits display artifacts and trace the development of prehistoric cultures and their replacement by modern tribes such as the Ute and the Navajo. A reproduction of the huge Barrier Canyon Mural pictograph shows early Native American art. Other exhibits illustrate Utah's mining history and feature specimens of the state's more than 600 minerals. A gift shop sells animal souvenirs for the kids, fossil and mineral specimens, books on Utah and natural history, and posters. A new, larger building in an adjacent space is under construction for the museum, due for completion in 2004.

The museum, 801/581-6927, is open 9:30 A.M.–5:30 P.M. Monday–Saturday and noon–5 P.M. Sunday and holidays; $6 adults, $3 children 3–12 and seniors 65 and up (special exhibits may cost more). It's on the University of Utah campus at 1390 E. President's Circle; turn in off University Street (1350 East) between 200 and 300 South Streets. Free validated parking is available in front.

Utah Museum of Fine Arts

This ambitious museum displays a little of everything, from 5,000-year-old Egyptian art to works by contemporary artists. Permanent exhibitions include art of China, India, Southeast Asia, Europe, Africa, pre-Columbia, and the early American West. Three large galleries host visiting exhibitions; there's also a pleasant café. The Museum of Fine Arts, 410 Campus Center Dr., 801/581-7332, is open 10 A.M.–5 P.M. Monday–Friday and noon–5 P.M. Saturday and Sunday; free. Free parking validation in university lots.

Red Butte Garden and Arboretum

Utah's largest botanical garden offers 30 acres of floral displays, ponds, waterfalls, and four miles of mountain nature trails in a 200-acre natural area. The garden visitors center features botanical gifts and books, and the Courtyard Garden is an excellent place for a family picnic. To reach the garden from I-15, take the Sixth South exit, which will take you east, then turn north two blocks to Fourth South and head east past where Fourth merges into Fifth South. After rising up a hill, take the left onto Wakara Way and continue east to the Red Butte Garden and Arboretum exit. The garden is open year-round with irregular hours and days. For times, call 801/581-4747. Entrance fees to the gardens are $5 adults, $3 seniors and children 2–17. Access to hiking trails in the natural area is free.

Fort Douglas Military Museum

Artifacts and historical photos take the visitor back to the days of the Nauvoo Legion, the Mormon Battalion, and U.S. Army life in Utah during pioneer days. In late 1862, Colonel Patrick Connor marched to this site with his California-Nevada volunteers and built Camp Douglas. Officially the post defended the mail route and kept check on local tribes of Native Americans. Connor also felt it necessary to keep an eye (and cannon) on the Mormons, whom he and other federal officials distrusted. The colonel wasted no time in seeking Native Americans to fight. In January 1863, just months after his arrival, Connor's troops ambushed several hundred Shoshoni on the Bear River in northern Cache Valley. The event advanced Connor's career but ranks as one of the bloodiest slaughters in the history of U.S.–Native American conflicts. Later, in a more peaceable mood, the colonel and some of his soldiers pioneered the development of Utah's minerals near Park City and elsewhere in the territory.

Fort Douglas Museum's exhibits show the unique histories of Fort Douglas and other military bases in Utah. A World War I room includes photos of German POWs once interned here. Other exhibits illustrate the big military buildup during World War II, when Utah even had a naval base. The Fort Douglas Museum, 32 Potter St., 801/581-2151, is open noon–4 P.M. Tuesday–Saturday; free.

The museum building, officers' row, and some of the other structures at Fort Douglas date from the 1870s and 1880s and are built in an architectural style termed Quartermaster Victorian. Pick up a walking-tour leaflet of the fort at the museum; a map shows the nearby post cemetery, where Colonel Connor, soldiers, and German POWs are buried. Fort Douglas, formerly used by the military as administration and recruitment offices, is now part of the University of Utah; turn north on Wasatch Drive from 500 South and travel one-half mile to the museum.

"This Is the Place" State Park

Brigham Young gazed onto the Salt Lake Valley for the first time from this spot, it's believed, and spoke the famous words, "This is the right place. Drive on." Exactly 100 years later, on July 24, 1947, a crowd gathered to dedicate the massive *This Is the Place* monument. Twelve-foot bronze statues of Brigham Young flanked by Heber C. Kimball and Wilford Woodruff stand atop a central pylon. The park has a pleasant picnic area, and the monument honors not only the Mormon pioneers but also the Catholic missionaries from Spain, fur trappers and traders, government explorers, and California immigrants who contributed to the founding of an empire in "the top of the mountains." Sculptures, bas-reliefs, and plaques around the base of the monument illustrate Utah's beginnings. A visitors center contains a mural depicting major events on the migration of the "Saints" from Nauvoo, Illinois, to their promised land. An eight-minute narration recounts the journey; narration in a foreign language can be requested, too.

"This is the Place" State Park is southeast of the University of Utah near the mouth of Emigration Canyon, at 2601 Sunnyside Ave., 801/582-1847 (recording). The visitors center is open 9 A.M.–5 P.M. Monday–Saturday; the park is open from dawn to dusk daily. Free.

Old Deseret, in the grounds near the monument, re-creates a Utah pioneer village. During the summer it comes alive with farming and craft demonstrations and wagon rides. Most of the dozen buildings that were moved here are original, some of the first in the valley. Some notable structures include Brigham Young's forest farmhouse, the 1847 Levi Riter cabin, and the Charles Rich house, designed in the 1850s for polygamous family living.

Old Deseret is open 10 A.M.–5 P.M. daily Memorial Day–Labor Day. Admission is $6 adults, $4 children and seniors; a family pass is available for $20.

Hogle Zoo

Utah's state zoo, an especially popular spot with the kids, is on the eastern edge of town and across from "This Is the Place" State Park. Children like to ride the miniature train ($1; closed in winter) and see exhibits in the Discovery Center. Many of the large-animal enclosures have natural settings; here you'll see the familiar elephants, rhinos, and hippos. The apes and monkeys carry on almost all the time, though mornings are best to hear the songs of the white-handed gibbons of Southeast Asia. Exhibits on tropical, temperate, and desert zones contain deadly cobras and vipers, aardvarks, Australian kookaburras, brightly colored birds in a walk-in aviary, and dozens of other exotic species. The cats include lions, leopards, tigers, and ocelots.

Though zoos don't normally display taxidermied animals, Hogle Zoo's unusual "liger" can be seen in the cat area. Shasta the liger was born of a Bengal tigress and an African lion father, the result of a mating that couldn't happen in nature because the animals' territories don't overlap. Hogle Zoo, 2600 E. Sunnyside Ave. (one-half mile east of Wasatch Dr.), 801/582-1631, www.hoglezoo.com, is open 9 A.M.–5 P.M. daily. Entrance fees are $7 adults, $5 children 3–12 and seniors 65 and over. Snack bars and strollers are available.

SOUTH OF DOWNTOWN
Liberty Park

This large park is the jewel of the city's public park system and contains abundant recreational facilities in addition to an excellent aviary, an arts center, and 80 acres of grass and shady boulevards. A fun addition to the park is a conceptual "map" of northern Utah that re-creates the rivers, lakes, and mountains as a series of fountains and wading pools.

The Children's Garden—playground, amusement park, snack bar, and large pond with rental boat—sits in the southeast corner of the park (all closed in winter). The tennis center on the western side of the park offers 16 lighted courts and instruction; an outdoor swimming pool adjacent to the tennis center is open in summer. Liberty Park is southeast of downtown and bordered by 900 and 1300 South and by 500 and 700 East.

Birds have taken over the southwest corner of Liberty Park. **Tracy Aviary** houses over 400 individual birds of 135 species and offers the "Birds of a Feather" show, with trained free-flying birds such as falcons. Birds on display include majestic golden and bald eagles, showy flamingos and peacocks, the hyacinthine macaw (the world's largest parrot), the golden pheasant of China, and hundreds of other feathered friends. Emus from Australia prance across fields while ducks, geese, swans, and other waterfowl keep to the ponds. You'll also get to meet Utah's only native vulture, the turkey vulture.

The "Birds of a Feather" show is presented during the summer at 11 A.M. and 1 P.M. Tuesday–Friday, 11 A.M., 1 and 3 P.M. Saturday, and at 1 and 3 P.M. Sunday and holidays; shows are also scheduled during weekends in spring and fall. Tracy Aviary is in Liberty Park at 589 East 1300 South, 801/596-8500; enter the aviary from the east side. The aviary is open daily 9 A.M.–6 P.M. in summer and 9 A.M.–4:30 P.M. the rest of the year; adults pay $4, children 4–12 and seniors $2.50.

The Chase Mill, just north of the aviary entrance, was built by Isaac Chase in 1852 and is one of the oldest buildings in the valley. Free flour from the mill saved many families during the famine of 1856–1857. The interior is closed to the public but you can view the exterior and an old millstone. Formal gardens lie north of the mill.

Chase's adobe brick house (built 1853–1854), farther to the north, has been restored. Go inside to see exhibits of the **Chase Home Museum of Utah Folk Art,** sponsored by the Utah Arts Council. On display is contemporary Utah folk art, including quilts, rugs, woodcarvings, ethnic arts, and Native American works. You'll find horseshoe pits to the north of the Chase house. The museum, 801/533-5760, is open noon–5 P.M. weekends mid-April–mid-October and daily Memorial Day–Labor Day; free.

Westminster College

The Salt Lake Collegiate Institute, founded in 1875 by the Presbyterian Church as a boys preparatory school, became Westminster College about the turn of the 20th century. By 1944 it had grown to be a four-year college, and in 1974 it became independent. Converse Hall, constructed in 1906 as the first building on the present campus, is a registered national historic site.

This private four-year college, at 1840 South 1300 East, 801/484-7651, provides a liberal-arts education with training in business, computer science, education, and nursing. Post-graduate programs are offered in business and education. Westminster College has approximately 2,300 students and 100 faculty members. Shaw Center, in the middle of the campus, serves as a student meeting place with snack bar, cafeteria, and small bookstore. Concerts, theater performances, poetry series, lectures, art exhibits, and other cultural activities are open to the public.

International Peace Gardens

With wishes for world peace, the Salt Lake Council of Women created this unusual garden in the northwest corner of Jordan Park. Members of Salt Lake City's various ethnic and national groups were invited to design and plant a garden that reflected their cultural heritage. Currently, nearly 25 groups have taken part; you'll find Dutch windmills, pagodas, and Buddhist temples scattered around the grounds. The Peace Gardens, near 900 West and 1000 South, are a lovely place for a stroll in summer.

NORTH OF DOWNTOWN
Bountiful-Davis Art Center

Exhibits by Utah artists and art classes take place at this gallery, 745 S. Main in Bountiful

SALT LAKE CITY

(84010), 801/292-0367, www.ulct.org/bountiful/bdac. It's open 5–9 P.M. Monday, 10 A.M.–6 P.M. Tuesday–Friday, and 2–5 P.M. Saturday; closed Sunday and holidays. Free. A gift shop is open during gallery hours. The gallery is eight miles north of Salt Lake City; take I-15 north to Salt Lake/Woods Cross Exit 318, go east 0.3 mile on 2600 South to 500 West (which becomes Main Street), then turn left (north) 0.2 mile.

Mid-August, the art center sponsors the Bountiful Summerfest International, with folk dance troupes from all over the world, arts and crafts, and ethnic food. The festival takes place in the city park and in the street behind the art center.

Utah Botanical Center

These gardens, operated by Utah State University in Logan for research and as a demonstration area, are undergoing a great transition. Formerly located in Farmington, they were dislocated by highway renovations and have only begun to be replanted in the new location, near Kaysville. The expanded gardens address issues such as the compatibility of increased urbanization with limited water supplies, diminishing public open space, and a shrinking resource base for native plants, wildlife, and wetlands. From the Kaysville exit off I-15, head south along the frontage road to the gardens. For updates on the progress of the new gardens, see www.usu.edu/ubc or call 801/451-3204.

Arts and Entertainment

Salt Lake City offers a wide variety of high-quality arts and cultural institutions; classical and religious music venues are particularly noteworthy. Some of the "lower" forms of art and entertainment, such as alternative music clubs and dance bars, have taken a little longer to get a toe-hold in the city, but there's a lot more going on here than you might think at first glance.

Local publications are the best places to check for information on what's happening. The *City Weekly* is the largest and most comprehensive free newspaper, with lots of arts and entertainment coverage. Good listings for restaurants, too.

Another good source is the *Salt Lake Visitors Guide* (available free at the Salt Lake Convention and Visitors Bureau). The daily papers, *Deseret News* and *Salt Lake Tribune*, both have listings in their Friday "weekend" and Sunday "art and entertainment" sections. The visitors center website at www.visitsaltlake.com also has a lengthy listing of events and entertainment options.

Tickets to most concerts and performances are available from **Fastix** at 801/355-ARTS.

Venues of Note

Most of Salt Lake City's top-flight music and arts performances take place in a handful of venues, themselves world-class facilities worthy of a visit. When you know the dates of your visit to Salt Lake City, contact the following concert halls and performance spaces to find out what's going on while you're here.

The city's main performance space is the **Capitol Theatre,** 50 West 200 South, 801/534-6364, a glittering vaudeville house from the turn of the 20th century that's been refurbished into an elegant concert hall. The **Abravanel Concert Hall,** between the Salt Palace and Temple Square at 123 W. South Temple, 801/533-5626, has fantastic acoustics and is home to the Utah Symphony and other classical music performances. The new **Rose Wagner Performing Arts Center,** 138 West 300 South, 801/323-6800, has three performance spaces and is home to several local dance and theater troupes.

In **Temple Square,** the Mormon Tabernacle and the Assembly Hall host various classical and religious musical concerts including performances by the famed Mormon Tabernacle Choir; call 800/537-9703 for information. The **Promised Valley Playhouse,** 132 S. State, 801/364-5696, was built in 1905 and has been used as a vaudeville hall, a movie palace, and, now, one of the city's leading stages for theater performances.

CLASSICAL MUSIC AND DANCE

From its modest beginnings in 1940, the **Utah Symphony,** www.utahsymphony.org, has grown to be one of the best-regarded orchestras in the country. Each season, the symphony performs in the glittering Abravanel Hall in Salt Lake City and travels to Snowbird, Deer Valley, Ogden, Provo, Logan, and other cities. Abravanel Hall and ticket offices are at 123 W. South Temple; call 801/533-5626 for information or 801/355-ARTS for tickets.

The **Utah Opera Company,** www.utahopera.org, founded in 1978, stages four operas during its October–May season. The Utah Opera and the Utah Symphony now share administrative offices and contact information (see above).

Another center for classical music and performance is the **University of Utah.** The university's Symphony Orchestra, Chamber Orchestra, jazz ensembles, opera, bands, and ballet, dance, and choral groups present regular concerts and performances on and off campus; the season runs September–May. Call the university's Public Relations office at 801/581-6772, or check the website at www.utah.edu/artsmuseums.

Ballet West began in Salt Lake City in 1963 as the Utah Civic Ballet, but as the group gained fame and began traveling widely it chose its present name to reflect its regional status. This versatile group's repertoire includes classical, modern, and foreign works. Most Utah performances take place at downtown's Capitol Theatre, September–April. For information, call 801/323-6900; for tickets call 801/355-ARTS, or check www.balletwest.org.

The professional **Ririe-Woodbury Dance Company,** 801/323-6801, www.ririewoodbury.com, has one of the most active dance programs outside New York City. The varied repertoire includes mixed media, eye-catching choreography, and humor. The group also shares its expertise by teaching production and dance skills to students and professionals. Ririe-Woodbury Dance Company is based at the Rose Wagner Performing Arts Center, as is the **Repertory Dance Theatre,** a professional company focusing on classical American and contemporary dance. For information, call 801/534-1000.

CONCERT SERIES AND MUSIC FESTIVALS

The **Concert Series at Temple Square** presents hundreds of performances a year for the public; all are free. The LDS Church sponsors the varied musical fare to provide a common meeting ground of great music for people of all faiths. You might hear chamber music, a symphony, operatic selections, religious choral works, piano solos, organ works, a brass band, or a percussion ensemble. Programs last about an hour and usually take place at 7:30 P.M. Friday and Saturday evenings in either the Assembly Hall or the tabernacle. Organists present 25-minute **Organ Recitals** in the tabernacle at noon (and at 2 P.M. in summer) Monday–Saturday and at 2 P.M. Sunday. The **Mormon Tabernacle Choir** sings in the tabernacle on Sunday mornings at 9:30 A.M. (be seated 15 minutes before) for a 30-minute radio broadcast. You're also welcome to attend rehearsals by the Mormon Tabernacle Choir on Thursday evenings at 8 P.M. At the same hour on Wednesday evenings, the Mormon Youth Symphony rehearses in the tabernacle, and on Tuesday evenings the Youth Chorus rehearses. Schedules of all musical events are posted in Temple Square, or call 801/240-3318 or 801/240-2534.

The **Madeleine Arts & Humanities Program** is held in the historic Cathedral of the Madeleine, 331 E. South Temple, 801/328-8941. This series of choral, organ, and chamber music concerts takes place on Sunday evenings throughout the spring and summer. Lectures, theatrical performances, and dance concerts are also held. All events are free.

In June, the **Gina Bachauer International Piano Competition** takes over Salt Lake City. More than 60 young pianists from around the world gather to perform a week-long series of performances both as solos (early in the competition) and with the Utah Symphony (only the finalists). The winners compete for recording contracts, a Steinway piano, and thousands of dollars in cash. It's a good chance to enjoy the musicianship of tomorrow's rising piano stars and to savor the thrill of musical competition. For information, call 801/521-9200, or check the website at www.bachauer.com.

Summer Concerts and Festivals: Local parks and public spaces are makeshift concert halls in summer. Check local media or the visitors center for details on the following ongoing concert series. **Gallivan Center Concerts and Films** feature free noontime concerts on weekdays, plus free live music concerts on Wednesday and Thursday evenings. **Monday in the Park Concerts** are free concerts at the Chase Home Museum in Liberty Park. **Creekside Concerts** are held outdoors every Saturday evening in summer at Westminster College, 1840 South 1300 East, 801/832-2437.

The Utah Symphony also offers an extensive summer series of concerts at Wasatch Front ski areas, a short evening's drive from downtown Salt Lake City. For information, call 801/533-5626 or check the website at www .utahsymphony.org.

THEATER

Pioneer Theatre Company, 801/581-6961, one of Salt Lake City's premier theater troupes, offers a seven-show season running September–May. The company performs a mix of contemporary plays, classics, and musicals. Although the company operates from the University of Utah's **Pioneer Memorial Theatre,** 300 South and University Street, it is not part of the university itself. The Pioneer Memorial Theatre is also the site of University of Utah student productions and the Young People's Theatre, which produces plays for children.

The city's cutting-edge theater group is the **Salt Lake Acting Company.** This well-established troupe doesn't shy away from controversy: their excellent production of Tony Kushner's *Angels in America* raised eyebrows and stirred strong reactions. Besides presenting new works from around the world, the company is also committed to staging plays by local playwrights; there are performances year-round. This professional troupe has two theater spaces at 168 West 500 North; for information, call 801/363-0526 or 801/355-ARTS for tickets.

The **Grand Theatre,** on the Salt Lake City Community College campus at 1575 S. State St., 801/957-3459 or 801/957-3263, is home to a year-round program of theatrical performances by both student and semiprofessional troupes. The **Hale Centre Theater,** 3333 S. Decker Lake Dr. (2200 South), 801/984-9000, offers family-oriented musicals and stage plays throughout the year.

For something spoofier, the **Off Broadway Theatre,** 272 S. Main, 801/355-4628, is the place for "improv" competitions, Broadway comedies, and topical farces. At the **Desert Star Playhouse,** 4861 S. State, 801/266-7600, you'll find old-fashioned melodramas and cabaret-style comedy skits.

NIGHTLIFE

Nearly all nightclubs and music bars that serve alcohol in Salt Lake are private clubs, and you'll end up paying a temporary membership charge (usually $5) in addition to the cover charge (even if you don't have a drink). Clubs open to the public (no membership needed) are so noted. The best way to check out the club scene is to pick up a copy of *City Weekly,* a free and widely available news and entertainment weekly.

If you're just looking for a beer and a chance to chat with the locals, try one of the brewpubs listed in the Food section. There's no membership charge at Salt Lake brewpubs.

Monk's House of Jazz, 19 East 200 South, 801/350-0950, is the city's premier jazz club. The **Tabernacle Social Club,** 201 East 300 South, 801/519-8900, is a hipper-than-thou piano bar, with an updated lounge act that features dueling pianos, sing-alongs and karaoke on Sundays and Tuesdays.

To explore the live-music club scene, start at the **Zephyr,** 301 S. West Temple, 801/355-CLUB. The Zephyr is perhaps SLC's premier music club, with live music (often national acts) performing in an intimate, friendly setting. The **O'Shucks Bar & Grill,** 22 East 100 South, 801/596-8600, combines a comfortable pub atmosphere with nightly live music, mostly acoustic. If you're looking for a singles-oriented, collegiate crowd, some danceable live music, and high spirits, check out the **Port O' Call,** 78 West 400 South, 801/521-0589.

If you want to check the local band scene, head to the **Dead Goat Saloon,** 165 S. West Temple, in Arrow Press Square, 801/328-GOAT (open to the public), or to the **Urban Lounge,** 241 South 500 East, 801/746-0557.

If you just want to dance, SLC offers a number of options. The most popular dance clubs are **DV8,** 115 S. West Temple, 801/539-8400, both a disco and a dance-band venue, and **ClubAxis,** 108 South 500 West, 801/519-AXIS, which has a DJ and cutting-edge music, with live bands on Saturday nights; Friday evening is Gay Night. **Area 51**, 400 West 451 South, 801/534-0819, has theme nights (Gothic, Techno, DiverseCity, etc.).

Salt Lake City isn't known for its vibrant gay scene, to put it mildly, and what gay life there is here is pretty well disguised. A good place to start the evening is **The Trapp,** 102 South 600 West, 801/531-8727, with a nice outdoor deck and a cruisy atmosphere.

MOVIES

First-run multiplexes are spread around downtown Salt Lake City; check the daily newspapers for listings. The city is lucky to have the Salt Lake Film Society, which sponsors a "year-round film festival" with art and foreign films at the **Broadway Centre,** 111 East 300 South, 801/321-0310, and the **Tower Theatre,** 876 East 900 South, 801/328-1645. The **Utah Film and Video Center,** 20 S. West Temple (Salt Lake Art Center), 801/534-1158, also screens independent documentaries, animation, and experimental films.

Brewvies, 677 South 200 West, 801/355-5500, is a brewpub/cinema combo where you can buy an ale and a burger and watch a first-run or cult favorite film.

For a selection of major release first-run movies, check out the following multiplexes in the downtown area: **Megaplex 12 at The Gateway,** 165 S. Rio Grande, 801/325-7500, **Crossroads Cinema,** 50 S. Main, 801/355-3883, and

Trolley Corners Theatre, 515 South 700 East, 801/364-6183.

SPORTS
Pro Sports

Utah professional sports fans love their **Utah Jazz,** which are usually strong contenders in the NBA's Western Division. The team plays at the Delta Center at 300 West and South Temple. Tickets are hard to come by at the last minute, but it's worth a call to the team's box office, 801/355-SEAT, to inquire. Otherwise, you'll need to rely on scalpers or ads in the classifieds. The **Salt Lake Singers,** 801/485-3800, is the AAA affiliate of baseball's Anaheim Angels. Games are played at the impressive Franklin Quest Field April–September; it's hard to imagine a more astonishing backdrop to a game of baseball than the craggy Wasatch Front. The **Utah Grizzlies,** 801/988-8000, are Salt Lake City's International League ice-hockey team. They play at the E Center, at 3200 S. Decker Street.

University of Utah

University athletic teams compete in football, basketball, baseball, softball, tennis, track and field, gymnastics, swimming, golf, skiing, and other sports. Contact the University of Utah Athletics Dept. at 1825 E. South Campus Dr., 801/581-UTIX.

Bonneville Raceway Park

For roaring engines, smoking tires, and checkered flags, visit the raceway in West Valley City, 6555 West 2100 South, 801/250-2600, during its April–October season.

EVENTS

Concerts, festivals, shows, rodeos, and other special events happen here nearly every day, and the Salt Lake Convention and Visitors Bureau, 90 S. West Temple, 801/521-2822, can tell you what's going on. Also check the Visitors Bureau's *Salt Lake Visitors Guide,* for some of the best-known annual happenings:

SALT LAKE CITY

In April, the annual **World Conference of the Church of Jesus Christ of Latter-day Saints** is held the first weekend of the month at Temple Square. The church president (believed to be a prophet of God) and other church leaders give guidance to members throughout the world. (Hotel rooms are in short supply at this time.) Call 801/240-2531 for more information.

Cinco de Mayo is celebrated in May with a party and concerts at Gallivan Center on the week of May 5. For information, call 801/538-FAIR. A larger celebration of multiculturalism comes the third weekend of the month, when the grounds of the Salt Lake City and County Building at State Street and 400 South erupt with the **Living Traditions Festival.** Enjoy dances, food, and entertainment of the many different cultures that make up the Utah mosaic. For more information, call 801/596-5000.

The **Scottish Festival & Highland Games** starts June off on a lively step with manly contests, bagpipe music and dancing, and ethnic food; held at Murray Park. Call 801/969-7030 for more information. The **Utah Arts Festival,** 801/322-2428, www.uaf.org, takes place the last weekend in June and includes lots of music, dance, literary readings, art demonstrations, craft sales, and food booths. The event is held at Library Square.

The summer's single largest festival is in July. The **Days of '47 Celebration** commemorates the arrival of Mormon pioneers here on July 24, 1847. The city celebrates with three parades, including the huge 24th of July Pioneer Parade (the day is a state holiday), a marathon, lots of fireworks, and the year's biggest rodeo, held at the Delta Center. For information, call 801/247-8545.

The **Greek Festival** in September celebrates Greek culture with food, music, folk dancing, and tours of the historic Holy Trinity Greek Orthodox Cathedral. The festival is held at the Hellenic Center at 300 South 300 West on the weekend after Labor Day. Call 801/328-9681 for more information. The **Utah State Fair** is a celebration of the state's agricultural heritage and features rodeos, livestock shows and judging, art and craft exhibits, musical entertainment, and

a midway, all at the state fairgrounds, North Temple and 1000 West, 801/538-8441.

SHOPPING

As in most large U.S. cities, shoppers in Salt Lake take much of their business to suburban malls. Cottonwood Mall, at Highland and Murray Holiday Roads south of the city, and Valley Fair Mall, at I-215 Exit 18 southwest of the city, are two popular malls, each containing more than 100 stores. Salt Lake City also boasts several unique shopping areas and unusual stores, including some excellent boutique centers and two large downtown malls. *Remember that many shops will be closed on Sunday.*

The Gateway

Just west of downtown, on the site of the former rail yards, The Gateway (801/456-0000) was built in the run-up to the 2002 Winter Olympics as a destination boutique shopping mall, entertainment center, and condo development. The shops, restaurants, and entertainment venues line a winding pedestrian street that is designed to resemble a developer's idea of Olde Worlde. Here you'll find chain stores such as Abercrombie & Fitch, J. Crew, Barnes & Noble, and Virgin Megastore, plus the Megaplex 12 cinema, 801/325-7500, and an impressive selection of restaurants and bars. The Gateway is between 400 and 600 West, between 200 South and North Temple.

Trolley Square

Salt Lake City's most unusual shopping center came about when developers cleverly converted the city's old trolley barn. Railroad magnate E. H. Harriman built the barn in 1908 as a center for the city's extensive trolley system. The vehicles stopped rolling in 1945, but their memory lives on in Trolley Square. Inside, you'll see several trolleys, a large stained-glass dome, salvaged sections of old mansions and churches, and many antiques. More than 100 shops and restaurants call this gigantic barn home. Watch movies at Cineplex-Odeon Theatres (four screens, 801/363-1183) and Flick 2 (two

© W. C. MCRAE

The Gateway is Salt Lake City's newest shopping venue.

SALT LAKE CITY

screens, 801/521-6113). Trolley Square is open daily, including Sunday afternoons, at the corner of 500 South and 700 East, 801/521-9877. **Trolley Corners,** across the street at 515 South 700 East, is a smaller shopping area with shops, restaurants, and Trolley Corners Theatres, 801/364-6183.

Crossroads Plaza

Located at 50 South Main across from Temple Square in the heart of downtown, 801/531-1799, this modern shopping center on four levels has more than 100 shops, fast-food restaurants, banks, and Crossroads Cinemas (three screens, 801/355-3883). Waldenbooks on the main floor and B. Dalton Bookseller on the second level have good selections of Utah books. Crossroads Plaza is open daily, including Sunday afternoons.

ZCMI Mall

What may have been America's oldest department store, Zion's Cooperative Mercantile Institution, downtown at the corner of South Temple and State, 801/321-8743, began in 1869 as a church-owned operation. The old facade graces the Main Street side, but the more than 90 shops and restaurants inside are new, and the ZCMI store itself is now called Meier & Frank, a May Company department store. ZCMI Mall is open Monday–Saturday.

TP Gallery

Crafts and art by Native Americans are featured here. Look for beadwork and leather items (Utes), jewelry (Navajo, Hopi, and Zuni tribes), pottery (Hopi and New Mexico Pueblo tribes), kachina dolls (Hopi), baskets (Papago), sand paintings, books, and cassettes. The gallery, downtown at 252 S. Main St., 801/364-2961, is open Monday–Saturday.

Recreational Equipment, Inc. (REI)

If you suddenly realize you need a new tent pole, some zip-off pants-into-shorts, or any other gear for hiking, camping, bicycling, skiing, river running, rock climbing, and travel, swing by this large store. Gear can be rented, too. The book section is a good place to look for regional outdoor guides. Topo maps cover the most popular hiking areas of Utah. Open daily at 3285 East 3300 South, 801/486-2100.

Gardner Village

This attractive shopping village in West Jordan, 12 miles south of downtown Salt Lake City, offers a restaurant and craft shops in the refurbished Gardner Mill, built in 1877. Old houses and cabins have been moved to the grounds and restored for additional shops. Step into the silo to dine at **Archibald's Restaurant,** 801/566-6940 (American and continental food), open daily for lunch and dinner (and Saturday and Sunday for breakfast). The village also has a small museum of historic exhibits, 801/566-8903. Take I-15 Midvale Exit 301 (7200 South), turn west, and follow signs to the Gardner Mill at 1100 West 7800 South.

Bookstores

Sam Weller's Zion Book Store, 254 S. Main, 801/328-2586, claims to be one of the West's largest, with more than half a million new and used books covering many topics. If you're a book lover, you'll want to check out the impressive selection of quality used books. **Borders Books and Music** right downtown in the Cross-roads Plaza, 50 S. Main, 801/363-1271, has a good selection of general reading and Utah books. **Deseret Book Co.** 36 S. State (ZCMI Mall), 801/328-8191 (and other locations), specializes in LDS literature, but it also has many general reading and Utah books. The **University of Utah's Bookstore,** 801/581-6326, has a varied selection on many subjects.

Recreation

Salt Lake City's stunning physical location at the base of the craggy, snow-covered Wasatch Mountains gives tangible evidence of the region's stellar recreational and sporting opportunities. Even on a short visit to the Salt Lake area, you'll want to get outdoors and enjoy a hike or a bike ride up a mountain canyon. You won't be alone: The city's newest immigrants, young professionals, are as attracted to the city's right-out-the-back-door access to the great outdoors as to the region's vibrant economy.

Even on a short visit to the Salt Lake area, you'll want to get outdoors and enjoy a hike or a bike ride up a mountain canyon.

Skiing has always been Utah's biggest recreational draw, and as host of the 2002 Winter Olympics the Salt Lake City area drew the attention of international skiing and winter sports lovers. Summer visitors will find lots to like after the snow melts: Most ski areas remain open for warm-weather recreation, including mountain biking, hiking, trail rides, tennis, and plain old relaxing. The U.S. Forest Service manages Mill Creek and Big and Little Cottonwood Canyons as part of the Wasatch National Forest. Located just east of the city, these canyons provide easy access to hiking and biking trail systems and to popular fishing streams.

DOWNHILL SKIING

Utah's "Greatest Snow on Earth" lies close at hand. Within an hour's drive from Salt Lake City you can be at one of seven downhill areas in the Wasatch Range, each with its own character and distinctive skiing terrains. (Coverage of the individual resorts follows in the Northern Wasatch Front chapter.) The snow season runs from about mid-November to April or May. Be sure to pick up the free *Utah Ski Vacation Planner* from Ski Utah, Inc., 150 West 500 South, Salt Lake City, UT 84101, 801/534-1779 or 800-SKI-UTAH, fax 801/521-3722, or from most tourist offices in Utah. Or check out the website at www.skiutah.com. The planner lists most Utah resorts and has diagrams of the lifts and runs, lift ticket rates, and detailed information on lodging. Call 801/521-8102 for Utah snow conditions.

Salt Lake City–area ski resorts are grouped quite close together. Although they are in different drainages, Solitude and Brighton ski areas in Big Cottonwood Canyon and Snowbird and Alta ski areas in Little Cottonwood Canyon, they all share the high country of the Wasatch Divide with Park City, Deer Valley, and The Canyons ski areas. There is no easy or quick route between the three different valleys, however, and traffic and parking can be a real hassle. Luckily, there are plenty of options for convenient public transport between Salt Lake City and the ski areas and between the resorts themselves.

Alternatively, you can ski between the various ski areas with **Ski Utah Interconnect,** which provides a guide service for backcountry touring between Wasatch Front ski areas. Skiers should be experienced and in good physical condition because of the high elevations (around

10,000 feet) and the need for some walking and traversing. Touring is with downhill equipment. On Monday, Wednesday, Friday, and Sunday, tours start at Park City Mountain Resort and ski through Solitude, Brighton, Alta, and Snowbird via the backcountry terrain between them. On the other three days (Tuesday, Thursday, and Saturday), the trip starts at Snowbird and goes through Alta, Brighton, and Solitude. The cost of $150 a day includes the guide's services, lunch, and all lift tickets. For details, contact Ski Utah, Inc., 801/534-1907, www.skiutah.com/resorts/interconnect.

Transportation to Ski Areas

Salt Lake City's public bus system, the UTA, 801/287-4636, www.utabus.com, has regularly scheduled service to the four resorts on the west side of the Wasatch Range: Solitude, Brighton, Snowbird, and Alta. You can get on the buses downtown (they connect with the TRAX light rail), at the University of Utah, or at the bottoms of the canyons. A couple of early-morning buses run up to the ski areas every day; return buses depart the ski areas around 5 P.M.

Lewis Brothers Stages offers a Ski Express from the Salt Lake City Airport and downtown hotels to all Wasatch Front ski areas, including Park City, Deer Valley, The Canyons, Brighton, Solitude, Snowbird, and Alta. Book a $56 round-trip ticket through a hotel or call Lewis Brothers directly at 801/359-8677 or 800/826-5844. Lewis Brothers also operates the Canyon Jumper, which connects Park City to Snowbird, Alta, Solitude, and Brighton. Optional ski packages include transportation and lifts at a discount. Similar services are offered by other transportation companies, including All Resort Express, 435/649-3999 or 800/457-9457, and Park City Transportation, 435/649-8567 or 800/637-3803.

CROSS-COUNTRY SKIING

During heavy snowfalls, Salt Lake City parks and streets become impromptu cross-country ski trails, and any snowed-under Forest Service road in the Wasatch Range is fair game for Nordic

skiers. The Mill Creek Canyon road is a favorite. If you don't mind cutting a trail or skiing ungroomed snow, ask at ski rental shops for hints on where the backcountry snow is good.

Otherwise, there are numerous organized cross-country ski areas in the Salt Lake City area. The Mountain Dell Golf Course in Parley's Canyon (off I-80 toward Park City) is a favorite place to make tracks. There are cross-country facilities at Alta and Solitude (see the Northern Wasatch Front chapter) as well as at the White Pine Touring Center in Park City.

HIKING, JOGGING, AND BIKING

The four miles of trails outside **Red Butte Garden** east of the University of Utah are a quiet place for a walk or a jog (see the University of Utah and Vicinity section). The hiking trails wind through wildflower meadows and past old sandstone quarries. You don't need to pay the admission to the gardens proper to hike the trails.

Joggers also favor the shady oasis of **Liberty Park** and the rolling terrain of **Sugarhouse Park**. (See Parks in the Other Sports and Recreation section for more information.)

Mill Creek Canyon

For hiking trails in the nearby Wasatch Range, simply drive up Mill Creek or Big or Little Cottonwood Canyon and look for trailheads. Contact the Wasatch-Cache National Forest Recreation Information, in the REI store at 3285 East 3300 South, 801/466-6411, for maps and advice. Also see the Big Cottonwood Canyon and Little Cottonwood Canyon sections in the Northern Wasatch Front chapter.

Great mountain biking, plentiful picnic areas, and many hiking possibilities lie along Mill Creek just outside Salt Lake City. The canyon entrance is at Wasatch Boulevard and Mill Creek Road (3800 South). You may bring your dog along, too—this is one of the few canyons where pets are welcome. In fact, odd-numbered days are designated "leash-free" days in Mill Creek Canyon. However, these off-leash regulations are fiercely contested and may change. Obey the posted regulations when you begin your hike. Bicycles are

SALT LAKE CITY

only allowed in Mill Creek Canyon on even days—days when dogs must be leashed.

Picnic sites are free and available on a first-come, first-served basis; most lack water. The first one, **Church Fork Picnic Area,** is three miles in at an elevation of 5,700 feet; **Big Water Picnic Area** is the last, 8.8 miles up at an elevation of 7,500 feet. A $3 usage fee is charged to visitors in Mill Creek Canyon.

Salt Lake Overlook on Desolation Trail is a good hiking destination for families. The trail climbs 1,200 feet in two miles for views of the Salt Lake Valley. Begin from the lower end of Box Elder Picnic Area (elev. 5,760 feet) on the south side of the road. Energetic hikers can continue on Desolation Trail beyond the overlook to higher country near timberline and go all the way to Desolation Lake (19 miles). The trail runs near the ridgeline separating Mill and Big Cottonwood Canyons, connecting with many trails from both canyons. Much of this high country lies in the Mount Olympus Wilderness. See Mt. Aire and Park City West 7.5-minute topo maps.

Alexander Basin Trail winds to a beautiful wooded glacial bowl below Gobblers Knob; the trailhead (elev. 7,080 feet) is on the south side of the road eight miles up Mill Creek Canyon, 0.8 mile beyond Clover Springs Picnic Area. The moderately difficult trail begins by paralleling the road northwest for a few hundred feet, then turns southwest and switchbacks one mile to the beginning of Alexander Basin (elev. 8,400 feet). The trail to Bowman and Porter Forks turns right here, but continue straight one-half mile for the meadows of the upper basin (elev. 9,000 feet). The limestone rock here contains many fossils, mostly shellfish. From the basin it's possible to rock-scramble to the summit of Gobblers Knob (elev. 10,246 feet). (The name comes from an attempt by mine owners to raise turkeys after their ore played out; the venture ended when bobcats ate all the birds.) See the Mt. Aire 7.5-minute topo map.

Bikers should continue to the end of the Mill Creek Canyon road, then set out on the Big Water Trail. The Great Western Trail (a 3,000-mile ridgetop trail, stretching from Canada to Mexico) intersects Big Water at 1.5 miles. Bikers can turn off of Big Water and follow the Great Western Trail to the ridge-top divide overlooking The Canyons Ski Resort. Here, the route turns south and follows the Wasatch Crest Trail along the ridge and around the head of the upper Mill Creek basin. To avoid conflicts with hikers, Big Water, Little Water, and the Great Western Trail are closed to mountain bikes on odd-numbered calendar days.

City Creek Canyon

In the city itself, a pleasant and relaxing route for a stroll or a jog follows **City Creek Canyon,** a shady, stream-filled ravine just east of the State Capitol. The road that runs up the canyon is now closed to most traffic and extends five miles from its beginnings at **Memory Grove,** just northeast of the intersection of E. North Temple and State Street, to Rotary Park at the top of the canyon.

Since pioneer days, people have obtained precious water from City Creek and enjoyed the diverse vegetation, wildlife, and scenery. Because City Creek is still part of the city's water supply, regulations prohibit dogs, horses, and overnight camping. A paved road through City Creek Canyon extends six miles past picnic areas to a trailhead.

Hikers and joggers may travel on the road every day. In summer (Memorial Day weekend–September 30), bicyclists may enter only on odd calendar days, motorized vehicles may drive up only on even calendar days and only with reservations (usually for a picnic); a gate at the bottom controls entry. No motorized vehicles are allowed the rest of the year, but bicycles can use the road daily then. A $3 charge applies if you drive through to the trailhead at the upper end (no reservation needed).

The big attraction for many visitors is a stop at one of the picnic areas along the road. Picnickers can reserve sites with the Water Department, 801/483-6797. Sites are sometimes available on a first-come, first-served basis (midweek is best). Picnic permits cost $3 and up depending on size of group. The entrance to City Creek Canyon is reached via Bonneville Boulevard, a one-way road. From downtown Salt Lake City, head east on North Temple, which becomes Second Avenue after crossing State Street, then turn left (north) 1.3 miles on B Street, which becomes Bonneville Boulevard after 11th Avenue, to City Creek Canyon Road. Returning from the canyon, you have to turn right on Bonneville Boulevard to the State Capitol. Bicyclists and joggers may approach City Creek Canyon from either direction.

A popular hiking destination from the trailhead at road's end (elev. 6,050 feet) is City Creek Meadows, four miles away and 2,000 feet higher. After 1.5 miles, you'll pass Cottonwood Gulch on the left; a side trail leads up the gulch to an old mining area. After another one-half mile on the main trail, a spring off to the right in a small meadow is the last reliable source of drinking water. During the next mile, the trail grows steeper and winds through aspen groves and then passes two shallow ponds. The trail becomes indistinct here, but you can continue one mile northeast to the meadows (elev. 8,000 feet); a topo map and compass help. For splendid views of the Wasatch Range, climb north one-half mile from the meadows up the ridge to where Davis, Salt Lake, and Morgan Counties meet. Hikers also enjoy shorter strolls from the trailhead along the gentle lower section of trail.

OTHER SPORTS AND RECREATION

Parks

Salt Lake City has lovely parks, many of which have facilities for recreation. For information about the city's park system, contact the Parks and Recreation office at 801/972-7800; for county park information, call 801/468-2560.

There are abundant reasons to spend time at **Liberty Park,** 801/538-2062, including the Tracy Aviary, the children's play area, and the acres of shade and lawn. The park also affords plenty of opportunity for recreation. The tennis center on the western side offers 16 lighted courts. The outdoor swimming pool adjacent to the tennis center is open in summer. During the sweltering Salt Lake summer, the shady boulevards provide a cool environment for jogging. You'll find horse-

shoe pits to the north of the park's historic Chase House. Liberty Park is southeast of downtown and bordered by 900 and 1300 South and by 500 and 700 East.

Mormon pioneers manufactured beet sugar at **Sugarhouse Park,** 801/467-1721, beginning in 1851; the venture later proved unprofitable and was abandoned. Today, expanses of rolling grassland in the 113-acre park are ideal for picnics, strolling, and jogging. The park has a playground and fields for baseball, soccer, and football. In winter, the hills provide good sledding and tubing. A lake attracts seagulls and other birds for bird-watching. Sweet smells rise from the Memorial Rose Garden in the northeast corner. Sugarhouse Park is on the southeast edge of Salt Lake City at 1300 East and 2100 South (access is from 2100 South).

Swimming Pools and Gymnasiums

Two of the best and most central outdoor public pools are at **Liberty Park,** 1300 South and 700 East, and **Fairmont Park,** 2361 South 900 East. Serious lap swimmers should check out the **Salt Lake City Sports Complex,** near the University of Utah at 645 S. Guardsman Way, 801/583-9713; it has a 25-meter indoor pool and a lovely 50-meter outdoor pool with great views of the mountains.

For an even bigger splash (at a far heftier price than the public pools listed above), try **Raging Waters,** 1200 West 1700 South, 801/972-8300, a water-sport theme park that features water slides and a Wild Wave pool. The children's area has waterfalls, geysers, a "dinosaur beach," and a small wave pool.

Tennis

Seventeen city parks have courts; call the Salt Lake City Parks and Recreation Department, 801/972-7800, for the one nearest you. **Liberty Park,** 1300 South and 500 East, has 16 courts.

Golf

Salt Lake City has plenty of places to tee off. The following lie close to town and are open to the public. **Bonneville** is an 18-hole, par-72 course east of downtown at 954 Connor St.

(2130 East off Sunnyside Ave. near the Hogle Zoo), 801/583-9513. **University** is a nine-hole, par-33 executive course on the University of Utah campus at 100 South 1900 East, 801/581-6511. **Mountain Dell** is a 36-hole, par-71 or -72 course east in Parleys Canyon; take I-80 East Canyon/Emigration Canyon Exit 134, 801/582-3812. Mountain Dell was the site of the Olympic cross-country ski competition in 2002. **Forest Dale** is a nine-hole, par-36 course at 2375 South 900 East (near Sugarhouse Park), 801/483-5420. **Nibley Park** is a nine-hole, par-34 course at 2730 South 700 East, 801/483-5418. **Glendale** is an 18-hole, par-72 course at 1603 West 2100 South, 801/974-2403. **Rose Park** is an 18-hole, par-72 course northwest of downtown at 1386 N. Redwood Rd., 801/596-5030.

Skating

Cottonwood Heights Recreation Center, 7500 South 2700 East, 801/943-3160, offers year-round ice-skating and lessons, indoor and outdoor pools, racquetball courts, and a weight room. Roller-skate at the Utah Fundome, 4998 South 360 West in Murray, 801/293-0800, and **Classic Roller Skating Centers,** 9151 South 255 West in Sandy, 801/561-1791.

Canoeing

A canoe trip through **Jordan River State Park** reveals birds and other wildlife in a peaceful setting that you wouldn't expect so close to downtown Salt Lake City. A green canopy of willow, Russian olive, and Siberian elm overhangs the river for much of its length. Canoeists can stop at the International Peace Gardens and other parks along the way. The state park office can advise on boating conditions and places to rent canoes, paddles, and life jackets. Park rangers enforce the rule that each boater must wear a Coast Guard–approved life jacket.

You'll need two cars or someone to pick you up at trip's end. Put-in is at 1200 West 1700 South (across from Raging Waters), take-out at 1000 North 1525 West; allow at least 2.5 hours (without stops) for the six-mile route. This is the only section of the river open to boats. The Jordan River State Park office is at 1084 N. Redwood Rd., Salt Lake City, UT 84116, 801/533-4496 (open Monday–Friday 8 A.M.–5 P.M.). It's a good idea to call the park before a trip to check on possible river obstructions. Off-season boating isn't recommended because of the greater likelihood of hazards blocking the way.

Rock Climbing

Rockreation, 2074 East 3900 South, 801/278-7473, offers instruction, equipment rental, and a massive rock gym with 6,700 square feet of climbing terrain. Day passes are available; there's also a weight and fitness room at the complex.

Equipment Rental

Utah Ski & Golf, 134 West 600 South, 801/355-9088, rents golf clubs in summer and ski equipment when the snow falls. Rent bicycles at **Canyon Bicycle,** 3969 S. Wasatch Blvd., 801/278-1500. For hiking, camping, climbing, and ski rentals, try **REI,** 3285 East 3300 South, 801/486-2100. Another all-sport rental outfit is **Wasatch Touring,** 702 East 100 South, 801/359-9361.

Accommodations

Salt Lake City has the best selection of accommodations in Utah, with many new hotels built for the 2002 Winter Olympics. Unless you're on a really tight budget, you'll probably be more comfortable if you avoid the cheapest motels along West Temple or State Street. Many of these older motor-court units have become residential lodgings, and the owners don't put much effort into upkeep. However, you should have a pleasant stay at all of the following accommodations.

There are several major lodging centers. Downtown Salt Lake City has the advantage of being close to Temple Square, Delta Center, the Salt Palace, and most other visitor attractions. South of downtown, near 600 South and West Temple, is a clutch of hotels and motels, including several business-oriented hotels. While these lodgings are only six blocks from the center of the city at Temple Square, remember that blocks are very long in SLC. Another cluster of hotels and motels is west along North Temple, the primary surface street leading to the airport. If your trip to Salt Lake City involves visiting students or conducting business at the university, there are a couple of good lodging options near the campus.

In general, room rates can be rather high, though quality is good. Because SLC is a major convention site and a winter recreation center, there really isn't much seasonal variation in the price of rooms. Reservations are strongly suggested, especially if you want to stay in central Salt Lake City.

The prices listed below are standard rack rates. You can frequently beat these prices by visiting the hotel's website to check for specials. Also, SLC often has a glut of hotel rooms, due to hotel overbuilding for the Olympics—63 new hotels were built in the Salt Lake area after the city won the Olympic nod. You can frequently find real deals on SLC lodgings at Internet booking sites, such as www.discounthotels.com and www.expedia.com.

If you have trouble locating a room, consider using the city's free reservation service by calling 800/847-5810 or visiting the website at www.visitsaltlake.com.

DOWNTOWN NEAR TEMPLE SQUARE
Under $50
There aren't many good budget-class accommodations in this prime area, but if cheap is what you're looking for, try the **Temple View Motel,** 325 North 300 West, 801/521-9525, slightly north of the city center; there are three kitchen units.

$50–75
You can find several good moderately priced motels near Temple Square. The **Howard Johnson Express Inn,** 121 North 300 West, 801/521-3450 or 800/541-7639, is an older but well-maintained motor-court motel with a pool, complimentary continental breakfast, and free HBO. The **City Creek Inn,** 230 W. North Temple, 801/533-9100 or 866/533-4898, www.citycreekinn.com, is a well-kept little motor court motel just two blocks from the temple. The **Travelodge at Temple Square,** 144 W. North Temple, 801/533-8200 or 800/255-3050, is kitty-corner to the temple. Besides standard rooms, it also has four two-bedroom units.

$75–100
Just east of Temple Square is the pleasant, well-maintained **Carlton Hotel,** 140 E. South Temple, 801/355-3418 or 800/633-3500, www.carltonhotel-slc.com. The Carlton offers a guest laundry, exercise room, sauna, hot tub, and in-room VCRs with free movies; there are also five suites.

Both of the following have family-style restaurants on premises. Overlooking Temple Square is the **Best Western Salt Lake Plaza Hotel,** 122 W. South Temple, 801/521-0130 or 800/366-3684, which offers a pool in addition to its great location. Directly across from Temple Square is the **Inn at Temple Square,** 71 W. South Temple,

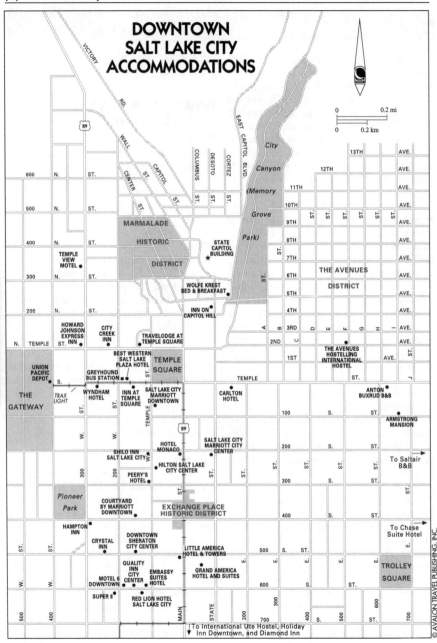

DOWNTOWN SALT LAKE CITY ACCOMMODATIONS

0   0.2 mi

0   0.2 km

801/531-1000 or 800/843-4668. Owned by the LDS Church, the inn was upgraded after the grand Hotel Utah was closed as a lodging. Rooms are very well appointed, and the entire facility is nonsmoking.

The first of SLC's historic older hotels to be refurbished into a natty, upscale lodging was the **Peery Hotel,** 110 West 300 South, 801/521-4300 or 800/331-0073. Its 1910 vintage style is preserved in the comfortable lobby, while the guest rooms are completely updated, nicely furnished, and quite spacious. There are two restaurants on the premises, as well as an exercise room.

$100–125

The **Shilo Inn Salt Lake City,** 206 S. West Temple, 801/521-9500 or 800/222-2244, is just south of the Salt Palace. In addition to the usual pool and fitness facilities it offers microwaves, refrigerators, and videocassette players in all rooms, free continental breakfast, restaurant and lounge, and a guest laundry.

One of SLC's best hotels, the **Hilton Salt Lake City Center,** 255 S. West Temple, 801/328-2000 or 800/222-TREE, is a huge complex with an indoor pool, two fine dining restaurants, a private club, fitness facilities, valet laundry, and convention facilities for small groups.

One block west of the temple is the **Wyndham Hotel,** 215 W. South Temple, 801/531-7500 or 800/553-0075. At this modern, 15-story hotel, you'll find a pool and conference, business, and exercise facilities; children under 12 stay free. Rack rates are high, but often discounts are available that bring that price down substantially.

Some of Salt Lake's most grand heritage homes sit on Capitol Hill, just below the State Capitol Building. Surely one of the most eye-catching is the red sandstone mansion now called the **Inn on Capitol Hill,** 225 N. State St., 801/575-1112 or 888/884-3466. Built in 1906 by a local captain of industry, the inn has 14 guest rooms decorated with period detail, but all with modern amenities like private bathrooms. Practically every room has views over all of Salt Lake City. Full gourmet breakfasts included.

The **Salt Lake City Marriott Downtown,** 75 S. West Temple, 801/531-0800 or 800/228-

9290, is directly across from the Salt Palace Convention Center. At this high-quality hotel there's an indoor/outdoor pool, sauna, fitness center, a good restaurant, lounge, and private nightclub (available to hotel guests). Weekend rates are often deeply discounted.

$150–175

The **Salt Lake City Marriott City Center,** 220 S. State St., 801/961-8700, was completed just before the Olympics; it sits above Gallivan Plaza, an urban park and festival space. A luxury-level business hotel, the Marriott has an indoor pool, recreation area, and a fine dining restaurant.

Over $200

Perhaps the grandest of all the fantastic homes on Capitol Hill is a three-story Georgian Revival mansion built in 1905 and now converted into the **Wolfe Krest Bed & Breakfast,** 273 N.E. Capitol Blvd., 801/521-8710 or 800/669-4525, www.wolfekrest.com. The inn's 13 rooms, all with private baths, are decorated with luxury fabrics, Oriental carpets, and antiques. Views over the city and City Creek Canyon are fantastic, as are the many-course breakfasts. Also of note: The proprietress is Mrs. Kay Malone, wife of former Utah Jazz star Karl.

SOUTH DOWNTOWN

Just south of the religious sites and convention areas downtown is a large complex of hotels and motels (mostly representatives of large chains) with rooms in almost every traveler's price range. These lodgings aren't entirely convenient for travelers on foot, but if you have a car or intend to ride buses (unfortunately, the free bus zone doesn't extend this far south, but the zone is just a short walk from these hotels), then these are some of the newest and nicest places to stay in the city.

Under $50

Directly south of downtown a couple of miles is the **International Ute Hostel,** 21 E. Kelsey Ave., 801/595-1645. Beds in dorm-style rooms are $15, private rooms are $35, and there's full access to kitchen facilities and common areas. Kelsey Avenue is the equivalent of 1160 South, just east off State Street.

$50–75

Diamond Inn, 1009 S. Main St., 801/355-4567 or 888/500-9192, isn't walking distance from downtown, but the TRAX light rail stops a block away. There's a pool, fitness facility, guest laundry, and free continental breakfast.

Motel 6 Downtown, 176 West 600 South, 801/531-1252 or 800/466-8356, has a pool. Pets are allowed at the **Super 8 Motel,** 616 South 200 West, 801/534-0808 or 800/800-8000. The **Salt Lake City Center Travelodge,** 524 S. West Temple, 801/531-7100 or 800/578-7878, offers nicely maintained rooms, all with coffeemakers and access to a heated pool and hot tub. Pets are accepted.

$75–100

The best location of all the south downtown motels is held by **Courtyard by Marriott Downtown,** 130 West 400 South, 801/531-6000. It's very central to all the restaurants and happenings in the city's fast-changing warehouse/loft district. There's a pool, hot tub, fitness facility, and airport shuttle.

If you're looking for comfortable rooms without breaking the bank, the **Little America Hotel & Towers,** 500 S. Main St., 801/363-6781 or 800/304-8970, is a great place to stay. This large lodging complex (with nearly 850 rooms) offers three room types. Courtside rooms and Garden Suites are scattered around the hotel's nicely manicured grounds, with most rooms overlooking a pool or fountain. Tower Suites are executive-level suites in a 17-story block offering some of SLC's best views. All guests share the hotel's elegant public areas, two pools, health club, and workout facility. The restaurant here is better than average, and there is free airport transport.

The **Quality Inn City Center,** 154 West 600 South, 801/521-2930 or 800/521-9997, offers a pool, fitness room, restaurant, guest laundry, and free airport shuttle.

One of the nicer-for-the-money hotels in this part of Salt Lake City is the **Crystal Inn,** at 230

Little America Hotel & Towers

West 500 South, 801/328-4466 or 800/366-4466. Rooms here are very large and nicely furnished; all come with refrigerators and microwaves. There's a free hot breakfast buffet for all guests. For recreation, there's an indoor pool, exercise room, sauna, and hot tub.

If you're in Salt Lake for an extended time, or are traveling with a family, consider the **Embassy Suites Hotel,** 110 West 600 South, 801/359-7800 or 800/362-2779. All suites have efficiency kitchens (with coffeemakers) and separate living and sleeping areas; there are two two-bedroom units. Facilities include a pool, sauna, exercise area, restaurant, and lounge.

Hampton Inn, 425 South 300 West, 801/741-1110 or 800/HAMPTON, offers a free continental breakfast and free local calls.

$100–125

Red Lion Hotel Salt Lake Downtown, 161 West 600 South, 801/521-7373 or 800/325-

4000, has a pool, spa, exercise facilities, room service, guest laundry, and free airport transportation. **Sheraton City Center Hotel,** 150 West 500 South, 801/532-3344 or 800/421-7602, is one of the city's best addresses for high-quality comfort and service. The lobby areas are very pleasant, and facilities include a great pool, exercise room, and spa. The rooftop restaurant and lounge are also notable. The Hilton offers free airport and downtown shuttles.

Holiday Inn Downtown, 999 S. Main, 801/359-8600 or 800/933-9678, is three blocks farther south than the other lodgings in this listing but offers facilities that make it stand out, such as a putting green, tennis courts, basketball court, and a playground for children in addition to the usual pool and exercise facilities. Besides, there's a free downtown shuttle service to whisk guests to the center of things (free airport transportation is offered as well). Rooms are very nicely appointed.

The **Hotel Monaco,** 15 West 200 South, 801/595-0000 or 877/294-9710, occupies a grandly renovated historic office building in a very convenient spot in the middle of downtown; on the main floor is **Bambara,** one of the most sophisticated restaurants in Utah. Rooms are sumptuously furnished with real élan: This is no anonymous business hotel in beige and mauve. Expect wild colors and contrasting fabrics, lots of flowers, and excellent service. Facilities include on-site fitness center, meeting rooms, plus concierge and valet services. Each room comes with two-line phones, CD stereo, in-room fax, printer, and copier, plus an iron and board. Pets are welcome, and if you forgot your own pet, the hotel will deliver a companion goldfish to your room. If you want to splurge on a hotel in Salt Lake, make it this one.

$150–175
Another addition to the Salt Lake hotel scene—

Salt Lake City contains a wealth of beautiful residential architecture. Early politicians, Mormon leaders, and wealthy merchants especially favored South Temple Street, east of downtown. Many of their mansions have been restored, and some are now high-quality B&Bs.

and to the skyline—is the new-in-2001 **Grand America Hotel and Suites,** 555 S. Main St., 801/258-6000 or 800/621-4505. This behemoth of a hotel is a full Salt Lake City block square (remember, that's 10 acres), and its 24 stories contain 775 rooms, over half of them suites. Rooms have luxury-level amenities; expect all the perks and niceties that modern hotels can offer.

EAST OF DOWNTOWN

There aren't many lodging choices in this part of the city, but this is a pleasantly residential area without the distinct urban jolt of much of the rest of central Salt Lake City.

This is also where most of the city's B&Bs are located. Salt Lake City contains a wealth of beautiful residential architecture, especially in the historic neighborhoods east of downtown and near the capitol. Early politicians, Mormon leaders, and wealthy merchants especially favored South Temple Street, east of downtown. Many of their mansions have been restored, and some are now high-quality B&Bs.

Most B&Bs have a range of room prices, so use the rate headings as just a guideline; most have suites at a higher price.

Under $50
The Avenues, one mile east of Temple Square, offers dorm rooms with use of a kitchen, TV room, and laundry. Information-packed bulletin boards list city sights and goings-on, and you'll meet travelers from all over the world. Year-round rates for the dorm are $17 per person (cost includes sheets), while private rooms are $34 (only half have private baths). Reservations (with first night's deposit) are advised in the busy summer-travel and winter-ski seasons. The hostel is on the corner of 107 F St. and 2nd Ave., Salt Lake City, UT 84103, 801/363-3855; open 8 A.M.–10 P.M. year-round. From downtown, head east on South

SALT LAKE CITY

Temple Street to F Street, then turn north two streets.

$50–75

The **Anton Boxrud Bed and Breakfast,** 57 South 600 East, 801/363-8035 or 800/524-5511, offers seven guest rooms (with a mix of private and shared baths) in a grand 1901 Victorian brick home. The house has been restored to its original splendor and features hardwoods, wood-paneled walls, stained glass, and period furnishings. There's also a hot tub, and breakfasts are notably good. Anton Boxrud B&B is a half-block south of South Temple on 600 East, near the governor's mansion.

The **Saltair B&B/Alpine Cottages and Condos,** 164 South 900 East, 801/533-8184 or 800/733-8184, www.saltlakebandb.com, is the oldest continuously operating bed-and-breakfast in Utah. Located in a pleasant neighborhood between downtown and the university, the property was built in 1903 and is on the National Register of Historic Places. In addition to the five comfortable and moderately priced rooms in the inn (with a mix of shared and private baths), there are two adjacent cottages available for families or for longer stays. Each of these totally renovated 1870s cottages comes with a full kitchen (though breakfast in the main inn is included), a fireplace, cable TV, and private phones; each sleeps up to four. Additionally, the Saltair has nine refurbished early-20th-century condos for rent on a weekly or monthly basis.

$75–100

The **Brigham Street Inn** is a fabulous Queen Anne mansion at 1135 E. South Temple, 801/364-4461 or 800/417-4461. When the architect-owners refurbished the home, they engaged 12 local designers and gave each a room to make over—the result is an eclectic showcase of sensitive historic renovation. There are nine guest rooms, each with private bath. One deluxe room has a private garden entrance, kitchen, and whirlpool.

The **Armstrong Mansion,** 667 East 100 South, 801/531-1333 or 800/708-1333, is another Queen Anne mansion converted to a comfortable B&B. Each of the 14 rooms has a private bath and is decorated with full Victorian flair.

$100–125

Right on the University of Utah's research park, the **Marriott University Park Hotel & Suites,** 480 Wakara Way, 801/581-1000 or 800/637-4390, is one of the city's best-kept secrets for luxurious lodgings in a lovely setting. You can't miss with the views: All rooms either overlook the city or look onto the soaring peaks of the Wasatch Range directly behind the hotel. Rooms are very nicely appointed—the suites are some of the nicest in the city. All rooms have minibars, refrigerators, and coffeemakers; there's a pool and exercise room, and bicycles are available for rent.

A block from the recent commercial development at Trolley Square is the **Chase Suite Hotel by Woodfin,** 765 East 400 South, 801/532-5511 or 800/237-8811. All rooms have separate sleeping and living spaces and come with full kitchens—just the thing if you're in town for a few days or traveling with a family. There's also a pool, hot tub, and sport court.

The **Anniversary Inn,** 460 South 1000 East, 801/363-4900 or 800/324-4152, caters to couples and newlyweds interested in a romantic getaway. All 32 rooms are imaginatively decorated according to theme: Beds may be in a covered wagon or a vintage rail car, and bathrooms may be in a "sea cave." Chances are good that your room will have its own private waterfall. You get to pick your suite from choices that include "the lighthouse," "the opera house," "South Pacific," and "Venice." These rooms aren't just filled with kitsch—they are luxury-class rooms, with big-screen TVs, hot tubs, stereos, and private bathrooms. Rates vary widely according to room. If you'd like to check out these clever theme rooms before signing up, call the inn for information on early afternoon tours, which are held daily except Sunday.

WEST DOWNTOWN TO THE AIRPORT

Nearly all of the following offer transportation to the Salt Lake City Airport. Hotels with the smallest addresses on W. North Temple are closest to downtown.

Under $50
Gateway Motel, 819 W. North Temple, 801/533-0603 or 877/388-8311, was spiffed up for the 2002 Winter Olympics. It's on the road to the airport but still quite close to downtown.

$50–75
Although it's on the road to the airport, the **Econo Lodge,** 715 W. North Temple, 801/363-0062 or 800/877/233-2666, is also convenient to downtown, as it's just west of the railroad overpass. The motel offers a courtesy car to downtown or the airport and has a pool and guest laundry. Of the many older motor-court motels along North Temple, perhaps the best-maintained is the **Overniter Motor Inn,** 1500 W. North Temple, 801/533-8300 or 800/914-8301, with an outdoor pool and clean rooms. Moderately priced rooms are also available at **Days Inn,** 1900 W. North Temple, 801/539-8538 or 800/329-7466, and at the **Motel 6 Airport,** 1990 W. North Temple; 801/364-1053, where there's a pool. Closer to the airport, the **Travelodge Airport Inn,** 2333 W. North Temple, 801/539-0438 or 800/578-7878, has a pool and guest laundry.

$75–100
The **Holiday Inn Airport,** 1659 W. North Temple, 801/533-9000, offers nicely furnished rooms, a restaurant and private club, and a pool and spa.

Practically next door to the terminal is the **Holiday Inn & Suites,** 5575 W. Amelia Earhart Dr., 801/537-7020 or 800/522-5575, with a pool and spa. At the **Airport Hilton,** 5151 Wiley Post Way, 801/539-1515 or 800/999-3736, rooms are very spacious and nicely furnished, and facilities include two pools, a putting green, sports court, and an exercise room and spa. The hotel even has its own lake.

$100–125
The **Radisson Hotel Salt Lake City Airport,** 2177 W. North Temple, 801/364-5800 or 800/333-3333, is a very attractive, lodge-like building with nicely furnished rooms. Guests receive a complimentary continental breakfast and newspaper, and in the evenings there's a "manager's reception" with free beverages. Facilities include a pool, spa, and fitness room. Suites come with a loft bedroom area. There's quite a range in room rates, though package rates and promotions can bring down the rates dramatically.

COMMERCIAL CAMPGROUNDS

Camp VIP offers tent and RV sites year-round with showers, swimming pool, game room, playground, store, and laundry. Rates are $22 for tents or RVs without hookups, $30 with. The campground is between downtown and the airport at 1400 W. North Temple, 801/328-0224. From I-15 northbound, take Exit 311 for I-80, go west 1.3 miles on I-80, exit north one-half mile on Redwood Road (Highway 68), then turn right another one-half mile on North Temple. From I-15 southbound, take Exit 313 and turn south 1.5 miles on 900 West, then turn right 0.8 mile on North Temple. From I-80 either take the North Temple exit or exit on Redwood Road (Highway 68) and go north one-half mile, then right one-half mile on North Temple.

Hidden Haven Campground, 18 miles east of Salt Lake City near Park City, 435/649-8935, has showers, store, laundry, and a trout stream. Tent and RV sites are open year-round; $14.50 without hookups, $19.75 with. Take I-80 Exit 143, then go east 1.6 miles on the north frontage road (or take Park City Exit 145 and go west one mile on the north frontage road).

Pioneer Village Campground, 16 miles north of Salt Lake City in Farmington, at Lagoon Amusement Park, 801/451-8100, is open mid-April–mid-October with showers, store, laundry, and discounts on rides; tent and RV sites cost $19 without hookups, $23–25 with. Take I-15's Lagoon exit and follow signs.

Cherry Hill Camping Resort, 18 miles north of Salt Lake City at 1325 S. Main in Kaysville, 801/451-5379, features a water slide, inner-tube ride, swimming pool, Pirates Cove (for young children), restaurant, miniature golf, and a variety of games, as well as a large campground with showers, store, and laundry. The season lasts mid-April–mid-October, though some activities operate only Memorial Day–Labor Day weekends. Tent or RV sites cost $19 without hookups, $23 with. Take I-15 Lagoon/Farmington Exit 327 and go north two miles on U.S. 89.

FOREST SERVICE CAMPGROUNDS

There are two campgrounds in Big Cottonwood Canyon about 15 miles southeast of downtown Salt Lake City. All have drinking water and cost $14 a night. **Spruces Campground** (elev. 7,400 feet, 9.1 miles up the canyon) is open early June–mid-October. The season at **Redman Campground** (elev. 8,300 feet) lasts mid-June–early October. It's between Solitude and Brighton, 13 miles up the canyon.

Little Cottonwood Canyon, about 19 miles southeast of downtown Salt Lake City, has two campgrounds with drinking water. **Tanners Flat Campground** (elev. 7,200 feet, 4.3 miles up the canyon) is open mid-May–mid-October; $14. Some sites can be reserved by calling 800/280-CAMP. **Albion Basin Campground** lies high in the mountains (elev. 9,500 feet) and is open early July–late September; $14. Go 11 miles up the canyon (the last 2.5 miles are gravel).

Some sites at each of the above campgrounds can be reserved by calling 877/444-6777.

Food

Travelers will be pleased with the quality of food to be found in Salt Lake City. If you've been traveling around the more remote areas of the state, the abundance of ethnic restaurants especially will be a real treat; the number of Chinese restaurants alone is astonishing.

Most of the following restaurants serve alcohol, though you'll need to ask specifically to see the drinks menu. At the time of publication, none of the restaurants in the listings below were private clubs (meaning that you would need to buy a membership to get in), but these things change. Several of the more popular restaurants have private clubs adjacent to the dining areas.

The free *Salt Lake Visitors Guide* also lists dining establishments. Dinner reservations are advisable at the more expensive restaurants. Also note that most restaurants are closed Sunday; if you're going to be in Salt Lake over the weekend, ascertain that your hotel has a restaurant, or you may be wandering the streets looking for an eating establishment that's open on the Sabbath.

COFFEEHOUSES AND BREAKFAST

If you've fallen victim to the nation's obsession with gourmet coffees, you'll discover that lattes and cappuccinos are more scarce in Utah than elsewhere because of Mormon strictures on caffeine. However, several fine coffeehouses exist in Salt Lake City, though at some distance from Temple Square. The **Salt Lake Roasting Co.,** 329 East 400 South, 801/363-7572, offers a wide selection of coffees, fresh baked European-style pastries, a vaguely "alternative" atmosphere, and a pleasant outdoor patio in good weather. At **Cup of Joe,** 353 West 200 South, 801/363-8322, the atmosphere is sleek and industrial; however, you'll also find comfortable couches and stacks of reading material. Joe's also serves lunchtime panini sandwiches and is open till midnight with entertainment—poetry readings, acoustic music, conversation clubs—most evenings.

For one of Salt Lake's favorite breakfasts, drive (or ride your bike) a couple of miles east of

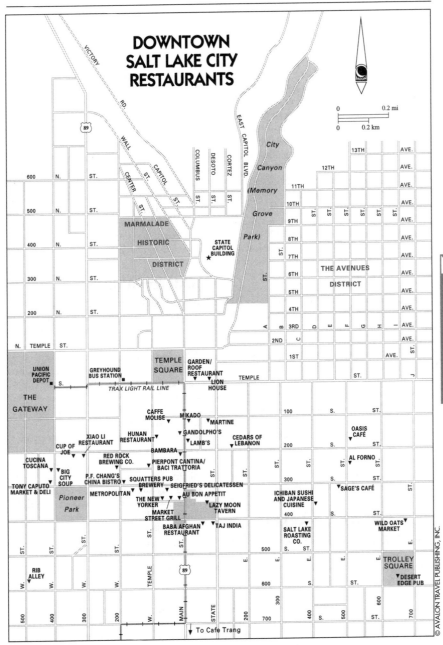

DOWNTOWN
SALT LAKE CITY
RESTAURANTS

SALT LAKE CITY

© AVALON TRAVEL PUBLISHING, INC.

the city to **Ruth's Diner,** 2100 Emigration Canyon, 801/582-5807. The restaurant's namesake was a cabaret singer in the 1920s who opened her own restaurant in 1931. Ruth's Diner has been in continuous operation ever since (the ads read "70 years in business . . . Boy am I tired!"). Ruth's is full of atmosphere and overlooks a rushing stream. It's a great place to go for an old-fashioned breakfast or a hearty lunch. Live music is featured at Sunday brunch. Another classic place for an old-fashioned breakfast is **Lamb's,** 169 S. Main, 801/364-7166, which hasn't changed its look or its menu since the 1930s. Lamb's is an easy walk from most downtown hotels.

Another pleasant place for a traditional breakfast is the **Park Cafe,** 604 East 1300 South, 801/487-1670. The Park is directly across from Liberty Park, which makes a great pre- or post-breakfast destination. Closer to downtown, in the Exchange District, the **Market Street Grill,** 48 Market St., 801/322-4668, is best known for its excellent seafood dinners but is also a favored spot for stylish and delicious breakfasts.

Brunch: If you're looking for Sunday brunch, most of the hotel restaurants have buffets, but for the brunch of champions, head to the lodges and resorts up nearby Wasatch Front canyons. The **Silver Fork Lodge,** 435/649-9551, 11 miles up Big Cottonwood Canyon, and the **Log Haven,** 801/272-8255, four miles up Mill Creek Canyon, are both favorite destinations for a scenic brunch, perhaps followed by a hike. The brunch at **La Caille at Quail Run,** at the mouth of Big Cottonwood Canyon, 801/942-1751, is where to head if you feel like putting on the Ritz.

DELIS AND FOOD MARKETS

Siegfried's Delicatessen, downtown at 69 West 300 South, 801/355-3891, closed Sunday, has a great selection of sausages, cold cuts, breads, pastries, and cheeses. A New York–style deli, **Gandolfo's,** 158 S. Main, 801/322-3354, offers favorites like meatball and pastrami sandwiches in a dining room hung with sports memorabilia. Another good place to stop to provision a picnic is **Tony Caputo Market & Deli,** 308 West Broadway, 801/531-8669, with great sandwiches, Italian-style sausage and cheese, loads of olives and other Mediterranean temptations, and a park nearby where you can have an impromptu picnic. **Carlucci's Bakery,** next door at 314 West 300 South, 801/366-484, offers European-style breads and pastries.

On summer Saturdays, the **Salt Lake Farmers Market** takes over Pioneer Park, at 300 South and 300 West. The market offers a wide variety of ethnic and to-go eating options, along with a selection of fresh fruits, vegetables, and baked goods.

Wild Oats Natural Food Market, 645 East 400 South, 801/257-9866, is an all-natural grocery store that also features a very good vegetarian café plus an expansive salad bar with lots of healthy carry-out options.

AMERICAN FARE

Lamb's, downtown at 169 S. Main, 801/364-7166, claims to be Utah's oldest restaurant; it started in Logan in 1919 and moved to Salt Lake City in 1939. You can still enjoy the classic 1930s diner atmosphere as well as the tasty food. The menu offers seafood, steak, chops, chicken, and sandwiches; Lamb's is an especially good place for breakfast. Dinner entrées range $13–15. Open for breakfast, lunch, and dinner; closed Sunday.

For moderately priced food and history of a different sort, try the **Lion House,** 63 E. South Temple, 801/363-5466. Built in 1856, this was one of Brigham Young's homes, where his 26 wives and 56 children spent most of their time. High-quality cafeteria-style meals are available for lunch and dinner in the basement dining room, formerly the household pantry.

For lunch soup and sandwiches, go to **Big City Soup,** 235 South 400 West, 801/333-SOUP. If fast food is more your style, then at least try the local purveyor: **Crown Burgers,** with many outlets throughout the Salt Lake area, is the local favorite for char-grilled burgers and good fries. Two convenient locations to downtown are at 377 East 200 South and 118 North 300 West.

Two excellent options for barbecue and soul food are **Sugarhouse Barbecue Co.,** 2207 South 700 East, 801/463-4800, with dry-rubbed ribs and pulled pork, and **Rib Alley,** 533 South 500 West, 801/359-9926, with Southern country cooking like barbecue ribs and catfish.

FINE DINING

Salt Lake City has a number of upscale restaurants where high rollers can flex their credit cards and eat world-class cuisine.

Metropolitan, 173 W. Broadway, 801/362-3472, is easily Salt Lake City's most ambitious restaurant, taking "fusion cuisine" to new lengths. In this high-design dining room (reserve tables near the fireplace-cum-water-sculpture), the foods of the world meet and mingle on your plate in preparations that are sometimes unexpected but always stylish. Seared venison medallions appear with tempura vegetables, venison-laced spring rolls, morel mushrooms, and a reduced sake sauce. A crabmeat Napoleon is served with caviar and fresh lobster sauce. Cuisine like this doesn't come cheap; expect to pay upwards of $10 for appetizers and $25–30 for entrées. Metropolitan is open nightly for dinner, Monday–Friday for lunch.

Bambara, in the Hotel Monaco, 202 S. Main, 801/363-5454, is another exciting addition to the Salt Lake dining scene. The menu emphasizes the freshest and most flavorful of local meats and produce, with preparations in a wide-awake New American style that equal parts tradition and innovation; entrées range $20–25. This is easily the most beautiful dining room in the city. Highly recommended.

Martine, 22 East 100 South, 801/363-9328, offers equally delicious food in a less formal atmosphere. The antique high-ceilinged dining room is coolly elegant, and the cooking and presentation subtly continental. You have a choice of ordering tapas-style—from $6.50 to $7.50 for lime and garlic calamari or tarragon halibut cakes with saffron aioli—or ordering full meals for $12–18. Another excellent spot for informal fine dining is **Third & Main,** 300 S. Main, 801/364-4600, with street-side dining, a

nice bar area, and classy New American cuisine at $14–22.

For classic French cuisine, **La Caille at Quail Run,** near Little Cottonwood Canyon at 9565 Wasatch Blvd., 801/942-1751, offers superb pastry, crepes, seafood, and meat dishes in an 18th-century rural French atmosphere. Vineyards, gardens, ponds, and manicured lawns surround the re-created French chateau—hard to believe it's Utah. Antique furnishings grace the dining rooms and halls. Expect to pay $30–40 per person for dinner. Dress is semiformal; reservations advised. Dinner is served daily, and brunch and a Basque-style dinner are served on Sunday.

VEGETARIAN

Even a meat-loving place like SLC offers a selection of dining options for vegetarians. **Sage's Café,** 473 East 300 South, 801/322-3790, serves satisfying vegetarian organic cuisine. Even the wine list emphasizes organic wines. **Oasis Café,** 151 South 500 East, serves an ambitious all-vegetarian menu that borrows tastes and preparations from around the world. **Evergreen House,** 755 State St, 801/328-8889, prepares all-vegetarian Chinese dishes. The café at **Wild Oats Market,** 645 East 400 South, serves a vegetarian menu.

BREWPUBS

Brewpubs are often the most convenient places in Utah to enjoy good food and drink as there's no private-club rigmarole. Each of the following pubs is open for both lunch and dinner.

The state's oldest brewpub is **Squatters Pub Brewery,** 147 W. Broadway, 801/363-2739. In addition to fine beers and ales, the pub serves sandwiches, burgers, and other light entrées in a handsome old warehouse. In summer, there's seating on the back deck.

Very popular and kind of a scene, the **Red Rock Brewing Company,** 254 South 200 West, 801/521-7446, offers pasta, salads, and sandwiches, including an excellent variation on the hamburger (baked in a wood-fired oven inside a bread pocket). There's often a wait to get in the door, but the food and brews are worth it. The Red Rock is unusual for Salt Lake in that it serves food late—till midnight on weekends.

Desert Edge Brewery, 801/521-8917, also known simply as "The Pub," is in Trolley Square at 700 East and 500 South. The menu is inexpensive, with sandwiches and salads available all day; some of the ales are cask-conditioned. In the evening, several zippy entrées, such as grilled salmon with spinach and chicken with citrus chipotle chili glaze appear on the menu; best of all, nothing costs more than $12. The atmosphere is retro industrial chic, and there's a second-floor outdoor veranda.

PIZZA

Gepetto's, near the University of Utah at 230 South 1300 East, 801/583-1013, presents pizza, lasagna, sandwiches, and salads. Live entertainment is offered Thursday–Saturday; open Monday–Saturday for lunch and dinner.

The Pie Pizzeria, downstairs from the University Pharmacy, 1320 East 200 South, 801/582-0193, offers New York–style hand-thrown pizza. Live music Monday and Tuesday evenings; open daily for lunch and dinner.

For pizza in more of a pub setting, try the gourmet pies at **Rusted Sun,** 2010 S. State St., 801/483-2120, with New York–style pizza and calzone, or the **Lazy Moon Pub,** 32 Exchange Place, 801/363-7600, which features live music and pleasant outdoor seating in addition to good boutique pizza.

STEAK AND SEAFOOD

Two sister restaurants with confusingly similar names offer the best fish and seafood in SLC. The **Market Street Grill,** downtown at 48 Market St., near Main and Broadway, 801/322-4668, features fresh seafood plus steak, prime rib, chops, chicken, and pasta. Adjacent is an oyster bar. Entrées run $14–22, though if you arrive before 7 P.M. you can order the early-bird specials for $12. Open daily for breakfast, lunch, and dinner and for brunch on Sunday.

Market Street Broiler, 260 South 1300 East, 801/583-8808, specializes in fresh fish and seafood, which you can enjoy in the dining room, pick up at the takeout counter, or purchase at the fresh fish market. Most of the fish is mesquite grilled; steaks, hickory-smoked ribs, and chicken are also available. An in-house bakery creates tempting pastries; open Monday–Saturday for lunch (daily in summer) and daily for dinner.

The New Yorker, 60 Market St., 801/363-0166, is yet another fine dining house in a historic storefront. Here the emphasis is on seafood and excellently prepared certified Angus beef and fresh American lamb. If you're not up to a full meal, there's also a café menu; or just go to the oyster bar and fill up on bivalves. The atmosphere is lively; it's in Salt Lake's financial district, so expect an audience of stock brokers and businessmen.

If you're looking for a steak-house atmosphere, Salt Lake City has several notable options. **Old Salt City Jail Restaurant,** two blocks east of Trolley Square near the University of Utah at 460 South 1000 East, 801/359-6090, offers steak, prime rib, and seafood in an authentic Old West jailhouse. Open daily for dinner. **Spencers,** in the downtown Hilton, 255 S. West Temple, 801/238-4748, has a big reputation as the city's best high-rolling steak house.

DINING WITH A VIEW

Some of the best views in the city are from the top of the 10-story Joseph Smith Memorial Building (the former Hotel Utah), 15 E. South Temple, where you'll find two excellent restaurants. The **Garden Restaurant,** 801/539-1911, offers unparalleled views onto Temple Square and downtown Salt Lake City. What's more, the restaurant is reasonably priced, offering sandwiches and salads for lunch ($8 and under) and steaks, seafood, and continental dishes at dinner (under $15). With even better views onto Temple Square, the **Roof Restaurant,** 801/539-1911, offers an upscale buffet (dinner only) with prime rib, salmon, ham, shrimp, salads, desserts, and all the trimmings. The price for this all-you-can-eat extravaganza is $27 adults, $16 children. Reservations are recommended; no alcohol is served.

MEXICAN AND SOUTHWESTERN

Red Iguana, 736 W. North Temple, 801/322-1489, is one of the city's favorite Mexican restaurants; it offers excellent south-of-the-border cooking with a specialty in Mayan and regional foods. Best of all, flavors are crisp, fresh, and earthy. The Red Iguana is very popular, so arrive early—especially at lunch—to avoid the lines. Entrées on the extensive menu average $10.

Miramar, 342 West 1300 South, 801/484-2877, serves traditional Mexican tortilla-based dishes, but its real focus is the excellent cuisine of other Latin and South American regions. Seafood dishes are a specialty. The food is authentic (for example, they offer *menudo*—tripe soup), so expect exciting and unusual flavors.

Right downtown, the **Pierpont Cantina,** 122 W. Pierpont, 801/364-1222, offers a large selection of traditional Mexican dishes plus salads, fajitas, and grilled meats. Nearly all entrées are priced under $10. Since it's located next to popular Baci Trattoria, the atmosphere is equally high-voltage, in an airy, wood-paneled room that rises in tiers toward the ribboned ceiling fans. There's seating outdoors in good weather. (Pierpont is an alley between 200 and 300 South.)

For the city's best Southwestern cooking plus scenic views, drive up Emigration Canyon two miles to the **Sante Fe Restaurant,** 2100 Emigration Canyon Rd., 801/582-5888. The menu is comprehensive and blends Creole, Mexican, and New Mexican flavors with worldly savvy. Dishes like *pollo asada* are served with jalapeño fettuccini ($13); shrimp come sautéed in lime juice and tequila with cilantro relish and succotash ($15).

For Mexican fast food, the local chain **La Frontera,** 1236 West 400 South, 801/532-3158, 1434 South 700 West, 801/974-0172, and other metro locations, serves burritos, enchiladas, tacos, *huevos rancheros,* and other Mexican favorites. Open daily for breakfast, lunch, and dinner.

CONTINENTAL

For something authentically French, go to **Au Bon Appetit,** 18 W. Market St., 801/519-9595, which offers a real Parisian bistro atmosphere and classic French fare for $14–18. In the same price range, **Cucina Toscana,** 307 W. Pierpoint Ave., next to Caputo's Market (the Italian soul of SLC), 801/328-3463, offers high-quality grilled meats, salads, and pasta in a coolly elegant dining room.

Right downtown at 55 West 100 South, **Caffe Molise,** 801/364-8833, offers a bistro atmosphere and tasty mid-priced Italian specialties. Pasta dishes are in the $10 range, with grilled chicken and beef dishes for $13–17. Another good value for classic Italian pasta dishes is **Al Forno,** 239 South 500 East, 801/359-6040.

Baci Trattoria, 134 W. Pierpont Ave., 801/328-1500, with its zippy, high-tech decor and lively clientele, is near both the Delta Center and the Salt Palace. Most nights it gets busy and boisterous, and the regulars like it that way. The food is good, including boutique pizza, updated pasta dishes for $12–18, grilled meats ranging from $15 for chicken preparations to $27 for three different veal dishes, and fresh fish specials nightly.

Many people feel that **Fresco Italian Cafe,** 1513 South 1500 East, 801/486-1300, is SLC's finest Italian eatery, if not the city's best overall restaurant. The pleasant setting features an intimate dining room entered through a garden, and the property is on a quiet street a few miles south of city center. The entrées are full-flavored yet subtle: cheese tortellini is served with fresh peas, roasted red peppers, sage, and tomato butter ($16), and the house specialty is grilled lamb medallions served with roasted garlic-rosemary demi-glace ($19).

MIDDLE EASTERN AND INDIAN

For something unusual, try **Baba Afghan Restaurant,** 55 East 400 South, 801/596-0786. Afghani food is like a mix of Indian and Middle Eastern cuisines. With entrées $9–12, it's a good value. There are a number of vegetarian dishes.

Cedars of Lebanon, downtown at 152 East 200 South, 801/364-4096, has exotic Mediterranean flavors from Lebanon, Morocco, Armenia, Greece, and Israel—many vegetarian items, too. Belly dancers enliven the scene on Friday and Saturday nights. Open Monday–Saturday for lunch and dinner.

Mazza, 1515 South 1500 East, 801/484-9259, is one of the city's top choices for Lebanese and Egyptian food, and the price is very reasonable for such high-quality food.

Tandoori and northern Indian cooking is the specialty at **Taj India,** 73 East 400 South, 801/596-8727. The nan breads are wonderful, and there is a large selection of vegetarian dishes. Near the university is a good Indian restaurant, the **Bombay House,** 1615 S. Foothill Dr., 801/581-0222, open for lunch and dinner. The **Star of India,** 177 East 200 South, 801/363-7555, is another favorite for tandoori-roasted meats and full-flavored curries.

ASIAN

An amazing number of Chinese restaurants dot Salt Lake City. Most feature rather old-fashioned Mandarin/American cooking. If you're looking for more spice, try the **Hunan Restaurant,** downtown in Arrow Press Square at 165 S. West Temple, 801/531-6677, which serves Sichuan-style preparations. Open Monday–Friday for lunch, daily for dinner.

Two restaurants bring updated Chinese food to Salt Lake City. At **P.F. Chang's China Bistro,** 174 West 300 South, 801/539-0500, in a historic building just south of the convention center, the cuisine is a split between traditional Chinese and modern ingredients cooked in a Chinese method. This is a busy place, so reservations are a good idea. Dinner entrées are $12–20. **Xiao Li Restaurant,** 307 West 200 South, in a vintage warehouse, prepares traditional northern Chinese cuisine but to a standard almost never observed in Western-influenced Asian restaurants. This is a good place to come if you want carefully prepared classics like orange chicken, sesame beef, or General Tso's chicken.

Thai food is popular in SLC. **Bangkok Thai,** 1400 S. Foothill Dr., 801/582-8424, is a ways from downtown, but worth the drive for intensely flavored red curries and other Thai specialties.

There are several good Japanese restaurants. At the **Happy Sumo,** in The Gateway at 153 S. Rio Grande St., 801/456-7866, traditional sushi mixes with eclectic pan-Asian dishes in a lively, upscale setting. The outdoor patio features live music most evenings. At **Mikado,** 67 West 100 South, 801/328-0929, specialties include shabu-shabu, steak teriyaki, sushi, and shrimp tempura. Open Monday–Saturday for dinner only; reservations recommended.

Ichiban Sushi and Japanese Cuisine, 336 South 400 East, 801/532-7522, is a transplant from Park City, where it had a huge reputation as a superlative sushi house. Its reputation has only grown since its move to Salt Lake, where it's currently housed in a converted Lutheran church.

Cafe Trang, south of downtown at 818 S. Main, 801/539-1638, is a top-rated Vietnamese restaurant with wonderful food, though don't expect much in the way of decor. Open daily for lunch and dinner.

Other Practicalities

INFORMATION
Tourist Offices
Volunteers at the **Salt Lake Convention and Visitors Bureau** downtown in the Salt Palace at 90 S. West Temple, Salt Lake City, UT 84101, 801/521-2822 or 800/541-4955, www.visitsaltlake .com, will tell you about the sights, facilities, and goings-on in town. The office also has many helpful magazines and brochures. Open 8 A.M.–5 P.M. (to 6 P.M. in summer) Monday–Friday and 9 A.M.–4 P.M. Saturday. At the airport, the Visitors Bureau has branches near the baggage claim areas in both Terminal 1 and Terminal 2, which are staffed only during the day.

The **Utah Travel Council**, www.utah.com, publishes a well-illustrated *Utah Travel Guide,* travel maps (both state maps and a series of five detailed maps covering the state), and other helpful publications. There are specialized guides to biking and rafting holidays as well. (You can also find these publications at the Salt Lake Convention and Visitors Bureau and local chambers of commerce.) The staff at the information desk provides advice and literature about Utah's national parks and monuments, national forests, Bureau of Land Management areas, and state parks as well as general travel in the state. You can stop by the Utah Travel Council offices in historic Council Hall, across the street from the capitol, or write Council Hall/Capitol Hill, Salt Lake City, UT 84114. Open 8 A.M.–5 P.M. Monday–Friday and 10 A.M.–5 P.M. weekends and holidays, 801/538-1900 or 800/200-1160, fax 801/538-1399.

Wasatch-Cache National Forest
Although visiting the Forest Service headquarters or a ranger station is always an option, travelers may find it easier to go to REI, 3285 East 3300 South, 801/486-2100, where the Forest Service has a recreation information kiosk. The staff here is often more customer-service oriented to outdoor reacreationalists than that found in ranger stations. A full selection of maps and printed material is available. The info center, 801/466-6411, is open 10:30 A.M.–7 P.M. Tuesday–Saturday.

The Wasatch-Cache National Forest **supervisor's office,** downtown on the eighth floor of the Federal Building, 125 S. State St., Salt Lake City, UT 84138, 801/524-3900, has general information and forest maps for all the national forests in Utah; some forest and wilderness maps of Nevada, Idaho, and Wyoming; and regional books. Open 7:30 A.M.–4:30 P.M. (to 5 P.M. in summer) Monday–Friday. The website is also a fountain of information: www.fs.fed.us/wcnf.

For detailed information on hiking and camping in the nearby Wasatch Range, visit the **Salt Lake Ranger District office,** 6944 South 3000 East, Salt Lake City, UT 84121, 801/943-1794. The district includes the popular Mill Creek, Big Cottonwood, and Little Cottonwood Canyons in the Wasatch Range, the Wasatch Range east of Bountiful and Farmington, and the Stansbury Mountains west of Tooele. Large reference books cover nearly every recreational activity and trail. The foresters here will likely have personal knowledge of the area you're heading to. It's open 8 A.M.–5 P.M. Monday–Friday.

Libraries
The large **city library** contains a wealth of reading material, a children's library, records, and audio- and videotapes. Special collections include Western Americana and Mormon history. Puppet shows and story hours entertain children. The architecture of the library building is striking and effective—full of natural light, it's a great place to read, then glance up at the mountains. Library hours are 9 A.M.–9 P.M. Monday–Thursday and 9 A.M.–6 P.M. Friday and Saturday. The main library is at 210 East 400 South, 801/524-8200. See the telephone blue pages or call for locations of the five branch libraries.

The **Marriott Library** at the University of Utah, 801/581-6085 (hours) or 801/581-8558 (information), ranks as one of the leading research libraries of the region. You'll find more

SALT LAKE CITY

than two million volumes and over 14,000 periodical titles inside. Special collections include the Middle East, United Nations, Western Americana, and Utah manuscripts. The large map collection has topo maps of all 50 states as well as maps and atlases of distant lands. Hikers can photocopy maps of areas they plan to visit. The public is welcome to use the library; a Library Permit Card can be purchased to use materials outside of the library. Open 7 A.M.–10 P.M. Monday–Thursday, 7 A.M.–5 P.M. Friday, and 9 A.M.–5 P.M. Saturday (shorter hours during summer and school breaks).

Media

The Salt Lake Tribune morning daily reflects the city's non-LDS viewpoints. The LDS-owned *Deseret News* comes out daily in the afternoon with a conservative viewpoint and greater coverage of LDS Church news. *Utah Highways* is a travel magazine reporting on back roads, hiking and biking, recreation, and other topics of interest to the Utah traveler. The free *City Weekly* describes the latest on art, entertainment, events, and social spots and covers local politics and issues.

Salt Lake City has good public radio stations. KUER 90 FM offers a good musical mix along with National Public Radio news. KCPW, at both 88.3 and 105.1 FM, offers more NPR news and programming as well as foreign news programs. KRCL, at 91 FM, is a community radio station with progressive news and locally produced programming.

SERVICES

The main **downtown post office** is at 230 West 200 South in the Expo Mart, 801/974-2200. The University of Utah has a post office in the bookstore.

Salt Lake City is a major regional banking center, and you'll have no trouble with most common financial transactions. As elsewhere in the world, ATMs are everywhere and make monetary exchange easy. If you are depending on foreign currency, consider changing enough for your trip around Utah while in Salt Lake City. Exchanging currency will be much more difficult in smaller, rural towns. Change foreign currency at **Wells Fargo** downtown at 79 S. Main, 801/246-1069.

Minor medical emergencies can be treated by **IHC**, just west of downtown at 55 N. Redwood Rd. and at six other area locations, 801/321-2490. Hospitals with 24-hour emergency care include **Salt Lake Regional Medical Center**, 1050 E. South Temple, 801/350-4111; **LDS Hospital**, Eighth Ave. and C St., 801/350-4111; **St. Mark's Hospital**, 1200 East 3900 South, 801/268-7111; and **University Hospital**, 50 N. Medical Dr. (1800 East), 801/581-2121. For a physician referral, contact one of the hospitals or the Utah State Medical Association, 801/355-7477.

For a 24-hour pharmacy, try the **Rite Aid** at 5540 South 900 East, 801/262-2981. If you're looking for a drugstore, check the phone book for **Smith's Pharmacy**; there are more than 25 in the Salt Lake metro area.

The **American Automobile Association** (AAA) offices are at 560 East 500 South, 801/541-9902.

USEFUL NUMBERS

Highway Emergency Assistance: 801/576-8606 or *71 (mobile phones).
Lawyer Referral Service (Utah State Bar Association): 801/531-9075.
Physician Referral Service (Utah State Medical Association): 801/355-7477.
Police (Salt Lake City): 801/799-3000.
Road Conditions: 801/964-6000.
Salt Lake Convention and Visitors Bureau (local travel information): 801/521-2822 or 800/541-4955.
Sheriff (Salt Lake County): 801/535-5441.
Utah Division of Wildlife Resources: 801/538-4700.
Utah Recreation/Ski Report: 801/521-8102.
Utah State Parks: 801/538-7220.
Utah Transit Authority (UTA): 801/287-4636.
Utah Travel Council (statewide travel information): 801/538-1030.

© SALT LAKE CITY CONVENTION AND VISITORS BUREAU/ ALAN YORGASON

TRAX light rail

TRANSPORTATION

Air

Salt Lake City International Airport is conveniently located seven miles west of downtown; take North Temple or I-80 to reach it. All major U.S. carriers fly into Salt Lake City. Salt Lake City is the western hub for Delta Air Lines, which is the region's air-transport leader.

SkyWest Airlines, 800/453-9417, Delta's commuter line, flies to Vernal, Cedar City, and St. George in Utah and to towns in adjacent states.

The airport has three terminals; in each you'll find a ground-transportation information desk, a cafeteria, motel/hotel courtesy phones, auto rentals (Hertz, Avis, National, Budget, and Dollar), and a ski-rental shop. Terminal 1 also houses Zion's First National Bank (currency exchange), an ice-cream parlor, and gift shops. Utah Information Centers are found in Terminals 1 and 2, 801/575-2800. Terminal 3 is dedicated to foreign arrivals and departures. Staff at the ground-transportation information desks will know the bus schedules into town and limousine services direct to Park City, Sundance, Provo, Ogden, Brigham City, Logan, and other communities. UTA Bus #50 is the cheapest way into town. It leaves the airport daily except holidays every hour from about 6:30 A.M. to about 11:30 P.M. (less frequently and only to about 5:30 P.M. on Sunday).

Train

Amtrak trains stop at a new depot at 340 South 600 West. The only train that currently passes through the city is the California Zephyr, which heads west to Reno and Oakland and east to Denver and Chicago four times a week. Call for fares, as Amtrak now prices tickets as airlines do, with advance-booking, special seasonal, and other discounts available. Amtrak office hours (timed to meet the trains) are irregular, so call first, 800/872-7245 (information and reservations).

Long-Distance Bus

Salt Lake City sits at a crossroads of several major freeways and has good **Greyhound** bus service. Generally speaking, buses go north and south along I-15 and east and west along I-80. One bus daily leaves from Salt Lake City for Yellowstone National Park (summer only). The Greyhound station is downtown at 160 W. South Temple, 801/355-9579 or 800/231-2222.

Tours

The **Gray Line,** 553 West 100 South, Salt Lake City, UT 84101, 801/521-7060 or 800/309-2352, offers a half-day city tour in the morning for $27 adults, $14 ages 5–12. Other trips feature excursions to the Great Salt Lake and to Olympic sites from the 2002 Winter Games. Gray Line will pick up at most large hotels. Three-day tours head south to Bryce, Zion, and Grand Canyon National Parks or northeast to Yellowstone and Grand Teton National Parks.

Local Bus and Light Rail

Utah Transit Authority (UTA) provides inexpensive bus and light rail train service in town and to the airport, the University of Utah, and surrounding communities. Buses go as far north as Ogden, as far south as Provo and Springville, and as far west as Tooele. The new TRAX light rail trains connect the Delta Center, the University of Utah, downtown Salt Lake City, and the southern suburbs. No charge is made for travel downtown within the "Free-Fare Square" area (bounded by North Temple, 400 South, West Temple, and 200 East). During the winter ski season, skiers can hop on the Ski Bus Service to Solitude, Brighton, Snowbird, and Alta ski areas from downtown, the University of Utah, and other locations. A bus route map and individual schedules are available at www.rideuta.com and from the ground transportation information desk at the airport, the Salt Lake Convention and Visitors Bureau downtown, Temple Square visitors centers, the Crossroads Mall, and the ZCMI Mall or by calling UTA at 801/287-4636 (BUS-INFO) 6 A.M.–7 P.M. Monday–Saturday. Free transfers are given on request when the fare is paid. On Sunday, only the airport, Ogden, Provo, and a few other destinations are served. UTA shuts down on holidays. Fares are $1.25 for two hours of travel on both TRAX or the buses; a day pass is $2.50.

Lewis Brothers Stages offers Red Horse Express service during ski season to Park City from the Salt Lake City Airport ($29 one-way, $56 round-trip). The Ski Express from Salt Lake City serves Solitude, Brighton, Snow-bird, Alta, and the Park City ski areas ($29 round-trip). The Canyon Jumper shuttle operates during the ski season connecting the Park City ski areas with Snowbird, Alta, Brighton, and Solitude ($31 round-trip). Ski packages with transportation and lift tickets can be purchased, too. Reservations 12 hours in advance are advised for these trips; 801/359-8677 (Salt Lake City), 801/649-2256 (Park City), or 800/826-5844.

Park City Transportation provides year-round service to Park City from downtown Salt Lake City and the airport starting at $29 one-way; ski shuttles depart from Salt Lake City and Park City in winter to Solitude, Brighton, Snowbird, Alta, Sundance, Snowbasin, and Powder Mountain ski areas; call a day in advance for reservations and to check if a passenger minimum applies—801/364-8472 (Salt Lake City), 801/649-8567 (Park City), or 800/637-3803.

Auto Rentals

All the major companies and many local outfits are eager to rent you a set of wheels. In winter you can find "skierized" vehicles with snow tires and ski racks ready to head for the slopes. Many agencies have an office or delivery service at the airport: Avis Rent A Car, Salt Lake International Airport, 801/575-2847 or 800/331-1212; Budget Rent A Car, 641 North 3800 West, 801/575-2586 or 800/527-0700; Dollar Rent-A-Car, 601 North 3800 West, Salt Lake International Airport, 801/575-2580 or 800/421-9849; Enterprise Rent-A-Car, 151 East 5600 South, 801/266-3777, 801/534-1888, or 800/RENT-A-CAR; Hertz, Salt Lake International Airport, 775 North Terminal Dr., 801/575-2683 or 800/654-3131; National Car Rental, Salt Lake City International Airport, 801/575-2277 or 800/227-7368; and Payless Car Rental, 1974 W. North Temple, 801/596-2596 or 800/327-3631.

Taxis

The following have 24-hour service: City Cab, 801/363-8400; Ute Cab, 801/359-7788; and Yellow Cab, 801/521-2100.

The Northern Wasatch Front

Immediately east of Salt Lake City, the Wasatch Range soars to over 11,000 feet. These mountains are characterized by their steep canyons and abundant snowfall, the combination of which makes for legendary skiing. Big Cottonwood Canyon, home to Solitude and Brighton ski and snowboard areas, is just south and east of the city; the next canyon south, Little Cottonwood, has Snowbird and Alta, two world-class ski resorts (snowboarding is permitted at Snowbird, but not at Alta). When the snow melts, the hiking here is every bit as great as the skiing and boarding.

About 45 minutes east of Salt Lake via I-80, and a thriving city in its own right, is Park City, home to three major ski areas: Park City Mountain Resort, The Canyons, and Deer Valley. Park City hosted many events during the 2002 Winter Olympics (the Cottonwood Canyon resorts stayed out of the Games) and is also well known as the site of the annual Sundance Film Festival.

Though the entire Northern Wasatch region is within commuting distance from Salt Lake, skiers who can afford the somewhat

The Canyons is an expansive ski area, with plenty of room to ski or snowboard.

THE NORTHERN WASATCH FRONT

Rockport Reservoir

2 mi

2 km

0

0

Red Butte Canyon

★ UNIVERSITY OF UTAH

"This is the Place" State Park

To Salt Lake City

Emigration Canyon

RUTH'S DINER, SANTA FE RESTAURANT

Parleys Canyon

MOUNTAIN DELL GOLF COURSE

65

Lambs Canyon

80

Wasatch

Range

Park City

248

DEER VALLEY SKI AREA

224

PARK CITY SKI AREA

CLOSED IN WINTER

224

Hailstone

40

Wasatch Mountain

State Park

224

Midway

Heber City

40

80

UTAH WINTER SPORT PARK

224

THE CANYONS SKI AREA

80

Desolation Lake

SILVER FORK LODGE

Guardsman Pass

BRIGHTON SKI RESORT

ALBION BASIN CAMPGROUND

LOG HAVEN RESTAURANT

Mill Creek

Gobbler's Knob 10,246 ft

Canyon

SOLITUDE SKI RESORT

SPRUCES CAMPGROUND

REDMAN CAMPGROUND

Brighton Lakes Trail

Cottonwood

Wasatch-cache

National

Forest

ALTA SKI AREA

SNOWBIRD TRAM ▲ Hidden Peak 11,000 ft

▲ Mt. Olympus 9,026 ft

152

Big

Canyon

Twin Peaks 11,328 ft

Cottonwood

SNOWBIRD SKI AREA

TANNERS FLAT CAMPGROUND

White Pine Lake

215

Little

210

Red Pine Lake

152

80

Maybird Lakes

Lone Peak 11,253 ft

© AVALON TRAVEL PUBLISHING, INC.

NORTHERN WASATCH FRONT HIGHLIGHTS

Riding the lift alone at Solitude
Taking a snowboarding lesson at Brighton
Skiing fresh powder at Alta
Crossing over from Alta to Snowbird's Mineral Basin
Riding the terrain park at Park City Mountain Resort
Skiing groomed corduroy at Deer Valley
Exploring the far reaches of The Canyons
Dining in Park City

pricey accommodations should try to spend at least a couple of nights at one of the many lodges, which range from Alta's friendly, down-home places to Deer Valley's equally friendly but ultra-chic digs.

When the snow melts, many of the resorts have summer operations, with lift-assisted mountain biking being the most popular activity. There are also hiking trails, picnic areas, and campgrounds across the region.

Even in the summer, nights can be cold in the mountains, and even in the winter, sunny days can bring warm afternoons where it's possible to unzip your parka and bask in the thin-aired glow.

Big Cottonwood Canyon

Cliffs towering thousands of feet form the gateway to Big Cottonwood Canyon. Skiers come in season to try the downhill slopes at Solitude and Brighton and to cross-country ski at the Solitude Nordic Center or on snow-covered campground loop roads. Enter the canyon from Wasatch Boulevard and 7000 South, about 15 miles southeast of downtown Salt Lake City. The 14-mile drive to Brighton Basin reveals splendid vistas at each turn while climbing to an elevation of 8,700 feet. Guardsman Pass Road turns off just before Brighton and winds up to Guardsman Pass (elev. 9,800 feet) at the crest of the Wasatches, then drops down into either Park City or Heber City on the other side; the mostly unpaved road is usually open late June–mid-October.

Eight picnic areas lie along Big Cottonwood Creek. You'll come first to **Oak Ridge Picnic Area,** one mile from the entrance, followed by **Dogwood Picnic Area** (elev. 5,200 feet), 1.1 miles from the entrance, and finally to **Silver Lake Picnic Area** (elev. 8,720 feet) near road's end, 14.5 miles up the canyon. Silver Lake offers full access to fishing and picnic sites. All picnic areas are first-come, first-served except the **Jordan Pines** group area (8.8 miles from the canyon entrance; has water), with picnic sites and campgrounds by reservation only; 800/280-CAMP.

SOLITUDE MOUNTAIN RESORT

The best thing about Solitude is reflected in its name—it's rarely crowded. Even on a snowy Saturday in February, it's often possible to ski right up to the base area lifts and hop on, with no line. The other thing that makes this ski area distinctive is the European-style village at the base area. The village square is closed to cars—day visitors park in a lot about a five-minute walk away and underground parking lots stow condo guests' vehicles—and the inn and several condos face onto the pedestrian area. From all the lodgings, it's only a short walk to the lifts.

Ski season at Solitude runs from about Thanksgiving until the third week in April, depending on snow.

History

This area was originally called Solitude by silver miners in the early 1900s. It became a ski area served by two chairlifts in 1957, and in 1989 the Emerald Express became Utah's first high-speed quad lift. Until the Creekside condominiums opened in 1995, Solitude was entirely a day-use area. Solitude is privately owned by one family; Intrawest was brought in to develop some of the lodgings but has no equity interest in the resort.

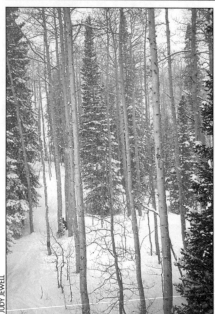

© JUDY JEWELL

Solitude's lifts may be slow, but they take skiers and snowboarders through some lovely aspen groves.

Terrain and Lifts

Skiers can choose from a wide variety of runs—there are plenty of nice wide blue cruisers, and, when conditions are favorable, gates open to expert terrain, including Honeycomb Canyon, containing over 400 acres of ungroomed powder skiing on the back side of the resort. The Honeycomb lift, a fixed quad that opened in 2002, made this challenging, largely natural area much more inviting than it had previously been. Pre-lift, the trip out of the canyon's bottom required a long return on a slow cat track; now, the lift runs from the canyon's bottom back to the top of the Eagle Express.

One of the nice things about Honeycomb Canyon is that, along with all the 50-degree-slope double-black-diamond tree runs, there's one run that's accessible to strong intermediate skiers and snowboarders. Woodlawn, a blue-black run, starts at the top of the Summit lift and goes right down the center of the canyon. There's one short, steep section and a lot of moguls before it reaches the bottom of the Honeycomb lift, but on a clear day with good snow conditions, it's a great challenge for an advancing skier. (In less than perfect conditions, it's terrifying and best left to experts.) Another good, challenging intermediate run is Dynamite, also starting at the top of the Summit lift.

Of the seven lifts, only one—Eagle Express—is a high-speed quad, which may partly explain why Solitude is not swamped with people. (The Powderhorn lift is especially long and slow.)

In all, there are over 1,200 skiable acres, rated 20 percent beginner, 50 percent intermediate, and 30 percent advanced. The green and blue runs are mostly clumped together, which makes it difficult for an expert and a novice to ski in the same area and meet up for lift rides together. The Eagle Express, which is the one high-speed quad, accesses a nice network of blue runs, and the Moonbeam lift has lots of options for beginners.

Adult lift tickets cost $44 (multiday and half-day tickets offer slight discounts, as do various frequent-skier deals). Seniors 60–69 pay $37; above age 70, $10. Lift tickets for children (7–13) are $24; age 6 and under free. If you're skiing here on your birthday (and have good ID), you'll pay only $22.

Lifts run 9 A.M.–4 P.M. daily. For more information, check www.skisolitude.com.

If you're interested in skiing between Solitude and Brighton, ask about the Solbright ticket ($59). From the top of Solitude's Summit lift, you can catch the Sol-Bright run over the Evergreen lift at Brighton.

Solitude has a ski school, rentals, and a program called Back Tracks, where ski patrollers take you on a backcountry tour outside area boundaries.

Solitude Nordic Center

Plenty of snow and nicely groomed tracks make this one of the best places in Utah for both traditional cross-country skiers and skate skiers. The 32 miles of groomed trails are relatively easy to ski, with level loops for beginners and rolling

DEALING WITH HIGH ALTITUDE

Suppose skiers leave their sea-level hometown at 5 P.M. on Thursday, fly to Salt Lake, and get the first tram up from the Snowbird base area at 9 A.M. on Friday. By 9:15, they're at 11,000 feet. No wonder they feel tired before they even start skiing.

It's hard to say who will be immobilized by the altitude. Men seem to have more problems than women, and athletes often feel worse than more sedentary people. But the altitude (and the dry air that goes along with it) can have a host of effects.

EFFECTS OF HIGH ALTITUDE

- Sleeplessness.
- Increased drug potency, especially with tranquilizers and sedatives.
- Increased UV radiation. People taking tetracycline are especially sensitive to the sun.
- Stuffy nose. The dry air can make your sinus tissues swell and feel stuffy. Antihistamines or decongestants just make the tissues swell more.
- Increased sensitivity to MSG.
- Increased flatulence.
- Slightly decreased fertility (decreased testosterone production in men; delayed ovulation in women).
- Slow-drying, thick nail polish.

TIPS

- Don't expect to go flat out all at once. Day two can be particularly rough . . . don't feel bad about knocking off early and taking a nap. Rest is good, even when sleep is difficult.
- Don't take it too easy. It's best to get some light exercise.
- Drink lots of water and avoid alcohol for the first two or three days.
- Decrease salt intake to prevent fluid retention.
- Breathe deeply.
- Wear sunglasses or goggles. It is easy to sunburn your eyes and damage their corneas.
- Use a vaporizer at night; most ski resorts have them in the rooms.
- Try not to arrive with a cold. (Ha!)
- If you're seriously prone to high altitude's ill effects, consult your doctor before your trip. Diamox, a prescription drug, stimulates the respiratory system and decreases fluid retention, easing the effects of high altitude.

---

terrain for more experienced skiers. Don't hesitate to try the gentle, mostly downhill ski from the Nordic Center lodge to the downhill skiing base area at Solitude. The best part about this run (at least for the lazy skier) is the free shuttle bus that'll ferry you back to the Nordic Center. It leaves every hour on the hour from the Stone Haus in the resort's village square.

The Nordic Center is in the Silver Lake Day Lodge, about two miles up the road from Solitude's downhill area, almost all the way to Brighton. It's open daily 9 A.M.–4:30 P.M. mid-November–mid-April. Trail fee is $10 ($7 after 12:30 P.M.), free for children under 10 and seniors 70 and over. The shop's staff offers rentals (touring, racing, telemark, and snowshoes), sales, instruction, day tours, and advice on backcountry touring and avalanche hazards. Tickets can also be purchased at Solitude ski area. For more information, see www.skisolitude.com or call 801/536-5774 or 800/748-4754, ext. 5774. The ski area is 12 miles up Big Cottonwood Canyon and only a 28-mile drive southeast of downtown Salt Lake City.

If you're not so fussy about skiing on groomed trails, explore the loop trails at **Spruces** campground, 9.1 miles up Big Cottonwood Canyon. These trails are also popular with snowshoers.

Summer Activities

Mountain Biking: Twenty miles of single-track within the resort area, plus easy access to nearby Wasatch National Forest roads and trails, make Solitude a fun place to bike. Bicycles are permitted on the Sunrise lift, which runs on weekends during the summer ($5 for one ride, $18 for the day). Rent mountain bikes at the Stone Haus in the village square.

Disc Golf: The 18-hole course is free, though you may want to ride the Sunrise lift to get to the first hole, which is at 9,000 feet (a pretty good hike up the mountain from the base area).

Accommodations

Most lodgings at Solitude are in the European-style ski village at the base of the slopes. One notable exception is the **Silver Fork Lodge,** 801/649-9551 or 888/649-9551, about a mile from Solitude at 11332 E. Big Cottonwood Canyon. The Silver Fork offers eight rustic B&B rooms starting at $135.

Over $200: The **Inn at Solitude** is a few steps away from the base area lifts. As ski resort hotels go, it's rather intimate, with 46 rooms, a fancy restaurant and private club bar, a spa, and other amenities. The **Village at Solitude Condominiums** offers condo units in three different developments: Creekside is right next to the base area lifts; Powderhorn is only a few steps farther; and Eagle Springs, while a slightly longer walk to the lifts, has access to Club Solitude's indoor pool and exercise room. All have fireplaces, full kitchens, TVs and VCRs, private decks, and come with one, two, or three bedrooms. Just outside the main village area are **The Crossings,** with larger townhouses, and **Alpine Creek,** with spacious one-bedroom units for a few dollars less than the in-village places. All of these places are owned and managed by Solitude Mountain Resort, www.skisolitude.com, 801/534-1400 or 800/748-4754.

Food

The Inn at Solitude's restaurant, **St. Bernard's,** is the place to go for an elegant (and expensive) dinner. The menu leans toward the Germanic—for instance, Weiner schnitzel is a specialty. **Creekside Restaurant** features very good Italian food, including wood-fired pizzas. It's open for lunch and dinner, closing for a couple of hours in between. The **Thirsty Squirrel,** a private club facing onto the square, is a popular après-ski pub, with typical bar food.

For a quick stand-up lunch, an espresso, or some basic groceries to take back to a condo kitchen, stop by the **Stone Haus,** right in the village square. During the summer, you'll be able to notice the distinctive grass roof—in the winter it's where cross-country skiers gather for a free shuttle back to the Nordic area.

Cross-country ski or snowshoe (approximately three-quarters of a mile) along easy trails to the trailside **Yurt,** 801/536-5709, for a five-course meal ($80). Only 20 people are seated each evening, and reservations are required (it's best to make them well in advance).

Outside the main resort complex, the **Silver Fork Lodge,** 11332 E. Big Cottonwood Canyon, 801/649-9551 or 888/649-9551, is popular for Sunday brunch and dinner.

Information

For information or weather reports, check out www.skisolitude.com, or call 801/534-1400 or 800/748-4754.

Transportation

From Salt Lake City, take I-80 East to I-215 South. Take I-215 to Exit 6 (6200 South) and follow 6200 South, which becomes Wasatch Boulevard. Follow the signs to Big Cottonwood Canyon; Solitude is 14 miles up Big Cottonwood Canyon.

UTA buses run between Salt Lake City and Solitude, with a couple of early-morning departures from downtown Salt Lake and a couple of late-afternoon return buses leaving from Solitude. Lewis Brothers Stages, 800/826-5844, and Canyon Transportation, 800/255-1841, also run buses up Big Cottonwood Canyon, with stops at both Solitude and Brighton.

BRIGHTON SKI RESORT

Brighton is a long-time favorite with local families for the excellent skiing and friendly, unpretentious atmosphere (no Euro-village resort atmosphere here—it's all about being on the mountain). It's also the most snowboard-friendly of the Cottonwood resorts and is the only place near Salt Lake with a real night-ski-

SKI UTAH INTERCONNECT

In the Wasatch, it's possible to ski five resorts in one day without crazy breakneck drives from one resort to another. If you look at the map, you'll see that Snowbird, Alta, Solitude, Brighton, and Park City Mountain Resort are not that far from each other and can be linked by backcountry routes.

Ski Utah Interconnect is a one-day guided backcountry tour for advanced skiers linking these five resorts. It takes legs of steel and the ability to ski ungroomed powder all day long. One caveat: You can't do this kind of backcountry skiing without a little hiking to reach those great bowls and chutes.

Four days a week (Monday, Wednesday, Friday, and Sunday), tours depart from Park City Mountain Resort and ski through Solitude Mountain Resort, Brighton Ski Resort, Alta Ski Area, and Snowbird Ski & Summer Resort via the backcountry terrain. From Snowbird, skiers are bused back to Park City.

On the other three days (Tuesday, Thursday, and Saturday), the trip starts at Snowbird and goes through Alta, Brighton and Solitude. (It doesn't work to ski from Solitude to Park City.)

Ski Utah Interconnect costs $150 per person, including guide service, avalanche beacons, lunch, lift tickets, and transportation back to the starting point. Both tours depart at 8:30 A.M. and are approximately eight hours. Reservations are recommended and can be made through Ski Utah, 801/534-1907.

ing program. The ski season runs November–late April.

History

Brighton is Utah's oldest ski resort, dating from 1936, when ski club members built a "skier tow" from half-inch wire rope and an old elevator drum. Two years later, a T-bar tow was erected, and in 1946 the area's first actual chairlift traveled up Mount Millicent. Brighton is now owned by Boyne, USA, which also owns Crystal Mountain Resort in Washington and Big Sky in Montana.

Terrain and Lifts

While 21 percent of the runs are beginner and 40 percent intermediate, Brighton does offer some difficult powder-bowl skiing and steep runs. Three high-speed quads (Great Western, Crest, and Snake Creek), one triple chairlift, and three double chairs climb as high as 10,500 feet for a 1,745-foot vertical descent to the base. In addition to the more than 60 runs and trails at Brighton, you can hop on the Sol-Bright run to visit Solitude ski area; a lift there will put you back on a trail to Brighton. Night skiing is offered Monday–Saturday.

Beginners and cautious intermediate skiers and boarders should venture onto the Majestic lift, which serves a good network of green and blue runs. More advanced folks will prefer the Millicent and Evergreen areas. One of the things that makes Brighton so popular with snowboarders (besides the fact that they're welcome here) is its lack of long runouts. It also has an open-backcountry policy, though it's unwise to head off into the backcountry unless you're with a Salt Lake native who grew up skiing and boarding here.

Brighton has a ski and snowboard school, rentals, ski shops, and three cafeterias. Many Utahns learned to ski at Brighton, and its snowboard classes are considered to be especially good.

Adults ski for $40 a day, $35 afternoon only, and $24 at night. Children 10 and under go free with a paying adult; seniors 70 and over pay only $10.

Accommodations

Under $100: The **Brighton Lodge,** below, offers hostel lodging at $90 per night.

$100–150: Room prices at the following Brighton accommodations vary considerably, depending on season, day of week, and room size. Each has entry-level rooms within this price range. Winter weekend rates can easily double these prices.

Adjacent to the slopes is resort-owned **Brighton Lodge,** which offers accommodations with a heated outdoor pool and spa; restaurant adjacent. Call 800/873-5512 for information. Just a short walk from the lifts, off the Brighton

Loop Road, **Brighton Chalets** rents out a range of cottages and chalets, 801/942-8824 or 800/748-4824, www.brightonchalets.com. Each chalet comes with a furnished kitchen, fireplace, and cable TV.

Food

Slopeside restaurants include the **Alpine Rose,** a good lunch spot; the **Brighton Chalet,** at the foot of Mt. Millicent; and **Molly Green's,** a private club.

Information

Contact Brighton Ski Resort at 801/532-4731 or 800/873-5512, www.skibrighton.com.

Transportation

Brighton is at road's end, two miles past Solitude in Big Cottonwood Canyon. From Salt Lake City, take I-80 East to I-215 South. Take I-215 to Exit 6 (6200 South) and follow 6200 South, which becomes Wasatch Boulevard. Follow the signs to Big Cottonwood Canyon; Brighton is 16 miles up Big Cottonwood Canyon.

UTA buses run between Salt Lake City and Brighton, with a couple of early-morning departures from downtown Salt Lake and a couple of late-afternoon return buses leaving from Brighton. Lewis Brothers Stages, 800/826-5844, and Canyon Transportation, 800/255-1841, also run buses up Big Cottonwood Canyon, with stops at both Solitude and Brighton.

HIKING BIG COTTONWOOD

Mineral Fork Trail follows an old mining road past abandoned mines, cabins, and rusting equipment to a high glacial cirque. Waterfalls, alpine meadows, wildflowers, and abundant birdlife make the steep climb worthwhile. The signed trailhead is on the south side of the road six miles up the canyon (0.8 mile past Moss Ledge Picnic Area). You'll climb 2,000 feet in three miles to the Wasatch Mine, whose mineralized water makes up much of

the flow of Mineral Fork Creek. Another two miles and 1,400 feet of climbing lead to Regulator Johnson Mine. A loop trip can be made by climbing the ridge west of Regulator Johnson (no trail) and descending Mill B South Fork Trail to Lake Blanche and the main road, coming out 1.5 miles west of the Mineral Fork Trailhead. See Mt. Aire and Dromedary Peak 7.5-minute topo maps.

Brighton Lakes Trail winds through some of the prettiest lake country in the range. Families enjoy outings on this easy trail, which begins in Brighton behind the Brighton Lodge. Silver Lake has a boardwalk giving full access to fishing docks. The first section follows Big Cottonwood Creek through stands of aspen and evergreens. The trail continues south across meadows filled with wildflowers, then climbs more steeply to Brighton Overlook, one mile from the start. Dog Lake, surrounded by old mine dumps, lies 200 yards to the south. Continue on the main trail one-half mile to Lake Mary, a large, deep lake below Mount Millicent. Lake Martha is another one-half mile up the trail. Another mile of climbing takes you to Lake Catherine, bordered by a pretty alpine meadow on the north and by the steep talus slopes of Sunset and Pioneer Peaks on the south. Total elevation gain for the three-mile hike to Lake Catherine is 1,200 feet. Hikers can also go another one-half mile to Catherine Pass and descend 1.5 miles to Albion Basin in Little Cottonwood Canyon. Sunset Peak (elev. 10,648 feet) can be climbed by following a one-half-mile trail from the pass. See the Brighton 7.5-minute topo map.

Campgrounds

At an elevation of 7,400 feet, **Spruces Campground** has sites 9.1 miles up the canyon. The campground is open with water and a fee early June–mid-October. Some sites can be reserved by calling 877/444-6777. **Redman Campground** lies 13 miles up the canyon, between Solitude and Brighton at an elevation of 8,300 feet; open mid-June–early October with water.

Little Cottonwood Canyon

The road through this nearly straight glacial valley ascends 5,500 feet in 11 miles. Splendid peaks rise to more than 11,000 feet on both sides. In winter and spring, challenging terrain attracts skiers to Snowbird and Alta ski areas. Enter Little Cottonwood Canyon from the junction of Highway 209 and Highway 210, four miles south of the entrance to Big Cottonwood Canyon.

Granite rock for the Salt Lake Temple came from quarries one mile up the canyon on the left. Here, too, are the Granite Mountain Record Vaults, containing genealogical and historical records of the LDS Church stored on millions of rolls of microfilm. Neither site is open to the public.

SNOWBIRD SKI AND SUMMER RESORT

When you drive up Little Cottonwood Canyon, Snowbird is the first resort you get to. It's about a 40-minute drive from the heart of downtown Salt Lake City. Aside from sheer convenience, Snowbird is known for its great snow—an average of 500 inches a year, and much of that classified as "champagne powder." It's a fun place to ski or board, with lots of varied terrain.

History

Snowbird's owner and developer, Dick Bass, is well known in mountaineering circles as the author of *Seven Summits,* his account of climbing the highest peak on every continent. He reportedly had the vision for the resort, including the deluxe Cliff Lodge, while he was holed up in a tent on Mount Everest. The soaring 11-story windowed atrium at the Cliff imparts a sense of openness that was so sorely lacking in that Everest tent. Along with open space and light, Bass also had a vision of a spa.

It was important to Bass to build an environmentally friendly resort, and much effort was taken to preserve trees and improve the quality of the watershed, which had been degraded by mining. Mine tailings were removed and lodges built in their place to avoid harming existing trees and vegetation.

Terrain and Lifts

Snowbird is on the west side of the Wasatch Range, with ski runs mostly on the north face of the mountains. There are three distinct areas to ski at this large and varied resort: Peruvian Gulch, Gad, and—on the back side—Mineral Basin. And, if 2,500 skiable acres aren't enough to keep you busy, you can buy a special lift ticket that allows skiing between Snowbird and neighboring Alta.

Plenty of lifts serve Snowbird, including three high-speed quads and a tram that can ferry up to 125 skiers up to the top of Peruvian Gulch at one time. The runs here are long, too, meaning that you don't have to hop a lift every few minutes. Unless it's a powder day (when all the locals call in sick and head for the mountains), lines are rarely a problem, especially midweek. The one place that does get crowded is the tram; lines can be quite long here, especially first thing in the morning and just after lunchtime. But the tram really is the way to get up the mountain quickly, with access to the best territory.

Twenty-seven percent of the runs are classed as beginner, 38 percent as intermediate, and 35 percent as advanced. Plenty of ungroomed areas lie in the backcountry, too. Snowbird's ski and snowboard schools and separate "bunny hill" make it a good place to learn. Seven double chairlifts, two quads, and a large aerial tram serve the 89 named runs. The longest run is 3.5 miles and drops 3,200 feet.

Intermediate-level skiers should pick up a copy of the free *Intermediate Experience Guide,* a pocket-sized guide detailing a full-day tour of Snowbird, with good maps and clear instructions. Experts will find enough terrain to keep busy for days, including traverses that lead to incredibly steep chutes.

Snowbird has gone to some lengths to attract snowboarders—there's a half-pipe under the

GETTING TO THE SLOPES

Don't assume that you'll need a rental car for your ski trip to Utah, even if you want to visit more than one resort. The cheapest way to arrange a ski trip is to stay in Salt Lake City and take the UTA bus, www.utabus.com, to the mountains. From downtown, take the TRAX light rail south to either the 7200 South or 10000 South station, then catch a bus to the slopes. Buses 92 and 93 travel up Big Cottonwood Canyon; 97 and 98 go up Little Cottonwood. Fares are about $2 each way; during the winter buses run throughout the day.

Another option is the Lewis Brothers Stages Ski Express, 801/359-8677, $19 round-trip from downtown hotels. Expect to hit the road shortly after 7 A.M.

Even easier is taking a bus—either public or private—to a ski resort where you'll stay in resort lodgings. From the airport, both Lewis Brothers and Canyon Transportation run regular shuttles to the ski areas (about $56 round-trip).

Once you get to your destination, don't feel like you're tied to your chosen ski area. It's easy to take UTA buses between Snowbird and Alta, or between Solitude and Brighton. For longer trips, Lewis Brothers' Canyon Jumper bus travels between Big and Little Cottonwood canyons and the Park City resorts (cost is about $20 one-way).

Mid-Gad lift and a fairly large terrain park near the Baby Thunder lift.

Skiers and snowboarders alike should be sure to check out the Mineral Basin area. Reach it by taking the tram to the top of Hidden Peak (11,000 feet), then heading over to the back side of the mountain. Two high-speed quads serve a great network of runs here.

Guided ski tours of about two hours (free with lift-ticket purchase) leave twice a day and tour mostly blue runs. Advanced skiers may take the Snowbird Mountain Experience, a five-hour guided excursion on steeper, more challenging terrain including powder and off-trail skiing (extra cost). A particularly popular program is First Tracks, which allows people to pay an extra $20 and ride the tram before it officially opens in the morning. A mountain guide then escorts this small group of First Tracks patrons down the mountain. Reserve at least a day in advance by calling 801/933-2222, ext. 4135.

Wasatch Powderbird Guides, 801/742-2800, offers helicopter skiing in the peaks above the regular runs; rates start at $525.

Snowbird also offers a number of **adaptive ski programs.** Sit-skis, mono-skis, and outriggers make skiing possible for athletes with mobility impairments. Instruction and programs are available for both children and adults.

In addition to its ski school, Snowbird offers rentals, a wide selection of shops, restaurants, snack bars, four lodges, swimming pools, health spa, and child-care services.

The exceptionally long season at Snowbird continues to mid-May, though many lifts close by May 1. Even confirmed Alta skiers head to Snowbird for their late spring skiing.

Standard adult lift tickets cost $56. Forgo the tram and your ticket price drops to $47; add access to Alta's lifts and you'll pay $64. Seniors pay $36, and two children 12 and under can ski free with each adult (lifts only; $15 for a pass that includes the tram). Half-day and multiday passes are also available.

Summer Activities

Snowbird offers a full array of family recreation and resort facilities to summer visitors. All lodging, spa, and recreational facilities remain open, as do all restaurants and retail outlets. The resort's summer emphasis is on fitness and outdoor activities. The Activity Center (near the tennis courts), 801/933-4147, rents mountain bikes and offers tours for hiking, climbing, backpacking, and mountain biking. A hiking map available at the center shows local trails and jogging loops. Guided hikes are available, and there's a nature trail adapted to guests with disabilities.

Tennis, mountain biking, hiking, and rentals are available. If you're looking to relax, there's also the Cliff Spa and Salon, with beauty and massage treatments. Snowbird is also the site of ongoing musical and arts events.

A summer favorite is the tram ride to Hidden Peak (elev. 11,000 feet) for a fantastic panorama of the Wasatches, the surrounding valleys, and the distant Uinta Mountains. Round-trip one-ride tickets are $10 adults, free for children under six.

Accommodations

All of Snowbird's accommodations are run by the resort; the best way to find out about the many options is simply to call the central reservation line, 800/232-9542, or check the website at www.snowbird.com. Prices vary wildly according to season, day of week, and view but are generally quite expensive during the winter.

Over $200: The poshest place to stay in Snowbird is the ski-in/ski-out **Cliff Lodge,** with 511 rooms, scores of incredible Oriental rugs, four restaurants, conference facilities, retail shops, a year-round outdoor pool, and a top-notch spa. The Cliff is swanky without being snobbish or stuffy—you don't have to look like the current season's Bogner catalog to fit in here (though many guests do). Standard winter room rates run $219–359, with package deals available.

The Cliff Spa offers all sorts of massage therapies, facials, no-polish manicures (nail polish takes forever to dry at this altitude), yoga and Pilates classes, a weight room, cardio equipment, and its own outdoor pool. A day pass to the spa permits access to the classes and workout facilities; people who aren't staying at the Cliff are perfectly welcome. It's best to reserve massages and other treatments at least a day or two in advance by calling 801/933-2225.

The **Lodge at Snowbird,** the **Inn,** and the **Iron Blosam Lodge** are the resort's three condominium complexes. Though they aren't quite as grand as the Cliff, they're perfectly nice, and quite practical places to stay (the three are pretty similar) with guest laundries, pools, steam and sauna, restaurants, and many kitchen units. All of these places are a short walk from the tram loading area. Most are one-bedroom units, with prices ranging $189–299; studio and efficiency rooms are sometimes available for less.

More condos are available through **Canyon Services,** P.O. Box 920025, Snowbird, UT 84092, 801/943-1842 or 800/562-2888. These upscale accommodations are found between Snowbird and Alta, and are available in four different complexes and in units with 2–5 bedrooms (winter rates start at about $350).

Food

Serious skiers will no doubt eat lunch either on the mountain at the **Mid-Gad Lodge** or at the **Forklift,** a sandwich-and-burgers joint near the base of the tram. And while these places are perfectly acceptable refueling stations, be aware that there are a couple of very good restaurants at Snowbird.

The **Aerie,** 801/933-2160 or ext. 5500, is the Cliff's fancy 10th-floor restaurant, serving what they call "New American cuisine" with fine sunset views of the mountains. New American or not, the seared tuna is fantastic. Entrées here start at about $20. If you'd like to partake of the Aerie's scenery but aren't up for such a splurge, check out the **sushi bar** in the Aerie's lounge. It's a friendly, casual atmosphere with really good fresh sushi and live jazz drifting over from the bar area. The Aerie also serves a big buffet breakfast.

The espresso bar in the Cliff's **Atrium,** 801/933-2140, has granola, bagels, and fruit. It's quick and has a splendid view of the mountain. The Atrium is also a pleasant place to relax at the end of the day, with a good après-ski menu of sandwiches, vegetarian chili, and other light snacks.

For a not-too-extravagant dinner, the **Keyhole Cantina,** 801/933-2025 or ext. 5100, has reasonably priced (but so-so) Southwestern-Mexican food and an astounding array of tequilas. It's tucked away in the bottom of Cliff Lodge.

In the Iron Blosam Lodge, **Wildflower Restaurant,** 807/933-2230 or ext. 1042, has very good Italian-inspired dinners. It's not quite as expensive or elegant as the Aerie, but the food and views are nearly as good.

Griff's General, ext. 4035, is a pretty decent mini-mart in the Snowbird Center. It's stocked well enough that you'll find something to cook up in a condo kitchen. There's also a liquor store on the premises.

Information

For reservations and information on the skiing and year-round resort facilities, contact Snowbird Ski and Summer Resort, Snowbird, UT 84092, 801/742-2222, www.snowbird.com. For a snow report, call 801/933-2100.

Transportation

The resort at Snowbird is six miles up Little Cottonwood Canyon and 25 miles southeast of downtown Salt Lake City. Snow tires are required November 1–May 1 (with tire chains in the car). During extremely heavy snowstorms the canyon may be temporarily restricted to vehicles with 4WD or chains.

It's easy to take UTA transit from Salt Lake to Snowbird. From downtown, take the TRAX light rail south to either the 7200 South or 10000 South station, then catch bus 97 or 98 to the slopes. The same buses continue up to Alta, providing an easy link between Snowbird and Alta. Buses run regularly and cost about $2 each way.

Canyon Transportation vans run regularly between the airport, Big and Little Cottonwood canyon resorts, and Park City ($27 one-way, or $50 round-trip from airport). Arrange through central reservations or call direct at 800/255-1841, from Salt Lake 801/255-1841. Lewis Brothers Stages, 800/826-5844, charges $56 per person, round-trip, between the airport and Snowbird or Alta. From downtown hotels, the Lewis Brothers Ski Express, 801/359-8677, costs about $19 round-trip to ski areas. If you want to head from Snowbird over to Park City, the Lewis Brothers' Canyon Jumper will take you there for $20.

Bird Area Shuttle Service (BASS) provides free shuttle service between the different areas of Snowbird during skiing hours.

ALTA SKI AREA

Alta has a special mystique among skiers. A combination of deep powder, wide-open terrain, charming accommodations, reasonable lift ticket

Alta's deep powder is for skiers only—no snowboarders allowed.

prices, and the polite but firm exclusion of snow-boards make it special, as does its clientele. Many Alta skiers have been coming here for years—it's not uncommon to share a lift with a friendly 70-year-old who, upon debarking the lift, heads straight for the steepest black run.

Do not come to Alta expecting to do anything but ski. There is no shopping, no nightlife, no see-and-be-seen scene.

Unlike Park City's resorts, there are no housing developments near Alta or Snowbird, which gives them a feeling of remoteness. The lack of development around Alta is largely due to Mayor Bill Levitt, owner of the Alta Lodge and mayor since 1972, who has fought developers all the way to the U.S. Supreme Court.

Dogs are not permitted in the town of Alta, unless they receive a special permit. Appeal to the powers-that-be at the town offices, if necessary.

History

The little town of Alta owes its original reputation to rich silver veins and the mining camp's rip-roaring saloon life. Mining started in 1865 with the opening of the great Emma Mine and peaked in 1872, when Alta had a population of 5,000 served by 26 saloons and six breweries. Crashing silver prices the following year and a succession of deadly avalanches ended the boom. Little remains from the old days except abandoned mine shafts, a few shacks, and the cemetery.

By the 1930s, only one resident was left—George Watson—who elected himself mayor. Watson ran a small tourist business known as the Alta Scenic Railway, providing rides in the canyon on a jitney, a car mounted on the old railroad tracks. In 1938 he deeded 1,800 acres to the U.S. Forest Service. (There is some present-day speculation that Watson didn't ever really own the deeded land, but he did take advantage of the tax breaks he got by handing it over.)

Ski enthusiasts brought Alta back to life. The Forest Service hired famous skier Alf Engen to determine Alta's potential as a site for a future ski area. In 1939, Alta's Collins chairlift became the second lift in the United States; detractors complained that the $1.50 per day lift tickets re-

served the sport just for the rich. (Some of the original Collins single chairs are still around; look for them in the Wildcat Base parking lot near the Goldminer's Daughter.)

For a closer look at Alta's colorful past, check out the Alta Historical Society's exhibit at the local community center/library, across the road from the Snowpine Lodge, 801/742-3522.

Terrain and Lifts

The first thing to know about Alta is that it's for *skiers;* snowboards aren't allowed. And, even though it's right next door to Snowbird, it feels totally different. Whereas Snowbird feels big and brawny, Alta has an almost European quality. To keep the slopes from becoming too crowded, Alta limits the number of skiers allowed. (It's rare that anyone is turned away; this mostly happens during the holidays and on powder-filled weekends.)

Lifts include one high-speed quad, a high-speed triple, six slower chairlifts, and five tow ropes. Even though Alta has the reputation of being an experts' ski area, there is a fair amount of very nice beginner territory. Of the more than 40 named runs, 25 percent are rated beginner, 40 percent intermediate, and 35 percent advanced. The longest run is 3.5 miles and drops 2,020 feet. Skiers should keep their eyes open as they ride the lifts—porcupines are a common sight in the treetops here.

A good strategy for skiing Alta's 2,200 acres is to begin the day skiing from the Albion Base on the east side of the resort, perhaps even warming up on the mile-long green Crooked Mile run near the Sunnyside lift before heading up the Supreme lift to fairly steep blue runs and some of Alta's famously "steep and deep" black runs. Later in the day, move over to the Wildcat side, after the sun has had a chance to soften the snow there.

Holders of the Alta-Snowbird pass can cut over to Snowbird's Mineral Basin area from the top of Alta's Sugarloaf lift. The cut-across is not difficult, and Mineral Basin is a fun place to ski.

Alta's season usually runs mid-November–April. Average total snowfall is about 500 inches

THE GREATEST SNOW ON EARTH

What makes Utah's snow so great? In a word, geography. Storms come in from the Pacific, pushed by cold jet-stream air across the Great Basin. When these storm clouds encounter the Wasatch peaks, the jet stream forces them upwards into even colder air, where they release their moisture. The extremely cold temperatures ensure that this moisture falls as light, dry snow.

Storm fronts often become trapped in the Salt Lake Valley, laden with moisture and too heavy to rise out of the Great Basin. These heavy clouds make it partway out of the basin, dump snow on the nearby mountains, then drop back to the Great Salt Lake where they pick up more moisture. This cycle continues until the storm weakens and the clouds release enough moisture to float over the tops of the mountains and continue eastward.

per year, and snow levels usually peak in March, with depths of about 121 inches.

Beginners can use the free rope tows beside Alta Lodge and Snowpine Lodge or the three beginners' lifts. Lift tickets cost $40 ($32 half day), $32 children 12 and under, $22 for the beginners' lifts. Seniors 80 and older ski free. The combined Alta-Snowbird pass costs $64.

Alta's Alf Engen Ski School, 801/359-1078, offers a wide variety of lessons; rentals and child-care services are also available. Guided snowcat skiing (and snowboarding) in the Grizzly Gulch backcountry is available for expert skiers and boarders with lots of off-trail experience. Five runs cost $200; call the ski school to reserve a spot.

Cross-Country Skiing

The **Alta Nordic Shop,** 801/742-9722, is at the base of the Wildcat lift, near the western end of groomed cross-country trails. These trails, groomed for both classic and skate skiing, are not the world's most exciting—they essentially parallel the tow rope that runs between the Wildcat and Albion lifts—but they're a good place to learn cross-country techniques or get your legs in shape at the beginning of the season. A Nordic Pass ($7, available at the Nordic Shop) is required to ski these groomed trails. The Nordic Shop also sells and rents cross-country gear and snowshoes, and provides lessons.

More ambitious cross-country skiers can head up the unplowed summer road to Albion Basin. Sno-Cats often pack the snow. The road begins at

the upper end of the Albion parking lot, then climbs gently to the top of Albion Lift, where skiers can continue to Albion Basin. Intermediate and advanced skiers can also ski to Catherine Pass and Twin Lakes Pass. Cross-country skiers may ski the beginner (green) Alta trails. Those heading for the backcountry should have proper equipment and experience; the Nordic Shop can advise on avalanche conditions.

Summer Activities

Alta doesn't offer any summer programs, though a number of area Forest Service trails attract hikers and bikers; lodges remain open.

Accommodations

Alta's accommodations are excellent though pricey: even bunk beds in a dorm room are over $100! Note, however, that room rates at most lodgings include breakfast and dinner. Rates at all the lodges are comparable, from about $115–150 for a dorm bed to $450–500 for a large room with a view. In summer, room rates drop by nearly half. The easiest way to find a room is simply to call **Alta Reservation Service,** 801/942-0404 or 888/782-9258, which can make reservations at all lodgings and arrange transportation and ski packages.

In Alta, one of the nicest and most central places to stay is the **Alta Lodge,** 801/742-3500 or 800/707-2582, www.altalodge.com, an old-fashioned ski lodge that oozes authenticity. Rates run from $120 (dorm bed) to $450 (large corner room) and include breakfast and dinner. Alta

Lodge, built in 1939, is not fancy. In fact, descending the four flights of wood-plank stairs from street level is a bit like entering a mine. Fortunately, at the bottom of this shaft guests are greeted by a friendly dog, engaging people, and a super-size bottle of SPF 45 sunscreen at the check-in window. The atmosphere is relaxed—walk through the maze of hallways at 5 P.M. and you may see a gray-haired woman in a skirted swimsuit, towel slung over her shoulder, heading off to the hot tubs. After hot-tubbing, the same woman will show up, beer in hand, at the Sitzmark Club, the lodge's lively bar. There are no televisions in the rooms at Alta Lodge, but a game room off the lobby has a big-screen TV and nightly videos. The lodge also has a good ski-and-play program for kids.

The most luxurious place to stay in town is **Alta's Rustler Lodge,** 801/742-2200 or 800/451-5223, www.rustlerlodge.com, with heated outdoor pool, fine-dining restaurant, and spacious rooms. But even here, there's no pretense. Aprésski, it's common to see guests wandering around the lobby swathed in their thick hotel bathrobes. The Alta Day Spa, at the Rustler, offers massage, facials, and full-body skin care; call the lodge to book an appointment.

Alta's oldest and least expensive place to stay is the **Snowpine Lodge,** 801/742-2000, www .thesnowpine.com. It was built as a WPA project in 1938, and its original design was a smaller version of Mount Hood, Oregon's Timberline Lodge, another WPA ski lodge. Since then, the Snowpine has been extensively remodeled, but it is still small, cozy, and a touch on the funky side. Like Alta Lodge, the Snowpine is an easy place to make friends—the lobby area, the outdoor hot tub, and the dining room are all very convivial.

The **Alta Peruvian Lodge,** 801/742-3000 or 800/453-8488, is another good choice, with its large heated outdoor pool and grand lobby. Like most of the other local lodgings, the Peruvian has a colorful history. In 1947 its owner acquired two hospital barracks from Brigham City, over 100 miles to the north, hauled them to Alta, and hooked them together. Though the original structure still stands, the lodge has been considerably updated and modernized. Rates run

from $150 (dorm bed) to $250 per person. Breakfast and a family-style dinner are included in the room rates.

The **Goldminer's Daughter Lodge,** 800/453-4573, www.skigmd.com, is right near the base of the Wildcat lift, near the large parking area, with easy ski-in, ski-out access. (All of Alta's lodgings have easy access from the slopes, but most are up-slope from the lifts, meaning that at the end of the day, you've got to be hauled back to your lodge on a tow rope.) While the Goldminer's Daughter doesn't have quite the history or ambience of many of Alta's lodgings, it's a shade less expensive and plenty comfortable.

Food

Since virtually all of Alta's lodges include breakfast and dinner for their guests, Alta does not have a highly developed restaurant scene. All of the lodge dining rooms are open to the public; of these, the Rustler and Alta Lodge are particularly good places for dinner.

Stop for lunch on the mountain at **Watson's Shelter,** mid-mountain near the Germania lift. It's a cafeteria with good soup and salads. Upstairs, **Collin's Grill.** 801/742-3333, is a sit-down restaurant.

Alta's one real restaurant of note is the **Shallow Shaft,** 801/742-2177, across the road from Alta Lodge. It's open for dinner only, with a Southwestern twist, including entrées such as cold-smoked salmon with a honey-lime-chipotle sauce. Prices are reasonable given the caliber of the food: $18–30, including salad and sides. The Shallow Shaft is one of Utah's best restaurants, and reservations are required.

Information

For more information, contact Alta Ski Area, P.O. Box 8007, Alta, UT 84092, 801/742-3333 (office) or 801/572-3939 (snow conditions), or visit www.alta.com. Alta Ski Area broadcasts weather and travelers' information at AM 530.

Transportation

Alta is eight miles up Little Cottonwood Canyon. Snow tires are required in the canyon November 1–May 1 (with tire chains in the car).

N. WASATCH FRONT

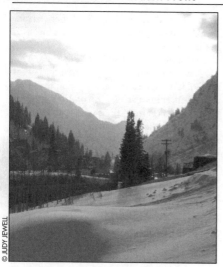

© JUDY JEWELL

the evening sky in downtown Alta

During extremely heavy snowstorms the canyon may be temporarily restricted to vehicles with 4WD or chains; occasionally it shuts down entirely.

Parking can be difficult in Alta. Pay attention to the No Parking signs, as parking regulations are enforced.

It's easy to take UTA transit from Salt Lake to Alta. From downtown, take the TRAX light rail south to either the 7200 South or 10000 South station, then catch bus 97 or 98 to the slopes. The bus ride from the 7200 TRAX station to Alta takes a little over an hour.

Canyon Transportation vans run regularly from the airport ($27 one way, or $50 round-trip), 801/255-1841 or 800/255-1841. Lewis Brothers Stages, 800/826-5844, charges $56 per person, round-trip, between the airport and Alta. From downtown hotels, the Lewis Brothers Ski Express, 801/359-8677, costs $19 round-trip to ski areas.

HIKING LITTLE COTTONWOOD

White Pine, Red Pine, and **Maybird Gulch Trails** lead to pretty alpine lakes. Red Pine and Maybird Gulch lie in the Lone Peak Wilderness.

All three trails begin from the same trailhead, then diverge into separate valleys. On any one of them, you'll enjoy wildflowers and superb high-country scenery. Start from White Pine Trailhead (elev. 7,700 feet) 5.3 miles up the canyon and one mile beyond Tanners Flat Campground. The trail crosses a bridge over Little Cottonwood Creek and contours west, then southwest to White Pine Fork. The effects of several avalanches can be seen along this section. The trails divide after one mile, just before crossing White Pine Fork; turn sharply left for White Pine Lake or continue straight across the stream for Red Pine Lake and Maybird Gulch. Red Pine Trail contours around a ridge, then parallels Red Pine Fork to the lake (elev. 9,680 feet)—a beautiful deep pool ringed by conifers and alpine meadows. Energetic hikers can rock-scramble along the stream another one-half mile (no trail) to Upper Red Pine Lake. The upper lake sits in a glacial cirque devoid of trees. Trout lurk in the waters, though the lake may remain frozen until late June. Maybird Gulch Trail begins two miles up Red Pine Trail from White Pine Fork and leads to tiny Maybird Lakes. From the trailhead, White Pine Lake is 3.5 miles (2,300-foot elevation gain), Red Pine Lake is the same (1,920-foot elevation gain), and Maybird Lakes are 4.5 miles (2,060-foot elevation gain). See the Dromedary Peak 7.5-minute topo map. This whole area is heavily used by hikers, so take great care with the environment. Please follow the Forest Service regulation that prohibits wood fires within one mile of the lakes.

Peruvian Gulch–Hidden Peak Trail gives you the advantage of hiking just one-way from either the top or bottom by using the Snowbird tram. From the top of Hidden Peak (elev. 11,000 feet), the trail crosses open rocky country on the upper slopes and spruce- and aspen-covered ridges lower down, then follows an old mining road down Peruvian Gulch. Elevation change along the 3.5-mile trail is 2,900 feet. The Dromedary Peak 7.5-minute topo map covers this area.

Cecret Lake Trail begins from the west side of Albion Basin Campground and climbs glacier-scarred granite slopes to a pretty alpine lake (elev.

9,880 feet) below Sugarloaf Mountain. Wildflowers put on colorful summer displays along the way. The trail is just one mile long and makes a good family hike; elevation gain is 360 feet. Continue another mile for fine views south to Mount Timpanogos from Germania Pass. It's no secret that early miners had trouble spelling Cecret Lake; you'll see two versions on maps!

Campgrounds

Tanners Flat Campground is 4.3 miles up the Little Cottonwood Canyon at an elevation of 7,200 feet; sites have water and a fee mid-May–early September, then no water or fee to mid-October. **Albion Basin Campground** lies 11 miles up the road near the head of the canyon at an elevation of 9,500 feet (the last 2.5 miles are gravel road); sites have water late June–early September, then no water or fee to late September or early October. Both campgrounds accept reservations through www.reserveusa.com or at 877/444-6777.

Park City

Park City is without a doubt the recreational capital of Utah. With three ski areas and the Olympic Winter Sports Park located in the valley, the city (pop. 7,370) is noted worldwide for its snow sports: The U.S. national ski team trains here, and many of the 2002 Winter Olympic competitions took place in the valley. In summer, guests flock to the resorts to golf and explore the scenic mountain landscapes on horseback, mountain bike, or foot.

However, there's a lot more to Park City than recreation: the well-heeled clientele that frequent the resorts have transformed this old mining town into the most sophisticated shopping, dining, and lodging center in Utah. However, such worldly comforts come at a cost. Condominium developments and trophy homes stretch for miles, encroaching on the beauty that brought people here in the first place.

Even if you're not a skier or hiker, plan to explore Park City's historic downtown. Late-19th-century buildings along Main Street and on the hillsides recall Park City's colorful and energetic past. Here you'll find a historical museum, art galleries, specialty shops, and fine restaurants. A busy year-round schedule of arts and cultural events (including the Sundance Film Festival), concerts, and sporting contests also help keep Park City hopping.

History

In October 1868, with winter fast approaching, three off-duty soldiers from Fort Douglas discovered a promising outcrop of ore on a hillside two miles south of the present town site. Their sample assayed at 96 ounces of silver per ton, with lesser values of lead and gold. Two years later, the Flagstaff Mine began operation at that first discovery, and development of one of the West's richest mining districts took off. What had been a peaceful valley with grazing cattle now swarmed with hordes of fortune hunters and rang with the sound of pickaxes. The famed Ontario Mine and dozens of other strikes soon followed. Silver from the Ontario—as much as 400 ounces in a ton—started the fortunes of U.S. Senator Thomas J. Kearns of Salt Lake City and George Hearst, father of publisher William Randolph Hearst. By 1880, Park City had grown into a substantial town with an ethnically diverse population of 10,000. The *Park Mining Record*, later the *Park Record*, began weekly publication that continues today. Scandinavian miners introduced skiing to the community, though the heavy 10-foot boards used then have little in common with today's equipment. A lively red-light entertainment district sprang up in Deer Valley Gulch, but it's long gone today.

The great hotel fire of 1898 nearly brought an end to the young city. The fire raced along Main Street, reduced 200 businesses and houses to ashes, and left much of the population homeless. Determined citizens immediately set to work rebuilding and constructed a new downtown within three months. Many of the businesses you see along Main Street date from that time. In the

N. WASATCH FRONT

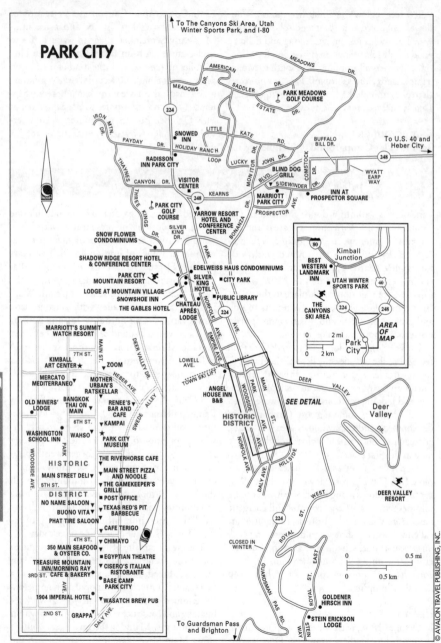

PARK CITY

To The Canyons Ski Area, Utah Winter Sports Park, and I-80

To U.S. 40 and Heber City

MOON

PARK MEADOWS GOLF COURSE

MEADOWS DR.
AMERICAN DR.
SADDLER DR.
ESTATE DR.
MEADOWS DR.

224

IRON MTN. DR.
PAYDAY DR.
THAYNES CANYON DR.
THREE KINGS DR.
SILVER KING DR.

SNOWED INN
LITTLE KATE RD.
HOLIDAY RANCH LOOP
LUCKY JOHN DR.
MONITOR DR.

BUFFALO BILL DR.
WYATT EARP WAY
248

RADISSON INN PARK CITY

VISITOR CENTER
224
248
KEARNS

BLIND DOG GRILL
SIDEWINDER DR.
COMSTOCK DR.

PARK CITY GOLF COURSE

MARRIOTT PARK CITY

INN AT PROSPECTOR SQUARE

SNOW FLOWER CONDOMINIUMS

YARROW RESORT HOTEL AND CONFERENCE CENTER

PROSPECTOR
BONANZA DR.
PARK

SHADOW RIDGE RESORT HOTEL & CONFERENCE CENTER

PARK CITY MOUNTAIN RESORT

LODGE AT MOUNTAIN VILLAGE
SNOWSHOE INN
THE GABLES HOTEL

EDELWEISS HAUS CONDOMINIUMS
CITY PARK
SILVER KING HOTEL
PUBLIC LIBRARY
CHATEAU APRÈS LODGE

NORFOLK
224
AVE.

EMPIRE AVE.

LOWELL AVE.

TOWN SKI LIFT

ANGEL HOUSE INN B&B

HISTORIC DISTRICT

SEE DETAIL

WOODSIDE
PARK
MAIN ST.

NORFOLK AVE.

DALY AVE.
HILLSIDE
WEST ST.

DEER VALLEY DR.

Deer Valley

DEER VALLEY RESORT

224

ROYAL ST. EAST
ROYAL ST.

CLOSED IN WINTER

GUARDSMAN PASS RD.
STEIN WAY

GOLDENER HIRSCH INN

STEIN ERICKSON LODGE

To Guardsman Pass and Brighton

Area of Map detail (inset):

80
Kimball Junction
BEST WESTERN LANDMARK INN
UTAH WINTER SPORTS PARK
40
THE CANYONS SKI AREA
224
248
Park City
AREA OF MAP

0   2 mi
0   2 km

0   0.5 mi
0   0.5 km

© AVALON TRAVEL PUBLISHING, INC.

Historic Main Street detail (inset):

MARRIOTT'S SUMMIT WATCH RESORT
KIMBALL ART CENTER ★
7TH ST.
MAIN ST.
ZOOM
DEER VALLEY DR.
HEBER AVE.
SWEDE ALLEY

MERCATO MEDITERRANEO
MOTHER URBAN'S RATSKELLAR
OLD MINERS' LODGE
BANGKOK THAI ON MAIN
RENEE'S BAR AND CAFE
6TH ST.
WASHINGTON SCHOOL INN
WAHSO
KAMPAI
PARK CITY MUSEUM
PARK AVE.
WOODSIDE AVE.

HISTORIC
THE RIVERHORSE CAFE
MAIN STREET DELI
MAIN STREET PIZZA AND NOODLE
5TH ST.
DISTRICT
THE GAMEKEEPER'S GRILLE
NO NAME SALOON
POST OFFICE
BUONO VITA
TEXAS RED'S PIT BARBECUE
PHAT TIRE SALOON
CAFE TERIGO

4TH ST.
350 MAIN SEAFOOD & OYSTER CO.
CHIMAYO
TREASURE MOUNTAIN INN/MORNING RAY CAFE & BAKERY
EGYPTIAN THEATRE
3RD ST.
CISERO'S ITALIAN RISTORANTE
BASE CAMP PARK CITY
1904 IMPERIAL HOTEL
WASATCH BREW PUB
2ND ST.
GRAPPA
DALY AVE.

N. WASATCH FRONT

early 1900s, Park City's mining economy began seeing more depressions than upswings. Mine flooding, labor troubles, and a big drop in metal prices during the Great Depression caused many residents to leave. By the early 1960s the town looked ready to fold up, but then the big skiing and resort boom brought it to life again.

Orientation

Park City lies in a mountain valley at an elevation of 7,000 feet on the eastern side of the Wasatch Range 31 miles east of Salt Lake City via I-80 and Highway 224. The principal exit for Park City is called Kimball Junction, and although Park City proper is seven miles south, the condominiums and shopping centers begin immediately. Just south of Kimball Junction is The Canyons Resort, with its mammoth new lodges, and the Utah Winter Sports Park, the ski-jump facility. In Park City proper, the Park City Mountain Resort is just west of downtown; most businesses stretch along historic Main Street. Two miles west of Park City is Deer Valley, both an upscale condo development and the state's most exclusive ski resort. Deer Valley's most expensive addresses are in Silver Lake Village, a development perched 1,000 feet above the town on a rocky bluff.

SIGHTS

No matter what else you do in Park City, spend an hour or two wandering along historic Main Street. Even with the inrush of galleries, gift shops, and trendy restaurants, there's still considerable Old West charm here.

Park City Museum

Drop in here to see historic exhibits on Park City's colorful past. The museum is in the old City Hall Building, 528 Main St., 435/649-6104, built in 1885 and rebuilt after the 1898 fire. Go downstairs to see the original jail, known as the "dungeon." It's open 10 A.M.–7 P.M. Monday–Saturday, noon–6 P.M. Sunday. Hours may vary in spring and fall; free.

Kimball Art Center

This large civic art center, at the corner of Heber and Park near the bottom of Main Street, 435/649-8882, exhibits works of noted artists and sponsors classes and workshops. Two galleries display monthly-changing shows of paintings, prints, sculptures, ceramics, photography, and other media. The gift shop has many items for sale. Open 10 A.M.–6 P.M. Monday–Thursday and Saturday, 10 A.M.–9 P.M. Friday, noon–6 P.M. Sunday. (Hours are more limited in the spring and fall.) Look for other art galleries along Main Street, too.

PARK CITY MOUNTAIN RESORT

The first great thing about Park City Mountain Resort is its convenience to downtown Park City: The Town Lift loads right above Main Street! The other thing skiers and snowboarders love about this place is its expanse. There's a lot of terrain, good bowl skiing for experts, and some of Utah's best terrain parks and pipes for snowboarders. In spite of all this space, the resort can get very crowded, especially on weekends and holidays. Lift tickets are also quite expensive here.

History

Though Park City locals began messing around on skis and building ski jumps in the 1930s, the resort didn't open until 1963. Skiers and snowboarders can check out signs erected by Park City Historical Society to mark old mining sites around the resort. Intermediate-level skiers and snowboarders can join a free two-hour Mountain History Tour, which leaves the Resort Plaza every day at 10 A.M. and the Summit Demo Center (near the top of the Silverlode and Bonanza lifts) daily at 1 P.M.

Park City Mountain Resort hosted all the snowboarding events and the men's and women's giant alpine slalom in the 2002 Winter Olympics. The resort is owned by Powder Corp.

Terrain and Lifts

Though many people access the ski area via the Town Lift, the main base area is actually about half a mile north, at the Resort Center.

This is where the main resort parking lot is, and from here, lifts can get you to various points on the mountain.

One high-speed quad, four six-passenger high-speed lifts, four quad chairs, five triple chairs, and four double chairs carry up to 27,200 skiers *per hour* high onto the eastern slope of the Wasatch Range. More than 100 trails range in length from one-quarter to 3.5 miles (16 percent easier, 45 percent more difficult, and 39 percent most difficult). Three terrain parks and two pipes are part of Park City's successful effort to attract snowboarders. Experienced skiers and boarders can enjoy the powder in five open bowls near the top of the mountain—a total of 650 acres. The total drop is 3,100 feet in elevation from the top of Jupiter Bowl to the Resort Center.

Blue runs dominate the lower and mid-mountain. Intermediate skiers and boarders will appreciate the hillside full of blue cruisers off the King Con high-speed quad; even beginners can get a nice long run from the mid-mountain (it's easy to get to by riding first the Town Lift, then Bonanza) by following the Home Run trail back to the Town Lift base.

The Jupiter and McConkey's lifts ferry expert skiers and boarders to a series of steeper bowls. Actually, the lifts get you to only a couple of areas near the bowls; after debarking the lifts, many people hike along the ridges to find just the right run down.

Mountain hosts are posted around this sprawling resort, helping visitors find their way back to the Town Lift base or over to the challenging Jupiter Bowl area. Expert skiers and snowboarders can join free Black Diamond tours at the Resort Plaza every Tuesday and Saturday at 9:30 A.M.

Park City ski area and the adjacent resort village offer night skiing, a ski school, rentals, ski shops, ice-skating, and restaurants (three are on the slopes).

Skiing at Park City Mountain Resort is one of several outdoor activities that people with disabilities can learn with the help of the **National Ability Center,** located on the edge of town. The center provides special equipment and in-struction at affordable rates, offers programs to people of all ages, and is open for summer programs as well. For more information, contact the center at 435/649-3991 (Voice/TDD), www.nac1985.org.

Ski season usually runs mid-November–mid-April. Lifts run 9 A.M.–4 P.M. Night skiing runs 4–9 P.M. late December–March on the Payday and First Time lifts.

Adult lift tickets cost $65 all day, $50 for the afternoon, $26 for night skiing. Children 12 and under go for $31 full day or half day, and $16 night. Senior rates are $36 for a full day (no other special senior rates).

Summer Activities

Although the Park City ski area shuts most of its lifts down for the summer, the resort remains open and maintains 30 miles of trails for mountain bikers, hikers, and horseback riders; for $9 you can ride up the Payday Lift with your bike or picnic hamper. A free map of designated mountain-biking trails is available from the resort, local bike shops, and grocery stores.

The ski area's **Alpine Slide** gives the thrill of a toboggan ride for summer visitors. A chairlift takes you to the start of a half-mile track that twists and winds down the hillside. No special skills are needed to ride the sled. Open noon–10 P.M. weekdays, 10 A.M.–10 P.M. weekends late May–late September (shorter hours after Labor Day); $9 adult per plunge, $3 children 2–6.

Even more frightening is the **ZipRider,** a cable ride that makes a 60-second, 500-foot plunge along 2,300 feet. At its highest point, the rider is suspended 110 feet off the ground. Price per ride is $15.

Drivers actually take control of **Mountain Sleds** (something like soapbox derby carts) for a trip down the Homerun trail. Price per ride is $25.

Other summer activities include a climbing wall, horseback rides, miniature golf, and hiking.

Information

Contact Park City Mountain Resort at P.O. Box 39, Park City, UT 84060, 435/649-8111 (office), 435/649-0493 or 800/222-7275 (lodging reservations). Or dial up the website at www .parkcitymountain.com. Check the snow report at 435/647-5449.

DEER VALLEY RESORT

This is the crème de la crème of Utah ski areas. Here you'll find good uncrowded skiing on immaculately groomed trails with all the extras of posh accommodations, gourmet dining, attentive service, and polished brass everywhere. Lift operators steady the chairs as you plunk your bottom down, mountain guides lead free tours, and, at the top of nearly every lift, a friendly green-parka-clad host points you to a run that's right for you. And, in spite of its reputation as being a cushy, glitzy area for spoiled rich folks, the skiing here can be great, and the people riding the lifts are by and large friendly and interesting.

Like Alta, Deer Valley prohibits snowboards.

History

Though a small ski area, Snow Park, operated in this area 1947–1965, Deer Valley itself did not open until 1981. The owners, Edgar and Polly Stern, wanted to provide a resort that was both easy to get to and more luxurious than other ski areas. The Sterns were soon joined by Roger Penske; the two families still own the resort.

Like Park City's other ski areas, Deer Valley was built on private land (as opposed to the Cottonwood areas, which are on U.S. Forest Service leases) and is fueled by development. It's rather like the typical golf course development, where expensive homes are built immediately adjacent to the area, meaning that you're frequently skiing past incredibly huge, expensive homes.

The 2002 Olympics slalom, mogul, and aerial events were held at Deer Valley.

Deer Valley Resort is the crème de la crème of Utah ski areas. Here you'll find good uncrowded skiing on immaculately groomed trails with all the extras of posh accommodations, gourmet dining, attentive service, and polished brass everywhere.

Terrain and Lifts

Deer Valley spans four mountains: Bald Eagle Mountain, Bald Mountain, Empire Canyon, and Flagstaff Mountain. Though the main base area and parking is at Snow Park, the mid-mountain Silver Lake area is much more of a hub. In fact, at the end of the day, you can't just ski straight down to the parking area; instead you must make your way to Silver Lake, take a short ride on the Homestake lift out of the valley, then ski down Bald Eagle Mountain to the base.

The slopes are served by 19 lifts, including one four-passenger high-speed gondola and seven high-speed quads, providing 88 runs, six bowls, and a vertical drop of 3,000 feet. The longest run is two miles. Fifteen percent of the skiing is rated easier, 50 percent more difficult, and 35 percent most difficult. Though Deer Valley has the reputation of coddling skiers, there's plenty of challenging territory for advanced skiers, especially in Empire Canyon.

Deer Valley is famous for its meticulously groomed trails. To find out what's been groomed, check the boards at the top of every mountain. Mountain hosts can also steer you to freshly groomed trails (or onto ungroomed powder).

The majestic Snow Park Lodge (elev. 7,200 feet) contains the ticket office, ski school, rentals, ski shop, child-care service, gift shop, and restaurant. You can drive 1,000 feet higher to Silver Lake Lodge, a major hub of activity on the mountain, with more restaurants and luxury hotels.

Mountain guides lead tours of the mountain at 9:30 and 10 A.M. from the Snow Park Lodge and at 1:30 P.M. from the Silver Lake Lodge.

Bald Eagle Mountain, near the Snow Park base, is the main beginners' area and served as the site for 2002 Olympic events. Aspiring slalom skiers can take a run on the Know You Don't slalom course; the Champion mogul course is also open to the public. Not surprisingly, the

White Owl run, site of the freestyle aerial jumps, is off-limits.

At 9,400 feet, Bald Mountain is steeper and more exposed; its intermediate and advanced runs have spectacular views but often get skied out in the afternoon. Find steep ungroomed trails in the Sultan and Mayflower areas.

On the right (west) side of Flagstaff Mountain (elev. 9,100 feet) the snow often holds up well, making its intermediate and beginner ski trails good bets for skiing later in the day. Blue runs off the Northside Express are good for intermediates. The Flagstaff area also has tree skiing and access to Ontario Bowl.

Empire Canyon (elev. 9,570 feet) has skiing for all abilities, including a family ski area off the Little Chief lift, challenging but skiable intermediate terrain, and some of the most advanced skiing at Deer Valley, including eight chutes and three bowls.

A mid-mountain course located on the Race Course ski run just above the Silver Lake Lodge offers a chance to race against the clock or another racer. Times are electronically displayed at the finish; $3 per run.

The classic last run of the day is Last Chance, which goes past some fairly amazing yard art all the way to the parking area. (Tired skiers can also board the Silver Lake Express from the top and ride it back to the Snow Park base.)

Deer Valley's season runs early December–mid-April. Lifts run 9 A.M.–4:15 P.M.

Adult lift tickets cost $69 full day, $48 afternoon; children 4–12 ski for $38 full day, $30 afternoon; seniors 65 and older pay $48 full day, $32 afternoon. To prevent overcrowded trails, Deer Valley restricts the number of skiers on the mountain and often needs to restrict ticket sales during Christmas, New Year's, and Presidents' Day weeks. If you're planning on skiing here during the holidays, reserve lift tickets a few days in advance by calling 800/558-3337.

Summer Activities

Mountain bikers, hikers, and sightseers can catch the Sterling lift up to the top of Bald Mountain 10 A.M.–5:30 P.M. Wednesday–Sunday, where they can explore more than 50 miles of trails running from the peak. Cost is $16 for a full-day pass, $9 for a single-ride bike pass, and $8 for hikers or sightseers. Riders must wear helmets. Instruction, rentals, and tours are available; call the resort at 800/424-3337 for more information. Summer is also the season for off-road cycling events, Utah Symphony concerts, and music festivals. For horseback rides, call Deer Valley Stables at 435/645-6530.

Accommodations

There is an abundance of condominium lodgings in Deer Valley, many almost immediately adjacent to the slopes. The best way to book lodgings is to contact Deer Valley Central Reservations, 435/645-6528 or 800/558-3337, www.deervalley.com, and let them guide you through the process. Another local booking service is Deer Valley Lodging, 800/453-3833, with lodges, condominiums, and private homes. Package deals are often available, but rates at Deer Valley lodgings are extremely high—it's hard to find a hotel room for less than $250, or a condo for under $350. But remember, you're only a couple of miles from Park City and about an hour from Salt Lake. It's worth skiing Deer Valley even if you can't afford to sleep here.

Accommodations are in two main areas: Snow Park, the Deer Valley base area, which is about one mile from downtown Park City, and the Silver Lake area, located mid-mountain approximately 3.2 miles from the Snow Park base area. Both Snow Park and Silver Lake lodges are themselves just day lodges.

Over $200: If money is no object, book a room at the luxurious **Stein Ericksen Lodge,** 7700 Stein Way, 435/649-3700 or 800/453-1302, mid-mountain in the Silver Lake area. The lodge is like a Norwegian fantasy castle built of log and stone. Rooms are exquisitely appointed, and there's a day spa with pool and fitness room. The restaurant here is one of the highest rated in the area. Expect to pay upwards of $600 during ski season.

Another extremely comfortable place is the **Goldener Hirsch Inn,** in exclusive Silver Lake Village at 7570 Royal St. East, 435/649-7770 or 800/252-3373, an Austrian style ski-in, ski-out inn with beautifully furnished rooms, hot tubs, a sauna, lounge, meeting facilities, and underground parking (about $400 a night and up). The restaurant here is also extremely good.

At the Snow Park Base, **The Lodges at Deer Valley** are condos with a year-round outdoor pool and hot tub; rates are $275 for a hotel room, $425 and up for condo apartments. These are joined by many, many other condos. Central reservations can help you select a place.

Food

The mid-mountain lodges here are unique because you can actually drive to them. In the **Silver Lake Lodge,** several cafeteria-style restaurants make for a quick lunch. On a sunny day, stretch out in the lawn chairs on McHenry's Beach, the big sunny spot in front of the lodge, with a grilled portabello mushroom sandwich. There are also a couple of small coffee shops on the mountain—they serve Deer Valley's trademark turkey chili and good cookies. For a sit-down lunch, après-ski snacks, or dinner, the **Royal Street Cafe,** in the Silver Lake Lodge, is a good bet.

If you take an informal survey of lift riders here, the most popular meal in Deer Valley seems to be the **Seafood Buffet** at the Snow Park Lodge, 435/645-6632, on weekday evenings. Both quality and quantity are unstinting, and it costs nearly $50.

For fine dining, the award-winning **Mariposa,** at Silver Lake Lodge, 435/645-6715, is a good bet, preparing "classic and current" cuisine; fresh fish, rack of lamb, steaks, chicken, and other meats receive internationally savvy sauces and preparations ($27–39). Open daily (winter only) for dinner (reservations suggested).

At the **Goldener Hirsch Inn,** in Silver Lake Village, 435/649-7770, dishes reflect both an Austrian heritage and New World pizzazz: Steaks are served with mushroom strudel ($32); sturgeon fillets are pan-seared ($28). At the Stein Ericksen Lodge, also at Silver Lake Village, 435/649-3700, the elegant **Glitretind Restaurant** serves contemporary European dinner cuisine ($25–35).

Information

Contact Deer Valley Central Reservations, 435/649-1000 or 800/558-3337 (skiing information and reservations) or 435/649-2000 (snow report). Deer Valley's general information number is 800/424-3337, and the website is www.deervalley.com. Deer Valley is 1.5 miles south of downtown Park City (33 miles east of Salt Lake City), and free shuttle buses connect the resort and the town.

THE CANYONS RESORT

Talk about infinitely expanding ski areas! (And in Utah, everyone is.) The Canyons Resort, Utah's largest and fastest-growing resort, now sports an entire city's worth of buildings near the bottom of the lifts. Over $33 million has been spent on expanding and renovating the resort. Lifts—including more high-speed lifts than other Utah resorts—reach up to seven separate peaks along the Wasatch Mountains, serving more than 3,700 skiable acres, making The Canyons one of the largest ski areas in the United States. At the base of the slopes are two of the largest lodge hotels in all of Utah. It's no surprise that, given all this development, ticket prices are pretty high.

History

From a fairly small local resort called Park West, this area morphed into Wolf Mountain, and then, in 1997, became The Canyons. The Canyons is owned and operated by American Skiing Company, which also owns a number of ski areas in New England and Steamboat in Colorado.

Though no Olympic events took place in The Canyons, the resort is extraordinarily proud of the fact that the *Today Show* was broadcast from the Grand Summit Lodge.

The Canyons expanded incredibly quickly, and its financial situation reportedly is tenuous. A huge, nearly completed property near the base is vacant, and a proposed golf course and skating rink are big question marks.

Terrain and Lifts

The Canyons is the first ski area you'll reach

Skiers survey the run at The Canyons ski area.

coming from Salt Lake City. The resort has 19 lifts, including an eight-passenger gondola and five high-speed quads. The 3,500 acres are spread out across eight mountains; the 125 ski trails are rated 14 percent beginner, 44 percent intermediate, 42 percent advanced and expert. The longest run is 2.5 miles and drops 3,100 feet. For snowboarders, there are six natural half-pipes and one constructed pipe. Many locals who once skied at Park City have shifted allegiances to The Canyons, mostly because of the less-crowded slopes here. However, if the snow is iffy, it's usually better to head over to the Cottonwood canyons; when conditions aren't absolutely favorable, The Canyons seems to have the worst snow of any of the Wasatch resorts.

To begin a day at The Canyons, ride the cabriolet from the parking area to the resort base. From the base, you'll have to wait in line for the Flight of the Canyons gondola, which soars over mountains, valleys, and terrain parks to the Red Pine Lodge, the mid-mountain base. From here, ski down to the Tombstone Express, ride that lift, and from there continue working your way south (left on the trail map) to the top of the Dream-scape lift, which lets out onto a mountainside full of nice blue runs.

Expert skiers and boarders can go from Tombstone to Ninety Nine 90. Check out the runs off Ninety Nine 90, a high-speed quad serving expert runs. The views from the top are breathtaking, the trails there send you meandering through gladed steeps, open bowls, and narrow chutes. You could spend a whole day there, especially after a big snowfall. Also, from there, you can access backcounty skiing on huge bowls way above the tree line. There is a short hike, but it's well worth it.

At the end of the day, ride up on the Super Condor Express, then cruise home on Upper Boa to Willow Drain, a long easy cruise marred only by an uphill walk at the end. (If you can't bear to walk, just ride the gondola back down to the base.)

The resort offers day care, supervised lunches, ski lessons, and rentals for the younger set. The Canyons includes a ski school, rental and sales shop, a half dozen restaurants (two mid-slope), and a free shuttle service from lodges and hotels in Park City.

The Canyons season runs November–April;

lifts are open 9 A.M.–4 P.M. weekdays, 8:30 A.M.–4 P.M. weekends.

Adult lift tickets cost $62, $50 half day; tickets for children 12 and under are $33, $32 half day.

Summer Activities

The **Flight of the Canyons Gondola** ($12 adult, $8 seniors, $6 children) lifts you up to the Red Pine Lodge, where you can eat lunch or embark on a day hike. The resort also can arrange backcountry horseback rides and hot-air balloon rides.

Accommodations

Over $200: A major portion of the expansion at The Canyons has been the building of **Grand Summit Lodge** and **Sundial Lodge,** which sit at the base of the ski slopes. Completed just in time for the Olympics, these enormous hotels are built to a scale unlike any other lodgings in Park City and vie with Canadian national park resorts in terms of grandness and scope. The Grand Summit offers fully furnished hotel rooms, suites, penthouses, and studio apartments. One-, two-, and three-bedroom units are available. Facilities include a full-service health club including indoor/outdoor pool, three on-site restaurants, and bar and brewpub. The lodge fronts directly onto the gondola loading platform. The Sundial Lodge is a luxury-level condominium development. All units have full kitchens, and nearly all have fireplaces and balconies. Make inquiries through the central reservation line, 888/226-9667, or at www.thecanyons.com.

Food

Mid-mountain, at the top of the gondola, the **Red Pine Lodge** is a good place to grab lunch without having to disrupt a day on the slopes. It serves the typical pizza, burgers, soup, and salad. Better food is served at the **Lookout Cabin,** a sit-down restaurant at the top of the Lookout lift.

Dinner is served mid-mountain at the **Viking Yurt.** To reach the yurt, dinner guests ride a sleigh up the ski runs, either directly to the yurt or to the Red Pine Lodge, where snowshoes or cross-county skis are doled out for the short trek to the yurt. The fixed-menu five-course gourmet dinner runs about $100. Reserve a spot at 435/615-9878 or www.parkcityyurts.com.

In the Grand Summit Lodge, **The Cabin,** 435/615-8060, is the elegant dinner restaurant. **Doc's,** just inside the lodge near the door to the gondola, is a popular lunch spot. If you're not staying at the lodge, it's nice to have an excuse to go inside, take a break, and enjoy its atmosphere. Either of these places is a bit of a splurge (The Cabin also serves breakfast—definitely a splurge at $10–15; it's very nice.)

Information

For skiing information, contact The Canyons, 4000 The Canyons Dr., Park City, UT 84098, 435/649-5400 or 800/754-1636, www.thecanyons.com. Call 435/615-3456 for a snow report, or 888/226-9667 for reservations.

The Canyons is 27 miles east of Salt Lake City via I-80 and Highway 224. A free shuttle bus runs between the resort area and Park City.

PARK CITY AREA WINTER RECREATION

Utah Olympic Park

Built for the 2002 Olympics, this was the site of the bobsled, luge, and ski jump competitions. It is now open daily to the public for guided tours of the competition sites, including visits the top of the K120 ski jump and the bobsled run for panoramic views of the surrounding country.

The mission of the park is now to train aspiring athletes. Visitors can often watch athletes train. During the summer, there are freestyle aerial shows on Saturdays as world-class athletes perform high-flying flips and twists before landing in a splash pool. On Sundays, there are ski jumping shows.

It's also possible to actually *do* something here, such as take the bobsled run (with a professional driver). Freestyle aerials, ski jumping, skeleton, and luge introductory camps are offered for all ages and ability levels.

The Olympic Park is open 9 A.M.–5 P.M. daily. Admission fees vary according the type of tour you choose. Adults pay $5–10, seniors and youth (13–17) $3–9, and children $2–8. The park is near The Canyons at 3000 Bear Hollow Dr., 435/658-4200.

White Pine Touring

Park City's cross-country ski center offers rentals, instruction, and guided snowshoe tours. It has a touring center and about 30 miles of groomed trails during the winter at the **Park City Golf Course,** Park Ave. and Thaynes Canyon Dr., 435/649-8701. The season runs mid-November–early April. Trail fee is $10 adults, $5 children 6–12, 6 and under free. Year-round office and shop is on Main St. at Heber Ave. in Park City, 435/649-8710.

Adventure Skiing

Snowcat skiing is available from **Park City Powder Cats,** 435/649-6596. Experienced skiers can explore the backcountry between the ski areas in Big and Little Cottonwood Canyons and Park City with **Ski Utah Interconnect,** which provides a guide service for extensive touring of Wasatch Front Ski Areas. Touring is with downhill equipment. Begin at Park City and move onto Brighton-Solitude-Alta-Snowbird ($150). For details, contact Ski Utah, Inc., 801/534-1907, www.skiutah.com.

Sleigh Rides

Riding a horse-drawn sleigh to a Western dinner or an evening of entertainment is quickly becoming a Park City tradition. One of the more elaborate activities is offered by **Snowed Inn Sleigh Company,** 435/647-3310, which takes guests on a sleigh ride into the forest, where cooks prepare a Dutch-oven meal; while you wait, singers entertain. Costs are $54 adults, $29 children; reservations are a must. Snowed Inn also offers daytime rides to its deer park.

Snowmobiling

Outfitters offer snowmobile tours around the Park City high country. You get to drive your own snowmobile and follow a guide into the backcountry; lunch and dinner excursions are the norm. **High Country Snowmobile Tours**

offers snowmobile excursions to Deer Valley's Silver Lake Lodge with a meal included for $115. For information or reservations call 435/645-7533 or 888/404-7669. **Snowest Snowmobile Tours,** 435/645-7669, runs tours on a large private ranch.

PARK CITY AREA SUMMER RECREATION

Mountain Biking

This is a favorite summer activity in the Park City area. Some of the local landowners, including ski resorts and mining companies, have offered access to their land and have even built trail sections at their own expense. Helmets are always required when riding on private land. The chamber of commerce publishes an annual summer booklet, *Park City Mountain Bike Trails,* which gives descriptions and maps of the trails open that summer. Both Deer Valley and Park City resorts keep a lift open for bikers and hikers during the summer. Deer Valley's 55 miles of single- and double-track trails are stunning; Park City has 35 miles of trails. The Canyons also offers gondola rides to mountain bikers; from there they can access many trails.

In addition, Park City is on the route of the **Historic Union Pacific Rail Trail,** which runs 29 miles from Echo Reservoir to Jordanelle Reservoir State Park.

Bikes are rented by nearly every resort and sports store. (See Equipment Rental.)

Golf

Park City has two 18-hole courses. The **Park City Municipal Golf Course** is at Park Ave. and Thaynes Canyon Dr., 435/615-5800. Designed by Jack Nicklaus, **Park Meadows Golf Club,** 2000 Meadows Dr., 435/649-2460, is one of the longest in the state—7,338 yards. Play the **Silver Putt Miniature Golf Course** at Park City Ski Area, 435/649-8111.

Hiking

The ski areas open their trails to hikers in summer; pick up a trail map and just head out. Deer Valley, Park City, and The Canyons resorts all offer lift-assisted hiking that takes walkers up to the high country without a painful foot ascent; see individual resorts for information. *Park City Trails,* by Raye Ringholz, describes many hiking and ski-touring possibilities in the area and offers a history and walking tour of Park City.

When hiking around Park City, stay clear of relics of the mining past that lie scattered about. You're likely to come across miners' cabins in all states of decay, hoist buildings, aerial tramway towers, rusting machinery, and great piles of mine tailings. Unlike other parts of the Wasatch Range, most of the land here belongs to mining companies and other private owners. Visitors need to keep a distance from mine shafts—which can be hundreds of feet deep—and respect No Trespassing signs.

Horseback Riding

For trail rides and riding lessons, contact **Park City and Deer Valley Stables,** with three locations in the Park City area, 435/645-7256 or 800/303-7256. Horseback rides are also available at The Canyons, 435/649-5400.

Ballooning

Though expensive, a flight aboard a hot-air balloon is an exhilarating experience. Balloons take off in the early morning year-round, weather permitting, and trips typically include a continental breakfast and post-flight champagne toast. Cost is $90 for 30 minutes, $150 for one hour with either **Park City Balloon Adventures,** 435/645-8787 or 800/396-8787, or **Morning Star Balloons,** 435/685-8555.

Fishing

Fly-fishing is a favorite pastime in the mountain streams and lakes of the Wasatch Mountains. The Weber and Provo Rivers are well known for their wily native cutthroat, wild brown, and rainbow trout and Rocky Mountain whitefish. Get your fishing license at **Park City Fly Shop,** 2065 Sidewinder Dr., 435/645-8382. For guide service and instruction, contact **Local Waters Fly Fishing,** 435/748-5329 or 800/748-5329.

Other Sports and Activities

Two-hour **rafting** trips down the Provo River Canyon are offered by **High Country Rafting,** 801/224-2500. Trips start at Frazier Park, 30 minutes from Park City, and cost $35 for adults, $15 for children. With similar prices, whitewater trips down the Weber River, north of Park City, are offered by **Park City Rafting. Boating, water-skiing,** and **sailboarding** are popular activities at the Jordanelle, Rockport, and Echo Reservoirs.

The **Norwegian Outdoor Exploration Center,** 435/649-5322, is a nonprofit organization offering cross-country ski and snowshoeing tours and hikes for people of all ages. For a schedule, check www.outdoorcenter.org.

The local yoga studio, **The Shop,** 1167 Woodside Ave., 435/649-9339, teaches Anusara yoga.

The **city park** next to the former miners' hospital (1904) has picnic tables, a playground, volleyball and basketball courts, and ball fields.

Prospector Athletic Club, at the Inn at Prospector Square, 2200 Sidewinder Dr., 435/649-6670, has an indoor pool, ski conditioning, racquetball and tennis courts, gym, weight room, saunas, hot tub, classes, and massage and physical therapies; open daily. **Park City Racquet Club,** 1200 Little Kate Rd., 435/615-5400, features two outdoor pools, indoor and outdoor tennis, racquetball, basketball, volleyball, aerobics, saunas, and massage.

Equipment Rental

Most sports stores in Park City rent skis and related equipment in winter and bicycles and camping gear in summer.

White Pine Touring, 201 Heber Ave. (Park City Golf Course), 435/649-8710, rents cross-country skis, mountain-climbing equipment, camping gear, and mountain bikes.

Gart Brothers Sporting Goods, in Holiday Village Mall, 1780 Park Ave., 435/649-6922 or 800/284-4754, carries downhill skis and equipment.

Cole Sport, 1615 Park Ave. and at Deer Valley and Park City Ski Areas, 435/649-4806 or 800/345-2938, rents downhill skis and equipment, snowboards, mountain bikes, in-line skates, and tennis rackets. There's also a downtown location at 518 Main St., 435/655-3032.

Jans Mountain Outfitters, 1600 Park Ave. and Wolf Mountain, Deer Valley, and Park City ski areas, 435/649-4949 or 800/745-1020, has downhill, telemark, and cross-country rentals, snowboards, mountain bikes, in-line skates, and fly-fishing gear.

ARTS AND ENTERTAINMENT
Musical Concerts

Summer is music-festival time in Park City. The Utah Symphony and other classical performers take the stage at Deer Valley's outdoor amphitheater for a summer concert series; for information call 435/649-1000. The Canyons, 801/536-1234, offers rock, country, and jazz concerts. The Park City International Music Festival offers chamber music at Kimball Art Center and Park City Community Church mid-July–mid-August; call 435/649-5309 for more information. And there are free concerts on Wednesday evenings 6–8 P.M. in summer at the City Park bandstand; call 435/655-8252.

Cinema

Catch first-release films at **Holiday Village Cinemas III** in Holiday Village Mall, 1776 Park Ave. (north edge of town), 435/649-6541. The **Park City Film Series,** 435/615-8291, offers art, foreign, and classic films at the Carl Winters Auditorium in the Park City Library, 1225 Park Ave.

Theater

The **Egyptian Theatre Company** puts on dramas, comedies, musicals, and children's theater year-round in the historic Egyptian Theatre, 328 Main St., 435/649-9371.

Nightlife

As you'd expect in a ski resort, nightlife centers on bars and dance clubs. The principal hangouts are on Main Street, though all the lodges and resorts and most of the larger hotels have bars and clubs of their own. The **No Name Saloon,** 447 Main St., 435/649-6667, has darts, pool,

and live music nightly; **The Phat Tire Saloon,** 438 Main St., 435/658-2699, has live music and a sports bar atmosphere. **Cisero's,** 306 Main St., 435/649-6800, has live music Wednesday–Saturday and a big-screen TV for sports. All are private clubs, requiring a small membership fee (usually around $5) to enter.

Mother Urban's Ratskellar, underground at 625 Main St., 435/615-7200, named for an early-1900s madam, is a colorful and friendly place with live jazz and blues and a European ratskellar atmosphere. Jazz and pop singers entertain nightly at the **Riverhorse Cafe,** 540 Main St., 435/649-3536. You can drink a microbrew and chat with friends at **Wasatch Brew Pub,** 250 Main St., 435/649-0900.

EVENTS

Contact the Park City Area Chamber/Bureau, 435/649-6100, for the latest news on happenings around town. Major annual events include in January the **Utah Winter Games,** which features alpine and Nordic skiing and ice-skating. January is also the month the stars come to town for the **Sundance Film Festival.**

In June, cyclists speed toward the finish line in the **Park City Pedalfest,** a major bicycle event including a road race, criterion, and time-trial stages.

The **Park City International Music Festival,** 435/649-5309, www.pcmusicfestival.com, presents concerts year-round with an emphasis on the festival's acclaimed summer concert series (throughout July at The Canyons).

Cowboys and cowgirls compete in the **Oakley Rodeo** Thursday–Saturday on the 4th of July weekend 15 miles east of Park City. In August, over 200 artists exhibit their work on Main Street for the **Art Festival. Summit County Fair** in nearby Coalville has a parade, rodeo, horse show, roping, demolition derby, entertainment, and exhibits. Golfers meet for the **Franklin Quest Championship,** a senior PGA tournament held at Park Meadows Golf Club.

September means the **Miners' Day Celebration** is here, including a parade and mucking and drilling contests over Labor Day weekend.

SUNDANCE INSTITUTE FILM FESTIVAL

Robert Redford began this noted film festival in 1981 as a venue for independent films that otherwise had a difficult time reaching the screen or a mass audience. In subsequent years, the Sundance Festival has become the nation's foremost venue for new and innovative cinema. The festival is held the second half of January, at the height of the ski season, so Park City is absolutely packed and then some (as the festival has grown, some films are now shown at the Tower Theatre in Salt Lake City). Definitely make plans well in advance if you want to attend any of the screenings or festival activities.

Tickets to the screenings can be hard to come by, especially for films with advance reputations or big stars; if you can't get tickets, put your name on waiting lists or join the lines at the theaters for canceled tickets. However, tickets to less well-known films are usually available at the last minute. If you are coming to Park City expressly to see the films, inquire about package tours that include tickets.

Park City is exciting during the festival, as the glitterati of New York and Hollywood descend on the town. You'll see movie stars, some wild clothing, and lots of deal-making. For information on the Sundance Festival, call its information number, 435/328-FILM, or check the website at www.sundance.org.

Dozens of balloons take flight over Park City for the **Autumn Aloft Hot-Air Balloon Festival.**

Ski areas open in November. In celebration, there's a big street dance, ski racing, and fireworks, usually near Thanksgiving.

Christmas in the Park presents carols, the lighting of a community tree, and a visit by Santa in December. Skiers descend the slopes with torches at Park City ski area for the **Christmas Eve Torchlight Parade.** In **Santa Claus on the Mountain,** Santa takes to skis to give treats to kids at Park City ski area. Well-known personalities compete in the **Celebrity Ski Classic** and the **Tournament of Champions** at Deer Valley in mid-December.

SHOPPING

Park City's primary shopping venue is historic Main Street, which is lined with upscale boutiques, gift shops, galleries, craft shops, and sporting-goods stores. Don't miss **Mountain Body,** upstairs at 608 Main St., 435/655-9342, with locally made lotions and salves for dry, high-altitude skin and a wide variety of spa treatments. **Dolly's Bookstore,** 510 Main St., 435/649-8062, has a good selection of books for all ages and interests. The **Factory Stores@Park City,** 6699 Landmark Dr., just south of I-80 Park City Exit 145, 435/645-7078, form a complex of about 50 factory outlets.

ACCOMMODATIONS

Park City offers more than 30 B&Bs and hotels, plus nearly 60 condo developments; guest capacity far exceeds the town's permanent population! Rates peak at dizzying heights during the ski season, when accommodations may also be hard to find. Most lodgings have four different winter rates, which peak at the Christmas holidays and in February and March; there are different rates for weekends and weekdays as well. Many lodgings have rooms in a wide range of prices (from hostel rooms to multiroom suites to penthouses), so remember that *the following price categories are for a standard double room in the winter high season.* Summer rates are usually about half of the rates below. During ski season, many lodgings ask for minimum stays—sometimes a weekend, sometimes a full week. Park City's hotel tax is 10.35 percent; add this to any rate you're quoted.

The following accommodations are mostly in addition to the lodges and hotels operated by and located at Deer Valley and The Canyons. For rooms at these resorts, contact the central reservation phone numbers mentioned in those sections.

The Park City Area Chamber of Commerce has an online lodging locator at www.parkcityinfo .com. A similar locator geared to skiers is at www.skiutah.com.

N. WASATCH FRONT

Reservation Services

Undoubtedly the easiest way to find a room or condo in Park City is to call one of the many reservation services; most also offer ski, golf, or other recreational packages. For reservations in Deer Valley condos and private homes, contact **Deer Valley Central Reservations**, 435/649-1000 or 800/558-3337, www.deervalley.com; it also represents some properties in Park City. Other Deer Valley properties are available through **Deer Valley Lodging**, 1375 Deer Valley, P.O. Box 3000 (84060), 435/649-4040 or 800/453-3833, www.deervalleylodging.com.

AAA Lodging & Ski Reservations, 435/649-2526 or 800/522-7669, www.ski-res.com, represents that rarity in Park City—a moderately priced accommodation. **Budget Lodging**, 435/649-2526 or 800/522-7669, books everything from hotel rooms to large condos.

Another good place to start your lodging search is **David Holland's Resort Lodging and Conference Services**, P.O. Box 905, Park City, UT 84060, 435/645-3315 or 800/SKI 2002, www.davidhollands.com. This service owns an assortment of inns, condos, and lodges in Park City and represents other units and private homes, which makes it able to offer a variety of prices and facilities.

$75–100

Base Camp Park City, 268 Main St., 888/980-7244, is Park City's hostel-style hotel. Each room has four bunks, with a bath down the hall and a shared kitchen and lounge. It is clean and has a helpful staff. Rates run $35 per bunk or $90 per room.

The **Chateau Après Lodge**, 1299 Norfolk Ave., 435/649-9372, is a short walk from the Park City Mountain Resort Base and has a dedicated following among serious skiers. The rooms are far from elegant, but this is really Park City's best deal on a private room. The breakfast buffet is a great place to meet other skiers.

$100–125

Out at the Kimball Junction freeway exit is the **Best Western Landmark Inn**, 6560 N. Landmark Dr., 435/649-7300 or 800/548-8824,

with a pool, spa, and a free ski shuttle. Also by the freeway and with similar facilities is the **Holiday Inn Express**, 1501 West Ute, 435/658-1600.

Near the Park City lifts, the **Edelweiss Haus Condominium Hotel**, 1482 Empire Ave., 435/649-9342 or 800/438-3855, has a mix of hotel-style rooms and one- and two-bedroom condos with full kitchens. The complex includes a swimming pool, hot tub, fitness room, sauna, and guest laundry.

As its name implies, the **Old Miners' Lodge**, 615 Woodside Ave., 435/645-8068 or 800/648-8068, started out as a miners' boardinghouse in 1889. The old inn was refurbished to period authenticity but with added luxuries—private baths in all rooms, a hot tub, and down comforters—which Utah's early miners likely had to do without. All rooms are individually decorated and named for characters from Park City's past. Stone steps lead to the lodge, and access to the inn may be difficult for guests with mobility problems.

Adjacent to the Park City Ski Area is the **Shadow Ridge Resort Hotel & Conference Center**, 50 Shadow Ridge St., 435/649-4300 or 800/451-3031. Shadow Ridge offers a mix of hotel-style rooms and kitchen-equipped condos with 1–3 bedrooms. Facilities include a heated outdoor pool, spa, sauna, and fitness center.

The **Inn at Prospector Square**, 2200 Sidewinder Dr., 435/649-7100 or 800/453-3812, is another upscale conference hotel and condominium complex; it also includes a full athletic club and Park City's best steak house, the Grub Steak. There are seven room types scattered through eight different buildings. The Prospector folks also run the **Snowshoe Inn**, 1415 Empire Ave., 435/649-7100 or 800/453-3812, a smaller inn near the base of Park City Mountain Resort.

$150–175

The comfortable and friendly **1904 Imperial Hotel**, 221 Main St., 435/649-1904 or 800/669-8824, began its life as a boardinghouse during Park City's mining boom. Today, the venerable structure has been carefully refurbished and now serves as a homey B&B inn with modern conveniences. All 10 rooms are decorated with period furnishings and have private baths. The hotel's Main Street address means that guests are in easy walking distance to restaurants, shopping, and nightlife. Prices vary quite a bit between seasons.

Also right downtown is the **Treasure Mountain Inn,** 255 Main St., 435/649-7334 or 800/344-2460. Treasure Mountain is a large complex of three buildings with several room types, all with kitchens. The Treasure Mountain has seen a lot of use, and during holidays its rates spike up to $200, but you can't argue with its location.

$175–200

Lodging options cluster around the Park City Mountain Resort lifts. Particularly handy for skiers and snowboarders are the **Lodge at the Mountain Village,** 1415 Lowell Ave., 435/649-0800 or 800/824-5331, and the pet-friendly **Gables Hotel,** 1345 Lowell Ave., 435/647-3160 or 800/443-1045; both are right at the base of the lifts. All guests have use of an indoor/outdoor swimming pool, hot tubs, saunas, steam rooms with massage, and free covered parking; the resort has shops, nightclubs, and good restaurants on the premises. The Gables offers simple hotel rooms, studios, and one-bedroom units complete with kitchens. The lodge offers studio to four-bedroom condo units.

Over $200

The new **Marriott's Summit Watch Resort,** 780 Main St., 435/647-4100 or 800/845-5279, is a cluster of condominium hotels at the base of Main Street near the Town Lift. They are easily the nicest lodging options in the downtown district, with rooms ranging from studios to two-room villas. All rooms have kitchen facilities and luxury level amenities; there's a central pool, and all the dining that downtown Park City offers is within a five-minute stroll.

The **Yarrow Resort Hotel and Conference Center,** 1800 Park Ave., 435/649-7000 or 800/927-7694, is just below historic Main Street and close to the ski lifts. This large, attractive

hotel offers high-quality rooms, a good restaurant, outdoor heated pool, hot tub, and exercise room. Some rooms have kitchens, and there are eight suites.

Despite its pedestrian name, the **Hotel Park City,** 2001 Park Ave., 435/940-5000, is quite glitzy, even by Park City standards. This all-suite hotel has deluxe in-room CD and DVD players, comfy leather sofas, sumptuous bathrooms, a heated outdoor pool, a spa and fitness center, and a good restaurant.

Angel House Inn B&B, 435/647-0338 or 800/264-3501, is a Victorian mansion built in 1889 and converted into an eight-room B&B. Rooms are decorated in period style but have private baths. Guests share a parlor with fireplace, TV, and VCR; the Angel House is just two blocks from Main Street. Rates drop to below $100 in the off season.

Another landmark Park City B&B is the **Washington School Inn,** 543 Park Ave., 435/649-3800 or 800/824-1672. The quarried limestone inn was built in 1889 as the town's elementary school; after a complete remodel in the 1980s, the old Washington School emerged as one of the most luxurious lodgings in Park City. There are 12 large standard rooms and three suites, all with private baths and each uniquely decorated. There's an indoor hot tub, sauna, and ski lockers. Children 12 and over are welcome. The inn closes for the month of May.

The **Silver King Hotel,** 1485 Empire Ave., 435/649-5500 or 800/331-8652, is a top-quality condominium hotel at the base of the Park City lifts, with studio, one-, and two-bedroom units. All units have full kitchens (including microwaves and dishwashers), washers and dryers, whirlpool tubs, and fireplaces; some rooms have private hot tubs. Facilities include year-round indoor/outdoor pool, ski lockers, covered parking, and sauna. The Silver King requests a five- to seven-day minimum stay during the ski season and weekend stays in summer.

Another deluxe condo hotel next to the lifts at Park City is **Snow Flower Condominiums,** 400 Silver King Dr., 435/649-6400 or 800/852-3101, with balconies, fully equipped kitchens, fireplaces, and jetted tubs. Facilities include

© JUDY JEWELL

Historic buildings along Park City's Main Street house upscale shops and restaurants.

outdoor soaking tubs and, in summer, tennis courts and a barbecue area.

Marriott Park Hotel & Convention Center, 1895 Sidewinder Dr., 435/649-2900 or 800/234-9003, is one of Park City's plushest hotels, located in a newer business development northeast of downtown. Designed with the small conference trade in mind, it offers swimming pool and spa facilities, two restaurants, and a lounge; in addition to hotel rooms, there are one- and two-bedroom units with kitchens.

The **Radisson Inn Park City,** 2346 Park Ave., 435/649-5000 or 800/333-3333, sits two miles below the lifts at Park City. Facilities include an indoor/outdoor pool, hot tubs, and sauna.

Campgrounds

Hidden Haven, 435/649-8935, offers seasonal tent and year-round RV sites with showers and laundry; guests may cast for trout in a stream running beside the campground. From I-80, take Park City Exit 145 and travel west one mile on the north frontage road. The campground is about six miles from Park City.

There are good public campgrounds in the Heber City area. Jordanelle and Wasatch Moun-

tain State Parks are both good places to pitch a tent in the summer. See the Central Utah chapter for details on these state parks.

FOOD

Park City has the greatest concentration of good restaurants in Utah. The five blocks of historic Main Street alone offer dozens of fine places to eat, and each of the resorts, hotels, and lodges offers more options, including moderately priced buffets. Note that many of the restaurants close in May and November—the so-called "mud season." On ski-season weekends, dinner reservations are strongly suggested.

American Fare and Steak Houses

A favorite place for a traditional breakfast is the **Morning Ray Cafe & Bakery,** in the Treasure Mountain Inn complex at 255 Main, 435/649-5686, with fresh pastries, omelets, and hotcakes served till noon. For lunch, there are salads and sandwiches. At night, the Morning Ray becomes the Evening Star, serving reasonably priced, reasonably healthy dinners. Another good choice for breakfast, bagels, and deli sandwiches is **Main Street Deli,** 525 Main St., 435/649-1110.

For a Western steak-house atmosphere, go to **Grub Steak Restaurant,** in the Inn at Prospector Square, 2200 Sidewinder Ave. (at Kearns Blvd.), 435/649-8060. The steaks, prime rib, grilled chicken, and seafood are excellent, and dinners come with a trip to the salad bar. Open Sunday for brunch, Monday–Friday for lunch, and daily for dinner. **Texas Red's Pit Barbecue,** 440 Main St., 435/649-7337, dishes out ribs, beef, pork, chicken, two-alarm chili, and catfish in a Western setting; open daily for lunch, dinner, and takeout.

American Regional Cuisine

New American cooking is the order of the day at **Zoom,** 660 Main St., 435/649-7614. The grilled meats are excellent, as are the trout and the lamb kebabs ($18–27). Lunch features boutique pizzas and sandwiches. Zoom has perhaps the nicest patio dining in Park City. Zoom is owned by Robert Redford, and the walls are festooned with photos from the Sundance Film Festival.

Renee's Bar and Cafe, 136 Heber Ave. #107, 435/615-8357, is a sophisticated but reasonably priced vegetarian restaurant with a bar specializing in martinis. The sleek bar dominates this restaurant, which serves vegetarian appetizers and entrées ($8–14), including tasty black bean and sweet potato tacos.

Seafood

One of Park City's best restaurants is the **Blind Dog,** 1781 Sidewinder Dr., 435/655-0800. Don't let its bland setting fool you; the food here is seriously good (entrées $18–35), and though crabcakes and sushi are favorites here, the Dog also makes a mean meatloaf.

Fresh seafood is flown in daily to **350 Main Seafood & Oyster Co.,** 350 Main St., 435/649-3140. Diners can choose the informal oyster bar

or opt for fine dining on daily fresh specials and house favorites like lobster thermidor, bouillabaisse, paella, and seafood pasta dishes ($20–30). Open daily for dinner only. The **Seafood Buffet** at Deer Valley's Snow Park Lodge, 435/645-6632, offers an outstanding smorgasbord of salmon, crab, grilled tuna, shrimp, and other fish as well as prime rib, vegetables, and desserts. Open Monday–Saturday during the ski season for dinner; $48 adults, $22 children under 12.

Park City has the greatest concentration of good restaurants in Utah. The five blocks of historic Main Street alone offer dozens of fine places to eat, and each of the resorts, hotels, and lodges offers more options, including moderately priced buffets.

Brewpubs

Park City's sole brewpub is **Wasatch Brew Pub,** 250 Main St., 435/649-0900. In addition to excellent beers and ale, the Wasatch offers sandwiches, fish and chips, and soups for lunch and grilled fish, chicken, and steaks for dinner. A lighter snack and appetizer menu is available throughout the day; in good weather, there's a patio for outdoor dining. Open for lunch and dinner.

Mexican and Southwestern

The **Baja Cantina,** at the Resort Center at Park City Ski Area, 435/649-2252, serves zippy, full-flavored Mexican lunches and dinners ($8–15) in a colorful and bustling dining room. It's a good place to revive yourself if you've skied until you're ready to drop.

One of Park City's most noted restaurants is **Chimayo,** 368 Main St., 435/649-6222, the area's leading purveyor of contemporary Southwest cuisine. Entrées like adobe chicken, herb-crusted trout, and piñon crabcakes make for exciting, highly flavored dining. Most entrées are $20–30; open daily for dinner only.

Asian

Bangkok Thai on Main, 605 Main St., 435/649-8424, has Thai barbecue ($14), curries ($13–15), and other specialties including many vegetarian options. Save room for the homemade coconut ice cream; open daily for dinner only. **Taste of Saigon,** 580 Main St., 435/647-0688, brings Vietnamese cuisine to Park City. A filling bowl of noodle soup is under $10. **Kampai,** 586 Main, 435/649-0655, has excellent sushi and an assortment of noodle dishes. Entrées range $15–23 in the evening.

One of the most exciting restaurants in Park City is **Wahso,** 577 Main, 435/615-0300. It's name is both Chinese and French (*oiseau,* meaning "bird"), as is the cuisine at this stylish, slightly formal restaurant. French sauces meet Chinese cooking techniques, and vice versa. It's a wonderful blend of cuisines; highly recommended. Entrées range $25–32.

Pizza and Italian

Davanza's Pizza, 1776 Park Ave. in the Holiday Village Mall, 435/649-9700, fixes old-fashioned pizza, subs, burgers, and salads; open Monday–Saturday (daily in ski season) for lunch and dinner, with free delivery in Park City and Deer Valley. For a choice of pizza or pasta in a pleasant dining room, try **Main Street Pizza & Noodle,** 530 Main St., 435/645-8878.

A good midrange Italian restaurant is **Buono Vita,** 427 Main St., 435/658-0999. It's a comfortable place for Italian comfort foods like fettuccini Bolognese and spaghetti carbonara ($9–15).

Cisero's Italian Ristorante, 306 Main St., 435/649-6800, offers a large selection of pasta dishes, veal, seafood, and chicken entrées ($12–20) and the house specialty, cioppino ($23); open daily for lunch and dinner.

If you enjoy sunny Mediterranean flavors, you're in luck. The following are among Park City's best restaurants. Plan to spend $25–30 for most entrées. At **Grappa,** 151 Main St., 435/645-0636, the cuisines of southern France and Italy meet in a lovely plant-filled dining room (and in summer, a beautiful deck) above the bustle of Main Street. Entrées range from wood-fired pizza to pasta (five-cheese mushroom lasagna) and horseradish-crusted salmon. The Mediterranean focus is even wider at **Mercato Mediterraneo,** 628 Park Ave., 435/647-0030, at the base of Main Street in a colorful, light-filled dining room. The menu is a tempting mélange of dishes from the sun-drenched cuisines of North Africa, Spain, Greece, southern France, and Italy. A selection that includes couscous, cassoulet, paella, seafood pasta, and wood-fired pizza precludes easy dining decisions.

International

The inspiration for the food at pleasant **Cafe Terigo,** 424 Main St., 435/645-9555, is Italian, but dishes such as seared duck breast with polenta, rosemary, and brandy and almond salmon with horseradish potatoes ($16–29) show that ingredients and techniques have been substantially updated. Open for lunch and dinner.

The Riverhorse Cafe, in the old Masonic building at 540 Main St., 435/649-3536, serves fresh fish and seafood, poultry, lamb, porterhouse steak, and pasta dishes ($18–32). The Riverhorse also features live musical entertainment; open daily for dinner.

Off the beaten path but worth searching out, **Chez Betty,** in the Copperbottom Inn at 1637 Short Line Dr., 435/649-8181, serves lovely, French-inspired dinners, including an excellent four-course chef's tasting menu ($39, or $59 with wine) and Sunday brunch ($11–22).

OTHER PRACTICALITIES

Information

A number of Main Street storefronts advertise "visitors information"; these places are almost invariably real estate offices, though they do have racks of brochures. For the best selection of info, and a genuinely helpful staff, visit the **Park City Area Chamber/Bureau** at 750 Kearns Ave., 435/658-4541 or 800/453-1360, www.parkcityinfo.com. There's a branch office in the Park City Museum, 528 Main Street. Park City's **public library,** 1255 Park Ave., 435/645-5600, has a good collection of regional books and maps; open 10 A.M.–9 P.M. Monday–Thursday, 10 A.M.–6 P.M. Friday and Saturday, and Sunday 1–5 P.M.

Services

The **post office** is downtown at 450 Main St., 435/649-9191. **Park City Family Health and**

Urgent Care provides care 24 hours a day at 1665 Bonanza Dr., 435/649-7640.

Guardian Angel, 435/783-2662, offers in-room licensed and bonded child care. Deer Valley, The Canyons, and Park City resorts all have day-care facilities at the lodges, or put the kids on skis and enroll them in the children's instructional programs offered at all resorts.

Transportation

Park City Transit operates a trolley bus up and down Main Street (about every 10 minutes daily) and has several bus routes to other parts of town including Park City, The Canyons, and Deer Valley ski areas (about every 10–20 minutes daily). All buses are free; pick up a transit guide from the chamber/bureau, on any of the buses, or by calling Park City Transit, 435/645-5130 (recording). Parking can be extremely difficult in downtown Park City, so it's a good idea to hop a bus.

Park City Transportation provides year-round service to downtown Salt Lake City and the SLC airport for $27 one-way; ski shuttles depart from Park City and Salt Lake City in winter to Brighton, Solitude, Snowbird, Alta, Sundance, Snowbasin, and Powder Mountain ski areas; call 24 hours in advance for reservations and to check if a passenger minimum applies; 435/649-8567 (Park City), 435/364-8472 (Salt Lake City), 800/356-7384 in Utah, or 800/637-3803 out of state.

Lewis Brothers Stages also makes regular runs between Park City and Salt Lake City Airport or downtown ($29 one-way, $56 round-trip). A shuttle during the ski season connects the Park City ski areas with Solitude, Brighton, Snowbird, Alta, and Sundance. Reservations two days in advance are advised for these trips; call 435/359-8677 (Salt Lake City), 435/649-2256 (Park City), or 800/826-5844.

Call **Park City Cabs,** 435/658-2227, for cabs.

The following rental outfits feature cars, 4X4s, and vans; most come with ski racks. Each will deliver cars to and pick them up from Park City area addresses: **All Resort Car Rental,** 435/649-3999 or 800/457-9457, or **Budget Rent-A-Car,** 435/645-7555.

North of Park City

Old ranching and mining communities dominate the mountain valleys that now serve as the I-80 and I-84 corridor east of Salt Lake City. The little towns out here don't offer much for the traveler, though Coalville does have inexpensive lodging alternatives to pricey Park City. The reservoirs here are popular with RV campers, boaters, and anglers.

Coalville and Vicinity

In 1858, when William Smith noticed that wheat that had spilled from wagons here had grown to maturity, he decided that this area would be a good place to settle. Smith returned the following spring with several families to begin farming. Coal mines discovered by the pioneers provided additional income and gave the community its name. Today coal has lost importance, but a large oil and gas field discovered in the 1970s holds future promise. Coalville (pop. 1,380), the Summit County seat, lies 19 miles northeast of Park City on I-80

near the confluence of Chalk Creek and the Weber (pronounced WEE-ber) River.

Accommodations under $75: Frugal skiers can choose to stay at unfussy motels in Coalville like **A Country Place,** 99 S. Main, 435/336-2451 or 800/371-2451, or **Moore's Motel,** 90 S. Main, 435/336-5991. Another good bet is the **Best Western Holiday Hills,** 210 South 200 West, 435/336-4444 or 866/922-7278, with a continental breakfast, indoor pool, and exercise room. **Holiday Hills RV Park,** just off I-80 Coalville Exit 164, 435/336-4421, offers tent and RV sites, showers, and a store.

Rockport State Park

Rockport Reservoir (1,189 surface acres) is tucked in the Weber River Valley 13 miles south of Coalville. Visitors enjoy fishing, water-skiing, sailing, windsurfing, and swimming. Anglers come to reel in rainbow, cutthroat, and German brown trout, and smallmouth bass. The Weber River above and below the lake also has good fishing for trout and whitefish. During freeze-up, December–April, anglers try their luck through the lake ice. Like most high-country lakes, Rockport (elev. 6,100 feet) is usually calm in the mornings and evenings but windy in the afternoons. The state park facilities are along the eastern shore and include a paved boat ramp, docks, three picnic areas with covered tables, eight primitive campgrounds, and the modern **Juniper Campground** (with showers). Reservations are recommended for Juniper Campground on summer weekends, though there's usually plenty of space in the primitive campgrounds. The main season runs April–October, but a camping area (no water) is kept open for winter visitors. Entrance fees are $9 for day use, $8–17 for camping. Anglers may park in highway pullouts on the lake's west side without charge. Contact the park at 9040 N. Highway 302, Peoa, UT 84061, 435/336-2241 (ranger), 435/538-7221 (Salt Lake City), or 877/444-6777 (reservations). Rockport State Park is 45 miles east of Salt Lake City; take I-80 Wanship Exit 156 and go south five miles on U.S. 189.

Echo Reservoir

This privately owned reservoir between Coalville and Echo averages about 1,000 surface acres. **Echo Resort,** 435/336-9894 or 336-2247, in a grove of large cottonwood trees on the eastern shore, has a paved boat ramp, picnicking, camping, and a snack bar. The resort has a second camping area two miles south. Fishing, mostly for rainbow and brown trout and channel catfish, is fair to good. Water-skiing and sailing are the most popular lake activities. Open early May–September. Take I-80 Coalville Exit 164 and go north 3.5 miles (or take I-80 Echo Exit 169 and go south two miles).

Morgan and Vicinity

Mormons settled here along the Weber River in 1852 and named their community after one of its members. The town (pop. 2,640) is the Morgan County seat and a center for farming, livestock raising, and dairying. Look for **Devil's Slide** 7.5 miles east of Morgan on the south side of I-84; the natural rock formation resembles a giant playground slide.

Lost Creek State Park

Steep hillsides covered with grass, sage, and groves of evergreens surround the 365-acre reservoir. Anglers catch mostly rainbow trout; winter visitors come to ice fish. The east arm has a paved boat ramp. Picnicking and camping are primitive; there are outhouses but no established sites, tables, drinking water, or fees. Elevation is 6,000 feet. For information, contact East Canyon State Park, 435/829-6866 (801/538-7221 in Salt Lake City). The road is paved to the dam, then turns to gravel. Take I-84 Devil's Slide/Croydon Exit 111, go northeast two miles past a cement plant to the small farming town of Croydon, then turn left 13 miles to Lost Creek Reservoir. Or take I-84 Henefer Exit 115 and turn northwest 4.5 miles to Croydon, then right 13 miles to the reservoir.

East Canyon State Park

East Canyon Reservoir is one of the closest mountain lakes to Salt Lake City (38 miles). It's also close to Ogden (33 miles) and Morgan (12 miles). The 600-acre lake is about six miles long and one-half-mile wide; elevation is 5,700 feet. Power boating, water-skiing, and angling are the most popular activities. Fishing is good for rainbow trout in the lake and in East Canyon Creek. You'll find a marina and most of the state park facilities at the lake's north end. The marina, 435/829-6157, is open late May–mid-September with a store, snack bar, boat storage, slips, and boat rentals (fishing boats with or without motors, canoes, personal watercrafts, paddle boats, and ski boats). A beach east of the marina is popular with swimmers and picnickers. The state park is open year-round; facilities at the north end of the lake include a paved boat ramp, picnic area, and campground (water and showers, but not much shade). Parking areas with outhouses are along the east side and at the south end. Day use fees are $7; camping runs $8–14. Camping reservations are recommended for summer weekends. The **park office** can be reached at 5535 S. Highway 66, Morgan, UT 84050, 435/829-6866 (801/538-7221 in Salt Lake City) or 877/444-6777 (reservations). **East Canyon Resort,** a quarter mile south of the reservoir, has a restaurant open to the public.

Northern Utah

Northern Utah is dominated by the sprawling metropolis of Salt Lake City. However, there are plenty of things to do and see in north Utah beyond the sights of the Utah state capital and seat of the LDS Church. One of the state's most famous features is the Great Salt Lake, a remnant of a network of Ice Age lakes that once covered the West. It's not exactly easy to visit the lake itself—and at certain times of the year, not exactly pleasant, but this is a one-of-a-kind destination that merits a detour.

The region has a rich railroad history. Ogden was born of the railroads, and the city's historic downtown is dominated by Union Station, now home to museums. The first transcontinental railway joined the Atlantic and Pacific coasts near here in 1869, at Promontory Summit. This windswept pass is preserved as the Golden Spike National Historic Site, with a visitors center and exhibits to beguile the student of history and the rails.

Logan is one of Utah's most pleasant towns, home to Utah State University and a profusion of summer festivals, including the Utah Opera Festival. The town's alpine setting and the surrounding dairy farms make the deserts and saline lakes of Utah seem far away.

Downtown Brigham City's arch welcomes visitors to the world's largest game bird refuge.

NORTHERN UTAH

Strevell

Clear Creek

Cedar Creek

Snowville

Yost

Sawtooth National Forest

Lynn

Raft River Mountains

Park Valley

Rosette

Kelton

Grouse Creek

LOCOMOTIVE
SPRINGS

Promontory

GOLDEN SPIKE NATIONAL
HISTORIC SITE ★

Grouse Creek Mountains

Hogup Mountains

Great

Desert

Lucin

Salt

Desert Peak
6,985 ft ▲

233

Montello

Lake

Carrington
Island

NEVADA

Silver Island Mountains

Lakeside Mountains

HILL AIR FORCE

RANGE

(NO PUBLIC ACCESS)

80

ALT.
93

Salt

Bonneville
Salt Flats

Wendover

80

NORTHERN UTAH

Great

ALT.
93

0   20 mi

0   20 km

Losepa

*Wasatch-Cache
National Forest*

Ferguson

WENDOVER BOMBING AND

GUNNERY RANGE

(NO PUBLIC ACCESS)

Stansbury Mountains

NORTHERN UTAH

The Great Salt Lake

Since its discovery by fur trappers in the 1820s, the lake has both mystified and entranced visitors. Early explorers guessed that it must be connected to the ocean, not realizing that they had come across a body of water far saltier. Only the Dead Sea has a higher salt content. When Mormon pioneers first tried evaporating the lake water, they found the residue bitter tasting—it's only 84 percent sodium chloride (table salt); the remaining 16 percent is sulfates and chlorides of magnesium, calcium, and potassium. Mining companies have extracted salt, magnesium, lithium, chlorine, gypsum, potassium sulfate, and sodium sulfate from the water, which yields up to 27 percent solids. The lake's northern arm, isolated by a railroad causeway, contains the highest mineral concentrations—about twice those of the southern arm. The lowest salt levels occur on the south and east sides at river inlets. Bacteria grow in such numbers that they sometimes give a red tint to water in the northern arm, as do the reddish-orange algae *Dunaliella salina.* The blue-green algae *Dunaliella viridis* occasionally give their own hue to the lake's southern arm. A tiny brine shrimp *(Artemia salina)* and two species of brine fly *(Ephydra sp.)* live in the lake, too. The harmless flies emerge from the lake near the end of their life cycle to lay eggs, then die several days later. Until recently, no fish had ever been found alive in the Great Salt Lake. By the spring of 1986, however, unusually heavy runoff from tributaries had diluted the lake so that small rainwater killifish could survive.

The lake has always been changing—rising with spring snowmelt, then falling due to evaporation that peaks in late summer and autumn. These annual variations result in differences in lake levels of six to as much as 18 inches. Long-term changes have affected the lake, too: Climate variations and diversion of river water for irrigation have caused a 21-foot difference between record low and high levels. Because the lake lies in a very shallow basin, its area has varied dramatically between 900 square miles at the lowest water level and 2,500 square miles at the

NORTHERN UTAH HIGHLIGHTS

Antelope Island State Park
Ogden's 25th Street and Union Station
Brigham City peaches and cherries
Golden Spike National Historic Site
Logan's historic city center
American West Heritage Center
Utah Festival Opera
Malted milk shakes at Logan's Bluebird Restaurant

highest. The record low surface elevation of 4,191 feet was reached in 1963, and the "experts" thought the lake might shrink to nothing. Unfortunately, at that time much construction was going on near the shore without thought that the waters could rise. The lake's previous record high had occurred in 1873, causing concern to Brigham Young and other church leaders. They devised a plan to pump lake water into the desert to the west, but receding levels eliminated the need for the pumping project.

Utahns haven't always been so lucky. In just five years, from 1982 to 1987, the lake rose 12 feet to record elevations. The spreading waters threatened to inundate parts of Salt Lake City, nearby towns and farms, the airport, rail lines, and I-80. High levels also upset the lake's ecology and ruined much of the surrounding marshland. Seven of the state's nine bird refuges were flooded including world-famous Bear River Migratory Bird Refuge. (For a poignant account of these times, read Terry Tempest Williams' memoir, *Refuge: An Unnatural History of Family and Place.*) An emergency session of the Utah Legislature in May 1986 authorized a pumping project with an initial price tag of $60 million to transfer water to the West Pond site in the Great Salt Lake Desert. From a peak elevation of 4,212 feet in January 1987, the lake level subsided, soon eliminating the need for pumping. With the current drought pushing the lake toward record lows, the Great Salt Lake continues to confound the experts.

Great Salt Lake State Park

Bathers have enjoyed hopping into the lake ever since the 1847 arrival of Mormon pioneers. Extreme buoyancy in the dense water makes it impossible for a bather to sink—no swimming ability is needed! But put your head underwater and you'll quickly realize that the salty water causes great irritation to the eyes, throat, and nose. During summer algae blooms, the odor of the water irritates the nose.

Beginning in the 1880s, several resorts popped up along the lake's east and south shores. Besides bathing, guests could enjoy lake cruises, dances, concerts, bowling, arcade games, and roller-coaster rides. **Saltair Resort** stood as the last and grandest of the old resorts. Completed in 1893, the Moorish structure rose five stories and contained a huge dance floor where as many as 1,000 couples could enjoy the orchestra's rhythms. A rail line from Salt Lake City ran out on a 4,000-foot pier to the resort, which stood on pilings over the water. After 1930, low water levels, the Great Depression, fires, and fewer visitors gradually brought an end to Saltair. Its buildings burned for the second time in 1970.

A developer has recently built a smaller replica of the Saltair Resort on the Great Salt Lake's southern shore near I-80 Exit 104. Despite floods of rising lake waters and wind damage, this Saltair is still open, though it is nowhere near as glamorous as the resort's earlier incarnations. The main structure has a smattering of gift shops (Christmas tree ornaments made of salt), food concessions, and a small museum; videos detail the history of the lake and promote the race course at Bonneville Salt Flats. A short causeway leads out into the lake, where you can get a good whiff of the brackish water. Saltair is also a popular site for concerts; for information on events, call 801/250-4400.

The adjacent **Great Salt Lake State Park beaches,** 801/250-1898, are popular in summer; free entry. Stop in at the nearby **Great Salt Lake visitors center,** 801/533-4083, to see a video and exhibits about the lake; free. A good selection of local travel information is available, too. Open 9 A.M.–4 P.M. daily year-round. From Salt Lake City, drive west nine miles on I-80,

hiking Antelope Island, the largest of the Great Salt Lake's eight islands take Exit 111 (7200 West), and follow the north frontage road west to the beaches; or take I-80 Exit 104 (Magna) and turn east on the north frontage road.

Salt Island Adventures, 801/252-9336, www.gslcruises.com, offers cruise-boat excursions on the Great Salt Lake. Cruises leave from the Great Salt Lake State Marina (I-80 Exit 104); options include a one-hour sightseeing tour ($12 adults, $10 seniors and children under 12); a six-hour lake tour ($64 adult, $62 seniors, and $37 children); and a sunset/dinner cruise ($48 adult, $46 senior, and $38 children).

Antelope Island State Park

Though just a short distance offshore from Salt Lake City, Antelope Island seems a world away. Its rocky slopes, rolling grasslands, marshes, sand dunes, and lake views instill a sense of remoteness and rugged beauty. An extension of the Oquirrh Mountains, Antelope Island is the largest of the lake's eight islands. It measures 15 miles long and 5 miles wide; Frary Peak (elev. 6,596 feet) rises in the center. Archaeologists have found prehistoric sites showing that Native Americanss came here long ago, perhaps on a land bridge during times of low lake level. In 1843, explorers John Frémont and Kit Carson rode their horses across a sandbar to the island and named it after the antelope (pronghorn) herds that the party hunted for food. In 1849, Brigham Young established a ranch here for the church's herds of cattle, sheep, and horses. Ranching has continued

to be a major activity, though the Mormons lost ownership of the island in 1884.

Antelope Island is home to over 500 bison, as well as deer, bighorn sheep, pronghorn, and other wildlife. The yearly bison roundup (late October) is a big event for both cowboys and visitors: The bison are driven to corrals on the north end of the island and given veterinary checkups. To keep the herd small enough to avoid overgrazing, some animals are culled out for sale or for hunt.

Thanks largely to its population of brine flies and shrimp, the Great Salt Lake attracts a wide variety of birds and is an important migratory stop. Antelope Island is a good place to look for eared grebes, avocet, black-necked stilts, willets, sanderlings, long-billed curlews, burrowing owls, chukars, and all sorts of raptors.

The entire island is a state park, accessible via a seven-mile paved causeway (entrance fee is $8 per vehicle). Antelope Island is a great place for mountain biking; park trails open to hiking, bicycling, and horseback riding allow access to much of the island. Campsites run $11 (including the toll and day-use fee) and can be reserved by calling 800/322-3770. Showers and restrooms are available in the swimming area in the northwest corner of the island. Take I-15 Exit 335 (two-thirds of the way north to Ogden), then drive nine miles west to the start of the causeway and the entrance booth. For information write to 4528 West 1700 South, Syracuse, UT 84075, or call 801/773-2941.

Ogden

Located at the northern edge of the Wasatch Front urban area, Ogden remains very much its own city even as it is engulfed by suburbs. Ogden was one of the West's most important rail hubs at the beginning of the 20th century, and in the downtown area vestiges of the city's affluence remain in the grand architecture and the impressive Union Pacific Depot.

Today, Ogden is Utah's third largest city, with a population of 65,500, housing over 125,000 people in the metro area. The city is worth exploring for its museums, historic sites, and access to scenic spots in the Wasatch Range, which looms precipitously just behind the city. Ogden Canyon, beginning on the east edge of town and leading into the Wasatch, leads up to lakes, campgrounds, hiking trails, and three downhill ski areas. Several 2002 Winter Olympic events took place in the Ogden area, including the downhill and super-G ski races and the men's and women's curling competition. Ogden lies 35 miles north of Salt Lake City off I-15.

History

Tribes of nomadic Shoshoni chose the confluence of the Weber and Ogden Rivers as a winter camp because of its relatively mild climate, good fishing and hunting, and plentiful grass for their horses. This same location, the site of present-day Ogden, was also used in the winter of 1825–1826 by a group of American fur trappers and their Native American wives and children. The Shoshoni maintained friendly relations with the new Americans and continued to camp in the area.

Peter Skene Ogden of the British Hudson's Bay Company explored and trapped in the upper reaches of the Ogden and Weber Valleys, but he never descended to the site of the city that bears his name. In 1846, Miles Goodyear established an out-of-the-way trading post and stockade here, one of the first permanent settlements in Utah, and named it Fort Buenaventura.

When Mormons arrived at the site of Salt Lake City in 1847, Goodyear, a former mountain man, felt too crowded, so he sold out to the Mormons and left for California. Captain James Brown of the Mormon Battalion, who negotiated the purchase, moved in with his family. In 1849, Brigham Young visited the site, then known as Brownsville, and thought it favorable for settlement. The following year he sent 100 families to found the town of Ogden. The pioneer community suffered floods, drought, early frosts, insects, cholera, and Native American attacks but managed to survive. At times residents had to supplement their meager harvests with the roots of sego lilies, thistles, and other wild plants.

Arrival of the transcontinental railroad in 1869 changed Ogden forever. Although the railroad's Golden Spike had been driven at Promontory Summit, 55 miles to the northwest, Ogden earned the title "Junction City" as lines branched from it through Utah and into surrounding states. New industries and an expanding non-Mormon population transformed the sleepy farm town into a bustling city. Today, Ogden serves as a major administrative, manufacturing, and livestock center for the intermountain West.

Orientation

Mormon pioneers laid out the city in their typically neat fashion but adopted an unusual street system. Streets running east-west are numbered, from 1st Street in the north of town to 47th Street in the south; streets running north-south commemorate U.S. presidents and other historical figures. The streets were laid out before the city had found its center—today, the intersection of 25th Street and Washington Boulevard is usually considered the center.

SIGHTS

Union Station Museums

Travelers thronged into the cavernous Union Station Building during the grand old days of railroading. Completed in 1924, it saw more than 120 trains daily during the peak World War II years. Now, though, Union Station

OGGDEN

To Brigham City (Golden Spike Fruitway) ↑

24TH ST.
WESTERN COLONY INN
2ND   ST.

OGDEN PLAZA

LA FERROVIA RISTORANTE
PEERY'S EGYPTIAN THEATRE
BANGKOK GARDEN

GROUNDS FOR COFFEE
BISTRO 258
25TH ST.

ROOSTER'S 25TH STREET BREWING COMPANY
GREYHOUND BUS STATION
OGDEN MUNICIPAL PARK

LINCOLN · GRANT · WASHINGTON

BEN LOMOND COMMUNITY POOL

OGDEN NATURE CENTER

To I-15 and Best Western High Country Inn
12TH   ST.
89
39
203

MILLSTREAM MOTEL
CANYON RD.
To Ogden Valley Ski Resorts
39

MOTEL 6 OGDEN
16TH ST.
ECCLES DINOSAUR PARK

LORIN FARR COMMUNITY POOL
PARK   BLVD.
EL MONTE GOLF COURSE
TIMBER MINE

Ogden   River
To Super 8, Best Rest Inn, Comfort Suites and Tamarack Restaurant
104

VALLEY DR.

PRAIRIE SCHOONER
20TH   ST.

21ST
21ST ST.
TRAVELODGE OGDEN
ST.

WILSON LN.
EXCHANGE RD.
22ND
TABERNACLE SQUARE
ST.
POLK · TAYLOR · FILLMORE

23RD
OGDEN CITY MALL
BLVD.   BLVD.

UNION GRILL
24TH
WEBER COUNTY MAIN LIBRARY
ST.

UNION STATION MUSEUMS
SEE DETAIL
89
25TH
ST.
203

Fort Buenaventura State Park
River
CAJUN SKILLET
26TH
OGDEN RANGER DISTRICT

POST OFFICE
ECCLES COMMUNITY ART CENTER
27TH
ST.

MARSHALL WHITE CENTER POOL
28TH
ST.

15
29TH
OGDEN COMMUNITY POOL
ST.

MADISON
30TH
POLK

31ST
MT. OGDEN PARK AND GOLF COURSE
79
32ND
MONROE · QUINCY
LAUREL ST.

OGDEN MUNICIPAL AIRPORT
DAYS INN OGDEN
JACKSON · VAN BUREN · HARRISON · TYLER · TAYLOR

WALL · LINCOLN · GRANT · ADAMS · JEFFERSON
36TH

To Hill Aerospace Museum
Weber River

WEBER STATE UNIVERSITY (ENTRANCE AND INFORMATION BOOTH)
WEBER STATE UNIVERSITY
SKYLINE DR.

26
RIVERDALE   RD.
89
0   1 mi
0   1 km
203
DEE EVENT CENTER/ ICE SHEET

BAVARIAN CHALET
COUNTRY HILLS

To I-84
BERCONI'S PASTA HOUSE
46TH ST.

© AVALON TRAVEL PUBLISHING, INC.

echoes mostly with memories. Visit the main lobby to see murals painted in 1978, when the city restored the station to its former glory. The South Mural shows workers of the Central Pacific (many of them immigrants from China) building the first transcontinental railroad from Sacramento; the North Mural pictures the Union Pacific crew laying its line from Omaha. Special shows and performances occasionally take place in the lobby or at the M.S. Browning Theatre.

Union Station, 25th St. and Wall Ave., 801/629-8444, houses the **Ogden-Weber Convention and Visitors Bureau Information Center,** 801/627-8288 or 800/ALL-UTAH, www .ogdencvb.org, supplier of local travel information; it's open 8 A.M.–8 P.M. Monday–Saturday and 10 A.M.–7 P.M. Sunday from Memorial Day weekend to Labor Day weekend and 8 A.M.– 5 P.M. Monday–Friday the rest of the year. In the same office, the **Forest Service Information Center,** 801/625-5306, provides recreation information for forested areas in the Wasatch Range; open 8 A.M.–4:30 P.M. Monday–Friday (and Saturday in summer). The station also houses the Union Grill Restaurant, a model train store, and a gift shop.

The museums and art gallery in the station are well worth a visit. A single ticket gives admission to all exhibitions—$4 adults, $2 children 3–12, and $3 ages 65 and over. Hours are 10 A.M.–5 P.M. Monday–Saturday (also 11 A.M.– 3 P.M. Sunday in summer).

The **Browning-Kimball Car Museum** displays a glittering collection of about a dozen antique autos ranging from a one-cylinder 1901 Oldsmobile to a 16-cylinder 1930 Cadillac sports sedan. Chicago gangsters once owned the 1931 Pierce Arrow, probably the museum's most famous car; note the built-in gun holster. Car exhibits rotate about three times a year. The Utah License-Plate Exhibit shows every tag from 1915, when they were first issued, to the present.

Wattis-Dumke Railroad Museum uses highly detailed dioramas to illustrate railroad scenes and construction feats. Eight model trains (HO scale) roll through the Ogden rail yard, wind through a model of the Sierra and Humboldt Palisades,

cross the Great Salt Lake on the Lucin Cutoff, and descend Weber Canyon. Exhibits and photos show railroading history and great trains, such as the "Big Boys," which weighed more than one million pounds and pulled heavy freights up the mountain ranges. A documentary film about the first transcontinental railroad is shown on request. Outside, just south of the station, you can visit giant diesel locomotives and some cabooses; ask for tour times.

The **Natural History Museum** displays beautiful rocks, minerals, and gemstones. Fossils reveal imprints of dinosaurs and other prehistoric life forms, and you can look at Native American artifacts and crafts. On display is a smoky quartz specimen weighing 19 pounds— over 44,000 carats—said to be the world's largest faceted stone.

Browning Firearms Museum (upstairs) contains the gun shop of and many examples of firearms invented by the Browning family. John M. Browning (1855–1926), a genius in his field, held 75 major gun patents. He developed the world's first successful automatic firearms, which used gases from the bullet to expel the old shell, load a new one, and cock the mechanism. The skillfully done exhibitions display both military and civilian handguns, automatic weapons, rifles, and shotguns. A 17-minute slide show illustrates the Browning family's story and advancement of firearms design.

The Gallery at the Station (also upstairs) displays paintings, sculpture, and photography in a former pigeon roost. Exhibitions rotate monthly.

Historic 25th Street

When Ogden was the railroad's main transport hub, 25th was the city's main street. Running like a wide boulevard between Washington Avenue and the palatial Union Pacific Depot, the street boasted the city's first grocery and hardware stores, blacksmith shops, livery stables, hotels, and restaurants, many of them run by immigrants attracted by the railroads. Most of the buildings were built for posterity in red brick and handsome vernacular styles.

After the city's residents came to rely less on the railway and more on the motor car, the city's orientation changed, and this historic precinct fell into disrepair and ill-repute. In the last decade, artists and small cafés have colonized the street because of its cheap rents, and a younger generation finds aesthetic value in the lovely historic commercial architecture. Twenty-fifth Street now serves as a combination of gallery and restaurant row, while still functioning as the city's bowery. It's a pleasant place for a stroll, and many of the shops and cafés are worth a detour. Pick up a brochure detailing histories of many of these buildings from the tourist office in Union Station.

On summer Saturdays, the **25th St. Farmer's & Art Market** takes over Ogden Municipal Park at 25th and Grant. Also in the park is the **Ogden Amphitheater,** with free events all summer, including free movies and classical music concerts on Monday nights.

Peery's Egyptian Theater
You can't miss the unusual facade of this venerable building near the corner of 25th Street and Washington Avenue. Looking suspiciously like an Egyptian sun temple, this old-time movie palace and vaudeville theater was built in 1924 in the "atmospheric" style during the fit of Egyptomania that followed the discovery of King Tut's tomb. After falling into disrepair for many years, the old theater was completely refurbished and serves as Ogden's performing arts center. The interior of the hall is equally astonishing, with a sun that moves across the ceiling, floating clouds, and glittering stars. With columns, hieroglyphs, and mummies everywhere, the theater looks like the set for *Aida*. The Egyptian, 2415 Washington Blvd., keeps very busy with a series of top-notch musical performances and regional theater productions. For information on current performances, call 801/395-3200 or 800/337-2690.

Adjacent to the Egyptian Theater is the **David Eccles Conference Center,** a handsome new building designed to harmonize architecturally with the theater. Together the conference center and the theater form the core of Ogden's convention facility.

Weber County Daughters of Utah Pioneer Museum and the Miles Goodyear Cabin
Drop in to examine the furnishings, clothes, and crafts of Mormon pioneers. Walk behind the museum to see the Goodyear cabin, probably the oldest non-Native American structure in Utah. It was built in about 1845 of cottonwood logs and later moved here from its original site near the Weber River. The cabin can be seen even when the museum is closed. Pioneer Museum, 2148 Grant Ave., in the former Weber Stake Relief Society Building (1902), 801/393-4460, is open 10 A.M.–5 P.M. Monday–Saturday Memorial Day–Labor Day; free.

Ogden Temple and Tabernacle
The modern temple of white cast stone and reflective glass has a central gold spire much like that of the Provo Temple. In fact, both temples were designed by the same architect. Dedicated in January 1972, the Ogden Temple contains 283 rooms on four levels and efficiently accommodates many people while retaining a reverent atmosphere; only Mormons engaged in sacred ordinance work may enter. The white-steepled Ogden Tabernacle, 2133 Washington Blvd. on Tabernacle Square, completed in 1956, sits just to the north. Visitors are welcome inside the tabernacle when it's open, 9 A.M.–5 P.M. Monday–Saturday in the summer.

Fort Buenaventura State Park
Miles Goodyear built the original Fort Buenaventura in 1846 to serve as a trading post and way station for travelers crossing the remote Great Basin region. Now a replica of the tiny fort provides a link with Utah's mountain-man past. Researchers excavated the original site and pored through historical documents so that reconstruction would be authentic. The location, dimensions, and materials used for the stockade and three cabins inside closely follow the originals. Volunteers often have displays and presentations inside the cabins daily in the summer and on weekends in spring and autumn. Special programs are scheduled throughout the year: mountain-man rendezvous on Easter and Labor

Day weekends and the pioneer skill show held on July 24. Check program schedules with the park office, 2450 South A Ave., 801/621-4808, or the Ogden-Weber Convention and Visitors Bureau Information Center, 801/392-5581. Trees and grass surrounding the fort provide a peaceful setting near downtown. The park has a picnic area and a pond popular for canoeing in summer (rentals are available). Open 8 A.M. until dark daily except in winter; $5 per vehicle or $1 per person to walk in. From downtown Ogden, take 24th Street west across the rail yard and Weber River, turn left on A Avenue, and follow signs to 2450 A Avenue.

Eccles Community Art Center

A series of monthly-changing exhibitions in this historic mansion display the best of regional paintings, sculpture, photography, and mixed media. The ornate mansion, 2580 Jefferson Ave., 801/392-6935, once owned by the philanthropic Eccles family (whose name attaches to many arts centers in northern Utah) is an attraction in itself. Turrets, cut glass, and carved woodwork decorate the brick and sandstone structure, built in 1893 in a Richardsonian-Romanesque style. The carriage house in back contains a sales gallery, and the grounds are used as a sculpture garden. Open 9 A.M.–5 P.M. Monday–Friday and 9 A.M.–3 P.M. Saturday; free.

Ogden Nature Center

The 127 acres of wildlife sanctuary on the outskirts of Ogden provide a place for children and adults to enjoy nature while learning. Hiking trails lead through woods, wetlands, and open fields. Deer, porcupines, muskrats, rabbits, snakes, and about 130 species of birds have been spotted here. Injured or orphaned animals are cared for at the center's rehabilitation center and then released into the wild. The new visitors center offers classes, workshops, displays, and activities year-round; the pillars used in construction are recycled from the railroad trestle that once spanned the Great Salt Lake. Visitors are welcome to use the picnic area. Call 801-621-7595 or write the center at 966 W. 12th St., Ogden, UT 84404, for information on summer camps and other children's programs or to arrange a tour. Open 9 A.M.–5 P.M. Monday–Friday, 10 A.M.–1 P.M. Saturday. Admission is $3 ages 12–64, seniors and children 3–11 $1.25. To get there, follow West 12th Street northwest from downtown.

Eccles Dinosaur Park and Museum

Paths at this leafy park lead to 115 life-size, realistic replicas of dinosaurs, making this a favorite with children. Exhibitions are based on the most up-to-date studies of paleontologists, and the replicas are created by the same folks who build "dino-stars" for Hollywood films. A 16,000-square-foot museum expands the services and facilities of the park. It includes 10,000 square feet of exhibit space, a large paleontology laboratory, offices, and a lecture hall that can be divided into classrooms. In summer, the complex, near the entrance to Ogden Canyon, 1544 E. Park Blvd., 801/393-DINO, is open 10 A.M.–8 P.M. Monday–Saturday and noon–6 P.M. Sunday with earlier closing the rest of the year; $4 adults, $3 seniors (62 and older), $2.50 ages 3–17.

Hill Aerospace Museum

Construction of Hill Field began in 1940, just in time to serve the aircraft maintenance and storage needs of the military during the hectic World War II years. The decades since have seen a parade of nearly every type of bomber, fighter, helicopter, trainer, and missile belonging to the U.S. Air Force. At Hill Aerospace Museum, five miles south of Ogden on I-15, 801/777-6818, about 50 of these can be seen close-up in outdoor and indoor exhibits, from the Stearman bi-wing trainer—which helped many servicemen and -women learn to fly during the late 1930s and early 1940s—to the super-fast (Mach 3.5) SR-71 *Blackbird* strategic reconnaissance plane. The Engine Room displays cutaway models of a 28-cylinder Pratt & Whitney R-4360 and several jet engines. Other exhibits inside include flight simulators, missiles, a Norden bombsight, uniforms, aircraft art, and model aircraft. Chances are you'll see jets from the adjacent Air Force base streaking overhead on training missions.

Open 9 A.M.–4:30 P.M. daily year-round; donation. To get there, take Roy Exit 341 and follow signs east.

WEBER STATE UNIVERSITY

Weber (WEE-ber) State University lies southeast of downtown on a bench of prehistoric Lake Bonneville; the Wasatch Range rises steeply behind. The university emphasizes undergraduate education, though the four-year school also offers a few graduate programs in education and business. The school began in 1889 as Weber State Academy under the LDS Church, became a state-supported community college in 1933, Weber State College in 1963, and Weber State University in 1991. It now operates on a four-quarter system with a student population of about 15,000 and faculty and staff of 1,200. The institution serves largely as a commuter university for Weber and Davis Counties. Visitors are welcome on campus for the **Museum of Natural History,** 801/626-6653, Collett Art Gallery, library, student union with bookstore, and cultural and sporting events. **Swenson Gymnasium,** on the south end of campus, 801/626-6466, provides swimming, racquetball, tennis, basketball, indoor track, and weightroom facilities to the public. **Wilderness Recreation Center,** next to Swenson Gymnasium, 801/ 626-6373, rents bicycles, whitewater kayaks, rafts, cross-country skis, camping gear, and other sports equipment; open 9 A.M.–5 P.M. Monday–Friday, 8 A.M.–5 P.M. Saturday, and 2–5 P.M. Sunday year-round. The Olympic curling competitions took place at the campus's new **Ice Sheet,** an ice rink and stadium; call 801/399-8750 for a public skating schedule.

Obtain a free parking permit and map at the **information booth** along the main entrance road off 3750 Harrison Boulevard. Campus tours can be arranged by calling 801/626-6844. A clock tower at the center of campus makes a handy landmark, so it's hard to get lost. The general information number for the university is 801/626-6000.

ENTERTAINMENT AND EVENTS

Ogden has a busy calendar of theater, dance, festivals, shows, and sporting events. To find out what's going on, contact the Ogden-Weber Convention and Visitors Bureau Information Center in Union Station, 801/627-8288 or 800/255-8824, www.ogdencvb.org.

In January, the **Winterfest/Hof Sister City Festival** celebrates winter and Ogden's German sister city, Hof, with ski and dogsled races and German food, music, and dancing.

June brings the **Taste of Ogden,** which takes place midmonth at Municipal Park and is a celebration of Ogden's restaurants.

Two of summer's biggest civic events are in July. **Pioneer Days** has a parade, rodeo, and crowning of Miss Rodeo Utah, while **Ogden Street Festival** takes over 25th Street with a 10K run, dog-trick contests, chili cook-off, and a huge garage sale in the lot in front of Union Station.

August brings the **Weber County Fair,** with horse shows and racing, livestock sale, and exhibits. Every Saturday morning, there's a lively **Farmer's Market** on historic 25th Street.

The **Golden Spike Bicycle Classic** is a road race of about 85 miles from Promontory Summit to Ogden the weekend after Labor Day in September. Late in the month is the **Greek Festival,** which celebrates Ogden's Greek heritage with food, dancing, and entertainment at the Greek Orthodox Church of the Transfiguration (674 42nd St.).

RECREATION

Year-round **swimming** is offered at Ben Lomond Community Pool, 1049 7th St., 801/625-1100; Ogden Community Pool, 2875 Tyler Ave., 801/625-1101; and Marshall White Center Pool, 222 28th St., 801/629-8346. The outdoor Lorin Farr Community Pool, 1691 Gramercy Ave., 801/629-8691, is open in summer. **Holiday Island Event Park,** 1750 South 1350 West, 801/394-3232, has water slides to provide still more ways to get wet in summer.

Tennis courts are located at many parks around the city; call the Ogden Parks Department, 801/629-8284, for the one nearest you. The Ogden City Recreation Department, 801/629-8253, organizes many sports and crafts programs for children and adults.

Gold's Gym, 550 25th St., 801/399-5861, features an indoor pool, track, weight room, basketball, racquetball, handball, and volleyball; daily admission or membership. Classic Skating Center Waterpark, 4181 Riverdale Rd.; 801/394-0822, has a roller-skating rink and water slides.

Hikers with time and a vehicle should head up into the Wasatch Range for **wilderness hikes** amongst the aspen forests and cliff-hung canyons; check with the Forest Service Information Center in Odgen's Union Station, 801/625-5306, for trail maps. However, the city of Ogden provides its own excellent trail system, the **Ogden River Parkway**. This 3.1-mile trail system links a number of the city's major parks and attractions along the Ogden River, including Eccles Dinosaur Park and the Utah State University Botanical Gardens. Join the trail at any number of points along Park Avenue, Big D Sports Park, the Botanical Gardens, or off Valley Drive.

Enjoy **golfing** at any of these courses: 18-hole Ben Lomond, 1800 N. U.S. 89, 801/782-7754; nine-hole El Monte, 1300 Valley Dr. at the mouth of Ogden Canyon, 801/629-8333; nine-hole Golf City Family Fun Center, 1400 East 5600 South, 801/479-3410 (also has a lighted 18-hole miniature golf course); 18-hole Mount Ogden Park and Golf Course, 1787 Constitution Way, 801/629-8700; nine-hole Nordic Valley, 15 miles east at 3550 Nordic Valley Way in Eden, 801/745-0306; 18-hole Schneiter's Riverside, 5460 S. Weber Dr., 801/399-4636; 18-hole Valley View, 2501 E. Gentile in Layton, 801/546-1630; 18-hole The Barn Golf Course, 305 W. Pleasant View Dr. in North Ogden, 801/782-7320; and 18-hole Wolf Creek, 15 miles east at 3900 N. Wolf Creek Dr. in Eden, 801/745-3365.

You'll find good **downhill skiing** in the Wasatch Range 15–19 miles east of Ogden at Nordic Valley, Snowbasin, and Powder Mountain; see Vicinity of Ogden. **Cross-country skiers** can use the easy set tracks in Mount Ogden Park and Golf Course at 30th and Taylor or head into the mountains for more challenging terrain. The Ogden Ranger District office of the U.S. Forest Service, 25th and Adams Ave., 801/625-5112, has a list of popular cross-country and snowshoeing areas; the *Wasatch Ski Touring and Hiking Map #3* published by Alpentech details routes near Ogden.

ACCOMMODATIONS

Rooms are relatively inexpensive in Ogden, which makes it a good base for exploring the area (remember, Salt Lake City is only 35 miles south).

Under $50
You'll find the city's cheapest rooms along Washington Boulevard, which was the main highway before the freeway went in. Quite a number of older motor-court motels still operate here, but caveat emptor: Some are in fairly grim shape, and for the same money you could find better values. If you're looking for an inexpensive room, try the **Millstream Motel,** 1450 Washington Blvd., 801/394-9425; almost half the rooms have kitchenettes and there's a restaurant on the premises. Right across the street is the new **Motel 6 Ogden,** 1455 Washington Blvd., 801/627-4560 or 800/466-8356, with a pool.

West of the freeway is the **Super 8 Motel of Ogden,** 1508 West 2100 South, 801/731-7100 or 800/800-8000.

$50–75
Closer to the center of the city is **Travelodge Ogden,** 2110 Washington Blvd., 801/394-4563, a nicely maintained older motel with a pool, guest laundry, and an exercise room. Pets are accepted for a $10 fee. For an affordable stay in the city center, try the **Western Colony Inn,** 234 24th St., 801/627-1332, with kitchenettes and nicely maintained motel rooms.

Most other Ogden midrange lodgings are located near freeway exits. At I-15 Exit 347 is the **Best Western High Country Inn,** 1335 W. 12th St., 801/394-9474 or 800/594-8979, with a pool, spa, and fitness room. Pets are accommodated, and there's a good restaurant in the motel.

At I-15 Exit 346 is **Best Rest Inn,** 1206 W. 21st St., 801/393-8644 or 800/343-8644, with a pool, 24-hour restaurant, and a convenience store. All rooms come equipped with microwaves and fridges.

The **Comfort Suites of Ogden,** 2250 South 1200 West, 801/621-2545 or 800/462-9925, has an indoor pool and fitness center; all rooms have efficiency kitchens and coffeemakers, and rates include continental breakfast.

$75–100

Near the city center is **Ogden Marriott Hotel,** 247 24th St., 801/627-1190 or 800/421-7599, with an indoor pool, hot tub, guest laundry, and a business center; there's a lounge and restaurant on the premises. A few blocks south of downtown is **Days Inn Ogden,** 3306 Washington Blvd., 801/399-5671 or 800/999-6841. This comfortable hotel offers nicely decorated rooms (some poolside rooms are quite large), a restaurant, and a private club. Facilities include an indoor pool, spa, and fitness room.

Since the post-Olympic closing of the landmark Ben Lomond Hotel in 2003, the only historic boutique hotel in Ogden is the **Ogden Plaza,** 2401 Washington Blvd, 866/394-9400, www.ogdenplazahotel.com, a grand art deco souvenir of the early 20th century. In addition to comfortable rooms and gracious formal lobby, guests are offered exercise facilities, a business center, and a fine-dining restaurant. The Plaza was completely renovated and refurbished for the Olympics—this is a charming place to stay, with frequent rate specials that bring the price down to near budget levels.

$150–200

For a unique lodging experience, consider the **Alaskan Inn,** six miles east of Ogden at 435 Ogden Canyon, 801/621-8600 or 888/707-8600, www.alaskaninn.com. A log lodge and cabin complex, the Alaska Inn sits along the banks of a mountain stream. Lodging is either in suites in the central lodge building or in individual log cabins. The decor—hand-hewn pine furniture, brass lamps, Western art—is rustic and elegant. Breakfast is included in the rates.

Campgrounds

Century Mobile Home and RV Park, 1399 W. 21st St. South (I-15 Exit 346, then one block west on Wilson Ln.), 801/731-3800, has showers, swimming pool, game room, store, and laundry. Sites are open year-round: $17 tents or RVs without hookups, $23 with. There are a number of more rural campgrounds up Ogden Canyon; see Vicinity of Ogden.

FOOD

Breakfast and Light Meals

The **Tamarack Restaurant,** 1254 W. 21st St., near I-15 21st St. exit, 801/393-8691, is good to know about; it's open 24 hours daily. If your idea of breakfast is strong coffee, fresh pastries, and the option of an omelet, plan on frequenting **Grounds for Coffee,** 126 1/2 25th St., 801/629-0909, the city's best coffee shop; there's often entertainment in the evening. The coffee shop is in a beautifully preserved 19th-century saloon along historic 25th Street.

Historic 25th Street

Quite a number of good restaurants line 25th Street, the slowly gentrifying Main Street of turn-of-the-20th-century Ogden. In addition to the following there are bakery cafés, a Greek restaurant, taverns with burgers, and home-style Mexican food.

One of the most youthful and lively places along 25th is **Rooster's 25th Street Brewing Company,** 253 25th St., 801/627-6171, a brewpub with good food (burgers, pizza, ribs, fresh fish, and sandwiches) and good microbrews. In summer there's a pleasant shady deck that's lightly misted to keep diners cool. Entrées range $8–15; open daily. **La Ferrovia Ristorante,** 234 25th St., 801/394-8628, offers an inexpensive selection of pasta, pizza, and calzone in the $10 range; dinner entrées edge up to $15. Open Tuesday–Saturday for lunch and dinner.

Bistro 258, 258 25th St., 801/430-4287, is probably Ogden's best fine-dining restaurant. The dishes are continental-influenced, though there's also a good selection of Utah beef. A house specialty is roasted balsamic herb chicken; filet mignon stuffed with spinach and Montrachet cheese is a stand-out. Open for dinner only; closed Sunday. Entrées range $11–21.

If you're looking for modern American-style food—grilled fish, gourmet sandwiches, and salads—head to the Union Pacific Station and try the **Union Grill,** 2501 Wall Ave., 801/621-2830. Dinner entrées range $11–16; closed Sunday.

Western-Theme Restaurants

For good beef, seafood, and American-style dining, Ogden has a number of interesting choices; entrées at the following three restaurants run $13–18. The **Graycliff Lodge,** 508 Ogden Canyon, five miles up Ogden Canyon on the left, 801/392-6775, serves old-fashioned steak, lamb, prime rib, and seafood in a romantic creekside setting; open for Sunday brunch and Tuesday–Sunday for dinner. **Prairie Schooner,** 445 Park Blvd., 801/392-2712, serves steak, prime rib, and seafood in an informal Western atmosphere (dine in a covered wagon); open daily for dinner. For another take on the Western theme, try the **Timber Mine,** 1701 Park Blvd., 801/393-2155, which serves steak and seafood to diners in a mine shaft; open daily for dinner.

Ethnic Restaurants

As befits a town at the base of towering mountains, Ogden has a good and very popular German restaurant, the **Bavarian Chalet,** 4387 Harrison Blvd., across from the Dee Event Center, 801/479-7561. All your German favorites are here, including schnitzels, sauerbraten, and strudels. This is one of the city's most beloved restaurants; reservations are suggested. Open Tuesday–Saturday for dinner.

Bangkok Garden, 465 E. 25th St. 801/621-4049, has a good selection of spicy Thai cuisine, and it also serves up high-quality Chinese cooking. Although it's not strictly ethnic, the **Cajun Skillet,** 2550 Washington Blvd., 801/393-7702, serves up spicy Louisiana fare that's quite a distance from the steak and potatoes that typifies standard Utah cooking.

OTHER PRACTICALITIES

Shopping

Ogden City Mall, downtown at 24th and Washington Blvd., 801/399-1314, is a giant indoor shopping area with five department stores and about 60 smaller shops and restaurants; open daily including Sunday afternoons. The **Newgate Mall,** in the southwest part of town at Wall Ave. and Riverdale Rd., 801/621-1161, has more than 60 stores and restaurants; open daily including Sunday afternoons. Obtain outdoor supplies for camping, backpacking, mountain biking, and skiing (and rentals for both downhill and cross-country) at **Alpine Sports,** 1165 Patterson, 801/393-0066.

Information and Services

The **Ogden-Weber Convention and Visitors Bureau Information Center** in Union Station at Wall Ave. and 25th St., Ogden, UT 84401, 801/627-8288 or 800/ALL-UTAH, can tell you about the sights, facilities, and goings-on for Ogden and surrounding communities, including Davis, Morgan, and Box Elder Counties; open 8 A.M.–8 P.M. Monday–Saturday and 10 A.M.–7 P.M. Sunday Memorial Day–Labor Day weekends, 8 A.M.–5 P.M. Monday–Friday the rest of the year.

Visit the **Forest Service Information Center** at Union Station or the **Ogden Ranger District office** of the U.S. Forest Service, 507 25th St. and Adams Ave., to find out about local road conditions (or call 801/625-5112 or 800/492-2400), camping, hiking, horseback riding, ski touring, snowshoeing, and snowmobiling. The district comprises the Wasatch Range from Kaysville to just south of Brigham City; both offices have maps and books for sale. They're open 8 A.M.–4:30 P.M. Monday–Friday (and Saturday in summer at Union Station).

Weber County's **main library,** 2464 Jefferson Ave., provides good reading; open 10 A.M.–9 P.M. Monday–Thursday, 10 A.M.–6 P.M. Friday–Saturday, and 1–5 P.M. Sunday (October–May). Call 801/627-6913 for information on the county's two branch libraries. Weber State University has the large **Stewart Library,** 801/626-6415 or

626-6403; hikers can make photocopies of topo maps; open during the semester 7:30 A.M.–midnight Monday–Thursday, 7:30 A.M.–8 P.M. Friday, 9 A.M.–5 P.M. Saturday, and noon–8 P.M. Sunday; open in summer and during school breaks 7:30 A.M.–8 P.M. Monday–Thursday, 7:30 A.M.–6 P.M. Friday, and 2–5 P.M. Saturday and Sunday.

Hospital care and physician referrals are provided by **McKay-Dee Hospital Center,** 3939 Harrison Blvd., 801/627-2800, and **Columbia Ogden Regional Medical Center,** 5475 South 500 East, 801/479-2111. Minor medical problems can be handled at **NowCare,** 698 12th, 801/394-7753. The downtown **post office** is at 2641 Washington Blvd., 801/627-4184.

Transportation

Utah Transit Authority (UTA) buses serve many areas of Ogden and head east to Huntsville and south to Salt Lake City and Provo; buses operate Monday–Saturday and offer some late-night runs. UTA has an **information booth** at its main downtown bus stop in Ogden Municipal Park at the corner of 25th and Washington Blvd., 801/621-4636; open noon–5 P.M. weekdays. **Greyhound** provides long-distance service from the terminal at 25th and Grant Avenue, 801/394-5573.

Air travelers use the **Salt Lake City International Airport**, just 35 miles away.

Yellow Cab, 801/394-9411, provides 24-hour taxi service.

Vicinity of Ogden

EAST OF OGDEN

Ogden Canyon

Cliffs rise thousands of feet above narrow Ogden Canyon, just barely allowing Highway 39 and Ogden River to squeeze through. In autumn, the fiery reds of maples and the golden hues of oaks add color to this scenic drive deep within the Wasatch Range. Ogden Canyon begins on the eastern edge of Ogden and emerges about six miles farther, at Pineview Reservoir in the broad Ogden Valley.

This fertile agricultural basin is a crossroads for recreationalists. In winter, skiers turn south from the reservoir to Snowbasin Ski Area and north to Nordic Valley and Powder Mountain ski areas. Summer visitors have a choice of staying at swimming beaches and campgrounds on the shore of Pineview Reservoir or heading to canyons and mountain peaks in the Wasatch. For recreation and road information, contact the Forest Service Information Center in Union Station, Wall Ave. and 25th St. in Ogden, 801/625-5306, or the Ogden Ranger District office, 507 25th St. and Adams Ave., 801/625-5112. Reach the canyon from Ogden by heading east on 12th Street (take I-15 Exit 347).

Pineview Reservoir

This many-armed lake on the Ogden River provides excellent boating, fishing, water-skiing, and swimming at an elevation of 4,900 feet. Campgrounds (with nightly rates $10–14), picnic areas, and marinas ring the shore of this four-mile-long reservoir. The Forest Service's **Anderson Cove,** a large campground with a swimming beach on the southern shore, is eight miles east of Ogden. The campground is open Memorial Day to Labor Day weekends; sites have drinking water but no showers. Reservations can be made for family and group sites by calling 877/444-6777. The **Jefferson Hunt Campground** is on the South Fork of the Ogden River where it meets Pineview Reservoir, one mile east of Anderson Cove; all sites and facilities are wheelchair accessible and have drinking water. For day-tripping, the **Bluffs Swim Area** offers sandy beaches and shaded picnic areas at Cemetery Point on the lake's east side ($5 per vehicle, $1 per pedestrian; day use only); a marina with boat ramp, docks, and snack bar is nearby ($4 boat launch); follow Highway 39 to the Huntsville turnoff (10.5 miles east of Ogden), then turn west two miles. **Middle Inlet** is another beach area 1.5 miles north of Huntsville ($4 per vehicle). **Port Ramp,** 801/745-8089, on the lake's western shore, has a boat ramp, small

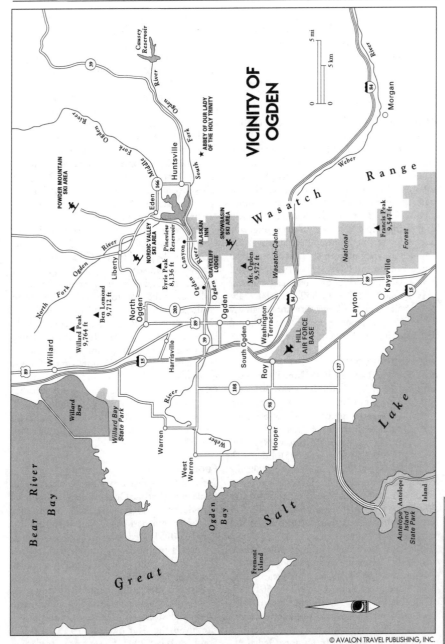

VICINITY OF
OGDEN

© AVALON TRAVEL PUBLISHING, INC.

store, dock, slips, fuel, and storage ($4 to launch or park); open daily late April–September. **North Arm Wildlife Viewing Trail** makes a 0.4-mile loop at the north end of the reservoir, where the North Fork of the Ogden River joins the reservoir; the trail, built especially for wildlife viewing, lies off Highway 162.

Abbey of Our Lady of the Holy Trinity

This community of 30 Trappist monks welcomes visitors to its chapel and reception room. The monks explain the monastery's work and sell locally produced bread, honey, and farm products. Although no tours are given, a slide show illustrates the religious life and work of the community. You may attend the Mass and chants held daily in the chapel. Quonset buildings, originally just temporary, have proved both practical and unique for nearly all the monastery's needs. The founders chose this location for its seclusion and beautiful setting. The abbey is four miles southeast of Huntsville at 1250 South 9500 East, 801/745-3784; follow signs for Monastery from Highway 39. The reception room is open 8 A.M.–noon and 1–5 P.M. Monday–Saturday.

Accommodations

$50–75: The **Jackson Fork Inn,** Hwy. 39 at milepost 18 (7345 East 900 South), 801/745-0051, offers rooms starting at $70, each with private baths and unique decor—not bad for a barn. On the northern arm of Pineview Reservoir is a charming log B&B, the **Snowberry Inn,** 1315 N. Hwy. 158 (P.O. Box 795), Eden, UT 84310, 801/745-2634. The inn overlooks the reservoir and provides access for water sports and swimming, while Ogden-area ski resorts are only 15 minutes away. All five guest rooms come with private baths; guests share a hot tub, billiard table, and TV room.

$75–100: Between Eden and Powder Mountain Winter Resort are several condominium developments. The **Wolf Creek Village,** 3720 N. Wolf Creek Dr., Eden, UT 84310, 801/745-0223 or 800/933-9653, has condos and an 18-hole golf course. In ski season, the rates are substantially more expensive.

Also see the **Alaskan Inn,** under Ogden Ac-

commodations, which is near the top of Ogden Canyon near Ogden Valley.

Campgrounds: The free **Maples Campground** (elev. 6,200 feet) is nestled among maples and aspens in the mountains near Snowbasin Ski Area. The season lasts late May–early September; no drinking water. Drive to the ski area's lower parking lot (marked Lower Shop), then turn west 1.5 miles on a gravel road.

Travel Highway 39 east from Huntsville to find eight Forest Service campgrounds within 10 miles. Most of these campgrounds have water; charges range $10–14. **Perception Park,** 7.5 miles east of Huntsville, was specially built to accommodate people with disabilities. Some sites can be reserved by calling 877/444-6777.

The free (first-come, first-served) **Weber County Memorial Park,** 801/399-8491, is one mile down the paved road to Causey Reservoir, a narrow crescent-shaped lake in the upper South Fork of the Ogden River. A paved road in the park crosses the river to individual sites; three group sites can be reserved through Weber County Parks and Recreation. Water is available late May–late September. Turnoff for Causey Reservoir is one mile east of Willows Campground on Highway 39. **Monte Cristo Campground** sits high in mountain forests of spruce, fir, and aspen at an elevation of 8,400 feet (between mileposts 48 and 49, 40 miles east of Ogden, 21 miles west of Woodruff on Highway 39); sites are open early July–late September with drinking water.

Food

Some of the Ogden area's favorite places to eat nestle in the bucolic Ogden Valley, just minutes from downtown Ogden. The **Jackson Fork Inn,** Hwy. 39 at milepost 18 (7345 East 900 South), 801/745-0051, used to be a dairy barn, though it's now a popular supper club with steaks, chicken, and pasta ($12–18), open for Sunday brunch and daily for dinner.

Also in the valley, the little town of Huntsville offers a couple of places to eat and Utah's oldest bar—in business since 1879— the **Shooting Star Saloon,** 7345 East 200 South, 801/745-2002. This is a favorite place to come for burgers; TV's *Good Morning America* once named it one of the top five places for burgers in the United States. Interesting graffiti in the restrooms.

A fun place to eat near Eden is **Eats of Eden,** 2529 N. Hwy. 162, 801/745-8618, serving good pizza, pasta, and sandwiches; open for lunch and dinner.

SNOWBASIN SKI AREA

Snowbasin was gussied up for the 2002 Winter Olympics and is now one of Utah's largest ski areas, with an excellent lift system, great panoramic views, and no crowds. Though it gets a bit less snow than the Cottonwood resorts, Snowbasin is well equipped with snow-making machines.

History

Skiers have been gliding down the varied terrain here since 1939. The resort is owned by R. Earl Holding, a Utah developer and president of Sinclair Oil; his other holdings include Sun Valley Resort in Idaho and the Little America chain of hotels. During the early stages of Olympic planning, Holding swung a land swap that many people still regard with disdain, trading land that was thought to have little value for a very nice, very developable parcel of Forest Service land, now the site of the base lodge. Snowbasin hosted the men's and women's downhill, super-G, and combined competitions during the 2002 Winter Olympics.

Terrain and Lifts

With more than 3,200 acres of terrain and relatively few other skiers and snowboarders, there's almost always room to roam here. The area is well covered with speedy lifts, meaning that you can spend more time skiing and less time standing in line or sitting on pokey chairlifts.

Four triple chairlifts and one double plus one quad and two gondolas and a short little tram serve 63 runs, of which 11 percent are rated beginner, 49 percent intermediate, and 40 percent expert; snowboarding is allowed. The longest run is three miles and drops 2,400 feet in elevation.

With 40 percent of trails marked with black diamonds, Snowbasin is clearly an expert skier's dream. The north side of the mountain (the John Paul area) has incredible expert terrain—long and *steep*. However, John Paul is sometimes closed for races. There are also extra-black chutes off the top of the Strawberry Express gondola.

But intermediate skiers can also have a good, non-terrifying time here. The Strawberry area in particular is full of nicely groomed long blue cruisers. Beginners will find only limited territory.

Snowbasin offers a ski school, ski shop, rentals, and three day lodges. Of particular note is the **outdoor ice rink** at Needles Lodge, at the top of the Needles gondola. Skating fee is $2, skate rentals $2; the ride up on the gondola for people who don't have regular lift tickets is $12 adult, $6 child 7–12.

Snowbasin's season usually lasts from Thanksgiving until mid-April.

Adult lift tickets cost $54 for a full day, $44 half day; children's rates are $33 full day, $26 half day; seniors pay $44/$29.

Cross-Country Skiing and Snowshoeing

Snowbasin maintains the Maples Nordic Loop, 11 miles of cross-country ski trails, groomed for both classic and skate skiers. This loop is west of the Grizzly Center and is free. Cross-country ski and snowshoe rentals are available at the Grizzly Center.

Accommodations and Food

There is no lodging at Snowbasin. Though most people drive up from Salt Lake City, the Ogden Valley lodgings are quite handy, and the Snowberry Inn B&B caters to skiers.

Dining options are pretty limited: You can eat at the base lodge or you can eat at the mountain-top Needles Lodge (it's open for both lunch and dinner) or John Paul Lodge.

Information

Contact Snowbasin at 3925 E. Snowbasin Rd., Huntsville, UT 84317, 801/620-1000 or 888/437-5488, www.snowbasin.com. Call 801/620-1100 for a snow report.

Transportation

From Ogden, take I-15 southbound and exit to I-84 eastbound (Exit 343). Proceed east on I-84 and exit at Mountain Green (Exit 92). Continue east on Old Highway and turn left on Highway 167 heading north (just east of the Sinclair station). Turn left on Highway 226 heading west and proceed approximately three miles to Snowbasin.

From the Salt Lake City area, take I-15 and U.S. 89 to I-84, then Highway 167.

OTHER OGDEN AREA SKIING

Nordic Valley Ski Area

This downhill ski area is the closest to Ogden and is especially popular with families (Monday is family night). Two double chairlifts serve 19 runs, of which 30 percent are beginner, 50 percent intermediate, and 20 percent expert. Elevation drop is 1,000 feet. You can ski at night, too—all runs are under lights Monday–Saturday until 10 P.M. Day skiing takes place Friday–Sunday and all school holidays. Nordic Valley's season runs early December–late March. Adult lift tickets cost $22 full day, $16 half day, and $12 night. Nordic Valley, P.O. Box 478, Eden, UT 84310, 801/745-3511, has a ski school, ski shop, and a day lodge. It's 15 miles northeast of Ogden; go through Ogden Canyon, turn left at Pineview Dam, and follow signs.

Powder Mountain Winter Resort

Two double chairlifts and one triple, plus one quad, reach two different peaks and serve more than 80 runs (10 percent beginner, 50 percent intermediate, and 40 percent expert). Three surface tows supplement the chairlifts. High elevations of 6,895–8,900 feet catch plentiful powder snow. You can ski at night from the Sundown lift until 10 P.M. Powder Mountain's season lasts mid-November–late April. Adult lift tickets cost $41 full day, $34 for half day and night skiing. Facilities include a ski school, ski shops, rentals, and three day lodges. Powder Mountain, P.O. Box 450, Eden, UT 84310, 801/745-3771 (recording) or 801/745-3772 (office), www.powdermountain .com, is 19 miles northeast of Ogden; drive

through Ogden Canyon, turn left at Pineview Dam, and follow signs. In summer, mountain bikers are free to use the trails, but there is no lift-assisted hiking or biking.

Accommodations: Condo developments are located between Eden and the resort along Highway 158 (see East of Ogden). At the ski area itself, you'll find rooms and suites at the **Columbine Inn,** 801/745-1414, and condos at **Powder Ridge MTA Resort,** 801/531-1666 or 800/272-UTAH. One-bedroom units begin at $125 a night during ski season.

NORTH OF OGDEN

Golden Spike Fruitway

Old U.S. 89 north to Brigham City passes many orchards. Fruit stands, open during the July to mid-September season, offer a bountiful supply of cherries, apples, peaches, pears, apricots, plums, berries, and vegetables.

Willard

This small community (pop. 1,540) is known for its fine pioneer houses. The city park has picnic tables and a playground. Willard lies at the foot of the Wasatch Range 11 miles north of Ogden on U.S. 89 (take I-15 Exit 360).

Willard Bay State Park

Two separate recreation areas along the eastern shore of Willard Bay provide opportunities for water sports, camping, and nature study. More than 200 species of birds have been observed near the park; common ones include the white pelican, California gull, snowy egret, Western grebe, killdeer, black-necked stilt, and American avocet; eagles visit in winter. Conditions are great for water-skiing and power boating, but only fair for sailing. Anglers catch channel catfish, smallmouth bass, bluegill, crappie, and walleye. Winter visitors find good ice fishing in the bay mid-December–late February. Only two miles of Willard Bay's 15-mile circumference are natural shoreline; dikes enclose nearly all of the bay to keep out saltwater from the Great Salt Lake just to the west. Canals carry water into the bay during winter and spring, then out for irrigation during the growing season. Park fees are $7 for day use, $14 for camping. Contact Willard Bay State Park at 900 West 650 North, P.O. Box A, Willard, UT 84340, 435/734-9494 (ranger) or 800/322-3770 (reservations).

North Marina features a sandy swimming beach, campground with showers, boat ramp, and dock. The developed campground's season is normally April 1 (or Easter, if it falls in March) through October, but an overflow area on the shore stays open year-round. Reservations are recommended on summer weekends and holidays. North Marina is just west of I-15 Willard Exit 360.

South Marina has a boat ramp, docks, and campground with showers. The area is set up mostly for day use, as the open grassy areas used for camping lack designated sites. The dikes on this part of the bay prevent beaches and lake views, but you won't be so crowded here on summer weekends, and the campground nearly always has room. South Marina is open April 1 (Easter if it falls in March) through October; no reservations are taken here. Access is from I-15 Exit 354; follow signs west 2.5 miles.

BRIGHAM CITY

Peaks of the Wasatch Range exceeding 9,000 feet form the backdrop to this city of 16,960 people 21 miles north of Ogden. Pioneers settled along Box Elder Creek in 1851, naming both the creek and the town for the trees growing here. Five years later they renamed their community to honor LDS Church president Brigham Young. Brigham City serves as Box Elder County seat and a center for surrounding fruit orchards, truck farms, and ranches.

Historic displays in the **Brigham City Museum-Gallery,** 24 North 300 West, 435/723-6769, show how residents lived in the 19th century. The art gallery features changing shows by local artists and artists from all over Utah; open11 A.M.–6 P.M.

Old U.S. 89 north to Brigham City passes many orchards. Fruit stands, open during the July to mid-September season, offer a bountiful supply of cherries, apples, peaches, pears, apricots, plums, berries, and vegetables.

Tuesday–Friday and 1–5 P.M. Saturday; free. The **Brigham City Depot,** 833 W. Forest, 435/723-2989, a late-19th-century railroad station, has been lovingly restored to its original condition, with separate waiting rooms for each gender and many antiques from railroading in the past.

Many people think the Mormon **Box Elder Tabernacle,** 251 S. Main St., 435/723-5376, is Utah's most beautiful building. Construction took place 1865–1890. Six years later the tabernacle burned; the present structure dates from 1897. Gothic-arched windows and doors, a soaring white steeple, and 16 smaller spires make the stone and brick structure distinctive. Non-Mormons are welcome; tours are conducted in the tabernacle 9 A.M.–9 P.M. daily May–October.

Events
During **Golden Spike Days** in May, the city has historic art exhibits in the museum, the Golden Spike Parade, and other festivities. Brigham City celebrates the harvest during **Peach Days** (the weekend after Labor Day) with a parade, entertainment, carnival, art show, Peach Queen Pageant, and a footrace.

Recreation
Box Elder Natatorium, 380 South 600 West, 435/723-2622, has an indoor pool, basketball court, and weight room at Box Elder High School. There's an outdoor swimming pool in **Pioneer Park** at 800 W. Forest, 435/723-2711. **John Adams Park,** 100 North and 500 East, has picnicking, playground, and tennis courts.

The 18-hole **Eagle Mountain Golf Course** is at 960 East 700 South, 435/723-3212.

Accommodations
Main Street, which runs north-south through Brigham City, is where most of the town's businesses are. Toward the south end, off I-15 Exit 364, is a clutch of motels and restaurants.

© BILL WEIR

Brigham City's Box Elder Tabernacle is one of Utah's most distinctive buildings.

Under $50: The **Galaxie Motel,** 740 S. Main St., 435/723-3439, is an older motor court motel with inexpensive rooms.

$50–75: For more comfort, try the **Howard Johnson Brigham City,** 1167 S. Main St., 435/723-8511, or 800/1 GO HOJO, with a pool, hot tub, and restaurant. The **Crystal Inn,** 480 Westland Dr., 435/723-0440 or 800/408-0440, offers all suite units with efficiency kitchens, complimentary continental breakfast, guest laundry, indoor pool; children under 16 stay free. For the business traveler, there are easily accessed modem jacks and three phones in each room.

Campgrounds: Golden Spike RV Park, 905 West 1075 South, 435/723-8858, offers camping sites for tents, vans, or campers plus RV hookups. Grounds include showers, store, and laundry; may close in winter. **Brigham City KOA,** four miles south of Brigham City on U.S. 89 (near I-15 Willard Exit 360), 435/723-5503, offers sites for tents and RVs with showers, pool, a store, and laundry; open March 1–November 15. Other nearby places to camp are at Willard Bay State Park (see North of Ogden) and Mantua Reservoir (see Vicinity of Brigham City).

Food

Amid the taco stands and fast-food restaurants along Main Street are a couple of unique places to eat. The **Idle Isle Restaurant,** 24 S. Main St., 435/734-2468, is an ice-cream parlor, candy store, and diner little changed from the 1920s when it first opened. At lunch, there's soup, homemade rolls, and various sandwiches on the menu; in the evening, all meals—good American-style dishes like roast pork and chicken-fried steak—come with a piece of pie. The atmosphere is splendid.

Another restaurant with an illustrious past is the **Maddox Ranch House,** 1900 S. U.S. 89, 435/723-8545, just south of Brigham City. Established during the 1940s, this restaurant is the epitome of the classic steak house. The dining room used to overlook a feedlot—how's that for atmosphere? Besides steaks, diners come for burgers and fried chicken—and they come from miles around to eat here; reservations are a good idea on weekends.

Information and Services

The **chamber of commerce,** 6 N. Main St., 435/723-3931, will answer your questions about the area and offers a three-hour tour of the historic city and surrounding area; open 9 A.M.– noon and 1–4 P.M. Monday–Friday.

Brigham City Community Hospital is at 950 South 500 West, 435/734-9471.

VICINITY OF BRIGHAM CITY
Bear River Migratory Bird Refuge

Millions of birds drop in to feed or nest in the freshwater marshes created by the intersection of the Bear River and the Great Salt Lake; about 60 species nest in the refuge. In pioneer days, reports told of flocks of waterfowl blackening the sky. Flooding in the late 1980s closed the area and displaced many birds until receding waters allowed it to reopen in 1990. A four-mile loop gravel road is open to visitors. Head west 15 miles on Forest Street from Brigham City on a partly paved road. The refuge office in town, 866 S. Main, in Breitenbeker's Plaza, Brigham City, UT 84302, 435/723-5887, offers a bird list, a short video shown on request, and information; open 8 A.M.–4:30 P.M. Monday–Friday.

Mantua Reservoir

This 554-acre reservoir beside the town of Mantua is popular for fishing, boating, and picnicking. From Brigham City, follow U.S. 89/91 east four miles up Box Elder Canyon. Visitors are welcome to view the native cutthroat and lake trout at **Mantua Fish Hatchery,** one mile southeast of Mantua; open 8 A.M.–5 P.M. daily. Exhibits show how the trout are obtained as eggs at Bear Lake and returned a year later after growing to a five-inch length. All of the one million trout produced annually go to Bear Lake.

The U.S. Forest Service's **Box Elder Campground** is just west of the reservoir. It's open with drinking water mid-May–late September ($10); some sites can be reserved by calling 877/444-6777. The adjacent picnic areas are free.

Inspiration Point

Beginning as Main Street in Mantua, unpaved Forest Route 084 leads south 14 miles to Inspiration Point (elev. 9,422 feet) and dizzying views across the Great Salt Lake and much of northern Utah; you can spy mountains in Nevada, Idaho, and Wyoming on a clear day. Limber pine grow near the summit and subalpine fir lower down. The road is rough in spots, though cars with good clearance can make it to the top in dry weather. Keep left at the three-way fork 2.5 miles from Mantua; see the Wasatch-Cache National Forest map. **Willard Basin Campground** (elev. 9,000 feet) lies two miles before Inspiration Point. It's open early June–mid-September; no water or fee. **Skyline Trail** begins from Willard Basin and winds south to the summit of Ben Lomond (elev. 9,712 feet) and other peaks, then to North Ogden Pass and finally Pineview Reservoir, 22 miles away. Or you could start hiking from Inspiration Point. Other trails branch off Skyline, too; see the Mantua, North Ogden, and Huntsville 7.5-minute topo maps. For more information, contact the **Ogden Ranger District office,** 507 25th St. and Adams Ave. in Ogden, 435/625-5112.

Tremonton

This agricultural center 15 miles northwest of Brigham City was settled in 1888 and named for Tremont, Illinois. The **North Box Elder County Museum,** 150 S. Tremont, 435/257-3371, displays historic exhibits and Native American artifacts. It's open in summer 8 A.M.–4 P.M. Monday–Friday, 9 A.M.–5 P.M. Monday–Friday the rest of the year; free. For information about the area, visit the **information desk** in the Tremonton Community Center, 150 S. Tremont, Tremonton, UT 84337, 435/257-3371.

Box Elder County Fair and Rodeo in late August features a parade, rodeo, horse pulling, livestock judging, and varied exhibits.

Bear River Valley Hospital provides medical services at 440 West 600 North, 435/257-7441.

Tremonton Accommodations
Under $50: The **Marble Motel,** 116 N. Tremont, 435/257-3524, is a small, homey motel in the center of town; it accepts pets and offers five two-bedroom units.

$50–75: Also in the town center is the redbrick **Sandman Motel,** 585 W. Main, 435/257-7149.

The large and modern **Western Inn,** is at I-84 Exit 40, 435/257-3399.

Belmont Springs

Hot springs have been developed into a swimming pool and hot tubs, a nine-hole golf course, and a campground. Volleyball and horseshoe equipment is available, too. Belmont Springs, 435/458-3200, lies 10 miles north of Tremonton and one mile south of Plymouth. The season at this small resort runs early May–early October; hours are 9 A.M.–9 P.M.—golf hours are 8:30 A.M. until dark. Admission to the pool and hot tubs is $4 adults, $2.50 children; camping costs $8 without hookups and $15 with (ask about tent rates).

Corinne

The location beside the Bear River and along the transcontinental railroad seemed ideal in 1869, when Corinne's founders laid out the town. Banks, freight companies, and mining concerns based themselves at the promising new site. A steamboat service began ferrying ore across the Great Salt Lake to a mill and smelter at Corinne. The population swiftly rose to the 2,000 mark as business boomed. Saloons, dance halls, and prostitutes entertained the largely non-Mormon population and prompted Brigham Young to declare the town off-limits to his followers. Corinne became the gentile capital of Utah and a center for political opposition to the Church of Jesus Christ of Latter-day Saints.

But the "curse of Corinne" kept the town from realizing its dreams. Receding lake levels grounded the steamboat business, a diphtheria epidemic killed many citizens, appeals for political support from the U.S. Congress failed, and, finally, the railroads chose the LDS city of Ogden as their junction point. Today Corinne is a sleepy farm town haunted by a few old buildings from its past. The Methodist Church, corner of S. Sixth St. and Colorado, dates from 1870 and is believed to be the first non-Mormon Church built in Utah. Corinne lies five miles west of Brigham City on the way to the Golden Spike National Historic Site.

Golden Spike National Historic Site

At 12:47 P.M. on May 10, 1869, rails from the East and the West met for the first time. People across the country closely followed telegraph reports as dignitaries and railway officials made their speeches and drove the last spikes, then everyone broke out in wild celebration. The joining of rails at this windswept pass in Utah's Promontory Mountains marked a new chapter in the growth of the United States. A transcontinental railroad at last linked both sides of the nation. The far western frontier would be a frontier no more. Swift-moving Army troops would soon put an end to Native American troubles. Vast resources of timber, mineral wealth, and farmland lay open to development.

History

The Central Pacific and Union Pacific Railroads, eager for land grants and bonuses, had been laying track at a furious pace and grading the lines far ahead. So great was the momentum that the grader crews didn't even stop when they met but laid parallel grades for 250 miles across Utah. Finally Congress decided to join the rails at Promontory Summit and stop the wasteful duplication of effort. A ragged town of tents, boxcars, and hastily built wooden shacks sprang up along a single muddy street. Outlaws and crooked gambling houses earned Promontory Summit an awful reputation as a real "hell-on-wheels" town. The party ended six months later when the railroads moved the terminal operations to Ogden. Soon only a depot, roundhouse, helper engines, and other rail facilities remained. The Lucin Cutoff across the Great Salt Lake in 1904 bypassed the long twisting grades of Promontory Summit and dramatically reduced traffic along the old route. The final blow came in 1942, when the rails were torn up for scrap to feed wartime industries.

Visitors Center and Events

The Golden Spike National Historic Site, au-

GOLDEN SPIKE CEREMONY

In grade school, many of us learned that when the Union Pacific and Central Pacific Railroads met, a solid-gold ceremonial stake was driven to mark the spot. One yearns to go to Promontory and pry out that golden spike. But the real story tells us the event was marked with no fewer than two golden spikes, both from California—a silver spike contributed by the state of Nevada and an iron spike with its body plated in silver and its cap plated in gold, courtesy of the state of Arizona.

A polished myrtlewood tie was placed at the site to receive the spikes, protecting the precious metals from the damage of driving them into the earth. At the ceremony, Central Pacific President Leland Stanford (founder of Stanford University) took the first swing at the final spike and missed it entirely—but did hit the tie. Union Pacific Vice President and General Manager Thomas C. Durant next tried his hand and missed not only the spike but the rail and the tie as well. A bystander was finally summoned from the crowd to tap the stake home.

Shortly after the formal ceremony concluded, the valuable spike and tie were removed and standard fittings were substituted to link the nation by rail.

thorized by Congress in 1965, re-creates the momentous episode of railroad history that took place here. The visitors center offers a few scant exhibits and programs that illustrate the difficulties of building the railroad and portray the officials and workers who made it possible. A short slide show introduces Promontory Summit's history. The 20-minute program, *The Golden Spike*, presents a more detailed account of building the transcontinental railroad. Rangers give talks several times a day in summer. An exhibit room has changing displays on railroading, and historic markers behind the visitors center indicate the spot where the last spike was driven.

The two locomotives that met here in 1869, Central Pacific's Jupiter and Union Pacific's 119,

succumbed to scrap yards around the turn of the 20th century. However, they have been born again in authentic replicas. Every day in summer the trains steam along a short section of track from the Engine House to the historic spot. You can't ride on the engines; they're here mostly for photo ops.

The annual Last Spike Ceremony reenacts the original celebration every May 10 with great fanfare. The Railroaders' Festival in August has special exhibits, a spike-driving contest, reenactments, handcar races, and entertainment. The visitors center (mailing address: P.O. Box 897, Brigham City, UT 84302), 801/471-2209, www.nps.gov/gosp, is open 9 A.M.–5:30 P.M. daily, closed Monday and Tuesday October 21–April 30 and Thanksgiving, Christmas, and New Year's Day. Admission is $7 per vehicle or $4 per adult, whichever is less. A sales counter offers a good selection of books on railroading, Utah history, and natural history, as well as postcards and souvenirs. Motels and restaurants are nearby in Brigham City and Tremonton. From the I-15 Brigham City Exit 368, head west on Highway 13 and Highway 83 and follow signs 29 miles.

Promontory Trail Auto Tour

Imagine you're riding the rails across Utah a century ago. This scenic drive follows the old grades past many construction feats of hardy railway workers. You'll see the parallel grades laid by the competing Union Pacific and Central Pacific, clearings for sidings, original rock culverts, and many cuts and fills. Wildflowers, grass-covered hills, and views over the blue Great Salt Lake appear much the same as they did to early train travelers. A booklet available at the visitors center describes the features and history at numbered stops on the drive. Allow about 75 minutes for the complete tour. If time is short, drive along just the west section (45 minutes) or the east section (30 minutes).

Big Fill Walk

An easy 1.5-mile round-trip at the east end of the driving tour leads farther down a railroad grade to the famous Big Fill and Big Trestle sites. Rugged terrain on this side of the Promontory

Mountains posed some of the greatest construction challenges to both lines. The Central Pacific tackled an especially deep ravine here with a massive fill, 170 feet deep and 500 feet long, requiring about two months of work by 500 men and 250 teams of animals. The Union Pacific, pressed for time, threw together a temporary trestle over the gorge, paralleling the Big Fill.

VICINITY OF GOLDEN SPIKE NATIONAL HISTORIC SITE
Promontory Point
This peninsula that juts into the Great Salt Lake has no connection with the first transcontinental railroad but does make a pleasant scenic drive. A paved road follows the eastern shore of the peninsula below the Promontory Mountains for 22.5 miles, then becomes gravel for the last 17.5 miles around to the west side. There are good views of the Great Salt Lake, the Wasatch Range, and the Lucin Cutoff railroad causeway. Lake Crystal Salt Co. at road's end was a salt extraction plant (it's no longer in operation). There's no hiking or camping on Promontory Point—the land has been fenced and signed No Trespassing. The

Promontory Point turnoff is six miles east of the Golden Spike visitors center.

Thiokol
Many buildings of this giant aerospace corporation lie scattered across the countryside about six miles northeast of the historic site. You're not likely to be allowed to tour the facility, but you can see a group of missiles, rocket engines, and a space-shuttle booster casing in front of administrative offices. Turn north two miles on Highway 83 at the junction with the Golden Spike National Historic Site road (eight miles east of the visitors center).

Promontory Branch of the Central Pacific Railroad
Adventurous motorists, mountain bikers, and hikers can follow sections of the historic railroad grade west 89 miles from Golden Spike National Historic Site to Lucin, near the Nevada border. Signs along the way describe histories of town sites, sidings, and natural features in this austerely beautiful land. You may see small herds of pronghorn. Only cemeteries, foundations, and debris remain at such former towns as Kelton

Morton Thiokol's plant near Promontory is one of Utah's many defense-related operations.

(1869–1942), Terrace (1869–1910), and historic Lucin (1875–1907).

Cars can make the 11-mile section of unpaved county road between the junction near Locomotive Springs (20 miles southwest of Snowville) and Kelton, but you'll need dry weather and a four-wheel drive, high-clearance vehicle for further sections of the railroad grade. If you are planning on exploring this remote region, contact the Bureau of Land Management's Salt Lake District office, 801/977-4300, or ask the staff at Golden Spike National Historic Site about road conditions. Sections of the road may be closed, and bridges and trestles that have not been maintained may be dangerous.

THE NORTHWEST CORNER

Raft River Mountains (Sawtooth National Forest)

Few Utahns know about these mountains in the northwest corner of the state, despite their pretty alpine scenery. Panoramic views from the top of the Raft River Range take in the Great Salt Lake, barren desert, farmlands, and mountains in Utah, Nevada, and Idaho. The range runs east-west—something of a rarity in the region. The summit ridge isn't what you'd expect, either—it's a long ridge of gently rolling grasslands. Bull Mountain (elev. 9,931 feet) crowns the range, though it's hard to pick out from all the other grassy knolls.

Hikers haven't yet discovered the range—you'll find pristine forests and canyons but no real trails. Aspen, Douglas and subalpine fir, and limber pine thrive in the canyons and on the northern slopes below the summit ridge. Ranchers run cattle on the top and in other meadow areas. A road that requires a four-wheel-drive vehicle climbs into the mountains from Yost.

Clear Creek Campground (elev. 6,400 feet) offers sites in a beautiful setting below the north slope of the Raft River Range. The roads leading to the campground also offer access to the range's best hiking. For information, contact the **Burley Ranger District office** of the Sawtooth National Forest, 2621 S. Overland Ave., Burley, ID 83318, 208/678-0430.

Park Valley

Travelers can easily cross the lonely country of Utah's northwest corner on paved Highways 42 and 30. Park Valley, south of the Raft River Mountains, has a small store and gas station, and a café (all closed Sunday).

Logan and Vicinity

Without question one of the most appealing towns in Utah, Logan (pop. 40,270) lies surrounded by the lush dairy and farmlands of the Cache Valley and by the lofty peaks of the Bear River Range. Of all the mountain communities in the American West that advertise their Swiss or Bavarian aspirations, Logan comes closest to actually looking alpine.

The town itself is built on stair-like terraces, which mark ancient shorelines of Lake Bonneville. Utah State University lends a youthful energy to the town, and residents are notably trim and attractive (the fact that some are performers from New York City doesn't hurt). Logan is also one of the state's festival centers: Theater, music, and performance series enliven the town in summer. As everywhere in Utah, the outdoors is never far away: The mountains provide abundant year-round recreation including scenic drives, boating on nearby Bear Lake, camping, fishing, hiking, and skiing.

History

Mountain men tramped through Utah's northernmost lands in search of beaver and other fur-bearing animals as early as 1819. They found good trapping near Cache Valley and stayed for several seasons, holding one rendezvous here and two at nearby Bear Lake. The fur trappers often stored their valuable pelts in a cache (French for "hiding place"), an underground pit for which the valley was later named.

LOGAN

To Smithfield
AMY'S MONGOLIAN BBQ
1400 N.
CACHE VALLEY MALL
LOGAN REGIONAL HOSPITAL
ROMNEY STADIUM
91
UTAH STATE
MUNICIPOOL
1000 N.
900 N.
500 600 700
THE SPECTRUM
LOGAN GOLF AND COUNTRY CLUB
HILLCREST AVE.
1500
EL SOL
800 N.
MOUNT LOGAN MIDDLE SCHOOL
700 N.
PARKING TERRACE
NORA ECCLES HARRISON MUSEUM OF ART
LOGAN RANGER DISTRICT (U.S FOREST
MAIN
600 N.
TAGGART STUDENT CENTER
UNIVERSITY
Lady Bird Park
100
ALTA MANOR SUITES
500 N.
MERRILL LIBRARY
400 300 200 100 200 300 400
OLD MAIN BUILDING
500 400
COMFORT INN
MANDARIN GARDEN
N.
RD.
89
To Logan Canyon and Bear Lake
300 N.
LOGAN LIBRARY
BEST WESTERN WESTON INN
N.
BOULEVARD
CANYON
Logan River
200
HISTORICAL MUSEUM/ TOURIST OFFICE
POST OFFICE
CAFFE IBIS
MORMON TEMPLE
N.
100 N.
CENTER
MORMON TABERNACLE
INN ON CENTER STREET/ ANNIVERSARY INN
ST.
Moon
CAFÉ SABOR
100
SEE DETAIL
BICENTENNIAL PARK
CENTRAL PARK
S.
WORTHINGTON PARK (LOGAN HIGH SCHOOL)
200
COMMUNITY RECREATION CENTER
S.
ST.
300 S.
DAYS INN
400
CACHE COUNTY FAIRGROUNDS
500
S.
RACE TRACK
600 S.
WILLOW PARK AND ZOO
91
0   1 mi
0   1 km
WESTERN PARK CAMPGROUND
SUPER 8 MOTEL
CRYSTAL INN
89
To Brigham City and Wellsville
To Hyrum and Providence

Detail:

BLUEBIRD RESTAURANT
CENTER ST.
LYRIC REPERTORY THEATRE
ELLEN ECCLES THEATRE
MAIN ST.
100 S. ST.
100 W. ST.
IAS RESTAURANT
BEST WESTERN AU H OTEL
200 S. ST.

Cold winters and hostile Native Americans discouraged permanent settlement in the area until 1856, when a small group of Mormons established Maughan's Fort (now Wellsville). Uncertainties caused by the "Mormon War" delayed the founding of Logan and other communities another three years. Farms, a dairy industry, and livestock raising begun in those early years continue to be an important part of Logan's economy today. High-tech industries have moved to the area in recent years, most notably the Utah State University Space Dynamics Lab, which designs projects for the space shuttle.

SIGHTS

Logan has a lovely little downtown filled with handsome architecture, lined with trees, and flanked by parks. A walk along Main Street is a pleasant diversion, with numerous shops to visit, including bookstores, recreation stores, old-fashioned shops, and the mandatory Bluebird Restaurant, a traditional soda fountain.

© BILL WEIR

A worker in period clothing demonstrates the traditional way to cut hay at the American West Heritage Center.

Mormon Temple and Tabernacle

The distinctive castellated temple rises from a prominent hill just east of downtown, at 175 North 300 East. After Brigham Young chose this location in 1877, church members labored for seven years to complete the temple. Architect Truman O. Angell, designer of the Salt Lake Temple, oversaw construction. Timber and blocks of limestone came from nearby Logan Canyon. Only Mormons engaged in sacred work may enter the temple, but visitors are welcome on the grounds to view the exterior.

The tabernacle also stands as a fine example of early Mormon architecture. Construction of the stone structure began in 1865, but other priorities—building the temple and ward meeting-houses—delayed dedication until 1891. The public may enter the tabernacle, which is downtown at Main and Center Streets.

At the **Cache Valley Historical Museum** (Daughters of Utah Pioneers Museum), 160 N. Main, 435/753-5139, exhibits show how Logan's early settlers lived. You'll see their tools, household furnishings, clothing, art, and photographs; open 10 A.M.–4 P.M. Tuesday–Friday in summer and by appointment the rest of the year; free. It is also the Cache Valley tourist office. More of Logan's history can be seen on a walking tour; ask for the self-guided, 45-minute *Logan's Historic Main Street* brochure at the tourist office.

Willow Park and Zoo

This small free zoo, 419 West 700 South, displays exotic birds such as an Andean condor, a golden pheasant, a mitered conure, and more familiar golden and bald eagles, peacocks, swans, and ducks. Animals you might meet include capuchin monkeys and coatimundis. Willow Park also has picnic areas and a playground in amongst its large shady trees. The zoo is open daily from 8 A.M. until dark year-round except on some holidays.

American West Heritage Center

This institution six miles southwest of Logan combines the function of a visitors center with the history and culture of the Old West. The center, 4025 S. Hwy. 89/91, 435/245-6050, www.americanwestcenter.org, closely tied to the popular **Festival of the American West,** is

NORTHERN UTAH

The Ellen Eccles Theatre is home to the Utah Festival Opera.

quite ambitious, and plans call for building a permanent living history installation that will highlight the lives and lifestyles of the native peoples of the Cache Valley as well as the fur-trapping explorers who arrived here in the 1840s. The center really comes alive in August when the festival hits: Mountain men clad in buckskin throw tomahawks, cowboy poets rhapsodize about the open range, and bonneted homestead wives give cooking lessons. (See Arts and Entertainment.) The Northern Utah Welcome Center serves as the focal point of the site and provides tourist information, an introduction to local history, and a gift shop; it's open 8 A.M.–5 P.M. Monday–Saturday year-round, except on winter holidays.

Adjacent to the center and incorporated into it is the **Ronald V. Jensen Living Historical Farm,** an outdoor museum that re-creates life on a Cache Valley family farm in 1917. Workers dress in period clothing to plow soil, thresh grain, milk cows, shear sheep, and butcher hogs. The men mostly worked in the fields while women stayed closer to home to cook, can, quilt, gather eggs from the henhouse, and pick vegetables from the garden. You'll see breeds of animals representative of early

farms, a lineup of steam tractors, a giant early gasoline tractor, and many other pieces of farm machinery. Buildings here include an 1875 farmhouse, summer kitchen, root cellar, smokehouse, blacksmith shop, horse barn, sheep shed, and a privy or two. Special demonstrations take place all through the year, usually on Saturday; these range from planting the garden to shearing the sheep and harvesting the grain. In fall, the cornfield is converted into a maze. The farm is open 10 A.M.–5 P.M. Monday–Saturday Memorial Day–Labor Day; $6 adults, $5 seniors, $4 children, or $20 family.

UTAH STATE UNIVERSITY

In 1888, a federal land-grant program opened the way for the territorial legislature to establish the Agricultural College of Utah. The school grew to become Utah State University (USU) in 1957 and now has eight colleges, 45 departments, and a graduate school. USU's "Aggies" number more than 20,000, led by 2,300 faculty and staff. The university has continued its original purpose of agricultural research while diversifying into atmospheric and space sciences, ecology, creative arts, social sciences, and other fields.

Attractions on campus include the **Nora Eccles Harrison Museum of Art,** 435/797-0163, one of the largest permanent collections of art in Utah; the student center; and several libraries. **Old Main Building,** with its landmark bell tower, was begun one year after the college was founded and has housed nearly every office and department in the school at one time or another. The oak-shaded campus sits northeast of downtown on a bench left by a northern arm of prehistoric Lake Bonneville.

> *People from all over Utah and the intermountain West come to Logan to take in an opera, a chamber music concert, or an evening of theater in this scenic alpine valley.*

A full schedule of concerts, theater, lecture series, art exhibits, and sports competitions fills the calendar. The University Relations Department can provide information on upcoming cultural events; contact them at 435/797-1158. Park free along streets off campus or for a small charge at the Parking Terrace on 700 North (between 800 and 900 East). Try USU's famous Traditional Aggie Ice Cream, available in the student center and at the USU Dairy Sales outlet, 8710 University Blvd., 435/797-2109.

ENTERTAINMENT AND EVENTS

One of the best reasons to visit Logan is to catch the community's high-quality arts and music festivals. People from all over Utah and the intermountain West come to Logan to take in an opera, a chamber music concert, or an evening of theater in this scenic alpine valley. The Cache Valley Tourism Council, 160 N. Main St., 435/752-2161, www.tourcachevalley.com, can fill you in on what's happening in the area.

Utah Festival Opera Company

This professional opera troupe, 435/750-0300 or 800/830-6088, www.ufoc.org, takes over the beautifully restored Ellen Eccles Theatre, 43 S. Main, in July and August. The fact that a small Utah agricultural college town has its own prominent opera company is slightly unusual. Two factors account for the opera and its hearty success. Michael Ballam, a Logan-area native and professional opera singer, decided in 1993 to start an opera company in Utah; at the same time, Logan's old movie palace and vaudeville hall, the Capitol Theatre, was remodeled and transformed into a world-class performing arts center. Renamed the Ellen Eccles Theatre, the theater has excellent acoustics and an intimate yet formal atmosphere that perfectly suited Ballam's operatic vision. Utah Festival Opera currently stages four performances during its month-long season. For more information, write P.O. Box 3489, Logan, UT 84323-3489.

Old Lyric Repertory Theatre

The Old Lyric, 28 W. Center, 435/797-1500 or 888/878-2931, provides a summer season of musicals, comedies, and dramas in a historic theater in downtown Logan at 28 W. Center. Visiting equity actors lead the shows produced by the Utah State University's drama department. Other Logan-area summer stock theaters also present light comedies and musicals.

Musical Events

Utah State University and Logan jointly sponsor a **Music in the Parks** series throughout the summer. The university also sponsors a **summer performing arts series,** which brings the Utah Symphony, dance troupes, and chamber musicians to the campus. For information on both series, call 435/797-0305. The **Capitol Arts Alliance,** 435/752-0026, brings in musicals, events, and performances to the Ellen Eccles Theatre throughout the year.

Festival of the American West

This unusual festival, 435/797-1143 or 800/225-FEST, www.americanwestcenter.org, is a full-strength celebration of Western heritage held the last week of July and the first week of August at the new American West Heritage Center in Wellsville, six miles south of Logan on Highway 89. Special festival tickets are necessary for entry; $15 adult, $13 seniors, $10 students 12 and over, and $8 children 3–11.

The festival and the center are a hybrid of a number of interesting ideas. The center and the Jensen Living Historical Farm (see above) are a living museum of farm life in the early 20th century.

In late July and early August, the center is the site of the eight-day Festival of the American West. There's a wide mix of events during the festival, ranging from shoot-outs and a mountainman encampment to a Dutch-oven cook-off; however, the various musical and arts events generally draw the biggest crowds. Cowboy poetry readings here bring together some of the most noted bards in the West, and there are also displays of Western art, performances of folk ballet, and concerts.

Other Events

The **Mendon May Day Festival** takes place 11 miles west of Logan and features a maypole dance and other festivities.

June brings the **Summerfest Art and Jazz Festival** to downtown Logan, which features works by local artists, concerts, food, and a home tour.

The **Cache County Fair and Rodeo** has agricultural and craft exhibits along with PRCA rodeo action at the fairgrounds in Logan during August. At the Clarkstor Ampitheatre, 21 miles northwest of Logan, the **Martin Harris Pageant** re-creates pioneer and Mormon history.

In Wellsville, seven miles southwest of Logan, **Wellsville Founders Day Celebration** on Labor Day in early September commemorates the first pioneers to settle in Cache Valley.

Cinema

Watch films at **Cache Valley 3,** Cache Valley Mall, 1300 N. Main, 435/753-3312 (recording); **Cinema Theatre,** 60 West 100 North, 435/753-1900; or the **Utah Theatre,** 18 W. Center, 435/752-3072.

RECREATION

Parks, Swimming, and Tennis

Willow Park, 450 West 700 South, is a good place for a picnic and has the added attractions of a small zoo, playground, volleyball courts, and a softball field. **Bicentennial Park** offers picnic spots downtown at 100 S. Main. Swim year-round at the indoor **Municipool,** 114 East 1000 North, 435/750-9890. The **Community Recreation Center,** 195 South 100 West, 435/750-9877, features tennis and handball/racquetball courts, basketball, volleyball, weight room, indoor track, table tennis, sauna, and whirlpool. **Tennis courts** are also available at Mount Logan Middle School, 875 North 200 East; Central Park, 85 South 300 East; and Worthington Park, Logan High School, 162 West 100 South.

Golf

The cool and verdant Cache Valley is especially suited to golf, and there are some dandy courses in the Logan area. Play at the 18-hole **Logan Golf and Country Club,** 710 North 1500 East, 435/753-6020; the **Logan River Golf Course,** 550 West 1000 South, 435/750-0123; the 18-hole **Birch Creek Golf Course,** 600 E. Center in Smithfield, seven miles north, 435/563-6825; or nine-hole **Sherwood Hills,** in Sardine Canyon, 13 miles southwest on U.S. 89/91, 435/245-6055. Sherwood Hills also offers a hotel, 435/245-6424, one indoor and two outdoor pools, horseback riding, cross-country ski trails, racquetball, and tennis.

Winter Sports

Ice-skating is popular in winter at Central Park, 85 South 300 East. The Logan Ranger District office, 435/755-3620, has lists of cross-country ski tours in the area.

The **Beaver Creek Lodge,** 28 miles east of Logan on Hwy. 39, 435/753-1707 or 435/753-1076, offers snowmobile rentals plus cross-country ski trails in winter. Just next door is the **Beaver Mountain Ski Area** (see the Logan Canyon section).

Equipment

Trailhead Sports, 117 N. Main, 435/753-1541, has hiking and camping gear, cross-country ski rentals and sales, canoe and kayak rentals and sales, and topo maps. Outdoor sporting goods are also sold at **The Sportsman,** 129 N. Main, 435/752-0211, and **Gart's Sporting Goods,** 585 N. Main, 435/752-4287.

ACCOMMODATIONS

$50–75

Logan's motels are generally well maintained and moderately priced. For a basic, inexpensive room, try the **Super 8 Motel,** 865 S. U.S. 89/91, 435/753-8883 or 800/800-8000. The **Days Inn,** 364 S. Main, 435/753-5623 or 800/325-2525, provides a pool, some kitchen rooms, and a guest laundry. Right downtown, the **Best Western Baugh Motel,** 153 S. Main, 435/752-5220 or 800/462-4154, offers large rooms, outdoor swimming pool, and exercise room. There's also a restaurant adjacent. Also downtown, **Best Western Weston Inn,** 250 N. Main, 435/752-5700 or 800/532-5055, has a pool, two hot tubs, a weight room, and a free breakfast. **Comfort Inn,** 447 N. Main, 435/752-9141 or 800/228-5150, has a guest laundry, complimentary continental breakfast, pool, hot tub, and exercise room. The **Crystal Inn,** 853 S. Main, 435/752-0707 or 800/280-0707, offers a pool, hot tub, and nicely furnished rooms with efficiency kitchens.

$75–100

South of Logan, near Wellsville and the American West Heritage Center, is the **Ramada Limited,** 2002 S. U.S. Hwy. 89, 435/787-2060 or 800/272-6232.

History and luxury meet at **Providence Inn B&B,** three miles south of Logan at 10 S. Main in Providence, 435/752-3432. The inn is listed on the National Register of Historic Places; parts of the building were built as a stone church in 1869. Each of the grandly refurbished 15 rooms offers a private bath, TV and VCR, and phone.

North of town, **Alta Manor Suites,** 45 East 500 North, 435/752-0808, offers units with fireplaces, full kitchens, and whirlpool baths in a handsome apartment-like structure.

$100–125

One of the more unusual places to stay in Logan is **Inn on Center Street/Anniversary Inn,** 169 E. Center, 435/752-3443, www.anniversaryinn.com, a complex of heritage homes with 22 theme rooms. Because this lodging was designed as a special occasion destination (hence the name), all rooms have private baths with jetted tubs and big-screen TVs, and breakfast is delivered to your room. No children; reservations only.

Campgrounds

To reach **Riverside RV Park,** 435/245-4469, turn east on 1700 South from U.S. 89/91, 435/245-4469; open year-round just south of town with showers and laundry. **Country Cuzzins RV Park,** 1936 N. Main, 435/752-1025, is open year-round with campsites, a laundry, convenience store, and hot showers; no tenting. **Hyrum State Park** offers camping, swimming, fishing, and boating seven miles south near the town of Hyrum (see the Hyrum State Park section), and the U.S. Forest Service operates many campgrounds beginning six miles east of town on U.S. 89 in Logan Canyon (see the Logan Canyon section).

FOOD

If you're looking for a cup of coffee, a pastry, or perhaps a salad for lunch, then head to **Caffe Ibis,** 52 Federal Ave., 435/753-4777. The atmosphere is pleasantly alternative, and the adjacent bakery and health food store are a nice plus.

Like any college town, Logan has a full array of pizza and fast-food places; most of them are along N. Main. **Mandarin Garden,** 432 N. Main, 435/753-5789, is the best of the many Chinese restaurants in town; open Monday–Friday for lunch, daily for dinner. At **Amy's Mongolian BBQ,** 1537 N. Main, 435/753-3338, you can enjoy Mongolian barbecue or a Chinese buffet, or order from the menu; open Monday–Saturday for lunch and dinner. For Mexican food, try **El**

Sol, 871 N. Main, 435/752-5743, open daily for lunch and dinner.

For something uniquely Loganesque, try the **Bluebird Restaurant,** 19 N. Main, 435/752-3155, a beautifully maintained soda fountain, chocolatier, and restaurant that appears unchanged from the 1930s. Open Monday–Saturday for breakfast, lunch, and dinner.

Also a Logan tradition, **Gia's Restaurant,** 119 S. Main, 435/752-8384, open Monday–Saturday for lunch and dinner, has an atmospheric dining room and is Logan's best bet for a traditional Italian meal; entrées cost $8–14.

For more up-to-date dining, ¡**Cafe Sabor!,** at the west end of Center Street at 600 W. Center, 435/752-8880, offers tasty Mexican and Southwest fare in Logan's old train depot. The tortillas and salsas are all made fresh on premises; there's outdoor dining on the shaded passenger platforms. Traditional Mexican dishes are $7–9; grilled chicken, fish, and beef entrées are $8–18.

A new dining room for high quality northern Italian cooking is **Le Nonne Ristorante Italiano,** 132 N. Main, 435/752-9577. The chef-owner hails from Tuscany, and the cuisine reflects cooking learned from his *nonne* (grandmothers). Open for lunch and dinner Monday–Friday, dinner only on Saturday.

OTHER PRACTICALITIES

Information and Services

The **Cache Valley Tourism Council,** downtown at 160 N. Main, Logan, UT 84321, 435/752-2161 or 800/882-4433, www.tourcachevalley.com, has maps and travel information for Cache and Rich Counties, including Logan and Bear Lake; it's open 8 A.M.–5 P.M. Monday–Friday (and sometimes Saturday in summer). To learn more of local history and architecture, ask for *Logan's Historic Main Street,* a brochure outlining a self-guided, 45-minute walking tour. For recreation information and maps of the surrounding mountain country, visit the **Logan Ranger District office,** on U.S. 89 at the east edge of town (1500 E. U.S. 89, Logan, UT 84321), 435/755-3620; it's open 8 A.M.–4:30 P.M. Monday–Friday (until 5 P.M. in summer and some Saturdays). The district covers Logan Canyon, the Bear River Range, and the Wellsville Mountains. Logan's **public library,** 255 N. Main, 435/750-9870, is open 10 A.M.–9 P.M. Monday–Thursday, 10 A.M.–6 P.M. Friday–Saturday. Good places for regional and general reading include the simply named **A Bookstore,** 130 North 100 East, 435/752-9089, and **The Book Table,** 29 S. Main, 435/752-3055.

Logan Regional Hospital provides 24-hour emergency care at 1400 North 500 East, 435/752-2050. The **post office** is at 151 North 100 West, 435/752-7246.

Transportation

Greyhound, 2500 North 900 West, 435/752-4921, runs buses daily south to Ogden and Salt Lake City and northeast to Idaho Falls (and West Yellowstone in summer). **Logan Cab,** 435/753-3663, provides taxi service. No scheduled airlines serve Logan.

VICINITY OF LOGAN

Hyrum City Museum

The attractive small town of Hyrum has a museum that houses exhibitions on local history, gems and minerals, and dinosaurs. Open 2–6 P.M. Tuesday, Thursday, and Saturday in the city offices at 83 W. Main, 435/245-6033.

Hyrum State Park

The Little Bear River feeds this popular 450-acre reservoir beside the town of Hyrum. Boaters come to water-ski, sail, or paddle across the waters. Sandy beaches dot the shore, though no lifeguards watch over the area. Fishing for bluegill, perch, and largemouth bass tends to be only fair, but trout fishing can be excellent. Anglers sometimes have good luck in the river just below the spillway during spring runoff. Winter visitors fish through the ice, ice-skate, and sail iceboats during freeze-up—about mid-December–late March.

The park has two developed areas on the north shore. The launch and campground area has picnic grounds, a beach, a boat ramp, docks, and the ranger office, but most park visitors head for the day-use area farther east along the shore for

VICINITY OF LOGAN

To Wyoming

Randolph

10 mi

10 km

Bear Lake State
Park East Shore

Bear Lake State
Park Marina

Bear Lake

Laketown

RENDEZVOUS
BEACH

Pickleville

Garden City

To Pocatello

Swan Peak
9,114 ft

BEAVER MOUNTAIN
SKI PARK

Tony Grove
Lake

Logan Canyon

Wasatch-Cache

National

Forest

HARDWARE
RANCH

Mount
Doubletop
9,873 ft

Mount
Naomi

Naomi Peak
9,979 ft

Mount Elmer
9,676 ft

Wilderness

Area

Logan

River

Logan Peak
9,713 ft

Blacksmith

Fork

Cove

Richmond

Smithfield

North Logan

Logan

Bear River

Cutler
Reservoir

Newton
Reservoir

Clarkston

To Idaho

Newton

RONALD V. JENSEN
LIVING HISTORICAL FARM

AMERICAN
WEST
HERITAGE
CENTER

Hyrum

Hyrum State
Park

Wellsville

Wellsville

Wilderness

Wellsville Cone
9,356 ft

Wellsville

Mtns.

Area

Wasatch-
Cache
National
Forest

Mantua
Reservoir

Mantua

To Bear River
Migratory Bird
Refuge

Brigham
City

To Ogden

NORTHERN UTAH

© AVALON TRAVEL PUBLISHING, INC.

picnicking, lying on the beach, and swimming. It's reached by a half-mile drive (follow signs) or a half-mile foot trail from the campground. The main season at Hyrum Lake (elev. 4,700 feet) runs mid-April–late September; water and outhouses are available off season at the campground. Day use costs $5, camping $14. Campground reservations are advised on summer weekends. The park makes a good base for exploring the Cache Valley area; rangers can suggest places to go and provide snowmobiling information. The ranger office, 405 West 300 South, Hyrum, UT 84319, 435/245-6866 (ranger) or 800/322-3770 (reservations), at the main entrance is open 8 A.M.–5 P.M. daily during the warmer months and 8 A.M.–noon the rest of the year. From Logan, drive south seven miles on the Hyrum Road (Highway 165), which branches off U.S. 89/91 on the south edge of town, or go southwest six miles on U.S. 89/91, then turn east three miles on Highway 101 and follow signs.

Hardware Ranch and Blacksmith Fork Canyon

The Utah Division of Wildlife Resources operates this ranch in the midst of the northern Wasatch Range to provide winter feed for herds of elk; call 435/753-6202 for general information. In winter, concessionaires offer sleigh rides for a closer look at the elk and wagon rides if there's not enough snow. A visitors center, 435/753-6202, with displays and a café, 435/753-6768, is also open in winter. You can also rent snowmobiles from the café. During the spring calving season, you might see newborn baby elk. You're not likely to see elk here in the summer months, but the drive in is still pretty.

The 16-mile paved road from Hyrum east to Hardware Ranch follows the scenic Blacksmith Fork Canyon past fishing spots (trout and whitefish), **Shenoah Picnic Area,** and **Pioneer Campground.** Pioneer's sites are open late May–late September with water; $10. Two small campgrounds, **Friendship** and **Spring,** are to the north along the Left Hand Fork of Blacksmith Canyon; they're open mid-May–late October (no water; $5 fee). An extensive snowmobile trail system extends from Hardware Ranch as far as Logan

Canyon to the north and the Monte Cristo area to the south, with many side trails.

LOGAN CANYON

From its mouth on the east edge of Logan, Logan Canyon, with its steep limestone cliffs, winds more than 20 miles into the Bear River Range, a northern extension of the Wasatch Mountains. Paved U.S. 89 follows the canyon and is a designated Scenic Byway. If you're looking for a daytrip out of Logan, just head up the canyon; you'll pass lots of picnic areas, campgrounds, fishing spots, and trailheads where you can easily spend a few blissful hours.

Steep slopes on the west rise to rolling plateau country across the top of the range, and moderate slopes descend to Bear Lake on the east. The route climbs to an elevation of 7,800 feet at Bear Lake Summit, from which there's a good view of the lofty Uintas of northeastern Utah. In autumn, maples of the lower canyon turn a brilliant crimson while aspens in the higher country are transformed to gold. Roadside geologic signs explain features in Logan Canyon. Picnicking is free at picnic areas, but you have to pay to picnic at some campgrounds.

A mile-by-mile guide to the canyon is available from the Cache Valley travel office in Logan. Contact the Logan Ranger District office for information on picnicking, camping, fishing, hiking, cross-country skiing, snowmobiling, and road conditions; it's open 8 A.M.–5 P.M. Monday–Friday near 1500 East and U.S. 89 in Logan, 435/753-2772. Some campsites can be reserved by calling 800/283-CAMP.

Skiing

Beaver Mountain Ski Area, 435/753-4822 (snow and road conditions) and 435/753-0921 (office, ski school, and lift tickets), operates three double chairlifts serving 22 runs, the longest of which is 2.25 miles and drops 1,600 vertical feet. A cafeteria, ski shop, rentals, and lessons are available at the day lodge. Adult lift tickets cost $28 full day, $22 half day; children under 12 and seniors over 65 ski for $22 full day, $13 half day. The ski area is open 9 A.M.–4 P.M. daily early December–late March. Go northeast 28 miles on U.S. 89, then north 1.5 miles on Highway 243.

Hiking

A number of easy to moderate hikes makes Logan Canyon a lovely and convenient destination for a little exercise and an eyeful of nature. Four miles up the canyon, **Riverside Nature Trail** winds along the Logan River between Spring Hollow and Guinavah Campgrounds, a 1.5-mile (one-way) stroll with good bird-watching opportunities. From Guinavah, you can loop back to Spring Hollow via the **Crimson Trail**; this more strenuous trail takes you up the limestone cliffs and down in another two miles. It takes its name from the autumn colors visible along the way. Five miles up is the **Wind Cave Trailhead.** Wind Cave, with eroded caverns and arches, is one mile and an 1,100-foot climb from the trailhead.

Jardine Juniper Trail begins at Wood Camp Campground, 10 miles up the canyon. The trail climbs 1,900 feet in 4.4 miles to Old Jardine, a venerable Rocky Mountain juniper tree. Still alive after 1,500 years, it measures about 27 feet in circumference and 45 feet high. The name honors a USU alumnus. A mile farther up the canyon is **Logan Cave,** a 2,000-foot-long cavern that hardy spelunkers can explore; bring at least two light sources.

At **Bear Lake Summit,** 30 miles from Logan, the **Limber Pine Nature Trail** originates at the parking area on the right and terminates at a massive limber pine 25 feet in circumference and 44 feet high. At one time this tree was thought to be the world's oldest and largest limber pine, but a forestry professor at USU discovered that it is really five trees grown together and "only" about 560 years old. The easy self-guided walk takes about an hour; Bear Lake can be seen to the east.

Accommodations

$75–100: A handsome timber and stone lodge, **Beaver Creek Lodge,** 435/753-1707 or 753-1076, not only offers rooms daily but also has horseback trail rides, snowmobile rentals, and cross-country ski trails in winter. The lodge is about 28 miles northeast on U.S. 89, just past the turnoff for Beaver Mountain Ski Area.

Campgrounds: There are 10 Forest Service campgrounds along U.S. 89 in Logan Canyon, so finding a place to pitch a tent shouldn't be difficult. The closest to Logan are **Bridger** and **Spring Hollow** Campgrounds, three and four miles respectively from town. Most campgrounds charge $10–14. You can reserve a campsite by calling 877/444-6777.

BEAR LAKE

More than 28,000 years ago, faulting in massive blocks of the earth's crust created a basin 50 miles long and 12 miles wide. Bear Lake filled the entire valley during the last ice age but has now receded to cover an area 20 miles long and 8 miles wide at an elevation of 5,900 feet. About half the lake lies in Utah and half in Idaho. The lake's famed turquoise color is thought to be caused by limestone particles suspended in the water.

The ecology of Bear Lake has been upset somewhat by an enterprising irrigation system. In recent centuries, Bear Lake has dwindled in size so greatly that Bear River, which once fed the lake, now totally bypasses it. The lake is kept from becoming saline by farmers who canal water from the river back to the lake during spring runoff and then pump it back into the river during the summer irrigation season.

Donald McKenzie, an early fur trapper, named the lake after the black bears once found here. Nomadic tribes and groups of trappers frequented the shores during the 1820s and held two large gatherings here. Mormons arrived beginning in 1863 to start farms and ranches.

In recent years, thousands of summer cabins have sprouted along the shore and hillsides to take advantage of the scenery and water sports. Bear Lake State Park offers a marina and campground on the west shore, a large camping area on the south shore at Rendezvous Beach, and undeveloped campgrounds on the east shore. For information on Bear Lake, dial up the website www.bearlake.org.

Bear Lake National Wildlife Refuge

This wetlands refuge occupies 17,600 acres of marshlands north of the lake and is a favored

BEAR LAKE MONSTER

When white settlers first arrived in the Bear Lake area, the local Native Americans warned them that a monster lived in the lake. The beast was described as being of the "legged serpent" variety and was said to have carried humans away. Few Native Americans of the area would bathe in the lake or camp nearby, but settlers scoffed—even after a few sightings by whites.

In 1868, no fewer than 20 people reported seeing the monster, all within a period of a few weeks. These included a few citizens of local repute and a wagonload of eight travelers. The monster gained fame and many believers, both in the area and beyond. Soon monsters were "spotted" in other lakes, including a 45-foot-long alligator that came out of the Great Salt Lake and smashed a campsite as the residents fled. This proliferation of tall tales began to cast doubts on the existence of Bear Lake's monster, and fewer sightings were reported.

There were even a few legends explaining the monster's demise. One farmer told of a huge creature from the lake that hungrily devoured part of his flock of sheep. As the surviving animals fled, the monster's eye caught a coil of barbed wire about the size and shape of huddled prey and swallowed it whole. By the farmer's account, the resulting pain drove the beast back into the lake and it was never seen again. Rangers at Minnetonka Cave offer another story. They maintain the monster was intimidated by the surrounding human population and sought refuge in the cave where it survived on cave popcorn and coral. In this version, the monster was felled by a collapsing cave wall, with all but a clenched claw buried under rubble. The existing trail was built over that rockfall and rangers today still point out a piece of flowstone just under the trail that strangely does resemble a large dragon claw.

stopping place for sandhill cranes, herons, white pelicans, egrets, and many species of ducks. Four species of fish evolved in Bear Lake that are not found any other place in the world. One of these, the Bonneville cisco, attracts anglers by the thousands. During spawning in January, nets are used to dip the small (6–8 inches long), tasty fish from the icy water. Ice fishing is very popular; fish sought year-round by anglers include the native Bear Lake cutthroat and Bonneville whitefish and the introduced rainbow and Mackinaw trout and yellow perch. Keep an eye out for the Bear Lake monster—a dark dragonlike creature 90 feet long that spouts water!

Bear Lake State Park

The 71,000 acres of Bear Lake give plenty of room to water-ski, sail, or fish. For state park information and campground reservations, write to P.O. Box 184, Garden City, UT 84028, or call 435/946-3343 or 800/322-3770 (reservations). The **marina,** one mile north of Garden City on U.S. 89, offers boat slips (protected by a breakwater), a boat ramp, a swimming area, picnic tables, a campground with showers, and ranger offices. Season is year-round; $7 day use, $14 camping. On busy summer weekends it's a good idea to have reservations for the marina or Rendezvous Beach area.

Rendezvous Beach, a wide sandy beach, attracts visitors to the lake's southern shore. The park has a day-use area with a boat-rental concession and several campgrounds with showers. Ask at the entrance station for recommended places to camp; some sites have lake views, some offer hookups, and some are set up mainly for RVs. Open early May–late September; $7 day use, $14 camping, $20 camping with hookups. Rendezvous beach is eight miles south of Garden City near Laketown.

Primitive campgrounds and day-use areas are located on the east side of Bear Lake. From south to north are **First Point, Second Point** (day use only), **South Eden, Cisco Beach, Rainbow Cove,** and **North Eden.** Sites stay open year-round; outhouses are provided, but only South Eden has drinking water. Fees are $4 day-use, $7 camping. First Point and Rainbow Cove offer boat ramps. Scuba divers like the steep underwater drop-offs near Cisco Beach. Turn north from Laketown.

Garden City and Vicinity

This small town (year-round pop. 300) on the east shore at the junction of U.S. 89 and Highway 30 comes to life in summer. You can learn about the area at a **tourist information center** at the highway junction; open 10 A.M.–6 P.M. daily May–September. **Pickleville Playhouse,** 2.8 miles south of Garden City, 435/946-2918 (Garden City) or 435/755-0961 (Logan), features family entertainment on summer evenings. A Western-style cookout precedes the show.

The town celebrates the harvest of its most famous crop during the **Raspberry Days Festival** on the first weekend in August with a parade, the crowning of Miss Raspberry, a Little Buckaroo Rodeo, crafts, and entertainment. The **Mountain Man Rendezvous** reenacts the big gatherings of fur trappers and Native Americans that took place at Bear Lake in the summers of 1826 and 1827; the modern event is held the second weekend of September at Rendezvous Beach in Bear Lake State Park; call 435/946-3343 for information.

Accommodations

$50–75: Bear Lake Motor Lodge, just south of the highway junction at 50 S. Bear Lake Blvd., 435/946-3271, is open year-round and has a restaurant. **Ideal Beach Resort,** 2144 S. Bear Lake Blvd. (3.3 miles south of Garden City), 435/946-3364 or 800/634-1018 in Utah, offers motel and condo accommodations (half-week or longer) year-round, plus camping and a restaurant. The Ideal also offers boat rentals, a beach, swimming pools, tennis, and miniature golf. The adjacent nine-hole **Bear Lake Golf Course,** 435/946-8742, is open to the public.

$100–125: Harbor Village Inn, 900 N. Bear Lake Blvd., 435/946-3448 or 800/324-6840, is open year-round and offers suites with full kitchens and fireplaces, plus use of tennis courts, lap pool, and hot tub.

Campgrounds: In addition to the state park campgrounds, there's the **Bear Lake KOA,** 0.8 mile north of Garden City on U.S. 89 near the state park marina, 435/946-3454. It offers a swimming pool, miniature golf, tennis, store, showers, cabins and laundry; it's open May–October.

Food

Each of the above three lodgings (Bear Lake Motor Lodge, Ideal Beach Resort, Harbor Village Inn) has its own restaurant. Additionally, **Bear Lake West** is 4.5 miles north of Garden City, just across the Idaho border (three miles south of Fish Haven), 208/945-2222, and has a nine-hole golf course and a steak and seafood restaurant, open in summer for Sunday brunch and Thursday–Saturday for dinner.

Minnetonka Cave

At the beginning of the 20th century a grouse hunter retrieved a fallen bird after climbing a steep slope and noticed a cave entrance. Returning a few days later with friends and lights, he discovered an extensive and beautiful cave. Now you can visit this cave with a U.S. Forest Service ranger as your guide through its nine rooms.

Wear comfortable shoes with good soles—the tour is 1,800 feet long and involves 484 stair steps (some of them muddy and slick), and the route is retraced on the way out. Wear a light jacket and long pants; the temperature is 40°F and the humidity gives the cold a bite. Tours last 60–90 minutes (depending on group size); from the cave's sign at St. Charles, Idaho, go west 10 miles to the cave entrance parking lot.

There are several Forest Service campgrounds along the route and a few designated free camping sites. Tours of the cave are given every half-hour 10 A.M.–5:30 P.M. daily mid-June–Labor Day; $5 adults, $4 children (6–15); call 208/245-4422 for information.

Randolph

The Rich County seat, Randolph (pop. 800), is a quiet rural town 19 miles south of Bear Lake. Farming and ranching have been the main activities here ever since Randolph H. Stewart led the first settlers here from Idaho in 1870. **Rich County Round-Up Days,** held in August, feature a rodeo, parade, and exhibits. No accommodations in town—just a drive-in.

West-Central Utah

Utah's Wild West remains nearly as wild as ever. Rugged mountain ranges and barren desert valleys have discouraged all but the most determined individuals. Explorers, pioneers in wagon trains, Pony Express riders, and telegraph linemen crossed this inhospitable land with only the desire to reach the other side. It took the promise of gold and silver to lure large numbers of people into the jagged hills. Fading ghost towns still show the industry of the early miners. Hardy ranchers also braved the isolation to grow hay and run their cattle and sheep. Shortage of water has always been the limiting factor to development. Travelers, however, can enjoy the solitude and the thrill of exploring a land little changed since white explorers first arrived. Roads provide surprisingly good access for such a remote region. Paved I-80, U.S. 50/6, and Highway 21 cross it, while dirt roads branch off in all directions. Following the Pony Express and Stage Route from Fairfield to Ibapah might be the most unique driving tour; you experience some of the same unfenced wilderness as did the tough young Pony Express riders. You can negotiate

Beehive-shaped charcoal kilns are just east of the ghost town of Frisco.

© BILL WEIR

WEST-CENTRAL UTAH

© AVALON TRAVEL PUBLISHING, INC.

WEST-CENTRAL UTAH HIGHLIGHTS

Great Salt Lake Desert
Bonneville Salt Flats
Oquirrh Overlook
Pony Express route
Cross-country hiking in remote mountain ranges

this and many other back roads by car in dry weather. For the adventurous, the wildly beautiful mountain ranges offer countless hiking possibilities—though you'll have to rough it. Hardly any developed trails exist.

THE LAND

Located in the Great Basin, west-central Utah consists of about equal amounts of valley and mountain terrain. Geologic forces have worked here on a grand scale. Great blocks of the earth's crust rising along faults formed the mountains— all of which run north-south. Volcanic activity has left well-preserved craters, cinder cones, and lava flows. The massive sandbars that once lined the southern shore of Lake Bonneville have blown northeastward to form impressive dunes at Little Sahara. Streambeds in west-central Utah actually drain into several different subbasins, the two largest of which are Great Salt Lake and Sevier Lake.

Clouds moving in from the Pacific Ocean lose much of their moisture to the Sierra Nevada and other towering mountain ranges in California and Nevada. By the time the depleted clouds reach west-central Utah, only the Deep Creek, Stansbury, and southern Wah Wah Mountains reach high enough to gather sufficient rain and snow to support permanent streams. Notable summits of the region include Ibapah (12,087 feet) and Haystack (12,020 feet) Peaks of the Deep Creek Range, Deseret Peak (11,031 feet) of the Stansbury Mountains, Swasey (9,669 feet) and Notch (9,655 feet) Peaks of the House Range, Frisco Peak (9,660 feet) of the San Francisco Mountains, and Crystal Peak (7,106 feet) of the Wah Wah Range.

Though west-central Utah is now one of the driest parts of the Great Basin, a far different scene existed some 10,000 years ago. Freshwater Lake Bonneville then covered 20,000 square miles—one-fourth of Utah. Forests blanketed the mountains that poked above the lake waters. With time, the giant inland sea gradually shrank to much smaller remnants such as the Great Salt Lake, leaving behind the glistening salt flats of the Great Salt Lake Desert. Rainfall variations over time have caused Sevier Lake, southwest of Delta, to fluctuate between being a dry lakebed and the state's third-largest body of water.

Climate

Precipitation averages 8–10 inches annually over most of the region, which ranges 4,000–6,000 feet in elevation. The rain and snow that do fall soon disappear because of the low humidity and abundant sunshine. Rainfall peaks in spring and again during the late summer–early autumn thunderstorm season. In this harsh semidesert, winter temperatures can drop into the subzeros, but the summer sun can send the thermometer climbing above 100 degrees. Visibility to 70 miles or more in the clean, dry air rewards mountain climbers with incredible views.

FLORA AND FAUNA

Vegetation in the valleys consists of sparse, low-growing plants such as saltbush, greasewood, black and bud sagebrush, shadscale, little rabbitbrush, Mormon tea, and grasses. Big sagebrush, juniper, and piñon pine grow higher up. The highest peaks support mountain shrubs, aspen, and a variety of conifers, including the long-lived bristlecone pine.

Availability of water determines the quantity and variety of wildlife. Of the larger animals, mule deer and pronghorn are most widespread. Elk can be found in mountainous areas east of Delta. Rocky Mountain bighorn sheep have been reintroduced in the Deep Creek Range. Herds of wild horses roam the Confusion and House Ranges. Other wildlife includes coyote, mountain lion, bobcat, kit fox, spotted and striped skunks, and black-tailed jackrabbit. Vast numbers of birds visit Fish Springs National Wildlife Refuge and other desert oases. Waterfowl and marsh birds stop over in greatest numbers during their early spring and late autumn migrations. Many smaller birds nest near water sources in late spring and early summer.

HISTORY

Native American Peoples

Paleo-Indians entered this region about 15,000 years ago to collect wild plants and to pursue the now-extinct mammoth and other big game. After 5,000 years or so, the drying climate and changing environment caused many of the large animals to disappear. Still nomadic, the groups adapted by relying more on small game and wild plant foods. New technologies including the bow and arrow, pottery, and small-scale agriculture distinguished the Fremont people around A.D. 550. When the Fremont culture faded, about 1300—perhaps because of drought and depletion of resources—the culturally distinct Shoshoni moved in. These nomadic hunters and gatherers proved well suited to the dry environment. It's likely the modern Goshute—or Gosiutes—and Utes descended from them.

Within the first decades of Utah's settlement by white people, all tribes suffered great losses of population and land. Even today the people struggle to adapt to modern ways. The Goshute once occupied northwest Utah and adjacent Nevada; they now live in the Goshute and Skull Valley Indian Reservations. The Utes had the greatest range of all of Utah's tribes, extending from west-central Utah into Colorado and New Mexico; they now have reservations in northeast Utah and southwest Colorado.

Explorers and Overland Trails

Imposing terrain and a scarcity of water discouraged early explorers from crossing the Great Basin region. In 1776, the Spanish became the first non-Indians to visit west-central Utah when members of the Dominguez-Escalante Expedition left the Utah Lake area and headed southwest, passing near the present-day towns of Delta and Milford.

Most American mountain men of the 1820s also kept to the Great Basin's edge—but not Jedediah Smith. With a party of 17 men, Smith set out in 1826 from northern Utah for Spanish California, searching for new fur-trapping areas. When Smith returned to Utah with two companions, the little group nearly perished in deep snows in the Sierra Nevada and from thirst in the desert.

Government explorer John C. Frémont named and made the first scientific studies of the Great Basin in 1845, putting to rest myths about the Great Salt Lake's monsters, whirlpools, and subterranean outlets to the Pacific.

In the following year, travelers began crossing the Great Basin as a shortcut to California. Horses and mules made the crossing safely, but the Donner-Reed wagon train met with disaster. Mud in the Great Salt Lake Desert slowed the group so much that they ran out of water and lost some of their wagons and oxen. The exhausted and demoralized group reached the Sierra Nevada late in the season, when snowstorms trapped and killed 40 of the 87 emigrants.

In 1859, Captain J. S. Simpson surveyed a military road to the south of the treacherous desert to connect Camp Floyd in central Utah with Carson Valley in western Nevada. Swift riders of the Pony Express used the road, known as the South-Central Overland Route, in 1860–1861, before the telegraph ended this brief chapter of American history. The Lincoln Highway, America's first designated transcontinental motoring route, included part of this road from 1910 to 1927.

Gold!

Prospectors found placer gold deposits in the early 1860s, though significant production had to wait for the arrival of the transcontinental railroad in 1869. Deposits of gold, silver, copper, lead, and zinc were found in quick succession. Major mining districts included Ophir, Mercur, and Tintic to the southwest of Salt Lake City; Gold Hill, Clifton, and Willow Springs in the far west of Utah; Detroit near Delta; and the San Francisco Mountains near Milford. Active gold mining continues in the Mercur, Tintic, and Detroit districts.

Military Reserves

Jet aircraft and helicopters occasionally break the silence in flights above the Wendover Bombing and Gunnery Range. Scientists and engineers at Dugway Proving Grounds work on chemical and biological weapons. The base received some notoriety in 1968 after 6,500 sheep died on neighboring ranches. The military never admitted that it had released toxic warfare chemicals, but it did compensate the ranchers. Just south of Tooele you'll see the neat rows of buildings across the vast Tooele Army Depot, which functions as a storage, maintenance, repair, and training center. In 1996, the Army began incineration of part of the U.S. chemical weapons cache at the depot.

Great Salt Lake Desert

Lake Bonneville once covered 20,000 square miles in Utah, Idaho, and Nevada; when the lake broke through the Sawtooth Mountains, its level declined precipitously, leaving the 2,500-square-mile Great Salt Lake and huge expanses of salt flats to its south and west. These salt flat remnants of Lake Bonneville are almost completely white and level and go on for over a hundred miles in some directions. It is commonly said that one can see the earth's curvature at the horizon, though this apparently takes a very discerning eye.

Other than the section traversed by I-80, most of the Great Salt Lake Desert is off-limits to ordinary travelers, as it is used by the military to test weapons of all sorts.

WENDOVER AND VICINITY

Wendover began in 1907 as a watering station during construction of the Western Pacific Railroad. The highway went through in 1925, marking the community's beginnings as a travelers' stop. Wendover Air Force Base got its start in 1940 and soon grew to become one of the world's largest military complexes. During World War II, crews of bombers and other aircraft learned their navigation, formation flying, gunnery, and bombing skills above the 3.5 million acres of desert belonging to the base. Only after the war ended did the government reveal that one of the bomber groups had been training in preparation for dropping atomic bombs on Japan. Little remains of the base—once a city of nearly 20,000 people. Hill Air Force Base, near Ogden, continues to use the vast military reserve for training air crews.

Wendover now has the tacky grandiosity of a Nevada border town.

Bonneville Salt Flats International Speedway

A brilliant white layer of salt left behind by prehistoric Lake Bonneville covers more than 44,000 acres of the Great Salt Lake Desert. For much of the year, a shallow layer of water sits atop the salt flats. Wave action planes the surface almost

© BILL WEIR

Built for speed: Race fans gather at the Bonneville Salt Flats.

perfectly level—some say you can see the curvature of the earth here. The hot sun usually dries out the flats enough for speed runs in summer and autumn. Cars began running across the salt in 1914 and continue to set faster and faster times. Rocket-powered vehicles have exceeded 600 miles per hour. Expansive courses can be laid out; the main speedway is 10 miles long and 80 feet wide. A small tent city goes up near the course during the annual **Speed Week** in August; vehicles in an amazing variety of styles and ages take off individually to set new records in their classes. The salt flats, just east of Wendover, are easy to access: take I-80 Exit 4 and follow the paved road five miles north, then east. Signs and markers indicate if and where you can drive on the salt. Soft spots underlain by mud can trap vehicles venturing off the safe areas. Take care not to be on the track when racing events are being held!

> *The hot sun usually dries out the flats enough for speed runs in summer and autumn. Cars began running across the salt in 1914 and continue to set faster and faster times. Rocket-powered vehicles have exceeded 600 miles per hour.*

Silver Island Mountains

These rugged mountains rise above the salt flats northeast of Wendover. You can visit them and their rocky canyons on a 54-mile loop drive. Take I-80 Exit 4, go north 1.2 miles, turn left 0.8 mile on a gravel road, then turn right at the sign for the Silver Island Mountains. The road loops counterclockwise around the mountains, crosses Lebby Pass, and returns to the junction near I-80. Another road goes north from Lebby Pass to Lucin in the extreme northwest corner of Utah. High-clearance vehicles do best on these roads, though cars can often negotiate them in dry weather. The Northern Utah map in the Utah Travel Council series shows approximate road alignments and terrain.

Danger Cave

Archaeologists from the University of Utah discovered thousands of prehistoric artifacts in this cave. The five distinct layers of debris—the oldest dating back at least 10,000 years—have provided a wealth of new information on the region's early inhabitants. During field work in the 1950s, a huge piece of the cave's ceiling came crashing down. No one was hurt, but "Danger Cave" seemed an appropriate name. No exhibits or signs exist, so there's not much to see. If you'd like to visit the cave anyway, take I-80 Exit 4, turn north 0.4 mile, turn left (west) 1.4 miles on a paved road, then turn right (northwest) 1.8 miles on a gravel road (keep left past the gravel pits) to the cave. The road curves southwest along the face of the Silver Island Mountains. The cave entrance is easy to locate, about 200 feet from the road. You'll find excavation work and the collapsed ceiling in the large room, which was once home to ancient Native Americans. A bit farther down the road is another undeveloped cave once used by off-duty military personnel for recreation. The cave floor was paved with concrete and a jukebox was powered by a generator to create a dance area that could be used even during blackouts. Juke Box Cave and Danger Cave are both part of an undeveloped Utah state park.

Metaphor: The Tree of Life

Twenty-five miles east of Wendover on I-80, a weird roadside sculpture juts up from the salt flats. The 87-foot-tall sculpture was created in the early 1980s by Swedish artist Karl Momen. Conceived as "a hymn to our universe whose glory and dimension is beyond all myth and imagination," it may fall short of that rhapsodic goal, but it is just about the only *thing* along this stretch of road.

Practicalities

This desert town has a split personality—half the town lies in Utah and half in Nevada. On both sides you'll find accommodations and restaurants where you can take a break from long drives on I-80. Five casino hotels, eight motels, and two campgrounds offer places to stay. Six casinos on the Nevada side provide a chance to lose your money in the usual gambling games. Most of the town's visitor facilities line Wendover Boulevard, also known as State Highway, which parallels the interstate. Lodgings are cheaper on the Utah side. The **Day's Inn,** 685 E. Wendover Blvd., 435/665-2215 or 800/329-7466, which runs about $70, is the nicest and most expensive place on the Utah side. The other lodgings are all well less than $50; to really pinch pennies, the **Bonneville Inn,** 375 Wendover Blvd., 435/665-2500, is okay for a cheap motel, and it has an indoor pool.

For information about the area stop in at the **Nevada-Wendover Welcome Center,** on the Nevada side at 937 Wendover Blvd. (P.O. Box 2468, Wendover, NV 89883), 702/664-3414 or 800/426-6862. It's open 8:30–11:30 A.M. and noon–5 P.M. daily; look for the World War II Memorial capped by a B-29 model in front. Major annual events near Wendover include the **Wendover Bordertown Bike Challenge,** held over three days in late April or early May for both mountain and road bikes. During the **Land Speed Opener** in July, attempts are made to set new speed records. **Wendover Air Show** takes place in August or October, **Speed Week** in the third week of August, the smaller **World of Speed** in late September, and the **Bonneville World Finals** in mid-October at the Bonneville Salt Flats International Speedway.

SKULL VALLEY

Iosepa

Now a ghost town with little more than a cemetery, foundations, and a few houses, Iosepa once had a population of 226 Polynesian settlers. Devout Hawaiian Mormons who desired to live in the promised land of Utah began the settlement in 1889. All the good farmland around Salt Lake City had been taken, so the group wound up in this desolate valley west of the Stansbury Mountains. Undaunted by the harsh climate and scarcity of water, the Hawaiians laid out a townsite and named it Iosepa ("Joseph") after the sixth president of the LDS Church, Joseph F. Smith. Livestock was raised, crops and trees were

planted, and roses bloomed in the new desert home. The islanders celebrated Pioneer Day on August 28, the date they arrived in Skull Valley, with feasts of poi and roast pig. Not all harvests produced a profit, however, and life here was hard. Leprosy appeared in 1896, and its several victims were forced to live in a separate building—Utah's only known leper colony. News in 1916 of plans to build a Mormon temple in Hawaii brought a wave of homesickness, and within a year the struggling settlement disbanded.

Today Iosepa is a large ranch along the road 15 miles south of I-80 Timpie Springs Exit 77. There's no sign at the ranch, but it's the largest in the area, with four houses along the road and several farm buildings. The two small frame houses belonged to the original Hawaiian settlement; two other surviving buildings are farther back. Residents don't mind people visiting the old townsite, but ask first. To see the cemetery, turn east past a group of mailboxes and the northernmost house, go through a gate, then keep left at a fork. The cemetery, marked by six flagpoles, is three-quarters of a mile in; the road may be too rough for cars. Time and the elements have reduced the graves to mounds of gravel with just a few marble headstones. Their Hawaiian names seem out of place in this lonely desert valley.

Skull Valley Indian Reservation

From prehistoric times, the Goshute have ranged over this region to hunt and gather wild plant foods. And since the 1860s, they have been ranching and farming. If you've seen the hogans and sweat lodges in the Four Corners area, you'll find this reservation something of a change: There are no culturally distinctive houses or outbuildings here.

GRANTSVILLE

Here on the edges of the Great Salt Lake Desert, old buildings and tall Lombardy poplars reflect the pioneer heritage of this rural community, first settled in 1851 and named Willow Creek Fort. The museum in town offers a look

WHAT'S OUT THERE?

Two military installations—the Utah Training and Test Range and the Dugway Proving Ground—occupy much of the land in the Great Salt Lake Desert. They are both extremely high-security areas.

Utah Training and Test Range

The UTTR provides the huge amount of land necessary to train military air crews and test weapons. It is, put simply, a bombing range, with many mock targets erected for fighter pilots and their crews to practice on. The UTTR was created in 1979 for cruise missile testing. The large amount of land and airspace required for that purpose has made the UTTR a natural place to test smart munitions, long-range standoff weapons, remote controlled/unmanned air vehicles, boost-glide precision-guided munitions, air-to-air missiles, and autonomous loitering anti-radiation missiles.

The UTTR also has the largest overland contiguous block of supersonic authorized restricted air space in the continental United States. The airspace is situated over 2,624 square miles of Department of Defense land, of which 1,490 square miles are owned by the U.S. Air Force. The remainder is owned and managed by the U.S. Army at Dugway Proving Ground.

Though the UTTR quite obviously does not allow visitors, the Hill Aerospace Museum, located at the Hill Air Force Base just south of Ogden in the town of Roy is open to the public and has many displays of military aircraft (see the Northern Utah chapter).

Dugway Proving Ground

The primary mission of Dugway Proving Ground is to evaluate, test, and develop chemical defense; biological defense; incendiary, smoke and obscurant systems; and to conduct environmental technology testing. Dugway sells its services to all authorized customers, including United States and foreign governments, as well as nongovernmental organizations. In addition, Dugway is a major range and test facility for chemical and biological defense testing.

Dugway Proving Ground encompasses about 800,000 acres. In addition to chemical and biological defensive testing and environment characterization and remediation technology testing, Dugway is the Defense Department's leader in testing battlefield smokes and obscurants. The installation currently consists of more than 600 buildings with a total value of more than $240 million.

As if all this weren't enough, Dugway has developed a following among UFOlogists, who suspect that the base's secret status, underground facilities, and low profile make it the perfect place for sequestering of "alien artifacts" and other items of extraterrestrial origin.

at local history. Grantsville stretches along Highway 138 nine miles northwest of Tooele. For hiking and camping in the Stansbury Mountains, crowned by 11,031-foot Deseret Peak, head south 10 miles to South Willow Canyon Recreation Area.

Donner-Reed Pioneer Museum

Early residents built this one-room adobe schoolhouse within the old fort walls in 1861. Today it's a museum honoring the Donner-Reed wagon

train of 1846. These pioneers crossed the Great Salt Lake Desert to the west with great difficulty, then became trapped by snow while attempting to shortcut through the Sierra Nevada to California. Of the 87 people who started the trip, only 47 desperate people survived the harsh winter—by eating boiled boots and harnesses and the frozen flesh of dead companions. Museum displays include a large collection of guns and pioneer artifacts found abandoned on the salt flats, pottery, arrowheads, and other Native

American artifacts. Outside you can try out Grantsville's original iron jail and see an early log cabin, blacksmith shop, and old wagons. Another adobe building across the street served as a church and dates from 1866. The museum is open on request during the summer; free. To view the exhibits, visit or call Grantsville City Hall, at the corner of Park and Main, 435/884-3411, which is open Monday–Friday 8:30 A.M.–5 P.M. From the city hall, go two blocks west on Main to Cooley Street, then one block north to the museum.

Bonneville Seabase

Scuba divers can enjoy ocean-type diving in the middle of the mudflats. A natural pool here was found to have salinity so close to that of the ocean that marine creatures could thrive in it. Several dozen species have been introduced, including groupers, triggerfish, damsel fish, clown fish, and lobsters. The springs are geothermally heated, so winter cold is no problem. The original pool has been expanded and new pools were created by dredging. User fees run $15 per person; you can rent full equipment for scuba diving ($21) or snorkeling ($11). Bonneville Seabase is five miles northwest of Grantsville at 9390 W. Hwy. 138, 435/884-3874.

Practicalities

The **city park** at 100 E. Cherry Street offers picnicking, a playground, and a baseball diamond. Big events include the **Fourth of July** parade and fireworks (the show alternates between here and Tooele each year) and the **Tooele County Livestock Show and Rodeo** in mid-July.

STANSBURY MOUNTAINS

Not all of western Utah is desert, as a visit to this section of the Wasatch National Forest southwest of Grantsville will show. Trails lead to Deseret Peak and other good day-hiking and backcountry destinations. Grantsville Reservoir, South Willow Canyon Recreation Area, and trailheads into the Deseret Peak Wilderness are accessed via the South Willow

Canyon on the southeast slope of the Stansbury Mountains. Signs for Willow Creek Recreation Area on the west end of Grantsville will guide you south onto South Willow Road. Turn right onto a paved road after four miles and continue west up South Willow Canyon. For more information about the area, contact the Salt Lake Ranger District office, 6944 South 3000 East, Salt Lake City, UT 84121, 435/524-5042.

Follow the paved road only a few miles from the South Willow Road Junction to reach **Grantsville Reservoir,** popular for water sports, trout fishing, picnicking, and camping; campsites begin to appear after three miles. Reach an alternate part of the reservoir by continuing on the dirt road at the first curve. Five miles from South Willow Road is **South Willow Canyon Recreation Area,** on the east slope of the mountains—six small, free campgrounds along the South Fork of Willow Creek are open early June–mid-September; no drinking water. Cottonwood, box elder, Douglas fir, and aspen thrive in the canyon. Elevations range from 6,080 feet at the first campground to 7,400 feet at the last one, Loop, at the end of the road. Sites can be crowded on summer weekends.

More sites are available at the BLM's **Clover Creek Campground,** at the southern end of the Stansbury Mountains on a spring-fed creek. There's no developed water or fee. From Grantsville head out South Willow Canyon Road and continue past the recreation area turnoff to Highway 199 at Rush Valley. Turn right onto Highway 199 and travel west; the campground is eight miles from the junction with Highway 36.

Deseret Peak Wilderness Area

Hikers enjoy expansive views amidst alpine forests and glacial cirques in the Deseret Peak Wilderness Area in the central portion of the Stansbury Mountains. The moderately difficult 3,600-foot climb to the summit is 7.5 miles round-trip. Most of the way is easy to follow, though it's recommended that you carry the USGS topo maps Deseret Peak West and Deseret Peak East (7.5-minute) or Deseret Peak (15-minute). The trail begins at Loop Campground at the end of the road up South Willow Canyon and connects to make a loop to the summit. After three-quarters of a mile the main summit trail turns left and follows Mill Fork (the trail forking right leads to an alternate summit trail and North Willow Canyon). The main trail ascends two more miles through meadows, aspen, Douglas fir, limber pine, and a glacial cirque to a high ridge at 10,000 feet. Follow the ridge west three-quarters of a mile to Deseret Peak (elev. 11,031 feet). On a clear day atop the summit you can see much of the Wasatch Range on the eastern horizon, the Great Salt Lake to the north, Pilot Peak in Nevada to the northwest, the Great Salt Lake Desert to the west, and countless desert ranges to the southwest. To make a loop, follow the trail along the north ridge about 1.5 miles, contouring on the west side of three smaller peaks, then drop east a half mile into Pockets Fork. At the junction with the trail connecting North and South Willow Canyons, turn right 1.5 miles back to the trail junction in Mill Fork, three-quarters of a mile from the start.

For other trails and access roads in the Stansburys, see the topo and Wasatch-Cache National Forest maps. Only foot and horse travel are permitted in the wilderness area (west of Mack Canyon–Big Hollow Trail, north of Dry Canyon, and south of Pass Canyon).

Tooele

To sound like a native, pronounce the town's name "too-WILL-uh." Origin of the word is uncertain, but it may honor the Goshute chief Tuilla. The attractive town (pop. 22,500) lies 34 miles southwest of Salt Lake City in the western foothills of the Oquirrh (pronounced OH-ker) Mountains and has become a bedroom community for Salt Lake City workers. At its 4,900-foot elevation, Tooele offers fine views of the Great Salt Lake to the north and Tooele Valley and Stansbury Mountains to the west. Mormon pioneers settled here in 1849 to farm and raise livestock, but today the major industries are the nearby Tooele Army Depot—site of ongoing chemical-weapons incineration—the Dugway Proving Ground, and mining. Visitors wanting to know more about the region's history will enjoy the Tooele County Museum's exhibits on mining, smelting, and railroading; the pioneer mill and historic park at Benson Grist Mill; the Daughters of Utah Pioneers Museum of pioneer history in Tooele; and the Donner-Reed Pioneer Museum in nearby Grantsville. Other attractions in the area include a scenic drive and overlook in the Oquirrhs, the ghost town of Ophir, and hiking and camping in the South Willow Canyon Recreation Area in the Stansbury Mountains.

SIGHTS

Tooele Railroad Museum

A steam locomotive and a collection of old railroad cars surround Tooele's original (1909) train station. Step inside to see the restored station office and old photos showing railway workers, steam engines, and trestle construction. You might also meet and hear stories from retired railway men who volunteer as museum guides. Mining photos and artifacts illustrate life and work in the early days at Ophir, Mercur, Bauer, and other booming communities now faded to ghosts. Much of the old laboratory equipment and tools on display came from the Tooele Smelter, built by International Smelter & Refining Company in 1907–1909. The smelter processed copper, lead, and zinc until 1972. Ore came over the Oquirrh Mountains by aerial tramway from the Bingham Mine. More than 3,000 people worked here during the hectic World War II years. A highly detailed model shows the modern Carr Fork Mill, built near Tooele but used only 90 days before being dismantled and shipped to a more profitable site in Papua, New Guinea. Two railroad cars, once part of an air force mobile ballistic missile train, contain medical equipment and antique

TOOELE ARMY DEPOT

In the summer of 1996, the army began burning part of the nation's store of chemical weapons at the Tooele Army Depot, located 10 miles south of the town of Tooele and 55 miles from Salt Lake City. The simultaneous incineration of the U.S. and Soviet stockpiles of poison gas and blistering agents was part of an agreement reached by the two countries in the late 1980s.

The Tooele Army Depot holds the nation's single largest cache of chemical weapons, with 44 percent of the arsenal stored in underground bunkers called igloos. Part of the reason for burning the weapons, besides treaty requirements, is that there is a far greater risk of leakage and environmental damage in leaving the chemical agents in the present bunkers than there is in incinerating them. Tooele is on a major earthquake fault zone, and a large temblor could cause a release from the bunkers. As it is, about three weapons leaks a week are detected—though contained—in the current igloos.

The Tooele incinerator was the first to go into operation in the United States (eight chemical weapons depots are scattered across the country, and all will incinerate their weapons on site), and the plant is a prototype of the weapons-destruction factories to be erected elsewhere. The gases to be destroyed include sarin (the poison gas used by a Japanese cult in the notorious 1995 subway disaster), mustard gas, nerve gas, and lewisite, a skin-blistering agent.

The incineration of the chemical weapons has proved to be a hot issue, with many groups interested in public health and the environment seeking to prohibit operation of the burners. Opponents fear that the plants are unsafe and that there is a high risk of accidental release of toxins into the air. Proponents argue that there is a far greater risk to public health and the environment by leaving the chemical weapons in the bunkers.

The plant burned the first of its 1.1-million-item chemical weapon arsenal in August 1996. Within a week the plant had to close when traces of sarin were detected in the end-of-the-line air filters—the final stage before the air was released into the environment. After changing gaskets and fine-tuning the air pressure in the release chamber, the incineration began again after a week. Incineration continues today; during the summer of 2003, the Agency for Toxic Substances and Disease Registry, a public health agency of the U.S. Department of Health and Human Services, released an assessment of the effects of incineration, indicating that people residing near Tooele have not been, and are not currently being, exposed to site-related contaminants at levels that could result in adverse health effects.

furniture. Outside, kids can ride the scale railway (Saturday only), check out a caboose, or explore a replica of a mine. Tooele County Museum is open 1–4 P.M. Tuesday–Saturday Memorial Day–Labor Day weekends. Admission is by donation. From downtown Tooele go east a half mile on Vine Street; the museum is at 35 N. Broadway, 435/882-2836.

Daughters of Utah Pioneers Museum

Meet Tooele's pioneers through 128 framed pictures and see their clothing and other possessions at this downtown museum, 39 E. Vine St., just a half-block east of Main. The small stone building dates from 1867 and once served as a courthouse for Tooele County. The little log cabin next door, built in 1856, was one of the town's first residences. The Daughters of Utah Pioneers Museum (DUP) is open some Saturdays in summer and for groups on request; call the numbers on the front (the small DUP museums are run by volunteers and those who are on call to open the museums change from season to season and year to year).

Benson Grist Mill

Pioneers constructed this mill—one of the oldest buildings in western Utah—in 1854. Wooden pegs and rawhide strips hold the timbers together. E. T. Benson, grandfather of LDS president Ezra Taft Benson, supervised its construction for the LDS Church. The mill produced flour until 1938, then ground only animal feed until closing in the 1940s. Local people began to restore the exterior in 1986. Much of the original machinery inside is still intact. Antique farm machinery, a granary, log cabin, blacksmith shop, and other buildings stand on the grounds to the east. Ruins of the Utah Wool Pullery, which once removed millions of tons of wool annually from pelts, stand to the west. The mill and historic park are open regularly 10 A.M.–4 P.M. Monday–Saturday Memorial Day–Labor Day, though tours can be arranged other times on request. Benson Grist Mill is one block west of Mills Junction (Highway 36 at Highway 138), eight miles north of Tooele, four miles south of I-80 Exit 99, and 10 miles east of Grantsville, 435/882-7678.

Oquirrh Overlook

An overlook within the world's largest and oldest open-pit copper mine provides a close look at the nonstop excavation work taking place on the terraced slopes. Signs and exhibits explain the mining process. Prospectors discovered the mineral wealth in 1863, though the Mormon rancher for whom the canyon was named never took part in the mining. Most of the early production concentrated on gold, silver, and lead. Attention shifted to copper in 1906 as mining companies began excavation of an open-pit mine. Today, five billion tons of rock later, the pit measures 2.5 miles in diameter at its top and one-half mile deep. The "richest hole on earth" has yielded 12 million tons of copper and significant amounts of gold, silver, and molybdenum. Efficient mining, smelting, and refining techniques can make a profit even though Bingham Canyon ore now averages only 0.7 percent copper. Miners once lived in the town of Bingham Canyon, famed for being one street wide and seven miles long! Expanding operations gradually destroyed the town in the 1950s; by 1961 nothing remained. Company officials lived in the attractive town of Copperton, which survives today.

From the Oquirrh Overlook, you'll see not just the world's largest open-pit copper mine, but also panoramic views and canyon scenery. Views take in much of northern and western Utah: Great Salt Lake, Wasatch Range, Salt Lake City, Tooele Valley, and the Stansbury Mountains. The intricate patterns of the terraced **Bingham Canyon Copper Mine** lie directly below.

For a bird's-eye view of the mine from the crest of the Oquirrh Mountains, 10.5 miles from Tooele, head east on Vine Street and enter Middle Canyon. Forests of box elder and maple dominate the lower canyon, with firs and aspen farther up. After seven miles a picnic and parking area appears on the right. The pavement ends here, and large RVs and vehicles with trailers should not go beyond. The gravel road begins a steep one-mile climb with sharp curves to Butterfield Pass (elev. 8,400 feet). Turn left at the pass and continue 2.5 miles to the overlook (elev. 9,400 feet). Ice and snow close the road in winter.

The mine's visitors center is on the opposite side of the pit. To reach it, continue east at the pass and descend on a gravel road through Butterfield Canyon into the Salt Lake Valley; ask about conditions—this road is sometimes closed. After seven miles, the road meets a bend in a paved highway—though this junction may not be signed. Continue straight (east) 11 miles to I-15 (Exits 294 and 295) or turn left (north) five miles to Highway 48 and the Kennecott Bingham Canyon Copper Mine entrance, where the mine's visitors center, 801/322-7300 (recording), is located. Open 8 A.M.–dusk daily April–October; admission is $4 per car. Stop at the mine gate for a pass, then follow signs to the overlook.

ENTERTAINMENT AND EVENTS

Catch movies at the **Ritz,** 111 N. Main, 435/882-2273. Summer events in Tooele include the **Arts Festival** in early June. July 4 marks the opening of rodeo season with the **Bit 'N Spur Rodeo,** held at the rodeo grounds at 200 West and 600 North. A morning Fourth of July parade of cowboys, cowgirls, and public safety vehicles highlights the event; the location of the evening fireworks display alternates yearly between Tooele and Grantsville. A demolition derby and quarterhorse show draw a crowd to the Tooele City Recreation Complex for the **Tooele County Fair** in early August. In late September, Tooele hosts the **Festival of the Old West**, a Native American powwow and cultural event, and the long-running **Tooele Gem & Mineral Show.**

RECREATION

Sailboarding

Ten miles south of Tooele is the small town of Stockton on the shore of Rush Lake, where sailboarding has gained great popularity in recent years. Rush Lake's location between two mountain ranges and its proximity to Salt Lake guarantee sailboarders steady currents of south winds, with plenty of strong 8–15 mph blasts on hot days.

Mountain Biking

Soldier Canyon, six miles south of Tooele, draws mountain bikers. It's a four-mile climb to the mining ghost town of Jacob City, 9,000 feet above sea level.

Other Recreation

The **city park** offers picnicking, playground, and an indoor swimming pool (open year-round) at the corner of Vine and 2nd West, 435/882-3247. During the summer months it may be more fun to swim in the outdoor pool at the **Stansbury Park Golf Course,** 435/882-2426. **Elton Park** at Second North and Broadway has tennis courts and ball fields. **Middle Canyon** has a picnic area seven miles from town (head east on Vine Street). **Settlement Canyon** contains a small reservoir (a local fishing and swimming spot) one-half mile up and **Legion Park,** a picnic area, 1.5 miles up. Play golf at the nine-hole **Oquirrh Hills Golf Course** at Seventh and Edgemont on the east side of town, 435/882-4220, or the 18-hole course in **Stansbury Park** eight miles north on Highway 36, 435/882-4162.

PRACTICALITIES

Accommodations

$50–75: All motels lie conveniently along Main Street (Highway 36). On the north end, the **Villa Motel,** 475 N. Main, 435/882-4551 or 800/882-4551, has basic rooms at the lower end of the price range, some with kitchenettes. The **Best Western Inn Tooele,** 365 N. Main, 435/882-5010 or 800/448-5010, has an indoor pool, a spa, and a couple of rooms with kitchenettes. **American Inn and Suites,** 491 S. Main, 435/882-6100 or 800/228-5150, offers free full breakfasts, kitchenettes and efficiency kitchens, laundry facilities, and a pool and spa. Rates are discounted on weekends.

$75–100: The new **Hampton Inn,** 461 S. Main, 435/882-6102 or 800/HAMPTON, has a pool, hot tub, and free breakfast bar, and each room has an efficiency kitchen.

Camping: You won't find any developed campgrounds in town, but campers sometimes head east on Vine Street to Middle Canyon or southeast on Settlement Canyon Road (one-third mile south of Valleyview Motel) into Settlement Canyon. Other possibilities are the BLM **Clover Creek Campground** 20 miles southwest (go 12 miles south on Highway 36, then eight miles west on Highway 199) and the Forest Service campgrounds in **South Willow Canyon Recreation Area** and the **Grantsville Reservoir** 20 miles west of town (see the Stansbury Mountains section); none of the areas has water or a fee.

Food

Somewhat oddly in this prototypically Old West town, many of the good eating options are ethnic. Eat Chinese-Polynesian-American at the **Sun Lok Yuen,** 615 N. Main, 435/882-3003; open Monday–Saturday for lunch and dinner. **Tooele Pizza & Restaurant,** 21 E. Vine, 435/882-8035, also has Greek food; open Monday–Saturday for lunch and dinner. For Mexican try **Melina's Mexican Restaurant,** 29 N. Main, 435/843-8700; open for lunch and dinner.

Tracks, 1641 N. Main, 435/882-4040, a private club (with easy membership available), has some of the best food and the liveliest atmosphere in town (nothing fancy, but it's good bar food) and microbrews on tap.

Information and Services

The **Tooele Chamber of Commerce** can tell you about the sights and services here. Its office is upstairs in the Key Bank at 201 N. Main (Tooele, UT 84074), 435/882-0690 or 800/378-0690; open about 9 A.M.–4 P.M. Monday–Friday. The **public library** is at 128 W. Vine St., 435/882-2182; open Tuesday–Saturday.

The **post office** is downtown at 65 N. Main, 435/882-1429. **Mountain West Medical Center** has 24-hour emergency services at 2055 N. Main, 435/843-3600.

Transportation

Utah Transit Authority (UTA) buses connect Tooele with Salt Lake City and other towns of the Wasatch Front Monday–Saturday. The main bus stop is at Main and 4th South, 435/882-9031.

South of Tooele

OQUIRRH MOUNTAINS GHOST TOWNS

Ophir

Picturesque old buildings and log cabins line the bottom of Ophir Canyon, which once boomed with saloons, dance halls, houses of ill repute, hotels, restaurants, and shops. In the 1860s, soldiers under General Patrick Connor heard stories of Native Americans mining silver and lead for ornaments and bullets. The soldier-prospectors tracked the mines to this canyon and staked claims. By 1870 a town was born—named after the biblical land of Ophir, where King Solomon's mines were located. Much of the ore went to General Connor's large smelter at nearby Stockton. Later the St. John & Ophir Railroad entered the canyon to haul away the rich ores of silver, lead, and zinc and small amounts of gold and copper. Ophir's population peaked at 6,000, but, unlike most other mining towns of the region, Ophir never quite died. People still live here and occasionally prospect in the hills. The city hall and some houses have been restored, and the new **Ophir Gophir** sells groceries and refreshments, 801/882-9903, but canyon vegetation has claimed the rest of the old structures.

Paved roads go all the way into town. From Tooele, head south 12 miles on Highway 36 through Stockton, turn left five miles on Highway 73, then left 3.5 miles to Ophir. Tailings and foundations of a flotation mill built in 1930 are near the mouth of Ophir Canyon. The road to Ophir follows an old railroad grade; part of an abandoned passenger car still lies on the right just before the town. A gravel road continues up the canyon beyond Ophir, crossing Ophir Creek and weaving through forests of box elder and aspen before ending 2.5 miles farther. You can camp here, but you won't find any facilities. Hikers can continue upstream and ascend Lowe Peak (elev. 10,572 feet) and other summits in the Oquirrh Mountains.

Mercur Gold Mine

General Connor's soldiers also discovered silver in the canyon southeast of Ophir during the late 1860s. After a slow start, prospectors made rich strikes and the rush was on. The mining camp of Lewiston boomed in the mid-1870s, then busted by 1880 as the deposits worked out. Arie Pinedo, a prospector from Bavaria, began to poke around the dying camp and located the Mercur Lode of gold and mercury ore. He and other would-be miners were frustrated when all attempts to extract gold from the ore failed. Then in 1890, a new cyanide process proved effective, and a new boomtown arose around the Golden Gate Mill five years later. Though fire wiped out the business district in 1902, Mercur was rebuilt and had an estimated population of more than 8,000 by 1910. Only three years later, the town closed up when ore bodies seemed depleted. Mining revived in the 1930s and again in the 1980s. Thanks to strip mining, virtually nothing remains of this ghost town.

Other Ghost Towns

Stories of several other historic mining sites and the famous Ajax underground store make fascinating reading, but little remains at these sites. Good sources of information include *The Historical Guide to Utah Ghost Towns,* by Stephen L. Carr, and *Some Dreams Die: Utah's Ghost Towns and Lost Treasures,* by George A. Thompson.

PONY EXPRESS AND STAGE ROUTE

Relive some of the Old West by driving the Pony Express route across western Utah. The scenic route goes from spring to spring as it winds through several small mountain ranges and across open plains, skirting the worst of the Great Salt Lake Desert. Interpretive signs and monuments along the way describe how Pony Express riders rode swiftly on horseback to bring the country closer together. The 140 miles between Fairfield in the east and Ibapah near the Nevada border provide a sense of history and appreciation for the land lost to motorists speeding along I-80.

Allow at least a full day for the drive and bring food, water, and a full tank of gas. The Bureau of Land Management has campgrounds at Simpson Springs and south of Callao. No motels or restaurants line the road, but Ibapah has two gas station/grocery stores. You can travel the well-graded gravel road by car; just watch for the usual backcountry hazards of wildlife, rocks, and washouts. Adventurous travelers may want to make side trips for rockhounding, hiking, or visiting old mining sites. Always keep vehicles on existing roads—sand and mud flats can be treacherously deceptive!

You can begin your trip down the historic route from the Stagecoach Inn at Fairfield (from Salt Lake City or Provo, take I-15 to Lehi, then go 21 miles west on Highway 73). You can also begin at Faust Junction, 30 miles south of Tooele on Highway 36, or Ibapah, 51 miles south of Wendover off U.S. 93A. The BLM has an information kiosk and small picnic area 1.8 miles west of Faust Junction. For the latest road conditions and travel information, contact the BLM Salt Lake District office, 2370 South 2300 West, Salt Lake City, UT 84119, 801/977-4300. The following are points of interest along the route.

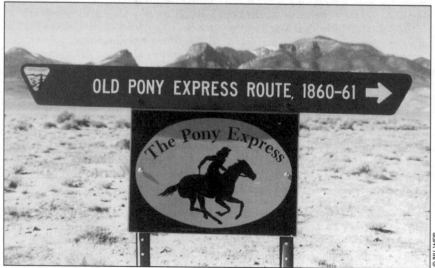

Visitors can follow the old Pony Express route through a lonely stretch of desert.

A BRIEF HISTORY OF THE PONY EXPRESS

In 1860, Pony Express officials put together a chain of stations between St. Joseph, Missouri, and Sacramento, California. Relays of frontier-toughened men covered the 1,838-mile distance in 10 days. Riders stopped at stations spaced about 12 miles apart to change horses. Only after changing horses about six times did the rider complete his day's work. Despite the hazards of frontier travel, only one mail pouch was ever lost, and Native American conflicts held up service for only a single month. Historians credit the daring enterprise with providing communications vital to keeping California aligned with the Union during the Civil War and proving that the West could be crossed in all kinds of weather—thus convincing skeptical politicians that a transcontinental railroad could be built. The Pony Express operated for only 18 months; completion of the transcontinental telegraph in October 1861 put the riders out of work. The company, which received no government assistance, failed to make a profit for its owners.

Stagecoach Inn at Fairfield

The inn was built for travelers in 1858 by John Carson, who had arrived as one of the first white settlers in the area around 1855. Now it's a state park. Inside the restored structure you can see where weary riders slept and sat around tables swapping stories. Stagecoach Inn is 36 miles northwest of Provo.

Simpson Springs

Native Americans had long used these excellent springs before the first white men came through. The name honors Captain J. H. Simpson, who stopped here in 1859 while leading an army survey across western Utah and Nevada. About the same time, George Chorpenning built a mail station here later used by the Pony Express and Overland Express companies. A reconstructed stone cabin on the old site shows what the station looked like. Ruins of a nearby cabin built in 1893 contain stones from the first station. Foundations of a Civilian Conservation Corps camp lie across the road. In 1939, the young men of the CCC built historic markers, improved roads, and worked on conservation projects. The BLM campground higher up on the hillside has water (except in winter) and good views across the desert. A $3 per-vehicle fee is charged; do not drink the water. Sparse juniper trees grow at the 5,100-foot elevation. Simpson Springs is 25 miles west of Faust Junction and 67 miles east of Callao.

Fish Springs National Wildlife Refuge

The Pony Express station once located here no longer exists, but you can visit the 10,000 acres of marsh and lake that attract abundant bird and wildlife. Waterfowl and marsh birds stop over in greatest numbers during their early-spring and late-autumn migrations. Many smaller birds nest here in late spring and early summer, though they're difficult to see in the thick vegetation. Opportunistic hawks and other raptors circle overhead. A self-guided auto tour makes an 11.5-mile loop through the heart of the refuge. Most of the route follows dikes between the human-made lakes and offers good vantage points from which to see ducks, geese, egrets, herons, avocets, and other water birds. The tour route and a picnic area near the entrance are open from sunrise to sunset; no camping is allowed in the refuge. Stop at the information booth near the entrance to pick up a brochure, see photos of birds found at the refuge, and read notes on the area's history. Fish Springs National Wildlife Refuge is 42 miles west of Simpson Springs and 25 miles east of Callao, 435/831-5353.

Boyd Pony Express Station

Portions remain of the station's original rock wall, and signs give the history of the station and the Pony Express. Find the station 13 miles west of Fish Springs and 12 miles east of Callao.

Callao

This cluster of ranches dates from 1859, when several families decided to take advantage of the desert grasslands and good springs here. The original name of Willow Springs had to be changed when residents applied for a post office—too many other Utah towns had the same name. Then someone suggested Callao (locally pronounced CAL-ee-o), because the Peruvian town of that name enjoys a similar valley-backed-by-high-mountain setting. Residents raise cattle, sheep, and hay. Children go to Callao Elementary School, one of the last one-room schoolhouses in Utah. Local people believe that the Willow Springs Pony Express Station site was located off the main road at Bagley Ranch, but a BLM archaeologist contends that the foundation is on the east side of town. Callao is 67 miles west of Simpson Springs and 28 miles east of Ibapah (via the Pony Express and Stage Route). A BLM campground at the site of a former CCC camp is four miles south beside Toms Creek; no water or fee. The tall Deep Creek Range rises to the west.

Canyon Station

To get here, follow signs for Sixmile Ranch, Overland Canyon, and Clifton Flat between Callao and Ibapah. The original station used by Pony Express riders was in Overland Canyon northwest of Canyon Station. Native Americans attacked in July 1863, burned the first station, and killed the Overland agent and four soldiers. The new station was built on a more defensible site. You can see its foundation and the remnants of a fortification. A signed fork at Clifton Flat points the way to Gold Hill, a photogenic ghost town six miles distant (see Vicinity of Ibapah). Canyon Station is north of the Deep Creek Range, 13 miles northwest of Callao and 15 miles northeast of Ibapah.

Ibapah

Pronounce Ibapah "EYE-buh-paw" to avoid sounding like a tourist! Ibapah is about the same size as Callao—little more than a group of some 20 ranches. **Ibapah Trading Post,** 435/234-1166, offers gas and groceries.

VICINITY OF IBAPAH

Continuing south a short way, the main road forks left to the Goshute Indian Reservation, while the right fork crosses into Nevada to U.S. 93 (58 miles) on the old Pony Express and Stage Route. From Ibapah you can also go north to Gold Hill ghost town (14 miles) and Wendover (58 miles) or south to U.S. 50/6 near Great Basin National Park via Callao, Trout Creek, and Gandy (90 miles).

Goshute Indian Reservation

The Goshute mastered living in the harsh desert by knowing of every edible seed, root, insect, reptile, bird, and rodent, as well as larger game. Their meager diet and possessions appalled early white settlers, who referred disparagingly to the Goshute as "diggers." Loss of land to ranchers and dependence on manufactured food put an end to the old nomadic lifestyle. In recent times the Goshute have gradually begun to regain independence by learning to farm and ranch. Several hundred members of the tribe live on the Goshute Indian Reservation, which straddles the Utah-Nevada border. Most of the reservation is off-limits to nonmembers without special permission.

The isolated Goshute Reservation has been in the national news in the last few years. Tribal elders have tentatively agreed to build a repository on their reservations for the nuclear waste from several out-of-state atomic energy generation facilities, in return for tens of millions of dollars in payments and infrastructure development. The federal government and Private Fuel Storage, a consortium of eight nuclear power companies, have worked out an agreement with the Goshute tribal leadership to lease reservation land for the nuclear storage facility, which could house up to 40,000 metric tons of highly radioactive fuel rods. The Utah governor—and a number of vocal Goshute opponents—have fought the facility's placement, and the whole matter is still intensely politically charged and unsettled.

Gold Hill

Miners had been working the area for three years when they founded Gold Hill in 1892. A whole treasure trove of minerals came out of the ground here—gold, silver, lead, copper, tungsten, arsenic, and bismuth. A smelter along a ridge just west of town processed the ore. But three years later Gold Hill's boom ended. Most people lived only in tents anyway, and soon everything but the smelter foundations and tailings was packed up. A rebirth occurred during World War I, when the country desperately needed copper, tungsten, and arsenic. Gold Hill grew to a sizable town with 3,000 residents, a railroad line from Wendover, and many substantial buildings. Cheaper foreign sources of arsenic knocked the bottom out of local mining in 1924, and Gold Hill began to die again. Another frenzied burst of activity occurred in 1944–1945, when the nation called once more for tungsten and arsenic. The town again sprang to life, only to fade just as quickly after the war ended. Determined prospectors still roam the surrounding countryside awaiting another clamor for the underground riches. Decaying structures in town make a picturesque sight. (Several year-round residents live here; no scavenging allowed.) Visible nearby are the cemetery, mines, railroad bed, and smelter site. The smaller ghost town of **Clifton** lies over the hill to the south but little remains; No Trespassing signs make visitors unwelcome. Good roads (partly dirt) approach Gold Hill from Ibapah, Wendover, and Callao.

DEEP CREEK RANGE

The range soars spectacularly above the Great Salt Lake Desert. Few people know about the Deep Creeks despite their great heights, diverse wildlife, and pristine forests. Ibapah Peak (elev. 12,087 feet) and Haystack Peak to the north (elev. 12,020 feet) crown the range. Glacial cirques and other rugged features have been carved into the nearly white granite that makes up most of the summit ridge. Prospectors have found gold, silver, lead, zinc, copper, mercury, beryllium, molybdenum, tungsten, and uranium. You'll occasionally run across mines and old cabins in the range, especially in Goshute Canyon. Of the six perennial streams on the east side, Birch and Trout Creeks still contain Lake Bon-

neville cutthroat trout that originated in the prehistoric lake; both creeks were closed to fishing at press time. Wildlife includes Rocky Mountain bighorn sheep (reintroduced), deer, pronghorn, mountain lion, coyote, bobcat, and many birds. Vegetation ranges from grass and sagebrush in the lower foothills to piñon pine and juniper, then to montane forests of aspen, Engelmann spruce, Douglas fir, white fir, subalpine fir, ponderosa pine, and limber pine. Bristlecone pine grows on some of the high ridges. Alpine tundra covers the highest peaks. The Deep Creek Range gets plenty of snow in winter, so the climbing season runs late June–late October. Aspen and some mountain shrubs put on colorful displays in September and early October. Streams in the range have good water (purify first), but the lower canyons are often polluted by the organisms that accompany cattle excrement. Carry water while hiking on the dry ridges.

Main Climbing Routes

Most of the canyons have roads into their lower reaches. Four-wheel-drive vehicles will be able to get farther up the steep grades than cars. Most hikers start up Granite or Indian Farm Creek and head for Ibapah or Haystack Peak. A trail along **Granite Creek** offers the easiest approach to Ibapah Peak, about 12.5 miles round-trip and a 5,300-foot elevation gain from the beginning of the jeep trail. The road to Granite Creek turns west off Snake Valley Road 10 miles south of Callao (7.8 miles north of Trout Creek Ranch). Keep left at a junction about one mile in, then follow the most-used track. The road enters Granite Canyon after three miles. The first ford of Granite Creek, a half mile into the canyon, requires a high-clearance vehicle; the second, 0.8 mile farther, may require four-wheel drive. The road deteriorates into a jeep track in another 0.6 mile at the border of Deep Creek Wilderness Study Area. Four-wheel-drive vehicles can climb the steep grade another two miles. Continue two miles on a pack trail to the beginning of a large meadow at the pass, then head cross-country 1.5 miles to the small peak (11,385 feet) just before Ibapah. A small trail on the east side of this peak continues three-quarters of a mile to the summit of

Ibapah. (This small trail probably once connected with the pack trail but is little used today.)

Impressive panoramas take in the rugged canyons and ridges of the Deep Creek Range below and much of western Utah and eastern Nevada beyond. Remains of a heliograph station sit atop Ibapah. Early mapmakers measured the highest point in the range at 12,101 feet and named it "Haystack." A later survey determined the correct height to be 12,087 feet and renamed the peak "Ibapah"; the second-highest peak was given the old Haystack name by default. Hikers can head cross-country two miles north from Ibapah to Haystack Peak (12,020 feet). The 7.5-minute Ibapah Peak topo map covers the entire hike to the summit of both peaks via Granite Creek.

Other Climbing Routes

Red Mountain (11,588 feet) can also be climbed from the pass above Granite Creek. The jeep trail to **Toms Creek** leads to a route to the head of the creek, from which Haystack Peak is about three miles south along the crest of the range; turnoff for Toms Canyon is 1.6 miles south of Callao and 8.4 miles north of the Granite Creek turnoff. A more direct route to Haystack Peak goes up through **Indian Farm Canyon.** Turnoff for this canyon is 4.3 miles south of Callao and 5.7 miles north of the Granite Creek turnoff. **Red Cedar Creek** in the heart of the Deep Creeks remains pristine—no trails, roads, or other developments. It's also very rugged; allow a day or two just to hike through one-way. Early ranchers mistook the Rocky Mountain juniper for red cedar. **Trout Creek** is another good hiking area. A trail goes most of the way up the valley.

Approaches to the peaks from the Goshute Indian Reservation have been used less because of travel restrictions and because this western slope is much drier. Probably the easiest way up from here is to drive though Goshute village to Fifteen Mile Creek and to hike the pack trail to the ridge between Ibapah Peak and Red Mountain, meeting the trail coming up from Granite Creek. To visit the west side you need to plan ahead and get permission from the Tribal Council, which meets once a month. Write to them at P.O. Box 6104, Ibapah, UT 84034, explaining the purpose of your trip, what you'll be doing, dates, roads and trails to be used, and the organization you're with, if any. Then, on arrival, check in at the tribal offices. For more information call the executive secretary at 435/234-1138 or the law enforcement office at 435/234-1139.

Information and Services

Hikers venturing into this remote range must be self-sufficient and experienced in wilderness travel. You'll need the 7.5-minute Ibapah Peak and Indian Farm Creek topo maps for the central part of the range, the 7.5-minute Goshute and Goshute Canyon maps for the northern part, and the 15-minute Trout Creek map for the southern part. The metric 1:100,000 Fish Springs quad covers the whole area, but with less detail. For firsthand information, contact the BLM House Range Resource Area, 35 East 500 North, Fillmore, UT 84631, 435/743-6811. The aged but good Sierra Club book *Hiking the Great Basin,* by John Hart, has detailed trail descriptions.

All approaches to the Deep Creeks involve dirt-road travel and generally sizable distances. Some of the ways in (to the Granite Creek Road Junction) start from Wendover and continue via Gold Hill (92 miles), from Provo via the Pony Express and Stage Route (158 miles), from Delta via the Weiss Highway (93 miles), and from U.S. 50/6 near the Utah-Nevada border via Gandy and Trout Creek (52 miles). Ibapah has the nearest gas and groceries (38 miles from the Granite Creek turnoff).

Eureka and Tintic Mining District

The lucky prospectors who cried "Eureka! I've found it!" had stumbled onto a fabulously rich deposit of silver and other valuable metals. Eureka sprang up to be one of Utah's most important cities and the center of more than a dozen mining communities. Much can still be seen of the district's long history—mine headframes and buildings, shafts and glory holes, old examples of residential and commercial architecture, great piles of ore tailings, and forlorn cemeteries. Exhibits at the Tintic Mining Museum in Eureka show what life was like. Paved highways provide easy access: from I-15 Santaquin Exit 248 (south of Provo) go west 21 miles on U.S. 6; from Delta go northeast 48 miles on U.S. 6; and from Tooele go south 54 miles on Highway 36.

History

Mormon stockherders began moving cattle here during the early 1850s to take advantage of the good grazing lands. Utes under Chief Tintic, for whom the district was later named, opposed the newcomers but couldn't stop them. Mineral deposits found in the hills remained a secret of the Mormons, as church policy prohibited members from prospecting for precious metals. In 1869, though, George Rust, a gentile cowboy, noted the promising ores. Soon the rush was on—ores assaying up to 10,000 ounces of silver per ton began pouring out of the mines. Silver City, founded in 1870, became the first of many mining camps. New discoveries kept the Tintic District booming. Gold, copper, lead, and zinc added to the riches. By 1910 the district had a population of 8,000 and the end was nowhere in sight. The hills shook from underground blasting and the noise of mills, smelters, and railroads. Valuable Tintic properties kept the Salt Lake Stock Exchange busy, while Salt Lake City office buildings and mansions rose with Tintic money. Mining began a slow decline in the 1930s but has continued, sporadically, to the present. Most of the old mining camps have dried up and blown away. Eureka and Mammoth drift on as sleepy towns—monuments to an earlier era.

The ghosts of former camps can be worth a visit, too, though most require considerable imagination to see them as they were. Do not go near decaying structures or mine shafts. You'll also find sites of towns that exist mostly as memories. Diligent searching through the sagebrush may uncover foundations, tailings piles, broken glass, and neglected cemeteries. Yet behind many of the sites linger dramatic stories of attempts to win riches from the earth. History buffs may want to look at the book *Faith, Hope and Prosperity: The Tintic Mining District,* by Philip Notarianni, available at the Tintic Mining Museum. Also see *The Historical Guide to Utah Ghost Towns,* by Stephen L. Carr, and *Some Dreams Die,* by George A. Thompson.

EUREKA

Mines and tailing dumps surround weather-beaten buildings. Eureka lacks the orderliness of Mormon towns; the main street snakes through the valley with side streets branching off in every direction. Few recent buildings have been added, so the town retains an authentic atmosphere from an earlier time. Eureka now has a population of about 600, down from the 3,400 of its peak years.

Tintic Mining Museum

The varied exhibits in this small museum will give you an appreciation of the district and its mining pioneers. A mineral collection from the Tintic area has many fine specimens. You'll see early mining tools, assay equipment, a mine office, courtroom, blacksmith shop, a 1920s kitchen, many historic photos, and displays that show social life in the early days. One display is dedicated to the influence of Jessie Knight, a Mormon financier and philanthropist. Knightsville, now a ghost town site near Eureka, gained fame as one of the few mining towns in Utah without a saloon or gambling hall. Knight also promoted mine safety and closed his mines for a day of rest on Sunday—both radical concepts at the time.

You'll find the museum galleries upstairs in City Hall (built in 1899) and next door in the former railroad depot (1925). The *Tintic Tour Guide* sold here describes a 35-mile loop to some of the nearby ghost towns and mines. The Tintic Mining Museum, 435/433-6842 or 435/433-6869, is open sporadically—usually on summer weekends and some weekdays and on request at other times. Admission is free.

Bullion-Beck Mine

A large timber headframe on the west edge of town beside the highway marks one of the most productive mines in the district. John Beck arrived in 1871 and began sinking a shaft. At first people called him the "Crazy Dutchman," but the jeers ended when he hit a huge deposit of rich ore 200 feet down. The present 65-foot-high headframe dates from about 1890; originally a large wooden building enclosed it.

EUREKA VICINITY GHOST TOWNS

Dividend

Emil Raddatz bought this property on the east slope of the Tintic Mountains in 1907, believing that the ore deposits mined on the west side of the Tintics extended to here. Raddatz nearly went broke digging deeper and deeper, but the prized silver and lead ore 1,200 feet below proved him right. After his 1916 discovery, a modern company town grew up complete with hotel, movie theater, golf course, and ice plant. The miners, whose wages had been paid partly in stock certificates, chose the name Dividend because they had been so well rewarded. Mining continued until 1949, producing $19 million in dividends, but today only foundations, mine shafts, and large piles of tailings remain. A loop road east of Eureka will take you to this site and other mining areas. Walking or driving off the road is forbidden because of mine shafts and other hazards. Though the road is paved, some sections are badly potholed and need to be driven slowly. From downtown Eureka, go east 1.5 miles on U.S. 6 and turn right on the Dividend road

(0.1 mile east of milepost 141); the road climbs into hills and passes the Eureka Lily headframe and mine on the left after 2.5 miles. Continue 0.3 mile to Tintic Standard #1 shaft on right, then 0.3 mile more to the site of Dividend and the #2 shaft (signed); the road ends at a junction 0.9 mile farther; turn left 0.7 mile to U.S. 6 (four miles east of Eureka). The Sunshine Mining Company currently operates the Burgin Mine about one mile east of Dividend.

Mammoth

Prospectors made a "mammoth" strike over the hill south of Eureka in 1870. The town of Mammoth, more mines, mills, and smelters followed. The eccentric mining engineer George Robinson built a second town, immodestly named after himself, one mile down the valley. Both towns prospered, growing together and eventually becoming just Mammoth. Nearly 3,000 people lived here when activity peaked in 1900–1910. Then came the inevitable decline as the high-grade ores worked out. By the 1930s, Mammoth was well on its way to becoming a ghost town. People still live here and have preserved some of the old buildings. The Mammoth glory hole and mine buildings overlook the town at the head of the valley. Ruins of smelters and mines cling to hillsides. From Eureka, go southwest 2.5 miles on U.S. 6, then turn left (east) one mile on a paved road. Upper and lower towns can now be distinguished.

Silver City

Optimistic prospectors named their little camp for the promising silver ore, but a city it was not to be. The cost of pumping water out of the mines cut too deeply into profit margins, and a 1902 fire nearly put an end to the town. At that point LDS financier Jessie Knight stepped in to improve the mines and rebuild the town. He also built a smelter and later a mill. Silver City reached its peak about 1908 before declining to ghost town status in the 1930s. You can't miss the giant piles of tailings (light colored) and slag (dark colored) from the smelter and mill at the old townsite. Extensive concrete foundations show the complexity and size of the operations. Sagebrush has reclaimed the rest of the town, of which only debris and foundations survive. Some diehards still mine and prospect in the area, though; a new mining operation is currently reprocessing the old smelter waste products. Silver City ghost town site lies 3.3 miles southwest of Eureka (0.8 mile past the Mammoth turnoff) just off U.S. 6.

SHEEPROCK MOUNTAINS

Black Crook Peak (elev. 9,275 feet) tops this little-known range northwest of Eureka. Sheeprock Mountain Trail (Forest Trails 051 and 052) follows the crest of the mountains for most of their length. Several other trails connect from each side. See the Uinta National Forest map and the 7.5-minute Erickson Knoll, Dutch Peak, Lookout Pass, and Vernon topo maps. Mining, which peaked in the early 1900s, still continues on a small scale for silver, lead, and zinc. Bald eagles winter here approximately December–March; their numbers appear to fluctuate with the rabbit population. Anglers can try for brook and brown trout in Vernon Reservoir and Vernon and Bennion Creeks.

The small **Little Valley Campground** is open May–November; no water or charge. Benmore Experimental Pastures, northeast of the mountains, date from 1933 as a cooperative state and federal program to develop techniques of restoring and managing rangelands. Although the Sheeprock Mountains are in the Wasatch National Forest, the Spanish Fork Ranger District office of the Uinta National Forest manages this area, known as the Vernon Division, 44 West 400 North, Spanish Fork, UT 84660, 435/798-3571. Follow Highway 36 northwest 17 miles from Eureka (or south 42 miles from Tooele) to a junction signed Benmore, just east of Vernon; turn south five miles to Benmore Guard Station, then left 2.5 miles for Vernon Reservoir. Little Valley Campground is off to the right in a side valley 2.3 miles past the reservoir. A road in via Lofgreen is a bit rough for cars. None of these roads are recommended in wet weather.

LITTLE SAHARA RECREATION AREA

Sand dunes have made a giant sandbox between Eureka and Delta. Managed by the BLM, the recreation area covers 60,000 acres of free-moving sand dunes, sagebrush flats, and juniper-covered ridges. Elevations range from about 5,000 to 5,700 feet. Varied terrain provides challenges for dune buggies, motorcycles, and four-wheel-drive vehicles. While off-road vehicles can range over most of the dunes, areas near White Sands and Jericho Campgrounds have been set aside for children. The Rockwell Natural Area in the western part of the dunes protects 9,150 acres for nature study.

The dunes originated 150 miles away as sandbars along the southern shore of Lake Bonneville roughly 10,000 years ago. After the lake receded, prevailing winds pushed the exposed sands on a slow trek northeastward at a rate of about 18 inches per year. Sand Mountain, however, deflected the winds upward, and the sand grains piled up into large dunes downwind. Lizards and kangaroo rats scamper across the sands in search of food and, in turn, are eaten by hawks, bobcats, and coyotes. Pronghorn and mule deer live here all year. Juniper, sagebrush, greasewood, saltbush, and grasses are the most common plants. An unusual species of fourwing saltbush (*Atriplex canescens*) grows as high as 12 feet and is restricted to the dunes area.

A visitors center near the entrance is open irregular hours. Three developed **campgrounds** with water (White Sands, Oasis, and Jericho) and a primitive camping area (Sand Mountain) are open all year. In winter, water is available only at the visitors center on the way in. Visitors to Little Sahara pay an entrance fee, which includes use of campgrounds. For more information or group camping permits, contact the BLM at 15 East 500 North, Fillmore, UT 84631, 435/743-6811.

The entrance road is 4.5 miles west of Jericho Junction, which lies 17 miles south of Eureka, 31 miles west of Nephi (I-15 Exits 222 and 228), or 32 miles northeast of Delta.

Delta to Milford

The barren Pahvant Valley along the lower Sevier River had long been considered a wasteland. Then, in 1905, some Fillmore businessmen purchased water rights from Sevier River Reservoir and 10,000 acres of land. The farm and town lots they sold became the center of one of Utah's most productive agricultural areas. Other hopeful homesteaders who settled farther from Delta weren't as fortunate. Thousands of families bought cheap land in the North Tract but found the going very difficult. Troubles with the irrigation system, poor crop yields, and low market prices forced most to leave by the late 1930s. A few decaying houses and farm buildings mark the sites of once-bustling communities. Farmers near Delta raise alfalfa seed and hay, wheat, corn, barley, mushrooms, and livestock. The giant coal-burning Intermountain Power Project (IPP) and the Brush Wellman beryllium mill have helped boost Delta's population to about 4,000. Miners have been digging into the Drum Mountains northwest of Delta since the 1870s for gold, silver, copper, manganese, and other minerals; some work still goes on there. The beryllium processed near Delta comes from large deposits of bertrandite mined in open pits in the Topaz and Spors Mountains farther to the northwest.

DELTA

For travelers, Delta (pop. 3,210) makes a handy base for visiting the surrounding historic sites, rockhounding, and exploring nearby mountain ranges. In downtown Delta, the **Great Basin Museum,** 328 West 100 North (turn north one block on 300 West from Main Street), 435/864-5013, presents a varied collection of pioneer photos and artifacts, arrowheads, a Topaz Camp

Beautiful rock, mineral, and fossil specimens await discovery in the deserts surrounding Delta. Sought-after rocks and minerals include topaz, bixbyite, sunstones, geodes, obsidian, muscovite, garnet, pyrite, and agate. Some fossils to look for are trilobites, brachiopods, horn coral, and crinoids.

exhibit, fossils, and minerals; antique farm machinery stands outside. The museum is open 10 A.M.–4 P.M. Monday–Saturday; free.

A **pioneer log cabin** (built 1907–1908), now on Main Street in front of Delta's municipal building, was the second house and the first post office in Melville, which was later known as Burtner and finally as Delta in 1910. Historical markers near the cabin commemorate the Spanish Dominguez-Escalante Expedition, which passed to the south in 1776, and the Topaz Camp for Japanese Americans interned during World War II.

Rockhounding

Beautiful rock, mineral, and fossil specimens await discovery in the deserts surrounding Delta. Sought-after rocks and minerals include topaz, bixbyite, sunstones, geodes, obsidian, muscovite, garnet, pyrite, and agate. Some fossils to look for are trilobites, brachiopods, horn coral, and crinoids. The chamber of commerce in Delta is a good source of local information.

You can see gemstones from the area at **West Desert Collectors,** 278 W. Main, 435/864-2175, and **Tina's Jewelry & Minerals,** 320 E. Main, 435/864-2444. Useful publications include *Guide to Rocks and Fossils,* available at the chamber of commerce, and *Collector's Guide to Mineral and Fossil Localities,* published by the Utah Geological and Mineral Survey (June 1977). A hat and plenty of water will add to your comfort and safety when enjoying the outdoors. Always be watchful when hiking to avoid rattlesnakes and mine shafts. Both are occasionally found in caves, where the dim light makes them harder to see.

Dig for trilobites and other marine fossils at **U-Dig Fossils,** a private quarry at 350 East 300

South, 435/864-3638. It's best to come prepared with work gloves, sturdy shoes, and protective eyewear; U-Dig provides hammers, buckets, and advice. One hour of digging goes for $6 adults 17 and older, $4 ages 8–16, free to children 7 and under. Open 9 A.M.–6 P.M. Monday–Saturday April 1–October 15. It's best to arrive by 4 P.M., because if business is slow, the quarry closes early.

Entertainment and Events

Catch movies at **T&T Twin Theatres** in Pendray Plaza (east end of town just north of U.S. 6 and U.S. 50 Junction), 435/864-4551.

Each February thousands of snow geese use the fields and waters between Clear Lake Wildlife Management Area and Delta as a rest stop on their northern migration. The first weekend in March the **Snow Goose Festival** celebrates these beautiful white birds. Other annual events include the **Fourth of July** fireworks and demolition derby, **Pioneer Day** (parade, rodeo, games) on July 24 in Hinckley, and **Millard County Fair** (parade, horse show, games, demolition derby, and street dance) at the fairgrounds on the east side of town in early August. In September enjoy the **Classy Chassy Car Show** and the **West Millard High School Rodeo** with hundreds of contestants.

Recreation and Shopping

The indoor **West Millard County Swimming Pool** is open year-round at the corner of 200 East and 300 North, 435/864-3133. A **city park** with picnic facilities and tennis courts is at the corner of Main and 100 West; restrooms are in the nearby municipal building. **Sunset View Golf Course,** 435/864-2508, offers nine holes three miles northeast of town on U.S. 6. **Gunnison Bend Park** west of town has picnicking, water-skiing, and fishing (catfish and largemouth bass); go west 2.5 miles on U.S. 50/6, then right two miles.

West Desert Collectors, 278 W. Main, 435/864-2175, has beautiful rocks, minerals, and fossils. **Tina's Jewelry & Minerals,** 320 E. Main, 435/864-2444, offers beautiful gems.

Accommodations

Under $50: All of Delta's motels are on or

close to Main Street. **Willden Motel,** 127 W. Main, 435/864-2906; **Diamond D Motor Lodge,** 234 W. Main, 435/864-2041; **Delta Inn Motel,** 347 E. Main, 435/864-4267; and the **Budget Motel,** a half-block south of Main on 350 East, 435/864-4533, each offer inexpensive, no-fuss rooms.

$50–75: At the east edge of town, the **Best Western Motor Inn Motel,** 527 E. Topaz Blvd. just north of U.S. 6, 435/864-3882 or 800/354-9378, has an indoor pool and allows pets.

Campgrounds: Antelope Valley RV Park, 760 W. Main, 435/864-1813, has showers and is open April–November; $12 tents, $14 RVs without hookups, $20 RVs with. **Oak Creek Campground** lies in a pretty wooded canyon in the Fishlake National Forest; sites have drinking water late May–early October; $7. Head east 14 miles on U.S. 50 and Highway 125 to Oak City, then turn right four miles on a paved road.

Food

Tops City Cafe, 313 W. Main, 435/864-2148, serves standard American fare daily for breakfast, lunch, and dinner. The **Rancher Motel,** 171 W. Main, 435/864-2741, has a café with American and Mexican food and a dining room upstairs serving steak and seafood; open daily for breakfast, lunch, and dinner. **Chef's Palace,** 225 E. Main, 435/864-2421, offers steak, seafood, chicken, and a salad bar; open Monday–Saturday for dinner only.

Delta Valley Farms has a family restaurant two miles northeast of Delta on U.S. 6; open Monday–Saturday for lunch. Call 435/864-3566 in advance if you'd like a tour of the cheese-making plant.

Information and Services

Delta Chamber of Commerce will tell you about services in town and sights in the surrounding area. The office is in the municipal building at Main and 200 West (80 North 200 West, Delta, UT 84624), 435/864-4316; open 10 A.M.–5 P.M. Monday–Friday. The **public library,** also in the municipal building, 435/864-4945, is open 2–8 P.M. Monday–Friday and 1–5 P.M. Saturday.

The **post office** is at the corner of 300 East and 100 South, 435/864-2811. **Delta Community Medical Center** provides emergency care at 126 S. White Sage Avenue (south off U.S. 50 on the east side of town), 435/864-5591.

BAKER HOT SPRINGS

Though Crater Springs Health Resort, north of Delta, has closed, local people still come here to soak in the hot springs. Water emerges from the ground at near boiling temperatures and flows into two surviving concrete tubs. The springs also feed shallow ponds that feature colorful mineral deposits and strange-looking algae growths. To reach the hot springs from Delta go northeast 11 miles on U.S. 6, turn left (west) 19 miles on the paved Brush Wellman Road, then right (north) seven miles on a dirt road along a large black lava flow. Springs are on the right. Ruts may make this dry-weather-only road difficult for cars. (You can save about nine miles from Delta if you can navigate the maze of farm roads between the west edge of Delta and Brush Wellman Road.) Adventurous motorists can also follow dirt roads from Baker Hot Springs north and east 35 miles to Little Sahara Recreation Area.

CANYON MOUNTAINS

East of Delta, the **Oak Creek Campground** lies along the creek amid Gambel oak, cottonwood, maple, and juniper on the west side of the mountains. Canyon walls cut by Oak Creek reveal layers of twisted and upturned rock. This Forest Service campground (elev. 5,900 feet) has water and a camping fee late May–early October. Groups can reserve a large area with amphitheater, sports area, and shelter. Oak Creek usually has good fishing for rainbow trout. Much of its flow comes from a spring at the upper end of the campground. From Delta go east 14 miles on U.S. 50 and Highway 125 to the small farming town of Oak City, then turn right four miles on a paved road. A gravel road continues upcanyon past the campground to other forest roads and hiking trails; see the Fishlake National Forest map. Unpaved roads also

provide access to the steeper east side of the Canyon Mountains. Fool Creek Peak tops this small range at 9,717 feet. For more information, contact the Fillmore Ranger District office at 390 S. Main in Fillmore (P.O. Box 265, Fillmore, UT 84631), 435/743-5721.

WEST OF DELTA
Topaz Camp

Topaz is easily Utah's most dispirited ghost town site. Other ghost towns had the promise of precious metals or good land to lure their populations, but those coming to Topaz had no choice—they had the bad fortune to be of the wrong ancestry during the height of World War II hysteria. About 9,000 Japanese—most of whom were American citizens—were brought from the West Coast to this desolate desert plain in 1942. Topaz sprang up in just a few months and included barracks, communal dining halls, post office, hospital, schools, churches, and recreational facilities. Most internees cooperated with authorities; the few who caused trouble were shipped off to a more secure camp. Barbed wire and watchtowers with armed guards surrounded the small city—which was actually Utah's fifth-largest community for a time. All internees were released at war's end in 1945 and the camp came down almost as quickly as it had gone up. Salvagers bought and removed equipment, buildings, barbed wire, telephone poles, and even street paving and sewer pipes. An uneasy silence pervades the site today. Little more than the streets, foundations, and piles of rubble remains. You can still walk or drive along the streets of the vast camp, which had 42 neatly laid-out blocks. A concrete memorial stands at the northwest corner of the site.

One way to get here is to go west six miles from Delta on U.S. 50/6 to the small town of Hinckley, turn right (north) 4.5 miles on a paved road (some parts are gravel) to its end, turn left (west) 2.5 miles on a paved road to its end in Abraham, turn right (north) 1.5 miles on a gravel road to a stop sign, then turn left three miles on a gravel road; Topaz is on the left.

Drum Mountains

Strange subterranean noises can sometimes be heard in these desert mountains; some say the sounds are like the thumps or rumblings of a drum. Prospectors began combing the parched hillsides in 1872 but did little mining development. Harry Joy and Charles Howard, mining engineers from Michigan, organized the Detroit Mining District here in 1879. They dug for gold, silver, and copper and built a smelter. Mining centered on the small town of **Joy**. Crumbling foundations are all that remain of the townsite, though you can find dilapidated mine buildings in nearby canyons. Western States Minerals has an active gold mine in the Drums. You can reach the mountains by continuing west from Topaz or from U.S. 6 on the paved Brush Wellman Road.

House Range

This range about 45 miles west of Delta offers great vistas, scenic drives, wilderness hiking, and world-famous trilobite fossil beds. Swasey Peak (elev. 9,669 feet) is the highest point. From a distance, however, Notch Peak's spectacular 2,700-foot face stands out as the most prominent landmark in the region. What the 50-mile-long range lacks in great heights, it makes up for in massive sheer limestone cliffs and rugged canyons. Precipitous drops on the western side contrast with a gentler slope on the east. Hardy vegetation such as juniper, piñon pine, mountain mahogany, and sagebrush dominates the dry slopes. Bristlecone pines grow on the high ridges of Swasey and Notch Peaks; the long-lived trees are identified by inward-curving bristles on the cones and by needles less than 1.5 inches long in clusters of five. Some of the high country also harbors limber pine, ponderosa pine, white fir, Douglas fir, and aspen.

Wildlife includes mule deer, pronghorn, chukar partridge, bald and golden eagles, and peregrine falcon. Wild horses roam Sawmill Basin to the northeast of Swasey Peak. Permanent water supplies are found only at a few scattered springs in the range. Limestone caves attract spelunkers, especially Antelope Spring Cave near Dome Canyon Pass (ask directions at the BLM office in Fillmore or from the Speleological Society of Utah). Council Cave on Antelope Peak (between Notch and Swasey Peaks) has an enormous opening, visible for more than 50 miles.

Mining in the range has a long history. Stories tell of finding old Spanish gold mines with iron tools in them that crumbled at a touch. More recent mining for tungsten and gold has occurred on the east side of Notch Peak. Outlaws found the range a convenient area to hide out; Tatow Knob (north of Swasey Peak), for example, was a favorite spot for horse thieves. Death Canyon got its name after a group of pioneers became trapped and froze to death; most maps now show it as Dome Canyon.

Driving in the House Range: The dirt roads here can be surprisingly good. Often you can zip along as if on pavement, but watch for loose gravel, large rocks, flash floods, and deep ruts that sometimes appear on these backcountry stretches. Roads easily passable by car connect to make a 43-mile loop through Marjum and Dome Canyon Passes. You'll have good views of the peaks and go through scenic canyons on the west side of both passes. Drivers with high-clearance vehicles can branch off on old mining roads or drive past Antelope Spring to Sinbad Overlook for views and hiking near Swasey Peak.

Shale beds near Antelope Spring have given up an amazing quantity and variety of **trilobite fossils** dating from about 500 million years ago. Professional collectors have leased a trilobite quarry, so you'll have to collect outside. Trilobites can also be found near Swasey Spring and near Marjum Pass. Flat-edged rock hammers work best to split open the shale layers.

During World War I, a hermit took a liking to the House Range and built a one-room cabin in a small cave, where he lived until his death. He entertained visitors with a special home brew. Walk a quarter mile up a small side canyon from the road to see the cabin, which is on the right side of the road that comes down to the west from Marjum Pass.

Several roads connect U.S. 50/6 with the loop through Marjum and Dome Canyon Passes. Going west from Delta on U.S. 50/6, you have the choice of the following turnoffs: after 10 miles, turn right 25 miles at the fork for the unpaved old U.S. 50/6; or after 32 miles, turn right 10 miles on a road signed Antelope Spring; or after 42 miles, turn right 16 miles on a road also signed Antelope Spring; or after 63 miles (30 miles east of the Utah-Nevada border), turn right 14 miles on a road signed Painter Spring.

Hiking in the House Range: Most hiking routes go cross-country through the wilderness. Springs are very far apart and sometimes polluted, so carry water for the whole trip. Bring topo maps and a compass; help can be a long way off if you make a wrong turn. Because of the light precipitation, the hiking season at the high elevations can last late April–late November. You can visit most destinations, including Swasey and Notch Peaks, on a day hike. These peaks offer fantastic views over nearly all of west-central Utah and into Nevada. For more information on the House Range, contact the BLM office at 35 East 500 North in Fillmore (P.O. Box 778, Fillmore, UT 84631), 435/743-6811.

The trip to **Swasey Peak** makes a good half-day hike and is usually done as a loop. Total distance for the moderately difficult trip is about 4.5 miles with a 1,700-foot elevation gain to the summit (elev. 9,669 feet). Drive to the Antelope Spring turnoff, 2.5 miles east of Dome Canyon Pass, and follow the well-used Sinbad Overlook road 3.3 miles, passing the spring and trilobite area, up a steep grade to a large meadow below Swasey Peak. Cautiously driven cars might be able to get up this road, though it's safer to park low-clearance vehicles and walk the last 1.5 miles. (Nonhikers with suitable vehicles will enjoy driving to Sinbad Overlook for views at the end of the road.) From the large meadow at the top of the grade, head northeast on foot up the ridge, avoiding cliffs to the left. After 1.25 miles you'll reach a low summit; continue one-half mile along the ridgeline, curving west toward Swasey Peak. To complete the loop, descend one-half mile to the northwest along a ridge to bypass some cliffs, then head southwest three-quarters of a mile to the end of Sinbad Overlook road.

From here it's an easy 1.5 miles by road back to the start; Sinbad Spring and a grove of ponderosa pines are about halfway. No signs or trails mark the route, but hikers experienced with maps shouldn't have any trouble. Topo maps for this hike are the 7.5-minute Marjum Pass and Swasey Peak. Route-finding is easier when hiking the loop in the direction described. You'll get a close look at the mountain mahogany on Swasey Peak—some thickets of this stout shrub have to be crossed; wear long pants to protect your legs.

The 2,700-foot sheer rock wall on the western face of prominent **Notch Peak** is only 300 feet shorter than El Capitán in Yosemite. Most hikers prefer the far easier summit route on the other side via Sawtooth Canyon. This moderately difficult canyon route is about nine miles round-trip and has a 1,700-foot elevation gain. Bring water, as no springs are in the area. Like the Drum Mountains, Notch Peak has a reputation for strange underground noises. The 15-minute Notch Peak topo map is needed as much for navigating the roads to the trailhead as for the hiking. First take Antelope Spring Road to the signed turnoff for Miller Canyon, 4.5 miles north of milepost 46 on U.S. 50/6 (42 miles west of Delta) and 11.5 miles south of old U.S. 50/6 (35 miles west of Delta). Turn west 5.3 miles on Miller Canyon Road, then bear left to Sawtooth Canyon at a road fork.

A stone cabin 2.5 miles farther on the right marks the trailhead. The cabin is owned and used by people who mine in the area. Follow a rough road on foot into Sawtooth Canyon. After three-quarters of a mile the canyon widens where two tributaries meet; take the left fork in the direction of Notch Peak. A few spots in the dry creekbed require some rock-scrambling. Be on the lookout for flash floods if thunderstorms threaten.

After about three miles the wash becomes less distinct; continue climbing to a saddle visible ahead. From there, a short but steep quarter-mile scramble takes you to the top of 9,655-foot Notch Peak and its awesome drop-offs. Other ways up Notch Peak offer challenges for the adventurous. The other fork of Sawtooth Canyon can be used, for example, and a jeep road through Amasa Valley provides a northern approach.

Confusion Range

The Confusions lie in a long, jumbled mass west of the House Range. The sparse vegetation consists largely of piñon pine, juniper, sagebrush, shadscale, and cheatgrass. Some Douglas fir grow on the King Top Plateau, the highest area in the Confusion Range, where elevations reach 8,300 feet. Shortages of water and feed allow only small numbers of wild horses, pronghorn, deer, and smaller animals to eke out an existence.

Fossil Mountain in the southeast part of the Confusions has an exceptional diversity of marine fossils, many very rare. Thirteen fossil groups of ancient sea creatures have been found in rocks of early Ordovician age (350–400 million years ago). Fossil Mountain stands 6,685 feet high on the west edge of Blind Valley. A signed road to Blind Valley turns south off U.S. 50/6 between mileposts 38 and 39 (54 miles west of Delta). Fossil Mountain is about 14 miles south of the highway.

SOUTH OF DELTA

Fort Deseret

What remains of this fort represents a fading piece of pioneer history. Mormon settlers hastily built the adobe-walled fort in only 18 days in 1865 for protection against Native Americans during the Black Hawk War. The square fort had walls 550 feet long and 10 feet high with gates in the middle of each side. Bastions were located at the northeast and southwest corners. Native Americans never attacked the fort, but it came in handy for penning up cattle at night. Parts of the wall and stone foundation still stand. From Delta go west five miles on U.S. 50/6, then turn left (south) 4.5 miles on Highway 257. The site is on the west side of the road near milepost 65, about 1.5 miles south of the town of Deseret.

Great Stone Face

A natural rock formation seven miles southwest of Deseret bears a striking resemblance to the Mormon prophet Joseph Smith. To see the profile you have to view the rock from the west.

From the town of Deseret, go south three miles on Highway 257, then turn right (west) four miles (should be signed) on a dirt road. A short hike at road's end leads up a lava flow to the stone face.

Clear Lake State Waterfowl Management Area

Lakes and marsh country offer ducks, Canada geese, and other birds a refreshing break from the desert. Roads cross Clear Lake on a causeway and lead to smaller lakes and picnic areas to the north. The Utah Division of Wildlife Resources manages the area. From the junction of U.S. 50/6 and Highway 257 west of Delta, go south 15.5 miles on Highway 257, then turn left (east) seven miles on a good gravel road.

Pahvant Butte

Locally known as Sugar Loaf Mountain, this extinct volcano rises 1,000 feet above the desert floor. Waters of prehistoric Lake Bonneville leveled off the large terrace about halfway up. Remnants of a crater, now open to the southwest, are on this level. Another terrace line is at the bottom of the butte. Hikers can enjoy the volcanic geology, expansive panoramas, and a visit to the curious ruins of a windmill. Construction of the wind-powered electric power station began in 1923 but was never completed. A large underground room and two concentric rings of concrete pylons give an eerie Stonehenge-like atmosphere to the butte.

Easiest way up is an old road on the south side that goes to the windmill site. From Clear Lake, continue east 3.3 miles to the second signed turn on the left for Pahvant Butte (Pahvant Butte Road: 3 miles, Sugarloaf Well #1: 8 miles). Turn left 3.5 miles at the sign, then turn left one-half mile on Pahvant Butte Road. Park before the road begins a steep climb. Daredevils in four-wheel drives have tried going straight up the slope from here, but the real road turns right and follows switchbacks 0.7 mile to the windmill site. This last 0.7 mile is closed to vehicles because of the soft volcanic rock, but it's fine for walking; elevation gain is about 400 feet. Pahvant Butte's highest point is about a half mile to the north and 265 feet higher; you'll have to find your own way across if headed there. Dirt roads encircle Pahvant Butte and go northeast to U.S. 50 and southeast to Tabernacle Hill and Fillmore. The Tabernacle Hill area provides good examples of volcanic features.

MILFORD

Miners on their way to Frisco and Newhouse crossed the Beaver River at a ford below a stamp mill, so Milford seemed the logical name for the town that grew up here. Most of Milford's businesses in the early days supplied the mining camps. Today the town serves as a center for the railroad, nearby farms, and a geothermal plant. Steam from wells at the Blundell Geothermal Plant, 13 miles northeast of town, produces electricity for Utah Power and Light. Travelers heading west will find Milford their last stop for supplies before the Nevada border. Milford (pop. 1,310) is at the junction of Highway 21 and Highway 257, 77 miles south of Delta and 32 miles east of Beaver. Baker, Nevada, is 96 miles northwest.

Recreation
The **city park** at 300 South and 200 West has a picnic area. An outdoor pool is behind the high school at 141 North 200 West, 435/387-2315. Milford's five-hole **golf course,** on the west edge of town (about 1000 South and 700 West), 435/387-2711 (city office), is open April–October.

Accommodations and Food
In Milford, the **Station Motel,** at the corner of 100 West and 500 South, 435/387-2481, has basic rooms, and the **Station Restaurant,** 435/387-2804, is open daily for breakfast, lunch, and dinner. On the west edge of town, the new, pet-friendly **Oak Tree Inn,** 777 W. Highway 21, 800/523-8460, has comfortable rooms with microwaves and refrigerators and a fitness center. Guests get a free breakfast next door at **Penny's Diner,** a pretty good 24-hour restaurant. **Pavilion Park** has a free camping area just beyond

the high school grounds on 300 West, open year-round with water.

Information and Services
The **post office** is at 458 S. Main. **Milford Valley Memorial Hospital** is at 451 N. Main, 435/387-2411. **Milford City office,** 302 S. Main (P.O. Box 69, Milford, UT 84751), 435/387-2711, can answer questions about the area 8 A.M.–3 P.M. Monday–Friday. During the summer you can obtain area information in the old caboose at 46 S. Main. The **public library,** 400 South 100 West, 435/387-5039, is open weekday afternoons.

Rock Corral Campground and Pass Road
The BLM has a campground and picnic area east of Milford in the Mineral Mountains, a popular area for rockhounding; no water or fee. From Highway 21 on the southeast edge of Milford, turn east 5.5 miles on Pass Road, then left (north) 5.2 miles. Returning to Pass Road, you can continue east 13.4 miles over the Mineral Mountains and loop back to Highway 21 between mileposts 102 and 103 4.8 miles west of Beaver. Pass Road has a gravel surface with a dirt section near the pass.

MINERSVILLE RESERVOIR PARK

The 1,130-acre reservoir here has good year-round fishing for rainbow trout and smallmouth bass (ice fishing in winter). Be sure to check with the rangers for information about fishing regulations for the park. Bait fishing is not allowed and there are special catch limits. Most people come here to fish, though some visitors go sailing or water-skiing. Park facilities include picnic tables, campsites (all with electric and water hookups), restrooms with showers, paved boat ramp, fish-cleaning station, and dump station. Fees are $4 for day use, $13 for sites in the campground with water and electric hookups. Reservations are a good idea on summer holidays. In winter the restrooms may be closed but water is available. For information or reservations, write P.O. Box 1531,

Beaver, UT 84713, or call 435/438-5472. Minersville Reservoir lies just off Highway 21 in a sage- and juniper-covered valley eight miles east of Minersville, 18 miles southeast of Milford, and 14 miles west of Beaver.

SAN FRANCISCO MOUNTAINS AND GHOST TOWNS

Frisco Peak (elev. 9,660 feet) crowns this small range northwest of Milford. The Wah Wah Valley and Mountains lie to the west. Silver strikes in the San Francisco Mountains in the 1870s led to the opening of many mines and the founding of the towns of Newhouse and Frisco. By 1920 the best ores had given out and both communities turned to ghosts. A jeep road goes to the summit of Frisco Peak.

Frisco

The Horn Silver Mine, developed in 1876 at the south end of the San Francisco Mountains, was the first of several prolific silver producers. Smelters, and charcoal ovens to fuel them, sprouted up to process the ore. A wild boomtown developed as miners flocked to the new diggings. The railroad reached Frisco in 1880 and later extended to nearby Newhouse. Frisco's population of 6,000 included quite a few gamblers and other shady characters. Twenty-three saloons labored to serve the thirsty customers. Gunfights became almost a daily ritual for a while, keeping the cemetery growing. But it all came to an end early in 1885, when rumblings echoed from deep within the Horn Silver Mine between shifts. The foreman luckily delayed sending the next crew down, and a few minutes later the whole mine collapsed with a deafening roar that broke windows in Milford, 15 miles away. Out of work, most of the miners and business people moved on. More than $60 million in silver and other valuable ores had come out of the ground in the mine's 10 frenzied years. Some mining has been done on and off since, but Frisco has died.

Today Frisco is one of Utah's best-preserved mining ghosts, with about a dozen stone or wood buildings surviving. A headframe and mine buildings, still intact, overlook the town from the hillside. Five beehive-shaped charcoal kilns stand on the east edge of Frisco. You can see the kilns and the townsite if you look north from Highway 21 (between mileposts 62 and 63) 15 miles west of Milford. Dirt roads wind their way in. A historical marker for Frisco is at the turnoff for the town; turnoff for the beehive kilns is 0.3 mile east. Hiking off the roads can be very dangerous near the old mines and time-worn buildings.

Newhouse

Prospectors discovered silver deposits in 1870 on the southwest side of the San Francisco Mountains but lacked the funds to develop them. Mining didn't take off until 1900, when Samuel Newhouse financed operations. A sizable town grew here as ore worth $3.5 million came out of the Cactus Mine. Citizens maintained a degree of law and order not found in most mining towns: Even the saloon and the working girls had to operate outside the community. Deposits of rich ore ran out only 10 years later and the town's inhabitants departed. The railroad depot was moved to a nearby ranch and other buildings went to Milford. Today, Newhouse is a ghostly site with about half a dozen concrete or stone buildings standing in ruins. Foundations of a smelter, mill, other structures, railroad grades, and lots of broken glass remain. A good dirt road turns north two miles to the site from Highway 21 (between mileposts 57 and 58) 20 miles west of Milford.

WAH WAH MOUNTAINS

Beyond the San Francisco Mountains, the Wah Wah Mountains extend south about 55 miles in a continuation of the Confusion Range. Elevation ranges from 6,000 to more than 9,000 feet. The name comes from a Paiute term for salty or alkaline seeps. Sparse sagebrush, juniper, and piñon pine cover most of the land. Aspen, white fir, ponderosa pine, and bristlecone pine grow in the high country. Mule deer, pronghorn, and smaller animals roam the mountains. Carry water, maps, and a compass into this wild country. Few people visit the Wah Wahs despite their pristine ecosystem. A 1986 BLM publication reported an estimated 155 visitor days per year for recreation in the Wah Wah Mountains Wilderness Study Area, which includes the northern and central parts of the range. That's an average of less than half a person per day!

Crystal Peak

This snow-white pinnacle in the north end of the Wah Wah Mountains stands out as a major landmark. The soft white rock of the peak is tuff from an ancient volcano thought to predate the block-faulted Wah Wahs. The best way to climb the peak (elev. 7,106 feet) is to ascend the ridge just south of it from the east, then follow the ridge northeast up the peak. Be careful of soft,

crumbly rock. See the 15-minute Crystal Peak topo map for details.

Central Section

The heart of the Wah Wahs has some fine scenery and opportunities for nature study. Rugged cliffs mark the west edge of the range. A good hiking route begins at about 6,600 feet in elevation at the end of a dirt road going up Pierson Cove. Follow the dry wash upstream a short way to a split in the drainage, then take the left fork north through a canyon. After about two miles you'll come out of the canyon onto a high plateau. For the best views, turn northwest and continue climbing three-quarters of a mile to the summit of an 8,918-foot peak. See the 7-minute Wah Wah Summit topo map for back roads and hiking routes.

Central Utah

In many ways, the geography and history of central Utah are extensions of the northern part of the state. The rugged Wasatch Range continues to act as an eastern boundary to the spread of the state's largest municipalities, which cluster at the base of the range. Here, smaller mountains and hills form a transition to the basin and range terrain to the west. The mountains of the Wasatch Range are steeper and higher than those to the north, perhaps even more majestic, and likely to be coated with snow. Just two years after the founding of Salt Lake City, Mormon pioneers began settling both this area and the Wasatch Plateau south of the range. Quiet Mormon villages occupy much of the lower country today.

Provo

Utah's second-largest city (pop. 105,000), Provo has a striking setting on the shore of Utah Lake beneath the west face of the Wasatch Range. The city is best known as the home of Brigham Young University (BYU), a large, dynamic school sponsored by the Church of Jesus Christ of Latter-day Saints. Museums and cultural events on the BYU campus make it a popular destination.

Provo also contains a rich architectural heritage. At the turn of the 20th century, this hardworking young city constructed its civic buildings with style and substance, and its residential areas

© JUDY JEWELL

Jordanelle State Park

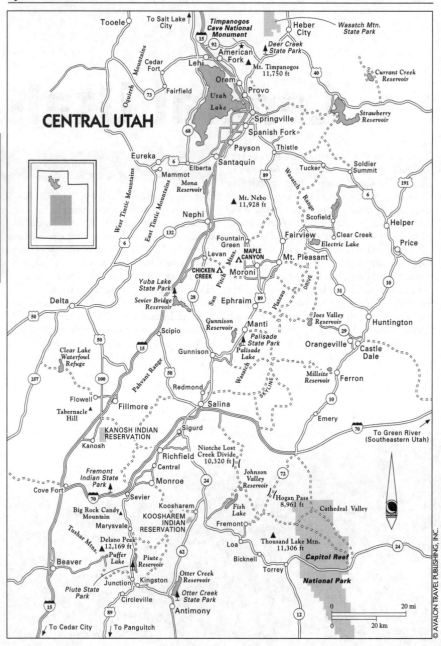

CENTRAL UTAH

CENTRAL UTAH

© AVALON TRAVEL PUBLISHING, INC.

The steep Wasatch Range rises immediately behind Provo's historic, tree-lined downtown.

are filled with Victorian mansions and vernacular workers' homes. The visitors center can provide two self-guided tour brochures to the city's historic architecture.

Provo boasts one of the most majestic views of any of the Wasatch Front cities, perhaps contributing to the city's consistently high marks in many publications' "livability" ratings. It also offers a university town's full selection of cultural and sporting events, easy access to water sports, fishing, hiking, and skiing, and a relatively low crime rate.

History

In 1776, members of the Dominguez-Escalante Expedition visited the Utah Valley, where Provo now sits, and sent back glowing reports of fertile soil, plentiful game, and beautiful countryside. The Spanish friars who led the group had hoped to return and establish missions for the local Native Americans, but political decisions prevented them from doing so. The expedition had friendly relations with the Utes (known here as the Timpanogotzis), as did most later mountain men and early Mormon settlers. Fur trappers included Etienne Provost, a French Canadian

who passed through in 1824 and 1825. His Anglicized name was adopted in 1849 when Mormons arrived in the Utah Valley to start their first settlement. Within the next two years, the communities of Lehi, Pleasant Grove, American Fork, Springville, and Payson also sprang up in the valley. Geneva Steel and other major industries established during the World War II years transformed the Provo area from an agrarian landscape to the major urban center it is today. The downtown business district, though, still features many distinctive buildings from the late 19th century and earlier.

BRIGHAM YOUNG UNIVERSITY

The university had a modest beginning in 1875 as the Brigham Young Academy, established under the direction of LDS Church president Brigham Young. Like the rest of Provo, BYU's population and size have grown dramatically in recent decades. BYU is one of the largest church-affiliated schools in the world. Students aren't required to be Mormons, but about 95 percent of the student body of 29,000 do belong to the LDS Church. High academic standards upheld by students and faculty have made the university a leader in many fields. Everyone attending the school must follow a strict dress and grooming code—something you'll notice immediately on a stroll across the modern campus.

Exhibits and concerts are held in the **Harris Fine Arts Center** (just north of the Wilkinson Center) and other locations on campus, 801/378-7444 (music ticket office) or 801/378-4322 (theater performances). BYU also goes all out to support its Cougars football and other athletic teams. Major sporting events take place in the 65,000-seat Cougar Stadium and the indoor 23,000-seat Marriott Center, 801/378-2981 (ticket office).

You're welcome to visit the more than 600 acres of BYU's vast campus. The **visitors center** provides literature and advice about things to see, events, and facilities open to the public. It's open 8 A.M.–5 P.M. Monday–Friday on the brow of the hill near the Maeser Building, south on Campus Dr., 801/378-4678. Campus tours, either walking or in small open-air vehicles, introduce the university; student guides point out features of interest and tell about student life and research work. The free tours last about 45 minutes and depart Monday–Friday 9 A.M.–4 P.M. by reservation; tours also depart the same days at 11 A.M. and 2 P.M. on a walk-in basis (no reservation needed) from the visitors center. Free parking is available in front of the center for those taking guided tours or needing information about the campus. Additional free visitors' parking (signed) is near the north end of Campus Drive, near the Wilkinson Center (east across the street), and north of the Museum of Art.

Wilkinson Center serves as the social center for BYU. The main level has a choice of cafeterias and snack bars (open Monday–Saturday for breakfast, lunch, and dinner), the Varsity Theater (current movies), an art gallery, lounge areas, and an information desk. The **Skyroom Restaurant** on the sixth floor, 801/378-2049, offers great views and fine dining (open Monday–Friday for lunch and Friday for dinner). The lower level has **Outdoors Unlimited**

CENTRAL UTAH HIGHLIGHTS

Timpanogos Cave National Monument
Alpine Scenic Loop
Sundance Resort
Heber Valley Historic Railroad
Picnic lunch at Fillmore's Territorial Statehouse State Park
Driving U.S. 89 through ranch country
Fremont Indian State Park
Staying lakeside at a Fish Lake cabin resort

(rentals of bicycles and equipment for camping, boating, snowshoeing, cross-country and downhill skiing, and other sports), 801/378-2708, and a **post office.** Some of the other recreation facilities are open only to university students, faculty, and staff.

The **BYU Bookstore** occupies three levels on the west side of the Wilkinson Center with a good selection of general books, textbooks, LDS titles, art supplies, and BYU clothing and souvenirs. The **Harold B. Lee Library,** just west of the bookstore, has an impressive collection of books and maps on five levels; the genealogical library on the fourth floor ranks second in size only to the one in Salt Lake City, which is the largest in the world; main collections are open 7 A.M.–midnight Monday–Saturday; 801/378-2926.

Small collections on campus include a series of salt- and freshwater aquariums in the basement of the Widtsoe Building, and Earth Science exhibits and a Foucault pendulum in the lobby and hallways of the Eyring Science Center. The Summerhays Planetarium in the Eyring Science Center, 801/378-4361, presents programs to the public for a small charge.

Museum of Art

This is one of the largest art museums in the West, displaying famous works of art including Rembrandt's *Raising of Lazarus,* Gifford's *Lake Scene,* and Andy Warhol's *Marilyn.* These are just of few of the museum's 14,000 works

© BILL WEIR

Students relax on campus at Brigham Young University.

ranging from Renaissance to modern, Asian to local. The building itself is a work of art, with a polished granite exterior, hardwood floors, and high-ceilinged galleries bathed in natural light. Special exhibits have entrance fees; otherwise, admission is free. Hours are 10 A.M.–9 P.M. Monday–Saturday; call 801/378-2787 for more information.

Monte L. Bean Life Science Museum

Mounted animals and dioramas realistically depict wildlife of Utah and distant lands. The exhibits not only identify the many species on display but also show how they interact within their environments. The Children's Discovery Room has cages of insects and small animals. Special presentations include movies, talks, workshops, and live-reptile, animal-adaptation, and other demonstrations; call for the schedule. The research library is southeast of the Marriott Center on 1430 North, 801/378-5051; open 10 A.M.–5 P.M. Monday–Friday. Natural history items can be purchased in the gift shop. Mu-

seum exhibits are open 1–9 P.M. Monday and 10 A.M.–5 P.M. Tuesday–Saturday; free.

Earth Science Museum

This small museum features excellent exhibits of dinosaurs and early mammals. A popular dinosaur video program both entertains and educates. A viewing window lets you observe researchers cleaning and preparing bones. The museum is at 1683 N. Provo Canyon Road (across from Cougar Stadium), 801/378-3680. Hours are 9 A.M.–5 P.M. Monday–Friday (till 9 P.M. on Monday) and noon–4 P.M. Saturday; free.

Museum of Peoples and Cultures

This museum's purpose is to communicate knowledge about both modern and ancient peoples of the world. Exhibits reflect research in the Great Basin in Utah, the American Southwest, Mesoamerica, South America, the Near East, and Polynesia. The museum, at the corner of 700 North and 100 East, 801/422-0020, is open 9 A.M.5 P.M. Monday–Friday; free.

OTHER PROVO SIGHTS
McCurdy Historical Doll Museum

Mrs. Laura McCurdy Clark, who started the collection, often used her dolls to teach history to students. The original collection has been expanded to about 4,000 dolls, representing U.S. presidents and their wives, other historical figures, and diverse nationalities. Private parties can be arranged here. The museum shop sells dolls, doll supplies, toys, and books. The doll museum is at 246 North 100 East, 801/377-9935; it's open noon–5 P.M. Tuesday–Saturday (1–5 P.M. January–March). Admission is $3 adults, $2 ages under 12.

Provo Tabernacle

Architect William Folsom, who designed the St. George and Manti Temples, patterned this English-style structure, at 100 S. University Ave., after a Presbyterian Church he had visited in Salt Lake City. Construction, begun in 1883, required 15 years. Organ recitals and other concerts take place here.

Provo Temple

This modern building of white cast stone incorporates floral elements and a central golden spire. It's particularly impressive lit up against the sky at night. Dedication took place in 1972 with 75,000 people in attendance. Church members carry out sacred work within the 283 rooms. Visitors can't go inside but are welcome to visit the landscaped grounds, at 2200 N. Temple Dr. (turn east on 2230 North from University Ave. or drive north on 900 East).

Utah Lake State Park

The largest body of fresh water completely within the state, Utah Lake is 24 miles long and 11 miles wide. Average depth is only 9.4 feet. Mountains form the skyline in all directions. Swans, geese, pelicans, ducks, and other migratory birds stop by. Best bird-watching is at the south end of the lake and near the Provo Airport. The state park provides recreation facilities on the east shore, just a short drive from downtown Provo. Boaters come for water-skiing, sailboarding, and fishing; four paved boat ramps, docks, and slips are available.

The swimming beach offers another way to cool off. Anglers catch white and black bass, channel catfish, walleyed pike, carp, and other warmwater fish during most of the year. The lake usually freezes over by late December and has good ice fishing; trout descend from the mountain rivers during this season. A visitors center has ice-skating in winter. The campground is open mid-March–October with water and showers; $7 per vehicle for day use, $17 for camping. The park is open year-round at 4400 W. Center, Provo, UT 84601, 801/375-0733 (recording), 801/375-0731 (office), or 800/322-3770 (reservations). Head west four miles on Center from downtown Provo or take the I-15 exit for West Center and go west three miles.

Springville Museum of Art

The museum started in the early 1900s as the collection of Springville High School, but when it began to receive gifts of major works from artists Cyrus Dallin and John Hafen, townspeople decided that a special building was needed.

They built this fine Spanish-style structure during the Depression with federal and LDS Church assistance. The town is now also known as "Art City" for its patronage. The permanent collection contains 1,200 American works including some of the best by early Utah pioneers and Native Americans as well as the state's modern artists. Eleven galleries display visiting exhibits downstairs; a permanent collection is housed upstairs. The annual April Salon is a major show of Utah contemporary artists. The museum is at 126 East 400 South in Springville, 801/489-2727. From Provo, drive seven miles south on U.S. 89 (S. State St.) or take I-15 Exit 263 and go east. The museum is open 10 A.M.–5 P.M. Tuesday–Saturday (until 9 P.M. on Wednesday) and 3–6 P.M. Sunday, closed Monday and state holidays and two weeks prior to the April Salon; free.

ENTERTAINMENT AND EVENTS

For current happenings not only in Provo but also in nearby towns, check with the Utah County Travel Council, 51 S. University Avenue, Ste. 111, 801/370-8393.

Brigham Young University has a busy calendar of cultural and sporting events; call 801/378-7444 (music ticket office), 801/378-4332 (theater performances), or 801/378-2981 (sporting events). Catch movies at **Carmike Cinemas,** 175 West 200 North, 801/374-6061; **Movies 8,** Plum Tree Shopping Center at 2424 N. University Parkway, 801/375-5667; or BYU's **Varsity Theatre,** Wilkinson Center, 801/378-3311.

In Orem, **SCERA** offers family entertainment movies year-round inside the Show House at 745 S. State and summer plays and musicals in an outdoor shell at 699 S. State; call 801/225-2560 (recorded info) or 801/225-2569 (office).

Major annual events in the area include **Art City Days,** which takes place in Springville in June. The **City of Orem Family Summerfest** presents a parade, talent show, 5K run, Dutch-oven cook-off, and other entertainment. Also in June, Sundance holds a **Bluegrass Festival.** Cowboys show their skills at the **Lehi Round-up and Rodeo.**

In July, Provo celebrates the Fourth with a **Freedom Festival** grand parade, freedom run, sports events, concerts, arts festival, and fireworks. **Provo Arts Festival** has performing and visual arts and special programs for kids. Springville presents groups of dancers from many countries in the **Springville World Folkfest**. **Pioneer Day** brings a parade and other entertainment to Provo and other towns on July 24. **Fiesta Days** in Spanish Fork has a parade, rodeo, pioneer activities, 10K run, and entertainment for three days near July 24. Highland lets loose in its **Highland Fling** with a parade, 10K run, carnival, fireworks, entertainment, and children's games.

In August, the **Utah County Fair** features a horse show, exhibits, and entertainment in Spanish Fork. The town of Payson puts on a **Scottish Festival**. Nationally recognized storytellers present traditional and new pieces in the **Timpanogos Storytelling Festival**.

RECREATION
Parks, Gyms, and Water Parks
North Park, 500 West 500 North, contains **Veterans' Memorial Pool & Waterslide Park** (801/379-6614), picnic areas, playground, and a **Daughters of Utah Pioneers Pioneer Museum** open 2–5 P.M. Monday–Friday in summer. **Fort Utah City Park** has picnic tables, a playground, and a replica of the fort built by Provo's first settlers; from downtown, head west on Center past the I-15 interchange and turn north one block on Highway 114 (2050 West). **Pioneer Park** has picnicking and a playground at Center and 500 West. **Provo Recreation Center** next to Provo High School at 1155 N. University Avenue, 801/379-6610, has an indoor pool, racquetball and volleyball courts, and weight rooms.

The big **Seven Peaks Resort Water Park,** 1330 East 300 North, 801/377 4FUN, contains two huge water slides, twisting tubes, and a variety of pools to cool off in; guests can also picnic or play games such as volleyball, basketball, softball, and horseshoes. Other attractions include ice-skating in winter and an 18-hole executive golf course. Open

late May–early September; admission is $16.50 ages 12–59, $12.95 ages 3–12, free for toddlers (ages 3 and under) and seniors (60 and over). Turn east on Center Street to its end and follow signs. **Trafalga Family Fun Center,** 168 South 1200 West in Orem (take I-15 Exit 274), 801/224-6000, features a water-tube slide, mini golf, bumper boats, and arcade games.

Other Recreation
Play golf at the 27-hole **East Bay Golf Course,** 801/373-6262 (turn east on East Bay Blvd. from South University Ave. near the I-15 interchange), or the nine-hole **Cascade Fairways Public Golf Course,** 1313 East 800 North in Orem, 801/225-6677.

In winter, skiers hit the slopes at **Sundance Ski Area,** 14 miles northeast of town, 801/225-4107. **Hansen Mountaineering,** 757 N. State, Orem, UT 84057, 801/226-7498, leads trips and provides instruction and sales for rock climbing, winter camping, and cross-country skiing.

ACCOMMODATIONS

Most of Provo's newer hotels and motels are chain motels that lie along South University Avenue, the long commercial strip that runs from I-15 Exit 266 to downtown. The downtown area offers older but well-maintained properties.

Under $50
Motel 6, 1600 S. University Ave., 801/375-5064 or 800/4-MOTEL-6, has a pool and a guest laundry and allows pets. The **Colony Inn Suites,** 1380 S. University Ave., 801/374-6800 or 800/524-9999, is an especially good deal, with suite-style rooms—all with kitchens and living and dining areas—for the price of a motel room. Facilities include a sauna, pool, and hot tub.

For a comfortable, inexpensive room downtown, try the **Provo Travelers Inn,** 469 W. Center, 801/373-8248. There's a pool, and some rooms have kitchenettes.

$50–75
The **Fairfield Inn by Marriott,** 1515 S. University Ave., 801/377-9500 or 800/228-2800,

has an indoor pool, spa, and a complimentary continental breakfast. In addition to the nicely furnished standard rooms, there are six suites with kitchens. The **Holiday Inn,** 1460 S. University Ave., 801/374-9750, is a new complex with a good restaurant, pool, and nicely furnished rooms.

The **Travelodge,** 124 S. University Ave., 801/373-1974 or 800/255-3050, is right in the center of town and has a pool. The Travelodge also has some larger family units that can sleep up to six. The **Best Western Colombian Motel,** 70 East 300 South, 801/373-8973 or 800/321-0055, has a pool.

Another clutch of motels sits north of downtown near the university. The **Days Inn,** 1675 North 200 West, 801/375-8600 or 800/325-2525, has a pool. The **La Quinta,** 1555 N. Canyon Rd., 801/374-6020, is nicely landscaped and has an indoor pool, spa, and a complimentary continental breakfast. The **Best Western Cottontree Inn,** 2230 N. University Pkwy., 801/373-7044 or 800/662-6886, has an indoor and outdoor pool, plus large rooms with lots of extras.

$75–100

Provo's finest hotel is the **Provo Marriott Park Hotel,** 101 West 100 North, 801/377-4700 or 888/825-3162, an upscale business and conference hotel. Rooms are large, very nicely appointed, and come with minibars and coffeemakers; facilities include a pool, spa, and weight room.

Campgrounds

Lakeside RV Campground, 4000 W. Center (just before Utah Lake State Park), 801/373-5267, has sites for tents and RVs with showers, pool, laundry, store, and canoe rentals; open year-round. **Provo KOA,** 320 North 2050 West (a quarter mile west of I-15 on Center, then one block north), 801/375-2994, has sites for tents and RVs with showers, pool, laundry, and store; open year-round. **Frazier Park** along the Provo River, five miles up Provo Canyon, 801/225-5346, welcomes tents and RVs with hookups and showers; closed in winter. **Deer Creek Park,** along the Provo River farther upstream near the dam for Deer Creek Reservoir, 801/225-9783, offers tenting sites or full hookups; showers available. Open April 15–October 15. You'll find Forest Service campgrounds near Provo along the Alpine Scenic Loop to the northeast, Squaw Peak Road to the east, and Hobble Creek–Diamond Fork Loop to the southeast.

FOOD

You'll notice a strong collegiate influence at Provo area eateries. Food tends to be fairly simple and cheap—liquor licenses, in the hometown of BYU, are rare. A drive along North University Drive reveals dozens of perfectly good fast-food restaurants.

Otherwise, with a couple of exceptions, the food scene here is rather restrained. **Good Earth Natural Foods,** 1045 S. University Ave., 801/375-7444, has a café (open Monday–Saturday for lunch and dinner), a bakery, and groceries. **Gandolfo's Deli,** 18 N. University, 801/375-3354, is a popular spot for sandwiches. One of Provo's few fine dining restaurants is **Ottavio's Ristorante Italiano,** 69 E. Center St., 801/377-9555, with a wide selection of excellent pasta and roast meat dishes ($12–18) served in a historic hotel lobby. In a side café is a coffee shop with fresh pastries that will enliven your Provo morning. Open daily for breakfast, lunch, and dinner; it also has a liquor license.

Tepanyaki Steak House, 1240 North 500 West, 801/374-0633, prepares Japanese cuisine daily for dinner. The **Bombay House,** 463 N. University Ave., 801/373-6677 is a good Indian restaurant with lunchtime buffet and Tandoori-baked meats. For a Latin American twist, go to **Tucano's Brazilian Grill,** 4801 N. University Ave., 801/224-4774.

If you're looking for Mexican food, consider driving south of Provo to Springville. There, **La Casita Mexican Restaurant,** 333 N. Main St., 801/489-9543, is the area's best bet for good traditional south of the border cooking; the restaurant has a liquor license.

OTHER PRACTICALITIES

Information and Services

Utah County Travel Council, 51 S. University Ave., Ste. 111, in the old county courthouse (P.O. Box 912, Provo, UT 84601), 801/370-8393 or 800/222-UTAH out of state, www .utahvalley.org, offers advice on sights and services in Provo and the Utah Valley; open Memorial Day–Labor Day weekends 8 A.M.–8 P.M. Monday–Friday and 10 A.M.–6 P.M. Saturday–Sunday, then 8 A.M.–5 P.M. Monday–Friday the rest of the year.

The U.S. Forest Service has three offices in the area. The **Uinta National Forest Supervisor,** 88 West 100 North, Provo, UT 84601, 801/377-5780, has general information about all districts in the forest and some books and maps for sale; open 8 A.M.–5 P.M. Monday–Friday. Contact the **Pleasant Grove Ranger District office,** 390 North 100 East, Pleasant Grove, UT 84062, 801/785-3563, for specific information about the Alpine Scenic Loop and other areas in the Uinta National Forest north of Provo; open 8 A.M.–5 P.M. Monday–Friday (plus Saturday 8 A.M.–5 P.M. in summer). The **Spanish Fork Ranger District office,** 44 West 400 North, Spanish Fork, UT 84660, 801/798-3571, covers the Uinta National Forest east and southeast of Provo and the Wasatch National Forest, Vernon Division, southwest of town; open 8 A.M.–5 P.M. Monday–Friday (8 A.M.–4:30 P.M. daily in summer).

Provo City Library, 425 W. Center, 801/379-6650, is open 9:30 A.M.–9 P.M. Monday–Thursday and 9:30 A.M.–6 P.M. Friday–Saturday. BYU's **Harold B. Lee Library,** just west of the Wilkinson Center, 801/378-2926, has an impressive collection of books and maps on five levels; open 7 A.M.–midnight Monday–Friday and 8 A.M.–midnight Saturday. The **BYU Bookstore** at the Wilkinson Center, 801/378-3584, has one of the best and largest selections in the state. For a good selection of books plus a coffee bar, head to **Borders Books,** 4801 N. University Blvd., 801/224-2720.

The **post office** is at 95 West 100 South, 801/275-8777. The **U.S. Forest Service** provides avalanche/mountain weather information during the snow season at 801/374-9770. **Utah Valley Regional Medical Center** is at 1034 North 500 West, 801/373-7850.

Transportation

Utah Transit Authority (UTA), 801/375-4636, provides local bus service in Provo and connects with Springville, Salt Lake City, Ogden, and other towns; buses don't run on Sunday and holidays except for a few lines on Sunday in Salt Lake City and Ogden. **Greyhound Bus,** 124 North 300 West, 801/373-4211, has at least two northbound and two southbound departures daily. **Amtrak** trains, 800/872-7245, serve Provo. **Yellow Cab,** 801/377-7070, provides taxi service. Scheduled airline flights leave from the Salt Lake City Airport.

Northwest of Provo

Hutching's Museum of Natural History

This amazingly diverse collection in the town of Lehi (LEE-high) began as a family museum. Highlights include pioneer rifles, Native American crafts, glittering minerals, ancient fossils, mounted birds of Utah, and colorful tropical shells. The museum is at 53 N. Center St. in Lehi (16 miles northwest of Provo on I-15), 801/768-7180; open 9:30 A.M.–5:30 P.M. Monday–Saturday; $3 adults, $1.50 children under 12.

Thanksgiving Point

Also near Lehi, this vast new park and entertainment center between Utah Lake and I-15 contains everything from a business park, golf course, formal garden, and paleontology museum to a petting zoo, plus loads of dining and shopping. Parts of the park are still under construction, but highlights include **The Barn,** which serves as a performance and special event space; **Farm Country,** a farm and petting zoo, complete with wagon rides and lots of tame animals doing what comes naturally; **Thanksgiving Gardens,** containing 55 acres of formal gardens plus a "waterfall amphitheater"; and a 200-acre, 7,728-yard **18-hole golf course.** The **Village at Thanksgiving Point** offers six restaurants and dining halls, and nearly 11 shops and stores.

Thanksgiving Point will either really appeal to you as a one-stop vacation wonderland or send you screaming in the other direction, in search of noncommercialized, unpackaged pastimes. However, one very good reason to make the stop is to visit the **Museum of Ancient Life,** which claims to be the largest dinosaur museum in the world. With over 122,000 square feet of exhibition space, this museum contains 60 complete dinosaur skeletons, with dozens of hands-on displays, research facilities, and a six-story IMAX theater. Most of the featured dinosaurs represent species that once strode across the alluvial sands of ancient Utah, including the first-ever displayed skeleton of a supersaurus, super-sized at 110 feet long.

The Thanksgiving Point compound is just west of I-15 Exit 287, 801/768-2300 or 888/672-6040. The facility is open 9 A.M. to 9 P.M. Monday–Friday and 9 A.M. to 10 P.M. Saturday. Admission rates are a complex system of individual and combo tickets; call up the website at www.thanksgivingpoint.com to check out the options. An adult admission to the Museum of Ancient Life is $9.50, children 3–12 are $7.50. An Adventure Passport ticket to most facilities (including the museum, theater, gardens, and farm) is $24 adult, $18 children.

Camp Floyd Stagecoach Inn State Park

A restored inn, an old U.S. Army building, and a military cemetery preserve a bit of pioneer history at Fairfield, a sleepy village on the other side of Utah Lake from Provo. John Carson, who had been one of the first settlers of the site in 1855, built a family residence and hotel three years later. About the same time, troops of the U.S. Army under Colonel Albert Johnston marched in and established Camp Floyd nearby. The soldiers had been sent by President Buchanan to put down a rumored Mormon rebellion. Upon finding that no "Mormon War" existed, the colonel led his men to this site so as not to intimidate the major Mormon settlements. Fairfield jumped in size almost overnight to become Utah's third-largest city, with a population of about 7,000—including the 3,000 soldiers. Even for the times, it was rowdy—17 saloons served the army men. The camp (later named Fort Crittenden) served no real purpose, however, and was abandoned in 1861 so that troops could return east to fight in the Civil War. Carson's hotel, later known as the Stagecoach Inn, continued to serve travelers on the dusty main road across Utah. Pony Express riders, stagecoach passengers, miners, sheepherders, and every other kind of traveler stopped here for the night until the doors closed in 1947.

Now the inn is a state park, furnished as in the old days and full of exhibits on frontier life. A shaded picnic area is beside it. The only surviving building of Camp Floyd has been moved across the street and contains a diorama of the fort and some excavated artifacts. Camp Floyd's well-kept cemetery is a three-quarter-mile drive west and south of Fairfield. The Stagecoach Inn is open 11 A.M.–5 P.M. daily from about Easter weekend

to the end of September. The season may be extended depending on visitation; it's a good idea to call ahead, 801/768-8932, especially if you are driving out just to see the exhibits. Admission is $5 per vehicle, $1 per individual. From Provo or Salt Lake City, take I-15 to Lehi and turn west 21 miles on Highway 73.

North of Provo

TIMPANOGOS CAVE NATIONAL MONUMENT

Beautiful cave formations reward visitors who hike the trail to the cave entrance on the north side of Mount Timpanogos. Branching helictites, icicle-like stalactites, rising stalagmites, and graceful flowstone formations appear snow white or in delicate hues of green, yellow, or red. Tunnels connect three separate limestone caves, each of which has a different character. The first was discovered by Martin Hansen in 1887 while he was tracking a mountain lion. Middle and Timpanogos Caves weren't reported until 1921–1922. Timpanogos Cave so impressed early explorers that a trail, lighting, and national monument protection came soon afterward.

Exhibits and a short slide show in the visitors center introduce the formation, history, and ecology of the caves. The staff provides information on special cave tours and on wildlife and plants of the area. A brochure available here identifies plants and trees along the trail to the caves and illustrates the geology and formation of the caves. Related books, hiking maps, posters, and slides are sold. Be sure to obtain tickets here for the cave tour before starting up the trail. Rangers schedule nature walks on the trail to the caves. There's a $3 per vehicle entry fee.

Allow about three hours for the complete trip, including 45–60 minutes for the cave tour. The three-mile round-trip hike from the visitors center to the caves is moderately difficult; you'll climb 1,065 feet to an elevation of 6,730 feet. Points along the way have fine views up and down American Fork Canyon and out onto the Utah Valley. People with breathing,

heart, or walking difficulties shouldn't attempt the trail; wheeled vehicles (including strollers) and pets aren't allowed. Rangers enforce safety rules that prohibit running, throwing rocks, or shortcutting; children under 16 must stay with their parents.

Ranger-led tours wind about one-third mile through the caves. Underground temperature is about 45°F all year, so bring a sweater or jacket. The caves close during winter because snow and ice make the trail too hazardous. The season lasts mid-May–mid-October; tickets are sold (in the visitors center only) 8 A.M.–3:30 P.M. (extended to 7 A.M.–5:30 P.M. in the peak summer season). On Saturday (all day), Sunday afternoons, holidays, and midsummer weekdays, you may have a long wait. Call ahead to check hours and find out how busy the caves are. Tickets can also be purchased two to three weeks in advance by calling and paying with a credit card. Tours often sell out mid-June–mid-August, when advance reservations are strongly recommended. Admission fees for the cave tours are $6 adults, $5 children 6–15, $3 for kids 3–5, and free for infants; Golden Age card holders pay $3.

A snack bar at the visitors center is open in summer. Picnickers can use tables across the road from the visitors center and at a site a quarter-mile west. The U.S. Forest Service has several campgrounds nearby. Contact the monument at R.R. 3, Box 200, American Fork, UT 84003, 801/756-5238. The visitors center is two miles up American Fork Canyon on the Alpine Scenic Loop (Highway 92). You can take I-15 American Fork Exit 279 if you're coming north from Provo or the I-15 Alpine Exit 287 if coming south from Salt Lake City.

ALPINE SCENIC LOOP

The narrow paved highway twists and winds through some of the most beautiful alpine terrain in Utah. Mount Timpanogos rises to 11,750 feet in the center of the loop and presents sheer cliff faces and jagged ridges in every direction. More than a dozen campgrounds and several picnic areas line the way. Anglers can try for trout in swift clear streams. Autumn brings brilliant golds to the aspen and scarlets to the maples. Winter snows close the loop at its higher elevations and attract skiers to Sundance Resort. The most scenic sections of the loop lie along American Fork Canyon and its South Fork, Provo Canyon and its North Fork, and on the high pass between these drainages. A drive on U.S. 89 or I-15 completes the approximately 40-mile loop. With a few stops, a full day can easily be spent on the drive. If you'd like to see Timpanogos Cave on the way, begin the loop there to avoid waiting in ticket lines, especially on weekend afternoons.

Most of the picnic areas and campgrounds lie along American Fork Canyon at elevations of

5,400 to 6,200 feet; their season begins in early May and lasts to late October. Higher recreation areas are **Granite Flat Campground** (elev. 6,800 feet), **Altamont Group Campground** (elev. 6,600 feet), **Timpooneke Campground** (elev. 7,400 feet), **Mt. Timpanogos Campground** (elev. 6,800 feet), and **Theatre in the Pines Picnic Area** (elev. 6,800 feet). The season runs from about Memorial Day weekend to the third week in September. Nearly all the recreation areas have water and charge a $13 fee (except Timpooneke and Mt. Timpanogos Campgrounds, which charge $10). Some areas can be reserved by calling 877/444-6777. **Pleasant Grove Ranger District office,** 390 North 100 East, Pleasant Grove, UT 84062, 801/785-3563, of the Uinta National Forest has information and maps for recreation areas along the Alpine Scenic Loop and for the Lone Peak and Mount Timpanogos Wildernesses; open 8 A.M.–5 P.M. Monday–Friday (daily in summer). (You'll pass the office if taking U.S. 89 and Highway 146 between Provo/Orem and the mouth of American Fork Canyon.)

Lone Peak Wilderness

The summit of Lone Peak rises to 11,250 feet on the divide between Little Cottonwood and American Fork Canyons. Despite its closeness to Provo and Salt Lake City, the wilderness (30,088 acres) offers good opportunities for solitude. Hikers sometimes spot mountain goats. A climb to the summit is a very strenuous day hike; many people prefer taking two days. Some routes have dangerous drop-offs and require mountaineering skills. Lower elevations have fine scenery as well as easier hiking. Lake Hardy (southeast of the summit) is a popular destination. Four main trailheads provide access to the wilderness: Bells Canyon from lower Little Cottonwood Canyon to the north, Draper Ridge to the west, Alpine to the south, and Granite Flat Campground (off American Fork Canyon) to the southeast. Topo

maps for the wilderness are the 7.5-minute Lehi, Draper, Dromedary Peak, and Timpanogos Cave. Trail descriptions are given in *Wasatch Trails, Volume Two,* by Daniel Geery, and *The Hiker's Guide to Utah,* by Dave Hall. Contact the Salt Lake City Ranger District office for hiking information on the north slope, the Pleasant Grove Ranger District office for the south side.

Mount Timpanogos Wilderness

The sheer cliffs of Mount Timpanogos tower 7,000 feet above the Utah Valley and present one of the most dramatic sights of the Wasatch Range. Trails to the heights lead past waterfalls, flower-filled alpine meadows, lakes, and permanent snowfields. One trail continues to the 11,750-foot summit for superb vistas of central Utah. The climb is strenuous, especially the last three miles, but requires no special skills. You'll see whole families—from grandchildren to grandparents—on this popular mountain. Even short hikes can be very rewarding. Take care to bring storm gear in case the weather suddenly turns bad. A shelter at Emerald Lake provides a refuge from storms. Hike either the **Timpooneke Trail** from Timpooneke Campground or the **Aspen Grove Trail** from the Theatre in the Pines Picnic Area; both trailheads lie just off the Alpine Scenic Loop. One-way distances to the summit are 9.1 miles on the Timpooneke Trail (4,350-foot elevation gain) and 8.3 miles on the Aspen Grove Trail (4,900-foot elevation gain). A hike on both trails (highly recommended) can be done with a car shuttle. If a trip to the summit sounds too ambitious, stick to the 12 miles between the trailheads via Emerald Lake (elev. 10,300 feet).

The **Summit Trail** branches off west of Emerald Lake, climbs a steep slope to the jagged summit ridge, then follows the ridge southeast to the top. A large snowfield and the deep blue waters of Emerald Lake lie directly below. Chunks of ice break off the snowfield and float in the lake dur-

> *The sheer cliffs of Mount Timpanogos present one of the most dramatic sights of the Wasatch Range. Trails to the heights lead past waterfalls, flower-filled alpine meadows, lakes, and permanent snowfields. One trail continues to the 11,750-foot summit for superb vistas of central Utah.*

ing even the hottest summer days. Local people often refer to the snowfield as a glacier, but technically it's just a snowfield. Some climbers continue southeast along the summit ridge and drop down onto the snowfield and slide or walk to Emerald Lake, but this can be a bit hazardous. Hiking season is mid-July–mid-October. In winter and spring, hikers must be equipped and experienced for snow travel. Topo maps are the 7.5-minute Timpanogos Cave and Aspen Grove, though you're not likely to need them unless snow covers the trails. The Pleasant Grove Ranger District office can advise on hiking conditions.

Cascade Springs

Crystal-clear water emerges amidst lush vegetation and flows down a long series of travertine terraces at this beautiful spot. The springs produce more than seven million gallons of water daily. Boardwalks (some accessible for people with disabilities) and short trails with interpretive signs allow a close look at the stream and pools. Trout can be seen darting through the water (though fishing is prohibited). Plantlife includes maple, oak, aspen, willow, water birch, box elder, cattails, watercress, and wildflowers. The drive to Cascade Springs is also very pretty, either from the Alpine Scenic Loop or from Heber Valley. A paved road (Forest Route 114) branches off the Alpine Scenic Loop near its summit (between mileposts 18 and 19) and winds northeast seven miles to the springs. An unpaved road, passable by car if the road is dry, begins on the west edge of Heber Valley and climbs high above the valley with good views, then drops down to the springs; turn west seven miles on Highway 220 from Highway 113 (between Midway and Charleston) and follow signs.

Sundance Resort

Since actor/director Robert Redford purchased this land in 1969, he has worked toward obtaining an ideal blend of recreation, the arts, and natural beauty. Sundance sponsors a wide selection of summer arts and music events; workshops, exhibits and artist residencies provide an intense artistic focus to this remote mountain Eden. Redford also founded the **Sundance Institute** in 1980 as a laboratory for independent filmmakers; the actual Sundance Film Festival is held in Park City.

Downhill skiing begins in mid-December and lasts into April. One quad, two double chairlifts, and two triple chairs take skiers high on the southeast slopes of Mount Timpanogos. The 41 runs on 450 acres provide challenges for people of all abilities; total elevation drop is 2,150 feet. Ski instruction, rentals, accommodations, restaurants, and packages are available at the resort. On weekends, adult lift tickets cost $40 full day, $30 half day; children 12 and under ski for $22 full day, $16 half day; weekday prices are discounted around $10. **Sundance Nordic Center** offers 24 miles of Nordic track, lessons, and rentals.

Accommodations: Cottages start at $205 in summer, $235 in winter; mountain houses start at $500 in summer, $850–1,000 in winter, all per day.

Food: Sundance has three dining facilities in the main compound, including the **Foundry Grill,** which serves breakfast, lunch, and dinner Monday–Saturday and brunch on Sunday. The **Tree Room** prepares elegant dinners daily. Reservations are recommended for all dining. Contact Sundance at R.R. 3, Box A-1, Sundance, UT 84604, 801/225-4100 (recording of summer theater, events, and winter skiing), 801/225-4107, or 800/892-1600 (office). The website is www.sundanceresort.com. The resort can be easily reached by taking U.S. 189 from Provo, Orem, or Heber City, then turning northwest 2.5 miles on Highway 92 (Alpine Scenic Loop).

Squaw Peak Road

This scenic drive follows the Wasatch Range east of Provo and offers many fine views over Utah Valley. The road turns south from U.S. 189 in Lower Provo Canyon, then climbs high into the mountains. Pavement ends after five miles at the turnoff for **Hope Campground** (has water late May–mid-October; $9; elev. 6,600 feet). The road continues south eight miles to **Rock Canyon Campground** (a group area with water late May–mid-October) and on to the Left Fork of Hobble Creek east of Springville for a total of 26 miles one-way. Squaw Peak Road has some rough spots in the middle section, but cars with good clearance can usually be driven through in dry weather. The Pleasant Grove Ranger District office can advise on camping, hiking, road conditions, and Rock Canyon group reservations.

Just west of Heber City, near the eastern flanks of the Wasatch Range, the town of Midway has sprouted a number of upscale resorts.

HEBER CITY

Its setting in a lush agricultural valley surrounded by high mountains has earned Heber City the title "Switzerland of America." Many of its people work at farming, raising livestock, and dairying—as their families have done since pioneer days. A massive snowslide blocked passage of the first settlers making their way up Provo Canyon in 1859, but they simply disassembled their wagons and portaged them to the other side. The town's name honors Heber C. Kimball, a counselor to church president Brigham Young. Heber City (pop. 5,870) makes a handy stop for travelers exploring the nearby Wasatch and Uinta Ranges or visiting the large Deer Creek and Strawberry Reservoirs. It also offers reasonably priced accommodations a short drive from Park City.

Heber Valley Historic Railroad
Ride a turn-of-the-20th-century train pulled by steam locomotive #618 past Deer Creek Lake into scenic alpine Provo Canyon. The round-trip to Vivian Park and back to Heber City takes 3.5 hours; adult fare is $24, senior $21, and children $14. A 90-minute trip goes to Soldier Hollow ($16, $13, $10). The depot is at 450 South 600 West, 435/654-5601.

Midway Fish Hatchery
Visitors are welcome at this state-run trout hatchery. It's open 8 A.M.–4:30 P.M. daily, one mile south of Midway just off Highway 113 (Charleston Rd.).

Soldier Hollow
Soldier Hollow, site of the 2002 Olympic and Paralympic cross-country skiing and biathalon events, offers 31 km of trails for mountain biking, hiking, camping, snowshoeing, biathlon, and cross-country skiing. Rentals (including rifles for biathlon practitioners) are available at the lodge. Trail fees run about $5 adults, $2 youth 12–17, free for children under 12.

Soldier Hollow occupies a corner of the huge Wasatch Mountain State Park. From Heber City, head west on 100 South to Midway. Take a left on Center Street (Highway 113) in Midway and head south for 3.5 miles to Soldier Hollow. For details about events, snow conditions, etc., call 435/654-2002.

Homestead Crater
Just northwest of the town of Midway, on the grounds of the Homestead Resort, is a large volcanic-like cone called the Crater. This geological curiosity is actually composed of travertine deposited by the local hot springs; water once flowed out of the top, but it's now piped to a 65-foot-deep, 95° pool deep in the Crater's belly. The Crater is accessible for scuba diving, snorkeling, bathing, and tours; swimmers and soakers pay $10 admission, $8 for guests of the Homestead Resort. Scuba classes and guided dives are more expensive; call 435/654-1102 or 800/327-7220 for reservations, which are required for scuba.

Events
Horse shows and rodeos take place through the summer in the Heber City area. A **powwow** in June brings tribes for dances and craft sales. The **Utah High School Rodeo Finals** are also held in June. **Wasatch Fair Days** features a parade, rodeo, exhibits, livestock show, entertainment, and demolition derby in early August. **Swiss Days** are celebrated with a parade, entertainment, food, and flea market on the Friday and Saturday before Labor Day.

Recreation
The **city park** at Main and 300 South has picnic tables and a playground. **Wasatch Community Pool** has indoor swimming and racquetball at Wasatch Middle School, 200 East 800 South

(turn east from Main onto 600 South, then right on 200 East), 435/654-3450. Wasatch County High School has **tennis courts** at 600 South and 200 East.

Accommodations

Heber City motels are generally very well-maintained and reasonably priced. A few miles west, in Midway, are several more expensive and luxurious resorts.

$50–75: All of the following have pools, and most also have spas with saunas and whirlpools. Rooms at the **National Nine High Country Inn,** 1000 S. Main, 435/654-0201 or 800/345-9198, are a good deal; all come with refrigerators and microwaves. The **Danish Viking Lodge,** 989 S. Main, 435/654-2202 or 800/544-4066, has a grassy playground, guest laundry, and two two-bedroom units. **Hylander Motel,** 425 S. Main, 435/654-2150 or 800/932-0355, is clean and attractive and has one suite. The **Swiss Alps Inn,** 167 S. Main, 435/654-0722, has a playground and two suites with full kitchens (rates here jump up to nearly $100 during ski season).

$75–125: In Midway, the **Kastle Inn,** 1220 Interlaken Ln., 435/654-2689, is a massive castle-like home with six guest rooms, all with private baths and TV/VCRs.

Over $125: Undoubtedly the most unique place to stay in the Heber City area is the **Homestead Resort,** 700 N. Homestead Dr. (Midway, UT 84049), 435/654-1102 or 800/327-7220. This hot-spring resort is three miles west of town near Midway and features mineral baths, swimming, and accommodations. The natural hot-spring water is believed to be good for the skin. The spacious grounds and stately buildings of the Homestead may remind you of an age long past, but the facilities are modern.

Golfers can play at the resort's 18-hole course. Stables offer horseback and hay rides (and sleigh rides in winter) and bicycle rentals, 435/654-1102 ext. 440. Rooms should be reserved well in advance, especially for summer weekends. The resort's own **Simon's** restaurant serves dinner and Sunday brunch in an elegant country setting (reservations are recommended), and **Fanny's**

Grill offers breakfast, lunch, and dinner daily; open year-round.

Another Midway resort, the **Blue Boar Inn,** 435/654-1400 or 888/650-1400, 1235 Warm Springs Rd., is right near an entrance to Wasatch Mountain State Park and the park's popular golf course. Each of the inn's 14 meticulously decorated rooms is devoted to a different poet or author; there's also a very good restaurant and a pub on site.

Food

American-style cafés line Main Street, along with plenty of fast food to serve the skiing crowds. One particularly good place to stop is the extra-convivial **Sidetrack Cafe,** 94 S. Main, 435/654-0563. Sandwiches are good here, and H&H bagels are flown in from New York. For something a little different, try **Yodels,** 79 E. Main St. in Midway, 435/654-5370, with Swiss and American cuisine for lunch and dinner Monday–Saturday. Another good bet in Midway is **Bella Sera,** 435/657-0100, 380 E. Main, where the focus is on Italian food; at the same address, **Bella Sera Pronto** serves pizza and sandwiches. **Simon's,** out at the Homestead Resort, 435/654-1102, serves top-notch steaks, prime rib, seafood, and high-quality American cuisine. Just down the road, the restaurant at the **Blue Boar Inn,** 1235 Warm Springs Rd., 435/654-1400 or 888/650-1400, is also highly regarded. They serve traditional dinners, such as steak, pork, and pasta, with innovative sauces.

Information and Services

The **Heber Valley Chamber of Commerce** has an information center at 475 N. Main (P.O. Box 427, Heber City, UT 84032), 435/654-3666; open 9 A.M.–5 P.M. Monday–Friday (also on Saturday and Sunday June–September). **Heber Ranger District office,** 2460 S. U.S. 40 (P.O. Box 190, Heber City, UT 84032), 435/654-0470, manages the Uinta National Forest lands east and southeast of Heber City. The staff provides literature and advice on camping, hiking, horseback riding, boating, fishing, cross-country skiing, snowmobiling, and back-road travel; open 8 A.M.–5 P.M. Monday–Friday (also some

Saturdays and Sundays June–September). The **Wasatch County Library,** 188 S. Main, 435/654-1511, is open Monday–Saturday.

The **post office** is at 125 East 100 North, 435/654-0881. **Wasatch County Hospital** is at 55 South 500 East, 435/654-2500.

VICINITY OF HEBER CITY
Wasatch Mountain State Park
Utah's largest state park encompasses 22,000 acres of valleys and mountains on the east side of the Wasatch Range. An excellent 27-hole golf course in the park has a pro shop and a café. Unpaved scenic drives lead north through Pine Creek Canyon to Guardsman Pass Road (turn right for Park City or left over the pass for Brighton), northwest through Snake Creek Canyon to Pole Line Pass and American Fork Canyon, and southwest over Decker Pass to Cascade Springs. Only a short nature trail has been developed, but you can set out on your own. Winter brings snow depths of 3–6 feet mid-December–mid-March. Separate cross-country ski and snowmobile trails begin near the golf course. **Homestead Cross-Country Ski Center,** 435/654-1102, provides equipment for both sports.

The large **Pine Creek Campground,** just north of the golf course at an elevation of 5,600 feet, has showers and hookups from late April or early May to late October. A 1.5-mile **nature trail** begins near site #21 on the Oak Hollow Loop in Pine Creek Campground. The staff offers **campfire programs,** usually on Friday and Saturday evenings, at the campground's amphitheater. **Little Deer Creek Campground** is a smaller, more secluded area in an aspen forest, open with water June–mid-September. It's also open earlier and later without water—check with the park office first; groups often reserve all the sites. You can get here by driving the seven-mile unpaved road to Cascade Springs, then turning north four miles on another unpaved road. The park visitors center, just before the golf course, has an information desk open 8 A.M.–5 P.M. daily year-round; P.O. Box 10, Midway, UT 84049, 435/654-1791 or 800/322-3770 (reservations). Make golf course reservations at 435/654-0532 (local) or 435/266-0268 (Salt Lake City). There's a $17–20 fee for camping. From Heber City, drive west three miles to Midway, then follow signs north two miles.

Just east of the Wasatch Range, the area outside Heber City has many ranches.

Deer Creek State Park

The seven-mile-long Deer Creek Reservoir lies in a very pretty setting below Mount Timpanogos and other peaks of the Wasatch Range. A developed area near the lower end of the lake has a campground with showers, picnic area, paved boat ramp, dock, and fish-cleaning station; elevation is 5,400 feet. **Island Beach Area,** 4.5 miles to the northeast, has a gravel swimming beach and a marina (open in summer with a store, snack bar, boat ramp, and rentals of fishing boats, ski boats, and personal watercraft); ice fishers can park here in winter. Rainbow trout, perch, largemouth bass, and walleye swim in the lake. Good winds for sailing blow most afternoons. You'll often see a lineup of catamarans at the sailboat beach near the campground and crowds of sailboarders at the Island Beach Area. Deer Creek State Park, P.O. Box 257, Midway, UT 84049, 435/654-0171 or 800/332-3770 for reservations (advised Memorial Day–Labor Day weekends), is open mid-April–late October. Admission fee is $9 per vehicle for day use (includes Island Beach Area), $14–20 per vehicle for camping at the campground area. The campground is just off U.S. 189 11 miles southwest of Heber City and 17 miles northeast of Provo.

Deer Creek Island Resort, at the Island Beach Area, 435/654-4779, has boat rentals (fishing, ski, sport) and a snack bar in summer; a restaurant offers fine dining Friday and Saturday evenings year-round. **Snow's Marina,** on Wallsburg Bay 1.2 miles northeast of the state park campground, has a small store, snack bar, boat ramp, RV park, and fishing-boat rentals (with or without motors). Snow's is open daily May–October.

Jordanelle State Park

This large reservoir upstream on the Provo River provides recreation for boaters and anglers. It's east of U.S. 40 six miles north of Heber. There are two recreation areas. **Rock Cliff Recreation Site** is at the upper end of the east arm of the reservoir and has splendid walk-in camping sites with restrooms and hot showers, a nature center, boardwalks with in-

A nature trail at Jordanelle State Park's Rock Cliff recreation area traverses a wetland.

terpretive displays, and pavilions for day use. Admission is $9 per carload, $4 per individual for day use; walk-in tent sites cost $14. **Hailstone Recreation Site** is a camping area with 230 campsites, restrooms and showers, day-use shaded pavilions, a modern marina with 80 boat slips, a general store, a laundry, and a small restaurant; tent sites are $14, full hookups are $17. Facilities include wheelchair access with raised tent platforms. The season is April–mid-October; contact Jordanelle State Park at P.O. Box 309, Heber City, UT 84032, 435/783-3030.

Heber Valley RV Park Resort, about six miles north of Heber City, 435/654-4049, offers camping sites, hot showers, a country store, and a launderette just below the Jordanelle Reservoir dam; open year-round.

© JUDY JEWELL

CENTRAL UTAH

Historic Union Pacific Rail Trail State Park

This state park consists of a multi-use, nonmotorized trail built to accommodate hikers, bicyclists, horseback riders, and cross-country skiers. The trail runs 27 miles from Echo Reservoir to Park City with trailheads and information kiosks at Echo Reservoir, Coalville, Wanship, Star Pointe, and Park City. Other staging areas will be added as well as spurs connecting to the Mormon Pioneer Historic Trail, Rockport Lake State Park, and the Jordanelle State Park's proposed trail system. There are campgrounds near the trailheads and spurs but not on the trails. The state park office can be reached at P.O. Box 309, Heber City, UT 84032, 435/645-8036.

Strawberry Reservoir

This 17,000-acre reservoir lies on a high rolling plateau 23 miles southeast of Heber City. Creation of the original Strawberry Reservoir began in 1906 as a federal reclamation project to divert water from the Colorado Basin west to the Utah Valley. Soldier Creek Dam (constructed in 1973) greatly increased the reservoir's size. A section of lake called "The Narrows" separates Strawberry Arm on the west from the smaller Soldier Creek Arm on the east. The water at this 7,600-foot elevation is cold for water-skiing, but hardy souls in wetsuits often brave it. Fishing is good all year (through the ice in winter) for rainbow and cutthroat trout and some brook trout and kokanee salmon. Several winter parking areas along U.S. 40 provide access for cross-country skiing, snowmobiling, and ice fishing. Check with the Heber Ranger District office, 435/654-0470, for information on recreation at the reservoir and in surrounding Uinta National Forest.

The **Strawberry Visitor Center/Fish Hatchery,** 435/548-2321, not only sells maps and books but also functions as a small museum with interactive displays explaining the history of the reservoir from its construction to its present-day fish-breeding programs. A 200-yard boardwalk with interpretive stations leads to the hatchery and an information kiosk. Open 9 A.M.–5 P.M. Monday–Thursday and 9 A.M.–6 P.M. Friday–Sunday from Memorial Day through the last weekend of October.

The U.S. Forest Service maintains four campgrounds and three marinas around the lake; all are open with water late May–late October; $11 without hookups, $20 (Loop B) with.

Other Recreation Areas in the Heber Ranger District

Whiskey Springs Picnic Area is located near the mouth of Daniels Canyon, eight miles southeast of Heber City on U.S. 40; water is available in summer. Elevation is 6,400 feet; signs along the short **Whiskey Springs Nature Trail** identify plants. **Lodgepole Campground** lies in upper Daniels Canyon, 16 miles southeast of Heber City on U.S. 40. The campground is open late May–late October with water; $14. Lodgepole pine and aspen grow at the 7,800-foot elevation.

Currant Creek Recreation Complex, on the southwest shore of **Currant Creek Reservoir** (elev. 8,000 feet), has a campground (with water late May–late October; $14 fee), paved boat ramp, fish-cleaning station, and fishing access for people with disabilities. Anglers catch rainbow, cutthroat, and brook trout; ice fishing is good in winter. **Currant Creek Nature Trail** begins from Loop D of the campground and climbs 400 feet in a 1.25-mile loop; signs tell about the ecology. The best way to get here from Heber City is to drive southeast 42 miles on U.S. 40 past Strawberry Reservoir, just before **Currant Creek Lodge** (motel and café, 801/548-2226), turn northwest 19.5 miles along Currant Creek on Forest Route 083. High-clearance vehicles can take a slow, scenic route over Lake Creek Summit (elev. 9,900 feet); from Heber City, head east 31 miles on Center Street, which becomes Lake Creek/Currant Creek Road (Forest Route 083).

Mill Hollow Campground sits on the shore of small Mill Hollow Reservoir at an elevation of 8,800 feet in an Engelmann spruce forest 37 miles from Heber City. It's open with water mid-June–late October; $14. The reservoir has trout fishing. Take U.S. 189 to Francis (northeast of Heber City), then Highway 35 and Forest Route 054 (gravel).

Wolf Creek Campground is located in an Engelmann spruce forest at 9,500 feet near Wolf Creek Pass 38 miles from Heber City. The campground is open with water early July–mid-October; $9. Group sites are also available.

From Heber City, drive north and east to Francis, then head southeast about 22 miles on Highway 35 (part gravel); this scenic road continues on to Hanna and Duchesne in northeastern Utah.

South of Provo Along I-15

HOBBLE CREEK–DIAMOND FORK LOOP

Pleasant canyon and mountain views line this 34-mile scenic drive east of Springville. The road is open about mid-May–late October and is normally fine for cars—all but about the middle eight miles are paved. Along the way you'll pass picnic spots, campgrounds, hiking trailheads, and fishing holes. Back roads branch off to Squaw Peak Road, Strawberry Reservoir, and other destinations. Hikers can choose from a trail network totaling about 100 miles. Contact the **Spanish Fork Ranger District office** for maps and recreation information at 44 West 400 North, Spanish Fork, UT 84660, 435/798-3571. Open 8 A.M.–5 P.M. Monday–Friday (daily in summer). Family and group sites at some campgrounds can be reserved by calling 877/444-6777; sites cost $9–10 a night. To drive the loop from Main Street in Springville (take I-15 Exit 263), head east three miles on 400 South to the mouth of Hobble Creek Canyon and follow Forest Routes 058 and 029.

NEBO SCENIC LOOP

This mountain drive loops off I-15 and winds into the heights of the southern Wasatch Range. You'll enjoy alpine forests, fine panoramas of the valleys below, and a close look at Mount Nebo—highest peak in the range. The entire 43-mile length from Payson to Nephi is paved; it's open mid-June–late October. In winter and spring, cross-country skiers and snowmobilers come up to glide across the snow. You can begin the drive from Payson in the north (I-15 Exit 254) or Nephi in the south (take I-15 Exit 222 or 228

and go east six miles on Highway 132). A partly paved road from Santaquin (I-15 Exit 248) goes southeast 11 miles via Santaquin Canyon to connect with the main drive.

More than 100 miles of trails lead into the backcountry. **Devil's Kitchen Geologic Area** lies at the end of a quarter-mile trail, 28 miles south of Payson; eroded layers of red-tinted river gravel and silt form spires and sharp ridges. **Mount Nebo Wilderness** is west of the drive and can be reached by several trails. Strong hikers can climb the south summit (elev. 11,877 feet) by trail on a day- or overnight trip. The higher north summit (elev. 11,928 feet) is two peaks farther north along a knife-edged ridge (no trail). *The Hiker's Guide to Utah,* by Dave Hall, has hiking descriptions for Mount Nebo and Santaquin Peak.

The U.S. Forest Service maintains recreation facilities, trailheads, and overlooks along the Nebo Scenic Loop. Contact the **Spanish Fork Ranger District office** for maps and information at 44 West 400 North, Spanish Fork, UT 84660, 435/798-3571; open 8 A.M.–5 P.M. Monday–Friday (daily in summer). If you're coming from the south, you can stop at the Forest Service's **Nephi Ranger District office,** 740 S. Main, 435/623-2735, for info on the scenic loop; open 8 A.M.–5 P.M. Monday–Friday. You can reserve sites at Payson, Blackhawk, Ponderosa, and Bear Canyon by calling 877/444-6777; sites cost $9–14.

NEPHI

This small town (pop. 4,520) serves as the commercial center for the region and the seat of Juab County. The first settlers arrived in 1851 and named the place for a patriarch in the Book of Mormon. Pleasant scents fill the air at the **Nephi Rose Garden,** one block east of Main on 100 North.

Recreation and Events

Nephi's annual events are the **Ute Stampede and Rodeo** in July and the **Juab County Fair** in August. The **city park** at Main and 500 North has picnic tables, a playground, and an outdoor pool. **Canyon Hills Park Golf Course,** 1200 East 100 North, 435/623-9930 (nine holes), lies up a canyon.

Accommodations

Under $50: The **Safari Motel,** 413 S. Main, 435/623-1071, has clean, inexpensive rooms plus a pool. The **Motel 6,** 2195 S. Main, 435/623-0666, is out by freeway Exit 222.

$50–75: You can't miss the **Whitmore Mansion Bed & Breakfast,** an ornate Eastlake/Queen Anne–style structure built in 1898 at 110 S. Main, 435/623-2047 or 877/709-8073. Five rooms are decorated with period antiques, and all have private baths.

Several modern motels lie just off I-15 Exit 222, including the **Super 8,** 1901 S. Main, 435/623-0888, and **Roberta's Cove Motor Inn,** 2250 S. Main, 435/623-2629 or 800/456-6460. Closer to downtown is the **Best Western Paradise Inn,** 1025 S. Main, 435/623-0624 or 800/524-9999.

Campgrounds: There's a very pleasant campground just east of Nephi. The **Nephi-KOA Horseshoe Ranch,** five miles east of town on Highway 132, 435/623-0811, has a pool, fishing, game room, and pleasant shady sites in a rural setting.

Food

The favorite place to eat in Nephi is **J.C. Mickelson's Restaurant,** at I-15 Exit 222, with good American-style home cooking. The area's best Mexican restaurant is **Mi Rancherito Restaurant,** 390 S. Main, 435/623-4391.

Information and Services

Central Valley Medical Center is at 549 North 400 East, 435/623-1242. The **Nephi Ranger District office,** 740 S. Main (Nephi, UT 84648), 435/623-2735, of the Uinta National Forest has information on the Nebo Scenic Loop; open 8 A.M.–5 P.M. Monday–Friday. The **public library** is at 21 East 100 North, 435/623-0822.

YUBA LAKE STATE PARK

Sevier Bridge Reservoir, 26 miles south of Nephi, is 22 miles long and 11,000 acres when full; its elevation is 5,014 feet. Minerals give the lake a turquoise tint that varies with the light. There's plenty of space for both water-skiers and anglers. Sailboarders often find good wind conditions here and warmer water in springtime than at most other Utah lakes. Anglers catch yellow perch, walleye, channel catfish, and northern pike; ice fishing, mostly for yellow perch, is done January–early March. North Sandy Beach (on the main road to the campground) and East Beach (reached from Highway 28) have the best swimming, but there's also a beach at the campground.

For many years the reservoir and state park were known as Yuba Lake, despite the fact that no such thing existed! The name "Yuba" refers to the dam, begun in 1902 and originally named "U.B." Farmers who helped to build the dam received water rights from the Deseret Irrigation Company in payment for their labor; if they stopped working they lost their stock—if they kept working they had to do additional work to pay for an assessment. An old song lamented that "U.B. damned if you do and U.B. damned if you don't."

The campground (with showers), picnic area, and a paved boat ramp lie on the west shore; take I-15 Exit 202 and follow signs 4.3 miles. North Beach is off to the left 2.2 miles in; a small store here is open on summer weekends. If driving to the campground from the south, you can save eight miles by taking the I-15 frontage road (west side) from Scipio. East Beach and Painted Rocks Pictograph Site, both on the east shore, can be reached by boat or from Highway 28 (an unpaved road from North Beach provides a shortcut to Highway 28). Boaters can also use a boat ramp near Painted Rocks Pictograph Site. The park and campground stay open all year, though the campground showers close November–March. It's a good idea to reserve campsites for summer weekends. If the campground is full, ask a ranger about other areas around the lake. Admission fees are $7 per vehicle for day use, $8 per vehicle for camping at Painted Rocks (no water), $8 per vehicle in the overflow area, or $14–17 per vehicle camping at the main campground; group day-use and camp areas can also be reserved. Write P.O. Box 159, Levan, UT 84639, or call 435/758-2611 (ranger) or 800/322-3770 (reservations).

FILLMORE

In 1851, Brigham Young and the Utah Territorial Legislature designated Fillmore as the territorial capital, even before the town was established. They chose this site in the Pahvant Valley because it lay in the approximate geographic center of the territory. Their plans didn't work out, but Fillmore (pop. 2,000) has become the center of a large agricultural region and the Millard County seat. A state historical museum in the Territorial Statehouse contains a wealth of pioneer history.

The city park in front of the Territorial Statehouse has picnic tables and a playground. An indoor swimming pool is just west of the statehouse. **North Park,** 500 N. Main, offers picnicking and a tourist information booth (open in summer).

Territorial Statehouse State Park

Completed in 1855, the statehouse is Utah's oldest government building. Architect Truman O. Angell designed the three-story sandstone structure, originally planned to have four wings capped by a large Moorish dome. Only the south wing was completed, though, because antagonism between the U.S. government and the Mormons blocked the appropriation of expected federal funds. Several legislatures met here, but only the fifth session, in 1855, stayed for its full term; the sixth and eighth sessions opened here, then quickly adjourned to Salt Lake City's better-suited facilities.

Rooms are furnished to represent a typical pioneer bedroom, parlor, and kitchen. Other exhibits display clothing, tools, and Native American artifacts. Lawbreakers spent time in the jail—one of the building's many uses. Historic photos and paintings show pioneer families and leaders of the church and government in early Utah. Open 9 A.M.–5 P.M. daily (to 6 P.M. in summer season); $3 adults, $1 ages 3–15, or $5 per vehicle. Guided tours can be arranged with advance notice at no additional charge. You can visit a pair of 1880s log cabins on the grounds; one has pioneer furnishings, the other a wagon. Peek in the windows of the restored 1867 Little Rock School House nearby. The cabins and schoolhouse can be opened on request. Rose gardens surround the statehouse, which is downtown at 50 W. Capitol Avenue (behind the Millard County Courthouse), 435/743-5316. Also part of this parklike complex are the municipal swimming pool and some lovely shaded picnic spots.

Accommodations

Under $50: Several motels lie along or near the I-15 Business Loop through town. The **Fillmore Motel,** 61 N. Main, 435/743-5454, has economy rooms and three two-bedroom units. The **Best Western Paradise Inn** is at I-15 Exit 167, 435/743-6895, and has a heated pool and a good restaurant, the **Garden of Eat'n.**

$50–75: The really unique place to stay in Fillmore is **Suite Dreams,** 172 North Main, 435/743-6862, a B&B inn with wraparound porches. The inn was built as a guesthouse, so rooms are large and well-furnished; each has a private bath. Suites have hot tubs, refrigerators, and king-size beds.

Campgrounds: Open year-round, **Wagons West RV Campground,** 545 N. Main, 435/743-6188, has showers, laundry, and a store; both tents and RVs welcome. **Fillmore KOA,** one-half mile off the south end of the business loop near I-15 Exit 163, 435/743-4420, has showers, laundry, and store.

Information and Services

An **information booth** is open in summer at North Park, 500 N. Main. **Millard County Tourism,** 460 N. Main (P.O. Box 1082, Fillmore, UT 84631), 435/743-6714, provides year-round information on the county and the

CENTRAL UTAH

Paiute ATV Trail; open variable hours. The **Fillmore Ranger District office,** 390 S. Main (P.O. Box 265, Fillmore, UT 84631), 435/743-5721, of the Fishlake National Forest has information about camping, fishing, hiking, horseback riding, and back-road travel in the nearby Pahvant Range and Canyon Mountains; open 8 A.M.–5 P.M. Monday–Friday. Visit the office of the **BLM's Warm Springs and House Range Resource Areas,** 35 East 500 North (P.O. Box 778, Fillmore, UT 84631), 435/743-5123, to learn about the valleys and rugged mountains of west-central Utah; open 7:45 A.M.–4:30 P.M. Monday–Friday.

The **public library** is at 25 South 100 West, 435/743-5314. **Fillmore Community Medical Center** is at 674 S. Highway 99, 435/743-5591.

VICINITY OF FILLMORE
Pahvant Range

These mountains east of Fillmore have seven summits over 10,000 feet; Mine Camp Peak (elev. 10,222 feet) is the highest. Elk, deer, and other wildlife live here. A network of trails and forest roads leads into the high country; contact the Fillmore Ranger District office for a Fishlake National Forest map, recreation information, and group campground reservations. Turn east six miles on 200 South from downtown Fillmore to reach four picnic areas along wooded Chalk Creek. They have water in summer; free. Elevations are 5,700–6,100 feet. Anglers catch rainbow and German brown trout in the creek. **Adelaide Campground** lies along Corn Creek farther south near Kanosh; open with water late May–early October; $9. Cottonwood, piñon pine, juniper, spruce, and maple grow at the 5,500-foot elevation. From the southernmost east-west street in Kanosh, turn east five miles on a gravel road (Forest Route 106). The road continues through pretty country and descends Mud Spring Hollow to I-70. Corn Creek has fishing for rainbow and German brown trout. Two recreation areas are in the northern part of the range: **Maple Hollow Picnic Area,** on the west side, has water late May–early October (elev. 6,900 feet); take the I-15 South Holden Exit 174 and go east six miles. Box elder, maple, oak, and fir trees grow in the hollow. **Maple Grove Campground** is open with water late May–early October (elev.

Cove Fort was built as a defense during the Black Hawk War.

6,400 feet); $7. Turn west four miles on the signed paved road from U.S. 50 (near milepost 47 between Scipio and Salina). Maple, water birch, oak, piñon pine, juniper, and aspen grow in the valley; Ivie Creek has fishing for rainbow trout.

Cove Fort

In 1867, during the Black Hawk War, LDS Church president Brigham Young ordered construction of this fort to protect travelers on the overnight journey between Fillmore and Beaver. Walls of volcanic basalt 13 feet high contained 12 rooms and a cistern and enclosed an area 100 feet square. Gunports at the two entrances and along the upper walls discouraged Native Americans from ever attacking the fort. Now furnished and restored to its 1877 specifications, the fort is open daily 10 A.M.–dusk about early April–mid-October; free. The south row of rooms contains the telegraph, stagecoach, post offices, dining room, kitchen, and laundry. North rooms constitute the sleeping accommodations. Outbuildings that have been reconstructed or relocated to the site include a barn, blacksmith shop, pigpen, and cabin. An icehouse is scheduled to be constructed. A picnic area is across the street. Volunteers of the LDS Church lead informal tours and relate the fort's history. Cove Fort stands near the junction of I-15 and I-70; take I-15 Exit 135 and go southeast two miles or take I-70 Exit 1 and go northwest one mile.

BEAVER

Mormon pioneers settled near the mouth of Beaver Canyon in 1856 to farm and raise livestock. Large flocks of sheep kept a woolen mill busy. The pastoral tranquillity came to an end four years later when prospectors discovered silver and gold in the San Francisco Mountains to the west. The flood of rambunctious miners, friction with the staid Mormon community, and fear of Native American attacks caused the community to call for federal troops. The army arrived in 1872, built a fort (later named Fort Cameron), and stayed until 1882. Today, Beaver (pop. 2,300) is a handy travelers' stop just east of I-15. Main Street (the I-15 Business Loop) has a good selection of motels and

TABERNACLE HILL

Volcanic eruptions in the desert 15 miles southwest of Fillmore have covered the land with cinder cones, a tuff ring, a collapsed caldera, spatter cones, pit craters, pressure ridges, and squeeze-ups. The first eruptions occurred 12,000–24,000 years ago, when Lake Bonneville covered the region. Explosive cinder and ash eruptions built a circular ring of tuff 3,000 feet across and 200 feet or more high, which rose above the lake waters. In a second period of eruptions 11,000–12,000 years ago, molten lava filled the tuff ring and spilled out to the north, forming a seven-square-mile island of black lava in the receding lake. About two-thirds of the tuff ring survives today. When viewed from the north, it resembles the Mormon Tabernacle in Salt Lake City—hence the name Tabernacle Hill. The collapsed caldera inside is 1,000 feet across and 60 feet deep. Two spatter cones near the hill represent the last gasps of the final eruption. A lava-tube cave, most of which lies west of the caldera, can be traced (on the surface) for about a mile. Bats live in some of the cave sections. You can enter the cave where its roof has collapsed, though rockfalls commonly block the passages. Watch for Great Basin rattlesnakes when exploring the caves and other features here.

You can visit Tabernacle Hill any time of the year, but in summer try to visit early in the day. From Fillmore, go west six miles on 400 North (Highway 100) to Flowell, turn left (south) one mile, turn right two miles (pavement ends), turn left (south) 3.5 miles at the junction (the other road continues to cinder pits). Continue on the main track toward Tabernacle Hill in the distance; at a major gravel road, turn west, then immediately turn south again on a narrow dirt road—Tabernacle Hill is 2.5 miles farther. You may have to walk the last two miles, depending on road conditions. Tabernacle Hill can also be reached from Meadow, eight miles to the southeast. The BLM office in Fillmore, 435/743-5123, has maps and information helpful in exploring this and other areas of Utah's Great Basin.

restaurants. Center Street (Highway 21) goes west to Minersville State Park (fishing and boating) and the desert country of west-central Utah. An entirely different world lies just to the east on Highway 153 (200 North St.)—wooded canyons, alpine lakes, and a ski area in Utah's third-highest mountain range, the Tushars.

Historic Buildings

More than 200 historic houses of architectural interest lie scattered around town. You'll see many of them by driving along the side streets. A large stone building remaining from Fort Cameron still stands on the east edge of town across the highway from the golf course. The old **Beaver County Courthouse,** with an ornate clock tower, represents the architectural splendor of its period. Building started in 1877, and the courthouse served Beaver County from 1882 until 1975. It now houses a historical museum; drop by noon–6 P.M. Tuesday–Thursday between Memorial Day and Labor Day weekends to see pioneer portraits, historic documents, an 1892 wedding cake, other artifacts, and mineral specimens. Visit the courtroom on the top floor, then head down to the dungeonlike jail cells in the basement (check out the graffiti). The adjacent Historical Park, on Center one block east of Main, has a statue of Philo T. Farnsworth (1906–1971), the "Father of Television," who was born in a log cabin near Beaver.

Recreation and Events

City parks offer picnic tables and playgrounds at Main and Center and at 400 East and 300 North. The second park also contains the indoor **Municipal Swimming Pool,** 435/438-5066. **Tennis courts** are at the rodeo grounds on the east edge of town. Play golf at the nine-hole **Canyon Breeze Golf Course** on the east edge of town, 435/438-2601. There's good **rockhounding** in the Mineral Mountains northwest of town and in other areas to the west; a brochure that describes collecting sites is available from many local businesses.

Beaver City Birthday celebrates with historic programs on February 6. **Summer Theater** performances take place late June–late July in the Opera House Civic Center across from the old county courthouse. **Horse races** run through the summer. Beaver celebrates **Pioneer Day** on July 24 with a parade, fireworks, rodeo, horse racing, and games. The **Beaver County Fair** is held in August at the fairgrounds near Minersville to the west.

Accommodations

Under $50: A dozen motels lie along the business route through town between I-15 Exits 109 and 112. For an inexpensive room, try the **Delano Motel,** 480 N. Main, 435/438-2418 or 800/537-2165, a well-maintained older motel. The **Sleepy Lagoon Motel,** 882 S. Main, 435/438-5513, is an attractive motel with nice landscaping and a small pond.

$50–75: Best Western's **Butch Cassidy Inn,** 161 S. Main, 435/438-2438, and **Paradise Inn,** 1451 North 300 West, 435/438-2455, are both very pleasant and have pools and spas. The **Beaver Super 8,** 626 West 1400 North, 435/438-3888, and the **Days Inn,** 645 N. Main, 435/438-2409, are both new and comfortable.

Campgrounds: At the north edge of town, **Beaver KOA** has showers, store, laundry, and pool (take I-15 Exit 112, go south 0.6 mile on the business loop, then turn left on Manderfield Rd.), 435/438-2924; open February–November. **Beaver Canyon Campground,** on the east side of town at 1419 E. Canyon Road (200 North), 435/438-5654, has showers, laundry, and a Mexican restaurant (open daily for dinner); open May–October. **United Beaver Camperland** offers showers, store, laundry, and pool at the south edge of town (near I-15 Exit 109), 435/438-2808; open year-round. **Minersville State Park** has a campground 14 miles west on Highway 21. The Tushar Mountains have good camping, too (see the Tushar Mountains section).

Food

You'll find good old-fashioned American food at **Arshel's Cafe,** 711 N. Main, 435/438-2977. A fixture in Beaver since the 1930s, this is the kind of diner where you ought to save room for homemade pie after your meal. Also good for standard American food is the **Garden of Eat'n**

Restaurant, at Paradise Inn, 435/438-2455, on the north edge of town.

Information, Services, and Transportation

Foresters at the **Beaver Ranger District office,** 575 S. Main (P.O. Box E, Beaver, UT 84713), 435/438-2436, provide information on camping, fishing, hiking, and road conditions in the forest lands of the Tushar Mountains to the east; open 8 A.M.–5 P.M. Monday–Friday. The **Beaver County Visitor Information Center,** P.O. Box 272, Beaver, UT 84713, 435/438-2975, can tell you more about sights and services in the area.

The **public library** is located at 55 W. Center, 435/438-5274. The **post office** is at 20 S. Main, 435/438-2321. **Beaver Valley Hospital** provides medical care at 85 North 400 East, 435/438-2531.

The **Greyhound Bus** stops at El Bambi Cafe, 935 N. Main, 435/438-2229.

THE TUSHAR MOUNTAINS

Although higher than the Wasatch Range, the Tushars remain relatively unknown and uncrowded. Travelers on surrounding highways get glimpses of their rocky summits, but people who hurry by rarely appreciate their size and height. Delano Peak (elev. 12,169 feet) crowns the Tushars and is the highest point in central Utah. From Beaver, Highway 153 (200 North Street) winds into the alpine country of the Fishlake National Forest to a ski area, campgrounds, fishing spots, and hiking trails. (The first 19 miles are paved, followed by 21 miles of dirt.) The road takes you through meadows and forests before making a steep descent to the town of Junction on U.S. 89. Forest Route 137 branches off Highway 153 10 miles from Beaver to Kents Lake, Anderson Meadow, and other pretty areas, then returns to the highway to complete a scenic loop (54 miles round-trip from Beaver). Drivers with high-clearance vehicles can journey amidst the summits on the Kimberly/Big John Road Backway between Highway 153 and the Kimberly Scenic Drive; much of this trip goes above timberline with spectacular views of peaks above

and canyons below. For recreation information and road conditions, visit the Beaver Ranger District office at the corner of 200 North and 100 East in Beaver, 435/438-2436.

Camping and Picnicking

Camping fees at the following campgrounds range $9–14. From Beaver, the first campground and picnic area reached is **Little Cottonwood,** six miles east on Highway 153. Sites are open with water late May–early September; elevation is 6,500 feet. **Ponderosa Picnic Area** (elev. 7,000 feet) is 2.5 miles farther up Beaver Canyon on Highway 153 in a grove of ponderosa pine; it has water in summer. Little Cottonwood and Ponderosa lie along the rushing Beaver River, which has trout fishing. **Mahogany Cove Campground** overlooks Beaver Canyon 12 miles east of town on Highway 153; open with water late May–early October. Its name comes from the abundant curl-leaf mountain mahogany; other trees at the 7,500-foot elevation include ponderosa pine, Gambel oak, juniper, and cottonwood. **Puffer Lake,** 21 miles from town on Highway 153, is set among forested hills of spruce, fir, and aspen at 9,700 feet. The lake, privately owned by **Puffer Lake Resort** on the other side of the highway, 435/864-2751, has trout fishing, primitive camping, and a primitive boat ramp. The resort offers boat rentals, a small store, and cabins during warmer months.

To reach additional campgrounds or to drive the scenic loop, turn southeast on Forest Route 137 at a junction 10 miles east of town (near milepost 10 on Highway 153). The first eight miles are on a good gravel road (to Anderson Meadow), then there are seven miles of dirt road to Highway 153; the last half is passable when dry by cars with good clearance, but it can be too rough for RVs. **Little Reservoir Campground** is less than a mile in on Forest Route 137; sites are in a ponderosa pine forest at 7,350 feet. It's open with water late May–early October. The reservoir here covers only three acres but often has good trout fishing. **Kents Lake Campground** overlooks Kents Lake five miles in on Forest Route 137. Sites are in a forest of spruce, fir, and aspen at 8,800 feet; open with water mid-June–early October. The 100-acre lake offers trout fishing. **Tushar Lakeside Campground** is a county-managed group area below Kents Lake, 435/438-2975. **Anderson Meadow Campground** lies in high forests and meadows overlooking Anderson Meadow Reservoir at 9,500 feet, eight miles in on Forest Route 137. It's open with water mid-June–early October. The reservoir has trout fishing. **La Baron Reservoir** is another popular fishing spot four miles farther (12 miles in on Forest Route 137), but it has only primitive camping; its elevation is 9,900 feet. Three miles farther you'll return to Highway 153; turn right for City Creek Campground and the town of Junction, left for Puffer Lake, Elk Meadows Resort, and Beaver.

The gravel and dirt section of Highway 153 from the town of Junction on U.S. 89 makes a relentless five-mile climb from the valley to the mountains—you'll need to use low gears going up and have good brakes coming down. This drive isn't recommended for trailers or RVs. The east side of Highway 153 is open late June until sometime in October. **City Creek Campground** is near the bottom of the grade; from the turnoff five miles northwest of Junction, follow a side road in for one mile. Sites lie along City Creek in a diverse forest of cottonwood, aspen, ponderosa pine, piñon pine, Gambel oak, and juniper at an elevation of 7,600 feet. Open with water from Memorial Day weekend to Labor Day weekend; free.

Hiking

Relatively few hikers have discovered this area, but good trails for hiking and horseback riding lead into the high country. Contact the Beaver Ranger District office in Beaver for details. Three peaks of the Tushars rise above 12,000 feet and make good climbing destinations—Delano Peak (elev. 12,169 feet), Mount Belknap (12,139 feet), and Mount Baldy (12,082 feet). Each involves an ascent of about 2,000 feet and can be reached on a day hike. (Strong hikers have climbed all

three in one day!) Delano can be climbed by a route up its southwest slope, Belknap by a trail up its southeast side, and Baldy by a route from Blue Lake up its southeast side. (All three trails are reached from the Big John Flat Road, which turns north from Highway 153 between mileposts 16 and 17.) When dry, the dirt road is often okay for cars. Other climbing routes are possible, too. Hikers can reach the top of Delano Peak in just an hour via the southwest route; follow the Big John Flat Road past Big John Flat and park at the pullout between Griffith and Poison Creeks, 5.6 miles north of Highway 153. The hike begins at an old jeep track marked by a sign saying it's closed to vehicles; follow the jeep tracks, then just head up the grassy slope to the summit. You're likely to see deer, hawks, and summer wildflowers on any hike in the area. Topo maps for the peaks are the 15-minute Delano Peak or the 7.5-minute Delano Peak, Mt. Brigham, Mt. Belknap, and Shelly Baldy Peak maps.

Elk Meadows Ski and Summer Resort

The resort offers skiing and year-round accommodations in the Tushars 18 miles east of Beaver. Ski season normally begins on Thanksgiving and lasts to mid-April. The ski area has 36 runs up to 2.5 miles long and with a vertical drop of 1,400 feet; 20 percent of the runs are rated beginner, 50 percent intermediate, and 30 percent advanced. Three double chairs, one triple chair, a Poma, and a T-bar serve the slopes. Lift tickets cost $37 adults all day, $25 morning or afternoon, $20 seniors or children all day, $12 half day.

Free shuttle buses serve the ski area. The resort offers a ski school, rentals, races, several restaurants, and condominium-style accommodations. Lodging costs run $80–300 depending on room, day of week, and season. Contact Elk Meadows Resort at P.O. Box 511, Beaver, UT 84713, 435/438-5433 or 888/881-SNOW. The website is www.elkmeadows.com.

South of Provo Along U.S. 89

SKYLINE DRIVE

This scenic back road, nearly all of which is unpaved, follows the crest of the Wasatch Plateau for about 100 miles between U.S. 6 in the north and I-70 in the south. Few people travel the entire length, however, preferring to do shorter sections reached from the many access roads. Much of the drive lies above 10,000 feet in vast meadows and alpine forests; above Ferron Reservoir, you'll reach the drive's summit at High Top (elev. 10,897 feet). Major attractions include sweeping vistas, fishing, hiking, horseback riding, and winter sports.

Probably the four most popular recreation areas on the plateau are **Scofield State Park, Huntington Canyon (Highway 31), Joes Valley Reservoir,** and **Ferron Reservoir.** Cars can normally reach Skyline Drive from these places when the roads are dry. The easiest access to the drive is paved Highway 31 between Fairview on the west and Huntington on the east; the road is kept clear in winter so that cross-country skiers, snowmobilers, and ice fishers can reach the plateau. Other roads may be too rough for low-clearance vehicles and even occasionally closed to all traffic; it's best to check with the Forest Service offices when planning a trip. A snowbank on Skyline Drive near Jet Fox Reservoir (east of Manti) often blocks traffic until middle or late July. The rest of the drive can usually be traveled mid-June to middle or late October. The drive may not be signed at either end; the north end is off U.S. 6 at a highway rest area near Tucker (between mileposts 203 and 204); the south end is reached from I-70 Ranch Exit 71. You'll need the Manti–La Sal forest map (Sanpete, Ferron, and Price Ranger Districts) and, for the southern end, the Fishlake Forest map. Nearly the entire drive is in the Manti–La Sal National Forest. Get recreation information and road conditions from the **supervisor's office** at 599 W. Price River Dr., Price, UT 84502, 435/637-2817. District offices are **Price Ranger District office** (same address and phone as the supervisor's office) for the northeastern part of the Wasatch

Plateau; **Ferron Ranger District office,** P.O. Box 310, Ferron, UT 84523, 435/384-2372, for the southeastern part of the plateau; and **Sanpete Ranger District office,** 540 N. Main, Ephraim, UT 84627, 435/283-4151, for the western half of the plateau.

FAIRVIEW

Mormon farmers settled on the grasslands of the upper San Pitch (or Sanpete) River Valley in 1859, giving their community its original name of North Bend. Many pioneer buildings can still be seen in town. The unusual Fairview Museum of History and Art is worth a visit. Fairview (pop. 1,640) lies 42 miles south of Provo on U.S. 89; turn east on Highway 31 to reach the alpine lands of the Wasatch Plateau.

Fairview Museum of History and Art

Many of the varied exhibits show a sense of humor. You'll see stern-faced pioneer portraits, furniture, clothing, tools, telegraph and telephone equipment, mounted wildlife, Native American crafts, geology displays, and artwork. Noted Utah sculptor Dr. Avard Fairbanks donated much of the art including *Love and Devotion,* which depicts Peter and Celestia Peterson, Fairview residents who were married for 82 years. A large threshing machine and other antique farm equipment are outside. The museum is open 10 A.M.–6 P.M. Monday–Saturday and 1–6 P.M. Sunday mid-May–mid-October; free. It's located in a former elementary school (built in 1900) at 85 North 100 East; from U.S. 89, turn east one block on 100 North, 435/427-9216.

Accommodations and Food

Under $50: Stay at the **Skyline Motel,** 236 N. State, 435/427-3312, with basic and clean rooms. Across the street is the town's sole eatery.

San Pitch Mountains

This small range rises northwest of Ephraim. **Maple Canyon Campground** (elev. 6,800 feet)

on the east side has pretty scenery but no water (or fee). You can hike from the campground up **Maple Canyon Trail** along the middle fork or up **Left Fork Maple Canyon Trail.** The trails can be done as a loop using a section of forest road. Maple Canyon is 3.75 miles west of Freedom. **Chicken Creek Campground** (elev. 6,200 feet) is on the west side of the range; open early May–early October with water and a $7 fee. Head east four miles from Levan. A rougher forest road continues southeast past the campground and over to Wales, four miles south of Freedom. Although the San Pitch Mountains lie within the Uinta National Forest, they are administered by the Manti–La Sal National Forest; visit the Sanpete Ranger District office in Ephraim for information. See the Fishlake National Forest map for ways to reach the campgrounds.

EPHRAIM

The first settlers arrived in 1854 and named this place after a tribe mentioned in the Book of Mormon. A fort guarded against Native American attacks during the first six years. Pioneer structures that date back more than a century can be seen on Ephraim's side streets. Turkey-raising is big business here and in nearby towns.

Ephraim (pop. 4,490) celebrates the **Scandinavian Festival** in May (Memorial Day weekend) with historic town tours, pioneer demonstrations, craft sales, and a fun run.

Snow College

One of the nation's leading junior colleges, Snow College began in 1888 as a Mormon academy. Today it's a state school with about 2,100 students and 75 faculty members. You're welcome to attend plays, concerts, and lecture series on campus; call 435/283-4021, ext. 616 (public relations), for cultural events and general information. Many sports facilities at the Activity Center, 300 East and Center, 435/283-7000, are open to the public, too, including an indoor pool, track, basketball, racquetball, tennis, and fitness center. The Badgers football team won the junior college national championships in 1985; call the Activity Center for schedules of their games and other sporting events. Union Building has a snack bar and bookstore at 100 East and Center. The library is at 250 E. Center, 435/283-4021, ext. 364. For more information about Snow College, visit or write the Administration Building at 150 E. College Avenue, Ephraim, UT 84627.

Accommodations

Under $50: For inexpensive, no-fuss rooms, stay at **Iron Horse Motel,** 670 N. Main, 435/283-4223, or **Travel Inn Motel,** 330 N. Main, 435/283-4070, which has its own restaurant.

$50–75: Ephraim Homestead Bed & Breakfast has an 1860s log cabin and two cozy rooms with shared bath in an upstairs barn. This old homestead, which was a typical Mormon farm, sits on half an acre of gardens at 135 West 100 North, 435/283-6367. Another landmark pioneer home turned B&B is the **W. Pherson House B&B,** 244 S. Main St., 435/283-8286 or 800/944-4197. Built in 1895, it was the home of one of the town's early bankers.

Campgrounds: Turn east 8.5 miles on 4th South for **Lake Hill Campground** (elev. 8,400 feet), open with water mid-June–mid-September; $11. Beyond Lake Hill Campground lie other areas of the Wasatch Plateau—the road continues to Skyline Drive.

Information and Services

The **post office** is at 45 East 100 North, 435/283-4189. **Ephraim Medical Clinic** is at 9 East 100 North, 435/283-4076. **Sanpete Ranger District office,** 540 N. Main, Ephraim, UT 84627, 435/283-4151, has recreation and road information for the western half of the Wasatch Plateau and for the San Pitch Mountains; open 8 A.M.–noon and 12:30–4:30 P.M. Monday–Friday.

MANTI

This town (pop. 2,640) dates from November 1849 and is one of the oldest in Utah. Brigham Young named it for a place mentioned in the Book of Mormon. An estimated 100 buildings built before 1880 can be seen on the side streets;

Manti possesses some of the state's most splendid pioneer-era architecture. Manti is the Sanpete County seat.

The **Mormon Miracle Pageant** in July portrays the history of the Book of Mormon and of the pioneers and early church leaders. The very popular production takes place at night on Temple Hill; a large cast provides lots of action. **Sanpete County Fair** is held in August. A **city park** at 300 West 200 North, 435/835-4961, has picnic tables, playground, and an outdoor pool.

Manti Temple

This temple, on a small hill, has a commanding position over the town. Brigham Young dedicated the site in April 1877, just three months before his death. Workers labored 11 years to complete construction, using locally quarried blocks of oolitic limestone. The temple architecture combines several 19th-century styles in a rectangular plan similar to the first Mormon temples in the Midwest.

Accommodations

Under $50: The town's best motel is **Manti Country Village,** 145 N. Main, 435/835-7666 or 800/452-0787, which has its own restaurant, a commodity in curiously short supply in the Sanpete Valley.

$50–75: Given the town's wealth of period architecture, it's no wonder that the best places to stay are historic B&Bs. **Manti House Inn,** 401 N. Main, 435/835-0161 or 800/284-4006, provides bed-and-breakfast accommodations in an 1880 pioneer house; workers who built the temple stayed here in the 1880s. The **Yardley Inn,** 190 West 200 South, 435/835-1861 or 800/858-6634, is a turn-of-the-20th-century English-style home. All five rooms and one suite have private baths; two rooms have fireplaces. **Cedar Crest Inn** is in a rural mountain setting on the left about one mile before Palisade State Park, south of town, 435/835-6352, and offers seven bed-and-breakfast guest rooms and an elegant restau-

The town of Manti dates from November 1849 and is one of the oldest in Utah. An estimated 100 buildings built before 1880 can be seen on the side streets; Manti possesses some of the state's most splendid pioneer-era architecture.

rant for guests (closed Sunday). If you prefer a modern B&B, try the **Legacy Inn,** 337 North 100 East, 435/835-8352, a new Victorian-style house. There are four guest rooms (two with private baths) and a family suite.

Campgrounds: In the Manti–La Sal National Forest, **Manti Community Campground,** seven miles east on 500 South/Manti Canyon Rd., is open with water early June–early October and has a trout fishing pond (elev. 7,400 feet). Fee is $8. The road continues nine miles to Skyline Drive.

Information and Services

The **post office** is at 140 N. Main, 435/835-5081. **Manti Medical Clinic** is at 159 N. Main, 435/835-3344. Manti's **public library** is downtown at 2 S. Main, 435/835-2201.

VICINITY OF MANTI
Palisade State Park

People have been enjoying themselves at 70-acre Palisade Lake since 1873. A pleasure resort here once featured a dance hall and a steam excursion boat. Now a state park, the lake lies six miles south of Manti, then two miles east. Only nonmotorized craft may be used. Canoeing and sailboarding are popular here. Canoes can be rented at the park. Anglers catch rainbow and cutthroat trout. The swimming beach and fishing conditions are best early in the season, before the water level drops. Cottonwoods shade the picnic area and campground. The campground is open with showers early April–late October. Restrooms close in winter, but self-contained campers can still stay here. Admission fees are $5 per vehicle for day use, $14 per vehicle for camping. Contact the park at P.O. Box H, Manti, UT 84642, 435/835-7275 (ranger) or 800/322-3770 (reservations). Campground reservations are a good idea on summer weekends.

M

CENTRAL UTAH

The nine-hole **Palisade Golf Course,** just beyond the state park entrance, 435/835-4653, has a clubhouse, pro shop, and driving range.

Gunnison Reservoir, three miles west of the state park, has good water-skiing and fishing for bass and perch; there are no developed facilities here, though people use the shore to launch boats (the west shore is best)—ask directions in Manti. **Nine Mile Reservoir** has a fine reputation for rainbow and other trout; the small lake is west of U.S. 89 and two miles south of Sterling.

Gunnison

The name honors Captain John Gunnison, an Army surveyor killed by Native Americans in 1853 near Sevier Lake. Gunnison (pop. 2,100) is an agricultural center with two motels, a campground, and several places to eat. An information booth is open in summer in the park on North Main.

Accommodations

$50–75: The lodging options at **Palisade Lodge,** 4.5 miles south of Manti, 435/835-5413, range from budget to deluxe. Recreation facilities include a pool, water slide, racquetball court, weight room, spas, and sauna.

SALINA

Salina (pronounced suh-LINE-uh by locals) is a Spanish word for "salt mine," one of which is found nearby. The first pioneers arrived in 1863, but Native American conflicts forced them to evacuate the site from 1866 to 1872. Today, Salina is a handy travelers' stop, strategically located at the junction of U.S. 89 and I-70. You'll find more than half a dozen motels and places to eat downtown and near the I-70 interchange.

Accommodations

Under $50: Downtown, **Henry's Hideway,** 60 N. State St., 435/529-7467 or 800/354-6468, is a nicely maintained motor court with pool.

$50–75: The **Victorian Inn B&B,** 190 W. Main St., 435/529-7342 or 800/972-7183, is a refurbished Victorian mansion with wonderful moldings and stained glass. There are three guest rooms, all with private baths. Out by the freeway exit is **Shaheen's Best Western Motel,** 1225 S. State St., 435/529-7455 or 800/528-1234, with a small pool, guest laundry, and coffee shop. Another good stop is the **Scenic Hills Budget Host Inn,** 75 East 1500 South, 435/529-7483 or 800/283-4678, with a 24-hour Denny's restaurant adjacent.

Campgrounds: Butch Cassidy Campground, 1100 S. State, between I-70 Exit 54 and downtown, 435/529-7400, offers sites for tents and RVs with showers, store, and laundry. **Salina Creek R.V. Camp,** behind the Texaco Station at 1385 S. State (near I-70 Exit 54), 435/529-3711, costs $18 with hookups; it has showers, store, and laundry.

Food

There are a number of restaurants at the freeway exit, but for a more unique experience, drive downtown to **Moms Café,** 10 E. Main St., 435/529-3921, with good home cooking in a vintage storefront.

Information and Services

Salina Medical Clinic is at 310 W. Main, 435/529-7411. The **public library,** at 90 W. Main, 435/529-7753, is open 1:30–6 P.M. Monday–Friday and noon–2 P.M. Saturday. The **city pool** is behind the library.

Vicinity of Salina

The **Redmond Clay and Salt Company** operates an open-pit salt mine three miles north of Redmond; you're welcome to watch the operations from an overlook that is open Monday–Friday 8 A.M.–4:30 P.M. For more information, contact the mine office at 6005 North 100 West, 435/529-7402. Watch for the company's "Real Salt" brand salt in local gift shops and stores.

From I-70 east of Salina, you can turn north on back roads to Skyline Drive and the Wasatch Plateau or head south into the alpine country of the Fish Lake Mountains. The small **Gooseberry Campground** lies along Gooseberry Creek in an aspen forest of the Fish Lake Mountains; elevation is 7,800 feet. Open with water late

May–early November; free. Take I-70 Gooseberry Road Exit 61 and go south 10 miles (six miles of pavement, then four miles of gravel). Snowmobiling is popular in this area during winter. The road continues south, climbing steadily through forests and meadows to **Niotche–Lost Creek Divide** (elev. 10,320 feet) in another 10 miles, then winds down to Johnson Valley Reservoir, where pavement continues to Fish Lake.

RICHFIELD

The seat of Sevier County and the center of a large agricultural region, Richfield (pop. 6,800) has a dozen motels, a good selection of restaurants, and other services for travelers; most are along the I-70 business route. This is by far the best-equipped town for travelers for some hundreds of miles.

See some local history in the museum exhibits inside the **Ralph Ramsey House,** 57 East 200 North (behind the courthouse); hours vary, so call 435/896-6439 (city offices) to schedule a visit. The stuccoed-adobe structure dates from 1873–1874. Before settling in Richfield, Ralph Ramsey carved the original eagle for the famous gate beside Brigham Young's residence in Salt Lake City.

Events

Sevier County Fair in August presents entertainment, livestock shows, 4-H exhibits, and a demolition derby. September is a busy month with the **Rocky Mountain ATV Jamboree,** the **Fishlake Mountain Bike Festival,** the **Fall Festival of the Arts,** and the **Gathering of the Clans,** which features highland games and activities.

Recreation

The **city park** at Main and 300 North (where U.S. 89 makes a bend) has covered picnic tables, playground, and an information booth (open in summer). An indoor/outdoor **swimming pool** sits at 600 West 500 North, 435/896-8572. **K-C Waterslide,** 995 South 100 East, 435/896-5334, offers another way to get wet in summer. **Cove View Municipal Golf Course** has nine holes on the southwest edge of town (take S. Airport Rd. from S. Main), 435/896-9987.

Accommodations

$50–75: Almost all of Richfield's motels string along S. Main Street. **Budget Host Knights Inn,** 69 S. Main, 435/896-8228 or 800/525-9024, has some kitchen units, and small pets are okay. **Best Western Appletree Inn,** 145 S. Main St., 435/896-5481 or 800/528-1234, offers large rooms, including five two-bedroom units that can sleep up to eight. **Quality Inn,** 540 S. Main St., 435/896-5465, has some kitchen units, an exercise room, and a free breakfast voucher for an adjoining restaurant. The **Days Inn,** 333 N. Main, 435/896-6476 or 888/275-8513, and the **Super 8,** 1575 N. Main, 435/896-9204, are both north of town. Each of the above listings has a pool.

Campgrounds: Open year-round, **J.R. Munchies RV Park,** 745 S. Main, 435/896-9340, charges $11 for RVs without hookups, $16 with, and has a store, showers, and laundry. **Richfield KOA,** 600 South 600 West, 435/896-6674, is also open all year with spaces for tents and RVs; $17 without hookups, $21 with. The KOA has a pool, store, showers, and laundry.

Food

The steak house restaurant at the **Days Inn,** 333 N. Main, 435/896-6476, is one of the best in town. The **Little Wonder Café,** 101 North Main St., 435/896-8960, is the place to go for old-fashioned breakfasts and home-style meals. **Pepperbellys Restaurant,** 680 S. Main St., 435/896-2097, is a lively Mexican-style restaurant with a '50s-theme dining room.

Information and Services

For travel info, visit the **information booth** in an 1888 former hardware store moved to the city park at Main and 400 North (open 10 A.M.–7 P.M. Monday–Saturday in summer) or contact the **Sevier County Travel Council,** 250 N. Main (Richfield, UT 84701), 435/893-0457 or 800/662-8898; open year-round 9 A.M.–5 P.M. Monday–Friday. The **Richfield Ranger District office** of the Fishlake National Forest has recreation and road information for the mountain country south and east of town and sells maps and books; the **supervisor's office** has general information on the entire forest. Both offices are open 8 A.M.–5 P.M. Monday–Friday at 115 East 900 North (Richfield, UT 84701), 435/896-9233. The **BLM District office,** across the street from the USFS offices at 150 East 900 North (Richfield, UT 84701), can give you information about recreation areas controlled by the BLM for much of this part of Utah; open 7:45 A.M.–4:30 P.M. Monday–Friday. The **public library** is open Monday–Saturday afternoons and evenings in a Carnegie building (built in 1913–1914) at 83 E. Center, 435/896-5169.

The **post office** is at 93 N. Main, 435/896-6231. **Sevier Valley Hospital** is at 1100 N. Main, 435/896-8271.

VICINITY OF RICHFIELD
Paiute All-Terrain Vehicle Trail
ATVers enjoy this 200-mile scenic loop trail and its many side trips in the scenic Pahvant Range, the Tushar Mountains, and the Monroe Mountains surrounding Richfield. Trail users travel among cool mountains, rugged canyons, and desert country. The trail is multi-use and can be enjoyed by mountain bikers, hikers, horseback riders, and even those with four-wheel-drive automobiles. Not all of the trail is suitable for each mode of travel; some parts are rough, others are narrow. Obtain up-to-date information before starting. Access points include Beaver, Richfield, Fillmore, Fremont Indian State Park, Kanosh, Piute State Park, Marysvale, and Circleville—and more access points are planned. Information and a brochure are available from the Fishlake National Forest office (see Information and Services under Richfield) and local tourist and state park offices. Information kiosks are also being built at the access points. **Millard County Tourism** also offers travel info on the entire trail; open 9 A.M.–5 P.M. Monday–Friday at 460 N. Main in Fillmore, UT 84631, 435/743-6714.

Monrovian Park
A paved road leads southeast from Monroe into this park in a pretty canyon. Cottonwoods and Gambel oaks shade picnic areas along gurgling Monroe Creek. Drinking water is available in summer. Four trails from the park area wind up onto the high Sevier Plateau above. Most spectacular is the trail that goes up Monroe Creek from the picnic areas, then follows Third Left Hand Fork to Scrub Flat Trail (six miles one-way); you'll have to do some wading. A narrow unpaved road with steep grades also climbs into the mountains. The Richfield Ranger District office in Richfield has detailed information about exploring this area. To reach the park, head south on Main Street in Monroe and follow signs four miles.

FREMONT INDIAN STATE PARK
The prehistoric Fremont people had lived over much of Utah, but archaeologists weren't aware of this group's identity until 1931. Artifacts discovered along the Fremont River in central Utah indicated that the Fremont was a distinct culture. The largest excavated site was discovered in Clear Creek Canyon during construction of I-70 in 1983. The Five Finger Ridge Village site probably had more than 150 occupants at its peak, around A.D. 1100; more people lived nearby in the canyon. The Fremont farmed in the canyon bottom and sought game and wild plant foods. They lived in pit houses and stored surplus food in carefully constructed granaries. More than 500 rock-art panels in the canyon depict the religious and hunting aspects of Fremont life in a cryptic form. Nothing remains at the village site, located across the canyon; workers constructing I-70 cut most of the ridge away to use as fill after the scientific excavations had been completed. Only an experienced eye can spot pithouse villages after nearly 1,000 years of weathering, so there was little to see at this village site anyway.

Visitors Center
The park's visitors center, dedicated in 1987, has excellent displays of artifacts found during ex-

cavations. Many aspects of Fremont life remain a mystery, but exhibits present ideas of how they could have lived here. Children can use a Fremont mano and metate to grind corn. A 16-minute video program introduces the Fremont, their foods, events that may have caused their departure, and the excavation of Five Finger Ridge Village. The exhibit area also has short video programs on the Fremont. Models illustrate pit-house construction and how Five Finger Ridge Village may have looked. A full-size replica of a pit house includes audio explanations of the functions of the dwelling.

Three loop trails begin outside the visitors center. Pick up a pamphlet inside for the Show Me Rock Art and Discovery Trails; keyed to numbered stops, the pamphlets provide more insight into Fremont life, partly by using Hopi legends. **Show Me Rock Art Trail** (200 yards) leads past fine petroglyphs; the trail is level and graded and can be used by people with strollers or wheelchairs. **Discovery Trail** (200 yards) goes to more rock art and climbs a short way above the visitors center. **Canyon Overlook Trail** (1,000 feet) ascends about 500 feet above the visitors center for fine views of the canyon and surrounding mountains; this starts as a nature trail but continues another mile. Park staff can tell you of 10 other trails and rock-art sites in the area, too. New trails are currently under construction, and all park trails allow mountain-bike travel. Volunteers and rangers lead walks in summer.

You can purchase related books, maps, rock-art posters, petroglyph replicas, Native American crafts, T-shirts, and postcards in the center. Video programs are shown on request. Park staff will take groups to other sites in the canyon; call or write at least a week in advance to 15500 Clear Creek Canyon Rd., Sevier, UT 84766, 435/527-4631. Open daily 9 A.M.–6 P.M. in summer and daily 9 A.M.–5 P.M. the rest of the year; closed on winter holidays; $5 per vehicle. The park is near I-70 Exit 17 in Clear Creek Canyon, five miles west of U.S. 89 and 16 miles east of I-15. Two picnic areas are on the frontage road east of the visitors center. You can camp at Castle Rock Camp-

ground. A short scenic drive follows the old highway nine miles through Clear Creek Canyon between the visitors center and I-70 Ranch Exit 8.

VICINITY OF FREMONT INDIAN STATE PARK
Castle Rock Campground

Clear Creek cut its canyon through tuff—a soft rock formed of hot volcanic ash from eruptions in the Tushar Mountains area. Erosion has carved towering buttresses and narrow canyons at Castle Rock, just off the main canyon. Campsites lie in a cottonwood and oak forest beside Joe Lott Creek. The campground is open with drinking water during the warmer months; $11. Register at the state park visitors center. Take I-70 Fremont Indian State Park Exit 17, turn onto the south frontage road, and follow it 1.3 miles.

Kimberly Scenic Drive

This unpaved 16-mile road climbs to about 10,000 feet on the north slopes of the Tushar Mountains. You'll enjoy good views and cool forests of aspen and fir. Old Kimberly, a ghost-town site and once the center of the Gold Mountain Mining District, is reached about halfway. Miners started the town in 1888. Gold production peaked around the turn of the century, then dropped off after 1907; production has been only sporadic since. Little remains of the town, but you'll see mine shafts, tailings, mill ruins, and foundations. Prospectors haven't given up hope—more recent mining equipment can be seen along the road, too. Cars with good clearance can usually negotiate the road if it's dry; ask locally or check at the Beaver Ranger District office of the Fishlake National Forest, corner of 190 North and 100 East in Beaver, 435/438-2436. Take I-70 Exit 17, turn west on the north frontage road and follow it under I-70; the drive ends at Marysvale on U.S. 89. Kimberly Scenic Drive connects with the Kimberly/Big John Road Backway (Forest Route 123) above Marysvale and winds through the alpine forests, rocky slopes, and meadows of

CENTRAL UTAH

the Tushar Mountains to Highway 153 (high-clearance vehicles recommended). See the Fishlake National Forest map.

Big Rock Candy Mountain

This multicolored mountain, made famous in a song by Burl Ives, rises above the Sevier River. Cold mineral springs high on the mountainside are claimed to be very healthful and a cure for many ailments. The water, usually diluted before drinking, has a slight lemonade tang but no scent.

JUNCTION

This tiny village (pop. 138) near the confluence of the south and east forks of the Sevier River is the Piute County seat. The entire county contains only 1,329 inhabitants. It's one of the smallest and most mountainous in the state, but local people say that if all the mountains were ironed out, the county would be one of Utah's largest! The outlaw Butch Cassidy grew up in this country and learned his first lawless ways here by altering cattle brands. The rustic cabin the Cassidys once called home still stands 2.5 miles south of Circleville (between mileposts 156 and 157 on U.S. 89). The bright red county courthouse dates from 1902–1903; drop in on weekdays for tourist information.

The **"biggest little rodeo in the world"** is held in July in Marysvale. The **Piute County Fair** takes place in August.

Accommodations

Under $50: This isn't a fancy place, but the **Junction Motel** is on the south edge of town, 435/577-2629, with basic rooms. Two rooms have sitting rooms and fireplaces, and sleep up to six people. The motel is open April–late November.

Campgrounds: Fat's Country Cafe and RV Park, 435/577-2672, is one block west from the courthouse; no showers. **City Creek Campground** is five miles northwest on Highway 153, then right one mile; sites lie along wooded City Creek at an elevation of 7,600 feet. The campground is open with water from Memorial Day weekend to Labor Day weekend; free.

VICINITY OF JUNCTION

Vehicles with stout engines can follow Highway 153 up a long grade into the Tushar Mountains to Puffer Lake (18 miles) and other scenic spots, then descend to Beaver (40 miles); pavement ends just outside Junction, then there's 25 miles of dirt road before pavement begins again. This road isn't recommended for trailers or RVs. (See the Tushar Mountains section.)

Piute State Park

The 3,300-acre Piute Reservoir is one of the largest in central Utah. It's relatively undeveloped, however, with just an outhouse or two, a place to launch boats, and some docks. Anglers catch rainbow trout here. The lake also has plenty of room for water-skiers. The park has no drinking water, established sites, or fee. Contact Otter Creek State Park for more information. From the town of Junction, drive north six miles on U.S. 89 and turn right 1.4 miles at the sign (near milepost 172).

Otter Creek State Park

Otter Creek Reservoir has some of the best trout fishing in Utah; it's 6.5 miles long and one-half to three-quarters of a mile wide (2,500 acres). Bird-watching is often good—especially in winter for raptors and swans and in spring for waterfowl and songbirds. Shore fishing can be productive in spring and autumn, but in summer you really need a boat because of moss near the shore and because the fish move to deeper waters. The park stays open all year and offers ice fishing and ice-skating in winter. The campground area at the south end of the lake (elev. 6,400 feet) has showers, tables with windbreaks, boat ramp, dock, and a fish-cleaning station. Boats with motors can be rented just outside the park. You can make reservations for the developed sites, or you can nearly always find a slot in the adjacent overflow areas. People also camp and fish at Fisherman's Beach, Tamarisk Point, and South Point on the west shore; no water or charge (BLM land). Entrance fees at the state park are $5 per vehicle for day use, $14 per vehicle for camping, or $11 per vehicle for camping at overflow areas. Contact the park at P.O. Box 43, Antimony, UT 84712, 435/624-3268 or 435/322-3770 (reservations). From the town of Junction, go two miles south on U.S. 89, then turn east 13 miles on Highway 62. **Otter Creek RV Park Marina,** across the highway, 435/624-3292 or 800/441-3292, offers RV sites ($9 without hookups, $15 with), a café (open daily for breakfast, lunch, and dinner), showers, boat rentals, and fishing supplies; it's open March–October.

Fish Lake and Vicinity

This large lake and the surrounding mountain country comprise an alpine setting of great beauty. You'll see expansive vistas, pristine meadows, sparkling streams, and dense forests on drives through the area. Hikers can reach more remote spots, such as the 11,633-foot summit of the Fish Lake Hightop Plateau. Part of what's intriguing about Fish Lake is the mix of ecosystems: sagebrush plateaus meet up with aspen forests at the water's edge.

Fish Lake formed when a block of the earth's crust dropped along faults. The water that filled the basin created one of Utah's largest natural lakes—six miles long and one mile wide. Anglers fish for lake (Mackinaw) and rainbow trout and splake (a hybrid of mackinaw and eastern brook trout). Swimming isn't recommended due to the cold water (50°F). Summers are cool at this 8,800-foot elevation. Heavy winter snows provide recreation for snowmobilers and cross-country skiers.

The lake and surrounding country lie in the Loa Ranger District of the Fishlake National Forest. The **Forest Information Center** in Fish Lake Lodge, 435/638-1033, is open daily in summer and sells or dispenses books, maps, and pamphlets. You can also contact the district office for the latest camping, fishing, hiking, and road conditions at 138 S. Main, Loa, UT 84747, 435/836-2811; it's open all year 8 A.M.–4:30 P.M. Monday–Friday. Paved Highway 25 branches off Highway 24 (31 miles southeast of Richfield, 14 miles northwest of Loa) and climbs seven miles over a pass to the lake; the road is usually kept open year-round.

FISH LAKE CAMPGROUNDS AND RESORTS

Most of the Forest Service campgrounds lie just off Highway 25 along the lake's west shore. Dispersed camping isn't permitted near Fish Lake; head farther into the backcountry if you'd like an undeveloped spot. The camping season runs about late May–late October; all the campgrounds along the lake have water and charge an $10 fee. Picnic areas are free (groups can reserve for a charge). Half of the campsites and the group areas can be reserved by calling 877/444-6777. Recreation sites, with distances from the junction of Highway 25 and Highway 24, are:

Doctor Creek (seven miles; in an aspen grove on the southwest shore; group areas can be reserved; has a dump station)

Twin Creek Picnic Area (8.8 miles; day use only; a ranger station is opposite the turnoff)

Mackinaw Campground (nine miles; in an aspen grove overlooking the lake)

Bowery Creek Campground and Picnic Area (10 miles; in an aspen grove overlooking the lake)

Joe Bush Fishermen Parking (10.7 miles)

Pelican Promontory (12 miles; turn left one mile for a panoramic view; not suitable for low-clearance vehicles)

Frying Pan Campground (14.5 miles; on the edge of an aspen grove near Johnson Valley Reservoir)

Tasha Equestrian Campground (14.7 miles, then one-half mile in; under construction; for people with horses)

Piute Parking Area (14.8 miles; access to the reservoir).

At the junction just past the reservoir, you can turn north along Sevenmile Creek on Forest Route 640 to I-70 and Salina (36 miles) or south on Forest Route 036 to a boat ramp on Johnson Valley Reservoir (one mile), Fremont River (three miles), and Loa (20 miles). Both drives have exceptional scenery and go past many good spots for fishing and primitive camping; the roads are usually okay for cars.

Accommodations

Fish Lake Resorts operates both the **Fish Lake Lodge** and **Lakeside Resort,** and each offers accommodations, a store, and a marina on the lake's southwest shore. The marinas rent fishing and pontoon boats and provide boat ramps, slips, bait, tackle, and boat gas. However, the accommodations are quite different at each of the resorts. At **Lakeside Resort,** 7.3 miles in on Highway 25, where the highway first meets the lake, 435/638-1000, free-standing cabins cost $85–140 for double occupancy (slightly more on weekends and holidays); some are open all year. RV sites with hookups are open May 15–October 15 at $20. **Fish Lake Lodge,** 1.2 miles beyond Lakeside Resort, 435/638-1000, is a huge, rambling log structure built in 1932; full of character, it has a dining area, dance hall, and a small store open Memorial Day weekend–Labor Day. "Rustic" (older) cabins open Memorial Day weekend to the end of hunting season start at $50. New cabins are available all year and cost $85 (both cabin styles are more on weekends and holidays). The rustic dining room in the lodge has lake views and is open daily for breakfast and dinner. Showers are available to the public for a small fee. Accommodations for Lakeside Resort and Fish Lake Lodge can be reserved year-round by contacting Fish Lake Resorts, 10 E. Center, Hwy. 25, Richfield, UT 84701, 435/638-1000.

Bowery Haven Resort lies near Fish Lake about 10 miles in on Highway 25, Fish Lake, UT 84701, 435/638-1040 (in-season) or 435/943-7885 (off-season). The resort's season lasts late May–late October. Amenities include a marina (fishing boat rentals, ramp, slips, and supplies), cabins ($85 for a cabin with plumbing, and half that for a "rustic" cabin), motel rooms (starting at $75), RV park ($20 with hookups—no tents; has showers and laundry), café (open daily for breakfast, lunch, and dinner), and a small store.

THOUSAND LAKE MOUNTAIN

This high plateau rises above the Fremont River to an elevation of 11,306 feet at Flat Top. Panoramas from the rim take in the wooded valleys surrounding Fish Lake to the west and the colorful rock formations and canyons of Cathedral Valley in Capitol Reef National Park to the east. Roads and trails provide access to viewpoints and fishing lakes on the plateau. Forest roads lead to the heights from Highway 72 on the west and from the middle desert and Cathedral Valley on the east. Thousand Lake Mountain may have been misnamed—its lakes number far fewer than a thousand. Some people think that a mapmaker in the 1800s accidentally switched names between this and Boulder Mountain to the south, which has far more lakes. For more information, contact the Loa Ranger District office in Loa; maps are the 15-minute Torrey topo and the Fishlake National Forest.

Elkhorn Campground

This small campground makes a good base for hikes to lakes and the Flat Top summit. It's open with water mid-June–late September; no charge. Meadows and a forest of aspen, fir, and spruce surround the sites; elevation is 9,300 feet. From the north edge of Loa, turn east and north 12 miles on Highway 72 to Forest Route 206 and follow it eight miles to the campground. The winding mountain road is unpaved but passable by cars in dry weather. Desert View Overlook, three miles before the campground, has a fantastic view of Cathedral Valley and beyond. The road to Elkhorn Campground can also be approached from I-70 via Highway 72; this paved road climbs over Hogan Pass (elev. 8,961 feet), past meadows, groves of aspen, and fine views of Cathedral Valley and the surrounding country.

Only vehicles with high clearance can drive up directly from Cathedral Valley via Forest Routes 020 and 022.

LOA

Pioneers settled here in the mid-1870s. A former Mormon missionary who had served in Hawaii suggested the town's unusual name. A commemorative marker next to the 1897 Loa Tithing House, on Center Street one block west from Main, has a rock from Mauna Loa. The small town (pop. 490) is the Wayne County seat and a handy base for exploring the Fish Lake area to the north. The **Wayne County Fair** on the third weekend in August has a parade, rodeo, exhibits, barbecue, and games.

Loa's courthouse and **post office** are at the junction of Main and Center; step inside the courthouse to see a small rock and mineral collection in the lobby. The **Loa Ranger District office,** 138 S. Main, Loa, UT 84747, 435/836-2811, has camping, fishing, hiking, and road condition information for the Fishlake National Forest lands north and east of town; there's also regional travel info. The office is open 8 A.M.–4:30 P.M. Monday–Friday. You can visit the brook and rainbow trout at **Loa Fish Hatchery,** 2.2 miles north of town; go north on Main and keep straight on the county road where Highway 24 curves to the left. The hatchery is open 8 A.M.–4:30 P.M. daily; call 435/836-2858 before coming out.

Accommodations

$75–100: The best place to stay in Loa is the **Road Creek Inn,** 90 S. Main, 435/836-2485 or 800/338-7688. Its restaurant features trout (from the inn's own trout farm), steak, and sandwiches (open daily for dinner). The building was Loa's old hotel; its 12 guest rooms have been refurbished in period style and are now offered B&B style. The owners are part of a ranch family and can also provide horseback riding, cattle drives, and other guest ranch activities. There are also a couple of older motels in town.

CENTRAL UTAH

Northeastern Utah

Northeastern Utah has an extremely diverse landscape comprising barren desert, deep canyons, high plateaus, and the lofty Uinta Mountains. Thousands of well-preserved bones unearthed in the region tell of a time about 140 million years ago when dinosaurs roamed the land in a relatively moist subtropical climate amid tree ferns, evergreens, and ginkgo trees. You can inspect the skeletons of these creatures in excellent museums in Vernal, Price, and Castle Dale, and visit bone excavations at Dinosaur National Monument and Cleveland-Lloyd Dinosaur Quarry.

The high country of the Uinta Mountains offers some of Utah's most scenic alpine scenery. Kings Peak tops the range at 13,528 feet—the highest point in the state. Anglers seek trout and arctic grayling in the countless lakes and streams of the Uintas. Trails provide access for hiking and pack trips into the High Uintas Wilderness at the heart of the range. Other popular recreation areas include Flaming Gorge National Recreation Area, Dinosaur National Monument, the Wasatch Plateau, and the San Rafael Swell. Anglers and boaters have a choice of many large reservoirs, seven of which are

Mirror Lake, a lovely reflecting pool, is often snowed in until mid-June.

NORTHEASTERN UTAH

Evanston

WYOMING
UTAH

Lonetree

Flaming
Gorge Lake

**Flaming Gorge
National Recreation Area**

Manila

Dutch John

MIRROR LAKE
HWY.

Sheep Creek

318

Uintas   Mountains

Spirit Lake

Oaks Park
Reservoir

44

191

Trial
Lake

▲ Kings Peak 13,528 ft
Highest Point in Utah

High Uintas
Wilderness

Red Fleet
Reservoir

Kamas

Mirror
Lake

32

150

35

Moon Lake

Steinaker
Reservoir

DINOSAUR
QUARRY

DINOSAUR
NATIONAL
MONUMENT

Tabiona

UINTAH AND OURAY

Altonah

121

Vernal

Lapoint

Jensen

40

87 87

121

Roosevelt

Starvation
Reservoir

Bottle Hollow
Reservoir

Ft. Duchesne

45

Dinosaur

HARPERS
CORNER RD.

Fruitland

Altamont

40 191

Myton

Pelican
Lake

40

Starvation
State Park

Duchesne

88

OURAY NATIONAL
WILDLIFE REFUGE

To
Spanish
Fork

Strawberry Reservoir

INDIAN RESERVATION

Ouray

Rangely

Bonanza

6

Tucker

Summit
9,100 ft

Ashley National
Forest

White River

Soldier Summit

Green

DRIVE

96

191

NINE MILE
CANYON

Scofield
Res.

Scofield

Kenilworth

Book

HILL CREEK EXTENSION

Helper

Price

Roan

Cliffs

Desolation Canyon

SKYLINE

31

Wellington

Sunnyside

123

East Carbon
City

UINTAH AND OURAY

Roan

Cliffs

Mack

Huntington
Reservoir

124

Cliffs

Book

To Grand
Junction, CO

Joes
Valley
Res.

Huntington

Cleveland

6

INDIAN RESERVATION

70

Colorado River

29

Orangeville

Cedar
Mountain

NEFERTITI

COLORADO
UTAH

Millsite
Res.

Castle
Dale

Ferron

191

SEGO

Ferron
Reservoir

Green River

Thompson

10

Emery

70

Green River

191

Arches
National
Park

128

To Salina

0   25 mi

0   25 km

24

San Rafael River

MOON

To Hanksville

To Moab

NORTHEASTERN UTAH HIGHLIGHTS

Backpacking the Uinta Mountains

Mirror Lake Highway

Utah Field House dinosaur collection in Vernal

Rafting the Green River's Split Mountain Gorge

Flaming Gorge National Recreation Area

Dinosaur Quarry at Dinosaur National Monument

College of Eastern Utah Prehistoric Museum in Price

Nine Mile Canyon Backcountry Byway

Wedge Overlook in the San Rafael Swell

state parks. River-runners enjoy lively rides down the Green River through Red, Lodore, Whirlpool, Split Mountain, Desolation, and Gray Canyons.

You'll see two spellings in this region—Uinta and Uintah—both of which are pronounced "yoo-IN-tuh." Geographical terms (Uinta Mountains, Uinta Basin) don't have an "h"; political divisions (Uintah County and Uintah and Ouray Indian Reservation) usually do.

CLIMATE

In summer, the valleys have average highs of about 90°F, which drop to the low 50s at night. Valley temperatures plummet in winter to about 30° during the day and 5° at night. The Wasatch Plateau and Uinta Mountains experience cool weather year-round. Above 10,000 feet, summer highs rarely exceed 70° in the day and drop to the 30s and 40s at night; freezing weather may occur at any time of year. Winter in the mountains brings highs in the 20s and lows well below zero. Annual precipitation changes dramatically with elevation, from about eight inches in the desert to 40 inches in the high country. Snowfall is widespread in winter and very heavy in the mountains.

HISTORY

Native Americans

Paleo-Indians trekked across this land beginning at least 15,000 years ago. About A.D. 550, the Fremont culture emerged as a distinct group. The Fremont ranged widely in search of wild foods and places to grow their corn, beans, and squash. By 1300, however, the tribe had mysteriously disappeared, leaving behind village sites, artifacts, and intriguing rock art.

Nomadic Utes moved in at about the same time that the Fremont culture faded away, but the Utes seemed to have no knowledge of their more sophisticated predecessors. Utes guided the Spanish Dominguez-Escalante Expedition through the Uinta Basin south of the Uinta Mountains in 1776 and were the first Native American group encountered by the Mormons in Utah. Mountain men traded with the tribe during the 1820s and 1830s on beaver-trapping expeditions. Neither the Utes nor the mountain men, however, made permanent homes in the Uinta Basin.

Early White Settlement

In the 1870s and early 1880s, the LDS Church sent out calls for members to colonize lands east of the Wasatch Plateau. Though at first the land looked harsh and barren, crops and orchards eventually prospered with irrigation. Nevertheless, it was some time before the first families took a liking to this country. Mrs. Orange Seely of the Castle Dale area is credited with saying, "The first time I ever swore was when we arrived in Emery County and I said, 'Damn a man who would bring a woman to such a God-forsaken country!'" Individual families also came out on their own and started isolated farms and ranches in the Uinta Basin and along the eastern edge of the Wasatch Plateau to the south. Much of the land proved too dry or rugged for any use and remains in its natural state even today. Discoveries of coal in 1877 and oil in 1900 attracted waves of new people to the sleepy Mormon settlements east of the Wasatch Plateau. Immigrant miners fresh from Europe brought a new cultural diversity to the region.

Uinta Mountains

This outstanding wilderness area contains lofty peaks, lush grassy meadows, fragrant coniferous forests, crystal-clear streams, and thousands of tiny alpine lakes. The Uintas, unlike most other major ranges of the United States, run east-west. Underground forces pushed rock layers up into a massive dome 150 miles long and 35 miles wide. Ancient Precambrian rocks exposed in the center of the range consist largely of quartzite (metamorphosed sandstone). Outcrops of progressively younger rocks are found away from the center. Glaciers have carved steep ridges and broad basins and left great moraines. Barren rock lies exposed across much of the land, including the peaks and high ridges.

Trees, from 10,000 feet to timberline (about 11,000 feet), include limber pine, Engelmann spruce, and subalpine fir. Lower slopes (7,000–10,000 feet) support dense unbroken forests of lodgepole pine (the most common tree in the Uintas), aspen, Douglas fir, white fir, blue spruce, and scattered stands of ponderosa pine. Elk, moose, mule deer, and Rocky Mountain goat (reintroduced) come here to graze in summer. Also foraging for food are black bear, mountain lion, coyote, bobcat, raccoon, porcupine, badger, pine marten, snowshoe hare, marmot, and pika. Anglers seek out arctic grayling and native cutthroat, Eastern brook, rainbow, German brown, and golden trout. Aerial stocking keeps even the most remote lakes swimming with fish. Your luck at a lake or stream can range from lousy to fantastic, depending on when it was last stocked and how many other anglers have discovered the spot.

The remote setting of the Uinta Mountains has protected much of the forests from the ravages of logging. The central part received protection in 1931 as a primitive area and designation in 1984 as the High Uintas Wilderness. Four of Utah's major rivers have their source in these mountains: the Bear and Weber Rivers on the north slope and the Provo and Duchesne on the south slope. Despite their great heights, the Uintas

have a gentler terrain than the precipitous Wasatch Range. High plateaus and broad valleys among the peaks hold the abundant rain and snowfall in marshes and ponds, supporting large populations of wildlife and fish.

Visiting the Uintas

Winding over the western end of the range from the town of Kamas to the Wyoming border, Highway 150 offers splendid panoramas and access to fishing lakes and hiking trails. On the east, U.S. 191 and Highway 44 provide access to the Uintas and Flaming Gorge Reservoir from Vernal. Unpaved roads also lead to trailheads on all sides of the range. Developed and primitive campgrounds can be found along these highways and at other locations including many of the trailheads.

Most people prefer to visit the Uintas mid-June–mid-September. Campers should be prepared for cold nights and freezing rain even in the warmest months. Afternoon showers are common in summer. Arm yourself with insect repellent to ward off the mosquitoes, especially in July. Snow stays on the ground until well into June, and the meltwater can make trails muddy until early July. The lakes and campgrounds along Highway 150 become crowded on summer weekends and holidays, though you can usually get off by yourself on a short hike into the backcountry.

An extensive trail system with about 20 trailheads goes deep into the wilderness and connects with many lakes. A great number of trips are possible, from easy day hikes to rigorous treks lasting weeks. Climbers headed for the summits can take trails to a nearby pass, then rock-scramble to the top. Kings Peak attracts the most attention because at 13,528 feet it's the highest point in Utah. The shortest approach is from Henrys Fork Trailhead on the north, which requires three days of hiking for the 32-mile round-trip; elevation gain is about 4,100 feet. Southern approaches from Swift Creek or

NORTHEASTERN UTAH

HIGH UINTAS WILDERNESS

To Manila

To Lonetree, WY

To Evanston, WY

To Evanston, WY

To Mountain View, WY

To Lonetree, WY

To Evanston, WY

To Kamas

To Tabiona

To Duchesne

To Roosevelt

To Roosevelt

To Roosevelt

To Vernal

Beaver Meadow Reservoir

SPIRIT LAKE

Kabell Meadows

Fish Lake

Chepeta Lake

CHEPETA

HOOP LAKE

Island Lake

Fox Lake

Queant Pass

Fox

W. FORK OF WHITEROCKS

BEAVER CREEK

Rainbow Lake

Atwood Basin

Chain Lakes

UINTA

Beaver Lake

DEADHORSE PARK

HENRYS FORK

Farmer's Lake

SWIFT CREEK

CHINA MEADOWS

Henrys Fork Lake

Anderson Pass

Kings Peak 13,528 ft

Smith Fork Pass

Bluebell Pass

E. FORK BLACKS FORK

Red Castle Lake

Garfield Basin

CENTER PARK

High Line Trail

Moon Lake

LAKE FORK

W. FORK BLACKS FORK

Dead Horse Pass

Cleveland Pass

Brown Duck Basin

Allsop Lake

Rocky Sea Pass

Four Lakes Basin

Upper Stillwater Reservoir

BEAR RIVER

Naturalist Basin

ROCK CREEK

CHRISTMAS MEADOWS

West Basin

Grandaddy Basin

Hades Pass

GRANDVIEW

150

MIRROR LAKE

0   5 mi

0   5 km

Uinta Trailheads usually take an extra day. More than a dozen other peaks in the Uintas exceed 13,000 feet. No permits are needed for travel in the wilderness area, though it's recommended that you sign registers at the trailheads. Groups must not exceed 14 people. The High Uintas Wilderness, an area of about 450,000 acres, is closed to mechanized vehicles (including bicycles). Horses can use nearly all trails in the wilderness area. An exception is Bluebell Pass, which is impassable for them; other passes may be rough going depending on recent storms and trail maintenance. Winter snows close Highway 150 and the back roads, at which time snowmobilers and cross-country skiers come out to enjoy the snowy landscapes.

Information

The U.S. Forest Service manages the Uintas and surrounding forest lands. Northern and western parts are administered by the Wasatch-Cache National Forest, 8226 Federal Bldg., 125 S. State St., Salt Lake City, UT 84111, 435/524-5030. Most of the southern and eastern areas are part of the Ashley National Forest, 355 N. Vernal Ave., Vernal, UT 84078, 435/789-1181. For specific information, it's best to contact the district offices directly. In the Wasatch-Cache National Forest, contact the **Kamas Ranger District office,** P.O. Box 68, Kamas, UT 84036, 435/783-4338; for the western end of the range, including the Provo River drainage, contact **Evanston Ranger District office,** P.O. Box 1880, Evanston, WY 82931-1880, 435/642-6662 in summer or 307/789-3194 year-round; for the northern side including Smiths Forks and Henrys Fork drainages, contact the **Mountain View Ranger District office,** P.O. Box 129, Mountain View, WY 82939, 307/782-6555. In the Ashley National Forest, contact the **Flaming Gorge Ranger District office,** P.O. Box 278, Manila, UT 84046, 435/784-3445, about the northeastern side including Spirit Lake and Sheep Creek; the **Vernal Ranger District office,** 355 N. Vernal Ave., Vernal, UT 84078, 435/789-1181, for the southeastern end including Whiterocks River; the **Roosevelt Ranger District office,** 244 W. U.S. 40, P.O.

Box 333-6, Roosevelt, UT 84066, 435/722-5018, for the southern end including Lake Fork, Yellowstone, and Uinta drainages; and the **Duchesne Ranger District office,** 85 W. Main, P.O. Box I, Duchesne, UT 84021, 435/738-2482, for the southwestern end including Rock Creek and the North Fork of Duchesne drainages. All these offices have the forest maps and the High Uintas Wilderness topo map (1:75,000 scale). Hikers will find good trail descriptions in the books *High Uintas Backcountry,* by Jeffrey and Brad Probst; *Hiking Utah,* by Dave Hall; and *Utah Mountaineering Guide,* by Michael Kelsey. If you plan to do some serious fishing, a set of 10 booklets, *Lakes of the High Uintas,* published by the Utah Division of Wildlife Resources, provides detailed descriptions of lakes, kinds of fish stocked, trail access, and camping. Each booklet covers different drainages; they're available from the DWR office at 1594 W. North Temple, Salt Lake City, UT 8414, 801/537-3320, or from http://mapstore.utah.gov/wildpubs.

KAMAS AND THE MIRROR LAKE HIGHWAY (HIGHWAY 150)

Kamas

Pioneers settled on this spot at the mouth of Beaver Creek Canyon in 1857. Today, Kamas is the start of what is probably Utah's most spectacular alpine drive. The Mirror Lake Highway (Highway 150) begins here at an elevation of 6,500 feet and climbs to the crest of the western Uinta Mountains at Bald Mountain Pass (elev. 10,678 feet) before descending on the other side and continuing to Evanston, Wyoming.

Nearest motels are in Heber City (17 miles southwest) and Park City (19 miles west). The **Kamas Ranger District office** is at 50 E. Center (P.O. Box 68, Kamas, UT 84036), 435/783-4338. Open 8 A.M.–4:30 P.M. Monday–Saturday June–mid-September and Monday–Friday 8 A.M.–4:30 P.M. the rest of the year. The office has forest maps and detailed recreation information; staff can advise on road conditions, campgrounds, hiking, cross-country skiing, and snowmobiling.

The scenic Mirror Lake Highway has many campgrounds and hiking trails into the Uinta Mountains.

NORTHEASTERN UTAH

Mirror Lake Highway

You can drive this scenic highway mid-June–mid-October. A $3 daily recreation pass, available at the start of the highway and at several points along the way, is required if you're going to park and hike. Campgrounds tend to fill on summer weekends, but some campsites can be reserved by calling 877/444-6777 or visiting www.reserveUSA.com.

The first 25 miles of the highway are pretty, but relatively tame. Shortly after passing the Provo River Falls, the road climbs sharply and the views open up to include rugged mountain peaks.

Snowplows keep the highway cleared in winter to Soapstone, 15.5 miles from Kamas, to provide access for cross-country skiing and snowmobiling. Five trails used by both skiers and snowmobilers begin along the highway and at Soapstone. Skiers using snowmobile trails will find the most solitude on weekdays. **Beaver Creek Cross-Country Trail** begins from Slate Creek (six miles east of Kamas) and parallels the highway to Pine Valley Campground, a distance of 5.5 miles one-way with an elevation gain of 440 feet. This trail is easy; branching off from it are other ski trails rated intermediate and advanced. You can obtain information and brochures for these and other skiing areas from the Kamas Ranger District office. Mileages given below correspond to mileposts along the highway:

Mile 0.0: Heading east on Highway 150 from the junction with U.S. 189 in Kamas.

Mile 0.1: Kamas Ranger District office on the right.

Mile 3.3: Kamas Fish Hatchery on the right; visitors welcome 8 A.M.–4 P.M. daily.

Mile 3.7: Sign for Beaver Creek Nudist Ranch (someone's idea of a practical joke!).

Mile 6.1: Entering **Wasatch-Cache National Forest**; Slate Creek.

Mile 6.7: Yellow Pine Campground on the left. Sites are in a forest of ponderosa and lodgepole pine and juniper at an elevation of 7,200 feet; open late May–late October; no water; $6 fee. **Yellow Pine Creek Trail** begins just north of the campground and goes up the creek to Lower Yellow Pine Lake (elev. 9,600 feet; four miles one-way) and beyond; this is a good hike early in the season.

Mile 8.2: Beaver Creek Picnic Area on the right. Sites line both sides of Beaver Creek amid lodgepole pine and willow at 7,300 feet.

Mile 8.9: Taylor Fork ATV Campground on the right; **Taylor Fork-Cedar Hollow ATV Trail** begins here. Sites are along Beaver Creek in lodgepole pine and aspen at 7,400 feet; water early June–mid-September; $9 fee.

Mile 9.3: Shingle Creek Campground and Picnic Area on the right. Sites are in a mixed forest of aspen, pine, spruce, and fir at 7,400 feet; water early June–mid-September; $10 camping fee.

Mile 9.9: Shingle Creek Trail follows the creek upstream to East Shingle Lake (elev. 9,680 feet; 5.5 miles one-way) and Upper Setting Trail; this is a good early-season hike. Past the trailhead, the highway climbs over a small pass to the Provo River and follows it upstream.

Mile 10.5: Lower Provo River Campground is one mile south on Pine Valley Road. Sites are along the Provo River in a pine and spruce forest at 7,600 feet; water early June–mid-September; $10 fee. The nearby **Pine Valley Group Camping Area** is a group reservation area.

Mile 15.5: Soapstone Campground on the right. Sites are along the Provo River amid lodgepole pine at 8,200 feet; water early June–mid-September; $12 fee.

Mile 17.0: Shady Dell Campground on the right. Sites lie along the Provo River at 8,200 feet; water early June–mid-September; $10 fee.

Mile 17.7: West Portal of Duchesne Tunnel; a sign describes this six-mile conduit that brings water from the Duchesne River to the Provo River. **Duchesne Tunnel Camping Area** is a group reservation site; call 800/280-CAMP.

Mile 18.8: Cobblerest Campground on the right. Sites are near the Provo River in a pine and spruce forest at 8,500 feet; water mid-June–mid-September; $10 fee.

Mile 22.3: Slate Gorge Overlook on the right.

Mile 23.1: Upper Provo Bridge Camping Area on the right at 9,200 feet; open early July–early September with tables and outhouses but no water; available by group reservation only.

Mile 23.9: Provo River Falls Overlook on the left.

Mile 25.4: Trial Lake Campground is a quarter mile to the left on Spring Canyon Road. Sites are on the southeast shore of the lake in a pine and spruce forest at 9,500 feet; water early July–early September; $10 fee. There's a parking area near the dam for anglers. Spring Canyon Road continues past the dam to Washington and Crystal Lakes and Crystal Lake Trailhead. **Notch Mountain Trail** begins at Crystal Lake Trailhead, goes north past Wall and Twin Lakes, through the Notch to Ibantik and Meadow Lakes, to the Weber River (elev. 9,000 feet; 6.5 miles one-way), and to Bald Mountain Pass (elev. 10,678 feet; 10 miles one-way). The **Lakes Country Trail** starts at the Crystal Lake Trailhead and goes west past Island, Long, and other lakes before joining the Smith-Morehouse Trail after three miles.

Mile 26.4: Lilly Lake Campground to the left. Sites are in a spruce and fir forest at 9,800 feet; water early July–early September. Lilly, Teapot, and Lost Lakes lie within short walking distances.

Mile 26.7: Lost Creek Campground to the right. Sites are beside the creek in a spruce and pine forest at 9,800 feet; water early July–early September; $10 fee. Lost Lake is a short walk to the southwest.

Mile 29.1: Bald Mountain Pass (elev. 10,678 feet); **Bald Mountain Picnic Area and Trailhead** on the left. **Bald Mountain National Recreation Trail** climbs to the summit of Bald Mountain (elev. 11,947 feet) with great views all the way; the two-mile (one-way) trail climbs 1,269 feet, putting you in the midst of the Uinta Range's alpine grandeur. Expect a strenuous trip because of the high elevation and steep grades; carry rain gear to fend off the cold wind (even in summer) and possible storms. From the top, weather permitting, you'll enjoy panoramas of the High Uintas Wilderness, the Lakes Roadless Area, and the Wasatch Range. **Notch Lake Trail** also begins near the picnic area and connects with Trial Lake.

Mile 30.5: Moosehorn Campground on the left. Sites are on the east and north shores of Moosehorn Lake in a spruce and fir forest at 10,400 feet; water early July–early September; $10 fee. **Fehr Lake Trail** begins a quarter mile south and across the highway; it goes to Fehr Lake (one-half mile), Shepard Lake (1.5 miles), and Hoover Lake (1.5 miles).

Mile 31.2: Mirror Lake Campground and Picnic Area are a half mile to the right. This is the largest campground (91 sites) on the Mirror Lake Highway. Sites are near the lake in a forest of spruce, fir, and lodgepole pine at 10,200 feet; water early July–early September; $12 fee. Parking for picnicking and fishing costs $3. Anglers can park at the south end of the lake and at the Mirror Lake Trailhead. Boats can be hand-launched; no motors at all are permitted on the lake. **Highline and North Fork of the Duchesne Trails** lead from the trailhead to the High Uintas Wilderness.

Mile 32.1: Pass Lake Trailhead on the left,

NORTHEASTERN UTAH

across the highway from Pass Lake. **Lofty Lake and Weber Canyon Trails** begin here and connect with other trails. Weber Canyon Trail goes to Holiday Park Trailhead (elev. 8,000 feet; seven miles one-way), reached by road from Oakley.

Mile 33.9: Butterfly Lake Campground on the left. Sites are on the south shore of the lake in a spruce, fir, and lodgepole pine forest at 10,300 feet; water early July–early September; $10 fee.

Mile 34.2: Hayden Pass (elev. 10,200 feet); **Highline Trailhead** on the right. This is the closest point on the highway to the **High Uintas Wilderness.** The Highline Trail tends to be muddy, rocky, and heavily used. It winds east from here across the Uintas nearly 100 miles to East Park Reservoir north of Vernal. The highway makes a gradual descent from the pass along Hayden Fork of the Bear River. Contact the Evanston Ranger District offices for camping, hiking, and back-road travel in this area.

Mile 35.0: Ruth Lake Trailhead on the left; the lake is an easy three-quarter-mile hike west. There are only a few parking spots available.

Mile 38.9: Sulphur Campground on the right. Sites lie near the Hayden Fork of Bear River in a forest of lodgepole pine, fir, and spruce at 9,000 feet; water early June–mid-September; $9 fee.

Mile 41.8: Beaver View Campground on the right. Sites overlook Hayden Fork of Bear River from a lodgepole pine and aspen forest at 8,900 feet; a beaver pond and lodge can be seen near the entrance station; water early June–mid-September; $9 fee.

Mile 42.4: Hayden Fork Campground on the right. Sites lie along Hayden Fork of Bear River in a lodgepole pine and aspen forest at 8,900 feet; water early June–mid-September; $9 fee.

Mile 45.6: Stillwater Campground on the right. Sites are in a lodgepole pine and aspen forest at 8,500 feet, near where Hayden Fork and Stillwater Fork meet the Bear River; water early June–mid-September; $9 fee.

Mile 45.8: Christmas Meadow Road goes right four miles to **Christmas Meadow Campground** and **Stillwater Trailhead.** Sites overlook a large meadow from a forest of lodgepole pine at 9,200 feet; water early June–mid-September; $9 fee. Stillwater Trailhead, near the campground, is the starting point for hikes to lakes in Amethyst, Middle, and West Basins to the south. **Wolverine ATV Trailhead Campground** is 1.5 miles in on Christmas Meadow Road, then one mile off; it offers sites for ATVers at 9,000 feet near a trailhead for a Lily Lake loop. Open mid-June–mid-September; no water or fee.

Mile 46.5: Bear River Ranger Station on the right. Stop here for recreation information about the northwestern part of the Uinta Range. The office is open 8 A.M.–4:30 P.M. Monday–Thursday, 8 A.M.–6 P.M. Friday and Saturday, and 8 A.M.–5 P.M. Sunday and holidays. In season, the campground is open weekends only mid-May–late May, daily late May–mid-October, then weekends only again through late October; 435/642-6662. Off-season, contact the office in Evanston, Wyoming, P.O. Box 1880, Evanston, WY 82931-1880, 307/789-3194, one mile south of I-80 at 1565 Hwy. 150, Suite A.

Mile 47.5: A road turns right two miles to **Lily Lake.** Most of the route is unmaintained dirt road.

Mile 48.2: Bear River Campground on the left. Sites are along the Bear River just upstream from the East Fork confluence in a lodgepole pine and aspen forest at 8,400 feet; water early June–mid-September; $9 fee.

Mile 48.3: East Fork Bear River Campground on the left. Sites are along the Bear River just below the East Fork confluence in a lodgepole pine and aspen forest at 8,400 feet; water early June–mid-September; $9 fee.

Mile 48.6: Forest Route 058 goes right about 17 miles to **Little Lyman Lake Campground.** Sites are near the east shore of the lake in a lodgepole pine forest at 9,200 feet; water early June–mid-September; $7 fee. Lyman Lake is just a short walk away. **Meeks Cabin Reservoir and Campground** are two miles farther on Forest Route 058, then left about five miles on Forest Route 073. Sites here are along the southwest shore of the reservoir in a lodgepole pine forest at 8,800 feet; water early June–mid-September; $9 fee.

Mile 48.7: Leaving Wasatch-Cache National Forest. This is approximately the end of the scenic drive. The valley opens up and supports sagebrush and scattered aspen groves.

Mile 54.6: Wyoming border; highway becomes Highway 150. Evanston is 23 miles ahead with several motels and two large grocery stores.

Vernal

One of the oldest and largest communities in northeastern Utah, Vernal makes a handy base for travels to the many sights of the region. The perennial waters of Ashley Creek—named for mountain man William H. Ashley, who passed by in 1825—attracted the first settlers to the valley during the early 1870s. The small community went through a succession of names—Hatchtown, Ashley Center, and Ashley—before residents decided on Vernal in 1893.

Rugged terrain and poor roads isolated the area from the rest of Utah for years. In 1916, when a local businessman wanted to order a shipment of bricks from Salt Lake City for the facade of a new bank, he solved the problem of expensive shipping costs by having the bricks sent by parcel post! Freight cost $2.50 per hundred pounds while the postal service charged only $1.05. Other Vernal residents caught on to the post office's bargain rates and even started parcel-posting crops to market until the postal service changed its regulations. The Bank of Vernal, nicknamed the "Parcel Post Bank," still serves the town at the corner of Main and Vernal.

Growth of the oil industry in recent decades has been a mixed blessing because of its boom-and-bust cycles. Vernal is the Uintah County seat and has a population of 7,366.

SIGHTS

Utah Field House of Natural History State Park and Museum

This recently overhauled museum is a good place for both adults and children to learn about the dinosaurs that once roamed the Uinta Basin. Full-size models stalk or fly in the Dinosaur Gardens outside. The natural setting makes the strange creatures seem almost alive. Inside, the Geology and Fossil Hall has displays of 45-million-year-old skulls of ancient mammals, crocodiles, and alligators that once roamed across Utah. Other exhibits offer fossil specimens ranging in size from tiny insects to massive dinosaur bones. A geologic mural 36 feet across shows the structure of rock layers in northeastern Utah. Other exhibits trace Utah's Native Americans from the Desert Culture through Anasazi and Fremont groups to the modern Ute. The Natural History Hall, offers a close look at mounted wildlife of the state. The museum, 500 E. Main, 435/789-3799, is open 8 A.M.–9 P.M. daily Memorial Day weekend–Labor Day and 9 A.M.–5 P.M. daily in winter. Admission is $1, children 6 and under free.

Daughters of Utah Pioneers Museum

Get to know Vernal's pioneers here. The many historical photos and carefully labeled exhibits present a good idea of what life was like in the old days. The large collection includes a pioneer kitchen, spinning wheels, farm machinery, a buggy, old organs, clothing, guns, and a model of a Western town. You'll see Dr. Harvey Coe Hullinger's well-stocked medicine chest, last used in 1926 when he was 101 years old. One room of the museum is the stone tithing office, built in 1877. The Daughters of Utah Pioneers operate the museum, which is across the street from the Uintah Stake Temple at the corner of 200 South and 500 West; open 10–4 P.M. Tuesday–Saturday June–August, 10–4 P.M. Friday–Saturday during September, and at other times by request (ask at the Vernal Welcome Center).

Western Heritage Museum

This museum is at the Western Park Complex, 300 East and 200 South, 435/789-7399, Vernal's convention center, amphitheater, equestrian

VICINITY OF VERNAL

Dinosaurs come alive at the Utah Field House of Natural History.

center, and racetrack. This pioneer museum and art gallery places special emphasis on Utah's outlaw heritage (real or imaginary). Housed here is the gun used by Matt Dillon in the TV series *Gunsmoke.* Open 9 A.M.–5 P.M. Monday–Friday and 10 A.M.–2 P.M. Saturday in the off season. Admission is free.

Ladies of the White House Doll Collection

Head for the Uintah County Library, 155 E. Main St. (next door to the Utah Natural History Museum) to view a display of dolls fashioned after each first lady. Each wears a hand-sewn reproduction of the dress she wore at the Inaugural Ball. Open 10 A.M.–9 P.M. Monday–Thursday, 10 A.M.–6 P.M. Friday and Saturday.

Dry Fork Petroglyphs

Several panels of famous petroglyphs are located along a sharp sandstone bluff about 10 miles northeast of Vernal. Considered to be some of the best rock art in the United States, what makes these carvings so notable is the fact that they contain dozens of nearly life-sized human figures, many with elaborate headdresses and ornamentation. The significance of these murals is unknown, though they were probably carved by the Fremont and are reckoned to be between 1,200 and 1,600 years old.

To reach the Dry Fork Petroglyphs (also called the McConkie Petroglyphs), drive west from Vernal on Main and turn north on 500 West. Follow the main road when it turns to the left onto Highway 121 and continue until the junction with 3500 West. Turn right (north) and follow this road for 6.8 miles. Watch for signs, and follow a private ranch access road to the marked parking area.

The petroglyphs are on private property, and a donation of $2 per vehicle is asked; there are no toilet facilities. Be sure to stay on the trails, and don't get immediately discouraged—the best of the carvings are about 15 minutes into the cliff-side hike. This area is very rich in petroglyphs, and you could easily spend hours wandering along the cliffs.

ENTERTAINMENT AND EVENTS

See movies at **Cinema 5,** 1400 W. U.S. 40, **Vernal Theatre,** 40 E. Main, or **Sunset Drive-In,** open in summer on W. U.S. 40. Call the Movie Information Line, 435/789-6139, to find out what's playing at the theaters.

In June, the **Outlaw Trail Festival** brings in some wild characters for shooting events, a bank robbery, trail rides on old outlaw paths, musicals, Western art competition, oil-painting workshop, and a song-writing contest.

The **PRCA Dinosaur Roundup Rodeo** in mid-July pits man against beast. It's Vernal's biggest event of the year and includes a parade and country music showdown. A parade celebrates **Pioneer Day** on the 24th.

The **Uintah County Fair** comes to town in August.

RECREATION

River Tour Outfitters

River trips down the Green River's Split Mountain Gorge through Dinosaur National Monument provide the excitement of big rapids and the beauty of remote canyons. Experienced rafters will enjoy the challenge of the Class III–IV run down the Cross Mountain Gorge in the Yampa River. One-day and longer trips are offered by **Hatch River Expeditions,** 221 North 400 East, 435/789-4316 or 800/342-8243, www.hatchriver.com; **Adrift Adventures,** P.O. Box 192, Jensen, UT 84035, 435/789-3600 or 800/824-0150, www.adrift .com; and **Dinosaur River Expeditions,** 540 E. Main, Vernal, UT 84078, 435/781-0717 or 800/247-6197, www.dinoadv.com. Expect to pay about $65 for day trips and about $150 per day for longer excursions; children usually get discounts.

The well-regarded **National Outdoor Leadership School** runs 12–16-day courses for young people (the average age is 18) in Desolation Canyon; its Vernal base is at 3101 East 2500 South, 435/781-0305, www.nols.edu.

Other Recreation

Wildwaters has water-tube fun in summer at 1155 E. U.S. 40, 435/789-5281. An outdoor **swimming pool** sits next to Independence Park at 170 South 600 West, 435/789-5775. Play **tennis** or **baseball** at the city park, corner of 400 North and 900 West. Golf at the 18-hole **Dinaland Municipal Golf Course,** 675 South 2000 East, 435/781-1428.

ACCOMMODATIONS

$50–75

Vernal offers high-quality lodgings; you can't go wrong at any of the following.

Well south of town along U.S. 191 is the **Weston Plaza Hotel,** 1684 W. U.S. 40, 435/789-9550, with an indoor pool and hot tub. If you're coming in from the east on U.S. 40, watch for the **Split Mountain Motel,** 1015 E. U.S. 40, 435/789-9020, a handy place to stay if you want to visit the water slide at Wildwaters. It's also one of the only places in town that allows pets.

The rest of Vernal's motels are closer to the center of things (such as they are in Vernal). **Sage Motel,** 54-56 W. Main St., 435/789-1442 or 800/760-1442, has comfortable rooms with refrigerators and microwaves, is pet-friendly, and is one of Vernal's least expensive lodgings. **Rodeway Inn,** 590 W. Main, 435/789-8172 or 800/228-2000, has kitchenettes and laundry facilities. **Days Inn,** 260 W. Main, 435/789-1011 or 800/328-1011, has a pool, kitchenettes, and laundry.

The downtown **Weston Lamplighter Inn,** 120 E. Main St., 435/789-0312, has a pool and in-room microwaves and refrigerators. It's within easy walking distance of the dinosaur displays at the Utah Field House.

$75–100

Vernal's two Best Westerns are just a little fancier than other lodgings in town. The **Best Western Antlers Motel,** 423 W. Main, 435/789-1202 or 800/528-1234, has a pool, hot tub, and fitness room; and **Best Western Dinosaur Inn,** 251 E. Main St., 435/789-2660 or 800/528-1234, has a pool, hot tub, and exercise room.

Vernal has one B&B, the **Landmark Inn,** 288 East 100 South, 435/781-1800 or 888/738-1800. This attractive brick house is just far enough off Main Street to be simultaneously quiet and convenient; rooms have TVs and private baths and start at about $75.

Campgrounds

Two state park campgrounds north of Vernal are located on reservoirs, making them popular swimming and boating spots: **Steinaker State Park,** eight miles north of Vernal on U.S. 191, and **Red Fleet State Park,** 12 miles north on U.S. 191. Open April–October, these lakeside parks are popular places for fishing and water sports; call 435/789-4432 for information. There's more camping 20 miles north in the Ashley National Forest and east at Dinosaur National Monument (23 miles).

Closer to town, **Vernal KOA** is near the Weston Plaza Hotel at 1800 W. Sheraton, 435/789-8935 or 800/KOA-7574. Facilities include cabins, a pool, store, showers, laundry, playground, and miniature golf; open April–October. **Campground Dina** is on the north side of town at 930 N. Vernal Ave., 435/789-2148 or 800/245-2148. It has showers, store, laundry, and miniature golf; open May–October. **Fossil Valley RV Park,** 999 W. U.S. 40, 435/789-6450, has showers and laundry; open April–November.

FOOD

Most of Vernal's restaurants are good, but pretty standard small-town establishments. So, it's easy to get excited about **Spoof's,** a coffee shop at 38 E. Main, 435/789-1154, and the **Dinosaur Brew Haus,** 550 E. Main, 435/781-0717, a casual spot with Utah microbrews, burgers, and salads. Right downtown, the **Wired Cow Café,** 490 W. Main, 435/789-2739, has good coffee, pastries, sandwiches, and ice cream concoctions.

Curry Manor, 189 S. Vernal Ave., 435/789-2289, is Vernal's gourmet restaurant, housed in a fine old brick home, and open for lunch

and dinner. It's worth heading 3.5 miles north of town to **Stella's Kitchen,** 3340 N. Vernal, 435/789-5657, for made-from-scratch home-cooking; open for three meals a day, seven days a week. On the road to Dinosaur National Park, **Naples Country Café,** 1010 S. Hwy 40, 435/789-8870, is a good place for breakfast or a sandwich.

Many of the motels have their own restaurants, which serve up familiar American fare. Several other American restaurants are worth noting. Right downtown, the **Seven-Eleven Ranch Restaurant,** 77 E. Main, 435/789-1170, is open daily except Sunday for breakfast, lunch, and dinner and serves a Saturday chuckwagon dinner. West of town, **Niki's,** 2750 W. Hwy. 40, 435/781-8239, is another popular steak house (it also serves seafood).

For an easy, informal lunch or dinner downtown, **La Cabaña,** 56 W. Main, 435/789-3151, has good Mexican food; open Monday–Saturday for lunch and dinner. Vernal's other Mexican restaurant, **Casa Rios,** is quite good and just north of downtown at 2015 W. Hwy. 40, 435/789-0103.

OTHER PRACTICALITIES

Information

The staff at the **Vernal Welcome Center,** 435/789-4002, next to the Utah Field House Museum at 235 E. Main, can fill you in on the many attractions of "Dinosaurland" and offers a short video program showing highlights of the region and other parts of Utah. A series of self-guided tour brochures has maps and mileages of suggested trips. The center is open 8 A.M.–7 P.M. daily in summer and 9 A.M.–5 P.M. daily the rest of the year. You can also contact the **Dinosaurland Travel Board** for tourist info and events at 800/477-5558, 55 E. Main, Vernal, UT 84078, www.dinoland.com.

Foresters at the **Vernal Ranger District office** of the Ashley National Forest, 355 N. Vernal Ave. (Vernal, UT 84078), 435/789-1181, can tell you about scenic drives, camping, hiking, cross-country skiing, and snowmobiling in the eastern Uinta Mountains. Open 8 A.M.–5 P.M.

Monday–Friday. The **Ashley National Forest supervisor's office** (at the same address and phone) has general information about the Flaming Gorge, Roosevelt, and Duchesne Districts. The **Bureau of Land Management Vernal District office,** 170 South 500 East (Vernal, UT 84078), 435/781-4400, offers information on the John Jarvie Historic Ranch in the northeast corner of the state and areas south of Vernal, such as Pelican Lake and the White River; land-use maps and brochures on recreation areas are available. Open 7:45 A.M.–4:30 P.M. Monday–Friday.

For detailed fishing and hunting information, stop at the **Utah Division of Wildlife Resources** on the second floor of the courthouse building, 152 East 100 North (Vernal, UT 84078), 435/781-9453; open 8 A.M.–5 P.M. Monday–Friday. The **Uintah County Library** is at 155 E. Main, 435/789-0091; **Bitter Creek Books,** 684 W. Main, 435/789-4742, offers a selection of regional and general titles and topo maps.

Services

The **post office** is near the corner of Main and 800 West, 435/789-2393. **Ashley Valley Medical Center** provides hospital care at 151 West 200 North, 435/789-3342. Camping and fishing supplies are available at **Basin Sports,** 511 W. Main, 435/789-2409. **Altitude Cycle,** 580 E. Main, 435/781-2595, is a good bike shop and sells a trail guide to local mountain-bike trails. (Find capsule trail information at www.altitudecycle.com.)

Transportation

Greyhound buses stop at 72 South 100 West, 435/789-0404 or 800/231-2222, and travel each way between here and Salt Lake City and east to Denver via Vernal. Rent cars from **All Save Car Rentals,** 2145 South 1500 East, 800/440-5776. Catch a cab from **Vernal Cab,** 435/790-1212. **Skywest Airlines,** 800/634-3000, has scheduled flights between Vernal and Salt Lake City three times daily.

North of Vernal

WILDLIFE THROUGH THE AGES SCENIC BYWAY

This scenic interpreted route follows U.S. 191 and Highway 44 north from Vernal to Flaming Gorge Reservoir. As the road climbs, you cross 19 geologic formations—an exceptionally thick geologic layer cake—revealing rock layers from the period of the creation of the Uinta Mountains and on through the periods of erosion that followed. The 30-mile drive begins four miles north of town on U.S. 191; a tour map at a pullout shows the formations to be seen ahead. *Wildlife through the Ages* brochures are available at the Vernal Welcome Center and Forest Service and BLM offices. Signs on the drive identify and briefly describe each formation from the Mancos (80 million years old) to the Uinta Mountain Group (one billion years old).

STEINAKER STATE PARK

Water sports, camping, and picnicking at the park's 750-acre Steinaker Reservoir make this a popular place in summer. Anglers catch large-mouth bass, rainbow trout, and a few brown trout. Water-skiers have plenty of room on the lake's two-mile length. Warm weather brings bathers to a swimming beach near the picnic area. Scuba divers find the best conditions from mid-summer to late autumn, when visibility is up to 30 feet. In winter, visitors come to ice fish or cross-country ski. The campground (elev. 5,500 feet) is open with drinking water all year; no showers or hookups. Other facilities include two covered pavilion areas and a paved boat ramp. The park charges $5 per vehicle for day use, $11 per vehicle for camping. From Vernal, go north six miles on U.S. 191, then turn left two miles; 435/789-4432 or 800/322-3770 (reservations).

RED FLEET STATE PARK

Colorful cliffs and rock formations, including three large outcrops of red sandstone, inspired the name of Red Fleet Reservoir. You can hike three-quarters of a mile or take a boat to see a dinosaur trackway. Anglers catch largemouth bass, rainbow trout, and some brown trout and bluegill. Like the larger Steinaker Reservoir, Red Fleet stores valuable water for irrigation and municipal use. A developed area offers covered picnic tables, water, restrooms, a fish-cleaning station, and a paved boat ramp; open year-round. Charges are $5 per vehicle for day use, $11 per vehicle for camping; call 435/789-4432 or 800/322-3770 (reservations) for more information. From Vernal, go north 10 miles on U.S. 191 to milepost 211, then turn right two miles on a paved road to its end.

JONES HOLE NATIONAL FISH HATCHERY

Make the long drive to Jones Hole either to see the mass production of trout or to marvel at the scenery. Canyon walls tower 2,000 feet above Jones Hole, and springs supply water for the young trout raised here that will later go to Flaming Gorge Reservoir and other areas. You can view the hatchery operation 7 A.M.–3:30 P.M. daily or see the outdoor raceways at any time during the day. The visitors center has exhibits on the trout and the Jones Hole area. Tours can be arranged on weekdays with at least one day's notice. The fragile eggs usually aren't on display, but you can see the newly hatched fish swimming in tanks inside the buildings and maturing fish in outdoor raceways. The hatchery produces about three million rainbow, brown, brook, and cutthroat trout annually. Call 435/789-4481 for information. Jones Hole is 38 miles northeast of Vernal via paved roads; head east on 500 North and follow the signs over Diamond Mountain Plateau.

Diamond Mountain is believed to be the site of a hoax played in the 1870s—two men salted the area with genuine diamonds, then sold out for a fortune; one culprit was caught, the other escaped. Unpaved roads connect Jones Hole Road with U.S. 191 and Browns Park. Hatchery staff discourage visits mid-November–mid-March because ice and drifting snow can make driving hazardous; it's best not to come then unless you call ahead, have four-wheel drive, and are prepared for winter camping.

An easy hiking trail begins below the raceways and follows Jones Hole Creek four miles to the Green River in Dinosaur National Monument. Hikers enjoy the spectacular canyon scenery, lush vegetation, a chance to see wildlife, and some Fremont pictographs. The creek has good fishing; special regulations (posted) include use of artificial lures and flies only. You may camp midway on the trail near the confluence with Ely Creek by first obtaining a backcountry permit from Dinosaur National Monument. Ely Creek has good places to camp and explore. The trail begins at an elevation of 5,550 feet and descends 500 feet to the Green River in Whirlpool Canyon.

JOHN JARVIE RANCH

Browns Park, along the Green River in Utah's northeast corner and adjacent to Colorado, has always been remote. The Wild Bunch and other outlaws often used the area as a hangout. John Jarvie settled here in 1880 and stayed until his death in 1909. He ran a store, post office, and ferry and still had time to take care of the ranch and do some prospecting. A guided tour of the restored ranch takes in the original 1880s corral, blacksmith shop and tools, farm implements, crude dugout, stone house, and other structures. Jarvie's store has been reconstructed and filled with shelves of canned goods, dried food, pots and pans, tools, harnesses, barbed wire, and other necessities of late-19th-century ranch life. Exhibits also show artifacts dug up from the original store site.

The John Jarvie Ranch is open 8 A.M.–5 P.M. daily May–October; free. Call 435/885-3307 for information (or call the BLM office in Vernal, 435/781-4400). Winter visits are possible, too; call first to find out road conditions. Boaters on the Green River can easily stop off to see the ranch; a sign marks where to pull in. You can camp at **Bridge Hollow Recreation Site,** one-quarter mile downstream from the ranch (water available), and **Indian Crossing Recreation Site,** one-quarter mile upstream from the ranch (no water); the ranch also has drinking water.

Trucks or cars with good clearance can drive to the ranch on an unpaved road through scenic Crouse Canyon; this route branches off Jones Hole Road 26 miles from Vernal, goes north past Crouse Reservoir and into the canyon, winds west through hills and parallels the Green River (though the river is hard to see from the road), crosses a bridge over the swift-flowing Green, and turns left 0.3 mile; distance from Jones Hole Road is 28 miles. Another way in is to go north from Vernal on U.S. 191 to 0.7 mile past the Wyoming border and turn right 22 miles on a gravel road; a steep 14 percent grade into Browns Park makes climbing back out difficult for RVs and other underpowered vehicles. A third approach is from Maybell, Colorado, on CO 318 (paved until the Utah border); this is the best road, especially in winter. Colorado 318 also provides access to Browns Park National Wildlife Refuge, a stopover point for migratory waterfowl in spring and autumn and a nesting habitat for ducks and Great Basin Canada geese. A gravel tour road goes through the refuge.

ASHLEY NATIONAL FOREST (VERNAL DISTRICT)

The southeastern part of the Uinta Mountains has very pleasant mountain country with scenic drives, fishing, hiking, camping, picnicking, and winter sports. Contact the U.S. Forest Service office in Vernal for road conditions and recreation information. Roads at the higher elevations open about the beginning of June and are often passable through October. Most roads to the campgrounds and reservoirs are okay for cars. Some areas may be closed to vehicle use because of

wet conditions, wildlife habitat, sheep ranges, or erosion problems. One handy campground is **Lodgepole,** offering sites with water late May–early September at an elevation of 8,100 feet; it's 30 miles north of Vernal on U.S. 191 on the way to Flaming Gorge NRA. Sites are $13; some can be reserved at www.reserveamerica.com or by calling 877/444-6777. Nearby, **Red Springs** is another roadside campground.

Anglers will find rainbow trout in most of the lakes and streams. Brown trout and native cutthroat trout live in some areas. Most hiking trails are rocky with some steep sections; carry topo maps. Trails lead into the High Uintas Wilderness from Chepeta Lake and West Fork of Whiterocks trailheads; road distances to the trailheads are relatively long, then there's a hike of about 6–7 miles to the wilderness boundary. In winter, three cross-country ski trails lead west from U.S. 191 into the Grizzly Ridge and Little Brush Creek areas; signed trailheads are about 25 miles north of Vernal. Most of these trails are rated intermediate to advanced, though some sections are good for beginners, too. Snowmobilers have an extensive network of trails that mostly follow forest roads.

RED CLOUD LOOP SCENIC DRIVE

This 74-mile loop winds through scenic canyons and mountains northwest of Vernal. Allow about half a day for just the drive. Side roads go to East Park and Oaks Park Reservoirs, campgrounds, fishing streams, and hiking areas. Aspen trees put on a brilliant display in autumn. About half the drive follows unpaved forest roads, so it's a good idea to check road conditions first with the U.S. Forest Service office in Vernal. Cars with good clearance can usually make the trip if the roads are dry. Drive 20 miles north from Vernal on U.S. 191 (or 15 miles south from the junction of U.S. 191 and Highway 44 in Flaming Gorge NRA) and turn west on the paved East Park Reservoir Road at the sign that says Red Cloud Loop. Signs then show the rest of the way. The Vernal Welcome Center's brochure *Red Cloud Loop* describes points of interest.

It's easy to find a campsite along Red Cloud Loop. **East Park Campground,** at East Park Reservoir (elev. 9,000 feet), has water; go 20 miles north of Vernal on U.S. 191, then 10 miles north-west on forest roads (all but the last mile is paved). Other campgrounds include **Oaks Park, Paradise Park, Kaler Hollow,** and **Whiterocks.** Of these, only Whiterocks has drinking water.

Flaming Gorge National Recreation Area

The Flaming Gorge Dam impounds the Green River just south of the Wyoming border, backing up a reservoir through 91 miles of gentle valleys and fiery red canyons. The rugged land displays spectacular scenery where the Green River cuts into the Uinta Mountains—cliffs rising as high as 1,500 feet, twisted rock formations, and sweeping panoramas. Although much of the lake lies in Wyoming, most of the campgrounds and other visitor facilities, as well as the best scenery, are in Utah. Some of northeastern Utah's best mountain biking can be found around the Flaming Gorge area. Boating on the clear blue waters of the lake or the river below is one of the best ways to enjoy the sights. Water-skiers have plenty of room on the lake's 66 square miles. Swimming is popular, too, as is scuba diving: **Atlantis Divers,** 206 West Main St., Vernal, 435/789-3616 or 800/894-3616, is the best resource for diving in the reservoir. Anglers regularly pull trophy trout and smallmouth bass from the lake and trout from the river. Rafting the lively Green River below the dam offers a thrilling ride that anyone with care and proper safety equipment can take—no special skills are needed. Be sure you're properly equipped before setting out. The U.S. Forest Service and private concessions offer boating facilities and about two dozen campgrounds in the recreation area.

Peace, quiet, and snow prevail in winter. Dedicated anglers still cast their lines into the Green River or fish through the lake ice. Cross-country skiers and snowmobilers make their trails through the woods. Campgrounds are closed, though snow campers and hardy RVers can stop for the night in parking areas.

Staff and volunteers at the **Flaming Gorge Ranger District/Manila Headquarters office** can answer your questions year-round at the junction of Highway 44 and Highway 43 in the center of Manila, P.O. Box 279, Manila, UT 84046, 435/784-3445. The office also sells forest and topo maps and some books; open 8 A.M.–4:30 P.M. daily in summer and 8 A.M.–4:30 P.M. Monday–Friday the rest of the year.

Information centers at Flaming Gorge Dam and Red Canyon Overlook have exhibits, video programs, maps, and literature. Flaming Gorge NRA can be easily reached by heading north 35 miles on U.S. 191 from Vernal. In Wyoming, head south on Highway 530 from the town of Green River or U.S. 191 from near Rock Springs.

Look for groups of graceful pronghorn in the open country east of the lake at Antelope Flat (north of Dutch John) and in the Lucerne area on the west side. Other wildlife in the area includes deer, elk, moose, mountain lion, black bear, bighorn sheep, fox, bobcat, mink, and eagle.

Admission to the Flaming Gorge National Recreation Area is $2 per vehicle per day. The official website is www.fs.fed.us/r4/ashley/fg_html_aw.html.

The rugged land displays spectacular scenery where the Green River cuts into the Uinta Mountains—cliffs rising as high as 1,500 feet, twisted rock formations, and sweeping panoramas.

FLAMING GORGE DAM AND VISITORS CENTER

Nearly a million cubic yards of concrete went into this dam, which was completed in 1962. The structure rises 502 feet above bedrock and is 1,285

NORTHEASTERN UTAH

feet long at the crest. The dam is open for self-guided tours daily from about the first weekend in April to the last weekend in September and for guided tours daily about early May–late September. Tours last 20–30 minutes and are free; check hours at the visitors center on the west end of the dam. You'll descend inside for a look at the three giant generators in the power-plant room, then go one floor below to where a shaft connects the turbine and generator of one of the units.

The visitors center has a large 3-D map of the area, exhibits, and video programs; books and maps are on sale and staff will answer your questions. Open 9 A.M.–5 P.M. Thursday–Monday year-round, and daily with extended hours in summer. The dam and visitors center are 6.5 miles northeast on U.S. 191 from the junction with Highway 44, or 2.8 miles southwest of Dutch John.

RED CANYON VISITORS CENTER

Sheer cliffs drop 1,360 feet to the lake below. The visitors center and nearby viewpoints offer splendid panoramas up and down the canyon and to the lofty Uinta Mountains in the distance. A fully accessible nature trail connects the overlooks and has signs about the ecology. Exhibits inside describe local wildlife and flora, geology, Native American groups that once lived here, and early history and settlement of the area. Books and maps are for sale at an information desk; the staff answers visitor questions and offers video programs. Open 10 A.M.–5 P.M. daily Memorial Day weekend to mid-September. The visitors center is 3.5 miles west on Highway 44 from the junction with U.S. 191, then three miles in on a paved road. Three very nice campgrounds are near the visitors center: **Red Canyon, Canyon Rim,** and **Greens Lake.**

SHEEP CREEK CANYON GEOLOGICAL AREA

Canyon walls on this scenic loop drive reveal rock layers deformed and turned on end by immense geological forces. The earth's crust broke along the Uinta North Fault and the south side rose 15,000 feet relative to the north. Fossils of trilobites, corals, sea urchins, gastropods, and other marine animals show that the ocean once covered this spot before the uplifting and faulting. Rock layers of yet another time preserve fossilized wood and tracks of crocodile-like reptiles. Nongeologists can appreciate the drive, too. The road through Sheep Creek Canyon is paved but has some narrow and rough places; it's closed in winter. The 13-mile loop branches off Highway 44 south of Manila between mileposts 14 and 15 and rejoins Highway 44 at milepost 22; the loop can be done in either direction. The *Wheels of Time* geology brochure, available at visitors centers and the Manila headquarters, describes geologic formations at marked stops. Three picnic areas line the drive—two in the lower part of the canyon and one in Palisades Memorial Park upstream where the road climbs out of the canyon. Camping in the canyon has been restricted ever since a flash flood in 1965 killed a family of seven; Palisades Memorial Park marks the site. Only dispersed camping is allowed along the drive and only October 1–May 15. Two primitive campgrounds (outhouses but no water or established sites) lie just off Highway 44 along lower Sheep Creek a short way from the entrance to the scenic loop.

SWETT RANCH

Oscar Swett homesteaded near Flaming Gorge in 1909, when he was just 16 years old, then built up a large cattle ranch in this isolated region. With the nearest store days away, Oscar ran his own blacksmith shop and sawmill and did much of the ranch work; his wife Emma tended the garden, made the family's clothing, raised nine children, and helped with the ranch chores. You can experience some of the early homestead life on a visit to the ranch by joining Forest Service tours from Memorial Day to Labor Day Thursday–Monday 9 A.M.–5 P.M. (check hours at the visitors centers). The house, cabins, spring house, root cellar, blacksmith shop, horse barn, cow shed, many other outbuildings, and farm machinery have been preserved. Drive north 0.3 mile on U.S. 191 from the Highway 44 junction (or south 1.6 miles from Flaming Gorge Lodge), then turn west and follow signs 1.3 miles on a gravel road.

BOATING ON FLAMING GORGE RESERVOIR

Watch for strong winds on the reservoir; they can whip up large waves without warning—even on a clear day. Rock reefs may appear and disappear as the lake level changes. Three marinas along the lake's length offer rentals, fuel docks, and supplies. Free paved boat ramps at these and several other locations are maintained by the Forest Service. **Cedar Springs Marina**, P.O. Box 337, Dutch John, UT 84023, 435/889-3795, near the dam at the lower end of the lake, rents boats (fishing, ski, and pontoon) and fishing gear and has a fuel dock, slips, store, scenic tours, and guided fishing trips; open April–October. Turnoff for the marina is 1.7 miles west of Flaming Gorge Dam on U.S. 191.

Lucerne Valley Marina, P.O. Box 10, Manila, UT 84046, 435/784-3483, provides services on the broad central section of the lake near Manila; the marina has boat rentals (fishing, ski, pontoon, and houseboats), fishing gear rentals, a fuel dock, slips, store, and guided fishing trips; open mid-March–mid-November. The marina is eight miles east of Manila on paved roads.

Buckboard Marina is on the west shore in Wyoming, 22.5 miles northeast of Manila on Highway 43/530, or 23.5 miles south of Green River on Highway 530. Services include boat rentals (fishing, ski, and pontoon), fishing gear rentals, a fuel dock, slips, store, scenic tours, and guided fishing trips; contact the marina at Star Route 1, Green River, WY 82935, 307/875-6927 or 800/824-8155.

THE GREEN RIVER BELOW FLAMING GORGE DAM

The Green bounces back to life in the Little Hole Canyon below the dam and provides enjoyment for boaters, anglers, and hikers.

Float Trips: Anyone in good shape with a raft, life jacket (must be worn), a paddle (and a spare), bailing bucket, and common sense can put in at the launch area just below the dam and float downriver to Little Hole (2.5 hours for seven river miles) or to Indian Crossing just above the John Jarvie Historic Ranch (5–8 hours for 14.5 river miles). It's also possible to continue 11 miles beyond Indian Crossing to Swallow Canyon take-out or 35 miles to Gates of Lodore; these runs are mostly flat and have troublesome sandbars at low water. Gates of Lodore marks the beginning of some big rapids in Dinosaur National Monument; you'll need permits and white-water experience here—or you can make prior arrangements to join a commercial river trip.

Visitors with canoes, kayaks, and dories can float all sections of the Green between the dam and Gates of Lodore, though river experience is needed for these craft. Have proper equipment before you get in and go. Raft rentals and shuttle services are provided by Flaming Gorge Lodge, 435/889-3773, and Flaming Gorge Recreation Services at the Dutch John Store, 435/885-3191. Rentals typically cost $50–90 per day, depending on the size of the raft; vehicle shuttles cost about $32 to Little Hole. Drivers can also drop their vehicles off at Little Hole and take an early-morning shuttle back to the starting point for about $10 per person.

Friday, Saturday, and holidays in summer often see large crowds on the river; you'll need reservations then for raft rentals and shuttles. For solitude, try to come Sunday to Wednesday. Guide services for boating and fishing trips can be contacted through the rental outfits. Life jackets (included with rentals) *must* be worn by all boaters—the water is too cold (57°F in summer, 40° in winter) to swim in for long. The 10 Class II rapids between the dam and Little Hole lend some excitement to the trip but aren't usually dangerous. Red Creek Rapid below Little Hole is a Class III rapid and can be difficult; scouting before running is recommended (many groups portage this one). Camping is permitted downstream from Little Hole at established primitive sites or dispersed sites. Bring drinking water or obtain some at Little Hole. No motors are allowed between the dam and Indian Crossing. Water flow varies according to power needs; allow more time if the flow is small. Call the Bureau of Reclamation, 435/885-3121, for present conditions.

The put-in is at the end of a 1.4-mile paved road (may not be signed) that turns off U.S. 191 one-third mile east of the dam. The parking area at the river is small and for unloading boats and passengers only. The main parking areas are 0.7 mile back up the road. Drivers can take either of two foot trails that descend from the parking lots to the river. The shuttle to Little Hole is only eight miles (paved) via Dutch John. The drive to Indian Crossing is much longer, 38 miles (25 of them unpaved); go north on U.S. 191 0.7 mile beyond the Wyoming state line, then turn east on a gravel road to Browns Park and follow signs; one section of this road has a 14 percent grade.

Fishing: Anglers can follow the **Little Hole National Recreation Trail** along the north bank of the Green River through Red Canyon for seven miles between the main parking area below the dam and Little Hole. Many good fishing spots dot the way. No camping, horses, ground fires, or motorized vehicles are allowed. The Green River downstream from the dam has a reputation for some of western America's best river fishing. Trophy catches have included 22-pound rainbow, 18-pound brown, and 14-pound cutthroat trout. Modifications to the dam allow the ideal temperature mix of warmer water near the lake's surface and cold water from the depths. Special regulations apply here to maintain the high-quality fishing (check for current regulations). Trout between 13 and 20 inches (the most prolific breeders) must be returned to the water; there's a three-fish limit (two under 13 inches, one over 20 inches), and only artificial lures and flies may be used. Anglers using waders should wear life jackets in case the river level rises unexpectedly; neoprene closed-cell foam waders are recommended for extra flotation and protection against hypothermia.

HIKING AND BIKING TRAILS

The **Canyon Rim Trail** is a popular 4.2-mile (one-way) hike or mountain-bike ride with trailheads at Red Canyon visitors center and the Greendale Overlook, a short distance from the junction of U.S. 191 and Highway 44. **Browne Lake** is a popular starting point for hikes outside the recreation area: Trail 005 goes to the **Ute Mountain Fire Lookout Tower,** a national historic site (two miles one-way); Trail 016 goes to **Hacking Lake** (seven miles one-way); Trail 012 goes to **Tepee Lakes** (five miles one-way) and **Leidy Peak** (elev. 12,028 feet; eight miles one-way); and Trail 017 goes to **Spirit Lake** (15 miles one-way). Browne Lake is 4.5 miles west on unpaved Forest Route 221 from the Sheep Creek loop drive, then 1.5 miles southeast on the Browne Lake road; see the Ashley National Forest map. Stop by Altitude Cycle in Vernal, 580 E. Main, 435/781-2595, for a guide to mountain-bike trails in northeastern Utah. Rentals are available at the Red Canyon Lodge; they also host the Dinotrax mountain-bike festival every August. Visitors centers and Forest Service offices have maps of hiking and mountain-bike trails and can suggest dirt roads suitable for either activity. The USGS topo maps are recommended, too.

DUTCH JOHN

Dutch John has always been a government town. It sprang up in 1957–58 to house workers during the construction of Flaming Gorge Dam and had a peak population of about 3,000. About 150 current residents work in various state and federal agencies.

Flaming Gorge Recreation/Dutch John Service, at the turnoff for Dutch John on U.S. 191, 435/885-3191, has a snack bar (open daily Memorial Day weekend–Labor Day), store (open early April–late October), raft rental and shuttle services, hot showers, and a gas station (open all year). **Flaming Gorge Flying Service,** at Dutch John Airport, 435/885-3338, offers raft rentals, river trips, guided fishing trips, shuttle service, hot showers, a launderette, and airplane fuel.

MANILA

The tiny town of Manila, just west of the recreation area, is the seat of Daggett County, the smallest and least-populated county in Utah. The name commemorates Admiral Dewey's capture of Manila in the Philippines, which occurred in 1898, while surveyors were laying out the Utah townsite. Manila is a handy, though rather bare-bones, base for travel in the Flaming Gorge area. The town is 63 miles northwest of Vernal and 46 miles south of Green River, Wyoming.

Food: Dine at the **Rainbow Inn,** W. Hwy. 43, 435/784-3117, open daily for breakfast, lunch, and dinner. Both gas stations in the center of town have small stores and snack bars.

ACCOMMODATIONS

$50–75: Flaming Gorge Lodge, seven miles southwest of Dutch John (Greendale, U.S. 191, Dutch John, UT 84023), 435/889-3773, offers motel rooms and condos all year (with reduced winter rates) and a restaurant serving breakfast, lunch, and dinner daily all year. The lodge also has a store, raft rentals, shuttles, and guided river fishing trips. The only remotely appealing place to stay in Manila is the **Vacation Inn,** W. Hwy. 43, 435/784-3259 or 800/662-4327, where all rooms have kitchenettes; open April–October.

Over $100: The nicest place to stay in the Flaming Gorge area is **Red Canyon Lodge,** 790 Red Canyon Rd., 435/889-3759, which sits beside the privately operated Green's Lake a short distance from the Red Canyon visitors center. The resort is open early April–late October (and winter weekends) and has rustic cabins and luxury duplex cabins (sleep up to six) with kitchens. A restaurant opens daily for breakfast, lunch, and dinner; a store offers groceries and fishing supplies, bike rentals, horseback riding, and boat rentals on Green's Lake.

Campgrounds: The camping season begins with the opening of Lucerne Valley Campground (eight miles east of Manila), usually on Easter Sunday. By Memorial Day, everything should be open. Campgrounds begin closing after Labor Day, though at least one is left open through October for hunters. If you're here early or late in the season, stop by or call the Manila Forest Service office or the Flaming Gorge Dam visitors center to find out what's available. Most campgrounds have water and charge a fee of $8–15. Group sites and single-family units in some areas can be reserved at www.reserveusa.com, or by calling 877/444-6777. Two primitive campgrounds (outhouses but no water or established sites) lie just off Highway 44 along lower Sheep Creek. Some primitive campgrounds on the lake can be reached only by boat or trail; these include Kingfisher, Island, Gooseneck, Hideout, and Jarvies Canyon. **Flaming Gorge KOA,** on W. Hwy. 43, 435/784-3184, has showers, laundry, pool, and playground; open May–October.

VICINITY OF FLAMING GORGE NRA

Spirit Lake has a beautiful setting in the high country of the Uintas. The lake (elev. 10,000 feet) offers fishing, boating, a campground, and a lodge. Hikers can take trails to nearby lakes (17 lie within three miles!) and to the High Uintas Wilderness. **Spirit Lake Campground** is in a fir, spruce, and lodgepole pine forest; open early June–late October.

Browne Lake has a small campground (elev. 8,200 feet; no water or fee) and fishing for native cutthroat trout. Several trails start nearby (see the Hiking and Biking Trails section). Browne Lake is 4.5 miles west on unpaved Forest Route 221 from the Sheep Creek loop drive, then 1.5 miles southeast on the Browne Lake road; see the Ashley National Forest map.

Ute Mountain Fire Lookout Tower (elev. 8,834 feet) has a good panorama of surrounding alpine lakes, Flaming Gorge Lake, and the Uintas. The tower has been restored as a historic site; ask at a visitors center for days and hours (it is staffed by volunteers and has irregular hours). Turn west one mile on Forest Route 221 from the Sheep Creek loop drive, then 1.5 miles south on Forest Route 005.

Dinosaur National Monument

The monument owes its name and fame to one of the world's most productive sites for dinosaur bones. More than 1,600 bones of 11 different dinosaur species cover a rock face at the quarry. The spectacular canyons of the Green and Yampa Rivers form another aspect of the monument. Harpers Corner Scenic Drive winds onto high ridges and canyon viewpoints in the heart of Dinosaur Monument. River-running allows a close look at the geology and wildlife within the depths and provides the bonus of thrilling rapids. Dinosaur National Monument straddles the Utah-Colorado border, but only the quarry, in the western end of the monument, has dinosaur bones.

Admission to the national monument costs $10 per vehicle for a seven-day pass, $5 for hikers, bicyclists, and motorcyclists. For supplementary information on Dinosaur National Monument, contact the Park Headquarters, 4545 E. U.S. 40, Dinosaur, CO 81610, 970/374-3000, www.nps.gov/dino.

THE LAND

From the original 80 acres reserved at the quarry in 1915, Dinosaur National Monument has grown to more than 200,000 acres of rivers, canyons, valleys, plateaus, and mountains. Elevations range from 4,750 feet at the Green River near the quarry to 9,006 feet atop Zenobia Peak of Douglas Mountain. The high country is part of the east flank of the Uinta Mountains, whose geology is graphically revealed in the deep canyons of the Green and Yampa Rivers. Wildlife inhabiting this rugged terrain includes mule deer, elk, pronghorn, Rocky Mountain bighorn sheep, mountain lion, black bear, coyote, bobcat, red and gray fox, badger, striped and Western spotted skunks, ringtail cat, raccoon, beaver, bat, and many species of rats and mice. Streamside vegetation consists largely of cottonwood, box elder, willow, tamarisk, and some black birch. Desert plants such as sagebrush, greasewood, shadscale, saltbush, and rabbitbrush grow

DINOSAUR COUNTRY

A fortunate combination of sand and water preserved the bones of dinosaurs, turtles, crocodiles, and clam shells from about 145 million years ago at this spot. River floods washed the carcasses onto a sandbar, where they were buried and preserved. Pressure from thousands of feet of additional sediments above gradually turned the sand to rock, and the bones within it were partially mineralized. Later, uplift of the Rockies and Uintas tilted the sandstone layer nearly on edge and exposed the overlying rocks to erosion.

In 1909, Earl Douglass, of the Carnegie Museum in Pittsburgh, suspected that dinosaur bones might be found here because similar rock layers had yielded fine specimens in Colorado and Wyoming. He was right. A discovery of eight brontosaurus tail bones in their original positions the following year became the first of many rewarding finds at the site. Douglass and other workers continued excavations until 1924, removing 350 tons of bones and attached rock that included 22 complete skeletons and parts of hundreds of other specimens. (Some of the best mounted skeletons can be seen at the Carnegie Museum.) After 1924, quarry work shifted emphasis from removing bones to exposing them in relief in their natural positions.

on the slopes at lower elevations. Middle elevations have piñon pine and juniper trees, serviceberry, buckbrush, and sagebrush. Douglas fir, aspen, ponderosa pine, spruce, and mountain mahogany thrive on the mountains and in the protective shade of the canyon walls. Annual precipitation averages about nine inches.

DINOSAUR QUARRY VISITORS CENTER

A large enclosure protects the quarry face from the elements and houses laboratories and visitor exhibits. Near the entrance, you pass a

DINOSAUR NATIONAL MONUMENT

© AVALON TRAVEL PUBLISHING, INC.

realistic stegosaurus before climbing a spiral ramp to the quarry observation deck. Exhibits illustrate the sandbar and Morrison scene and place the quarry in context within the span of geologic time. The rock layer is 8–12 feet thick and dates from the Jurassic period—about the middle of the age of dinosaurs. Workers have finished reliefing the quarry bones and have left them in place as a permanent exhibit. Roughly three-quarters of the bones come from sauropods—giant plant eaters with long necks and tails. All the bones appear in a jumble in the rock, just as they were deposited in the river sands long ago. One skeleton has a number marked on each bone; a diagram lets you figure out which piece is which. Models, artwork, and specimens on the lower level depict the variety of dinosaurs found here. Exhibits also show how workers remove bones from the rock and how they learn details about the dinosaurs' size, shape, diet, and muscle structure. Peek through windows of the pale-

ontology lab to see bones under study and the instruments used. In winter, you may see researchers at work here.

Staff will answer questions about the quarry and other places to see in the monument. Handouts available on request include information on backcountry roads, hiking, river-running, and Fremont rock art. A schedule posted during the main season lists times and places of ranger talks, nature walks, auto tours, children's programs, and campfire programs. A good selection of dinosaur and natural history books, posters, postcards, slides, topo and geologic maps, bird and mammal lists, and film is sold. The Dinosaur Quarry, 435/781-7700, is open 8 A.M.–4:30 P.M. daily (extended to about 7 P.M. Memorial Day–Labor Day weekends) and closed Thanksgiving, Christmas, and New Year's Day. From Vernal, drive east 13 miles on U.S. 40 to Jensen, then turn north seven miles on Highway 149. Parking space is in short supply during the busy summer season, so a free shuttle operates every 15 minutes between the quarry and a separate parking area during most of the day. The rest of the year you can drive all the way in, as can people with disabilities anytime. The privately owned **Dinosaur Quarry Gift Shop,** just outside the monument, has a snack bar; open summer only.

QUARRY TO JOSIE MORRIS CABIN DRIVE

Stop at the Dinosaur Quarry or a roadside pullout for the booklet *Tour of the Tilted Rocks,* which describes points of interest for an auto tour to the Cub Creek area. The drive goes 10 miles past the quarry turnoff to a historic ranch, passing sites of Fremont rock art and the Split Mountain and Green River Campgrounds on the way. A small overhang known as the **"Swelter Shelter"** contains some petroglyphs; the pullout is one mile beyond the quarry turnoff; a trail leads 200 feet to the cave. **Sound of Silence Nature Trail** begins on the left 1.9 miles past the quarry turnoff; this unusual nature trail makes a three-mile loop up Red Wash, enters an anfractuosity (a

Kids can learn how paleontologists re-create dinosaur skeletons at the Dinosaur Quarry.

© JUDY JEWELL

NORTHEASTERN UTAH

winding channel), crosses a bench and a ridge with fine panoramas, then descends through some slickrock back to Red Wash and the trailhead; you'll need the trail guide (best purchased at the quarry or headquarters) for this hike. Red Wash is also good for short strolls—just avoid it if thunderstorms threaten!

Continue on the drive to the Split Mountain Campground turnoff; the side road winds down one mile to the campground at the Green River. The Green River emerges from Split Mountain Canyon here after some of the roughest rapids on the whole river. **Desert Voices Nature Trail** begins at the campground entrance and makes a two-mile loop; a trail brochure available at the quarry, headquarters, or near the start describes plants and geology seen along the way—allow 1.5–2 hours.

Back on the main road, a Green River overlook is on the left 1.2 miles past the Split Mountain Campground turnoff. The road to Green River Campground is a short way farther on the left. **Placer Point Picnic Area** is 1.1 miles beyond the junction, just before a bridge across the Green River. The main road continues past a private ranch, then pavement ends. A road fork on the right 2.7 miles past the bridge goes to Blue Mountain (high-clearance vehicles and good maps needed); keep left for the Josie Morris Cabin. A **petroglyph panel** is on the left beside the road 0.7 mile beyond the road fork. Continue past this panel 0.2 mile and park in a pullout on the right (may not be signed) for a look at no fewer than seven lizard petroglyphs on the cliffs above and to the left; a steep climb up the slope (no trail) allows a closer view of these and other figures. Large shade trees surround the **Josie Morris Cabin** at the end of the road, 0.9 mile farther. Josie grew up in Browns Park during the 1870s and 1880s and settled here about 1914. She spent much of the next 50 years alone at the ranch, tending the fields, garden, cows, pigs, and chickens. She was in her 90s when she died as a result of a hip broken in a riding accident. You can visit her cabin, outbuildings, orchards, and a nearby box canyon.

MONUMENT HEADQUARTERS

A few exhibits and a 10-minute slide show (shown on request) introduce the monument's history, dinosaurs, and canyons. The staff offers handouts, books, and maps and will answer your questions. Open 8 A.M.–4:30 P.M. daily from Memorial Day weekend to Labor Day and 8 A.M.–4:30 P.M. Monday–Friday the rest of the year; 4545 U.S. 40, Dinosaur, CO 81610, 970/374-2216. The River Office here handles permits for groups running the Green or Yampa River within the monument. A self-guided scenic drive to Harpers Corner begins at the headquarters. You won't see any dinosaur exhibits in this part of the monument—the bones are only at the quarry area. From Vernal, go 35 miles east on U.S. 40 to the Colorado town of Dinosaur, then continue another two miles east to the monument headquarters. Dinosaur has a couple of small motels and places to eat.

HARPERS CORNER ROAD

This scenic drive begins at monument headquarters in Colorado and winds north past many scenic overlooks. The road opens in about early May and closes after the first big snowstorm in November although it's kept clear to Plug Hat Butte overlook, 4.3 miles in. A booklet available at the quarry and headquarters has good background material on the area and describes the sights at numbered stops along the way. The paved road is 31 miles long (one-way); allow about two hours for the round-trip or half a day if you also plan to hike the two nature trails. You'll pass three picnic areas along the way, but no water or campgrounds are available. The road climbs a series of ridges with fine views of much of the monument, including Island Park, Echo Park, and the canyons of the Green and Yampa Rivers. You'll see spectacular faulted and folded rock layers and a complete range of vegetation, from the cottonwoods along the rivers far below to aspen and firs of the highlands.

Plug Hat Nature Trail is an easy half-mile loop in a piñon-juniper forest at a stop 4.3 miles from the beginning of the drive. At Island Park

Overlook, about 26 miles along the drive, **Ruple Point Trail** heads west four miles (one-way) on an old jeep road to an overlook of the Green River in Split Mountain Canyon; carry water. The drive ends at Harpers Corner, a long and narrow peninsula. You can continue one mile on foot to the very tip by taking the **Harpers Corner Trail**; a brochure available at the start describes features visible from numbered stops. Cliffs on each side drop to a bend of the Green River at the beginning of Whirlpool Canyon, about 2,500 feet below. Echo Park, Steamboat Rock, and the sinuous curves of the Yampa River Canyon are visible, too. Allow 1.5–2 hours for the easy to moderately difficult walk. Binoculars come in handy for a better look at the geology and other features.

ECHO PARK

A rough dirt road branches off Harpers Corner Road 25 miles from monument headquarters and winds down more than 2,000 feet in 13 miles to Echo Park. The setting of Echo Park, near the confluence of the Green and Yampa Rivers, is one of the prettiest in the monument. The massive sandstone fin of Steamboat Rock looms into the sky across the Green River. Echo Park offers a campground, river access for boaters (permit needed), and a ranger station (open summer only). Cars with good clearance can often make this side trip, though it's better to have a truck. As with all dirt roads in Dinosaur National Monument, it shouldn't be attempted in any vehicle when it's wet. The clay surface becomes extremely slick after rains but usually dries out in 2–3 hours. Hikers can follow an unmarked route from Echo Park along the banks of the Yampa River to the mouth of Sand Canyon; go up Sand Canyon until it opens out, cut across benchland to Echo Park Road in lower Pool Creek Canyon, and follow the road back to Echo Park. High water levels on the Yampa can block the route from about late May to late June; you'll need to do some rock-scrambling in Sand Canyon. The loop is 6–8 miles long, depending on the route taken.

Drivers with high-clearance trucks can also explore the backcountry on **Yampa Bench Road,** which turns off eight miles down the Echo Park Road. Yampa Bench Road has views of the Yampa River Canyon and Douglas Mountain to the north and Blue Mountain to the south; allow 4–5 hours to drive the 38 miles between Echo Park Road and U.S. 40. It's always a good idea to get directions and the latest road conditions from a ranger before driving into the backcountry. Rains occasionally cut off travel, so carry extra water, food, and camping gear.

OTHER AREAS

Gates of Lodore, on the Green River, has a campground, a boat launching area for river-runners, and a ranger station—all open year-round. **Gates of Lodore Trail** follows the river downstream to the dramatic canyon entrance, an easy 1.5-mile round-trip; get a trail leaflet at the ranger station or the trailhead. Gates of Lodore is 108 miles from monument headquarters via U.S. 40, Highway 318, and 10 miles of gravel road.

Rainbow Park and **Ruple Ranch** are on the west shore of the Green River at opposite ends of Island Park. Both offer places to launch or take out river boats. Easiest access is from the quarry area; distances are 26 miles to Rainbow Park and about another five miles to Ruple Ranch via the rough and unpaved Island Park Road. Cars with good clearance may be able to drive in, but the road is impassable during wet weather.

HIKING IN THE MONUMENT

Any of the trails can easily be done on a day trip. The two longest—Jones Hole and Ruple Point—are each about eight miles round-trip and moderately difficult. The Echo Park–Sand Canyon route is a similar distance. Easier, self-guided nature walks are Red Rock (two miles round-trip), Plug Hat (half-mile round-trip), Harpers Corner (two miles round-trip), and Gates of Lodore (1.5 miles round-trip). Each trail is described elsewhere (see North of Vernal for visiting Jones Hole). Overnight trips are possible on the longer trails or on cross-country routes. Off-trail hikers must be able to navigate with map and compass and find (or carry) water and should have experience in desert travel over rugged terrain. One possibility is the three- to five-day hike from Echo Park to Gates of Lodore; before starting, though, you'll need to find river-runners to take you across the Yampa. Obtain the required backcountry permit for overnight hikes from rangers at monument headquarters or at the Dinosaur Quarry.

RIVER-RUNNING

Trips down the Green or Yampa River feature outstanding scenery and exciting rapids. All boaters in the monument must have permits or be with a licensed river-running company, even for day trips. A one-day trip on the Green gives a feeling for the river at a modest cost (see Recreation in the Vernal section). The most popular one-day run begins at Rainbow Park or Ruple Park; you bounce through the rapids of Split Mountain Canyon to take-outs at Split Mountain Campground. Longer trips usually begin on the Green at Gates of Lodore in the north end of the monument. Names of rapids like Upper and Lower Disaster Falls, Harp Rapids, Triplet Falls, and Hells Half Mile in Canyon of Lodore suggest that this isn't a place for inexperienced boaters.

In 1869, John Wesley Powell lost one of his four boats and many supplies at Disaster Falls on his first expedition. As a result, the rest of the trip was too hurried to make all the scientific studies he had planned. Powell's second trip, in 1871, also had trouble when another boat was upset here.

Canyon depths reach 3,350 feet, the deepest in the monument. Echo Park marks the end of Canyon of Lodore 19 river miles later. The Yampa River joins the Green here and noticeably increases its size and power. Whirlpool Canyon begins downstream with modest rapids for the next 17 miles, followed by an interlude of slow water at Island Park. The river picks up speed again on entering the warped walls of Split Mountain Canyon and roars through Moon-shine, S.O.B., Schoolboy, and Inglesby Rapids on the eight miles to Split Mountain Campground. From here, the Green flows placidly for the next 100 miles through open country.

The Yampa remains the last major undammed tributary of the Colorado River system. Snowmelt in the mountains of Colorado and Wyoming swells the Yampa to its highest and best levels May–mid-July. Most boaters put in at Deerlodge Park at the east end of the monument. The next take-out point is 46 miles downriver at Echo Park. A series of rapids culminates in Warm Springs Rapids, the Yampa's wildest. Where the water is shallow, boaters may have difficulties with sandbars and rocks.

Guided river trips are often best for first-time visitors. Contact the monument for a list of river concessionaires. Private groups planning a trip on the Green or the Yampa should write far in advance to the River Unit at monument headquarters; the office will let you know about equipment regulations and how to obtain the required permits. One-day permits are the easiest to obtain. Contact the River Unit at P.O. Box 210, Dinosaur, CO 81610, 970/374-2468. The *Dinosaur River Guide*, by Laura Evans and Buzz Belknap, has maps and descriptions of both rivers in the monument.

CAMPGROUNDS

Dinosaur National Monument has two pleasant riverside campgrounds: Green River and Split Mountain. They're within about a mile of each other. **Green River Campground,** which is open only in summer and has water and a $12 fee, is five miles east of the Dinosaur Quarry. **Split Mountain Campground** is open only November–March while nearby Green River Campground is closed; no water or fee. It's four miles east of Dinosaur Quarry, then one mile north on the Split Mountain Road.

There are several other campsites in the monument—one of the nicest is the **Echo Park Campground,** 38 miles north of Monument Headquarters, with water and several walk-in tent sites, $8. The last 13 miles of the road to Echo Park are unpaved and impassable when wet. RVs and trailers are not recommended. A small campground at **Gates of the Lodore** has a boat launch and drinking water (summer only). **Deerlodge Park Campground,** at the east end of the monument, sits just upstream from the Yampa River Canyon. Camping is primitive, with no designated sites, water, or fee; closed in winter. River trips on the Yampa usually begin here. The site is 53 miles from monument headquarters by paved roads. A primitive campground at **Rainbow Park** is 26 miles from Dinosaur Quarry on an unpaved road.

All campsites in the monument are available on a first-come, first-served basis.

VICINITY OF DINOSAUR NATIONAL MONUMENT

Stewart Lake State Waterfowl Management Area

Birders might want to make a short side trip south of Jensen to visit their feathered friends. Abundant vegetation in the water and on the shore of this shallow lake provides food and shelter for birdlife. Take the small paved road south 1.4 miles from Jensen, then, when the paved road curves right, keep going straight on the gravel road for 1.2 miles. The road is okay for cars but is too narrow for large rigs or trailers.

South of Vernal

NORTHEASTERN UTAH

OURAY NATIONAL WILDLIFE REFUGE

This desert oasis along the Green River provides a lush habitat for migratory and nesting waterfowl. Other birds and animals also find food and shelter in the brush, grass, marsh, and trees. A list compiled at the refuge names 206 bird species. More than 4,000 ducks nest in summer. Migratory populations peak in April and again in October. Some mallards and Canada geese winter along the Green River.

A self-guided auto tour loops through a variety of habitats on the 11,480-acre refuge. The tour begins at an information booth, 435/545-2522, which has a brochure and other literature, then follows gravel roads for nine miles past 12 numbered stops. Open daily all year during daylight hours; free. An observation tower gives a bird's-eye view of the marshlands. Hiking is permitted (take insect repellent). Some roads may close during spring flooding and autumn hunting, and those in the east part of the refuge may require four-wheel drive in wet weather. From Vernal, head southwest 14 miles on U.S. 40, turn south 14 miles on Highway 88, then turn into the refuge on a gravel road.

The White River has some of the best canoeing in Utah and is good for kayaking and rafting, too. The scenic ride through White River Canyon has only a few rapids, and they're easy.

OURAY NATIONAL FISH HATCHERY

Ouray National Wildlife Refuge was built with the goal of increasing the numbers of four endangered fish species: the Colorado squawfish, the humpback chub, the razorback sucker, and the longtail chub. (For more information about these fish, see the sidebar "Endangered Fish of the Colorado River Basin," in the Canyonlands National Park section of the Southeastern Utah chapter.) The fish hatchery has 18 ponds and a number of buildings. Forces of nature cause the fish to hatch in numbers much higher than the number that will survive. By collecting eggs and removing them from dangers in the stream, the hatchery ensures that more of the fish will reach maturity and reproduce.

PELICAN LAKE

Birds also stop in large numbers at this lake west of Ouray National Wildlife Refuge. The BLM has a campground (no water or fee) and a boat ramp on the south shore. From a junction northwest of the lake, go south on a narrow road (partly paved) that swings around the lake's west side to the campground and boat ramp. The lake has fishing for largemouth bass and bluegill. There's no swimming because of schistosomes (parasitic flatworms) in the water.

WHITE RIVER

The White has some of the best canoeing in Utah and is good for kayaking and rafting, too. The river originates in Colorado's White Mountains and meanders west to meet the Green River near the town of Ouray, Utah. The scenic ride through White River Canyon has only a few rapids, and they're easy. Trips can be a day to a week long, depending on where you put in and take out. Boating provides good opportunities for viewing wildlife. Groves of cottonwoods make pleasant places to camp. The best time to go is during spring runoff, mid-May–June. No permits are needed—the BLM gives boaters the responsibility for proper boating safety and clean camping. Launch point is at the Bonanza Highway Bridge (40 miles south of Vernal), and take-out is at the Mountain Fuel Bridge, 40 river miles downstream. The shuttle between the two bridges is only 20 miles on graded dirt roads. The trip can be extended by putting in at Cowboy Canyon, nine miles up-

river from Bonanza Highway Bridge on a very rough road, or by taking out at the confluence of the White and Green Rivers, 22 miles downriver from the Mountain Fuel Bridge. Both the confluence and Mountain Fuel Bridge take-outs are on Ute land; the tribe requires a permit to park or boat on its land (below Mountain Fuel Bridge). Contact the Utes at P.O. Box 190, Fort Duchesne, UT 84026, 435/722-5511. Bring life jackets, a spare paddle, insect repellent, and drinking water. Obtain information and a brochure on this trip from the BLM Vernal District office, 170 South 500 East, Vernal, UT 84078, 435/781-4400.

OTHER PLACES

The remote desert country south of Vernal has many sites of geologic or historic interest for those who enjoy exploring back roads. The BLM office in Vernal can suggest places to go. Fantasy Canyon contains eroded sandstone formations, but a high-clearance vehicle is needed to get in; contact the BLM for a map. The old Uinta Railway grade from Mack, Colorado, to the Utah ghost towns of Dragon, Watson, and Rainbow can be driven partway on a rough road. Gilsonite, a natural asphalt mined at these towns, provided the railway with most of its business. The narrow-gauge line operated 1904–1939 and had some of the steepest slick track and sharpest curves in the world.

West of Vernal

UINTAH AND OURAY INDIAN RESERVATION

The nomadic Utes moved into this part of Utah at about the same time that the older Fremont culture faded away, about 800 years ago, and practiced a hunting and gathering culture across much of the high-mountain basin country of Wyoming, Colorado, and Utah. The first white contact was with the Spanish missionary-explorer Dominguez-Escalante and his expedition in 1776, and the Utes were the first Native American group encountered by the Mormons in Utah.

Mountain men and trappers traded with the tribe during the 1820s and 1830s, though most whites figured that this land, seemingly short of water and most other resources, was worthless. Pressures of settlements elsewhere in Utah and Colorado gradually forced more and more Utes from their traditional lands into the Uinta Basin. In 1861, President Lincoln issued an executive order making nearly the entire Uinta Basin into the Uintah Indian Reservation—about 2,287,000 acres. By 1864, the U.S. Army had moved nearly all of the state's Utes onto the reservation. The Ouray Indian Reservation was established in 1881, then merged with the Uintah five years later.

Whites started having second thoughts, though, when they discovered coal and oil and realized the agricultural potential that irrigation held for the area. Much land was taken back. Beginning in 1905, heavily promoted homesteading programs brought in floods of settlers. The Utes recovered some cash awards for their lost lands during the 1950s and obtained the Hill Creek Extension south of the Uinta Basin. The reservation now covers approximately one million acres in the Uinta Basin, in the foothills of the Uinta Range and Tavaputs Plateau, and in the remote East Tavaputs Plateau.

The Ute tribe today consists of three bands: the Uintah (of Utah), the Whiteriver (moved from Colorado in 1880), and the Uncampahgre (moved from Colorado in 1882). About half of the current 2,900 Utes living on the reservation and in nearby towns belong to the Uncampahgre band; the rest are equally divided between the Uintah and the Whiteriver. Each band elects two members to the Ute tribal government. Tribal headquarters are east of Roosevelt at Fort Duchesne (pronounced doo-SHAYN), site of a U.S. Army base 1886–1912. A tribal museum at nearby Bottle Hollow Resort displays Ute artifacts and historic exhibits; you can also ask at the resort about Native American dances, powwows, and rodeos. In summer you might be able to see the Sun Dance, an important religious and social ceremony passed down from the Wind River Shoshoni. Other ceremonies are the Bear Dance (performed in spring) and the Turkey Dance (held on many social occasions).

Nontribal members must keep to the main roads on the reservation and purchase permits for most activities. Camping is allowed at the backcountry lakes open to fishing; you'll need either a fishing or a camping permit; boats need permits, too. Some lakes have boat ramps. A brochure with map and regulations also lists fishing areas and fees. Backcountry sites have outhouses and sometimes tables, but bring your own water. Small-game hunting is permitted with a tribal license. You'll need special permission to explore outside the permitted areas. Obtain permits at the Ute Indian Tribe Fish & Game Department in Fort Duchesne, 1.5 miles south of U.S. 40, P.O. Box 190, Fort Duchesne, UT 84026, 435/722-5511, or at sporting goods stores in Vernal, Price, Salt Lake City, and other towns.

Events

The July 4 **Northern Ute Indian Pow Wow and Rodeo** is the main annual event here; tribes from all over the West participate. Dances, rodeo action, craft displays, and food booths entertain the crowds. Other powwows, rodeos, and dances happen at different times of the year.

ROOSEVELT

President Theodore Roosevelt opened the way for settlement of whites on the Uintah and Ouray Indian Reservation by a proclamation in 1902. Three years later, grateful homesteaders named two of their new towns in his honor—Theodore (later renamed Duchesne) and Roosevelt. Today Roosevelt (pop. 4,300) is the largest town in Duchesne County and a supply center for surrounding agricultural and oil businesses and for the Utes. Roosevelt offers a good selection of places to stay and eat along the main highway (200 East and 200 North Streets downtown). The community is 30 miles west of Vernal and 146 miles east of Salt Lake City. Travelers can head north to Moon Lake and the High Uintas Wilderness. A scenic backcountry drive goes south to the many rock-art sites in Nine Mile Canyon (see the East of Price section).

Events

Festivities in the area on July 4 are the **Northern Ute Indian Pow Wow and Rodeo** at Fort Duchesne, **rodeos** in Neola and Tabiona, and a **Kid's Rodeo** in Altamont. **Altamont Longhorn Days & Rodeo** take place July 24. The **U.B.I.C. (Uintah Basin In Celebration)** in early August is Roosevelt's biggest annual event with parades, craft shows, and entertainment.

Recreation

The **city park** offers picnic tables, playground, and outdoor pool at 90 W. Lagoon, 435/722-4851. **Roosevelt Golf Course** has nine holes about 1.5 miles west of downtown, 435/722-9644. Catch movies at **Roosevelt Twin Theatre,** at 21 South 200 East, or **Uinta Theatre,** at 41 North 200 East; call 435/722-2095 for both places.

Accommodations and Food

Under $50: The **Frontier Motel,** 75 South 200 East, 435/722-2201 or 800/248-1014, has a swimming pool, hot tub, a pretty good restaurant, and some units with kitchenettes.

$50–75: Best Western Inn, one mile east on U.S. 40, 435/722-4644 or 800/528-1234, has a hot tub and swimming pool. Next door, **JB's** is a reliable family-style restaurant.

Information and Services

At the **Duchesne County Area Chamber of Commerce,** 48 South 200 East (P.O. Box 1417, Roosevelt, UT 84066), 435/722-4598, staff can tell you about points of interest in the area, events, and services. It's open 8 A.M.–5 P.M. Monday–Friday. Foresters at the **Roosevelt Ranger District office** of the Ashley National Forest know about camping, fishing, hiking, and road conditions on the forest lands north of town including the High Uintas Wilderness; forest maps, topo maps, and books are offered for sale; open 8 A.M.–noon and 1–5 P.M. Monday–Friday (8 A.M.–5 P.M. in summer). The office is on the west edge of town at 650 W. U.S. 40, 435/722-5018. The **public library,** next to the city park at 70 W. Lagoon, 435/722-4441, is open Monday–Saturday.

The **post office** is at 81 South 300 East. **Duchesne County Hospital** is at 250 West 300 North, 435/722-4691.

VICINITY OF ROOSEVELT
Guest Ranches and Resorts

A number of old-fashioned guest ranches operate in Ashley National Forest. The **U-Bar Wilderness Ranch,** P.O. Box 680846, Park City, UT 84068, 435/645-7256 or 800/303-7256, www.rockymtnrec.com, has been around since 1933, offering cabins, fly-fishing, horseback riding, and pack trips to those hankering to get away from it all. Lodging is in rustic one- or two-bedroom cabins ($75 double) or one cabin that can sleep 10. Meals are extra, but very reasonably priced. The ranch is 26 miles north of Roosevelt, up Highway 121 and Forest Route 118.

Anglers will love **LC Ranch,** just north of Altamont. The ranch was established in 1901 by an enterprising homesteader who decided to develop his holdings into a series of streams and ponds. Now a private reserve, the ranch contains 28 lakes and ponds filled with brookies, rainbow, and brown trout. Accommodations are in upscale "cabins" or a four-bedroom lodge decorated with over 30 trophy mounts; rates start at $75; meals are available. For information, contact LC Ranch/Western Rivers Flyfisher, 867 East 900 South, Salt Lake City, UT 84105, 435/454-3750 or 454-3090, www.lcranch.com.

The newest and most exclusive resort in the area is **Falcon's Ledge,** P.O. Box 67, Altamont, UT 84001, 435/454-3737, www.falconsledge.com. Falcon's Ledge was built originally to cater to fly fishers, upland game bird hunters, and falconers, though the luxury-level rooms and fine restaurant attract an increasing number of people who simply want to enjoy solitude and soft recreation. Rooms are located in a central lodge and are extremely comfortable; basic accommodations (without recreational options) are $165 per room. Breakfast is included, but other meals are by reservation only and are served family-style.

Ashley National Forest

Moon Lake is in the Uintas about 45 miles due north of Duchesne and 50 miles northwest of Roosevelt. Access roads are paved except for a seven-mile section crossing Native American lands. **Moon Lake Resort** offers cabins, boat rentals, store, mountain-bike rides, horseback rides, and guided pack trips June–Labor Day; write Mountain Home, UT 84051, 435/454-3142 (in-season). **Moon Lake Campground** (elev. 8,100 feet) is open with water from Memorial Day weekend to one week after Labor Day.

Major access points to the High Uintas Wilderness near Roosevelt are (from west to east): Lake Fork at Moon Lake (three trails), Center Park at the head of Hells Canyon, Swift Creek on the Yellowstone River (two trails), Uinta Canyon on the Uinta River, and West Fork of Whiterocks River. In winter, snowmobilers use trails in the Snake John area north of Whiterocks.

Five campgrounds are located along the Yellowstone River on Forest Routes 119 and 124 northwest of Roosevelt; elevations range from 7,700 feet at **Yellowstone Campground** to 8,100 feet at **Swift Creek Campground**; all have water and charge a fee from late May to the week after Labor Day.

Uinta Canyon and **Wandin** (no water) are along the Uinta River at an elevation of about 7,600 feet; take Highway 121 and Forest Route 118 north of Roosevelt.

The **Pole Creek (Elkhorn) Scenic Loop** on Forest Route 117 winds through canyons and atop ridges east of the Uinta River; some sections may be rough, though the drive is usually passable by cars with good clearance. **Pole Creek Campground** (elev. 10,200 feet) is at the north end of the loop; no water.

Big Sand Lake State Park

Good fishing attracts most of the visitors at this undeveloped park. The 390-acre reservoir has rainbow trout with some browns and cutthroats and lots of crayfish. People also come to water-ski and swim; ice fishers try their luck in winter. A boat ramp is on the southeast shore. No water or other services are available; free. The park ranger is based at Starvation State Park, near Duchesne, 435/738-2326. From Roosevelt, go southwest five miles on U.S. 40, turn west (then north) 10 miles to Upalco, continue straight (north) 0.7 mile where the main road curves left just past Upalco, then turn left 0.4 mile on a gravel road.

DUCHESNE

This small community (pop. 1,410) at the confluence of the Duchesne and Strawberry Rivers is the seat of thinly settled Duchesne (pronounced doo-SHAYN) County. The name is said to honor a French Catholic nun or a French fur trapper or to be a corruption of the name of an Indian chief. Ranching, farming, and the oil industry provide most of the employment. Main attractions for visitors are the High Uintas Wilderness and other sections of the Ashley National Forest, Starvation Lake, and fishing on the Duchesne and Strawberry Rivers.

Events and Recreation

Footprints through Duchesne on July 4 celebrates the area's homesteading with historic displays, fireworks, and entertainment. The **Duchesne County Fair,** usually on the third weekend of August, features a rodeo, parade, horse show, demolition derby, and other entertainment.

The **city park** at Main and 100 West, 435/738-2536, has picnic tables, playground, and an outdoor pool.

Accommodations

Under $50: The Inns of Duchesne comprises three separate properties, all run from its office at 23 W. Main, 435/738-2217 or 888/616-9100. Just stop by the main office and they'll sort you out. Prices at all the motels include continental breakfast. They can also set you up with an RV space.

Food

Country Kitchen Cafe, 540 W. Main, 435/738-2735, serves breakfast, lunch, and dinner daily except Sunday. **Cowan's Café,** 57 E. Main, 435/738-5609, serves breakfast, lunch, and dinner daily.

Information

People at the **Duchesne Ranger District office** of the Ashley National Forest have information on campgrounds, trailheads, and road conditions of the forest and the High Uintas Wilderness to the north and the Tavaputs Plateau to the south; forest maps, topo maps, and some books are sold. Offices are at 85 W. Main, 435/738-2482; open 8 A.M.–5 P.M. Monday–Friday (and Saturday 8 A.M.–4:30 P.M. Memorial Day–September).

VICINITY OF DUCHESNE

Guest Ranches

The **Rock Creek Guest Ranch,** P.O. Box 510060, Mountain Home, UT, 84051, 435/454-3332, offers pack trips into the High Uintah Primitive Area—fishing, hunting, and trail rides in a remote mountain setting 32 miles northwest of Altamont. The ranch offers many family-oriented activities as well, including chuckwagon meals, horseshoes, baseball, and easy hikes. Accommodations are in cabins (one bed $40; two beds $50), and meals are available

at the lodge or at special barbecue or Dutch oven picnics.

Uinta Mountains

Forest Route 144 turns north from Stockmore off Highway 35, then follows the Duchesne River North Fork to **Aspen Grove Campground** (elev. 7,000 feet), **Hades Campground** (elev. 7,100 feet), and **Iron Mine Campground** (elev. 7,200 feet). All three campgrounds have water and charge a fee from Memorial Day to one week after Labor Day; Iron Mine Campground also has a group reservation area. Forest Route 315 turns east from Defa's Ranch to **Grandview Trailhead,** an access point for the southwestern part of the High Uintas Wilderness; the grade is steep and rough, though cars with good clearance can make it in dry weather.

The **Rock Creek** area and **Upper Stillwater Reservoir** are reached by going north from Duchesne on Highway 87, turning north to Mountain Home, then west on Forest Route 134. The road is paved to the reservoir. **Miner's Gulch Campground,** 435/738-2482, is a group campground at an elevation of 7,500 feet; no water. Parking for anglers is across the road. **Yellow Pine Campground** nearby (elev. 7,600 feet) has developed sites with water and a dump station from Memorial Day to one week after Labor Day. **Upper Stillwater Campground** (elev. 7,900 feet) lies just south of Upper Stillwater Reservoir; sites are open mid-May–mid-October. **Rock Creek visitors center,** near Upper Stillwater Campground, has recreation and travel information in summer. **Rock Creek Trailhead** near the reservoir offers access into the High Uintas Wilderness.

Starvation State Park

The large Starvation Reservoir sits among rolling hills of high-desert country four miles west of Duchesne. Water-skiing is the biggest summer activity, followed by fishing, sailboarding, and sailing. Anglers catch walleye (a state record was taken here), smallmouth bass, and some largemouth bass and German brown trout. The marina is open mid-April–Labor Day with boat rentals (fishing, personal watercraft, and ski boats)

© JUDY JEWELL

Popular with anglers, boaters, and water-skiers, Starvation Reservoir is a good place to cool off.

and a store. A developed campground with pull-through and tent sites with showers overlooks the water. This exposed location can be windy. Continue past the campground turnoff for a picnic area near a sand beach. A second developed campground is just past the picnic area. There are four primitive camping areas around the reservoir; other facilities include a paved boat ramp, a fish-cleaning station, and a dump station. The park is open all year. The main season, Memorial Day weekend–Labor Day, is sometimes extended up to a month earlier and later; $5 for day use, $14 for camping. The campground usually has vacancies except on major holiday weekends. Showers and restrooms close during the off season, though outhouses are available. A paved four-mile road to the park turns off U.S. 40 just west of Duchesne. Address is P.O. Box 584, Duchesne, UT 84021, 435/738-2326 or 800/322-3770 (reservations).

Over the Mountains to Price

From Duchesne, U.S. 191 goes southwest 56 miles over the West Tavaputs Plateau to Price. The route follows the Left Fork of Indian Canyon to a pass at an elevation of 9,100 feet, then descends through Willow Creek Canyon to the Price River. Snow may close the road in winter. **Avintaquin Campground** (elev. 8,800 feet) is reached by a short gravel road from just south of the pass; sites nestle in a fir and aspen forest. The Bamberger Monument, between the pass and Price Canyon, commemorates construction of the highway by state prisoners in 1919; Governor Simon Bamberger gave the workers reduced sentences and other benefits for their efforts.

Price

In the beginning, Price was a typical Mormon community. Ranchers and farmers had settled on the fertile land surrounding the Price River in 1879. Four years later, everything changed when the railroad came through. A flood of immigrants from all over the world arrived to work in the coal mines and other rapidly growing enterprises. (An informal census taken in a pool hall at nearby Helper in the 1930s found 32 different nationalities in the room!) Coal mining has had its ups and downs in the last 100 years but continues to be the largest industry in the area. Price (pop. 8,400) is a modern city and a good base for exploring the surrounding mountains and desert. The highly recommended Prehistoric Museum and the Price Mural are in town; the Western Mining & Railroad Museum is in Helper to the north. Other places to visit lie tucked into the surrounding backcountry and include Nine Mile Canyon (rock-art and historic sites), Cleveland-Lloyd Dinosaur Quarry, San Rafael Swell, and many ghost-town sites. Roads wind up canyons to the cool forests and lakes on the Wasatch Plateau. Obtain information and maps for Carbon and Emery Counties at the Castle Country travel office (see Information). A walking-tour leaflet available at the office describes historic buildings in Price.

SIGHTS

College of Eastern Utah Prehistoric Museum

An excellent museum of natural and human history, this is a must-stop for anyone interested in the prehistoric creatures and people that lived in Utah thousands of years ago. Dramatic dinosaur displays include the skeletons of a fierce flesh-eating allosaurus, a plant-eating camptosaurus (not to be fooled with, either), a camarasaurus, a chasmosaurus, a prosaurolophus, and a stegosaurus. See bones of the huge Huntington Canyon mammoth recently discovered nearby, the colorful gemstones of the mineralogy

exhibits, and artifacts of the prehistoric Fremont and the modern Utes in the outstanding Native American collection. The power and mystery of prehistoric rock art is conveyed in a replica of the Barrier Canyon Mural. Contemporary art is on display in rotating exhibits. Kids can explore the hands-on displays in the Children's Room. The College of Eastern Utah operates the museum, at 155 E. Main, 435/613-5111 or 800/817-9949; open 9 A.M.–6 P.M. Monday–Saturday (also Sunday in spring and summer); $2 suggested donation. A gift shop offers regional and natural history books, fossils, T-shirts, and postcards.

Price Mural

Artist Lynn Fausett captured the history of Price and Carbon County in a colorful mural four feet high and 200 feet long. It extends around all four walls in the foyer of the Price Municipal Building, at the corner of Main and 200 East (enter from the east side). Open 8 A.M.–5 P.M. Monday–Friday; free. Look straight ahead for panels of the first settlers, Abram Powell and Caleb Rhodes. Follow the panels around to the right, past scenes of railroad workers, freight wagons, the first town hall in Price, religious leaders, the 1911 Fourth of July parade, and depictions of the coal-mining industry. A brochure available here gives details of each scene and identifies the self-portrait of the artist as a small boy. Fausett, a native of the area, used his own recollections and old photos for the project, which he worked on from 1938 to 1941. He also painted the Barrier Canyon Mural replica in the Prehistoric Museum and *The Pioneer Trek* at "This Is the Place" State Park near Salt Lake City.

ENTERTAINMENT AND EVENTS

Catch movies at **King Coal Theaters 3,** 1171 E. Main, **Price Theatre,** 30 E. Main, or **Crown Theatre,** 30 W. Main; call 435/637-2740 for recorded information. **Black Diamond Stampede Rodeo** provides plenty of action in June

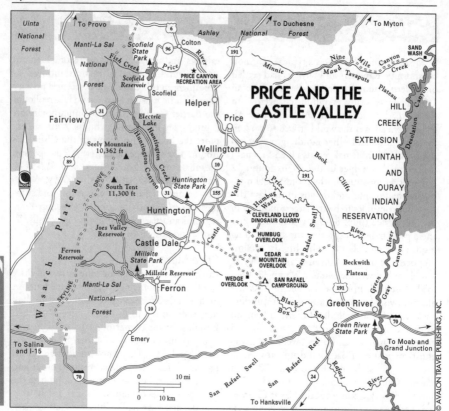

PRICE AND THE
CASTLE VALLEY

© AVALON TRAVEL PUBLISHING, INC.

at the Carbon County Fairgrounds. A **demolition derby** is also held in June. The **Greek Festival** in July features music, dancing, food, and tours of the Greek church. Wellington's **Pioneer Day** (July 24) festivities include a parade, rodeo, games, and food. **International Days and Carbon County Fair** in August celebrate the area's ethnic diversity with a parade, rodeo, agricultural exhibits, entertainment, contests, and food.

RECREATION

Washington Park, 250 East 500 North, 435/637-7946, has picnic areas, playground, indoor swimming pool, outdoor Desert Wave Pool, tennis, volleyball, basketball, and horseshoe courts. Two historic log cabins dating from the 1880s and a fitness track are across to the north in **Pioneer Park. South Price Park** offers a picnic area and tennis courts at 400 South and 100 East. **Carbon Country Club Golf Course,** four miles north of town on U.S. 6/191, 435/637-2388, has 18 holes.

ACCOMMODATIONS

Price has high-quality and inexpensive lodgings, which makes it a great base for exploration of this part of Utah.

Under $50

At the west end of Main Street is a shopping center complex that includes the **National 9**

Price River Inn, 641 W. Price River Dr. in Creekview Shopping Center, 435/637-7000 or 800/524-9999. Just to the north is the **Budget Host Inn,** 145 N. Carbonville Rd., 435/637-2424 or 800/283-4678; the local **Super 8** is at 180 North Hospital Dr., 435/637-8088 or 800/800-8000.

$50–75

Two of Price's nicest motels sit on the east end of town near a clutch of fast-food restaurants and the local supermarket mall. The **Greenwell Inn,** 655 E. Main, 435/637-3520 or 800/666-3520, has a pool, exercise room, and restaurant. The **Best Western Carriage House Inn,** 590 E. Main, 435/637-5660 or 800/528-1234 in Utah, has an indoor pool and hot tub. Out at freeway Exit 240 is the **Holiday Inn and Suites,** 838 Westwood Blvd., 435/637-8880 or 800/325-7466, with an indoor pool, sauna, and spa.

FOOD

A number of cafés and diners along Main Street serve standard American fare, but you'll have to venture slightly north and west of downtown to find **Grogg's Pinnacle Brewing Co.,** 1653 N. Carbonville Rd., 435/637-2924, the local brewpub, with burgers and sandwiches to accompany the hand-crafted beers. Find Greek food at the **Greek Streak,** 30 West 100 North, 435/637-1930.

Farlaino's Cafe, 87 W. Main, 435/637-9217, serves Italian and American cooking; open Monday–Saturday for breakfast and lunch and Wednesday–Saturday for dinner. **El Salto,** 19 S. Carbon Ave., 435/637-6545, brings excellent south-of-the-border flavor to town; open Monday–Saturday for lunch and dinner. Another spot with good Mexican food is **Ricardo's,** next to the Greenwell Inn at 655 E. Main, 435/637-2020.

OTHER PRACTICALITIES

Information and Services

Castle Country travel office offers literature and ideas for travel in Price and elsewhere in Carbon and Emery Counties; open 9 A.M.–5 P.M. Monday–Friday in the Prehistoric Museum at 155 E. Main, 435/637-3009 or 800/842-0789, www .castlecountry.com. The **Manti–La Sal National Forest** Supervisor's and Price District offices, across from the Creekview Shopping Center on the west edge of town (599 W. Price River Dr.), 435/637-2817, have information about recreation in the beautiful alpine country of the Wasatch Plateau to the west; all the Utah forest maps and some regional books are sold; open 8 A.M.–4:30 P.M. Monday–Friday (till 5 P.M. in summer).

The **Bureau of Land Management** has the Price River Resource Area and San Rafael Resource Area offices in Price; both have the same address and phone number: 125 South 600 West, 435/636-3600. Staff can tell you about exploring the San Rafael Swell, Cleveland-Lloyd Dinosaur Quarry, and Nine Mile Canyon and about boating the Green River through Desolation, Gray, and Labyrinth Canyons; land-use maps are sold. Open 7:45 A.M.–4:30 P.M. Monday–Friday. **Price City Library** is next to the Price Municipal Building at 159 E. Main, 435/637-0744; open Monday–Friday in summer and Monday–Saturday the rest of the year.

The **post office** is at the corner of Carbon Avenue and 100 South, 435/637-1638. **Castleview Hospital** is at 300 N. Hospital Drive on the west edge of town, 435/637-4800.

Transportation

Greyhound buses travel west daily to Salt Lake City and east to Denver from the stop at Phillips 66, 277 N. Carbonville Rd., 435/637-7153. **Amtrak** trains stop in nearby Helper on their runs between Denver and Salt Lake City, 800/872-7245.

North of Price

HELPER

In 1883, the Denver & Rio Grande Western Railroad began building a depot, roundhouse, and other facilities here for its new line. Trains headed up the long grade to Soldier Summit needed extra locomotives, or "helpers," based at the little railroad community, so the place became known as Helper. Miners later joined the railworkers, and the two groups still make up most of the current population of 2,500. The fine examples of early-20th-century commercial and residential buildings in downtown Helper have earned designation as a national historic site. The local economy has suffered downturns from layoffs in the railroad and coal industries, and this is reflected in the many vacant structures awaiting new owners.

The vacated structures have begun to attract artists who need inexpensive studio space, and an arts community has begun to take hold. The **Helper Arts Festival,** held the second week of September, showcases the local arts scene.

Western Mining and Railroad Museum

A venerable red caboose and examples of coal-mining machinery sit outside next to the museum in downtown Helper at 296 S. Main, 435/472-3009. Inside, you'll see two elaborate model railroad sets and photos of old steam locomotives in action. A mine room has models of coal mines (all are underground in this area) and equipment worn by the miners. Other exhibits illustrate Utah's two great mine disasters—the 1900 Scofield tragedy, in which 200 men and boys died, and the 1924 Castle Gate explosion, which killed 173. Other bits of history include ghost-town memorabilia, a Butch Cassidy exhibit, and a dentist's office. A company general store exhibit shows items that miners would buy with their company scrip. The new map room displays original maps showing hundreds of miles of tunnels. Video programs illustrate the area's mine and railroad history. The brick building

housing the museum dates from about 1914, when it was the Hotel Helper; from 1942 to 1982 it served as a YMCA for railroad men. Open 10 A.M.–6 P.M. Monday–Saturday May–September, 11 A.M.–4 P.M. Tuesday–Saturday October–April; donation.

PRICE CANYON RECREATION AREA

This pleasant spot in the woods makes a good stopping place for a picnic or a camp. From the turnoff 8.2 miles north of Helper, follow a narrow paved road three miles to the picnic area (free day use), a canyon overlook, and the campground (elev. 8,000 feet), which is open with water and a camping fee Memorial Day–late October. **Bristlecone Ridge Trail** begins at the far end of the campground loop and winds through a forest of Gambel oak, ponderosa pine, and mountain mahogany to a ridgetop. Grand views from the top take in surrounding mountains and Price and Crandall Canyons below. The moderately difficult hike is about two miles round-trip with an elevation gain of 700 feet. Bristlecone pines and lots of chipmunks live on the ridge.

SCOFIELD STATE PARK

The 3,000-acre reservoir lies in a broad mountain valley at an elevation of 7,600 feet. Anglers go after rainbow and cutthroat trout and crayfish. Water-skiers and boaters have lots of room to roam. The main campground is on the east shore with a picnic area, showers, dump station, boat ramp, docks, and fish-cleaning station. Madsen Bay area at the north end, near the turnoff for Mountain View, has a campground, restrooms, fish-cleaning station, and dump station. The Mountain View area on the northwest side of the lake offers picnic and camping areas near a boat ramp and dock. The lake is accessible all year, though the park shuts down off-season; restrooms and showers are open early May–late October. In winter, Scofield

GHOST TOWNS

Many coal-mining communities have bloomed and died in canyons and hillsides surrounding Helper. Most have fared poorly since they were abandoned, yet their picturesque ruins can be worth seeking out. The mines and decaying buildings are dangerous and shouldn't be entered—security staff enforces no-trespassing rules. One former company town has survived intact. Kenilworth's residents bought their houses at low prices when the mines closed and have continued to live here; the large company store, however, now stands vacant. Follow Helper's Main Street a short way south, then turn left (east) 3.8 miles on paved Highway 157. A small *Driving Tour Guide* describes coal mines and town sites in Carbon and Emery Counties; it's sold at the museum in Helper.

Scenic Spring Canyon has some of the best and most easily visited ghost towns. The paved road begins as "Canyon Street" in east Helper (across U.S. 6/191 from downtown Helper). You'll see railroad grades, mines, and ruins along much of the road's 6.7 miles. Sagebrush hides most of the Peerless ghost-town site, 2.8 miles in. Only foundations and a few buildings survive from this community, which peaked in the 1920s and '30s with a population of about 300, then died in the '50s. A tramway brought coal down from the mine high on the hillside. Spring Canyon is a total ghost; only a loading platform remains of a community that had up to 1,000 people during the '20s, '30s, and '40s. The site is near a junction 3.8 miles in; keep straight at the junction (the road to the right is still used by mining companies and is gated).

A large concrete loading facility on the right greets you on arrival at Standardville, 4.9 miles in. The formerly attractive, well-planned community had a population of 550 during its best years and set a standard for other mining towns. Mines nearby operated from 1912 until 1950. A ghostly two-story stone building, once the Liberty Fuel Company offices, marks the site of Latuda, 5.9 miles in. Several hundred people lived here from about 1920 to 1950; Latuda died completely in the late 1960s. Extensive ruins of the mine can be seen on the slopes to the left. Only foundations remain from Rains, once a town of 500, located 6.5 miles from Helper. A large stone ruin, once a store, stands at the site of Mutual, just beyond Rains. Most of the 250 or so residents lived to the north along a fork of Spring Canyon. You may have to park at the gate and walk a short distance on the road to Mutual.

NORTHEASTERN UTAH

Reservoir has excellent ice fishing. The State Division of Parks and Recreation grooms snowmobile trails nearby at Pond-Town Canyon (on the west side of the lake four miles north of the town of Scofield) and Left Fork of Whiteriver (near Soldier Summit). Cross-country skiing in the area is good, too, though no facilities or trails have been developed. Entrance fees are $6 for day use, $11–12 for camping; call 435/448-9449, or 800/322-3770 for reservations. The park nearly always has room except during major summer holidays. From Price, drive 23 miles north on U.S. 6, then turn left and follow Highway 96 for 13 miles. Other approaches are from Provo (66 miles) via Soldier Summit or from Highway 31 where it crosses the Wasatch Plateau to the south.

SCOFIELD

Two coal mines operate near this tiny mining town south of Scofield Reservoir. Production began in 1879 and peaked about 1920, when the town had a population of nearly 2,000. Utah's worst mining disaster took place nearby on May 1, 1900, at the Winter Quarters Mine, where about 200 men and boys perished in an explosion of coal dust. Weathered tombstones in the cemetery on the hill east of town still give testimony to the tragedy. A paved road continues south and west from Scofield to Highway 31 on the Wasatch Plateau. The **Lazy Anchor Campground,** with hot showers and laundry facilities, is open from snowmelt to first winter snows at the edge of town on the road from the lake, 435/448-9697.

FISH CREEK

The forest lands surrounding Scofield have plenty of places for dispersed camping. The **Fish Creek Trailhead,** west of the lake, is suitable for primitive camping. This is also the start of the 10-mile **Fish Creek National Recreation Trail.** From Scofield, go northwest 3.7 miles on a partly paved road, then turn left 1.5 miles at a fork up Fish Creek Valley. This last section of road is slippery when wet and may be too rough for cars at any time. The easy trail follows the creek through meadows and forests of aspen and evergreens. This is a good area to look for wildlife including moose, elk, mule deer, black bear, mountain lion, bobcat, and beaver. Anglers will find many places to cast a line; special fishing regulations (posted) apply in upper Fish Creek. The trail is good for both day- and overnight hikes; Skyline Drive is 13 miles upstream.

East of Price

Aside from a few ranches and coal mines, the rugged canyon country of the West Tavaputs Plateau remains largely a wilderness. Two especially good areas to visit here are Nine Mile Canyon (accessible by car) and Desolation and Gray Canyons of the Green River (accessible by raft or kayak). Adventurous drivers with high-clearance vehicles can explore other places, too; ask the BLM staff in Price about the back-country roads.

NINE MILE CANYON BACKCOUNTRY BYWAY

A drive through this scenic canyon takes you back in time to when Fremont Indians lived and farmed here, about 900 years ago. Although their pithouse dwellings can be difficult for a nonarchaeologist to spot, the granaries and striking rock art stand out clearly. The canyon is especially noted for its abundant petroglyphs and smaller numbers of pictographs. You'll also see several ranches and the ghost town of Harper. In the late 1800s and early 1900s; these roads through Nine Mile Canyon formed the main highway between Vernal and the rest of Utah.

Today the distances and dusty roads may discourage the more casual traveler. However, if you're interested in rock art or ancient America, then Nine Mile Canyon is an extremely scenic and compelling back road. Although the road is frequently rough and dusty, normal family cars should be able to make the trip with no problem as long as the road is dry.

Nine Mile Canyon is actually more than 40 miles long; the origin of its misleading name is unclear. The drive is about 120 miles round-trip from Price and takes most of a day. From Price, drive 10 miles southeast (three miles past Wellington) on U.S. 6/191 and turn north on 2200 East (Soldier Creek Road) at a sign for Nine Mile Canyon. The road passes Soldier Creek Coal Mine after 13 miles (pavement ends), continues climbing to an aspen-forested pass, then drops into the canyon.

Nine Mile Canyon can also be reached from the north, from near Myton (on U.S. 191) in the Uinta Basin, via Wells Draw and Gate Canyon. Gate Canyon is the roughest section and may be impassable after storms. Turnoff for the northern approach from U.S. 191 is 1.5 miles west of Myton; the turn is not well marked, so watch for signs to Pleasant Valley and turn south at 5500 Road. In about two miles, bear right at an unmarked intersection. You'll know you're on the right road if it soon turns into a graveled corduroy roadbed. It's 26 miles from U.S. 191 to the bottom of Nine Mile Canyon.

Obtain a brochure and road-log for Nine Mile Canyon in Price at the Castle Country tourist office, the Prehistoric Museum, or the BLM offices. It describes the various rock-art sites, ancient villages, and historic relics.

DESOLATION AND GRAY CANYONS OF THE GREEN RIVER

The Green River leaves the Uinta Basin and slices deeply through the Tavaputs Plateau, emerging

95 miles downstream near the town of Green River. River-runners enjoy the canyon scenery, hikes up side canyons, a chance to see wildlife, and visits to Fremont rock-art sites. John Wesley Powell named the canyons in 1869, designating the lower 36 miles Gray Canyon. Boaters usually start at Sand Wash, the site of a ferry that operated here from the early 1920s to 1952; a 42-mile road (36 miles unpaved) south from Myton is the best way in. Another road turns east from Gate Canyon near Nine Mile Canyon. Some people save the long 200-mile car shuttle by flying from the town of Green River to an airstrip on a mesatop above Sand Wash. Swasey Rapids, north of the town of Green River, is the most common take-out point. The last part of Gray Canyon, between Nefertiti and Swasey Rapids, is a good day trip. Although not as difficult as Cataract Canyon, Desolation and Gray Canyons do have about 60 rapids and riffles navigable by raft or kayak. Some are Class III and require river-running experience. Contact the BLM Price River Resource Area office in Price, 125 South 600 West, 435/636-3600, for information and the required permits. Open 7:45 A.M.–4:30 P.M. Monday–Friday. Commercial trips through the canyons are available; the BLM can give you names of the companies. The *Desolation River Guide,* by Laura Evans and Buzz Belknap, has maps and descriptions.

The Castle Valley and North San Rafael Swell

High cliffs of the Wasatch Plateau rise fortresslike to the west above Castle Valley, which is traversed by Highway 10 between Price and I-70 to the south. The wide band of the 10,000-foot-high uplands wrings all the moisture out of east-flowing storm systems, creating a rain shadow. However, perennial streams flow down the rugged canyons, enabling farmers to transform the desert into verdant orchards and fields of crops. To the east is the isolated and relatively unexplored canyon country of the San Rafael Swell.

Mormon pioneers didn't settle this side of the Wasatch Plateau until the 1870s, long after valleys on the other side of the plateau had been colonized. Water and good land began to run short by the time of the second generation of settlers, and many turned to jobs in nearby coal mines.

The barren mesas and badland formations, especially along the southern section of Highway 10, make for fine scenery. However, the real attraction of this area is the backcountry routes that lead to wild and undeveloped destinations. Unpaved roads lead west into the Wasatch Plateau, up steep canyons to lakes and pretty alpine country, to link up with Skyline Drive, or to cross the range to the Sanpete Valley and U.S. 89. Backcountry explorers can follow unpaved roads east to the San Rafael Swell, an area of great dramatic beauty and unparalleled recreational opportunity that has somehow avoided the fame and throngs of the state's other canyon country. Destinations included in this near-wilderness are dinosaur fossil quarries and remote vista points and trailheads.

HUNTINGTON

This small town at the mouth of Huntington Canyon dates from 1878 and has a population of 2,131. While it's not exactly a tourist town, from Huntington travelers can head west on paved Highway 31 and soon be in the cool forests and meadows of the Wasatch Plateau, or head east to the Cleveland-Lloyd Dinosaur Quarry and the San Rafael Swell.

Huntington State Park

The 250-acre Huntington Reservoir is a popular destination for picnicking, camping, swimming, fishing, and water-skiing. Lots of grass and shade trees and a swimming beach make the park especially enjoyable in summer. Boaters can use the boat ramp and docks. Anglers catch mostly largemouth bass and bluegill and some trout; crayfishing is good. The campground is open with showers March–October. Reservations are a good idea for summer weekends. In winter, the park is open for ice-skating and ice fishing. Fees are $5 for day use, $14 for camping. Located one mile north of town on Highway 10, 435/687-2491 (ranger) or 800/322-3770 (reservations).

Huntington Canyon

Highway 31 turns west up the canyon from the north edge of town. The giant Huntington power plant looks out of place in the agrarian landscape of the lower canyon. Beyond the power plant, **Bear Creek Campground** offers sites shaded by cottonwoods on the left near milepost 39 (8.8 miles in from Highway 10). It has water and a small fee in summer; elevation is 6,900 feet. The canyon narrows as the road climbs higher and enters groves of spruce, fir, and aspen. **Forks of Huntington Canyon Campground** sits in a side canyon among fir and spruce trees and has water and a camping fee early June–mid-September. The turnoff is on the left near milepost 30 (18 miles in from Highway 10); elevation is 7,600 feet. **Left Fork of Huntington Creek National Recreation Trail** begins at the end of the campground road and follows the creek up a pretty canyon. The trail offers easy walking and passes good trout-fishing spots; after four miles it comes to an open valley and connects with a jeep road.

Farther up the highway on the right, between mileposts 28 and 27 (20.5 miles in from Highway 10), **Old Folks Flat Campground** has sites in a spruce and aspen forest; open (water and fee) late May–early September. Reserve a site at www.reserveusa.com or 877/444-6777. **Electric Lake** offers rainbow and cutthroat trout fishing; a boat ramp is at the upper (north) end. The turnoff is on the right near milepost 14 (34 miles in from Highway 10), then eight miles in. **Skyline Drive** lies near the top of the plateau amidst expansive meadows and groves of fir and aspen. The junction for Skyline Drive to the south is on the left between mileposts 14 and 13; the turnoff for Skyline Drive to the north is five miles farther west along the highway. Roads branch off the northern section of Skyline Drive to Gooseberry Campground (1.5 miles), Flat Campground (4.5 miles), Electric Lake (six

miles), and Scofield (17 miles). **Gooseberry Campground** is near Lower Gooseberry Reservoir; take the north Skyline Drive turnoff and follow signs 1.5 miles; sites are open with water and a fee about mid-June–mid-September. Elevation is 8,400 feet. **Flat Canyon Campground** also provides a good base for fishing lakes of the high country; campsites are reached by a 5.5-mile paved road from the north Skyline Drive turnoff. The campground is open with water and a fee about mid-June–mid-September; elevation is 8,800 feet. Reservations can be made for either Flat Canyon or Gooseberry at www .reserveusa.com or 877/444-6777. From the campground, Boulger Reservoir is a quarter mile away, Electric Lake is two miles, and Beaver Dam Reservoir is two miles.

Other forest roads branch off the highway to more reservoirs and scenic spots; see the Manti–La Sal Forest map available from the Sanpete, Ferron, and Price Ranger District offices. Highway 31 continues 10 miles down the other side of the plateau to Fairview on U.S. 89. Snowplows keep Highway 31 open in winter, though drivers must have snow tires or carry chains November–March. Snowmobilers can use groomed trails on the plateau.

Accommodations and Food

In Huntington, the well-maintained **Village Inn Motel** has inexpensive rooms at 307 S. Main, 435/687-9888. **Coyote Moon Restaurant,** 685 North 400 East, 435/687-5566, is the best bet for a meal in Huntington.

CLEVELAND-LLOYD DINOSAUR QUARRY

You can learn more about dinosaurs and see their bones in an excavation here in the desert 22 miles east of Huntington or 30 miles south of Price via U.S. 6. Dinosaurs stalked this land about 147 million years ago, when it had a wetter and warmer climate. Mud in a lake bottom trapped some of the animals and preserved their bones. The mud layer, which later became rock of the Morrison Formation, has yielded more than 12,000 bones of at least 14 different dinosaur species at this site. Local ranchers discovered the bones and then interested the University of Utah, which started digs in 1928. Princeton University and Brigham Young University (which currently does excavations) also have participated in the quarry work.

Visitors Center

The BLM has built a visitors center, quarry exhibits, a nature trail, and picnic sites here. Inside the visitors center, you'll see exhibits on the dinosaur family tree, techniques of excavating and assembling dinosaur skeletons, and local flora and fauna. A fierce allosaurus skeleton cast gazes down on you. Related books, postcards, and posters can be purchased. The enclosed dinosaur quarry, about 100 yards behind the visitors center, contains excavation tools and exposed allosaurus, stegosaurus, camptosaurus, and camarasaurus bones. **Rock Walk Nature Trail** begins outside; a brochure available at the start outlines geology, dinosaurs, uranium mining, and ecology at numbered stops; allow 45 minutes. Usually the quarry can be visited 10 A.M.–5 P.M. on weekends beginning at Easter, then daily from Memorial Day weekend to Labor Day. Admission is $3 adults, $2 children; call 435/636-3600 for more information. The drive in is on graded dirt roads, though rains occasionally close them. From Price, drive south 13 miles on Highway 10 and turn left 17 miles on Highway 155 and follow the unpaved roads. From Huntington, go northeast two miles on Highway 10 and turn right 20 miles on Highway 155 and unpaved roads. Signs at the turnoffs from Highway 10 indicate the days and hours the quarry is open. If it's closed, there's nothing to see. Visitors are not allowed to collect dinosaur bones at the quarry or on other public lands; bones are of greater scientific value when researchers can examine them in place.

Humbug Overlook Driving Tour

A brochure available at the visitors center describes the plants and animals living in this desert country. The drive begins at the quarry and goes southeast seven miles to the rim of Humbug Canyon. Cars with good clearance can negotiate the road in dry weather. The **Jump Trail** winds

from the viewpoint down to the canyon floor, about a half-mile one-way.

Look for hoodoos on the canyon walls. They are formed when water erodes rock material down to a hard cap rock. The resulting formation often resembles a mushroom or a human head on a thin neck.

Cedar Mountain Driving Tour

The overlook atop Cedar Mountain has a great panorama to the south across the gently curved dome of the San Rafael Swell and the many canyons cutting into it. Distant ranges include the Wasatch Plateau (west), the Thousand Lake Mountains (southwest), the Henry Mountains (south), and the Book Cliffs (east). A picnic area is at the second overlook at the end of the drive. **Fossil Ledge Nature Trail** makes a quarter-mile loop from the picnic area. Distances to the second overlook are 39 miles from Price, 27 miles from Huntington, or 25 miles from Cleveland-Lloyd Dinosaur Quarry. A graded dirt road climbs about 2,000 feet in elevation through woodlands of juniper and piñon and ponderosa pine. Cars can easily drive the road in dry weather. A brochure describing points of interest along the way is available from the quarry visitors center or the BLM office in Price.

CASTLE DALE

The story goes that after founding the community in 1877, citizens applied for a post office for their town of Castle Vale, but the name was recorded wrong. Because they couldn't agree on which side of Cottonwood Creek to settle, two towns grew up here—Castle Dale (current pop. 1,660) on the north side and Orangeville (current pop. 1,400) on the south. Castle Dale has a good historical museum and is the seat of Emery County. A memorial in front of the courthouse honors the 27 miners who died nearby in the Wilberg Coal Mine fire on December 19, 1984.

Emery County Pioneer Museum

Period rooms depict life in the early days of Castle Valley settlements: a schoolroom, lawyer's office, country store, and kitchen. Pioneer rooms have farm and coal-mining tools and memorabilia of one-time outlaw Matt Warner. An art gallery exhibits local works. It's open 10 A.M.–4 P.M. weekdays and 1–4 P.M. Saturday all year; donations requested. The museum is at 93 East 100 North in Castle Dale City Hall, one block north of the courthouse at 100 North and 100 East, 435/381-5154.

Museum of the San Rafael

Exhibits at this museum, diagonally across the street from the courthouse at 64 North 100 East, 435/381-5252, include a paleontology room with life-size skeletons of dinosaurs, such as a 22-foot allosaurus. The dinosaurs displayed include only those species that have been found in Emery County. There are also exhibits of the prehistoric Fremont and Anasazi peoples, including a rabbit-fur robe, pottery, baskets, tools, jewelry, and the famous Sitterud Bundle (a bowmaker's kit). Admission is free, but donations are requested. Museum hours are 10 A.M.–4 P.M. weekdays and 1–4 P.M. Saturday.

Events and Recreation

Pioneer Day (July 24) is celebrated with a parade, rodeo, and games. **Castle Valley Pageant,** held in late July or early August, recounts the faith and trials of the pioneers who settled here; the pageant takes place on a hillside a short drive from town. The **Emery County Fair** is also in August; horse races are run in Ferron to the south, while the horse show, parade, and most exhibits are in Castle Dale.

The indoor **swimming pool** next to the city hall (one block north of the courthouse) is open May–September. The **city park,** between the courthouse and City Hall, has covered picnic tables. Castle Dale's **library** is next door to the city hall.

Accommodations and Food

The town's only lodging is the **Village Inn Motel,** 375 E. Main, 435/381-2309, with rooms for less than $50.

Big Moma's Pizza and Deli, 340 E. Main, 435/381-5080, offers pizza, spaghetti, and sandwiches Monday–Saturday for lunch and dinner.

THE HIGH COUNTRY WEST OF CASTLE DALE

Head northwest from town toward Joes Valley Reservoir on the paved road along Cottonwood Creek. After about 10 miles you'll reach a fork; an unpaved road turns right (north) along Cottonwood Creek to Upper Joes Valley (10 miles). The main road (Highway 29) enters Straight Canyon. Seely Creek below the dam in Straight Canyon has good fishing for German brown trout. Joes Valley Reservoir covers 1,170 acres in a large valley at the upper end of Straight Canyon, 16 miles from Castle Dale. A road turns off the highway at the north end of the lake and goes north to **Indian Creek Campground** (nine miles) and Highway 31 (21 miles). Indian Creek Campground is open with water late June–mid-September (fee); elevation is 9,000 feet.

Joes Valley Campground has two sections on the west shore of the reservoir; they have water mid-May–mid-September and charge a fee. One loop stays open all year (no water or charge off-season); elevation is 7,100 feet. Make reservations at www.reserveusa.com or 877/444-6777. **Joes Valley Marina,** about 20 miles west of Castle Dale, 435/381-2453, offers boat slips, rentals (fishing boats with motors, rowboats, and paddle boats), a café (breakfast, lunch, and dinner daily), a campground, and a small store; open mid-May–early November. Anglers catch rainbow and cutthroat trout in the lake. Lowry Fork to the north has good trout fishing in the spring. Water-skiing is popular on the lake, but winds are too erratic for reliable sailing. Pavement ends after the turnoff for Joes Valley Campground. A forest road continues west and climbs 13 miles to Skyline Drive (elev. 10,200 feet) at the top of the Wasatch Plateau. The clay road surface is usually fine for cars in dry weather but treacherously slippery when wet for *any* vehicle. The road from Castle Dale to the reservoir is kept open in winter for ice fishing and snowmobile access.

North Dragon Road turns south between the two sections of Joes Valley Campground and goes about 15 miles to a spectacular overlook above Castle Dale; the San Rafael Swell and the distant Henry, La Sal, and Abajo Mountains can be seen on a clear day. The road is unpaved (high-clearance vehicles recommended).

EXPLORING THE SAN RAFAEL SWELL (NORTHERN HALF)

About 65 million years ago, immense underground forces pushed rock layers into a dome about 80 miles long (north to south) and 30 miles wide. Erosion has exposed the colorful layers and cut deep canyons into this formation. I-70 divides the swell into roughly equal north and south halves. In the north, a 29-mile scenic drive passable by cars in dry weather branches off the road to Cedar Mountain and goes south past the Wedge Overlook, descends through Buckhorn Wash, crosses the San Rafael River, then winds across desert to I-70.

Much of the San Rafael Swell remains wild and remote. Seven sections of it are being considered for wilderness designation. The BLM's Price field office has information about travel and wilderness status in this unique land; the office is at 125 South 600 West in Price, 435/636-3600. Good books for travel and historical background on this little-known region are *Canyoneering the San Rafael Swell*, by Steve Allen, *Hiking Utah's San Rafael Swell*, by Michael Kelsey, and *Utah's Scenic San Rafael*, by Owen McClenahan. Allen's guide is by far the most detailed coverage of drives, hikes, and some rock climbs; Kelsey's book emphasizes history and hiking; McClenahan's mostly describes driving tours (about half of which can be done by car).

Wedge Overlook

An inspiring panorama takes in surrounding mountains and canyons and the 1,000-foot sheer drop into the "Little Grand Canyon." Rain and snowmelt on the Wasatch Plateau feed tributaries of the San Rafael River, which has cut this deep canyon through the San Rafael Swell. Downstream from the Little Grand Canyon, the river plunges through narrow canyons of the Black Boxes and flows across the San Rafael Desert to join the Green River. The signed turnoff for Wedge Overlook is on the way to

the San Rafael Bridge and Campground; see the Utah Travel Council's Northeastern Utah map for the different approaches from Price (23 miles), Huntington (15 miles), and Castle Dale (13 miles). Drive in 6.6 miles from the turnoff, keeping left at a fork near the beginning, to the first overlook, then continue to the left 0.9 mile for the best views at the end of the road. This area is fine for picnicking, but be sure to drive only on designated roads and camp only in designated campgrounds. Walk along the rim for other views.

San Rafael Campground

Continue 12 miles past the Wedge Overlook turnoff to the bridge and campground at the San Rafael River. The road descends into the main canyon via pretty Buckhorn Wash and crosses the bridge to the camping area. The cottonwood trees at the campground mysteriously died, giving the area a bleak appearance. Tables and outhouses are provided, but there's no water. From here the road continues south 20 miles to I-70 at Ranch Exit 129.

Floating the Little Grand Canyon

The 15-mile trip through this canyon provides one of the best ways to enjoy the scenery. The swift waters have a few riffles and small sand waves, but no rapids. Canoes, kayaks, and rafts can do the excursion in 5–6 hours with higher spring flows. An overnight trip will allow more time to explore side canyons. Best boating conditions occur during the spring runoff in May and June. Some people float through with inner tubes later in the summer. Life jackets should always be worn. No permits are needed for boating; the BLM in Price can advise on river flows and road conditions. Put-in is at Fuller's Bottom; the turnoff is near the one for the Wedge Overlook, then it's 5.4 miles to the river. Take-out is at the San Rafael Campground. Extremely dangerous rapids and waterfalls lie downstream from the campground in the Black Boxes; *don't* attempt these sections unless you really know what you're doing! Hikers can explore the canyons above and below the campground on day and overnight trips; autumn has the best temperatures and lowest water levels; wear shoes suitable for wading.

FERRON

The town's name honors a surveyor who visited the valley in preparation for Mormon settlement. Millsite State Park and Ferron Reservoir are on a scenic road that connects Ferron with Skyline Drive. Ferron (pop. 1,620) celebrates its pioneer heritage in September during **Peach Days** with horse races, a demolition derby, games, craft exhibits, a dance, and fireworks. The **Ferron Ranger District office** on the main highway at 115 West Canyon Rd., 435/384-2372, can help you plan a trip to the Wasatch Plateau. Open 8 A.M.–noon and 12:30–4:30 P.M. Monday–Friday.

Canyon Road to Skyline Drive

Turn west on Canyon Road beside the Ferron Ranger District office for a trip to Millsite State Park and the high country of the Wasatch Plateau. **Millsite State Park,** 435/384-2552 (ranger), 435/687-2491 (Huntington State Park), or 800/322-3770 (reservations), is four miles from town at an elevation of 6,200 feet. The 450-acre Millsite Reservoir is about twice the size of Huntington Reservoir and has the area's best sailing conditions and the most space for water-skiing. Anglers come to catch rainbow, cutthroat, and German brown trout. Ice fishing is done in winter. The park has picnic grounds, campground with showers (March–October), boat ramp, and dock. Facilities, except for show-

ers, stay open all year. Day use of the park costs $5, camping $14.

Millsite Golf Course, adjacent to the park, 435/384-2887, features nine challenging holes. Off-road vehicles are popular in the barren countryside near the reservoir.

Pavement ends past the state park, but a fairly good gravel road (narrow and winding in places) continues high into the mountains. Stop at **Ferron Canyon Overlook** (14 miles from town) for a panorama of Millsite Reservoir, the surrounding mountains and valleys, and the San Rafael Swell. Signs point out features and geology; elevation here is 8,200 feet. The road continues climbing to alpine country with pretty lakes and groves of fir and aspen.

Ferron Reservoir (28 miles from town) is the largest of the high-country lakes (57 acres). The Forest Service Campground is open mid-June–mid-September with water and a fee; elevation is 9,400 feet. Skyline Drive is only two miles beyond Ferron Reservoir. Turn north on the drive to a fine view of the reservoir and canyon to the east and valleys near Manti to the west. The highest point on Skyline Drive, at 10,897 feet, is just 0.8 mile beyond the viewpoint. **Twelve Mile Flat Campground,** about 1.5 miles south of the Ferron road junction and the only campground actually on Skyline Drive, is open with water mid- June–mid-September; fee. Elevation is 9,800 feet.

For additional information about outdoor activities in the area, or to buy books and maps, consult the U.S. Forest Service office at 115 West Canyon Rd., 435/384-2372 or 435/384-2505.

Southwestern Utah

Southwest Utah's climate and year-round recreation make this corner of the state seem more like an extension of Arizona—St. George is a major retirement mecca and golfing center—and its proximity to Nevada (the border is only nine miles away) lends a more worldly air to the region. The out-of-Utah feeling is enhanced by the locals' habit of referring to the region as "Dixie." Whatever the name, the scenery in this corner of Utah is astonishing, with two of the nation's most popular national parks and an abundance of recreational opportunities. In the same day, you can hike through serpentine canyons or flower-filled meadows, hit the slopes at the Brian Head Ski Area, glide on cross-country skis across a high plateau, explore the desert, or play a leisurely round of golf.

Zion and Bryce Canyon National Parks are part of the desert Southwest's grand circle of natural wonders, and in all but the depth of winter a steady stream of tourists

Zion–Mt. Carmel Highway

SOUTHWESTERN UTAH

To Junction →

← To Beaver

Grand Staircase–Escalante National Monument

Powell Point 10,188 ft

Pine Lake

Table Cliff Plateau

Glen Canyon National Recreation Area

Page

89

Lees Ferry

Colorado River

89A

Cottonwood Canyon

Lake Powell

GROSVENOR ARCH

Kodachrome Basin State Park

Henrieville

12

Tropic

Cannonville

63

Bryce Canyon National Park

12

Paunsaugunt Plateau

Paria River

Cliffs

Cliffs

White

Vermilion

Paria Canyon

Kaibab Plateau

89

A R I Z O N A

89A

Hatch

Panguitch

143

Markagunt Plateau

Mammoth Springs

Long Valley Junction

89

Parowan

Panguitch Lake

Cedar Breaks N.M.

Glendale

15

Brian Head

130

9

Mount Carmel

Kanab

89

Coral Pink Sand Dunes State Park

Fredonia

389

PIPE SPRING NATIONAL MONUMENT

Ashdown Gorge Wilderness

14

Navajo Lake

Orderville

Cedar City

Kanarraville

Kolob Terrace

STRAWBERRY POINT

Zion Lodge

Canaan Mountain

Springdale

Rockville

Zion National Park

Colorado City

56

15

Toquerville

La Verkin

Grafton

59

Hildale

20 mi

20 km

0

0

Enterprise

18

Pine Valley

Pine Valley Mountains

OAK GROVE

Virgin

Hurricane

18

BAKER DAM RECREATION SITE

RED CLIFFS RECREATION SITE

Washington

Veyo

Gunlock

Santa Clara

Shivwits

St. George

MOUNTAIN MEADOWS MASSACRE HISTORIC SITE

Enterprise Reservoir

56

Beaver Dam Mountains

15

N E V A D A

To Las Vegas, NV →

SOUTHWESTERN UTAH

© AVALON TRAVEL PUBLISHING, INC.

SOUTHWESTERN UTAH HIGHLIGHTS

Inspiration Point in Bryce Canyon
National Park

Best Friends Animal Sanctuary

Visiting *Gunsmoke* stage sets near Kanab

The Narrows in Zion National Park

Zion Lodge

Cedar City's Utah Shakespearean Festival

Driving the Markagunt Scenic Byway
(Highway 14 between Cedar City and
Long Valley Junction)

explore the region. If you're looking for higher culture, Cedar City offers a well-respected summer Shakespeare festival; at Kanab, you can visit sets used for vintage movie and TV Westerns.

THE LAND

The Mojave Desert, the Great Basin, and the Colorado Plateau meet here to create a unique combination of climates and ecosystems. Plants and wildlife normally found only in Arizona and southern California live in the arid plains and rocky ranges of the desert. The lofty cliffs of the Colorado Plateau rise east of the desert country with some of the most spectacular scenery on earth—the grandeur and colors have to be seen to be believed. Great faults break the Colorado Plateau into a staircase of lesser plateaus across southern Utah and into northern Arizona. Angular features of cliffs and canyons dominate the landscape. Volcanic cones and lava flows have broken through the surface, some in geologically recent times. Elevations range from 2,350 feet at Beaver Dam Wash to 11,307 feet atop Brian Head Peak.

Climate

No matter what the season, you can nearly always find pleasant temperatures in some part of this region. Ever since Brigham Young built a winter house at St. George to escape the cold and snow, people have been coming to take ad-

vantage of the mild climate. Midwinter temperatures at St. George (elev. 2,880 feet) may drop below freezing at night, but days are typically in the middle to upper 50s with bright sunshine. Spring and autumn bring ideal weather. Summer, when the highs often top 100°F at the lower elevations, is the time to head for the mountains and high plateaus. The alpine meadows and cool forests of the Beaver Dam Mountains, Cedar Breaks National Monument, and Bryce Canyon National Park provide a welcome refuge from summer heat. Precipitation ranges widely from place to place and from year to year, but most falls in winter/early spring and late summer. Annual precipitation averages 10.4 inches in St. George and more than 20 inches in the high country.

FLORA AND FAUNA

The land provides habitats for a great variety of plant and animal species. Sparse desert vegetation consists largely of big sagebrush, rabbitbrush, bitterbrush, blackbrush, yucca, cacti, and grasses. The distinctive Joshua tree, a member of the lily family, grows in the extreme southwestern corner of the state. Perennial streams support cottonwood, willow, velvet and single-leaf ash, tamarisk, rushes, and sedges. Creatures of the desert include the chuckwalla, Gila monster (a poisonous lizard), California king snake, and roadrunner. Above about 4,000 feet, woodlands of piñon pine and Utah juniper take over from the desert; you'll often find cliffrose, Utah serviceberry, live oak, and Gambel oak here, too. At about 7,000–8,000 feet, ponderosa pine, Gambel oak, and Rocky Mountain juniper are common. Thriving in the cool mountain air above 8,000 feet are Douglas fir, subalpine fir, Engelmann spruce, aspen, and wildflowers. Larger wildlife, such as mule deer, elk, mountain lion, and coyote, migrate with the seasons between the high and low country. More than 200 bird species have been spotted in the region. Raptors include bald and golden eagles, red-tailed and Cooper's hawks, peregrine and prairie falcons, and the American kestrel.

HISTORY

Native Americans

Beginning about 15,000 years ago, groups of Paleo-Indians traveled across the region to hunt and gather wild plants. Only scant evidence remains of their long stay here. Nomadic bands of Southern Paiutes—possible descendants of the Paleo-Indians—inhabited the region when the first white settlers arrived. The Paiutes befriended and guided the early explorers and settlers, but troubles soon began when they saw their lands taken over by farmers and ranchers. Unable to maintain their old lifestyle or defeat the newcomers, the Paiutes settled near the settlers' towns. They now have the Shivwits Reservation northwest of St. George and the Kaibab-Paiute Reservation in Arizona southwest of Kanab.

Explorers and Colonizers

In 1776, Spanish explorers of the Dominguez-Escalante Expedition were the first Europeans to visit and describe the region. They had given up partway through a proposed journey from Santa Fe to California and returned to Santa Fe along a route passing through the sites of present-day Cedar City and Hurricane.

In the first half of the 19th century, mountain men like Jedediah Smith and government surveyors such as John C. Frémont explored the land and learned about the Native Americans. In 1849–1850, LDS leaders in Salt Lake City took the first steps in colonizing the region when they sent an advance party led by Parley P. Pratt. Encouraging reports of rich iron ore west of Cedar Valley and of fertile land along the Virgin River convinced the Mormons to expand southward. Calls went out for members to establish missions, mine the iron ore, and supply iron products needed for the expanding LDS empire. Parowan, now a sleepy community along I-15, became the first settlement and Cedar City the second—both established in 1851. In 1855, a successful experiment in growing cotton along Santa Clara Creek near present-day St. George aroused considerable interest among the Mormons. New settlements soon arose in the Virgin River Valley. However, poor roads hindered development of the cotton and iron industries, most of which ended when cheaper products began arriving on the transcontinental railroad. Floods, droughts, disease, and hostile Native Americans discouraged some of Dixie's pioneers, but many of those who stayed prospered by raising food crops and livestock. The past 30 years have brought rapid growth to the region in the form of new industries, tourism, and retirement communities.

TOURS

Guided van tours of many of southwestern Utah's grandest sights are available from **Southern Utah Scenic Tours,** 435/867-8690 or 888/404-8687, www.utahscenictours.com. Tours depart from either Cedar City or St. George and go to Zion and Bryce National Parks, the North Rim of the Grand Canyon, and other beauty spots in the area. Theme tours include one that follows the legend of Butch Cassidy, one that visits the Western movie sets near Kanab, and another that visits a rural polygamist community! Custom tours are also available. Southern Utah Scenic Tours also offers a hotel reservation service.

Bryce Canyon National Park

A geologic fairyland of rock spires rises beneath the high cliffs of the Paunsaugunt Plateau. This intricate maze, eroded from a soft limestone, now glows with warm shades of reds, oranges, pinks, yellows, and creams. The rocks provide a continuous show of changing color through the day as the sun's rays and cloud shadows move across the landscape.

Visitors perceive a multitude of wondrous forms. Some see the natural rock sculptures as Gothic castles, others as Egyptian temples, subterranean worlds inhabited by dragons, or vast armies of a lost empire. The Paiute tale of the Legend People relates how various animals and birds once lived in a beautiful city built for them by Coyote; when the Legend People began behaving badly toward Coyote, he transformed them all into stone.

Bryce Canyon isn't a canyon at all, but the largest of a series of massive amphitheaters cut into the Pink Cliffs. In Bryce Canyon National Park, you can gaze into the depths from viewpoints and trails on the plateau rim or hike down moderately steep trails and wind your way among the spires. A 17-mile scenic drive traces the length of the park and passes many overlooks and trailheads. Off-road, the nearly 36,000 acres of Bryce Canyon National Park offer many opportunities to explore spectacular rock features, dense forests, and expansive meadows.

Cool temperatures prevail most of the year at the park's 6,600- to 9,100-foot elevations. Expect pleasantly warm days in summer, frosty nights in spring and autumn, and snow in winter. The visitors center, scenic drive, and a campground stay open through the year. Allow a full day to see the visitors center exhibits, enjoy the viewpoints along the scenic drive, and take a few short walks. Photographers usually obtain best results early and late in the day when shadows set off the brightly colored rocks. Memorable sunsets and sunrises reward visitors who stay overnight. Moonlit nights reveal yet another spectacle.

From Bryce Junction (on U.S. 89, seven miles south of Panguitch), turn east 14 miles on High-

way 12, then south three miles on Highway 63. Or, from Torrey (near Capitol Reef National Park), head west 103 miles on Highway 12, then turn south three miles (winter snows occasionally close this section). Both approaches have spectacular scenery. The park entrance fee of $20 per vehicle ($10 bicyclists) includes use of park shuttle buses during the summer months. Admission is good for seven days. A brochure available at the entrance station and visitors center has a map of major scenic features, drives, and trails.

The Hoodoos

The park's landscape originated about 60 million years ago as sediments in a large body of water—named Lake Flagstaff by geologists. Silt and calcium carbonate and other minerals settled on the lake bottom. These sediments consolidated and became the Claron Formation; a soft, silty limestone with some shale and sandstone. Lake Flagstaff had long since disappeared when the land began to rise as part of the Colorado Plateau uplift about 16 million years ago. Uneven pressures beneath the plateau caused it to break along fault lines into a series of smaller plateaus at different levels known as the "Grand Staircase." Bryce Canyon National Park occupies part of one of these plateaus—the Paunsaugunt. The spectacular Pink Cliffs on the east edge contain the famous erosional features known as the "hoodoos," carved in the Claron Formation. Variations in hardness of the rock layers result in these strange features, which seem almost alive. Water flows through cracks, wearing away softer rock around hard, erosion-resistant caps. Finally, a cap becomes so undercut that the overhang allows water to drip down, leaving a "neck" of rock below the harder cap. Traces of iron and manganese provide the distinctive coloring. The hoodoos continue to change—new ones form and old ones fade away. Despite appearances, wind plays little role in creation of the landscape; it's the freezing and thawing, snowmelt, and rainwater that dissolve weak layers, pry open cracks,

BRYCE CANYON NATIONAL PARK

SOUTHWESTERN UTAH

Grand Staircase–
Escalante National
Monument

Tropic

To Escalante

Cannonville

12

MOON

Pink Cliffs

Shakespeare
Pk. 7,850 ft

Creek

Bryce

Grand Staircase–
Escalante National

Yellow

Fairyland Canyon

Bryce Canyon

Pink Cliffs

Fairyland
Loop Trail

Bryce Canyon National Park

SHUTTLE BOARDING
AND PARKING AREA

Rim Trail

SEE DETAIL

VISITOR
CENTER

NORTH
CAMPGROUND

SUNSET
CAMPGROUND

Rim

Pink

Cliffs

12

Rim

Pink

Trail

To Panguitch, Hatch,
and Cedar City

East Fork Sevier River

Plateau

Paunsaugunt

Dixie

National

Forest

Tropic
Reservoir

SOUTHWESTERN UTAH

© PAUL LEVY

The erosive forces of water and ice formed Bryce's hoodoos.

and carve out the forms. The plateau cliffs, meanwhile, recede at a rate of about one foot every 50–65 years; look for trees on the rim that now overhang the abyss. Listen, and you might hear the sounds of pebbles falling away and rolling down the steep slopes.

Flora and Fauna

Bryce's plantlife changes considerably with elevation; higher elevations are moister than the lowlands and can support relatively lush vegetation. The warm, dry slopes beneath the canyon's rim, below about 7,000 feet, are dominated by piñon pine, Utah juniper, and Gambel oak.

Between 7,000–8,500 feet, Ponderosa pines rise majestically over greenleaf manzanita and other shrubs. You'll find these species in the area around the visitors center, campground, and lodge.

Blue spruce, white fir, Douglas fir, limber pine, bristlecone pine, and aspen thrive in the cool, moist conditions above 8,500 feet. It's easy to see these trees at Rainbow and Yovimpa Points, which are just above 9,100 feet.

Wildflowers put on a showy display from spring to early autumn. Springs and seeps below

the rim support pockets of water birch, bigtooth maple, willows, and narrow-leaf cottonwood.

Larger wildlife visit the higher elevations in summer, then move down out of the park as winter snows arrive. It's no shock that mule deer frequent Bryce's meadows, especially in morning and evening, but it's a little more surprising to see wild turkeys grazing there. Other residents include mountain lion, black bear, coyote, bobcat, gray fox, striped skunk, badger, porcupine, Utah prairie dog, yellow-bellied marmot, Uinta chipmunk, and golden-mantled ground squirrel. Beaver live near the park on the East Fork of the Sevier River. (*Paunsaugunt* is Paiute for "home of the beaver.") Despite the cool climate, you can find a few reptiles; look for the short-horned lizard, skink, and Great Basin rattlesnake.

Birds appear in greatest numbers May–October. Violet-green swallows and white-throated swifts dive and careen among the hoodoos in hot pursuit of flying insects. Other summer visitors are the golden eagle, red-tailed hawk, Western tanager, and mountain bluebird. Year-round residents include woodpeckers, owls, ravens, Steller's jay, Clark's nutcracker, and blue grouse.

Bryce's cliffs have become home to a thriving population of California condors. Six condors were released in the Vermilion Cliffs south of Bryce in 1996, and the population has grown to about 100. Peregrine falcons are another avian success story here; at least two pairs of these raptors nest in the park. Look for them from Paria View.

Although some wild creatures may seem quite tame, they must not be fed or handled—rodents may have diseases, and young deer contaminated with human scent might be abandoned by their mothers. Also, animals who become dependent on humans may die in winter when left to forage for themselves after the summer crowds have left.

History

Prehistoric Anasazi lived in the lower country surrounding Bryce and probably made frequent trips into what is now the park area to hunt game and gather piñon nuts and other wild foods. Nomadic groups of Paiutes later wandered into the area on seasonal migrations. Mormon pioneer Ebenezer Bryce homesteaded near the town site of Tropic in 1875, but the work of scratching a living from the rugged land became too hard. He left five years later for more promising areas in Arizona. The name of the park commemorates his efforts. He is remembered as saying of the area, "Well, it's a hell of a place to lose a cow."

A later settler, Ruben "Ruby" Syrett, recognized the tourist potential of the area and opened the first small lodge near Sunset Point in 1919, then Ruby's Inn in 1924. Enthusiasm for the scenic beauty led to creation of Bryce Canyon National Monument in 1923. The name changed to Utah National Park in the following year, then took its current name in 1928. Tours organized by the Union Pacific Railroad, beginning in the late 1920s, made Bryce well known and easily visited.

Park Shuttle Bus

In response to increased traffic congestion, decreased federal funding for infrastructure repair, and concern about environmental degradation,

the National Park Service (NPS) has instituted a shuttle service through Bryce Canyon Park. These tour buses depart from the front of Ruby's Inn (just outside the park entrance) every 15 minutes or so, and stop at all the major viewpoints along the main amphitheater, as well as at the campgrounds, the visitors center, and Bryce Canyon Lodge. Service is less frequent to Rainbow Point at the end of the park's 18-mile scenic drive. Passengers can take as long as they like at any viewpoint and catch a later bus. The shuttle bus service also makes it easier for hikers, who don't need to worry about car shuttles between trailheads.

Use of the shuttle bus system is not mandatory; you can still bring in your own vehicle. However, park officials note that there is generally one parking space for every four cars entering the park. The shuttle operates May 15–September 1, 7 A.M.–dark.

Visitors Center

From the turnoff on Highway 12, follow signs past Ruby's Inn to the park entrance; the visitors center is a short distance farther on the right. A brief slide show, screened on request, introduces the park. Geologic exhibits illustrate how the land was formed and how it has changed. Historic displays interpret the Paiutes, early explorers, and the first settlers. Trees, flowers, and wildlife are identified. Rangers present a variety of naturalist programs, including short hikes, mid-May–early September; see the posted schedule. The staff sells travel and natural history books, maps of the park and adjacent Dixie National Forest, posters, postcards, slides, and film. Open daily all year (except Christmas) 8 A.M.–4:30 P.M., with extended hours during the warmer months. Contact the park at Bryce Canyon, UT 84717, 435/834-5322, www.nps.gov/brca.

Special hazards you should be aware of include crumbly ledges and lightning strikes. People who have wandered off trails or gotten too close to the drop-offs have had to be pulled out by rope. Avoid cliffs and other exposed areas during electrical storms, which are most common in late summer.

SCENIC DRIVE

From elevations of about 8,000 feet near the visitors center, the scenic drive gradually winds 1,100 feet higher to Rainbow Point. About midway you'll notice a change in the trees from largely ponderosa pine to spruce, fir, and aspen. On a clear day, you can enjoy vistas of more than 100 miles from many of the viewpoints. Because of parking shortages on the drive, trailers must be left at the visitors center or campsite. Visitors wishing to see the rest of the viewpoints may choose to walk on the Rim Trail.

Fairyland Point

To reach the turnoff (just inside the park boundary), go north 0.8 mile from the visitors center, then east one mile. Whimsical forms line Fairyland Canyon a short distance below. You can descend into the "fairyland" on the **Fairyland Loop Trail** or follow the **Rim Trail** for other panoramas.

Sunrise and Sunset Points

These overlooks are off to the left about one mile past the visitors center; they're connected by a half-mile paved section of the **Rim Trail.** Panoramas from each point take in large areas of Bryce Amphitheater and beyond. The lofty Aquarius and Table Cliff Plateaus rise along the skyline to the northeast; you can recognize the same colorful Claron Formation in cliffs that faulting has raised about 2,000 feet higher. **Queen's Garden Trail** from Sunrise Point and **Navajo Loop Trail** from Sunset Point provide different experiences within the amphitheater.

Inspiration Point

It's well worth walking the three-quarters of a mile south along the **Rim Trail** from Sunset Point or driving a bit more than a mile to Inspiration Point to see a fantastic maze of hoodoos in the "Silent City." Weathering along vertical joints has cut many rows of narrow gullies, some more than 200 feet deep.

Bryce Point

This overlook at the south end of Bryce Amphitheater has memorable views to the north

and east. It's also the start for the **Rim, Peekaboo Loop,** and **Under-the-Rim Trails.** From the turnoff two miles south of the visitors center, follow signs 2.1 miles in.

Paria View

Cliffs drop precipitously into the headwaters of Yellow Creek, a tributary of the Paria River. You can see a section of Under-the-Rim Trail winding up a hillside near the mouth of the amphitheater below. Distant views take in the Paria River Canyon, White Cliffs (of Navajo sandstone), and Navajo Mountain. The plateau rim in the park forms a drainage divide. Precipitation falling west of the rim flows gently into the East Fork of Sevier River and the Great Basin; precipitation landing east of the rim rushes through deep canyons in the Pink Cliffs to the Paria River and on to the Colorado River and the Grand Canyon. Take the turnoff for Bryce Point, then keep right at the fork.

Farview Point

The sweeping panorama takes in a lot of geology. You can see levels of the Grand Staircase that include the Aquarius and Table Cliff Plateaus to the northeast, Kaiparowits Plateau to the east, and White Cliffs to the southeast. Look beyond the White Cliffs to see a section of the Kaibab Plateau that forms the north rim of the Grand Canyon in Arizona. The overlook is on the left nine miles south of the visitors center.

Natural Bridge

This large feature lies just off the road on the left, 1.7 miles past Farview Point. The span is 54 feet wide and 95 feet high. Despite its name, this is an arch, formed by weathering from rain and freezing, rather than by stream erosion like a true natural bridge. Once the opening reached ground level, runoff began to enlarge the hole and to dig a gully through it.

Agua and Ponderosa Canyons

You can admire sheer cliffs and hoodoos from the Agua Canyon overlook on the left, 1.4 miles past Natural Bridge. With a little imagination, you might be able to pick out the Hunter and the

Rabbit below. Ponderosa Canyon overlook, on the left 1.8 miles farther, offers a panorama similar to that at Farview Point.

Yovimpa Point and Rainbow Point

The land drops away in rugged canyons and fine views at the end of the scenic drive, 17 miles south of the visitors center. At an elevation of 9,105 feet, this is the highest area of the park. Yovimpa and Rainbow Points lie only a short walk apart yet offer different vistas. **Bristlecone Loop Trail** is an easy one-mile loop from Rainbow Point to ancient bristlecone pines along the rim. **Riggs Spring Loop Trail** makes a good day hike; begin from either Yovimpa Point or Rainbow Point and descend into canyons in the southern area of the park. **Under-the-Rim Trail** starts from Rainbow Point and winds 22.5 miles to Bryce Point; day-hikers could make a 7.5-mile trip by using the Agua Canyon Connecting Trail and a car shuttle.

HIKING

Hikers enjoy close-up views of the wonderfully eroded features and gain a direct appreciation of Bryce's geology. Because almost all of the trails head down off the canyon's rim, they're moderately difficult, with many ups and downs, but the paths are well graded and signed. Hikers not accustomed to the 7,000- to 9,000-foot elevations will find the going relatively strenuous and should allow extra time. Be sure to carry water and drink frequently—staying well hydrated will give you more energy.

Wear a hat and sunscreen to protect against sunburn, which can be a problem at these elevations. Don't forget rain gear because storms can come up suddenly. Always carry water for day trips because only a few natural sources exist. Ask at the visitors center for current trail conditions and water sources; you can also pick up a free hiking map at the visitors center. Snow may block some trail sections in winter and early spring. Horses are permitted only on Peekaboo Loop. Pets must stay above the rim; they're allowed on the Rim Trail only between Sunset and Sunrise Points.

VISITING BRYCE CANYON IN WINTER

Though Bryce is most popular during the summer months, it is especially beautiful and other-worldly during the winter, when the rock formations are topped with snow. And, since Bryce is so high (the elevation ranges 8,000–9,000 feet), winter lasts a long time, often into spring break.

The main park roads and most viewpoints are plowed, and the Rim Trail is an excellent, easy snowshoe or cross-country ski route. **Paria Ski Trail** (five-mile loop) and **Fairyland Ski Trail** (2.5-mile loop) are marked for snowshoers and cross-country skiers. Snowshoes are loaned free of charge at the visitors center with deposit of a credit card whenever snow depth measures 18 inches or more at the visitors center. Rent cross-country ski equipment just outside the park at Ruby's. Miles of snowmobile trails are groomed outside the park.

During the winter, most of the businesses around the park entrance shut down. The notable exception is Ruby's Inn, which is a wintertime hub of activity. During the winter months, rates drop precipitously—most rooms go for less than $50 January–March.

Ruby's Inn hosts the Bryce Canyon Winter Festival during Presidents Day weekend in February. The three-day festival has free cross-country skiing and snowshoeing clinics, demos, and tours. This is also the time and place to pick up tips on ski archery and winter photography.

Overnight hikers can obtain the required $5 backcountry permit at the visitors center (camping is allowed only on the Under-the-Rim and Riggs Spring Loop Trails). Backpack stoves must be used for cooking; wood fires are prohibited. Although there are several isolated springs in Bryce's backcountry, it's prudent to carry at least one gallon of water per person per day. Ask about the location and flow of springs when you register for the backcountry permit.

Don't expect much solitude during the summer on the popular Rim, Queen's Garden, Navajo Loop, and Peekaboo Loop Trails. Fairyland Loop

Trail is less used, and the backcountry trails are almost never crowded. September and October are the choice hiking months—the weather is best and the crowds smallest, although nighttime temperatures in late October can dip well below freezing.

Rim Trail

This easy trail follows the edge of Bryce Amphitheater for 5.5 miles between Fairyland and Bryce Points; the elevation change is 540 feet. Most people walk just sections in leisurely strolls or use the trail to connect with five others. The half-mile section near the lodge between Sunrise and Sunset Points is paved and nearly level; other parts are gently rolling.

Fairyland Loop Trail

This trail winds in and out of colorful rock spires in the northern part of Bryce Amphitheater, a somewhat less-visited area one mile off the main park road. Although the trail is well graded, remember the 900-foot climb you'll make when you exit. You can take a loop hike of eight miles from either Fairyland Point or Sunrise Point by using a section of the **Rim Trail**; a car shuttle saves three hiking miles. The whole loop is too long for many visitors, who enjoy short trips down and back to see this "fairyland."

Queen's Garden Trail

A favorite of many people, this trail drops from Sunrise Point through impressive features in the middle of Bryce Amphitheater to a hoodoo resembling a portly Queen Victoria. The hike is 1.5 miles round-trip and has an elevation change of 320 feet, which you'll have to climb on the way back. This is the easiest excursion below the rim and takes about 1.5 hours. Queen's Garden Trail also makes a good loop hike with the **Navajo** and **Rim Trails;** most people who do the loop prefer to descend the steeper Navajo and climb out on Queen's Garden Trail for a 3.5-mile hike. Trails also connect with the **Peekaboo Loop Trail** and go to the town of Tropic.

Navajo Loop Trail

From Sunset Point, you'll drop 520 feet in three-

quarters of a mile through a narrow canyon. At the bottom, the loop leads into deep, dark **Wall Street**—an even narrower canyon one-half mile long—then returns to the rim; the total distance is about 1.5 miles. Other destinations from the bottom of Navajo Trail are **Twin Bridges, Queen's Garden Trail, Peekaboo Loop Trail,** and the town of Tropic. The 1.5-mile trail to Tropic isn't as scenic as the other trails, but it does provide another way to enter or leave the park; ask at the visitors center or in Tropic for directions to the trailhead.

Peekaboo Loop Trail

This enchanting walk is full of surprises at every turn—and there are lots of turns! The trail is in the southern part of Bryce Amphitheater, which has some of the most striking rock features. You can start from Bryce Point (6.5 miles round-trip), from Sunset Point (5.5 miles round-trip via Navajo Trail), or from Sunrise Point (seven miles round-trip via Queen's Garden Trail). The loop itself is 3.5 miles long with many ups and downs and a few tunnels. The elevation change is 500–800 feet, depending on the trailhead you choose. This is the only trail in the park where horses are permitted; remember to give horseback travelers the right-of-way and, if possible, to step to higher ground when you allow them to pass.

Under-the-Rim Trail

The longest trail in the park winds 22.5 miles below the Pink Cliffs between Bryce Point in the north and Rainbow Point in the south. Allow at least two days to hike the entire trail; the elevation change is about 1,500 feet with many ups and downs. Four connecting trails from the scenic drive allow you to travel the Under-the-Rim Trail as a series of day hikes, too. Another option is to combine the Under-the-Rim and **Riggs Spring Loop** trails for a total of 31.5 miles.

The **Hat Shop,** an area of delicate spires capped by erosion-resistant rock, makes a good day-hiking destination; begin at Bryce Point and follow the Under-the-Rim Trail for about two miles. Most of this section is downhill (elevation change of 900 feet), which you'll have to climb on the way out.

BRISTLECONE PINE

S omewhere on earth, a bristlecone pine tree may be the planet's oldest living organism. The trees here, although not the world's oldest, are up to 1,700 years old. (A bristlecone in California is nearly 4,800 years old.) These twisted, gnarly trees are easy to spot in the area around Rainbow Point because they *look* their age.

What makes a bristlecone live so long? For one, its dense, resinous wood protects it from insects, bacteria, and fungi that kill many other trees. It grows in a harsh, dry climate, where there's not a lot of competition from other plants. During droughts that would kill most other plants, the bristlecone can slow down its metabolism until it's practically dormant, then spring back to life when conditions are less severe. Although the dry desert air poses its own set of challenges, it also keeps the tree from rotting.

Besides its ancient look, a bristlecone pine can be recognized by its distinctive needles—they're packed tightly, five to a bunch, with the bunches running along the length of a branch, giving it a bottlebrush-like appearance.

Bristlecone Loop Trail

The easy one-mile loop begins from either Rainbow or Yovimpa Point and goes to viewpoints and ancient bristlecone pines along the rim. These hardy trees survive fierce storms and extremes of hot and cold that no other tree can. Some of the bristlecone pines here are 1,700 years old.

Riggs Spring Loop

One of the park's more challenging day hikes or a leisurely overnighter, this trail begins from Rainbow Point and descends into canyons in the southern area of the park. The loop is about nine miles long, with an elevation change of 1,625 feet. Of the three backcountry campgrounds along the trail, the Riggs Spring site is most conveniently located, about halfway around the loop. Great views of the hoodoos, lots of aspen trees, a couple of pretty meadows, and great views off to the east are some of the highlights of this hike. Day hikers may want to take a shortcut bypassing Riggs Spring, saving three-quarters of a mile.

Mossy Cave Trail

This easy trail is not on the main park road; it's just off Highway 12, northwest of Tropic, near the east edge of the park. Hike up Water Canyon to a cool alcove of dripping water and moss. Sheets of ice and icicles add beauty to the scene in winter. The hike is only one mile round-trip with a small elevation gain. A side trail, just before the cave, branches right a short distance to a little waterfall; look for several small arches in the colorful canyon walls above. Although the park lacks perennial natural streams, the stream in Water Canyon flows even during dry spells. Mormon pioneers labored three years to channel water from the East Fork of the Sevier River through a canal and down this wash to the town of Tropic. Without this irrigation, the town might not even exist. From the visitors center, return to Highway 12 and turn east 3.7 miles toward Escalante; the parking area is on the right just after a bridge (between mileposts 17 and 18). Rangers schedule guided walks to the cave and the waterfall during the main season.

MOUNTAIN BIKING

Although mountain biking is prohibited on trails inside the national park, just a few miles west of the park entrance Red Canyon's bike trails are spectacularly scenic and exhilarating to ride. See Vicinity of Bryce Canyon for information on Red Canyon.

Ruby's Inn provides a shuttle service for Red Canyon mountain bikers.

HORSEBACK RIDING

If you'd like to get down among the hoodoos, but aren't sure that you have the energy to hike back up to the rim, consider letting a horse help you along.

SOUTHWESTERN UTAH

The park offers guided rides near Sunrise Point, and both two-hour ($30) and half-day ($45) trips are offered. Both rides descend to the floor of the canyon; the longer ride follows the Peekaboo Loop Trail. Riders must be at least seven years old and weigh no more than 220 pounds; the horses and wranglers are all used to novices.

TOURS

Ruby's Inn, a hotel, restaurant, and recreation complex at the park entrance, is a good place to take measure of the opportunities for organized recreation and sightseeing excursions in and around Bryce Canyon. The lobby is filled with outfitters who are anxious to take you out on the trail; you'll find each of the following there, along with other vendors who organize hayrides, barn dances, and chuckwagon dinners. **Red Canyon Horseback Rides,** 435/468-8660, has horseback riding near Bryce Canyon May–October. There's a choice of half-day ($45) and whole-day ($79 including lunch) trips. Shorter rides (as well as half- and full-day trips) are offered by **Scenic Rim Trail Rides,** 435/834-5341, ext. 217, which also operates out of Ruby's. An hour-long ride is $19. Ruby's also sponsors a rodeo nightly Monday–Saturday at 7 P.M. across from the inn.

You can also explore the area around Bryce Canyon on a noisier steed. Guided all-terrain vehicle (ATV) tours of Red Canyon are offered by **Great Western ATV,** 435/834-5200 or 800/432-5383. A one-hour trip is $29, a three-hour trip is $69.

If you'd like to get a look at Bryce and the surrounding area from the air, you can choose to take a scenic flight-seeing tour from **Bryce Canyon Airlines,** 435/834-5341, which offers both plane and helicopter tours. There's quite a range of options, from a 15-minute trip to a nearby mesa ($35) to a 2.5-hour trip that takes in the Grand Canyon ($295).

ACCOMMODATIONS

Travelers can have a hard time finding accommodations and campsites April–October in both the park and nearby areas. Advance reservations at lodges and motels are a good idea; otherwise, plan to arrive by late morning. Bryce Canyon Lodge is the only lodging in the park itself—you'll need to make reservations months in advance to get a room in this historic landmark. Other motels are clustered near the park entrance road. A larger selection of lodgings and dining options is found in Tropic, 11 miles east on Highway 12.

The park's two campgrounds operate on a first-come, first-served basis; arrive by noon in the main season to be assured of a spot.

Reach the **Bryce Canyon Information Line,** an area motel reservation service, at 435/444-6689.

Under $50

To find lodgings for less than $50 during the high summer season, head about 17 miles west of the park, to the U.S. 89 and Highway 12 junction, where the **Bryce Junction Inn,** 435/676-2221 or 800/437-4361, is a standard motel with rooms topping out at about $50.

$50–75

Other hotels are clustered on Highway 12, right outside the park boundary. Many of these have seen a lot of use over the years, usually without a lot of attendant upkeep. The **Foster's Motel** has plain vanilla motel rooms for right around $50. It's four miles west of the park entrance at 1150 Hwy. 12, 435/834-5227 or 800/372-4750, www.fostersmotel.com.

One of the newest lodgings, and a good value for the area, is the **Bryce View Lodge,** near the park turnoff and across the road from Ruby's Inn, 435/834-5180 or 888/279-2304, www.bryceviewlodge.com. Rooms in the handsome lodge-like buildings start at about $55. Six miles west of the park turnoff, the **Bryce Canyon Pines Motel,** 435/834-5441 or 800/892-7923, www.brycecanyonmotel.com, has rooms and cottages ranging $65–95, a seasonal covered pool, horseback rides, and a restaurant open daily for breakfast, lunch, and dinner early April–late October.

$75–100

At **Bryce Canyon Resort,** near the junction of

Hwy. 12 and Hwy. 63, 435/834-5351 or 800/834-0043, recently renovated rooms start at about $85 per night. Rooms in the old building are $69, with simple cabins running about $50.

$100–125

Set among ponderosa pines a short walk from the rim, the **Bryce Canyon Lodge** was built in 1923 by a division of the Union Pacific Railway; a spur line once terminated at the front entrance. The lodge has lots of charm and is listed on the National Register of Historic Places. It also has by far the best location of any Bryce-area accommodation; it's the only lodging in the park itself.

Hotel rooms start at $110 and run to $130 for a suite; western cabins are $120. The lodge is open April–October. Activities include horseback rides, park tours, evening entertainment, and ranger talks; a gift shop sells souvenirs. Try to make reservations for accommodations as far in advance as possible (eight months advised) with Xanterra Parks & Resorts, 14001 E. Iliff Ave., Ste. 600, Aurora, CO 80014, 650/372-1705 or 800/834-5351 (Bryce Canyon Lodge), in-season. You can also make reservations at the website www.xanterra.com.

The large, resort-like **Best Western Ruby's Inn** offers many year-round services on Hwy. 63 just north of the park boundary (Bryce, UT 84764), 435/834-5341 or 800/468-8660, www.rubysinn.com. The hotel features two indoor pools and a spa; rooms start just under $100. Kitchenettes and family rooms are also available; pets are okay. Ruby's Inn is more than just a place to stay, however. This is one of the area's major centers for all manner of recreational outfitters, dining, entertainment, and shopping.

Campgrounds

The park's two campgrounds both have water, provide some pull-through spaces, and cost $10. Try to arrive early for a space during the busy summer season because both campgrounds usually fill by 1 or 2 P.M., and only group areas may be reserved. The **North Campground** is on the left just past the visitors center. The best sites

here are just a few yards downhill from the Rim Trail, with easy hiking access to other park trails. The **Sunset Campground** is about 2.5 miles farther on the right, across the road from Sunset Point. Sunset has campsites accessible to people with disabilities.

Groceries, camping supplies, and coin-operated showers and a laundry room are available mid-April–late September at the **General Store,** between North Campground and Sunrise Point. During the rest of the year, you can go outside the park to Ruby's Inn for these services.

The Dixie National Forest has three Forest Service campgrounds in scenic settings among ponderosa pines. Often they'll have room when campgrounds in the park have filled. Group sites can be reserved, but the rest are available on a first-come, first-served basis. All sites have water and cost $8–10. The **Pine Lake Campground** lies at 7,700 feet just east of Pine Lake in a forest of ponderosa pine, spruce, and juniper. Sites are open mid-June–mid-September. From the highway junction north of the park, head northeast 11 miles on Highway 63 (gravel), then turn southeast six miles.

King Creek Campground is on the west shore of Tropic Reservoir, which has a boat ramp and fair trout fishing. Sites are at 8,000 feet and are usually open May–late September. Head seven miles south of Highway 12 down the gravel East Fork Sevier River Road, 2.8 miles west of the park turnoff. To reach the **Red Canyon Campground,** turn off Highway 12 four miles east of U.S. 89. It's at 7,400 feet, below brilliantly colored cliffs, and stays open from late May–late September. Contact the Powell Ranger District office in Panguitch, 435/676-8815, for more information on Kings and Red Canyon Campgrounds and at the Escalante Ranger District office in Escalante, 435/826-5400, for Pine Lake.

Private campgrounds in the area are $20 and up per night. **Ruby's Inn Campground,** at the park junction, 435/834-5301, is open early April–late October, with spaces for tents and RVs; showers and a laundry room are open all year. They've also got a few tepees ($23 per day) and bunkhouse-style cabins ($40 per day, no bedding provided). All of the considerable facilities at Ruby's are available to camping patrons. **Bryce Canyon Pines Campground,** four miles west of the park entrance, 435/834-5441 or 800/892-7923, has an indoor pool, a game room, groceries, and shady sites.

FOOD

The dining room at the **Bryce Canyon Lodge,** 435/586-9476, offers a varied menu with moderate prices; open daily in season for breakfast, lunch, and dinner (reservations advised for dinner). With 12 hours advance notice, you can order a box lunch.

The Ruby's Inn **Canyon Diner,** 435/834-5341, is one of Bryce Canyon's better restaurants; open for breakfast, lunch, and dinner daily. Casual lunch and dinner fare is served in the inn's snack bar April–October. Also check at Ruby's for seasonal chuckwagon meals, accompanied by singers and Western entertainment.

Bryce Canyon Resort, near the turnoff for the park, 435/834-5351 or 800/834-0043, has an on-site restaurant that features steak and barbecue and is open daily for breakfast, lunch, and dinner. Two miles west of the park turnoff is **Foster's,** 435/834-5227, a long-standing institution with old-fashioned diner food.

SERVICES

The **general store** at Ruby's has a large stock of groceries, camping and fishing supplies, film and processing, Native American crafts, books, and other souvenirs. The **Bryce post office** is at the store, too. Horseback rides, helicopter tours, and airplane rides are arranged in the lobby (see the Horseback Riding and Tours sections). In winter, cross-country skiers can rent gear and use trails located near the inn as well as in the park. Snowmobile trails are available (snowmobiles may not be used within the park). Western-fronted shops across from Ruby's Inn offer trail rides, chuckwagon dinners, mountain-bike rentals, souvenirs, and a petting farm. **Rodeos** take place in the nearby arena nightly Monday–Saturday in-season.

Vicinity of Bryce Canyon National Park

RED CANYON

The drive on Highway 12 between U.S. 89 and the turnoff for Bryce Canyon National Park passes through this well-named canyon. You may think that it should have been included in the national park because the brightly colored rocks belong to the same Claron Formation that's exposed at Bryce; however, because it's not part of the park, the trails at Red Canyon are open to the kinds of recreation that is prohibited in the park, principally mountain biking and ATV riding. In fact, this canyon is becoming very popular as other Utah mountain-biking destinations become overpopularized; however, many trails are restricted to foot traffic.

Staff members at **Red Canyon Visitors Center** can tell you about the trails, as well as scenic backcountry roads, that wind through the area; books and maps are sold. The visitors center is open daily about 8 A.M.–6 P.M. during the warmer months; it's between mileposts 3 and 4 on Highway 12, one-quarter mile west of Red Canyon Campground. You can contact the Powell Ranger District office in Panguitch for information year-round, 435/676-8815. (For details about Red Canyon Campground, see Accommodations in the Bryce Canyon section.)

Hiking

The U.S. Forest Service maintains many scenic hiking trails that wind back from the highway to give you a closer look at the geology. The following are open to hikers only. **Pink Ledges Trail,** the easiest and most popular, loops one-half mile past intriguing erosional features from the Red Canyon Visitors Center. Signs identify some of the trees and plants; the elevation gain is 100 feet. The **Birdseye Trail** winds through formations and connects the visitors center with a parking area on Highway 12 just inside the forest boundary, 0.8 mile away. **Buckhorn Trail** begins from site number 23 in Red Canyon Campground and climbs one mile for views of erosional forms and Red Canyon; the campground is on the south side of Highway 12 between mileposts 3 and 4. The **Tunnel Trail** ascends 300 feet in 0.7 mile for fine views of the canyon. The trail begins from a pullout on the south side of Highway 12 just west of a pair of tunnels, crosses the streambed, then climbs a ridge to viewpoints on the top. Ask at the visitors center for other good area trails worth exploring.

Mountain Biking

For tame pedalers, a spanking new, paved bike trail parallels Highway 12 for five miles through Red Canyon. Parking lots are located at either end of the trail.

True mountain bikers will eschew the pavement and head to **Casto Canyon Trail,** a 17-mile one-way trail that winds through red-rock formations and forest. The route starts and ends along Highway 12. If you don't have a shuttle vehicle at each of the trailheads, you'll need to pedal back another eight miles along the paved roadside trail to retrieve your vehicle. Start at Tom Best Road, just east of Red Canyon. You'll climb up through forest, turning onto Berry Spring Creek Road and then Cabin Hollow Road. When the trail starts heading into Casto Canyon, five downhill miles traverse wonderful red-rock scenery. When you reach the Casto Canyon Trailhead, you can choose to return to Highway 12, or you can pedal out to Highway 89 and Panguitch. Much of the trail is strenuous; take water along because there's no source along the way. Several side trails along the way can make this into a shorter ride; see the Forest Service brochure on Red Canyon trails.

POWELL POINT

Even in a state with many superb viewpoints, Powell Point (elev. 10,188 feet) is outstanding. Yet surprisingly few people know about this lofty perch at the southern tip of the Table Cliff Plateau, a southwestern extension of the Aquarius Plateau. Its light-colored cliffs stand about 15 air miles northeast of Sunset Point in Bryce

© JUDY JEWELL

SOUTHWESTERN UTAH

The Red Canyon bike path, just north of Bryce Canyon National Park, provides smooth sailing for road bikers.

Canyon National Park. Getting to Powell Point involves a bit of adventure. You can drive a car with good clearance within 4.3 miles of the point; high-clearance vehicles can go to within 0.6 mile. From the highway junction north of the national park, drive northeast 11 miles on Highway 63 (gravel), turn southeast six miles to Pine Lake, continue east six miles on Forest Route 132 up onto the plateau, then look for the one-lane dirt road on the right to Powell Point; high-clearance vehicles can turn in 3.7 miles to the Powell Point Trailhead. If you're not equipped for driving this rough road, you'll still find it good for hiking or mountain biking. The road ends where the ridge becomes too narrow for it; a clearing here is fine for camping (no facilities).

A foot trail continues 0.6 mile to the very end of Powell Point. The route passes through an extremely weather-beaten and picturesque forest of bristlecone and limber pine. Panoramic views begin well before trail's end; at the point itself it feels as though you're at the end of the world. Much of southern Utah and northern Arizona stretches out below to the far horizon. The colorful cliffs of the Claron Formation lie directly underfoot; take care near the crumbly cliff edges. Avoid Powell Point if thunderstorms threaten. (Note the many lightning scars on trees here!) The **Escalante Ranger District office,** 435/826-5400, may have current road conditions to Powell Point.

TROPIC

Mormon pioneer Ebenezer Bryce homesteaded near the town site of Tropic in 1875, but he left for Arizona five years later. Other pioneers settled six villages near the upper Paria River between 1876–1891. The towns of Tropic, Cannonville, and Henrieville still survive. Tropic lies just 11 miles east of Bryce Canyon National Park, visible from many of the park's viewpoints. Travelers think of Tropic primarily for its cache of motels lining Main Street (Highway 12); several pleasant B&Bs also grace the town. A **log cabin** built by Ebenezer Bryce has been moved to a site beside the Bryce Pioneer Village Motel; ask to see the cabin's small collection of pioneer and Native American artifacts. A **tourist booth** in the center of town is open daily early May–late October, about 11 A.M.–7 P.M.

Accommodations

$50–75: The basic motel rooms at **Doug's Place Country Inn,** 435/679-8600 or 800/993-6847, www.dougsplace.net, are part of a complex that includes a restaurant and a store. Rooms top out at $65 during the peak summer season. In the same price range, **Bryce Valley Inn,** 435/679-8811 or 800/442-1890, www.brycevalleyinn.com, has rooms in an attractive wood-fronted, Western-look motel. Pets are okay for a fee. On the south end of town, the **Bryce Pioneer Village Motel,** 435/679-8546 or 800/222-0381, www.bpvillage.com, has motel rooms and several cabins (one with kitchen); there's also a campground.

At the **Bryce Canyon Inn,** 435/679-8502 or 800/592-1468, the tidy new cabins are nicely furnished and cost $65 during high season. Also new are the **Bryce Country Cabins,** 80 S. Main St., 435/679-8643 or 888/679-8643, www.brycecountrycabins.com. The cabins overlook a meadow, and each has a private bath. One-half mile south of town is the log cabin–style **Francisco's Farm Bed & Breakfast,** 51 Francisco Ln., 435/679-8721 or 800/642-4136, which offers rooms in a farmhouse, all with private baths.

$75–100: A few blocks from the highway, the **Bryce Point Bed & Breakfast,** 61 North 400 West, 435/679-8629 or 888/200-4211, www.brycepointlodging.com, is a large home with very nice rooms, all with private baths, TVs and VCRs, and views out every window. All rooms have private entrances. There's also a guest cabin. The attractive **Bullberry Inn B&B,** 435/679-8820 or 800/249-8126, www.bullberryinn.com, has wraparound porches, and guest rooms have private baths and rustic-style furniture. At **Canyon Livery B&B,** 660 West 50 South, 435/679-8780 or 888/889-8910, every room has a private bath, balcony, and views of Bryce Canyon.

Over $100: The **Stone Canyon Inn** 435/679-8611 or 866/489-4680, www.stonecanyoninn

.com, just west of Tropic with views onto Bryce, has comfortable, uncluttered rooms starting at about $100.

Food

Hoo Doos Restaurant is part of Doug's Place Country Inn, 435/679-8632, and serves Mexican food, Texas-style barbecue, and steaks. It's open for breakfast, lunch, and dinner daily and is licensed to sell liquor. The **Hungry Coyote Restaurant,** at the Bryce Valley Inn, 435/679-8811, has a liquor-licensed restaurant with an outdoor mesquite barbecue area. Open for three meals daily.

Along U.S. 89: Panguitch to Kanab

PANGUITCH

Pioneers arrived here in 1864, but hostile Utes forced evacuation just two years later. A second attempt by settlers in 1871 succeeded, and Panguitch (Big Fish) is now the largest town in the area.

Panguitch is one of the more pleasant towns in this part of Utah, with an abundance of reasonably priced motels and a couple of good places to eat. It's also a good hub for exploring the many scenic highlights of south-central Utah.

The early-20th-century commercial buildings downtown have some of their original facades. On side streets you can see sturdy brick houses built by the early settlers. Stop by the **Daughters of Utah Pioneers Museum** in the old bishop's storehouse at 100 East and Center to see historic exhibits of Panguitch. Open Monday–Saturday about 4–8 P.M. in summer and by appointment the rest of the year; phone numbers to volunteers are on the door.

The **Paunsagaunt Wildlife Museum,** 250 East Center St., 435/676-2500, in the old Panguitch public school, is a taxidermy collection of more than 400 animals from western North America displayed in dioramas resembling their natural habitats. Displays also include stuffed animals from Africa, India, and Europe. It's actually quite well done, and kids seem to love it. There's a good collection of Native American artifacts. Admission is $4 adult, children 6–12 $2.50.

Events and Recreation

Major annual events include a **Quilt Walk** in early June, **Fourth of July** celebrations (parade, fireworks, and FFA junior rodeo in town; fireworks at Panguitch Lake), **Pioneer Day** on July 24 (parade and rodeo), and **Garfield County Livestock Show and Fair** in mid-August.

The **city park** on the north edge of town has picnic tables, a playground, tennis courts, and a tourist information cabin. A **swimming pool** is at 250 E. Center by the high school, 435/676-2259.

Accommodations

Under $50: The **Adobe Sands,** 390 N. Main St., 435/676-8874 or 800/497-9261, is a perfectly acceptable budget motel, open May–October. The **Blue Pine Motel,** 130 N. Main St., 435/676-8197 or 800/299-6115, is an attractive place that permits pets.

$50–75: The **Bryce Way Motel,** 429 N. Main St., 435/676-2400 or 800/225-6534, has a heated indoor pool. The **Color Country Motel,** 526 N. Main St., 435/676-2386 or 800/225-6518, has an outdoor pool and clean, well-maintained rooms. The **Bryce Canyon Motel,** 308 N. Main St., 435/676-8441, is well-kept and has kitchenette rooms. The **Panguitch Inn Motel,** an old downtown hotel at 50 N. Main St., 435/676-8871 or 800/331-7407, is open seasonally May–October.

Along U.S. 89, the **Best Western New Western,** 180 E. Center St., 435/676-8876 or 800/528-1234, has a swimming pool and hot tub, plus laundry facilities. Rooms here hover around $75 during the high summer season.

$75–100: Seven miles south of Panguitch, at the junction of Highways 89 and 12, is a large faux-Western complex called the **Western Town Resort,** 435/676-8770 or 888/687-4339, www.westerntownresort.com. The resort looks like a

SOUTHWESTERN UTAH

vintage frontier town, with trading posts, country stores, and stables, but most of the buildings, in fact, offer motel accommodations. Western Town, which is gradually evolving toward being a full-service resort, offers a saloon and dance hall (complete with a huge display of the Book of Mormon, free for the taking), a restaurant, guided horseback rides, and cowboy-style activities.

Campgrounds: Open year-round, **Hitch-N-Post Campground,** 420 N. Main, 435/676-2436, offers spaces for tents and RVs and has showers and a laundry room. The **Big Fish KOA Campground,** 555 S. Main, 435/676-2225, on the road to Panguitch Lake, is open April 15–October 15 with a pool, a recreation room, a laundry room, and showers; $20 tents, $25 for RVs, and $46 for cabins. The closest public campground is on Highway 12 in Red Canyon.

Food

The **Flying M Restaurant,** 580 N. Main, 435/676-8008, is a favorite for hearty breakfasts and standard American fare. For mesquite-grilled meats, try **Cowboy's Smokehouse Bar-B-Q,** 95 N. Main St., 435/676-8030. Traditional Italian favorites, with several vegetarian options, are dished up at **Grandma Tina's Spaghetti House,** 523 N. Main St., 435/676-2377. Tina also serves breakfast, including espresso and deep-fried scones (actually like tasty, not-too-sweet doughnuts).

Believe it or not, there's a tavern in Panguitch! The **Trails End Saloon,** 535 N. Main St., 435/676-2235, serves beer (including local microbrews) and wine coolers. During the summer, there's often live music on weekend evenings.

Information and Services

The **information center** in the city park, 435/676-8131 or 800/444-6689 (Bryce Canyon Information Line), offers brochures and suggestions for services in Panguitch and travel to Bryce Canyon National Park and other scenic destinations nearby. Open daily early May–late October, 9 A.M.–5 P.M.; closed in winter. Contact the **Garfield County Travel Council** year-round at P.O. Box 200, Panguitch, UT 84759, 435/676-8421. The **Powell Ranger District office** of the U.S. Forest Service has information on

campgrounds, hiking trails, fishing, and scenic drives in the forest and canyons surrounding Bryce Canyon National Park; open Monday–Friday 8 A.M.–4:30 P.M. at 225 E. Center (U.S. 89), 435/676-8815, or write P.O. Box 80, Panguitch, UT 84759.

The **post office** is at 65 North 100 West, 435/676-8853. **Garfield Memorial Hospital** provides medical services at 224 North 400 East, 435/676-8811 (hospital), 435/676-8842 (clinic).

HATCH

The Hatch family started a ranch in the upper Sevier River Valley during the early 1870s. Colorful cliffs of the Paunsaugunt Plateau contrast with the blue sky to the east. Stop in at the **Daughters of Utah Pioneers Museum** to learn about the pioneers and see their artifacts; it's usually open summer afternoons (except Sunday), or you can call the telephone numbers posted on the front door to reach a volunteer; turn west one block at the sign in the center of town. **Garfield Information Center,** just south of town, is open daily 9 A.M.–5 P.M. early May–late October with literature and advice for travel in Garfield County.

Accommodations

About $50: None of the following places is fancy by any stretch of the imagination, but they are a good value. **New Bryce Motel,** 227 North Main, 435/735-4265, has an on-site restaurant. It's open about mid-March–late November. **Riverside Motel and Campground** is just north of town, 435/735-4223 or 800/824-5651, and has sites for tents and RVs year-round; it also offers a store, laundry, showers and trout fishing in the Sevier River. Rooms are even less expensive at the **Dream Catcher Motel,** 216 N. Main, 435/735-4098, which also has a café (open daily for breakfast, lunch, and dinner); open late March–September.

Mammoth Creek Hatchery

This is one of about 11 state hatcheries producing trout and other game fish. You're welcome to visit during daylight hours. Indoor areas house the eggs and fry; larger fish swim in the outdoor raceways. Go one mile south of Hatch on U.S. 89 and turn west two miles on a paved road at the sign. An unpaved road continues to Mammoth Cave and other attractions on the Markagunt Plateau.

LONG VALLEY

Highway U.S. 89 follows the East Fork of the Virgin River past a series of small Mormon towns north of Kanab. Nearly all travelers visiting the national parks of the region will pass through this forested valley. Most of the towns in Long Valley offer a handful of motels, campgrounds, and restaurants.

Long Valley Junction

The junction (elev. 7,200 feet) marks the divide between the East Fork of the Virgin River to the south and the Sevier River to the north. Turn west on Highway 14 to visit Cedar Breaks National Monument and the alpine country of the Markagunt Plateau. Continue south 13 miles for Glendale or north 13 miles on U.S. 89 for Hatch.

Glendale

The original settlers named their community Berryville in 1864. A small fort helped protect against Navajo raids, but continued conflicts forced all the valley's inhabitants to leave by 1866. A new group arrived in 1871 and renamed the site Glendale after the town in Scotland.

Orderville

Orderville began as an experiment in communal life in 1875 as part of the Mormon United Order. Everyone worked on cooperative farms and industries, divided income according to need, shared meals at a common table, and met twice daily for worship. The experiment succeeded admirably for about 10 years, longer than in any other Mormon town. A combination of internal disagreements and external pressures eventually convinced community leaders to end the United Order and to return its property to private ownership. The **Orderville DUP Museum** contains

pioneer artifacts; open on request (call the telephone numbers posted on the door to reach a designated volunteer).

Mt. Carmel

This agricultural community, a few miles north of Mt. Carmel Junction, was first settled in 1865 as Winsor. Threats by Navajo and Paiutes forced its abandonment a year later and it wasn't reestablished until 1871, when it was named Mt. Carmel for a mountain in Israel. The Elkhart Cliffs of white Navajo sandstone rise to the east.

Mt. Carmel Junction

Highway 9 turns west here from U.S. 89 to Zion National Park.

Accommodations

The following accommodations along U.S. 89 from Long Valley Junction to Mt. Carmel Junction are listed north to south under each price category.

Under $50: Inexpensive accommodations in Orderville are offered by the **Parkway Motel,** 435/648-2380, and the **Hummingird Bed & Breakfast,** 102 Frost Ln., at the south end of town, 435/648-2415.

Clean basic rooms in Mt. Carmel Junction are available at the **Golden Hills Motel,** 435/648-2268 or 800/648-2268. The on-site **Golden Hills Restaurant** serves breakfast, lunch, and dinner daily.

$50–75: The historic **Smith Hotel** (1927), on Main St. north of Glendale, 435/648-2156 or 800/528-3558, has been restored as a bed-and-breakfast; all rooms have baths.

$75–100: In Glendale, **The Eagle's Nest B&B,** 500 West Lydia's Canyon Rd., 435/648-2200 or 800/293-6378, is a very attractive modern home with four guest rooms; all rooms have private baths and two have fireplaces. The proprietors are world travelers, and the home is filled with folk art from every continent.

The **Arrowhead B&B** in Mt. Carmel, at White Cliffs Ranch, 2155 S. State St., 435/648-2569 or 888/821-1670, has four attractive rooms in a ranch home surrounded by meadows and grassland. You'll enjoy the swimming pool,

THE UNITED ORDER OF ENOCH

T he United Order of Enoch was an attempt by Brigham Young to remedy several ills caused by an economic boom in the church community. The arrival of the railroad had brought some forms of prosperity to the Mormons, especially in allowing the development of mining. But the railroad also brought in a rougher class of folk who had no intention of emulating the quiet, industrious lifestyle of the Mormons, and it allowed the import of commercially produced goods at cheaper prices than could be had locally. Both factors spelled trouble for a church seeking self-sufficiency.

As Joseph Smith had envisioned in his Law of Consecration, the United Order was proposed as a policy of communal living in which members would commit all their privately owned goods toward a common end. Many members had surrendered their property in the early days of the church, but the troubled times the church found in the east had thwarted the success of true communal villages. In the 1870s, church leaders felt the time had come.

When Brigham Young reactivated the United Order, it took life in several forms. The earliest and one of the most successful was the Brigham City Cooperative (BCC), started by Lorenzo Snow in 1864. BCC was a cooperative general store that met with great success, expanding over the years to 40 departments. The store was run on investments by voluntary members who received dividends based on their contributions. So successful was this venture that its business was barely touched by the Panic of 1873.

Branches of the order offered full communal living in which members ate in a communal dining hall, wore uniform clothing, and worked in community-owned facilities. In such a commune, all private possessions were surrendered upon membership. The most successful commune of this type may have been Orderville, where travel-weary settlers went about living the United Order in its most idealistic form.

Orderville's effort was largely a success, but citizens from surrounding communities openly scoffed at the spartan life of the commune. Mormon children were gradually swayed by the taunts of their peers, which led to a "trouser rebellion." One story tells of a Mormon youth who sought permission and money to buy pants more fashionable than the standard communal issue. When he was denied on the grounds that his present pair was still serviceable, he took to work, earned the money himself, and promptly purchased a pair in the fashionable store-bought style. He was taken before the commune's elected board, which lauded his enterprise but decreed that every youth had to have the new pants or no one would. It was considered wasteful to replace pants that were still wearable, so youngsters were soon busy at the community grindstone wearing out the seats of their britches.

Younger members of the Orderville commune also suffered in that, unlike their elders, they didn't receive shares in the community when relinquishing their property. They were paid only a wage with no dividends—$.75 a day until they reached 18, $1.50 thereafter. Eventually, the younger population trickled away, seeking higher-paying jobs in the surrounding area.

Most communal attempts, though, lasted less than a year, crippled primarily by human nature. Wealthy residents didn't wish to relinquish their property, dissatisfaction with the distribution of goods was common, and residents were often lured away by employment and business opportunities outside the commune. The Orderville community lasted 11 years, during which time its communal property nearly quadrupled in value. In that, it can be considered something of a success.

hot tub, and pool table. Each room has a TV and VCR.

In Mt. Carmel Junction, **Best Western Thunderbird Motel,** 435/648-2203, features a good restaurant, nine-hole golf course, a pool, and large attractive rooms with balconies. Its **Thunderbird Restaurant** serves breakfast, lunch, and dinner daily.

Guest Ranch: Coral Canyons Ranch, three miles south of Mt. Carmel Junction, 800/469-3789, www.gowildwest.com, is a working ranch that takes in guests. You're free to tag along with the hands as they do ranch work, or you can simply relax and enjoy the peaceful surroundings. Organized activities like cattle drives and backcountry tours are also available. B&B rates are $99 per night; working ranch stays, which include three meals plus horseback riding, are $149 per day.

Campgrounds: Glendale KOA, five miles north of Glendale, 435/648-2490, has sites for tents and RVs, cabins, a pool, a store, horseback rides, laundry, and showers; open May–September. **Bauer's Canyon Ranch RV Camp,** on Hwy. 89 in Glendale, 435/648-2564, offers hot showers and laundry facilities; open March–October. **Tortoise and the Hare Campground,** one mile north of Orderville, 435/648-2312, has RV sites, with showers and laundry; open early April–late October.

Kanab and Vicinity

Striking scenery surrounds this small town in Utah's far south. The Vermilion Cliffs to the west and east glow with a fiery intensity at sunrise and sunset. Streams have cut splendid canyons into surrounding plateaus. The Paiutes knew the spot as *Kanab* ("place of the willows"), which still grow along Kanab Creek. Mormon pioneers arrived in the mid-1860s and tried to farm along the unpredictable creek. Irrigation difficulties culminated in the massive floods of 1883, which in just two days gouged a section of creekbed 40 feet below its previous level. Ranching proved better suited to this rugged and arid land.

Hollywood discovered this dramatic scenery in the 1920s and has filmed more than 150 movies and TV series here since. Famous films shot hereabouts include movies as different as *My Friend Flicka,* *The Lone Ranger,* and *The Greatest Story Ever Told.* The TV series *Gunsmoke* and *F Troop* were shot locally. Film crews have constructed several Western sets near Kanab, but most lie on private land and are difficult to visit. The Paria set east of town, however, is on BLM land and open to the public.

> *Hollywood discovered the dramatic scenery surrounding Kanab in the 1920s and has filmed more than 150 movies and TV series here since. Famous films shot hereabouts include movies as different as* My Friend Flicka, The Lone Ranger, *and* The Greatest Story Ever Told.

While most park visitors see Kanab (pop. 5,500) as a handy stopover on trips to Bryce, Zion, and Grand Canyon National Parks and the southern reaches of the Grand Staircase–Escalante National Monument, there are a few interesting sites around town that may warrant more than a sleep, eat, dash-out-of-town visit.

SIGHTS
Frontier Movie Town
The owners assembled this movie-set replica in Kanab to show tourists a bit of Hollywood's Old West. Some of the buildings have seen actual use in past movies and TV shows. Many small exhibits display Western and movie memorabilia; there's a selection of Western costumes available if you feel like getting gussied up as a cowboy or showgirl. Shops sell handicrafts and snacks. Local tour information is available, too.

On most nights there's a Dutch-oven cookout at Frontier Movie Town, along with light

SOUTHWESTERN UTAH

entertainment and a shootout; $20 for everything. Open April–October about 9 A.M.–11 P.M. Turn in off W. Center between Brandon Motel and Gift City, 435/644-5337; free.

Best Friends Animal Sanctuary

Located in Angel Canyon just north of Kanab, this is one of the more unusual destinations in Utah. The scenic canyon was formerly the set for several Western movies and TV shows (including *The Outlaw Josie Wales* and *Rin Tin Tin*), and several of the sets are still standing. However, the canyon is now home to Best Friends Animal Sanctuary, the largest no-kill animal shelter in the country. Best Friends takes in unwanted or abused "companion animals"—pets, farm animals, or other abandoned or neglected creatures—and gives them a permanent home on the preserve's 350 acres. Most animals are rehabilitated and are given new homes. Around 1,800 animals live at the sanctuary at any given time.

Ninety-minute tours of the facility are offered, several times a day. Call 435/644-2001 for reservations. Donations gladly accepted. The tour also visits some of the movie sets and features a short talk on the natural history of the canyon.

Squaw Trail

This well-graded trail provides a close look at the geology, plantlife, and animals of the Vermilion Cliffs just north of town. Allow about an hour on the moderately difficult trail to reach the first overlook (two miles round-trip with a 400-foot elevation gain) or 90 minutes to go all the way up (three miles round-trip with an 800-foot elevation gain). Views to the south take in Kanab, Fredonia, Kanab Canyon, and the vast Kaibab Plateau. At the top, look north to see the White, Gray, and Pink Cliffs of the Grand Staircase. The trailhead is at the north end of 100 East near the city park. Pick up a trail guide at the information center (brochures may also be available at the trailhead or BLM office). Bring water. Try to get a very early start in summer.

Moqui Cave

This is a natural cave that's been turned into a tourist attraction with a large collection of Native American artifacts. Most of the arrowheads, pottery, sandals, and burial items on display have been excavated locally. A diorama re-creates an Anasazi ruin located five miles away in Cottonwood Wash. Fossils, rocks, and minerals are exhibited, too, including what's claimed to be one of the largest fluorescent mineral displays in the country. The collections and a gift shop lie within a spacious cave that stays pleasantly cool even in the hottest weather. Open daily except Sunday early March–mid-November; summer hours are 9 A.M.–7 P.M., with shorter hours in spring and autumn; $4 adults, $3.50 seniors, $3 children 13–17, and $2 ages 6–12. The cave is five miles north of Kanab on U.S. 89, 435/644-8525.

Kanab Heritage House

This 1895 Queen Anne–style Victorian house reflects the prosperity of two of Kanab's early Mormon residents. Henry Bowman built it, but he lived here only two years before going on a mission. He sold the property to Thomas Chamberlain, who led a busy life serving as a leader in the Mormons' United Order and caring for his six wives and 55 children. (There's a family photo in the sitting room.) A guide will show you around the house and explain its architectural details. Photos, furnishings, and artifacts give an idea of what life was like in early Kanab. The town had no stores when the house was built, so each family grew its own vegetables and fruit. The grape arbor, berry bushes, and trees here represent those grown during pioneer times; fruit is free for the picking to visitors. The house is usually open for tours in summer Monday–Friday 4–8 P.M.; free admission. You might be able to visit at other times by appointment; call the number posted on the front of the house to reach a volunteer. Located one block off U.S. 89 at the corner of Main and 100 South.

ENTERTAINMENT AND EVENTS

In summer, free musical concerts are held at the city park gazebo, at the center of town. Wednesdays bring an ongoing local talent show. One of summer's largest events is the

Southern Utah Fiddle Championship, which is held annually in mid-July. An even more unique Kanab event is the **Greyhound Gathering** in mid-May, when hundreds of greyhound owners converge on the town. Events include a parade, a race, and a howl-in. The Greyhound Gang, a nonprofit organization dedicated to the rescue, rehabilitation, and adoption of ex-racing greyhounds, hosts this unlikely festival. Contact the visitors center for more information.

SHOPPING

Alderman & Son Photo, 19 W. Center, 435/644-5981, supplies film and camera needs (including repairs) beyond what you would expect in a town of this size. The shop almost qualifies as an antique camera museum.

Find a good selection of books, camping gear, and clothing, along with a little coffee bar, at **Willow Creek Books & Coffee,** 263 South 100 East, 435/644-8884.

Denny's Wigwam, 78 E. Center, 435/644-2452, is a landmark Old West trading post with lots of quality Western jewelry, cowboy hats and boots, and souvenirs. Danny's also hosts elaborate chuckwagon meals and entertainment, but usually only for bus tours. If a shindig is already scheduled, you can sometimes join the festivities by paying for an individual ticket.

ACCOMMODATIONS

Lodging reservations are a good idea during the busy summer months. All of the motels and campgrounds are on U.S. 89, which follows 300 West, Center, 100 East, and 300 South through town.

Under $50

The **Canyonlands International Youth Hostel,** one-half block off U.S. 89 at 143 East 100 South, 435/644-5554. is a small, motel-like complex, with rooms converted to simple dorm-style accommodations. Facilities include a kitchen, a laundry room, a TV room, a patio, a lawn, locked storage, and a reference library

of regional maps and books. Open year-round; check-in is 9 A.M.–11 P.M. No hostel card is required.

Riding's Quail Park Lodge, 125 U.S. 89 North, 435/644-5094 or 800/644-5094, has a pool and accepts pets. The same people own the nearby **Bob-Bon Inn,** 236 U.S. 89 North, 435/644-5094 or 800/644-5094, a nicely renovated motel.

Aiken's Lodge National 9 Inn, 79 W. Center, 435/644-2625 or 800/524-9999, has a pool; closed January and February. The **Sun-N-Sand Motel,** 347 South 100 East, 435/644-5050 or 800/654-1868, has a pool, a spa, and kitchenettes. The **Brandon Motel,** 223 W. Center, 435/644-2631 or 800/839-2631, has a pool, kitchenettes, and accepts pets.

$50–75

The one lodging in Kanab that varies from the usual motor-court formula is the **Parry Lodge,** 89 E. Center, 435/644-2601 or 800/748-4104. Built during Kanab's heyday as a movie-making center, the Parry Lodge was where the stars stayed; 60 years later, this is still a pleasant place to spend the night. At the very least, you'll want to stroll through the lobby, where lots of photos of the celebrities who once stayed here are displayed. There are several two-bedroom units, a pool, and a good restaurant.

The **Treasure Trail Motel,** 150 W. Center, 435/644-2687 or 800/603-2687, has basic, clean rooms and a pool. The **Four Seasons Motel,** 36 North 300 West, 435/644-2635, has a pool and accepts pets. The **Super 8,** 70 South 200 West, 435/644-5500, has a heated pool.

$75–100

The **Best Western Red Hills Motel,** 125 W. Center, 435/644-2675 or 800/830-2675, has comfortable rooms and a pool, and is within a short walk of restaurants. (Rates drop substantially during spring, fall, and winter.) The **Holiday Inn Express,** one mile east of downtown at 815 E. U.S. 89, 435/644-8888 or 800/HOLIDAY (800/465-4329), offers a nine-hole golf course, a free breakfast bar, a pool, and a hot tub.

Campgrounds

The **Kanab RV Corral,** 483 South 100 East, 435/644-5330, has sites with hot showers, a pool, and a laundry open all year. The **Hitch'n Post RV Park,** 196 East 300 South, 435/644-2681 or 800/458-3516, has sites with showers open all year. The **Crazy Horse Campark,** 625 East 300 South, 435/644-2782, has sites with a pool, a store, a game room, and showers; open mid-April–late October.

Near the east entrance to Zion National Park, the **Zican Indian Store,** 435/648-2154, has a campground with hot showers, restrooms, and sites for tents and RVs.

The campground at **Coral Pink Sand Dunes State Park** has restrooms with showers, paved pull-through sites, and a dump station. It's a pleasant, shady spot, but it can hum with ATV traffic. Open all year, but the water is shut off late October–Easter; winter campers need to bring their own. Reservations are recommended for the busy Memorial Day–Labor Day season.

Just north of the state park, the BLM maintains **Ponderosa Grove Campground** on the north edge of the dunes; no water. From Kanab, head eight miles north on U.S. 89, turn west on Hancock Road (between mileposts 72 and 73), and continue 7.3 miles to the campground.

FOOD

The **Vermillion Café,** 4 E. Center, 435/644-3886, is the place for espresso drinks, pastries, and deli sandwiches. You can find a good selection of organic and natural foods, including deli items, at **Wildflower Health Foods,** 18 E. Center, 435/644-3200. The setting is casual and the food is simple but sophisticated, with a modern Southwest flair, at **Rocking V Café,** 97 W. Center, 435/644-8001.

The **Parry Lodge,** 89 E. Center, 435/644-2601, has a homey dining room featuring steak, seafood, and some international dishes; open daily for breakfast, lunch, and dinner (closed 2–6 P.M.). Photos of former movie-star guests decorate the walls. The **Chef's Palace Restaurant,** 176 W. Center, 435/644-5052, offers steak,

prime rib, and seafood; open daily for breakfast, lunch, and dinner.

For good, unfussy Mexican and American cooking, try the friendly **Nedra's Too,** 300 South 100 East in the Heritage Center, 435/644-2030, open daily for breakfast, lunch, and dinner; or **Houston's Trail's End Restaurant,** 32 E. Center, 435/644-2488, open daily for breakfast, lunch, and dinner.

The **Wok Inn,** 86 South 200 West, 435/644-5400, has Hunan and Sichuan cuisine; open weekdays for lunch and dinner and weekends for dinner only, closed in winter. The best place for Mexican food is **Escobar's,** 373 East 300 South, 435/644-3739. Beer is served; closed Saturday.

INFORMATION AND SERVICES

Staff members at the **information center,** 70 South 100 East (Kanab, UT 84741), 435/644-5033, offer literature and advice for services in Kanab and travel in Kane County; open year-round Monday–Saturday 8 A.M.–8 P.M. The **Grand Staircase–Escalante National Monument** has an information center at 318 North 100 East, 435/644-2672; open Monday–Friday 7:45 A.M.–4:30 P.M.

CORAL PINK SAND DUNES STATE PARK

Churning air currents funneled by surrounding mountains have deposited huge sand dunes in this valley west of Kanab. The ever-changing dunes reach heights of several hundred feet and cover about 2,000 of the park's 3,700 acres. Moviemakers have used the location for filming. Tiny particles of quartz make up the sand; the "coral pink" refers only to the color. Average summer temperatures at the 6,000-foot elevation range from about 55°F at night to 95° during the day; winter days have highs of about 55°, lows below freezing at night. Most wildlife is difficult to spot, though you may see tracks in the sand. Coyotes are often heard at night. Wildflowers put on a fine show in June and July. Different areas in the park have been set aside for hiking, off-road vehicles, and a campground with hot showers. If you see what looks like a family reunion, it might be just a man and his wives from the nearby polygamist settlements of Colorado City or Hildale!

From Kanab, the shortest drive is to go north eight miles on U.S. 89 (to between mileposts 72 and 73), turn left 9.3 miles on the paved Hancock Road to its end, then turn left (south) one mile on a paved road into the park. From the north, follow U.S. 89 3.5 miles south of Mt. Carmel Junction, then turn right (south) 11 miles on a paved road. The back road from Cane Beds in Arizona has about 16 miles of gravel and dirt with some sandy spots; ask a park ranger for current conditions. Entrance fees are $5 per vehicle for day use, $14 per vehicle for camping. Contact the park at P.O. Box 95, Kanab, UT 84741, 435/648-2800 or 800/322-3770 (reservations).

Day-Use Area

On the left just past the contact station, a short boardwalk leads into a protected section of the dunes; signs explain the geology and illustrate some animals and plants that live in this semiarid desert. Photographers and families can explore on foot and use the sheltered picnic area.

Riding the Dunes

Drivers of off-road vehicles can head for the sands from a trailhead between the day-use area and the campground. The thrills of traveling across the Sahara-like landscape attract motorcyclists, ATVers, and dune-buggy enthusiasts. Paddle-type tires work best on the soft sand. Park regulations ask drivers to attach an eight-foot whip with a flag to their vehicles, to observe

quiet hours 10 P.M.–9 A.M., and to avoid riding across vegetation. All vehicles must be registered for off- or on-highway use. It's a good idea to ride where other drivers can see you. Rangers have a complete list of regulations.

Campground

The pleasant campground sits in a piñon pine, juniper, and oak woodland. Facilities include restrooms with showers, paved pull-through sites, and a dump station. Ice, firewood, and off-road vehicle whips may be sold by park staff. Open all year, but the water is shut off late October–Easter; winter campers need to bring their own. Reservations are recommended for the busy Memorial Day–Labor Day season.

Other Areas

The canyon country surrounding the park has good opportunities for hiking and off-road vehicle travel; the BLM office in Kanab can supply maps and information. The BLM maintains **Ponderosa Grove Campground** on the north edge of the dunes; no water or fee. It's on the paved Hancock Road that turns off one mile north of the park or eight miles north of Kanab from U.S. 89 (between mileposts 72 and 73). The campground is two miles in from the road to the park and 7.3 miles in from U.S. 89. Drivers with four-wheel-drive vehicles can turn south on Sand Springs Road (1.5 miles east of Ponderosa Grove Campground) and go one mile to Sand Springs and another four miles to South Fork Indian Canyon Pictograph Site in a pretty canyon. Visitors may not enter the Kaibab-Paiute Indian Reservation, which is south across the Arizona state line, from this side.

Zion National Park

Zion is a magnificent park, with stunning, soaring scenery. The story here is really just all about rocks and water. Little trickles of water, percolating through massive chunks of sandstone, have created both dramatic canyons and markedly un-desert-like habitats, enabling an incredible variety of plants to find niches here.

When you visit Zion, the first thing to catch your attention will be the sheer cliffs and great monoliths of Zion Canyon reaching high into the heavens. Energetic streams and other forces of erosion created this land of finely sculptured rock. The large park spreads across 147,000 acres and contains eight geologic formations and four major vegetation zones. Elevations range from 3,666 feet, in lower Coalpits Wash, to 8,726 feet, atop Horse Ranch Mountain.

The highlight for most visitors is Zion Canyon, which is approximately 2,400 feet deep. The Zion Canyon visitors center, at the mouth of Zion Canyon, is on Highway 9 about midway between I-15 and U.S. 89. It's 43 miles northeast of St. George, 60 miles south of Cedar City, 41 miles northwest of Kanab, and 86 miles southwest of Bryce Canyon National Park. Large RVs and bicycles must heed special regulations for the long tunnel on the Zion–Mt. Carmel Highway (see the sidebar "The Zion–Mt. Carmel Tunnel"). Visitors short on time usually drop in at the visitors center, travel the Zion Canyon Scenic Drive, and take short walks on Weeping Rock or Riverside Walk Trails. A stay of two days or longer is better to take in more of the grand scenery and hike other inviting trails.

Zion Canyon Scenic Drive winds through the canyon along the North Fork of the Virgin River past some of the most spectacular scenery in the park. (During the spring, summer, and early fall, a shuttle bus ferries visitors along this route.) Hiking trails branch off to lofty viewpoints and narrow side canyons. Adventurous souls can continue on foot past the road's end into the eerie depths of the Virgin River Narrows in upper Zion Canyon.

The spectacular Zion–Mt. Carmel Highway, with its switchbacks and tunnels, provides access to the canyons and high plateaus east of Zion Canyon. Two other roads enter the rugged Kolob section northwest of Zion Canyon. The *Kolob*, a Mormon name meaning "the brightest star, next to the seat of God," includes wilderness areas rarely visited by humans. Kolob Canyons Road, in the extreme northwestern section of the park, begins just off I-15 Exit 40 at the **Kolob Canyons Visitors Center** and climbs to an overlook for great views of the Finger Canyons of the Kolob; the drive is 10 miles round-trip. Motorists with more time may also want to drive the Kolob Terrace Road to Lava Point for another perspective of the park; this drive is about 44 miles round-trip from Virgin (on Highway 9) and has some unpaved sections.

Zion's grandeur extends all through the year. Even rainy days can be memorable as countless waterfalls plunge from every crevice in the cliffs above. Spring and autumn are the choice seasons for the most pleasant temperatures and the best chances of seeing wildlife and wildflowers. From about mid-October–early November, cottonwoods and other trees and plants blaze with color. Summer temperatures in the canyons can be uncomfortably hot, with highs hovering above 100°F. It's also the busiest season. In winter, nighttime temperatures drop to near freezing and weather tends to be unpredictable, with bright sunshine one day and freezing rain the next. Snow-covered slopes contrast with colorful rocks. Snow may block some of the high-country trails and the road to Lava Point, but the rest of the park is open and accessible year-round.

An entry fee of $20 ($10 for bus passengers and bicyclists)—good for seven days—is charged at the East and South Entrance Stations year-round. Entrance for Kolob Canyons or Lava Point drives only is $10.

For up-to-date information on the park, check out the website www.nps.gov/zion, or call 435/772-3256. The mailing address is Zion National Park, Springdale, UT 84767.

© PAUL LEVY

The Three Patriarchs are landmark mountains in Zion National Park.

Geology

The rock layers at Zion began as sediments of oceans, rivers, lakes, or sand dunes deposited 65–240 million years ago. The soaring Navajo sandstone cliffs that form such distinctive features as the Great White Throne and the Three Patriarchs were originally immense sand dunes. Look for the slanting lines in these rock walls, which result from shifting winds as the sand dunes formed. Calcium carbonate in the sand piles acted as a glue to turn the dunes into rock, and it's also responsible for the white color of many of the rocks. The reddish rocks are also Navajo sandstone, but they've been stained by iron oxides—essentially rust.

Kayenta shale is the other main rock you'll see in Zion. For an up-close look, check out the streambed at Middle Emerald Pool. The rippled gray rock is Kayenta shale. This shale, which lies beneath Navajo sandstone, is much less permeable than the sandstone. Water can easily trickle through the relatively porous sandstone, but when it hits the impermeable Kayenta shale, it runs along the top surface of the rock and seeps out on the side of the nearest rock face. Weeping Rock, with its lush cliffside springs, is a good

place to see the junction between Navajo sandstone and Kayenta shale.

A gradual uplift of the Colorado Plateau, which continues today, has caused the formerly lazy rivers on its surface to pick up speed and knife through the rock layers. You can really appreciate these erosive powers during flash floods, when the North Fork of the Virgin River or other streams roar through their canyons. Erosion of some of the Virgin River's tributaries couldn't keep up with the main channel, and they were left as "hanging valleys" on the canyon walls. A good example is Hidden Canyon, which is reached by trail in Zion Canyon.

Faulting has broken the Colorado Plateau into a series of smaller plateaus. At Zion you are on the Kolob Terrace of the Markagunt Plateau, whose rock layers are younger than those of the Kaibab Plateau at Grand Canyon National Park and older than those exposed on the Paunsaugunt Plateau at Bryce Canyon National Park.

Although some erosive forces, like flash floods, are dramatic, the subtle freezing and thawing of water and the slow action of tree roots are responsible for most of the changes. Water seeps

SOUTHWESTERN UTAH

ZION NATIONAL PARK

© AVALON TRAVEL PUBLISHING, INC.

NAVAJO SANDSTONE

Take a look anywhere along Zion Canyon, and you'll see 1,600–2,200-foot cliffs of Navajo sandstone. The big walls of Zion were formed from sand dunes deposited during a hot, dry period about 200 million years ago. Shifting winds blew the sand from one direction, then another—a careful inspection of the sandstone layer reveals the diagonal lines resulting from this "cross-bedding." Recent studies by researchers at the University of Nebraska—Lincoln, printed in *Nature* magazine, conclude that the vast dunes of southern Utah were formed when the landmass on which they sit was about 15 degrees north of the equator, about the same location as today's Honduras. The shift patterns apparent in the sandstone—the slanting striations easily seen in cliff faces—were caused in part by intense monsoon rains, which served to compact and move the dunes each rainy season.

Eventually, a shallow sea washed over the dunes. Lapping waves left shells behind, and as the shells dissolved, their lime seeped down into the sand and cemented it into sandstone. After the Colorado Plateau lifted, rivers cut deeply through the sandstone layer. The formation's lower layers are stained red from iron oxides.

into the Navajo sandstone, accumulating especially in the long, vertical cracks in the cliffs. The dramatic temperature changes, especially in the spring and fall, cause regular freezing and thawing, slowly enlarging the cracks and setting the stage for more dramatic rockfalls. Erosion and rockfall continue to shape Zion Canyon. In 1995 a huge rockslide blocked Zion Canyon Scenic Drive and left hundreds of people trapped at the lodge for several days until crews were able to clear a path.

Flora and Fauna

Many different plant and animal communities live in the rugged terrain of deep canyons and high plateaus. Because the park lies near the meeting place of the Colorado Plateau, the Great Basin, and the Mojave Desert, species representative of all three regions can be found here.

Only desert plants can endure the long, dry spells and high temperatures found at Zion's lower elevations; they include cacti (prickly pear, cholla, and hedgehog), blackbrush, creosote bush, honey mesquite, and purple sage. Cacti and yucca are common throughout the park. Pygmy forests of piñon pine, Utah juniper, live oak, mountain mahogany, and cliffrose grow between about 3,900–5,600 feet.

Once you get above the canyon floor, Zion's plants are not so different from what you'd find in the Pacific Northwest. Trees such as ponderosa pine and Douglas fir can thrive here thanks to the moisture they draw from the Navajo sandstone. White fir and aspen are also common on high, cool plateaus. Permanent springs and streams support a profusion of greenery such as cottonwood, box elder, willow, red birch, horsetail, and ferns. Watch out for poison ivy in moist, shady areas.

Colorful wildflowers pop out of the ground—indeed even out of the rocks—at all elevations from spring through autumn. In early spring, look for the Zion shooting star, a plant in the primrose family found only in Zion. Here, its nodding pink flowers are easily spotted along the Emerald Pools trails and at Weeping Rock. You're also likely to see desert phlox, a low plant covered with pink flowers, and, by mid-May, golden columbine.

Mule deer are common throughout the park. Also common is a type of beaver called a "bank beaver," which lives along the banks of the Virgin River rather than in log lodges, which would be too frequently swept away by flash floods. (Even though these beavers don't build log lodges, they still gnaw like crazy on trees—look near the base of riverside trees near Zion Lodge for their work.) Other wildlife includes elk, mountain lion, bobcat, black bear, bighorn sheep (reintroduced), coyote, gray fox, porcupine, ringtail cat, black-tailed jackrabbit, rock squirrel, cliff chipmunk, beaver, and many species of mice and bats.

Birders have spotted more than 270 species in and near the park, but most common are red-tailed hawk, turkey vulture, quail, mallard, great horned owl, hairy woodpecker, raven, scrub jay, black-headed grosbeak, blue-gray gnatcatcher, canyon wren, Virginia's warbler, white-throated swift, and broad-tailed hummingbird. Zion's high cliffs are good places to look for peregrine falcons; try spotting them from the cliffside at Angel's Rest trail.

Hikers and campers will undoubtedly see northern sagebrush lizards, and hikers need to watch for western rattlesnakes, although these relatively rare reptiles are unlikely to attack unless provoked.

History

As early as A.D. 285, the Kayenta-Virgin branch of the Anasazi built small villages of sunken pit houses in what's now the park. Their culture gradually developed over the centuries with improved agriculture and crafts until they left the region in about 1200. Next came the Kaibab band of Southern Paiutes, who spent part of the year here on seasonal migrations. The Paiutes relied heavily on wild seeds for food, supplemented by hunting and some agriculture. White settlers and their livestock depleted the range and wildlife so much that the Paiutes had to abandon this old lifestyle.

Mormon pioneers pushed up the Virgin River Valley in 1859 and founded Grafton, the first of a series of towns south of the present-day park. In 1863, the Isaac Behunin family began farming in Zion Canyon and built a one-room cabin near where Zion Lodge now stands. Other families settled and farmed the canyon until the area was established as a national monument. The canyon's naming is credited to Isaac Behunin, who believed this spot to be a refuge from religious persecution. When Brigham Young later visited the canyon, however, he found tobacco and wine in use and declared the place "not Zion"—which some dutiful followers then began calling it! A scientific expedition led by John Wesley Powell in 1872 helped make the wonders known to the outside world. Efforts by Stephen T. Mather, first director of the National Park Service, and others led to designation of Mukuntuweap (Straight Canyon) National Monument in 1909 and the establishment of Zion National Park in 1919.

Park Shuttle Bus

By the late 1990s, visitors to Zion remembered the traffic nearly as vividly as they remembered the Great White Throne; throughout much of the summer, the canyon road was simply a parking lot for enormous RVs. To relieve the congestion, the National Park Service has instituted an April–October shuttle bus service through the canyon.

There are two bus lines: One line travels between Springdale and the park entrance, stopping within a short walk of every Springdale motel and near several large visitor parking lots; the other bus line starts just inside the park entrance at the visitors center and runs the length of Zion Canyon Road, stopping at scenic overlooks, trailheads, and Zion Lodge. Lodge guests may obtain a pass authorizing them to drive to the lodge, but in general, private vehicles are no longer allowed to drive up Zion Canyon.

This is less of a pain than it might seem. It's still fine to drive to the campgrounds; in fact, the road between the park entrance and the Zion–Mt. Carmel Highway junction is open to all vehicles. Buses run frequently, so there's rarely much of a wait, and most of the bus drivers are friendly and well-informed, offering an engaging commentary on the sights that they pass (even pointing out rock climbers on the canyon's big walls).

If you get to Zion before 10 A.M. or after 3 P.M., there may be parking spaces available in the visitors center lot. Midday visitors should just park in Springdale (at your motel or in a public lot) and catch a shuttle bus to the park entrance.

Riding the bus is free; its cost of operation is included in the park admission fee. Buses run as often as every six minutes 5:30 A.M.–11 P.M. (less frequently early in the morning and in the evening). No pets are allowed on the buses.

November–March, private vehicles are allowed on all roads, and the buses are out of service.

Zion Canyon Scenic Drive is a six-mile road that follows the North Fork of the Virgin River upstream. Impressive natural formations along the way include the Three Patriarchs, Mountain of the Sun, Lady Mountain, Great White Throne, Angels Landing, and Weeping Rock. The bus stops at eight points of interest along the way; you can get on and off the bus as often as you wish at these stops. The road ends at Temple of Sinawava and the beginning of the Riverside Walk Trail.

Visitors Center

The park's sprawling visitors center opened in 2000 between Watchman and South Campgrounds. The plaza outside the building features several interpretive plaques, including some pointing out environmentally sensitive design features of the visitors center. Inside, a large area is devoted to backcountry information; staff members can answer your questions about various trails, give you updates on the weather forecast, and help you arrange a shuttle to remote trailheads.

The busiest part of the visitors center is its bookstore, which is stocked with an excellent selection of books covering natural history, human history, and regional travel. Topographic and geologic maps, posters, slides, postcards, and film are sold here, too.

The best way by far to get a feel for Zion's impressive geology and variety of habitats is to take a hike with a park ranger. Many nature programs and hikes are offered late March–November; check the posted schedule. From Memorial Day to Labor Day, children's programs are held at Zion Nature Center near South Campground; ask at the visitors center for details. A Backcountry Shuttle Board allows hikers to coordinate transportation between trailheads.

The Zion Canyon Visitors Center is open daily 9 A.M.–5 P.M. in winter and 8 A.M.–8 P.M. in summer. For up-to-date information on the park, check out the website www.nps.gov/zion, or call 435/772-3256. The mailing address is Zion National Park, Springdale, UT 84767.

Zion Museum

The old visitors center reopened in 2002 as a museum of southern Utah's cultural history, with exhibits focusing on Native American and Mormon history. The museum is open daily 8 A.M.–7 P.M. in summer, with shorter winter hours. It's at the first shuttle stop after the visitors center.

EAST OF ZION CANYON

The east section of the park is a land of sandstone slickrock, hoodoos, and narrow canyons. You can see much of the dramatic scenery along the Zion–Mt. Carmel Highway (Highway 9)

THE ZION–MT. CARMEL TUNNEL

If your vehicle is more than 7 feet, 10 inches wide; 11 feet, 4 inches tall; or 40 feet long (50 feet with trailer), you will need a traffic control escort through the narrow, mile-long Zion–Mt. Carmel Tunnel. Vehicles this size are too large to stay in their lane while traveling through the tunnel, which was built in the 1920s, when autos were not only small, but few and far between. Nearly all RVs, buses, trailers, fifth-wheels, and some camper shells require an "escort."

Visitors requiring an escort must pay a $10 fee per vehicle in addition to the entrance fee. Pay this fee at either park entrance before proceeding to the tunnel. The fee is good for two trips through the tunnel for the same vehicle during a seven-day period.

Though the park service persists in using the term "escort," you're really on your own through the tunnel. Rather than having you follow an escort vehicle, park staff stop oncoming traffic, allowing you enough time to drive down the middle of the tunnel. April–late October, traffic control personnel are present at the tunnel 8 A.M.–8 P.M. daily. During the winter season, oversized vehicle passage must be arranged at the entrance stations, Zion Canyon visitors center, Zion Lodge, or by phoning 435/772-3256. Bicycles and pedestrians are not allowed in the tunnel.

between the East Entrance Station and Zion Canyon. Most of this region invites exploration on your own. Try hiking a canyon or heading up a slickrock slope (the pass between Crazy Quilt and Checkerboard Mesas is one possibility). Highlights on the plateau include views of the White Cliffs and Checkerboard Mesa (both near the East Entrance Station) and a hike on the Canyon Overlook Trail (it begins just east of the long tunnel). Checkerboard Mesa's distinctive pattern is caused by a combination of vertical fractures and horizontal bedding planes, both accentuated by weathering. The highway's spectacular descent into Zion Canyon goes first through a 530-foot tunnel, then a 5,600-foot tunnel, followed by a series of six switchbacks to the canyon floor. See the sidebar "The Zion–Mt. Carmel Tunnel" for vehicle size restrictions in the tunnel.

KOLOB CANYONS

North and west of Zion Canyon lies the remote backcountry of the Kolob. This area became a second Zion National Monument in 1937, then was added to Zion National Park in 1956. You'll see all but one of the rock formations present in the park and evidence of past volcanic eruptions. Two roads lead into the Kolob. The paved five-mile Kolob Canyons Road begins at the Kolob Canyons Visitors Center just off I-15 and ends at an overlook and picnic area; it's open all year. Kolob Terrace Road is paved from the town of Virgin (15 miles west on Highway 9 from the South Entrance Station) to the turnoff for Lava Point; snow usually blocks the way in winter.

Kolob Canyons Visitors Center

Although it is small and has just a handful of exhibits, this visitors center, 435/586-9548, is a good place to stop for information on exploring the Kolob region. Hikers can learn current trail conditions and obtain the permits required for overnight trips and Zion Narrows day trips. Books, topographic and geologic maps, posters, postcards, slides, and film are sold. Open daily 8 A.M.–4:30 P.M. (to 5 P.M. in summer). The visitors center and the start of Kolob Canyons Road lie just off I-15 Exit 40.

© PAUL LEVY

It's easy to see the uplift of these sedimentary rocks along Kolob Canyons Road.

Kolob Canyons Road

This five-mile scenic drive winds past the dramatic Finger Canyons of the Kolob to Kolob Canyons Viewpoint and a picnic area at the end of the road. The road is paved and has many pullouts where you can stop to admire the scenery. The first part of the drive follows the 200-mile-long Hurricane Fault that forms the west edge of the Markagunt Plateau. Look for the tilted rock layers deformed by friction as the plateau rose nearly one mile. **Taylor Creek Trail,** which begins two miles past the visitors center, provides a close look at the canyons (see the Hikes in Kolob Canyons section). Lee Pass, four miles beyond the visitors center, was named after John D. Lee of the infamous Mountain Meadows Massacre; he's believed to have lived nearby for a short time after the massacre. **La Verkin Creek Trail** begins at Lee Pass Trailhead for trips to Kolob Arch and beyond. Signs at the end of the road identify the points, buttes, mesa, and mountains. The salmon-colored Navajo sandstone cliffs glow a deep red at sunset. **Timber Creek Overlook Trail** begins from the picnic area at road's end and climbs one-half mile to the overlook (elev. 6,369 feet); views encompass the Pine Valley Mountains, Zion Canyons, and distant Mount Trumbull.

Lava Point

The panorama from Lava Point (elev. 7,890 feet) takes in the Cedar Breaks area to the north, the Pink Cliffs to the northeast, Zion Canyon Narrows and tributaries to the east, the Sentinel and other monoliths of Zion Canyon to the southeast, and Mount Trumbull on the Arizona Strip to the south. Signs help identify features. Lava Point, which sits atop a lava flow, is a good place to cool off in summer—temperatures are about 20°F cooler than in Zion Canyon. Aspen, ponderosa pine, Gambel oak, and white fir grow here. A small, primitive campground near the point offers sites during warmer months; no water or charge.

Kolob Reservoir

This high-country lake north of Lava Point has

good fishing for rainbow trout. An unpaved boat ramp is at the south end near the dam. People sometimes camp along the shore, although there are no facilities. Most of the surrounding land is private. To reach the reservoir, continue north 3.5 miles on Kolob Terrace Road from the Lava Point turnoff. The fair-weather road can also be followed past the reservoir to the Cedar City area. Blue Springs Reservoir, near the turnoff for Lava Point, is closed to the public.

HIKES IN ZION CANYON

The trails in Zion Canyon provide perspectives of the park that are not available from the roads. Many of the hiking trails require long ascents but aren't too difficult at a leisurely pace. Carry water on all but the shortest walks. Descriptions of the following trails are given in order from the mouth of Zion Canyon to the Virgin River Narrows.

Experienced hikers can do countless off-trail routes in the canyons and plateaus surrounding Zion Canyon; rangers can suggest areas. Rappelling and other climbing skills may be needed to negotiate drops in some of the more remote canyons. Groups cannot exceed 12 hikers per trail or drainage. Overnight hikers must obtain backcountry permits ($5) from either the Zion Canyon or Kolob Canyons Visitors Center. Some areas of the park—mainly those near roads and major trails—are closed to overnight use. Zion Lodge offers shuttle services for hikers, or you can check the Backcountry Shuttle Board at the visitors center.

Pa'rus Trail
Shuttle Stops: Visitors Center and Canyon Junction

This two-mile paved trail runs from the South Campground to the Canyon Junction shuttle bus stop. For most of its distance, it skirts alongside the Virgin River and makes for a nice early morning or evening stroll. Listen for the trilling song of the canyon wren, then try to spot the small bird in the bushes. The accessible Pa'rus Trail is the only trail in the park that's open to bicycles and pets.

Watchman Trail
Shuttle Stop: Visitors Center

From a trailhead north of Watchman Campground, the trail climbs 370 feet to a bench below Watchman Peak, the prominent mountain southeast of the visitors center. Views encompass lower Zion Canyon and the town of Springdale. The well-graded trail follows a side canyon past some springs, then ascends to the overlook; the distance is 2.4 miles round-trip and takes about two hours. Trees and plants line the way. In summer, it's best to get an early start. Rangers lead nature walks during the main season.

Court of the Patriarchs Viewpoint
Shuttle Stop: Court of the Patriarchs

A short trail from the parking area leads to the viewpoint. The Patriarchs, a trio of peaks to the west, overlook Birch Creek; they are (from left to right): Abraham, Isaac, and Jacob. Mount Moroni, the reddish peak on the far right, partly blocks the view of Jacob. Although the official viewpoint is a beautiful place to relax and enjoy the view, you can get an even better view by crossing the road and heading about one-half mile up the Sand Bench Trail.

Sand Bench Trail
Shuttle Stops: Court of the Patriarchs and Zion Lodge

This easy loop has good views of the three Patriarchs, the Streaked Wall, and other monuments of lower Zion Canyon. The trail is 1.7 miles long with a 500-foot elevation gain; allow about three hours. During the main season, Zion Lodge organizes three-hour horseback rides on the trail. (The horses churn up dust and leave an uneven surface, though, so hikers usually prefer to go elsewhere.) The trail soon leaves the riparian forest along Birch Creek and climbs onto the dry benchland. Piñon pine, juniper, sand sage, yucca, prickly pear cactus, and other high-desert plants and animals live here. Hikers can get off the shuttle at the Court of the Patriarchs Viewpoint, walk across the scenic drive, then follow a service road to the footbridge and trailhead. A 1.2-mile trail along the river connects the trailhead with Zion Lodge. In

warmer months, try to hike in early morning or late afternoon.

Emerald Pools Trails
Shuttle Stop: Zion Lodge

Three spring-fed pools, small waterfalls, and views of Zion Canyon make this climb worthwhile. You have a choice of three trails. The easiest is the paved trail to the Lower Pool; cross the footbridge near Zion Lodge and turn right 0.6 mile. The Middle Pool can be reached by continuing 0.2 mile on this trail or by taking a totally different trail from the footbridge at Zion Lodge (after crossing the bridge, turn left, then right up the trail). Together these trails make a 1.8-mile round-trip loop. A third trail begins at the Grotto Picnic Area, crosses a footbridge, and turns left 0.7 mile; the trail forks left to the Lower Pool and right to the Middle Pool. A steep 0.4-mile trail leads from the Middle Pool to Upper Emerald Pool. This magical spot has a white-sand beach and towering cliffs rising above. Allow 1–3 hours to visit the pools, and don't expect to find solitude; these relatively easy trails are quite popular.

West Rim Trail
Shuttle Stop: The Grotto

This strenuous trail leads to some of the best views of Zion Canyon. Backpackers can continue on the West Rim Trail to Lava Point and other destinations in the Kolob region. Start from Grotto Picnic Area (elev. 4,300 feet) and cross the footbridge, then turn right along the river. The trail climbs the slopes and enters the cool and shady depths of Refrigerator Canyon. Walter's Wiggles, a series of 21 closely spaced switchbacks, wind up to Scout Lookout and a trail junction—four miles round-trip and a 1,050-foot elevation gain. Scout Lookout has fine views of Zion Canyon. The trail is paved and well graded to this point. Turn right one-half mile at the junction to reach the summit of Angels Landing.

Angels Landing rises as a sheer-walled monolith 1,500 feet above the North Fork of the Virgin River. Although the trail to the summit is rough, chains provide security in the more exposed places. The climb is safe with care and good weather, but don't go if the trail is covered with snow or ice or if thunderstorms threaten. Children must be closely supervised, and people who are afraid of heights should skip this trail. Once on top, you'll see why Angels Landing got its name—the panorama makes all the effort worthwhile. Average hiking time for the round-trip between Grotto Picnic Area and Angels Landing is four hours, best hiked during the cooler morning hours.

Energetic hikers can continue 4.8 miles on the main trail from Scout Lookout to West Rim Viewpoint, which overlooks the Right Fork of North Creek. This strenuous 12.8-mile round-trip from Grotto Picnic Area has a 3,070-foot elevation gain. West Rim Trail continues through Zion's backcountry to Lava Point (elev. 7,890 feet), where there's a primitive campground. A car shuttle and one or more days are needed to hike the 13.3 miles (one-way) from Grotto Picnic Area. You'll have an easier hike by starting at Lava Point and hiking down to the picnic area; even so, be prepared for a *long* day hike. The trail has little or no water in some seasons.

Weeping Rock Trail
Shuttle Stop: Weeping Rock

A favorite with visitors, this easy trail winds past lush vegetation and wildflowers to a series of cliffside springs above an overhang. Thousands of water droplets glisten in the afternoon sun. The springs emerge where water seeping through more than 2,000 feet of Navajo sandstone meets a layer of impervious shale. The paved trail is a half-mile round-trip with a 100-foot elevation gain. Signs along the way identify some of the trees and plants.

Observation Point Trail
Shuttle Stop: Weeping Rock

This strenuous trail climbs 2,150 feet in 3.6 highly scenic miles to Observation Point (elev. 6,507 feet) on the edge of Zion Canyon. Allow about six hours for the round-trip. Trails branch off along the way to Hidden Canyon, upper Echo Canyon, East Entrance, East Mesa, and other destinations. The first of many switchbacks begins a short way up from the trailhead at Weeping Rock parking area. The junction for Hidden

Canyon Trail appears after 0.8 mile (see the Hidden Canyon section). Several switchbacks later, the trail enters sinuous Echo Canyon. This incredibly narrow chasm can be explored for short distances upstream and downstream to deep pools and pour-offs. **Echo Canyon Trail** branches to the right at about the halfway point; this rough trail continues farther up the canyon and connects with trails to Cable Mountain, Deertrap Mountain, and the East Entrance Station (on Zion–Mt. Carmel Highway). The East Rim Trail then climbs slickrock slopes above Echo Canyon with many fine views. Parts of the trail are cut right into the cliffs (work was done in the 1930s by the Civilian Conservation Corps). You'll reach the rim at last after three miles of steady climbing. Then it's an easy 0.6 mile through a forest of piñon pine, juniper, Gambel oak, manzanita, sage, and some ponderosa pine to Observation Point. Impressive views take in Zion Canyon below and mountains and mesas all around. The **East Mesa Trail** turns right about 0.3 mile before Observation Point and follows the plateau northeast to a dirt road outside the park.

Hidden Canyon
Shuttle Stop: Weeping Rock

See if you can spot the entrance to Hidden Canyon from below! Inside the narrow canyon await small sandstone caves, a little natural arch, and diverse plantlife. The high walls, rarely more than 65 feet apart, block sunlight except for a short time at midday. Hiking distance on the moderately difficult trail is about three miles round-trip between the Weeping Rock parking area and the lower canyon; follow the East Rim Trail 0.8 mile, then turn right 0.7 mile on Hidden Canyon Trail to the canyon entrance. Footing can be a bit difficult in places because of loose sand, but chains provide handholds on the more exposed sections. Steps chopped into the rock just inside Hidden Canyon help bypass some deep pools. Allow 3–4 hours for the round-trip; the elevation change is about 1,000 feet. After heavy rains and spring runoff, the creek forms a small waterfall at the canyon entrance. The canyon is about one mile long and mostly easy walking, although the trail fades away. Look for the arch on the right about one-half mile up the canyon.

Riverside Walk
Shuttle Stop: Temple of Sinawava

This is one of the most popular hikes in the park and, except for the Pa'rus, it's the easiest. The nearly level paved trail begins at the end of Zion Canyon Scenic Drive and winds one mile upstream along the river to the Virgin River Narrows. Allow about two hours to take in the scenery—it's a good place to see Zion's lovely hanging gardens. Countless springs and seeps on the canyon walls support luxuriant plant growth and swamps. Most of the springs occur at the contact between the porous Navajo sandstone and the less permeable Kayenta Formation below. The water and vegetation attract abundant wildlife; keep an eye out for birds and animals and their tracks. At trail's end, the canyon is wide enough for only the river. Hikers continuing upstream must wade and sometimes even swim (see The Narrows section). Late morning is the best time for photography. In autumn, cottonwoods and maples display bright splashes of color.

The Narrows
Shuttle Stop: Temple of Sinawava

Upper Zion Canyon is probably the most famous backcountry area in the park, yet it's also one of the most strenuous. There's no trail and you'll be wading much of the time in the river, which is usually knee- to chest-deep. In places, the high, fluted walls of the upper North Fork of the Virgin River are only 20 feet apart, and very little sunlight penetrates the depths. Mysterious side canyons beckon.

Hikers should be well prepared and in good condition—river hiking is more tiring than that over dry land. The major hazards are flash floods and hypothermia. Finding the right time to go through can be tricky: spring runoff is too high, summer thunderstorms bring hazardous flash floods, and winter is too cold. That leaves just part of early summer (mid-June–mid-July) and early autumn (mid-September–mid-October) as the best bets. You can get through the entire 16-mile (one-way) Narrows in about 12 hours, although two days is best to enjoy the beauty of the place. Children under 12 shouldn't attempt hiking the entire canyon.

Don't be tempted to wear river sandals or sneakers up the Narrows because it's easy to twist an ankle on the slippery rocks. If you have a pair of hiking boots that you don't mind drenching, they'll work, but an even better solution is available from Zion Adventure Company, in Springdale at 36 Lion Blvd., 435/772-1001, www.zionadventures.com. They rent specially designed river hiking boots, along with neoprene socks, walking sticks, and, in cool weather, dry suits. They also provide a valuable orientation to hiking the Narrows. Boots, socks, and sticks rent for $16 per day, $25 for two days; with a dry suit the package costs $35 per day, $55 for two days.

Talk with rangers at the Zion Canyon Visitors Center before starting a trip; they also have a handout with useful information on planning a Narrows hike. You'll need a permit for hikes all the way through the Narrows—even on a day trip. No permit is needed if you're just going partway in and back in one day, although you must first check conditions and the weather forecast with rangers. Permits are required for overnight hikes; get them from the backcountry desk at the visitors center the day before you plan to hike or the morning of your hike (from 8 A.M.–noon). Only one-night stays are allowed. No camping is permitted below Big Springs. Group size for hiking and camping is limited to 12 (of the same affiliation, family, etc.) on the *entire* route.

A hike downstream saves not only climbing but also the work of fighting the river currents. In fact, the length of the Narrows should only be hiked downstream. The upper trailhead is near Chamberlain's Ranch, reached by an 18-mile dirt road that turns north from Highway 9 east of the park. The lower trailhead is at the end of the Zion Canyon Scenic Drive. The elevation change is 1,280 feet.

A good half-day trip begins at the end of the Gateway to the Narrows Trail and follows the Narrows 1.5 miles upstream to Orderville

Canyon, then back the same way. Orderville Canyon makes a good destination in itself; you can hike quite a ways up from Zion Canyon.

During the summer, Springdale Cycles offers a daily shuttle to Chamberlain's Ranch, leaving from the Mean Bean Coffee House at 6:30 A.M. Make shuttle reservations between 9 A.M.–6 P.M. on the day before you want to ride. The fee is $25 per person; a flat rate of $100 applies if fewer than four people are signed up. Call 800/776-2099 for information and reservations.

HIKES EAST OF ZION CANYON
Canyon Overlook Trail
You can't take the shuttle bus to this fun hike; it starts on the road east of Zion Canyon and features great views from the heights without the stiff climbs found on most other Zion trails. Allow about one hour for the one-mile round-trip; elevation gain is 163 feet. A booklet available at the start or at the Zion Canyon Visitors Center describes the geology, plantlife, and clues to the presence of wildlife. The trail winds in and out along the ledges of Pine Creek Canyon, which opens into a great valley. Panoramas at trail's end take in lower Zion Canyon in the distance. A sign at the viewpoint identifies Bridge Mountain, Streaked Wall, East Temple, and other features. The Great Arch of Zion—termed a "blind arch" because it's open on only one side—lies below; the arch is 580 feet high, 720 feet long, and 90 feet deep. The Canyon Overlook Trail begins across from the parking area just east of the longer (west) tunnel on the Zion–Mt. Carmel Highway.

HIKES IN THE SOUTHWEST DESERT
Huber Wash
From the parking area on Highway 9, this trail heads 2.5 miles up Huber Wash, through painted desert and canyons. One of the highlights of hiking in this area, besides the desert scenery, is the abundance of petrified wood. There's even a logjam of petrified wood at the 2.5-mile mark, where the trail ends in a box canyon, decked

with a hanging garden. If you're up to a tricky climb over the petrified logjam, you can climb up and catch the Chinle Trail, then hike five miles back to the road on that trail. The Chinle Trail emerges onto Highway 9 about 2.5 miles east of the Huber Wash Trailhead.

During the summer, this area of the park can be extremely hot, and in the early spring, it's often too muddy to hike. Thus, this is the ideal autumn hike. Even then, it'll be quite warm. Remember to bring plenty of water.

The Huber Wash Trailhead is about six miles west of the park entrance on Highway 9, near a power substation. Because the trail starts outside the park, it's not necessary to pay the park entrance fee if all you want to do is hike in this area.

HIKES IN KOLOB CANYONS
Taylor Creek Trail
This is an excellent day hike from Kolob Canyons Road. The easy-to-moderate trail begins on the left two miles from the Kolob Canyons Visitors Center and heads upstream into the canyon of the Middle Fork of Taylor Creek. Double Arch Alcove is 2.7 miles from the trailhead; a dry fall 0.2 mile farther blocks the way (water flows over it during spring runoff and after rains). A giant rockfall occurred here in June 1990. From this trail you can also explore the North Fork of Taylor Creek. A separate trail along the **South Fork of Taylor Creek** leaves the drive at a bend 3.1 miles from the visitors center, then goes 1.2 miles upstream beneath steep canyon walls.

Hiking to Kolob Arch
Kolob Arch vies with Landscape Arch in Arches National Park as the world's longest natural rock span. Differences in measurement techniques have resulted in a controversy regarding which is longer: Kolob Arch's span has been measured variously at 292–310 feet, while Landscape Arch's measures at 291–306 feet. Kolob probably takes the prize because its 310-foot measurement was done with an accurate electronic method. Kolob's height is 330 feet and its vertical thickness is 80 feet. The arch makes a fine destination for a

backpacking trip. Spring and autumn are the best seasons to go; summer temperatures rise into the 90s and winter snows make the trails hard to follow.

You have a choice of two moderately difficult trails. **La Verkin Creek Trail** begins at Lee Pass (elev. 6,080 feet) on Kolob Canyons Scenic Drive, four miles beyond the visitors center. The trail drops into Timber Creek (intermittent flow), crosses over hills to La Verkin Creek (flows year-round; some springs, too), then turns up side canyons to the arch. The 14-mile round-trip can be done as a long day trip, but you'll enjoy the best lighting for photos at the arch if you camp in the area and see it the following morning. Carry plenty of water for the return trip; the 800-foot climb to the trailhead can be hot and tiring.

You can also hike to Kolob Arch on the **Hop Valley Trail,** reached from Kolob Terrace Road. The Hop Valley Trail is seven miles one-way to Kolob Arch with an elevation drop of 1,050 feet; water is available in Hop Valley and La Verkin Creek. You may have to do some wading in the creek, and the trail crosses private land (don't camp there).

HIKES FROM LAVA POINT

Two trails—West Rim and Wildcat Canyon— begin from Lava Point Trailhead in the remote West Rim area of the park. You can reach the trailhead via the Kolob Terrace Road or by hiking the one-mile **Barney's Trail** from site 2 in the Lava Point campground.

The **West Rim Trail** goes southeast to Zion Canyon, 13.3 miles one-way with an elevation drop of 3,600 feet (3,000 of them in the last six miles). Water can normally be found along the way at Sawmill, Potato Hollow, and Cabin Springs.

The **Wildcat Canyon Trail** heads southwest five miles to a trailhead on Kolob Terrace Road (16 miles north of Virgin); the elevation drop is 450 feet. This trail lacks a reliable water source. You can continue north and west toward Kolob Arch by taking the four-mile **Connector Trail** to **Hop Valley Trail.**

Snow blocks the road to Lava Point for much of the year; the usual season is May or June to early November. Check road conditions with the Zion Canyon or Kolob Canyon Visitors Center. From the South Entrance Station in Zion Canyon, drive west 15 miles on Highway 9 to Virgin, turn north 21 miles on Kolob Terrace Road (signed Kolob Reservoir), then turn right 1.8 miles to Lava Point.

A special hike for strong swimmers is the **Left Fork of North Creek,** a.k.a. **"The Subway."** This challenging nine-mile day hike involves, at the very least, lots of route-finding and many stream crossings.

Like The Narrows, the Left Fork can be hiked either partway up, then back down (starting and ending at the Left Fork Trailhead) or, with a shuttle, from an upper trailhead at the Wildcat Canyon Trailhead downstream to the Left Fork Trailhead. The "top-to-bottom" route requires rappelling skills and at least 60 feet of climbing rope or webbing. It also involves swimming through several deep sections of very cold water.

Obviously, the Left Fork is not for everyone. Even though it is in a day-use-only zone, the Park Service requires a special permit, which, unlike other Zion backcountry permits, is available ahead of time through a somewhat convoluted lottery process. Prospective hikers should visit the park's website, www.nps.gov/zion, click the In Depth button, then click the Backcountry link. From there you will be instructed to email or fax (435/772-3426) information about your planned trip, including the size of your party and three choices of dates when you would like to hike. Trip dates are awarded by lottery. Only 50 permits are issued per day. If you're planning this hike at the last minute, try calling 435/772-0170 to see if there are any openings. The Left Fork trailhead is on Kolob Terrace Road 8.1 miles north of Virgin.

BIKING

One of the fringe benefits of the Zion Canyon shuttle bus is the great bicycling that's resulted from the lack of automobile traffic. It used to be way too scary to bike along the narrow, traffic-choked Zion Canyon Scenic Drive, but now it's a joy.

On the stretch of road where cars are permitted—between the visitors center and Canyon Junction (where the Zion–Mt. Carmel road meets Zion Canyon Scenic Drive)—the two-mile, paved Pa'rus Trail is open to bikers as well as pedestrians and makes for easy, stress-free pedaling.

If you decide you've had enough cycling, every shuttle bus has a rack that can hold two bicycles. Bike parking is plentiful at the visitors center, Zion Lodge, and most trailheads.

Bike rentals are available in Springdale at Springdale Cycles, 932 Zion Park Blvd., 435/772-0575 or 800/776-2099; and at Bike Zion, 1458 Zion Park Blvd., 435/772-3929 or 800/475-4576.

ROCK CLIMBING

Rock climbers come to scale the high Navajo sandstone cliffs; after Yosemite, it's the nation's most popular big-wall climbing area. For route descriptions, pick up a copy of *Desert Rock,* by Eric Bjørnstad, or *Rock Climbing Utah,* by Stewart M. Green. Both books are sold at the visitors center bookstore. Check to make sure your climbing area is open—some are closed to protect wildlife.

If watching the climbers at Zion gives you a hankering to scale a wall, the Zion Adventure Company, in Springdale at 36 Lion Blvd., 435/772-1001, www.zionadventures.com, runs day-long climbing clinics for beginning and experienced climbers. Because no outfitters are permitted to operate inside the park, these classes are held near St. George.

HORSEBACK RIDING

Trail rides leave from the corral near Zion Lodge and head down the Virgin River. A one-hour trip ($20) goes to the Court of the Patriarchs, and a half-day ride ($45) follows the Sand Bench Trail. Riders must be at least seven years old and weigh no more than 220 pounds.

ACCOMMODATIONS AND FOOD

Zion Lodge

The rustic lodge, 435/586-9476, sits in the heart of Zion Canyon, three miles up Zion Canyon Scenic Drive. Zion Lodge provides the only accommodations and dining places within the park. It's open year-round; reservations for rooms should be made as far in advance as possible. During high season, all rooms are booked months ahead. Double rooms begin at $120; cute cabins are $128.

The moderately priced restaurant offers a varied American menu daily for breakfast, lunch, and dinner. Picnic lunches can be ordered in advance by calling 435/772-3213, ext. 160. A snack bar serves fast food (closes in winter). Zion Lodge organizes horseback rides along the Virgin River (one hour) and Sand Bench Trail (three hours). Tours in open-air vehicles provide narrated sight-

ZION CANYON FIELD INSTITUTE

Delve a little more deeply into Zion's natural and human history by taking a workshop with the Zion Canyon Field Institute. Workshops run 1–3 days and focus on such topics as: bighorn sheep, bats, photography, native plants, nature sketching, and backcountry skills. Some of the workshops are service projects, which give participants the chance to learn about Zion while working on a project that benefits the park. These service projects are far more interesting than many service projects, and include such workshops as participating in an archaeological survey or studying the abundance and distribution of mountain lions in the park.

The Field Institute's programs are very reasonably priced, about $50 for a one-day workshop, $100 for a three-day program (photography workshops are a bit more expensive). Lodging and meals are not included.

For details on upcoming workshops, call 435/772-3264 or 800/635-3959 or check the schedule at www.zionpark.org.

seeing trips in Zion Canyon; they run several times daily between Memorial Day and Labor Day weekends. The lodge also has evening programs, a post office counter (open Monday–Saturday), and a gift shop. Make reservations for Zion Lodge by writing Xanterra Parks & Resorts, 1400 E. Iliff Ave., Ste. 600, Aurora, CO, 80014, or call 303/297-2757. Reserve online at www.xanterra.com.

Zion Canyon Campgrounds

Campgrounds in the park often fill up on Easter and other major holidays. During the summer, they're often full by early afternoon, so it's best to arrive early in the day. The **South** and **Watchman Campgrounds,** both just inside the South Entrance, have sites for $14 with water but no showers; Watchman has some sites with electrical hookups for $16. Reservations can be made in advance for Watchman Campground at 800/365-2267 or http://reservations.nps.gov. One of the campgrounds stays open in winter.

South Campground is a bit smaller and more oriented to tent camping than Watchman, and it has easy access to the Pa'rus Trail, but tenters

shouldn't eschew Watchman; loops C and D are for tents, and sites D-20 and D-33 are two of the nicest campsites you'll find in the park.

Some of the pioneers' fruit trees in the campgrounds are still producing; you're free to pick your own. Additional campgrounds lie just outside the park in Springdale (see the Springdale section).

Kolob Canyon Campgrounds

The Kolob section of the park doesn't have a campground. The nearest one within the park is Lava Point Campground (see Hikes from Lava Point). The **Redledge Campground,** in Kanarraville, is the closest commercial campground to the Kolob Canyons area; go two miles north on I-15, take Exit 42, and continue 4.5 miles into downtown Kanarraville, 435/586-9150. The campground is open year-round with a store, showers, and a laundry room. The tiny agricultural community was named after a local Paiute chief. A low ridge south of town marks the southern limit of prehistoric Lake Bonneville. Hikers can explore trails in Spring and Kanarra Canyons within the **Spring Canyon Wilderness Study Area** just east of town.

Vicinity of Zion National Park

SPRINGDALE AND VICINITY

Mormons settled this tiny town (pop. 470) in 1862, but with its location just outside the park's south entrance, Springdale is geared more toward serving park visitors than the typical Mormon settlement. Its many high-quality motels and B&Bs, as well as frequent shuttle bus service into the park, make Springdale an appealing base for a visit to Zion. Farther down the road toward Hurricane are the little towns of Rockville and Virgin, both of which are quickly becoming B&B suburbs of Springdale.

Zion Canyon Giant Screen Theatre

You *know* you should be in the park itself, not looking at movies of it on a six-story-tall screen. But, assuming you've been out hiking all day and

need a little rest, come here to meet the Anasazi, watch Spanish explorers seek golden treasure, witness the hardships of pioneer settlers, enter remote slot canyons, and join rock climbers hundreds of feet up vertical cliff faces. The feature program is *Treasure of the Gods,* but there's nearly always a big-screen version of a Hollywood movie showing as well (don't expect to see current hits; all the movies are a few years old). Shows start on the hour 11 A.M.–8 P.M. May–October and on the odd hours between 11 A.M.–7 P.M. the rest of the year; $8 adults, $5 children under 12. Call 435/772-2400 or 888/256-FILM (888/256-3456) for more information.

O.C. Tanner Amphitheater

The summer highlight at this open-air theater is a series of musical concerts held on Saturday evenings throughout the summer. The amphitheater is just outside the park entrance; call 435/652-7994 for information.

Accommodations

$50–75: The most reasonably priced lodgings in Springdale are the motel rooms at **Zion Canyon Campground,** 479 Zion Park Blvd., 435/772-3237. Budget travelers should also consider **Zion Park Motel,** 865 Zion Park Blvd., 435/772-3251, with clean basic rooms and a small pool. **Canyon Ranch Motel,** 668 Zion Park Blvd., 435/772-3357, is another good value, with individual cottages—some with kitchenettes—scattered around a grassy, shaded courtyard.

El Río Lodge, 995 Zion Park Blvd., 435/772-3205 or 888/772-3205, offers rooms in a green, shady location with a sundeck. The **Pioneer Lodge Motel,** 838 Zion Park Blvd., 435/772-3233, has a restaurant, a pool, and a spa. Various room styles are available, including a three-bed unit (about $80) and a three-bedroom apartment ($170).

Under the Eaves B&B, 980 Zion Park Blvd., 435/772-3457, features homey guest rooms, two with shared bath, in a vintage home. It's also possible to pay a bit more and get a kitchenette room here. Children over 10 welcome.

$75–100: **Flanigan's Inn,** 428 Zion Park Blvd., 435/772-3244 or 800/765-7787, is a very comfortable place to stay, with a restaurant, a pool, a day spa, and a complimentary breakfast buffet. The **Driftwood Lodge,** 1515 Zion Park Blvd., 435/772-3262 or 800/528-1234, has a pool and a spa.

Harvest House B&B, 29 Canyonview Dr., 435/772-3880, is an expertly run B&B in the center of Springdale with an old-fashioned porch and a hot tub. The four guest rooms, all with private baths, are nicely decorated. **Red Rock Inn,** 998 Zion Park Blvd., 435/772-3139, offers lodgings in newly constructed individual cabins, all with canyon views. Full-breakfast baskets are delivered to your door.

For a B&B with a Western difference, try the **Snow Family Guest Ranch,** 633 E. Hwy. 9, in Virgin, 800/308-7669. Located on 12 acres, the ranch raises horses and offers nine guest rooms to travelers. Children are accepted with prior arrangement only; no pets.

$100–125: Probably the nicest place to stay in Springdale is the new **Desert Pearl Inn,** 707 Zion Park Blvd., 435/772-8888 or 888/828-0898, a very handsome lodgelike hotel perched above the Virgin River. Much of the wood used for the beams and the finish moldings was salvaged from a railroad trestle made of century-old Oregon fir and redwood that once spanned the north end of the Great Salt Lake. The rooms are all large and beautifully furnished, with a modern look.

The new **Best Western Zion Park Inn,** 1215 Zion Park Blvd., 435/772-3200 or 800/934-7275, is an attractive complex with a good restaurant, a swimming pool, a gift shop, and some of the nicest rooms in Springdale. In addition to regular rooms, there are various suites and kitchen units available.

Just outside the south gates to Zion, the **Cliffrose Lodge,** 281 Zion Park Blvd., 435/772-3234 or 800/243-8824, sits in five acres of lovely, well-landscaped gardens with riverfront access. The rooms are equally nice, and there's a pool and a laundry room.

The **Novel House Inn at Zion,** 73 Paradise Rd., 435/772-3650 or 800/711-8400, is a newly constructed B&B with 10 guest rooms, each decorated with a literary theme and named after an author (including Mark Twain, Rudyard Kipling, and Louis L'Amour). All rooms have private baths and great views, and are in the $100–120 range.

Campgrounds: The **Zion Canyon Campground,** 479 Zion Park Blvd., 435/772-3237, offers cabins, new motel rooms, tent sites (no dogs allowed in tent sites), and RV sites; facilities include a store, pizza parlor, game room, laundry room, and showers.

Food

Just outside the park entrance, near the Springdale shuttle stop, **Sol Foods,** 435/772-0277, is a short walk from either park campground and a good place for a salad or sandwich. There's also a computer with Internet access.

Mean Bean Coffee, 932 Zion Park Blvd., 435/772-0654, is the hip place to hang in the morning. Besides coffee drinks, they serve a few pastries. For a more substantial breakfast, or lunch to go, head across the way to **Oscar's Café,** 948 Zion Park Blvd., 435/772-3232. **Tsunami Juice and Java,** just outside the park at 180 Zion Park Blvd., 435/772-3818, has what its name implies and that little something extra—showers! (Showers are $4.)

Panda Garden Chinese Restaurant, 805 Zion Park Blvd., 435/772-3535, serves surprisingly good Chinese cuisine daily for lunch and dinner. Also good, and reasonably priced, is **Zion Pizza and Noodle,** 868 Zion Park Blvd., 435/772-3815, a fun place with a good selection of microbrews. The American-style menu at the **Bumbleberry Inn,** 897 Zion Park Blvd., 435/772-3224, includes bumbleberry pies and pancakes; open Monday–Saturday for breakfast, lunch, and dinner.

The following restaurants all offer full liquor service: The **Spotted Dog,** at Flanigan's Inn, 428 Zion Park Blvd., 435/772-3244, has varied Southwestern and traditional American offerings; open daily for breakfast, lunch, and dinner. The **Pioneer Restaurant,** 828 Zion Park Blvd., 435/772-3009, serves American food, with vegetarian specialties; open daily for breakfast, lunch, and dinner.

Find Springdale's best meals at the **Bit & Spur Restaurant,** 1212 Zion Park Blvd., 435/772-3498, a Mexican restaurant with a menu that goes far beyond the usual south-of-the-border concoctions. (Keep your fingers crossed that sweet-potato tamales will be the evening's special!) Open for dinner only. Across the street, the **Switchback Grille,** 1215 Zion Park Blvd., 435/772-3200, offers wood-fired pizza, rotisserie chicken, and steaks and seafood in a pleasantly bland atmosphere. There's patio seating in good weather; open for three meals daily.

Information and Services

Just off Zion Park Boulevard, the folks at **Zion Adventure Company,** 36 Lion Blvd., 435/772-1001, offer an incredibly valuable service to people who want to explore Zion to its fullest. Their rental packages (most notably water hiking boots and dry suits) and their advice have made hiking the Virgin River Narrows safer and more accessible. They also offer rock-climbing and canyoneering classes and try to teach people to learn how to explore safely and adventurously on their own.

If you're looking to rent a bike or go on a guided bike tour (outside the park boundaries), stop by **Springdale Cycle Tours,** 932 Zion Park Blvd., 435/772-0575 or 800/776-2099. **Bike Zion,** 1458 Zion Park Blvd., 435/772-3929, also rents mountain bikes, including some fancy full-suspension models.

People traveling with their dogs are in a bit of a dilemma when it comes to visiting Zion. No pets are allowed on the shuttle buses, and it's absolutely unconscionable to leave a dog inside a car here in the warmer months. Fortunately, the **Doggy Dude Ranch,** 435/772-3105, provides high-quality daytime and overnight boarding on Highway 9 in Rockville.

The **Zion Canyon Medical Clinic,** 435/772-3226, provides emergency services approximately May–October; take the turnoff for the O.C. Tanner Amphitheater. The **post office** is in the center of town on Zion Park Boulevard, 435/772-3950. You may also want to check out the many art galleries, rock shops, and gift shops along Zion Park Boulevard. Campers who left that crucial piece of equipment at home should visit **Zion Outdoors,** downstairs at 868 Zion Park Blvd., 435/772-0630.

GRAFTON

Grafton is one of the best-preserved and most picturesque ghost towns in Utah. Photos of the deserted site grace the covers of no fewer than three books on ghost towns of Utah. Mormon families founded Grafton in 1859 near the Virgin River at a spot one mile downstream from the present site, but a big flood two years later convinced them to move here. Hostilities with the Paiutes during the Black Hawk War forced residents to depart again for safer areas from 1866 to 1868. Floods and irrigation difficulties made life hard even in the best of times, and

© BILL WEIR

An adobe schoolhouse stands in the ghost town of Grafton.

the population declined in the early 1900s until only ghosts remained.

Moviemakers discovered Grafton and used it for *Butch Cassidy and the Sundance Kid,* among other films. You may notice a few fiberglass chimneys and other "improvements." A schoolhouse, store, houses, cabins, and outbuildings still stand. One story goes that the Mormon bishop lived in the large two-story house with wife number one while wife number two had to settle for the rough cabin across the road—probably not an amicable situation! Grafton's cemetery is worth a visit, too; it's on the left at a turn 0.3 mile before the town site. A monument commemorates three settlers killed by Native Americans in 1866. Many of Grafton's families now live in nearby Rockville; they tend the cemetery and look after the old buildings. From Springdale, follow Highway 9 southwest two miles to Rockville and turn south 3.5 miles on Bridge Road (200 East). The last 2.6 miles are unpaved but should be okay for cars

in dry weather; keep right at a road junction 1.6 miles past Rockville.

CANAAN MOUNTAIN

The rocky hills south of Springdale and Rockville offer fine scenery for back-road drives or hikes. The **Smithsonian Butte National Back Country Byway,** a 7.6-mile dirt road from the Grafton road, climbs into the scenic high country south of the Virgin River and continues to Highway 59 (near milepost 8) between Hurricane and Hildale on the other side; follow the directions to Grafton but turn left at the road junction 1.6 miles past Rockville. Panoramas take in Zion National Park, Smithsonian Butte, Canaan Mountain, and the rugged countryside all around. You can also find good places to hike or camp along the way. Cars with good clearance can usually make this trip if the road is dry.

Canaan Mountain (elev. 7,200 feet), a wilderness study area south of Springdale, rises more than 2,000 feet above the surrounding land. The summit is a plateau of rolling slickrock, pinnacles, balanced rocks, and deep fractures similar to the plateaus of Zion National Park. High cliffs on three sides give you the feeling of being on an island in the sky. **Eagle Crags Trailhead** (elev. 4,400 feet) near Rockville provides access from the north past the Eagle Crags, a group of towering sandstone monoliths. **Squirrel Canyon Trailhead** (elev. 5,100 feet) near Hildale is the starting point for hikes from the south via Water or Squirrel Canyon. See the USGS 7.5-minute topo maps Springdale West, Springdale East, Smithsonian Butte, and Hildale. Contact the BLM office in St. George, 435/688-3200, and use *Hiking Utah,* by Dave Hall, for hiking information.

HURRICANE AND VICINITY

Legend has it that in the early 1860s a group of pioneers was descending the steep cliffs above the present town site when a strong wind came up; Erastus Snow compared it with a hurricane and named the place Hurricane Hill. (By the way, locals pronounce the town's name as HUR-uh-kun.) A canal to bring water from the Virgin River to Hurricane Bench took 11 years of hard work to build, beginning in 1893, but it allowed farming in the area for the first time. Settlers founded the town in 1906. Many retirees and winter visitors live here now, and the area is quickly turning into a suburb of St. George complete with a lush golf course.

Enjoy the small but select collection of pioneer and Native American artifacts on display at the **Hurricane Valley Heritage Park and Museum** at 35 W. State St., 435/635-3245; you can also obtain local and area information from the well-informed staff; open Monday–Friday 9:30 A.M.–5:30 P.M. and Saturday 10 A.M.–5 P.M.

Recreation

Inner Light Yoga Center, 134 S. Main, 435/645-3981, offers several classes a week.

Sky Mountain Golf Course, 1000 North 2600 West, 435/635-7888, is one of the state's most highly regarded golf courses. The setting is spectacular, with the Hurricane Cliffs looming behind; volcanic outcrops jut up through the fairways, making for unique natural obstacles. This par-72 course has 18 holes; facilities include a clubhouse with full rental options.

Accommodations

Under $50: The **Dixie Hostel,** situated in a gracious old stucco building downtown at 73 S. Main St., 435/635-9000, offers inexpensive dorm-style lodgings and private rooms; guests have access to a laundry and kitchen. Linens and a light breakfast are included.

$50–75: The **Super 8,** 65 South 700 West, 435/635-0808 or 800/800-8000, offers a pool and sauna. **Lamplighter Inn,** 280 W. State, 435/635-4647, has an outdoor pool and a hot tub. The **Days Inn,** 40 North 2600 West, 435/635-0500 or 800/325-2525, has an indoor pool and complimentary continental breakfast. The **Comfort Inn,** 43 N. Sky Mountain Rd., 435/635-3500 or 800/635-3577, has a pool and hot tub.

Campgrounds: The best bet for tent campers is **Quail Creek State Park,** 6.5 miles west of town, then two miles north, 435/879-2378;

it's on a reservoir with swimming access. **Brentwood RV Resort,** 4.5 miles west of town, 435/635-2320 or 800/447-2239, is open year-round with a nine-hole golf course, indoor pool, tennis courts, recreation room, and showers; a restaurant, bowling alley, water slide, and mini golf course are across the street. **Quail Lake RV Park,** six miles west of town, 435/635-9960, is open year-round with pool, spa, store, and showers.

Food

Turn off busy State Street and away from its chain restaurants to find **Main St. Cafe,** 138 S. Main, 435/635-9086. Here you'll find good breakfasts and lunches, served either inside, in a gallery-like space, or outside, on quiet Main Street.

THE DINOSAUR TRACKWAYS AND OLD FORT PEARCE

Both of these sites illustrate periods of Utah's past. They're easily visited on a scenic backroad drive through the desert between Hurricane and St. George. Most of the road is unpaved and has some rough and sandy spots, but it should be okay for cautiously driven cars in dry weather. From Hurricane, drive south eight miles on 700 West, then turn west 8.5 miles to the dinosaur trackways turnoff and another two miles to the Fort Pearce turnoff. From St. George, head east on 700 South and follow the road as it turns south; turn left (east) 2.1 miles on a paved road immediately after crossing the Virgin River, turn left 3.5 miles on another paved road after a curve, then turn left (east) 5.6 miles on an unpaved road to the Fort Pearce turnoff (or another two miles to the dinosaur trackways turnoff). Signs for Warner Valley and Fort Pearce point the way at many, but not all, of the intersections.

A group of dinosaur trackways documents the passage of at least two different species more than 200 million years ago. The well-preserved tracks, in the Moenave Formation, may have been made by a 20-foot-long herbivore weighing an estimated 8–10 tons and by a carnivore half as long. No remains of the dinosaurs themselves have been found here.

The name of Old Fort Pearce honors Captain John Pearce, who led Mormon troops of the area during the Black Hawk War with Utes 1865–1869. In 1861, ranchers had arrived in Warner Valley to run cattle on the desert grasslands. Four years later, however, Native American troubles threatened to drive the settlers out. The Black Hawk War and periodic raids by the Navajo made life very precarious. Springs in Fort Pearce Wash—the only reliable water for many miles—proved the key to domination of the region. In December 1866, work began on a fort overlooking the springs. The stone walls stood about eight feet high and were more than 30 feet long. No roof was ever added. Much of the fort and the adjacent corral (built in 1869) have survived to the present. Local cattlemen still use the springs for their herds. Petroglyphs can be seen a quarter mile downstream from the fort along ledges on the north side of the wash.

St. George

Southern Utah's largest town lies between lazy bends of the Virgin River on one side and rocky hills of red sandstone on the other. In 1861, more than 300 Mormon families in the Salt Lake City area answered the call to go south to start the Cotton Mission, of which St. George became the center (hence the frequently used term "Dixie" to describe the area). The settlers overcame great difficulties to farm and to build an attractive city in this remote desert. Brigham Young chose the city's name to honor George A. Smith, who had served as head of the Southern (Iron) Mission during the 1850s. (The title "Saint" means simply that he was a Mormon—a Latter-day Saint.) Visits to some of the historic sites will add to your appreciation of the city's past; ask for the brochure *St. George Historic Walking Tour* at the chamber of commerce. The warm climate, dramatic setting, and many year-round recreation opportunities have helped make St. George (pop. 49,660) the fastest-growing city in the state. Local boosters claim that this is where Utah's summer sun spends the winter.

SIGHTS

St. George Temple and Visitors Center

Visible for miles, the city's gleaming white temple rises from landscaped grounds in the center of St. George. In 1871, enthusiastic Mormons from all over the territory gathered to erect the temple.

Dedicated on April 6, 1877, the structure was the church's first sacred house of worship in the West. The St. George Temple is the oldest active Mormon temple in the world. It's constructed of stuccoed stone in a castellated Gothic Revival style; a cupola with a weather vane caps the structure. Sacred ceremonies take place inside, so no tours are offered, but you're welcome to visit the grounds to admire the architecture. The temple is especially impressive at night when it's lit up against the black sky. A visitors center on the northeast corner of the grounds has short films and videos introducing the Mormon religion; it's open daily 9 A.M.–9 P.M. (8 A.M.–10 P.M. in summer). The visitors center and temple are at 250 East 400 South, at the corner of 200 South, 435/673-5181.

St. George Tabernacle

When Brigham Young visited the Cotton Mission after its first year, he found the community afflicted with difficulties and low morale. Soon after, he ordered construction of a tabernacle to help rally the members. The task, paid for with tithes, took 13 years to complete. Builders used local red sandstone for the walls and placed a slender white steeple on the roof, reminiscent of a New England church. Tour guides explain some of the tabernacle's history and construction details. The 20-minute film *Windows of Heaven,* shown on request, dramatizes the revelation received here in 1899 by church president Lorenzo Snow. Guides offer

To Snow Canyon, Veyo, Gunlock Reservoir, and Pine Valley Mountains

DIXIE RED HILLS GOLF COURSE

SUNSET BLVD.

18

SCALDONI'S

PAULA'S CAZUELA

To Jacob Hamblin Home, Saldoni's Gourmet Grill, Snow Canyon, and Gunlock Reservoir

ST. GEORGE

To Washington, Zion National Park, and Cedar City

SKYLINE DR.

600 N.

400 W.

500 N.

400 N.

DIAGONAL ST.

300 N.

MAIN ST.

200 N.

PIONEER PRIMITIVE PARK

WESTON'S ECONOLODGE

TRAVELODGE EAST

DAYS INN THUNDERBIRD

INDUSTRIAL RD.

HIGHLAND DR.

TWIN LAKES GOLF COURSE

RED CLIFFS DR.

OUTBACK STEAKHOUSE

RED CLIFFS MALL

BUREAU OF LAND MANAGEMENT OFFICES

ST. GEORGE BLVD.

SINGLETREE INN

SUN TIME INN

CHALET MOTEL

MOTEL 6

EXIT 8

RAMADA INN

TABERNACLE

SEE DETAIL

BEST WESTERN TRAVEL INN

ST.

100

200

W.

300 W.

200 W.

100 W.

200

300

400

300 N.

100

200

300

400

500

600

700

800

900

1000

600 S.

700 S.

APPLEBY'S

VERNON WORTHEN PARK

DIXIE COLLEGE

15

200 S.

300 S.

400 S.

DIXIE CENTER

0   0.5 mi

0   0.5 km

SULLIVAN'S ROCOCO INN & STEAKHOUSE

AIRPORT DR.

500 S.

600 S.

700 S.

★ ST. GEORGE TEMPLE

DIXIE REGIONAL MEDICAL CENTER

AIRPORT

HOLIDAY INN RESORT HOTEL

18

RIVER RD.

SWIMMING POOL

PANCHO AND LEFTY'S

RANCH INN

900 S.

THE BLUFFS INN AND SUITES

BEST WESTERN ABBEY INN

J.C. SNOW PARK

BUDGET 8 MOTEL

CRYSTAL INN

15

INDIAN HILLS DR.

Santa Clara River

HILTON DR.

PINE VALLEY RANGER DISTRICT OFFICE (U.S. FOREST SERVICE)

EXIT 6

Virgin River

ST. GEORGE GOLF CLUB

SOUTHGATE GOLF COURSE

To Virgin River Gorge and Las Vegas, NV

AN OLDE PENNY FARTHING INN

SEVEN WIVES INN BED & BREAKFAST

BRIGHAM YOUNG WINTER HOME ★

ANCESTOR SQUARE

MAIN

100

200 N.

POST OFFICE

ANCESTOR INN

CHAMBER OF COMMERCE/ DUP PIONEER MUSEUM

ST. GEORGE   BLVD.

PAINTED PONY/HOME GROUNDS/J.J. HUNAN CHINESE RESTAURANT/ PIZZA FACTORY

BEAR PAW COFFEE

BEST WESTERN CORAL HILLS

200 W.

GREENE GATE VILLAGE HISTORIC BED & BREAKFAST INN

ST GEORGE TABERNACLE/ WASHINGTON COUNTY LIBRARY

TABERNACLE   ST.

© AVALON TRAVEL PUBLISHING, INC.

N

SOUTHWESTERN UTAH

free tours daily 9 A.M.–6 P.M.; occasional concerts (free) and other presentations take place, too. The tabernacle is downtown at Main and Tabernacle Sts., 435/628-4072.

Brigham Young Winter Home

Late in life, Brigham Young sought relief from arthritis and other aches and pains by spending winters in Dixie's mild climate. This also gave him an opportunity to supervise more closely the affairs of the church here, especially construction of the temple. A telegraph line connected Young's house with Salt Lake City. He moved here late in 1873 and returned each winter until his death in 1877. The carefully restored adobe house contains furnishings of the era, including some that belonged to Young. Fruit and mulberry trees grow in the yard; mulberry leaves once fed the silkworms of the short-lived pioneer industry. Free tours begin at Young's office on the east side of the house, which is at 67 West 200 North, 435/673-2517. Open daily 9 A.M. (8 A.M. in summer) until sunset.

Brigham Young's winter home is one of downtown St. George's main attractions.

© JUDY JEWELL

Jacob Hamblin Home

No one did more to extend the Mormons' southern settlements and keep peace with the Native Americans than Jacob Hamblin. He came west in 1850 with four children (his first wife refused to come) and settled in the Tooele area with wife number two. At Brigham Young's request, Hamblin moved south in 1856 and helped build the Santa Clara Fort. He built the present sandstone house after floods washed away the fort in 1862. Almost always on the move serving on missions, Hamblin had little time for home life. He moved to Kanab in 1870, then to Arizona and New Mexico. Even so, he had four wives and managed to father 24 children. The kitchen, work areas, and living rooms provide a good idea of what pioneer life was like. Free tours offer a view of the house and tell of activities that once took place here. The house is in the village of Santa Clara, four miles northwest of St. George, 435/673-2161; open daily 9 A.M. until sunset.

Daughters of Utah Pioneers Museum

Drop in to see hundreds of pioneer portraits and the tools and clothing used by early settlers. The spinning wheels and looms on display served in the mission's cotton and silk industries. Open Monday–Saturday 10 A.M.–5 P.M.; donation requested. The museum, staffed by the Daughters of Utah Pioneers, is at 145 North 100 East, behind the old county courthouse, 435/628-7274.

Dixie State College of Utah

A giant "D" on a hillside to the west watches over the "Home of the Rebels" and the surrounding town. The school began in 1911 as the St. George Stake Academy, founded by the LDS Church. Dixie College is now a four-year college operated by the state. The approximately 5,000 students meet on a three-semester system.

Visitors are welcome to attend cultural and sporting events and to use many of the facilities. The Fine Arts Building (700 East and 100 South) has exhibits inside, but you'll find the biggest work outside on the south wall. A mosaic more than 15 feet high and 127 feet long depicts the region's history from the days of the Fremont people to Mormon settlement. To find out what's going on at Dixie College, visit the administration building (700 East and 200 South) or call 435/652-7800 (box office).

ENTERTAINMENT AND EVENTS

The staff at the **St. George Visitors Center,** 435/628-1658, and at the **Washington County Travel and Convention Bureau,** 800/634-5747, will fill you in on upcoming events, including concerts at Dixie Center and the tabernacle and the many small sporting events that take place in St. George.

Major annual events include the **Dixie Invitational Art Show,** which hosts regional artists in February; it begins President's Day weekend at the Fine Arts Building on Dixie College campus.

September brings the **Lions Dixie PRCA Round-Up Rodeo.** In October, the **Huntsman World Senior Games** presents a wide variety of Olympic-type competitions for seniors; you'll be amazed at the enthusiasm and abilities. Also in October, the **St. George Marathon** attracts about 4,000 runners from all over the United States.

GOLF

With one private and eight public golf courses in the area, St. George enjoys a reputation as Utah's winter golf capital. Red sandstone cliffs serve as the backdrop for **Dixie Red Hills,** 1250 North 645 West, on the northwest edge of town, 435/634-5852, a nine-hole, par-34 municipal course. **Green Spring Golf Course,** 588 N. Green Spring Dr. (just west of I-15 Washington Exit 10), 435/673-7888, has 18 holes (par 71) and a reputation as one of the finest courses in Utah. The nine-hole **Twin Lakes Golf Course,** 660 N. Twin Lakes Dr. on the northeast edge of town (take the I-15 west frontage road, Highland Dr.), 435/673-4441, is one of the area's most picturesque courses.

Professionals favor the cleverly designed **Sunbrook Golf Course,** 2240 Sunbrook Dr. off Dixie Downs Rd., between Green Valley and Santa Clara, 435/634-5866: 27 holes, par 72. **St. George Golf Club** has a popular 18-hole, par-73 course south of town in Bloomington Hills, 435/634-5854. **Southgate Golf Course,** 1975 S. Tonaquint Dr. on the southwest edge

of town, 435/628-0000, has 18 holes and a 70 par. The adjacent Southgate Game Improvement Center, 435/674-7728 can provide golfers with computerized golf swing analysis plus plenty of indoor practice space and lots of balls.

Entrada, 2511 W. Entrada Trail, 435/674-7500, is an 18-hole course fast on its way to becoming St. George's most respected. The Johnny Miller–designed course is northwest of St. George and incorporates natural lava flows, rolling dunes, and arroyos into its design. The 18-hole course **Sky Mountain** is northeast of St. George in nearby Hurricane (see Vicinity of St. George).

OTHER RECREATION

Vernon Worthen Park, 400 East and 200 South, offers shaded picnic tables, a playground, and tennis courts. **J.C. Snow Park,** 400 East and 900 South, has picnic tables and a playground (but little shade). **Pioneer Primitive Park** overlooks the city from the north; in desert country just off Skyline Drive, it has a few picnic tables. The outdoor public **swimming pool,** 250 East 700 South, 435/634-5867, features a hydro slide; open Memorial Day–Labor Day. **Tennis** players may use the public courts at Dixie College and Vernon Worthen Park. The city's **Leisure Services Department,** 435/634-5860, offers a wide range of activities for adults and youth, including classes (art, music, sports), field trips, and lectures.

SPAS

St. George is now home to two major spa resorts and recreation centers. Both are outside of St. George, in gorgeous natural settings. **Green Valley Spa,** 1871 West Canyon View Dr., 435/628-8060 or 800/237-1068,www.greenvalleyspa.com, is a major fitness, sports, health, and beauty spa resort with all-inclusive rates. Facilities are numerous and of a very high quality, and include six pools, tennis and racquetball courts, a fully-equipped gym with an array of fitness classes, tennis instruction, golf club privileges, plus hiking and climbing in neighboring canyons. There's also a whole catalog of beauty and rejuvenation treatments, ranging from massage, wraps, and aromatherapy to Native American medicine ceremonies and Shamanic card divination. Lodging is in the Coyote Inn, a luxury condominium development that flanks a parklike pool and garden area. Three spa meals daily are included in the rates. Green Valley Spa requires a three-night minimum stay, with seven-day packages also available. Rates, which include all meals, most recreation, and one treatment per day, run $375–400 per day, based on a five-to seven-day stay.

Slightly less grandiose and sportier, the **Red Mountain Spa,** 202 N. Snow Canyon Rd., 800/407-3002, www.redmountainspa.com, focuses more exclusively on outdoor recreation, fitness, and wellness. Facilities include numerous swimming and soaking pools, a fitness center and gym, tennis courts, salon, spa, conference rooms, plus access to lots of hiking and biking trails. The base rate includes hiking, mountain biking, a wide range of fitness classes, lodging, and all meals. Treatments for relaxation and beauty include massage, facials, body polishing, and aromatherapy; these involve additional costs. Accommodations are in a series of lodge-like hotel structures or in luxury casitas. Prices, which include all meals, lodging, and use of most spa facilities and recreation, range $200–450 per day, depending on lodging type. Good deals are often advertised on the spa's website.

ACCOMMODATIONS

St. George offers a large number of places to stay and eat. Motel prices stay about the same year-round, though they may drop if business is slow in summer. Considering the popularity of this destination, prices are reasonable and quality is high. Golfers should ask about golf-and-lodging packages. Most lodgings sit along the I-15 business route of St. George Boulevard (Exit 8) and Bluff Street (Exit 6). As for food, almost every fast-food place known to humanity is available just off the interstate on St. George Boulevard.

Under $50

Many of St. George's less expensive lodging choices operate at I-15's Exit 8 or on St. George Boulevard as it heads west to downtown. Right at the freeway exchange you'll find **Motel 6,** 205 North 1000 East, 435/628-7979 or 800/466-8356, with a pool; pets okay. The **Travelodge East,** 175 North 1000 East, 435/673-4621 or 800/578-7878, has some kitchenettes and a pool; small pets okay.

Heading toward downtown, the **Sun Time Inn,** 420 E. St. George Blvd., 435/673-6181 or 800/237-6253, has kitchenettes and a pool. The **Chalet Motel,** 664 E. St. George Blvd., 435/628-6272 or 888/628-6272, offers some efficiency kitchens, two three-bed rooms, and a pool. **Weston's Econolodge,** 460 E. St. George Blvd., 435/673-4861, has a pool and a spa, and small pets are okay.

In the heart of downtown, the **Ancestor Inn,** 60 W. St. George Blvd., 435/673-4666 or 800/866-6882, has an indoor pool and a location on the edge of Ancestor Square.

Near Exit 6 off I-15, the **Budget 8 Motel,** 1230 S. Bluff St., 435/628-5234 or 800/275-3494, offers a pool and a spa.

$50–75

East of the Exit 8 interchange is the **Ramada Inn,** 1440 E. St. George Blvd. (right beside the Factory Outlet Mall), 435/628-2828 or 800/713-9435; facilities include an outdoor pool and hot tub. A complimentary continental breakfast is included; rooms are close to $75. The **Days Inn Thunderbird,** 150 North 1000 East, 435/673-6123 or 800/527-6543, has a pool, hot tub, sauna, fitness center, and free continental breakfast, and pets are okay.

The **Best Western Travel Inn,** 316 E. St. George Blvd., 435/673-3541 or 800/528-1234, has an outdoor pool and indoor spa; children under 12 stay free. The **Singletree Inn,** 260 E. St. George Blvd., 435/673-6161 or 800/528-8890, has a pool, hot tub, and free continental breakfast; pets okay with $5 fee. Special golf package rates.

Close to downtown is one of St. George's best, the **Best Western Coral Hills,** 125 E. St. George

Blvd., 435/673-4844 or 800/542-7733, a very attractive property with indoor and outdoor pools and two spas, an exercise room, and a complimentary continental breakfast. Children under 12 stay free.

Leave the freeway at I-15 Exit 6 to find another selection of motels. The **Crystal Inn,** 1450 S. Hilton Inn Dr., 435/628-0463 or 800/662-2525, is located on a golf course and has beautiful public areas, nicely appointed guest rooms, a pool, and a sauna.

Most rooms at **The Bluffs Inn and Suites,** 1140 S. Bluff St., 435/628-6699 or 800/832-5833, are suites with efficiency kitchens. Facilities include a pool and spa; pets okay. Two-night minimum for stays during Easter weekend and some special events. **Best Western Abbey Inn,** 1129 S. Bluff St., 435/652-1234 or 888/222-3946, is new, and all rooms have microwaves and refrigerators. There's an outdoor pool, indoor spa, recreation/fitness facilities, and a free hot breakfast.

The **Ranch Inn,** 1040 S. Main, 435/628-8000 or 800/332-0400, offers suite-like rooms with efficiency kitchens; there's a guest laundry, pool, and indoor hot tub.

$75–100

The **Holiday Inn Resort Hotel & Convention Center,** 850 S. Bluff St., 435/628-4235 or 800/457-9800, is a large complex with a "Holidome" complete with indoor and outdoor pools, whirlpool, recreation/fitness facilities, tennis court, and putting green. Children under 18 stay free.

Just across from Brigham Young's winter home, the **Seven Wives Inn Bed & Breakfast,** 217 North 100 West, 435/628-3737 or 800/600-3737, offers rooms in two historic homes. The simpler rooms run about $90; suites are over $100. All 13 guest rooms have private baths and are decorated with antiques. Children are welcome, and guests share a swimming pool.

Also located in St. George's historic district is **An Olde Penny Farthing Inn,** 278 North 100 West, 435/673-7755. Built in the 1870s as a pioneer home, the handsome structure has been beautifully restored as an inn

with five guest rooms, each individually decorated with period furnishings and fine art; all have private baths.

You'll find an entire compound of pioneer-era homes at the **Green Gate Village Historic Bed & Breakfast Inn,** 76 W. Tabernacle, 435/628-6999 or 800/350-6999. Nine beautifully restored homes offer a variety of lodging options—groups or families can rent an entire home. Many rooms come with kitchens and private baths, some with private whirlpools; there's a pool for the enjoyment of all guests. Some pets are okay, and children are welcome.

Campgrounds

The best camping in the area is at **Snow Canyon State Park,** 435/628-2255 or 800/322-3770 (reservations), in a pretty canyon setting, with showers. Go 12 miles north on Highway 18, then left two miles; $14 without hookups, $17 with hookups.

Right in St. George, **McArthur's Temple View RV Resort,** 975 S. Main, 435/673-6400 or 800/776-6410, is near the temple district and has a pool, a laundry room, and showers. East of town is **Settlers RV Park,** 1333 East 100 South (near I-15 Exit 8), 435/628-1624, with a pool and showers; RVs only.

Farther north, near I-15 Washington Exit 10, you'll find **St. George Campground & RV Park,** 2100 E. Middleton Dr., 435/673-2970, with tent sites, a pool, a laundry room, and showers; and **Redlands RV Park,** 650 W. Telegraph, 435/673-9700 or 800/553-8269, with a pool, a store, a laundry room, and showers.

FOOD

For a major recreation and retirement center, St. George is curiously lacking in unique places to eat. Almost every chain restaurant can be found here, but don't expect a bevy of local fine-dining houses. Some exceptions are listed as follows. You'll also find it bizarrely difficult to find restaurants that stay open late; even in high season, most restaurants close by 9 P.M.

The best place to head for lunch or dinner is Ancestor's Square, a trendy shopping development at the intersection of St. George Boulevard and Main Street. **Painted Pony,** 435/634-1700, has good Southwestern food. Dine Chinese at **J.J. Hunan Chinese Restaurant,** 435/628-7219. Pick up pizza at **Pizza Factory,** 435/628-1234. In the center of the square, the tiny **Home Grounds** is housed in the old jail and serves good coffee and tea.

Just across St. George Boulevard, **Bear Paw Coffee,** 75 N. Main St., 435/634-0126, is one of the few places in town to hang out and drink coffee. Breakfasts are large and delicious.

Unless noted, all of the following serve wine and cocktails. **Pancho & Lefty's,** 1050 S. Bluff St., 435/628-4772, serves Mexican lunch and dinners in a semiformal atmosphere. For Mexican food with a view, try **Paula's Cazuela,** 745 W. Ridgeview Dr. on the northwest edge of town, 435/673-6568, a hilltop restaurant serving fine Mexican fare for lunch and dinner.

For formal dining and spectacular views, head west toward the airport for **Sullivan's Rococo Inn & Steak House,** 511 Airport Rd., 435/628-3671; prime rib, steak, and seafood are the specialties. At **Scaldoni's Gourmet Grill,** in the Phoenix Plaza Mall, 929 W. Sunset Blvd., 435/674-1300, you can mix and match pastas with a wide variety of sauces. Dine in historic splendor at **Bentley House Restaurant,** at Green Gate Village, 76 W. Tabernacle, 435/656-3333, which offers fine dining in a restored pioneer home (no alcohol, reservations required).

INFORMATION AND SERVICES

The **St. George Chamber of Commerce** can tell you about the sights, events, and services of southwestern Utah; it has brochures of accommodations, restaurants, a historic walking tour, and area ghost towns; open Monday–Friday 9 A.M.–5 P.M. and Saturday 9 A.M.–1 P.M. The office is in the old county courthouse (built 1866–1876) at 97 E. St. George Boulevard (St. George, UT 84770), 435/628-1658.

For recreation, see the **Pine Valley Ranger District office,** 196 E. Tabernacle (St. George, UT 84770), 435/652-3100, for information on fishing, hiking, and camping in the Dixie National Forest north of town; maps of the forest and Pine Valley Wilderness are available. Open Monday–Friday 8 A.M.–5 P.M. The **Bureau of Land Management** oversees vast lands in Utah's southwest corner and the Arizona Strip; open Monday–Friday 7:45 A.M.–4:30 P.M. The offices for Dixie Resource Area, 435/688-3200, and the Shivwits and Vermilion Resource Areas of the Arizona Strip, 435/628-4491, are at 345 E. Riverside.

The **post office** is at 180 N. Main, 435/673-3312. The **Dixie Regional Medical Center** provides hospital care at 544 South 400 East, 435/634-4000 (physician referral number is 801/628-6688). You can exchange foreign currency at **First Security Bank,** 410 E. Tabernacle, 435/574-6600.

TRANSPORTATION

Skywest Airlines, 800/453-9417, has direct flights to Salt Lake City six times daily and to Las Vegas twice daily.

Rent automobiles in town from **Budget,** 116 W. St. George Blvd., 435/673-6825 or 800/527-0700; or **Enterprise,** 652 E. St. George Blvd., 435/634-1556. **National,** 435/673-5098 or 800/227-7368, and **Avis,** 435/627-2002 or 800/230-4898, are at the airport.

Greyhound buses, 435/673-2933, depart from McDonald's at 1235 S. Bluff St. for Salt Lake City, Denver, Las Vegas, and other destinations. The **St. George Shuttle** will take you to Las Vegas in a 15-passenger van for $20 from 850 S. Bluff St. (Holiday Inn); call 435/628-8320 for schedule.

Vicinity of St. George

Some good scenic drives begin at St. George. Whether you're short on time or have all day, a good choice is the 24-mile loop through Snow Canyon State Park via Highway 18, the park road (Highway 300), and Santa Clara. The old highway to Littlefield, Arizona, makes a 67-mile loop with I-15; this route follows former U.S. 91 through the pioneer settlement of Santa Clara and the sparsely settled Shivwits Reservation and over a 4,600-foot pass in the Beaver Dam Mountains to Littlefield; the I-15 section goes through the spectacular Virgin River Gorge upstream from Littlefield. In summer, the cool forests of the Pine Valley Mountains, 37 miles northwest of town, are an especially attractive destination: You can make a 130-mile drive with many possible side trips by circling the mountains on Highway 18, Highway 56, and I-15. Zion National Park, with its grandeur and color, is about 40 miles northeast of St. George. Adventurous motorists may want to try some of the unpaved roads through the desert east and west of St. George.

Snow Canyon is a remarkably wild and scenic state park just outside St. George.

SNOW CANYON STATE PARK

North of St. George, Snow Canyon State Park is a great place to explore and enjoy the desert scenery. Red-rock canyons, sand dunes, volcanoes, and lava flows have formed an incredible landscape. Walls of Navajo sandstone 50–750 feet high enclose five-mile-long Snow Canyon. Hiking trails lead into the backcountry for a closer look at the geology, flora, and fauna. Common plants are barrel, cholla, and prickly pear cacti, yucca, Mormon tea, shrub live oak, cliffrose, and cottonwood. Delicate wildflowers bloom mostly in the spring and autumn, following the wet seasons, but cactus and the sacred datura can flower in the heat of summer. Wildlife includes sidewinder and Great Basin rattlesnakes, Gila monster, desert tortoise, kangaroo rat, squirrel, cottontail, kit fox, coyote, and mule deer. You may find some Native American rock art, arrowheads, bits of pottery, and

ruins. Many of the place-names in the park honor Mormon pioneers. Snow Canyon was named for Lorenzo and Erastus Snow—not for the rare snowfalls. Cooler months have the best weather; summers are too hot for comfortable hiking except in early morning. Highway 18 leads past an overlook on the rim of Snow Canyon and to the paved park road (Highway 300) that drops into the canyon and follows it to its mouth and the small town of Ivins. Snow Canyon is about 12 miles northwest of St. George. It's reached either by Highway 18—the faster way—or via Santa Clara and Ivins. Each vehicle is charged a $5 day-use fee.

Hiking Trails

The **Hidden Piñon Trail** (also signed as Nature Trail) begins across the road from the campground entrance, then weaves among sandstone hills and lava flows to the Varnish Mountain

ST. GEORGE AND THE PINE VALLEY MOUNTAINS

Newcastle

To Cedar City

56

18

Enterprise

Irontown

Enterprise
Reservoir

Dixie

New Harmony

B u l l   V a l l e y   M o u n t a i n s

National

Pine

MOUNTAIN MEADOWS MASSACRE
HISTORIC SITE

BAKER DAM
RECREATION SITE

River

PINE VALLEY
RECREATION
AREA

Mountain

Pine Valley

Valley

Santa   Clara

Veyo

Wilderness

OAK GROVE
CAMPGROUND

P i n e   V a l l e y   M o u n t a i n s

Kanarra   Creek

15

Gunlock

18

17

Forest

SILVER REEF
GHOST TOWN

To Zion
National
Park

Gunlock Lake
State Park

Snow
Canyon
State Park

RED CLIFFS
RECREATION SITE

Leeds

9

La Verkin

River

SHIVWITS

TUACAHN
AMPHITHEATER

Snow Cyn.

Shivwits

Ivins

RED
MOUNTAIN SPA

Quail Creek
State Park

Virgin

Hurricane

PAIUTE

59

RESERVATION

Santa Clara

17

JACOB HAMBLIN
HOME

Washington

H u r r i c a n e   C l i f f s

To Las Vegas, NV

GREEN
VALLEY
SPA

St. George

River

0   25 mi

0   25 km

Virgin

15

OLD FORT
PEARCE

DINOSAUR
TRACKWAYS

A R I Z O N A

Overlook above Snow Canyon. At the overlook, desert varnish on sandstone has turned the rock jet black. The easy trail is 1.5 miles round-trip and has a small elevation gain; some sections cross rough rocks and deep sand. It's an easy scramble from the overlook area to the canyon floor below. **West Canyon Trail** is the longest in the park; it begins near the stables (0.7 mile south of the campground) and goes northwest along an old road up Snow Canyon to West Canyon. (You can also take cross-country hikes into other canyons passed on the way.) The trail is seven miles round-trip with a small elevation gain. **Lava Tubes Trail** winds across a lava field to an area of lava caves (one mile round-trip). The caves formed when molten lava broke out of the partly cooled flow and left rooms and tunnels behind. Artifacts indicate that Native Americans took shelter in the chambers. The trailhead is 1.5 miles north of the campground. The steep and strenuous **Volcano Trail** ascends a cinder cone northeast of Snow Canyon. The 1,000-year-old volcano is on the east side of Highway 18 one mile north of the turnoff for Snow Canyon. Near the park entrance, the 0.5-mile **Jenny's Trail** leads to a slot canyon; this trail is closed April–May.

North of St. George, Snow Canyon State Park is a great place to explore and enjoy the desert scenery. Red-rock canyons, sand dunes, volcanoes, and lava flows have formed an incredible landscape.

Practicalities

Set within the canyon, the **campground** at Snow Canyon State Park stays open all year with water, showers, and hookups. Sites cost $14; $17 with hookups. Camping reservations are especially recommended for spring and autumn weekends; during the summer it's very hot here and attracts few campers. Contact Snow Canyon State Park at P.O. Box 140, Santa Clara, UT 84765, 435/628-2255 or 800/322-3770 (reservations). **Snow Canyon Riding Stables,** 435/628-6677, offers horseback riding, campfire breakfasts, and Western shows year-round; you can arrange overnight pack trips in the Pine Mountains in summer.

TUACAHN AMPHITHEATER

Tuacahn is an outdoor amphitheater that seats 1,900 set among 1,500-foot-high red-rock cliffs northwest of St. George. Tuacahn offers a two-show summer theater season mostly featuring Broadway musicals. Recent performances have included *The Wizard of Oz* and *The King and I.* A new indoor performance space, the Haffen Theatre, features more intimate comedies and dramas. A Dutch-oven dinner is available before each production as well as free backstage tours. The show runs daily except Sunday mid-June–early September, and ticket prices—including dinner—run $25–35 ages 12 and over, $15–25 for children under 12. The amphitheater is northwest of St. George near the south entrance to Snow Canyon State Park. Call 800/746-9882, or check out the website www.tuacahn.org, for information and reservations.

VEYO AND VICINITY

Veyo Resort

Warm-water springs feed a swimming pool in this pretty spot. The family resort here, 435/574-2744, has picnic tables and a snack bar; it's open from about the last weekend in March to Labor Day. Take the Veyo Pool Resort Road from Highway 18 southeast of town. The little village of Veyo lies along the Santa Clara River 19 miles northwest of St. George.

Gunlock Lake State Park

The 266-acre reservoir is set among red and gray hills 10 miles southwest of Veyo. A parking area, docks, and paved boat ramp lie just off the road near the dam. The red-sand beach across the lake can be reached by boat or by a short walk across the dam. Largemouth bass, channel catfish, bluegill, and the odd trout swim in the waters. Open all year; no water or charge. Check with Snow Canyon State Park for current info at P.O.

Box 140, Santa Clara, UT 84765, 435/628-2255. Gunlock Lake can be reached from St. George via Veyo or by the slightly shorter route through Santa Clara.

Baker Dam Recreation Site

This 50-acre reservoir on BLM land is on the Santa Clara River upstream from Veyo. Anglers come for the rainbow and brown trout. An established campground is just before the dam; drive across the dam to undeveloped camping areas and a boat ramp. Open all year; no water or charge. Go north four miles on Highway 18 from Veyo, then turn right a half mile on a paved road (between mileposts 24 and 25).

HIGHWAY 18 NORTH TO ENTERPRISE

Mountain Meadows Massacre Historic Site

A short trip from Highway 18 west of the Pine Valley Mountains leads to the site of one of the darkest chapters of Mormon history. The pleasant valley had been a popular rest stop for pioneers about to cross the hot desert country to the west. In 1857, a California-bound wagon train whose members had already experienced trouble with Mormons of the region was attacked by an alliance of Mormons and local Native Americans. About 120 people in the wagon train died in the massacre. Only some small children

too young to tell the story were spared. The closely knit Mormon community tried to cover up the incident and hindered federal attempts to apprehend the killers. Only John D. Lee, who was in charge of Indian affairs in southern Utah at the time, was ever brought to justice. After nearly 20 years and two trials, authorities took him back to this spot to be executed by firing squad. Many details of the massacre remain unknown. The major causes seem to have been a Mormon fear of invasion, aggressive Mormons and Native Americans, and poor communications between the Mormon leadership in Salt Lake City and southern Utah. A monument now marks the site of the tragedy; turn west one mile on a paved road from Highway 18 between mileposts 31 and 32.

Enterprise Reservoirs

Rainbow trout lurk in the lower and upper reservoirs. Larger Upper Enterprise Reservoir has a paved boat ramp and easier access. Nearby **Honeycomb Rocks Campground** (elev. 5,700 feet) has water and a camping fee roughly Memorial Day–October. Its name describes the outcrops of porous volcanic rock. The open country here supports mostly grass, sage, and some ponderosa pine and Gambel oak. Drive to the town of Enterprise, 41 miles northwest of St. George (47 miles west of Cedar City), then follow paved roads 11.5 miles west and south.

Pine Valley Mountains

A massive body of magma uncovered by erosion makes up the Pine Valley Mountains. Vegetation ranges from piñon pine and juniper woodlands on the lower slopes to ponderosa pine and aspen at the middle elevations to Douglas fir, subalpine fir, Engelmann spruce, and limber pine in the heights. Signal Peak (elev. 10,365 feet) tops the range, much of which has been designated the Pine Valley Mountain Wilderness Area.

Pine Valley

In 1856, pioneers arrived at Pine Valley (elev. 6,600 feet) to harvest the extensive forests and raise livestock. Lumber from Pine Valley helped build many southern Utah settlements and even went into Salt Lake City's great tabernacle organ. The town's picturesque white chapel was built in 1868 by Ebenezer Bryce, who later homesteaded at what's now Bryce Canyon National Park. The chapel is open for tours daily 11 A.M.–5 P.M. from Memorial Day weekend to Labor Day. Most of today's residents come up only in summer for the cool mountain air.

Pine Valley Recreation Area

Continue three miles on the paved road past Pine Valley to the picnic areas, campgrounds, and trails in Dixie National Forest. At Pine Valley Reservoir, 2.3 miles up on the right, you can fish for rainbow and some brook trout. There's also fair fishing in the Santa Clara River upstream and downstream. **Ponderosa Picnic Area** is 0.4 mile farther on the right; free for day use. Turn right just past the picnic area for **Pines Campground, Lower Pines Picnic Area,** and **Brown's Point Trailhead.** Continue straight for **Blue Springs** and **South and North Juniper Campgrounds** and for **Whipple Trailhead.** Each campground has water and a fee during the May 20–October 31 season. Elevation is 6,800 feet. All campsites fill up most days in summer; try to arrive early or make reservations then. Reservations can be made by calling 877/444-6777 for individual sites at Blue Springs

Campground, the group campground at Upper Pines, and group picnic areas. The **Pine Valley Ranger District office,** 196 E. Tabernacle, St. George, 435/652-3100, can advise on camping and other recreation here.

Pine Valley Wilderness

The 50,000-acre wilderness has the best scenery of the Pine Valley Mountains, but it can be seen only on foot or horseback. A network of trails from all directions leads into the wilderness. The road from Pine Valley provides access to the **Whipple Trailhead** and **Brown's Point Trailhead** on the east side of the wilderness area. Trails are usually open mid-June into October. **Summit Trail** is the longest (35 miles one-way) and connects with many other trails. Several loops are possible, though most are too long for day hikes. **Whipple National Recreation Trail** is one of the most popular for both day- and overnight trips; it ascends 2,100 feet in six miles to Summit Trail. **Brown's Point Trail** also climbs to Summit Trail, but in four miles. Strong hikers can use the Brown's Point and Summit Trails to reach the top of Signal Peak on a day hike; the last part of the climb is a rock-scramble. Generally, the trails from Pine Valley are signed and easy to follow; trails in other areas may not be maintained. Take topo maps and a compass if you're going for more than a short stroll. The Pine Valley Ranger District office has a recreation map that shows trails and trailheads. *The Hiker's Guide to Utah,* by Dave Hall, describes a 15-mile loop in the Pine Valley Mountains.

NORTH OF PINE VALLEY MOUNTAINS

Irontown

This is one of Utah's best-preserved 19th-century iron smelter sites. The original Iron Mission near Cedar City had poor success during its brief life in the 1850s. In 1870, though, more extensive ore deposits farther west at this site encouraged another attempt at iron-making.

Daily production rose to nearly five tons, and a town of several hundred workers grew up around the smelter. Profits began to decline in the 1880s when cheaper iron from the eastern states flooded in. The town soon died, though mining has since continued on and off in the vicinity. A brick chimney, stone foundations of the smelter, and a beehive-shaped charcoal kiln show the layout of the operation. Look around in the sagebrush for remnants of the town site and pieces of slag and iron. Drive 16 miles west from Cedar City or 30 miles east from Enterprise to the signed turnoff on Highway 56 (just west of milepost 41), then turn southwest 2.7 miles.

EAST OF PINE VALLEY MOUNTAINS

Leeds

This small community has two exits on I-15; southbound traffic on I-15 must use Exit 23 on the north side of town. Northbound traffic on I-15 must take Exit 22 south of town. **Leeds RV Park,** 435/879-2450, has RV sites with hookups and showers (no tents); turn east on Center at the sign.

Silver Reef

This is probably Utah's most accessible ghost town. In about 1870, prospectors found rich silver deposits in the sandstone here, much to the surprise of mining experts who thought such a combination impossible. The town grew up several years later and boomed 1878–1882. The population peaked at 1,500 and included a sizable Chinese community. Then a combination of lower silver prices, declining yields, and water in the mines forced the operations to close one by one, the last in 1891. Other attempts at mining have since been made from time to time, including some uranium production in the 1950s and '60s, but the town had died.

The **Wells Fargo Building,** which once stood in the center of town, is now Silver Reef's main attraction. Built of stone in 1877, it looks as solid as ever. **Jerry Anderson Art Gallery** and the small **Silver Reef Museum** occupy the interior;

open Monday–Saturday 9 A.M.–5 P.M., 435/879-2254. Encroaching modern houses detract a bit from the setting, but the ghosts are still here. Stone walls and foundations peek out of the sagebrush. A short walk on the road past the building takes you to the ruins and tailings of the mills that once shook the town with their racket. Take I-15 Leeds Exit 22 or 23 and follow signs 1.3 miles on a paved road.

Oak Grove Campground

On the east side of the Pine Valley Mountains, Oak Grove (elev. 6,800 feet) is in a forest of Gambel and shrub live oak, ponderosa pine, and some spruce. The small campground has water about Memorial Day–October. Leeds Creek has trout fishing, but dense shrubbery along the banks can make access difficult. **Oak Grove Trail** winds three miles from the campground to Summit Trail in the Pine Valley Mountain Wilderness. Take I-15 Leeds Exit 22 or 23 and go northwest nine miles. The unpaved road may be rough, especially late in the season; it's usually passable by cars but isn't recommended for trailers.

Red Cliffs Recreation Site

Weather-sculpted cliffs of reddish-orange sandstone rise above this pretty spot. The seasonal Quail Creek emerges from a canyon, flows through the middle of the campground, then goes on to Quail Creek Reservoir two miles away. The campground and picnic area (elev. 3,240 feet) is open all year with water and a camping fee. **Desert Trail** starts on the left near the beginning of the campground loop and follows the creek a half mile into the canyon. Idyllic pools and graceful rock formations line the way. You'll need to do some wading to continue upstream past trail's end. A shorter (quarter-mile round-trip) but more rugged trail begins near the end of the campground loop and crosses slickrock to Silver Reef Lookout Point. Here there's a good panorama of the area, though you can't actually see Silver Reef ghost town. Take I-15 Leeds Exit 22 or 23, go south three miles on the frontage road, then turn west 1.7 miles on a paved road. Long trailers may drag on dips at stream crossings.

Quail Creek State Park
Barren rock hills surround the 590-acre reservoir at this park. Most of the water comes from the Virgin River, but Quail Creek also contributes its share. Curiously, the reservoir has two dams to hold back the waters. The state park on the west shore offers a campground (water but no showers or hookups), swimming beach, paved boat ramp, and docks. Anglers come for the largemouth bass, rainbow trout, catfish, and bluegill. Other popular activities include water-skiing, personal watercrafting, and sailboarding. The park stays open all year; $6 per vehicle for day use, $11 per vehicle for camping. For information, contact the park at P.O. Box 1943, St. George, UT 84770, 435/879-2378 or 800/322-3770 (reservations). If coming from the north, take I-15 Leeds Exit 23 and follow the frontage road south 3.4 miles, then turn left 1.5 miles; from the south, take I-15 Hurricane Exit 16, go east 2.6 miles on Highway 9, then north two miles on a paved road.

Cedar City

Cedar City (pop. 20,530), known for its scenic setting and its summertime Utah Shakespearean Festival, is a handy base for exploring a good chunk of southern Utah. Just east of town rise the high cliffs of the Markagunt Plateau—a land of panoramic views, colorful rock formations, desolate lava flows, extensive forests, and flower-filled meadows. Also on the Markagunt Plateau is the Cedar Breaks National Monument, an immense amphitheater eroded into the vividly hued underlying rock. Within an easy day's drive are Zion National Park to the south and Bryce Canyon National Park and Grand Staircase–Escalante to the east. Cedar City is just east of I-15, 52 miles northeast of St. George and 253 miles southwest of Salt Lake City; take I-15 Exit 57, 59, or 62.

History
Cedar City began as a mission in 1851 to supply the Mormon settlements with much-needed iron products. Church leaders, upon hearing of promising iron ore and coal deposits, decided to launch the first major colonizing effort since the settlement of the Salt Lake area. The first wagon loads of families and supplies left Provo in December 1850 for Parowan, 18 miles northeast of present-day Cedar City. Other settlers arrived at Cedar City late the following year. All had to start from scratch. Farmers planted crops to feed the new communities while miners and engineers laid plans for iron-manufacturing industries. Hard winters, crop failures, floods, and shortages of skilled workmen nearly doomed the whole project. The final blow came when Johnston's Army and others brought cheaper iron from the East. Only a small amount of iron was produced, and operations ceased in 1858. Sizable quantities of iron ore did exist, though; large-scale mining west of Cedar City began in the 1920s, peaked in 1957, and has tapered off in recent years.

Paiutes have lived here since before pioneer days. Sponsorship by the Mormon community allowed them to remain when the federal government forced most other tribes in the state to move onto reservations. There's a Paiute village in the northeastern part of Cedar City. The tribe puts on the Paiute Restoration Gathering in mid-June.

SIGHTS
Southern Utah University
The towns of southern Utah eagerly sought a branch of the state's teacher training school after it had been authorized in 1897 by the Utah legislature. A committee awarded the school to Cedar City, and classes began the same year in a borrowed church building. Some people say that Cedar City was chosen because it was the only one of the candidate towns without a saloon or pool hall! This satellite school inevitably became a four-year university with 6,000 students and today offers major fields of study in education, arts and letters, science, and business. The attractively

SOUTHWESTERN UTAH

Detail (inset)

200 WEST ST.
100 WEST ST.
CENTER
MAIN ST.
BOOMER'S
ROCK CHURCH
STRATFORD COURT HOTEL
CHINA GATE RESTAURANT
COLLEGE AVE.
100 EAST ST.
BARD'S INN BED & BREAKFAST
ADRIANA'S RESTAURANT
BEST WESTERN EL REY MOTEL
PIZZA FACTORY

Cedar City

CEDAR CITY

TRAVELODGE MOTEL
NICHOLS CANYON RD.
LEFTY'S CANTINA
FIDDLERS CANYON RD.
NORTH FIELD RD.
N. CEDAR BLVD.
MAIN ST.
BULLDOG RD.
AIRPORT RD.
CEDAR CITY REGIONAL AIRPORT
15
N. FIELD RD.
KITTY HAWK WY.
Coal Creek
COAL CREEK RD.
LA FIESTA
Iron Mission State Park
VISITORS CENTER
INDUSTRIAL RD.
56
COMFORT INN
ECONOLODGE
400 N. ST.
GODFATHER'S PIZZA
ABBEY INN
200 N. ST.
HOLIDAY INN
BEST WESTERN TOWN & COUNTRY INN
ESCOBAR'S
CENTER ST.
ADAMS MEMORIAL THEATRE
SEE DETAIL
RANDALL JONES THEATRE
SOUTHERN UTAH UNIVERSITY
200 S. ST.
14
200 S. ST.
W. ST.
BIG YELLOW INN B&B
SUPER 7 MOTEL
RODEWAY INN
400 S. ST.
ZION INN
SULLIVAN'S CAFÉ
300 S. ST.
300 E. ST.
1100 W. ST.
CEDAR REST MOTEL
600 S. ST.
HUNAN RESTAURANT
800 S. ST.
MAIN ST.
MOON
CROSS HOLLOW RD.
BAKER HOUSE BED & BREAKFAST
DAYS INN
15
GREEN'S LAKE DR.

0   0.5 mi
0   0.5 km

© AVALON TRAVEL PUBLISHING, INC.

landscaped campus occupies 104 acres just west of downtown.

Braithwaite Fine Arts Gallery presents changing exhibits in the Braithwaite Fine Arts Center, one block north of the intersection of 200 South and 400 West, 435/586-5432. It's open during the Shakespearean Festival Monday–Friday 10 A.M.–7:30 P.M., Saturday and Sunday 1–5 P.M.; open the rest of the year Monday–Thursday and Saturday 10 A.M.–7:30 P.M., Friday 10 A.M.–5 P.M. The Utah Shakespearean Festival is the main summer event on campus. The scheduling office, 435/586-1989, can tell you of upcoming convocations and other cultural happenings. Sports facilities open to the public include an indoor swimming pool, tennis and racquetball courts, and gym at the Physical Education Building, 600 West 200 South, 435/586-7815. Contact the college through campus information, Southern Utah University, Cedar City, UT 84720, 435/586-7700.

Iron Mission State Park Museum

This large museum dedicates itself to the history of the cultures that have lived in and developed Iron County, and to pioneer efforts to mine and process iron. Exhibits illustrate the Iron Mission's early hardships and the first iron production on September 30, 1852. Past members of the Iron Mission cast the old community bell on display. A diverse array of carriages is the museum's main attraction. You'll see everything from a bullet-scarred Overland stagecoach to an elegant Clarence carriage. All the sleighs, utility wagons, hearses, and many other forms of 19th-century transport have been meticulously restored. Also displayed are artifacts of prehistoric and modern tribes. Pioneer memorabilia include clothing, furniture, saddles, and a bathtub. A large collection of horse-drawn farm machinery sits out back. The museum, 589 N. Main, 435/586-9290, is open Monday–Friday 9 A.M.–5 P.M.; closed major holidays. Park admission is $4 per vehicle.

Rock Church

Depression-era residents needed a new LDS Church building but lacked the money to build one. Undaunted, they set to work using local materials and came up with this beautiful structure composed of many different types of rocks. Skilled craftspeople made the metal lamps, carpets, Western red cedar pews, and most other furnishings. Open for tours daily in summer; free admission. It's at the corner of Center and 100 East.

EVENTS AND RECREATION

Utah Shakespearean Festival

Cedar City's lively festival presents three Shakespearean plays each season, choosing from both well-known and rarely performed works. Most of the action centers on the Adams Shakespeare Theatre, an open-air theater-in-the-round, which is closely designed after the original Globe Theatre in Elizabethan London. The indoor Randall Jones Theatre presents the "Best of the Rest"—works by other great playwrights such as Chekhov, Molière, and Arthur Miller. In all, eight plays are staged late June–mid-October.

Costumed actors stage the popular Greenshow each day before the performances with Elizabethan comedy skits, Punch and Judy shows, period dances, music, juggling, and other good natured 16th-century fun. Another activity, the Royal Feaste, presents a pre-performance Elizabethan-style dinner (a feast with no silverware!) and entertainment from Tudor times ($30 per person, reservations required). Backstage tours of the costume shop, makeup room, and stage show you how the festival works. At literary seminars each morning, actors and Shakespearean scholars discuss the previous night's play. Production seminars, held daily except Sunday, take a close look at acting, costumes, stage props, special effects, and other details of play production.

The Greenshow and seminars are free, but you'll have to pay for most other events. Tickets cost $15–40, and it's wise to purchase them well in advance; however, last-minute theater-goers can usually find tickets to *something;* call 435/586-7790 for more information. Detailed brochures listing activities and dates of performances are available from the Utah Shakespearean Festival,

SOUTHWESTERN UTAH

Cedar City, UT 84720, 435/586-7878 or 800/PLAYTIX (800/752-9849) (box office), www.bard.org.

The theaters are on the Southern Utah University campus near the corner of Center and 300 West. Rain occasionally dampens the performances (the Elizabethan theater is open to the sky), and plays may move to a conventional theater next door, where the box office is located.

Other Events

Other events and festivals include the **Canyon Country Western Arts Festival** in March. The highlights are the readings by cowboy poets; there's also a display of Western art and music events.

In June, the local Native American community sponsors the **Paiute Restoration Gathering** with a parade, dances, traditional games, native food, and a beauty pageant on the second weekend in June. Mid-June brings **Groovefest,** a blues and bluegrass festival.

Utah athletes compete in the **Utah Summer Games** during late June; events, patterned after the Olympic games, begin with a torch relay and include track and field, 10K and marathon runs, cycling, boxing, wrestling, basketball, tennis, soccer, karate, and swimming.

Everyone dresses up in period clothing in July for the **Utah Midsummer Renaissance Faire** of 16th-century entertainment, crafts, and food. **Pioneer Day** honors Utah's early settlers with a parade and games in town on July 24. Dances by the **American Folk Ballet** portray America's southern and Western folk history.

In August, mountain men and Native Americans set up camp for black-powder shoots and games in the **Jedediah Smith High Mountain Rendezvous** in the mountains above Cedar City.

The season ends in November, when Cedar City celebrates its birthday on the 11th with games and pioneer crafts in **Iron Mission Days.**

Recreation

The main **city park** has picnic tables, playground, and horseshoe courts at Main and 200 North. The **municipal swimming pools** at 400 Harding Avenue (400 West 100 North), 435/586-2869, have indoor and outdoor areas and a hydrotube. Look for **tennis courts** at Canyon Park (on Highway 14, three blocks east of Main). From this park the new, paved Coal Creek walking and biking trail leads four miles up the desert canyon.

ACCOMMODATIONS

Cedar City is popular with visitors, so it's best to reserve a room at least a day or two in advance during the summer. There are two major concentrations of motels. A half dozen large chain hotels cluster around I-15 exits, together with lots of fast-food restaurants and strip malls. Downtown, along Main Street, are even more motels, ranging from classy new resortlike hotels to well-maintained budget motels. You can easily walk from most of the downtown motels to the Shakespearean Festival. Most of Cedar City's B&Bs are also within a stroll of the festival grounds.

Note that the following prices are for the high summer festival season. Outside of high season, expect rates to drop about one-third.

Under $50

Downtown, the **Zion Inn,** 222 S. Main, 435/586-9487, is one of Cedar City's best budget choices, with kitchenettes in some rooms. The **Super 7 Motel,** 190 S. Main, 435/586-6566, has a free continental breakfast and accepts pets.

$50–75

The following motels string along Main Street in downtown Cedar City. The **Travelodge Motel,** 2555 N. Main, 435/586-7435 or 800/348-8216, is a good deal with a pool and spa; pets are okay. The **Cedar Rest Motel,** 479 S. Main, 435/586-9471, offers basic rooms; small pets are okay. The **Rodeway Inn,** 281 S. Main, 435/586-9916 or 800/424-4777, has a pool, a sauna, and a spa; pets are okay.

The **Best Western El Rey Inn,** 80 S. Main, 435/586-6518 or 800/528-1234, offers suites, a restaurant, a pool, a sauna, and a spa. All rooms at the **Stratford Court Hotel,** 18 S. Main,

435/586-2433 or 877/688-8884, are nonsmoking; this nice hotel has an outdoor pool, free passes to a local gym, and a complimentary continental breakfast.

Out at I-15 Exit 59, the **Comfort Inn,** 250 North 1100 West, 435/586-2082 or 800/627-0374, has a pool, a spa, some kitchenettes, and a complimentary continental breakfast. Near the same exit, the **Holiday Inn,** 1575 West 200 North, 435/586-8888 or 800/432-8828, also offers a pool, a good restaurant, a spa, and a sauna; pets are okay.

At I-15 Exit 57, the **Days Inn,** 1204 S. Main, 435/867-8877 or 888/556-5637, has an indoor pool and complimentary continental breakfast. At Exit 52, the **Econolodge,** 333 North 1100 West, 435/867-4700 or 888/326-6613, has an outdoor pool and a hot tub.

$75–100

One of the best places to stay in Cedar City is the **Best Western Town & Country Inn,** 200 N. Main, 435/586-9911. It is a sprawling complex with nicely furnished rooms and suites, indoor and outdoor pools, and spas. Rooms have microwaves and refrigerators; several restaurants are adjacent. The **Abbey Inn,** 940 West 200 North, 435/586-9966 or 800/325-5411, offers a pool and kitchenettes.

Bed-and-breakfast inns and Shakespeare seem to go hand-in-hand. The **Bard's Inn Bed & Breakfast,** 150 South 100 West, 435/586-6612, two blocks from the Shakespearean Festival, has seven guest rooms, all with private baths, plus there's a two-bedroom cottage. Open during the festival season only.

For a more rural touch, the **Willow Glen Inn Bed & Breakfast,** 3308 N. Bulldog Rd., 435/586-3275, offers a three-bedroom inn plus two cottages (with a total of six guest rooms) on a 10-acre farm five miles north of downtown Cedar City, I-15 Exit 62; some baths are shared.

$100–125

The **Baker House Bed & Breakfast,** 1800 Royal Hunte Dr., 435/867-5695 or 888/611-8181, www.bakerhouse.net, is a few minutes' drive from the festival, but the rooms here are some of the most luxurious in Cedar City, and most have great views. There are five guest rooms in this modern Queen Anne mansion, all with private baths, fireplaces, and TVs.

The **Big Yellow Inn B&B,** 234 South 300 West, 435/586-0960, is an elegant Georgian revival home a block from the Shakespearean Festival with 11 guest rooms, all with air-conditioning and private baths.

Campgrounds

Cedar City KOA, 1121 N. Main, 435/586-9872 or 800/562-9873, is open all year with cabins, showers, a playground, and a pool, and can accommodate tents as well as RVs. **Country Aire RV Park,** 1700 N. Main, 435/586-2550, is open all year with showers and a pool; no tent sites.

East of Cedar City on Highway 14 are a handful of campgrounds in the Dixie National Forest. The closest, **Cedar Canyon,** is 12 miles from town, in a pretty canyon along Cow Creek. It's at 8,100 feet and open with water early June–mid-September.

FOOD

Family restaurants dominate Cedar City's cuisine. **Sullivan's Cafe,** 301 S. Main, 435/586-6761, is a favorite for casual family dining. **Boomer's,** 5 N. Main St., 435/865-9665, serves burgers, shakes, fries, and American standards. Upstairs is **Boomer's Pasta Garden,** a sister restaurant with a selection of pasta dishes.

At the **Pastry Pub,** 86 W. Center, 435/867-1400, expect pastries, sandwiches, and coffee; it's as close to a coffee shop as you'll find in Cedar City.

For Cantonese-style food, there's **Hunan Restaurant,** 501 S. Main, 435/586-8952, and **China Garden Restaurant,** 64 N. Main, 435/586-6042, whose giant sign you surely won't miss in downtown Cedar City. You can have a drink with your Mexican food at **Lefty's Cantina,** 2107 N. Main, 435/586-4741, and **La Fiesta,** 900 N. Main, 435/586-4646. For pizza, try the **Pizza Factory,** 124 S. Main, 435/586-3900, open Monday–Saturday, or

Godfather's Pizza, 241 N. Main, 435/586-1111, in the old train station.

The following fine-dining restaurants each serve wine and cocktails. Adriana's Restaurant, 164 South 100 West, 435/865-1234, has an English atmosphere with fine dining and is open in summer Monday–Saturday for lunch and dinner; call for hours off-season. East of Cedar City on Highway 14 is a dramatic desert canyon with two of the area's finest restaurants; both are open for dinner only. Five miles east of town is the Western-style Milt's Stage Stop, 435/586-9344, serving steak, prime rib, and seafood. The steak-house atmosphere is a bit more formal at Rusty's Ranch House, two miles east on Highway 14, 435/586-3839, in a dramatic canyon setting.

OTHER PRACTICALITIES
Information and Services
Iron County Travel Council, 581 N. Main, 435/586-5124, www.scenicsouthernutah.com, has literature and advice on travel in the area; open Monday–Friday 8 A.M.–7 P.M. and Saturday 9 A.M.–1 P.M. in summer, then Monday–Friday 8 A.M.–5 P.M. the rest of the year. Cedar City Ranger District office, 1789 Wedgewood Ln., 435/865-3200, of the Dixie National Forest has information on recreation and travel on the Markagunt Plateau. The BLM's Cedar City District office, just off Main at 176 E. DL Sargeant Dr. on the north edge of town, 435/586-2401, can tell you about the BLM lands in southwestern Utah, including Beaver River, Dixie, Kanab, and Escalante Resource Areas; open Monday–Friday 7:45 A.M.–4:30 P.M.

Cedar City Public Library, 136 W. Center, 435/586-6661, is open Monday–Thursday 9 A.M.–9 P.M., Friday and Saturday 9 A.M.–6 P.M. Mountain West Bookstore, 77 N. Main, 435/586-3828, sells books on Utah history, travel, general reading, and LDS titles. At the south end of town, Cedarhouse Books, 576 S. Main, 435/867-6267, has a good selection of books and a small coffeeshop.

The Renaissance Square and South Main Mall shopping centers are on South Main at the south edge of town. Camping and other outdoor supplies are sold at Ron's Sporting Goods, 138 S. Main, 435/586-9901, and Gart Bros. Sporting Goods, 606 S. Main, 435/586-0687. Valley View Medical Center, 595 South 75 East, 435/586-6587, provides hospital care. The post office is at 333 N. Main, 435/586-6701.

Transportation
Skywest Airlines has flights between Cedar City Municipal Airport and Salt Lake City, 800/453-9417. Rent a car from National, at the airport, 435/586-4004, or at National's office at the Town and Country Inn, 200 N. Main, 435/586-9900. Speedy Rentals, 650 N. Main, 435/586-7368, rents vans, cars, pickups, and motor homes.

Greyhound Bus, 1355 S. Main (the C-Mart Texaco station near the south I-15 interchange), 435/586-1204, offers service twice daily to Salt Lake City, Denver, St. George, Las Vegas, and other destinations.

PAROWAN

Although just a small town, Parowan (pop. 2,570) is southern Utah's oldest community and the seat of Iron County. Highway 143 turns south from downtown to the Brian Head Ski Area, Cedar Breaks National Monument, and other scenic areas on the Markagunt Plateau. To the west lies Utah's desert country. Accommodations in town offer a less expensive alternative to those in Brian Head. Iron County Fair presents a parade, rodeos, horse races, exhibits, and entertainment during the Labor Day holiday. In April, cowboys come to Parowan for the Iron County Cowboy Days & Poetry Gathering.

Stop by the Parowan visitors center, 75 N. Main, 435/477-8190, open Monday–Friday 9 A.M.–4 P.M. The public library is across the street at 16 S. Main, 435/477-3391. Parowan is 18 miles northeast of Cedar City and 14 miles north of Brian Head; take I-15 Exits 75 or 78.

Parowan Gap Petroglyphs
Native Americans have pecked many designs into the rocks at this pass 10.5 miles northwest of

Parowan. The common route for Native Americans and wildlife hunting the Red Hills crossed this gap, and it may have served as an important site for hunting rituals. The rock art's meaning hasn't been deciphered but it probably represents the thoughts of many different tribes over the past 1,000 or more years. Geometric designs, snakes, lizards, mountain sheep, bear claws, and human figures are all still recognizable. You can get here on a good gravel road from Parowan by going north on Main and turning left 10.5 miles on the last street (400 North). Or, from Cedar City, go north on Main (or take I-15 Exit 62), follow signs for Highway 130 north 13.5 miles, then turn right 2.5 miles on a good gravel road (near milepost 19). You'll find an interpretive brochure and map at the BLM offices in Cedar City.

Accommodations

Under $50: The **Ace Motel,** 72 N. Main, 435/477-3384, is a basic motel and it allows pets.

$50–75: The **Days Inn,** 200 South 600 W. Holyoak Lane (I-15 business route), 435/477-3326 or 888/530-3138, has new rooms and an on-site restaurant. **Swiss Village Inn,** 580 N. Main, 435/477-3391 or 800/528-1234, has a pool, spa, and restaurant.

Over $100: Splurge in Parowan at the nicely restored **Victorian Rose Country Inn,** 7 N. Main, 435/477-1555.

Campgrounds: Sportsmen's Country RV Park is at 492 N. Main, 435/477-3714. Tent campers should head a few miles out of town to the Markagunt Plateau.

Food

Parowan Cafe, 33 N. Main, 435/477-3593, is open Monday–Saturday for breakfast, lunch, and dinner. **Pizza Barn,** 595 West 200 South, 435/477-8240, serves pizza and pasta daily for dinner. For great ribs, go to **Hideaway Restaurant,** 215 South 600 West, 435/477-8646. **La Villa,**13 S. Main St., 435/477-1541, serves Mexican food.

The Markagunt Plateau

Markagunt is a Native American name for "highland of trees." The large, high plateau—much of the land is between 9,000 and 11,000 feet in elevation—consists mostly of gently rolling country, forests, and lakes. Black tongues of barren lava extend across some parts of the landscape. Cliffs at Cedar Breaks National Monument are the best-known feature of the plateau, but the land also drops away in the colorful pink cliffs farther southeast.

Two Scenic Byways cross this highly scenic area. Highway 14 climbs up a very dramatic cliff-lined canyon from Cedar City, reaching vista points over Zion National Park before dropping onto Long Valley Junction on Highway 89. Highway 143 departs from Parowan, climbing steeply up to lofty Brian Head with its ski and recreation area, past Panguitch Lake, and down to Panguitch in the Sevrier Valley. Brian Head is southern Utah's most popular ski area, and in summer the lifts carry mountain bikes up to ele-

vations of nearly two miles, allowing gear heads to explore high mountain glades and meadows.

Popular activities on the Markagunt include fishing, hiking, mountain biking, downhill and cross-country skiing, and snowmobiling. Contact the Cedar City Ranger District of the Dixie National Forest, 1789 Wedgewood Ln., 435/865-3200, for a forest map and information on exploring the area. In summer, volunteers or foresters staff the visitors center on Highway 14 opposite the Duck Creek Campground turnoff.

MARKAGUNT SCENIC BYWAY (HIGHWAY 14)

Starting at Cedar City's eastern boundary, Highway 14 plunges into a narrow canyon flanked by steep rock walls before climbing up to the top of the Markagunt Plateau. This is a very scenic route, passing dramatic rock cliffs and

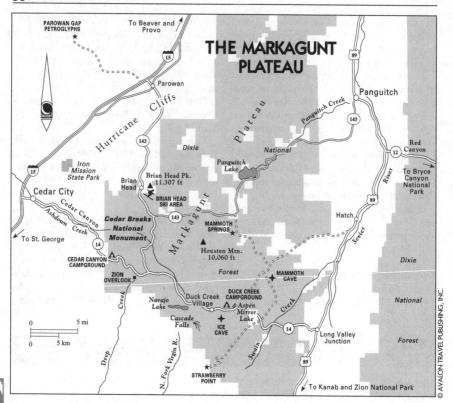

THE MARKAGUNT PLATEAU

© AVALON TRAVEL PUBLISHING, INC.

pink rock hoodoos that echo the formations at Zion and Bryce Canon National Parks. This isn't a quick drive, especially if you get caught behind a lumbering RV. But the scenic qualities of the canyon and the incredible vistas—which extend across Zion and down into Arizona—will amply repay your patience. The route also passes a number of wooded campgrounds and small mountain resorts. Due to their elevations—mostly 8,000–9,000 feet—these high mountain getaways are popular when the temperatures in the desert basin towns begin to bake. The route ends at the Long Valley Junction, at Highway 89, 41 miles from Cedar City.

Zion Overlook

A sweeping panorama takes in the deep canyons and monuments of Zion National Park to the south. Zion Overlook is 16.5 miles east of Cedar City on the south side of the road.

Bristlecone Pine Trail

This easy half-mile loop, graded for wheelchair access, leads to the rim of the Markagunt Plateau and excellent views. A dense spruce and fir forest opens up near the rim, where storm-battered limber and bristlecone pines cling precariously near the edge. You can identify the bristlecone pines by their short-needled, "bottlebrush" branches. The trailhead is 17 miles east of Cedar City on the south side of Highway 14.

Highway 148 Junction

Eighteen miles east of Cedar City is the junction with Highway 148, which leads north to Cedar Breaks National Monument. The route climbs up to elevations well over 10,000 feet and is usually open late May–mid-October. (See the Cedar Breaks National Monument section.)

Navajo Lake

Lava flows dammed this unusual 3.5-mile-long lake, which has no surface outlet. Instead, water drains through sinkholes in the limestone underneath and emerges as Cascade Falls (in the Pacific Ocean drainage) and Duck Creek (Great Basin drainage). From a pullout along the highway 24 miles east of Cedar City, you can sometimes see three of the sinkholes at the east end; a dam prevents the lake from draining into them. Anglers catch rainbow trout and occasionally some eastern brook and brown trout; ice fishing is possible in winter. You can hand-launch small boats at Navajo Campground or from boat ramps at Navajo Lake Lodge and Behmer Lodge & Landing. Take the Navajo Lake turnoff, 25.5 miles east of Cedar City, for the campgrounds, marina, and lodge along the south shore.

Virgin River Rim Trailhead

This trail stretches about 38 miles along the rim between Deer Haven Group Campground and Strawberry Point. Beautiful panoramas of Zion National Park and the headwaters of the Virgin River reward trail users. You can also reach it at Te-Ah Campground, from Navajo Lake via short (one-half to three-quarter mile) spur trails and at the start of the Cascade Falls National Recreation Trail. The entire length is open to hikers and mountain bikers. Off-highway vehicles can use the section from Deer Haven to Te-Ah Campground.

Cascade Falls National Recreation Trail

Splendid views and a waterfall make this an exciting trip. The easy trail is 1.1 miles round-trip with some ups and downs. It begins at the south rim of the Markagunt Plateau, drops a short way down the Pink Cliffs, then winds along the cliffs to the falls. The falls gush from a cave and bounce their way down to the North Fork of the Virgin River and Zion Canyon. The flow peaks during spring runoff. Take the Navajo Lake turnoff from Highway 14, go 0.3 mile, then turn left three miles on a gravel road to its end.

Duck Creek Campground

Turn north from Highway 14 at Duck Lake, about 28 miles east of Cedar City. The creek and lake adjacent to the campground offer trout fishing. You'll see why Duck Lake got its name. A **visitors center,** staffed by the Dixie Interpretive Association, is open daily 10 A.M.–5 P.M. in summer across the highway from the campground turnoff. **Singing Pines Interpretive Trail,** just east of the visitors center, makes a half-mile loop—an amusing information sheet introduces the forest trees through songs. **Old Ranger Interpretive Trail** makes a one-third-mile loop from Duck Creek Campground; look for a large pullout on the left where the main campground road makes a curve to the right (near the amphitheater); the information sheet explains the forest through the eyes of an old-time forest ranger. Pick up information sheets for both trails from the visitors center. The **Lost Hunter Trail** makes a three-mile loop from the same trailhead in Duck Creek Campground to the top of Duck Creek Bench; elevation gain is about 600 feet with many fine views. Reserve a campsite at www.reserveusa.com or 877/444-6777.

Ice Cave

Cool off inside this small cave, where the lava rock insulates ice throughout the summer. The road may be too rough for cars—ask conditions at the visitors center. Turn south on the dirt road beside the visitors center, keep left at the fork 0.2 mile in, keep right at another fork 0.8 mile farther, and continue 0.4 mile to the cave at the end of the road; signs mark the way.

Aspen Mirror Lake

Trout and scenic beauty attract visitors to this pretty reservoir. The turnoff is on the north side of Highway 14 about midway between Duck Creek Campground and Duck Creek Village. Park, then walk the level trail about one-quarter mile.

Duck Creek Village

Hollywood has used this area since the 1940s to film such productions as *How the West Was Won*, *My Friend Flicka*, and the *Daniel Boone* TV series. This handsome village—a collection of lodges, cabins, and log-built homes—lies at the edge of a large meadow (elev. 8,400 feet) about 30 miles east of Cedar City. The surrounding countryside is excellent for snowmobiling, a popular winter sport here. A big snowmobile race takes place on the weekend closest to Valentine's Day. Cross-country skiing is good, too, on meadow, forest, and bowl terrain. The snow season lasts about late November–late March. Blue Pine Tours, at Pinewoods Resort, 800/848-2525, offers snowmobile tours and rentals, as well as cross-country skiing and snowshoe rentals. In summer, Blue Pine Tours rents mountain bikes and ATVs.

Food: The **Pinewoods Restaurant,** 435/682-2512, prepares prime rib, steak, seafood, and other fare all year; open for breakfast, lunch, and dinner Friday–Monday. The **Duck Creek Village Inn,** 435/682-2565, offers American fare three meals a day year-round.

Strawberry Point

A magnificent panorama takes in countless ridges, canyons, and mountains south of the Markagunt Plateau. You can spot Zion National Park and even the Arizona Strip from this lofty perch (elev. 9,016 feet). Erosion has cut delicate pinnacles and narrow canyons into the Pink Cliffs on either side below the viewpoint. Turn south from Highway 14 between mileposts 32 and 33 (32.5 miles east of Cedar City) onto a gravel road and go nine miles to its end. A 500-foot path continues to Strawberry Point. Take care near the edge—the rock is crumbly and there are no guardrails.

Accommodations

Under each category, the accommodations are listed from west to east along Highway 14.

$50–75: Navajo Lake Lodge, at the west end of the lake, 702/646-4197, has cabins, a small café, store, boat rentals, and boat ramp. Open Memorial Day weekend–late October.

In Duck Creek Village, **Meadow View Lodge** on Highway 14, 435/682-2495 or 877/384-0361, rents lodge rooms and cabins all year. They also rent snowmobiles and ATVs. **Falcon's Nest,** 60 Movie Ranch Rd., 435/682-2556 or 800/240-4930, offers A-frame cabins with kitchens; adjacent is the Duck Quick Cafe. Two-night minimum on weekends (three nights on holidays). Open year-round.

$75–100: To reach the rest of Duck Creek Village, drive one mile east, then a half-mile south. The **Inn at Cedar Mountain,** 435/682-2378 or 800/897-4995, has condo-style rooms for up to eight people, open all year. Rates include a continental breakfast. **Pinewoods Resort,** 121 Duck Creek Ridge Rd., 435/682-2512 or 800/848-2525, offers two-bedroom condominiums in a log lodge; open year-round. All units have fireplaces and kitchens, and pets are okay.

Campgrounds: Sites in the **Cedar Canyon Campground** (elev. 8,100 feet) lie along Crow Creek among aspen, fir, and spruce in a pretty canyon setting. Open with water early June–mid-September; 12 miles east of Cedar City on Highway 14.

The U.S. Forest Service maintains **Spruces** and **Navajo Campgrounds** along the lake and **Te-Ah Campground** 1.5 miles west; all have water and charge a fee mid-June–mid-September; expect cool nights at the 9,200-foot elevation. Aspen, spruce, and fir grow along the lake.

Duck Creek Campground, north from Highway 14 at Duck Lake, has sites (elev. 8,600 feet) that are open early June–mid-September with water and a fee.

BRIAN HEAD–PANGUITCH LAKE SCENIC BYWAY 143 (HIGHWAY 143)

Beginning in Parowan, Highway 143 very quickly climbs up to nearly 10,000 feet, ascending some of the steepest paved roads in Utah in the process (some of the grades here are 13 percent). The terrain changes from arid desert to pine forests to alpine aspen forests in just 14 miles.

At an elevation of 9,850 feet, Brian Head is the highest municipality in Utah, with a year-round population of 95. The town takes its name from the flat-topped peak towering above to the east. Originally called Monument Peak, it got its present (misspelled) name in 1890 when its founders decided to honor the famed orator and politician William Jennings Bryan. Winter skiers like Brian Head for its abundant snow, challenging terrain, and good accommodations. Summer visitors come to enjoy the high country and to plunge down the slopes on mountain bikes. The beautiful colors of Cedar Breaks National Monument lie just a few miles south. Panguitch Lake, to the east, receives high ratings for its excellent trout fishing.

Brian Head Peak

You can drive all the way to Brian Head's 11,307-foot summit by car when the road is dry, usually July–October. Panoramas from the top take in much of southwestern Utah and beyond into Nevada and Arizona. Sheep graze the grassy slopes below. From Brian Head, follow the highway about two miles south, then turn left (northeast) three miles on a gravel road to the summit. The stone shelter here was built by the Civilian Conservation Corps in the 1930s.

Brian Head Resort

Brian Head comes alive during the skiing season, late November–late April. While it's not Utah's most exciting ski area, it's a good place to bring a family. There are two main areas at Brian Head: Navajo Peak, good for beginners and families, and Giant Steps, with more advanced runs. Snow cats transport more daring skiers to thrilling chutes and bowls on Brian Head Peak. A total of five triple and one double lift carry skiers up to elevations of 10,920 feet; the resort has 53 runs and 500 skiable acres, with a vertical drop of 1,707 feet. Thirty percent of the terrain is rated beginner, 40 percent intermediate, and 30 percent advanced. The resort also features several terrain parks, 20 rails, and a half-pipe for snowboarders. Lift tickets cost $38 adults full day, $33 half day; children 12 and under and seniors ski for $25 full day, $20 half day (rates go up during the holidays,

with adult tickets going for $42). There's a limited amount of night skiing available during the holidays; $10. Rentals, lessons, shops, and children's day care are available. For more ski information contact Brian Head Resort, Brian Head, UT 84719, 435/677-2035 or 800/272-7426, www .brianhead.com.

Cross-Country Skiing

Brian Head Cross-Country Center (in Cedar Breaks Lodge), 435/677-2012, grooms about 70 miles of trails in the area; ask for its map. The short **North Rim Trail** goes to overlooks in Cedar Breaks National Monument. Experienced skiers with maps and compasses can head out on backcountry routes to the summit of Brian Head Peak and many other areas. There is no fee for use of the trails; rentals are available at the lodge.

Mountain Biking

Brian Head's second season is during the summer and fall, roughly June–October, when the area comes alive with mountain bikers taking advantage of great terrain and discounted accommodations. Brian Head Resort opens itself to bikers as a mountain-bike park, complete with chairlift and trailhead shuttle services, bike wash, rentals, and repair services. They supply free maps (preview the routes and print maps from www .brianhead.com). Thrifty bikers can come away with some really good deals by shopping area hotels for mountain-bike lodging packages, which combine a few days of lodging with lift tickets, shuttle service, and sometimes even food and bike rentals. Bike-oriented summertime events in Brian Head include a late-July bike festival and mountain-bike races in August, September, and March. Mountain-bike rentals are available from Brian Head Resort, 435/677-2035.

Cedar Breaks National Monument

The northern entrance to this showcase of spectacular erosion (see the Cedar Breaks National Monument section) is two miles south of Brian Head on Highway 143.

Panguitch Lake and Vicinity

This 1,250-acre reservoir sits in a volcanic basin

surrounded by forests and barren lava flows. The cool waters have a reputation for outstanding trout fishing, especially for rainbow. Some German browns can also be caught in the lake and downstream in Panguitch Creek. Recently, the lake has gained popularity for ice fishing. Resorts line the lakeshore; many are venerable older fishing lodges with basic lodging in free-standing cabins; a couple are more upscale. Panguitch Lake is increasingly popular as a site for resort homes, as a glance at the dirt-moving equipment and piles of building supplies makes apparent.

Panguitch Lake lies along Highway 143 about 16 miles southwest of Panguitch and 14 miles northeast of Cedar Breaks National Monument. The lake has public boat ramps on the south and north shores.

Mammoth Springs

Moss and luxuriant streamside vegetation surround the crystal-clear spring waters at this beautiful spot. Mammoth Springs is about 5.5 miles south of Panguitch Lake. The last two miles are on gravel Forest Route 068. See the Dixie National Forest map (available at the Pine Valley and Cedar City Ranger District offices). A footbridge leads across the stream to the springs.

Mammoth Cave

Step a few feet underground to explore the inside of a lava flow. When this mass of lava began to cool, the molten interior burst through the surface and drained out through a network of tunnels. A cave-in revealed this section of tunnel, which has two levels. One of them you can follow through to another opening. The lower tunnel (with the large entrance) goes back about a quarter mile. To explore beyond that or to check out other sections, you'll have to stoop or crawl. Bring at least two reliable, powerful flashlights; the caves are very dark. Mammoth Cave is about 14 miles south of Panguitch Lake. Roads also lead in from Duck Creek on Highway 14 and Hatch on U.S. 89. You'll need the forest map to navigate the back roads, though there are some signs for Mammoth Cave.

Accommodations

Lodgings and campgrounds along Highway 143 are concentrated around Panguitch Lake, and there are a number of accommodations that serve Brian Head.

$50–75: On the west shore of Panguitch Lake, the **Rustic Lodge,** 186 S. West Shore Rd., 435/676-2627 or 800/427-8345, offers handsome kitchen-equipped cabins in a forested glen. Unfortunately, the resort is not directly on the lake (the lodge and cabins face onto a pasture) but this is otherwise a very pleasant place to stay. Campsites available also. Additional amenities include a boat moorage and boat rentals, a restaurant and pub, and laundry facilities. Two-night minimum on summer weekends. **Deer Trail Lodge,** northwest of the lake on Clearcreek Canyon Rd., 435/676-2211 or 866/676-2211, offers new creekside cabins in a steep canyon; again, unfortunately, these pleasant cabins are some distance from the lake itself. The resort also offers a restaurant (serving breakfast, lunch, and dinner daily) and campsites. Take West Shore or North Shore Rd. to Clear Creek Canyon Road, then turn west a half mile.

Bear Paw Lakeview Resort is on the east shore of Panguitch Lake at 905 S. Highway 143, 435/676-2650 or 888/553-8439, and has lakeview cabins and an RV park. There's also a small store, on-site restaurant, post office, and boat and mountain-bike rentals. Open early May–mid-November.

$75–100: A few resorts are actually on Panguitch lake. The nicest is **Aspen Cove** on the north shore, 435/676-8988 or 866/497-5581, a handsome log lodge right on the lake, overlooking a small marina. Also in the lodge is a good restaurant (open daily for breakfast, lunch, and dinner), small store, and a boat rental office.

Blue Springs Lodge is the Panguitch area's newest resort, near the general store at 225 N. Shore Rd., 435/676-2277 or 800/YUR-LODGE. Also a ways from the lake, this resort comprises modern log cabins with kitchens. Most can sleep six adults. The location—right on Highway 143—is about the only downside.

$100–125: Rates at Brian Head are steep during the ski season, though most places offer skiers vacation-package discounts. Several reservations services can help you book a condo: try **Brian Head Resort Reservation Service,** 435/677-2042 or 800/845-9781, www .brianheadtow.com, or **Brian Head Central Reservations,** 800/272-7426. **Brian Head Condo Reservations,** 435/677-2045 or 800/722-4742, offers units near both the Giant Steps and Navajo Mountain lifts in five large condo developments. Most units come with two bedrooms and two baths, full kitchen, plus a wood-burning fireplace. Prices for one-bedroom condos start at about $100 (double) in summer; during the ski season expect to pay at least $125.

The most upscale lodging choice in Brian Head is **Cedar Breaks Lodge,** 223 Hunter Ridge Rd., 435/667-3000 or 888/ATCEDAR, www.cedarbreakslodge.com, at the base of Navajo Peak on the north (lower) side of town. All rooms come with jetted tubs, a refrigerator, in-room coffee, and cable TV; kitchens are available in some rooms. There's also an indoor pool, two hot tubs, a steam room, sauna, day spa, and fitness center. Lodging choices range from hotel rooms to three-bedroom suites.

Campgrounds: The U.S. Forest Service has three campgrounds at Panguitch Lake; all are open with water early June–mid-September. **Panguitch Lake North Campground,** on the southwest side of the lake, has developed sites in a ponderosa pine forest at an elevation of 8,400 feet. **Panguitch Lake South Campground,** across the highway, is more suited for small rigs and tents. **White Bridge Campground** (elev. 7,900 feet) lies among cottonwoods and junipers along Panguitch Creek four miles northeast of the lake.

Three miles down West Shore Rd. off Highway 143, **Panguitch Lake General Store and RV Park,** near the turnoff for West Shore Road, 435/676-2464, has an RV park with hookup sites for self-contained RVs. The store is open all year and sells groceries, gas, gifts, and fishing supplies.

Food

At the Brian Head Mall, **Bump & Grind** serves coffee and deli items, 435/677-3111. Next door, **Xtreme Pizza** serves lunch to the ski crowd.

At Cedar Breaks Lodge, there are three dining rooms. The **Cedar Breaks Café** is open for breakfast and dinner, the **Double Black Diamond Steak House** serves Western-style fine dining in the evening only, and **Cedar Breaks Private Club** offers drinks and casual dining.

For food on the slopes, **Brian Head Station** serves breakfast and lunch daily during the ski season next to chairs #4 and 6, 435/677-2035. Typical ski-area grills operate in both the Navajo and Giant Steps Lodges; the Navajo Lodge also has a dinner restaurant, the **Lift House.**

Information

You can reach **Brian Head Chamber of Commerce** at P.O. Box 190325, Brian Head, UT 84719, 435/677-2810. Or check out the website at www.brianheadutah.com. The **post office** is in Brian Head Mall, near the center of town.

CEDAR BREAKS NATIONAL MONUMENT

Erosion on the west edge of the Markagunt Plateau has carved a giant amphitheater 2,500 feet deep and more than three miles across. A fairyland of forms and colors appears below the rim. Ridges and pinnacles extend like buttresses from the steep cliffs. Cottony patches of clouds often drift through the craggy landscape. Traces of iron, manganese, and other minerals have tinted the normally white limestone a rainbow of warm hues. The intense colors blaze during sunsets and glow even on a cloudy day. Rock layers look much like those at Bryce Canyon National Park and, in fact, are the same Claron Formation, but here they're 2,000 feet higher. Elevations range from 10,662 feet at the rim's highest point to 8,100 feet at Ashdown Creek below. In the distance beyond the amphitheater, you can see Cedar City and the desert's valleys and ranges. Dense forests broken by large alpine meadows cover the rolling plateau country away from the rim. More than 150 species of wildflowers brighten the meadows during summer; the colorful display peaks during the last two weeks in July.

A five-mile scenic drive leads past four spectacular overlooks, each with a different perspective. Avoid overlooks and other exposed areas during thunderstorms, which are common on summer afternoons. Heavy snows close the road most of the year. You can drive in only from about late May until the first big snowstorm of autumn, usually sometime in October. Winter visitors can come in on snowmobiles (unplowed roads only), skis, or snowshoes from Brian Head (two miles north of the monument) or from Highway 14 (2.5 miles south). Cedar Breaks National Monument is 24 miles east of Cedar City, 17 miles south of Parowan, 30 miles southwest of Panguitch, and 27 miles northwest of Long Valley Junction. Nearest accommodations and restaurants are two miles north in Brian Head.

Visitors Center and Campground

A log cabin contains exhibits and an information desk. The exhibits provide a good introduction to the Markagunt Plateau and identify local rocks, wildflowers, trees, animals, and birds. Related books, topo and forest maps, posters, slides, and film are sold. The staff offers nature walks, geology talks, and campfire programs; see the schedules posted in the visitors center and at the campground. Open daily 8 A.M.–6 P.M. about June–mid-October. A $3 per-vehicle entrance fee is collected near the visitors center; there's no charge if you're just driving through the monument without stopping. The small campground to the east has water and a $12 fee; camping is first-come, first-served. The campground is open about June–mid-September. There's a picnic area near the campground. Contact the monument at 2390 W. Hwy. 56, Ste. 11, Cedar City, UT 84720-4151, 435/586-9451, www.nps.gov/cebr.

Hiking Trails

Two easy trails near the rim give an added appreciation of the geology and forests here. Allow extra time while on foot—it's easy to get out of breath at these high elevations! Regulations prohibit pets on the trails. **Spectra Point/Wasatch**

Rampart Trail begins at the visitors center, then follows the rim along the south edge of the amphitheater to an overlook. The hike is four miles round-trip with some ups and downs. Weather-beaten bristlecone pines grow at Spectra Point, about halfway down the trail.

Alpine Pond Trail forms a two-mile loop that drops below the rim into one of the few densely wooded areas of the amphitheater. The trail winds through enchanting forests of aspen, subalpine fir, and Engelmann spruce. You can cut the hiking distance in half with a car shuttle between the two trailheads or by taking a connector trail that joins the upper and lower parts of the loop near Alpine Pond. Begin from either Chessmen Ridge Overlook or the trailhead pullout 1.1 miles farther north. A trail guide is available at the start or at the visitors center.

ASHDOWN GORGE WILDERNESS

Experienced hikers can explore this wilderness in the Dixie National Forest and enter Cedar Break National Monument's lower valleys. Although no trails within the monument itself wind from the rim down to the bottom, you can take **Rattlesnake Creek Trail** from a trailhead on the rim just outside the monument's north boundary. The rugged trail drops 3,400 feet in nine miles, following Rattlesnake and Ashdown Creeks to the lower trailhead on Highway 14 about seven miles east of Cedar City. Upon reaching Ashdown Creek, you have a choice of heading several miles upstream into the monument or entering the depths of Ashdown Gorge downstream. Check the weather forecast beforehand to avoid getting caught in a flash flood within the gorge. Hikers must be good at map reading and keeping an eye out for the next cairn or tree blaze. Rattlesnake and Ashdown Creeks usually have water, though it can be silty or polluted by livestock. You may have to do some wading in the gorge. Topo map is the 7.5-minute Flanigan Arch or 15-minute Cedar Breaks. Check with staff at Cedar Breaks National Monument or Cedar City Ranger District for current trail conditions.

South-Central Utah

The south-central region of Utah is dominated by three vast tracts of public land, the Grand Staircase–Escalante National Monument (GSENM), Capitol Reef National Park, and the Glen Canyon National Recreation Area, at the heart of which lies Lake Powell. While these public lands are not as famous as the brand-name national parks of southern Utah, they have much to offer travelers—particularly those people who love backcountry and solitude.

GSENM extends across 1.9 million acres of Utah public lands managed by the Bureau of Land Management and represents a unique combination of archaeological, historical, paleontological, geological, and biological wonders. Capitol Reef National Park is for the connoisseur of Utah backcountry—it's not the first park you may plan to visit, but it's the one that you will focus on as you hone your enthusiasm for the desert outback. Glen Canyon National Recreation Area encompasses the rugged canyons leading to the Colorado River's Glen Canyon, which was once considered the equal of the Grand Canyon for drama and beauty. The canyon now slumbers beneath the waters of Lake Powell, a magnet for boating and water sports.

© JUDY JEWELL

Red rock pillars are a hallmark of Kodachrome Basin State Park.

SOUTH-CENTRAL UTAH

To Salt Lake City

To Green River

70

89

62

24

Thousand Lake Mountain ▲

Capitol Reef National Park

Fremont

Bicknell

River

Torrey

Teasdale

Grover

15

12

To Las Vegas, NV

Boulder Mountain ▲

Aquarius Plateau

Boulder

BURR TRAIL

Waterpocket

0   10 mi

0   10 km

Panguitch

Box-Death Hollow Wilderness

Escalante Petrified Forest State Park ▲

Escalante

★ CALF CREEK RECREATION AREA

Circle Cliffs

12

Table Cliff Plateau

MOON

Harris Wash

HOLE-IN-THE-ROCK

Escalante

Bryce Canyon National Park

Tropic

Henrieville

Kodachrome Basin State Park ▲

Kaiparowits Plateau

Straight Cliffs

ROAD

Coyote Gulch

Paunsaugunt Plateau

SKUTUMPAH RD.

Paria River

COTTONWOOD CYN. RD.

MOST REMOTE SPOT IN CONTINENTAL U.S. ★

DANCE HALL ROCK ★

Pink Cliffs

89

JOHNSON CANYON

White Cliffs

Vermilion Cliffs

Buckskin Mountain

The Cockscomb

PARIA MOVIE SET/ OLD PAHREAH ▲

Grand Staircase–Escalante National Monument

Lake Powell

To Zion National Park and Las Vegas, NV

Kanab

89

PARIA CANYON RANGER STATION ▲

Big Water

Fredonia

89A

To Grand Canyon National Park (North Rim)

Vermilion Cliffs National Monument

Paria Canyons

WAHWEAP MARINA

To Page, AZ

SOUTH-CENTRAL UTAH HIGHLIGHTS

Highway 12 from Tropic to Torrey

Calf Creek Recreation Area

Hiking the Escalante River canyons

The Boulder Mountain Lodge

Burr Trail

Hiking and photographing Coyote Gulch

Picking apples at Fruita

Hiking the Grand Gulch in Capitol Reef National Park

Dinner at the Café Diablo in Torrey

Houseboating on Lake Powell

Just about the only human aggregation in this vast swathe of wilderness is the town of Escalante. Just 10 years ago, Escalante was just a country village that served the needs of local ranchers and the occasional hardened German hiker who disappeared off on foot to explore the canyons of the Escalante River. Today, with the sudden celebrity of the GSENM, Escalante has become a center for New Age eco-tourism and adventure sports—can the roar of bus coach tourism be far behind?

For the moment Escalante is still a pleasant little town, and to reach the wild and picturesque landscapes of the GSENM, Capitol Reef, and Glen Canyon still requires hiking boots, a high-clearance vehicle, or a boat—and a little time.

However, even casual travelers can enjoy traveling through this fantastic landscape of desert and rock. Highway 12, which begins near Bryce Canyon National Park and continues along the wild canyon and slickrock country of the Grand Staircase–Escalante National Monument, is one of the most scenic roads in Utah.

Grand Staircase–Escalante National Monument

This new national monument contains a vast and wonderfully scenic collection of slickrock canyonlands and desert, prehistoric village sites, Old West ranch land and arid plateaus, and miles of back roads linking stone arches, mesas, and abstract rock formations. The monument even preserves a historic movie set! (Think vintage Westerns.)

The 1.9-million-acre Grand Staircase–Escalante National Monument (GSENM) contains essentially three separate districts: On the eastern third are the narrow wilderness canyons of the Escalante River and its tributaries. In the center of the monument is a vast swath of arid rangeland and canyons called the Kaiparowits Plateau, with few developed destinations—before use of all-terrain vehicles (ATVs), dune buggies, and power dirt bikes was limited, these canyons and bluffs were a popular playground for off-road enthusiasts. The western third of the monument edges up against the Grey, White, and Pink Cliffs of the Grand Staircase. These thinly treed uplands are laced with former Forest Service roads. The GSENM is the largest land grouping designated as a national monument in the lower 48 states.

There's little dispute that the **Escalante canyons** are the primary reason people visit the monument. The river and its tributaries cut deep, winding slot canyons through massive slickrock formations, and hiking these canyon bottoms is an extremely popular adventure. This multiday trek is a right of passage for many devoted hikers, but you don't have to be a hardened backcountry trekker to enjoy this landscape: Two backcountry roads wind through the area, and some day hikes are possible.

The other districts offer less well-defined opportunities for adventure. Backcountry drivers and long-distance mountain bikers will find mile after mile of desert and canyon to explore. **Grosvenor Arch,** with double windows, is a popular back-road destination. At the southern edge of the park, along the Arizona border, is another rugged canyon system that's popular with long-distance hikers. The **Paria River**

Canyon is even more remote than the Escalante, and hiking these slot canyons requires experience and preparation.

After an unsteady start, the monument is beginning to feel like a single unit, and not just a cobbled-together assemblage of public land. The basic elements of internal infrastructure, such as consistent signage and helpful maps, are now in place, and with five visitors centers/ranger stations in operation, it now feels like its own entity. It's an evolving project, however, and be sure to inquire at the visitors center or the official website about conditions, restrictions, and new recreational opportunities before setting out.

The Land

This desert landscape once sat at the verge of a vast inland sea. About 300 million years ago, sandy dunes rose hundreds of feet above the waves, then sank below sea level and were covered by water. Thick layers of sediment built up one on top of the other, turning the sand dunes to stone. During the last 50 million years, powerful forces within the earth slowly pushed the entire region one mile upward. The ancestral Colorado River began to carve the deep gorges seen today near Glen Canyon. In turn, the tributaries of the Colorado, such as the Escalante, were also forced to trench deeper and deeper in order to drain their watershed.

The most characteristic rocks in the monument are the ancient dunes, turned to stone called slickrock, which make up many of the sheer canyon cliffs, arches, and spires of the region. Delicate cross-bedded lines of the former dunes add grace to these features. Forces within the restless plateau have also buckled and folded rock layers into great reefs as long as 100 miles. Weathering then carved them into rainbow-hued rock monuments. The aptly named Cockscomb, visible from Cottonwood Canyon Road, which cuts through the center of GSENM, is an example of these massive rock wrinkles.

Flora and Fauna

The dry conditions and thin or nonexistent soils limit both plant and wildlife in the Escalante region. Annual plants simply wait for a wet year before quickly flowering and spreading their seeds. Piñon pines, junipers, and other plants often adapt by growing in rock cracks that concentrate moisture and nutrients. Small mammals such as mice, wood rats, rock squirrels, and chipmunks find food and shelter in these outposts of vegetation. Even meager soils permit growth of hardy shrubs like blackbrush, greasewood, sagebrush, rabbitbrush, and Mormon tea. Prickly pear and other types of cacti do well in the desert, too.

Wildlife you might see in the semiarid desert are mule deer, desert bighorn sheep, pronghorns, coyotes, bobcats, foxes, skunks, porcupines, and many species of rodents. Ravens, eagles, hawks, owls, falcons, magpies, and smaller birds fly overhead. Watch out for the poisonous rattlesnakes and scorpions, although these shy creatures won't attack unless provoked.

History

Anasazi and Fremont people lived in the Escalante area from about A.D. 1050 to 1200. You can spot their petroglyphs, pictographs, artifacts,

© PAUL LEVY

Slot canyons abound in the Grand Staircase–Escalante National Monument.

SOUTH-CENTRAL UTAH

storage rooms, and village sites while you're hiking in the canyons of the Escalante River and its tributaries. High alcoves in canyon walls protect small stone granaries; check the floors of sandstone caves for things left behind—pieces of pottery, arrowheads, mats, sandals, and corncobs. (Federal laws prohibit removal of artifacts; please leave *everything* for the next person to enjoy.) You can visit an excavated Anasazi village, along with a modern replica of the original, 27 miles east in Boulder.

Southern Paiute arrived in the 1500s and stayed until white settlers took over. The nomadic Paiute had few possessions and left little behind despite their long stay. Mormon colonists didn't learn about the Escalante region until 1866, when Captain James Andrus led his cavalry east from Kanab in pursuit of Paiutes. Reports of the expedition described the upper Escalante, which was named Potato Valley after the wild tubers growing there.

Major John Wesley Powell's expedition down the Green and Colorado Rivers in 1869 had failed to recognize the mouth of the Escalante River; it seemed too shallow and narrow for a major tributary. In 1872, a detachment of Powell's second expedition led by Almon H. Thompson and Frederick S. Dellenbaugh stumbled across the Escalante on an overland journey. After some confusion they realized that an entire new river had been found, and they named it for Spanish explorer and priest Silvestre Valez de Escalante. The elusive river was the last to be discovered in the contiguous United States. Mormon ranchers and farmers arrived in the upper valleys of the Escalante in 1876 from Panguitch and other towns to the west, not as part of a church-directed mission but simply in search of new and better lands.

The sleepy town of Escalante served the needs of local farmers and ranchers for nearly a century, until 1996 when President Bill Clinton created the Grand Staircase–Escalante National Monument out of existing state and federal lands. The resulting political flap, and hardening local sentiments against outsiders and environmentalists, have not eased the creation of an ecotourism Eden in this desert backcountry.

GRAND STAIRCASE– ESCALANTE NATIONAL MONUMENT

To Torrey

Capitol Reef National Park

Boulder Mountain

Dixie

National   Forest

Anasazi State Park

Box-Death Hollow Wilderness Area

Boulder

BURR TRAIL

NOTOM-BULLFROG RD.

WOLVERINE LOOP TRAIL

THE GULCH

Escalante Petrified Forest State Park

DEER CREEK CAMPGROUND

CALF CREEK RECREATION AREA

ESCALANTE INTERAGENCY VISITOR CENTER

Escalante

ESCALANTE BRIDGE

LITTLE DEATH HOLLOW

Escalante   River

12

Tropic

CEDAR WASH RD.

HOLE-IN-THE-ROCK RD.

Escalante

HARRIS WASH

Glen Canyon

DEVILS GARDEN ★

EGYPT

National

Canyons

Recreation Area

Henrieville

Cannonville

Kodachrome Basin State Park

LEFT HAND COLLET RD.

EARLY WEED BENCH

DRY FORK

SHEEP CREEK

UPPER HACKBERRY CANYON

GROSVENOR ARCH

Straight Cliffs

Fiftymile Bench

RED WELL

WILLIS CREEK

Kaiparowits

CHIMNEY ROCK

Paria

COTTONWOOD CANYON RD.

FORTYMILE RIDGE TRAIL

River

The Cockscomb

Grand Staircase–Escalante

SMOKY MOUNTAIN RD.

HURRICANE WASH

DANCE HALL ROCK

HOLE-IN-THE-ROCK RD.

WILLOW GULCH

PARIA MOVIE SET/ OLD PAHREAH

LOWER HACKBERRY CANYON

Plateau

Burning Hills

HOLE-IN-THE-ROCK

Staircase

National   Monument

DANGLING ROPE MARINA

PARIA RANGER STATION

89

Bigwater

Lake Powell

★ Rainbow Bridge Nat'l Monument

WHITE HOUSE CAMPGROUND/ TRAILHEAD

BIG WATER VISITOR CENTER

WIRE PASS

Buckskin Gulch

UTAH

ARIZONA

WAHWEAP MARINA

GLEN CANYON DAM

NAVAJO INDIAN RESERVATION

Paria   Plateau

Page

98

LEES FERRY

89

To Tuba City, AZ and Flagstaff, AZ

SOUTH-CENTRAL UTAH

© AVALON TRAVEL PUBLISHING, INC.

Visitors Centers

The headquarters of the GSENM is in Kanab, quite distant from the heart—or even the boundaries—of the monument itself. This is the best office to contact by mail or phone before you set out: **GSENM Headquarters,** 318 North 100 East, Kanab, UT 84741, 435/644-4600, www .ut.blm/monument. The office is open daily 7:30 A.M.–5:30 P.M. March 15–November 15. In winter, the office is open Monday–Friday, 8 A.M.–4:30 P.M.

The regional visitors centers are good to stop by for information and advice before setting out. These include the following:

Escalante Interagency Visitors Center, 755 W. Main, Escalante, UT 84726, 435/826-5499, is open daily 7:30 A.M.–5:30 P.M.; winter hours are Monday–Friday 8 A.M.–4:30 P.M.

Cannonville Visitors Center, 10 Center St., Cannonville, UT 84718, 435/679-8981; open daily 8 A.M.–4:30 P.M. March 15–November 15.

Anasazi State Park, 460 N. Hwy. 12, Boulder, UT 84716, 435/335-7382, is open daily 9 A.M.–5 P.M.

Paria Contact Station, Hwy. 89, 44 miles east, Kanab, UT 84741, is open daily 8:30 A.M.–4:15 P.M. March 15–November 15.

Another visitors center opened in 2003 near Big Water, Utah, along U.S. 89 at the southern edge of the monument.

Monument Access

There is currently no entrance fee for visiting the monument. Free permits are required for all overnight backcountry camping or backpacking. There is a fee to camp in the monument's three developed campgrounds.

Hikers in the Paria Wilderness area are required to buy a permit (this includes Paria Canyon and Coyote Buttes), as are hikers at Calf Creek Recreation Area.

Only two paved roads pass through the monument, both in an east-west trajectory. Highway 12, on the northern border of the park, links Bryce Canyon and Capitol Reef National Parks with access to the Escalante canyons. This is one of the most scenic roads in Utah—in fact, *Car and Driver* magazine rates this route as one of

the 10 most scenic in all of the United States. Its innumerable swallow-your-gum vistas and geologic curiosities will keep you on the edge of your car seat.

U.S. 89, which travels along the southern edge of the monument between Kanab and Lake Powell, is not exactly a slouch when it comes to scenery either. It is also the access road for the North Rim of the Grand Canyon in Arizona. Three fair-weather dirt roads, each with a network of side roads and trails, cut through the rugged heart of the monument, linking the two paved roads. Before heading out on these back roads, check with a visitors center for conditions; high-clearance vehicles are recommended.

SIGHTS ALONG HIGHWAY 12

This tour proceeds west to east, from Bryce Canyon National Park and Tropic along the north edge of the monument to the towns of Escalante and Boulder. Stop at the **Cannonville Visitors Center,** 10 Center St., 435/679-8981, for information about back-road conditions and hikes in this part of the monument. Two back-country roads depart from Cannonville, leading to remote corners of the monument.

Johnson Canyon/Skutumpah Road

This route links Cannonville with U.S. 89 just east of Kanab (46 miles one-way). The unpaved portions of this road are usually in good condition, except after rains, when the bentonite soils that compose the roadbed turn to goo. In good weather, cars can usually make the journey. The road follows the Pink and White Cliff terraces of the Grand Staircase, with access to some excellent and comparatively undersubscribed-to hiking trails. Several steep slot canyons make for excellent canyoneering. At the junction of Glendale Bench Road, turn west to reach Glendale, farther north on U.S. 89. The lower 16 miles of Johnson Canyon Road are paved.

Cottonwood Canyon Scenic Back Road

This 46-mile route also connects Cannonville with U.S. 89 but passes through quite different

THE POLITICS OF ESTABLISHING THE NATIONAL MONUMENT

In September 1996, President Bill Clinton declared 1.9 million acres of south-central Utah a national monument, ending a decades-old debate about preserving the wilderness canyons in this part of the Southwest. The federal government's move sought to prevent the establishment of coal mines in the area, which had been planned by a Dutch resource-extraction consortium. The monument was formed by combining existing public land into a single administrative unit: The land now preserved as Grand Staircase–Escalante National Monument consists of land formerly supervised by the Bureau of Land Management (BLM), the Forest Service, and the state of Utah. The responsibility for administering the new monument was assigned to the BLM.

Preservation of the canyons as a national monument angered the Republican Utah legislative delegation and many others in this deeply conservative state. They were angry that they were not consulted about the formation of the monument, and they argued that the federal government should not interfere with local agriculture and the existing community. The move pleased environmentalists and backcountry recreationalists, however, who feared that the existence of a mining operation, no matter how environmentally sound, would destroy the area's unique scenic splendor and ancient Anasazi art and ruins.

Feelings pro and con about the monument can still run deep around Escalante and southern Utah, but a whole new breed of business is springing up to address the needs of the tourists and recreationalists who flock here. For people who have adapted to the changing economic and environmental forces, hostility to the monument and the crowds it attracts is subsiding.

The irony in all of this is that so far, in terms of land usage, very little has changed for either the farmers and ranchers who have leased these federal lands for generations or for the hikers and bikers who want to explore the wilds of this canyon country. The BLM has moved slowly to reassess access to the land and is trying to preserve the land's tradition as a multiuse area (with ranchers retaining grazing leases on federal land). Certain restrictions are in place, but these mostly affect the use of all-terrain vehicles (ATVs) and non-street-legal vehicles (off-road vehicles, dune buggies, and certain kinds of dirt bikes). Certain primitive roads will not receive regular maintenance. You will hear rumors aplenty about other restrictions being considered, but drastic changes do not seem imminent.

As has always been the case, the major considerations in planning a trip to this area remain the weather and the condition of the roads, not the anger of the locals or the machinations of the federal government.

terrain and landscapes. One of the most scenic backcountry routes in the monument, Cottonwood Canyon Road not only offers access to dramatic Grosvenor Arch, but it also passes along The Cockscomb, a soaring buckle of rock that divides the Grand Staircase and the Kaiparowits Plateau. Cottonwood Creek, which this road parallels, is a normally dry streambed that cuts through the angular rock beds of The Cockscomb. Several excellent hikes lead into the canyons and narrows, where the Paria River, Hackberry Canyon, and Cottonwood Creek all meet, about 20 miles south of Cannonville. Check at the Cannonville Visitors Center for information about road conditions. Although the road is sometimes passable for cars, several road crossings are subject to washouts after rainstorms, and the northern portion is impassable even to four-wheel-drives when wet because of the extremely unctuous nature of the roadbed. Check conditions before setting out if you plan to go beyond Grosvenor Arch.

SOUTH-CENTRAL UTAH

Kodachrome Basin State Park

Visitors come to this basin southeast of Bryce Canyon National Park to see not only colorful cliffs but also strange-looking rock pillars that occur nowhere else in the world. Sixty-seven rock pillars (here called "sand pipes") found in and near the park range in height from six to nearly 170 feet. One theory of their origin is that earthquakes caused sediments deep underground to be churned up by water under high pressure. The particles of calcite, quartz, feldspar, and clay in the sand pipes came from underlying rock formations, and the pipes appeared when the surrounding rock eroded away. Most of the other rocks visible in the park are Entrada sandstone: The lower orange layer is the Gunsight Butte Member, and the white layer with orange bands is the Cannonville Member.

Signs name some of the rock features. "Big Stoney," the phallus-shaped sand pipe overlooking the campground, is so explicit that it doesn't need a sign! An article, "Motoring into Escalante Land," by Jack Breed, in the September 1949 issue of *National Geographic,* brought attention to the scenery and renamed the area "Kodachrome Flat," for the then-experimental kind of Kodak film used by the expedition. The state park makes a worthwhile stop, both as a day trip to see the geology and as a pleasant spot to camp. A $5 per-vehicle day-use fee is charged. The park also offers several good half-day hiking trails.

To reach the park, drive to Cannonville and follow signs to Cottonwood Canyon Road for nine miles on paved roads. Adventurous drivers can also approach the park from U.S. 89 to the south via Cottonwood Canyon Road (35 miles) or Skutumpah Road through Bull Valley Gorge and Johnson Canyon (48 miles). These routes may be impassable in wet weather but may be okay for cars with good clearance in dry weather.

Scenic Safaris operates guided horseback and horse-drawn coach rides in the park. You can arrange rides at **Trailhead Station,** a small store in the park that sells groceries and camping supplies early April–late October, or contact P.O. Box 278, Cannonville, UT 84718, 435/679-8536 or 435/679-8787.

The state park's campground sits in a natural amphitheater at an elevation of 5,800 feet. It's open all year, has restrooms, showers, a dump station, and sites for $17. During the winter, restrooms and showers may close, but pit toilets are available. The campground usually has room except on summer holidays. For information or reservations, contact the park at P.O. Box 238, Cannonville, UT 84718, 435/679-8562 or 800/322-3770.

© JUDY JEWELL

Utah has excellent and varied state park campgrounds; Kodachrome Basin is one of the best.

Grosvenor Arch

Just one mile off the Cottonwood Canyon, a side road leads to the magnificent Grosvenor Arch. In fact, there are two arches here, jutting like flying buttresses out of a soaring cliff. The larger of the two openings is 99 feet across. The 1949 National Geographic Society Expedition named the double arch in honor of the society's president. The turnoff is 10 miles from the state park turnoff and 29 miles from U.S. 89. This is a good spot for a picnic.

Escalante Petrified Forest State Park

This pleasant park just northwest of Escalante offers camping, boating, fishing, picnicking, hiking, a visitors center with displays of petrified wood and dinosaur bones, and a chance to see petrified wood along trails. Rivers of 140 million years ago carried trees to the site of present-day Escalante and buried them in sand and gravel. Burial prevented decay as crystals of silicon dioxide gradually replaced the wood cells. Mineral impurities added a rainbow of colors to the trees as they turned to stone. Weathering has exposed this petrified wood and the water-worn pebbles and sand of the Morrison Formation. For a look at some colorful petrified wood, follow the **Petrified Forest Trail** from the campground up a hillside wooded with piñon pine and juniper. At the top of the 240-foot-high ridge, continue on a loop trail to the petrified wood; allow 45–60 minutes for the one-mile round-trip. **Rainbow Loop Trail** (three-quarters of a mile) branches off the Petrified Forest Trail to more areas of petrified wood.

The **campground** stays open all year, offering drinking water and showers but no hookups. The adjacent 139-acre Wide Hollow Reservoir offers fishing, boating, and bird-watching. Canoe rentals are $5 per hour or $20 per day. The park is 1.5 miles west of Escalante on Highway 12, then 0.7 mile north on a gravel road; $7 per vehicle for day use, $17 per vehicle to camp. Contact P.O. Box 350, Escalante, UT 84726, 435/826-4466 (ranger) or 800/322-3770 (reservations).

Escalante

The town of Escalante, 38 miles east of Bryce Canyon and 23 miles south of Boulder, has all services and is headquarters for explorations of the Escalante River canyons. The Escalante Interagency Office, 755 W. Main St., 435/826-5499, provides information on local hikes and road conditions. For more information on lodging and services, see the Escalante section.

Smoky Mountain Road

From Escalante, it's 78 miles south to Big Water, just shy of Lake Powell, along Smoky Mountain Road. This road is in rougher condition than other cross-monument roads. Be sure to check out conditions before setting out; four-wheel-drive vehicles are required. As this route passes across the Kaiparowits Plateau, the landscapes are bleak and arid. Then, the road drops precipitously down onto a bench where side roads lead through badlands to Lake Powell beaches. Big Water is 19 miles from Page, Arizona, and 57 miles from Kanab.

Hole-in-the-Rock Road

The building of this road by determined Mormons was one of the great epics in the colonization of the West. Church leaders organized the Hole-in-the-Rock Expedition to settle the wild lands around the San Juan River of southeastern Utah, believing that a Mormon presence would aid in ministering to the Native Americans there and prevent non-Mormons from moving in. In 1878, the Parowan Stake issued the first call for a colonizing mission to the San Juan, even before a site had been selected.

Preparations and surveys took place the following year as 236 men, women, and children received their calls. Food, seed, farming and building tools, 200 horses, and more than 1,000 head of cattle would be taken along. Planners ruled out lengthy routes through northern Arizona or eastern Utah in favor of a straight shot via Escalante that would cut the distance in half. The expedition set off in the autumn of 1879, convinced that they were part of a divine mission.

Yet hints of trouble to come filtered back from the group as they discovered the Colorado River crossing to be far more difficult than first believed. Lack of springs along the way added to their worries. From their start at Escalante, road builders progressed rapidly for the first 50 miles, then slowly over rugged slickrock for the final six miles to Hole-in-the-Rock. A 45-foot sheer drop below this narrow notch was followed by three-quarters of a mile of extremely steep slickrock to the Colorado River. The route looked impossible, but three crews of workers armed with picks and blasting powder worked simultaneously to widen the notch and to construct a precarious wagon road down to the river and up cliffs on the other side.

SOUTH-CENTRAL UTAH

The job took six weeks. Miraculously, all of the people, animals, and wagons made it down and were ferried across the Colorado River without a serious accident. Canyons and other obstacles continued to block the way as the weary group pressed on. Only after six months of exhausting travel did they stop at the present-day site of Bluff on the San Juan River.

Today, on a journey from Escalante, you can experience a bit of the same adventure the pioneers knew. Except for scattered signs of ranching, the land remains unchanged. If the road is dry, vehicles with good clearance can drive to within a short distance of Hole-in-the-Rock. The rough conditions encountered past Dance Hall Rock require more clearance than most cars allow. Bring sufficient gas, food, and water for the entire 126-mile round-trip from Escalante.

The turnoff from Highway 12 is five miles east of Escalante. In addition to rewarding you with scenic views, Hole-in-the-Rock Road passes many side drainages of the Escalante River to the east and some remote country of the Kaiparowits Plateau high above to the west. Staff members at the information center just west of Escalante can give current road conditions and suggest hikes.

Metate Arch and other rock sculptures decorate **Devil's Garden,** 12.5 miles down Hole-in-the-Rock Road. Turn west 0.3 mile at the sign to the parking area because you can't really see the "garden" from the road. Red- and cream-colored sandstone formations sit atop pedestals or tilt at crazy angles. Delicate bedding lines run through the rocks. There are no trails or markers—just wander about at your whim. The Bureau of Land Management (BLM) has provided picnic tables, grills, and outhouses for day use. No overnight camping is permitted at Devil's Garden.

Dance Hall Rock (38 miles down Hole-in-the-Rock Road) jumped to the fiddle music and lively steps of the expedition members in 1879. Its natural amphitheater has a relatively smooth floor and made a perfect gathering spot when the Hole-in-the-Rock group had to wait three weeks at nearby Fortymile Spring for road work to be completed ahead. Dance Hall Rock is an enjoyable place to explore and only a short walk from the parking area. Solution holes, left from water dissolving in the rock, pockmark the Entrada sandstone structure.

At road's end (57 miles from Highway 12), continue on foot across slickrock to the notch and views of the blue waters of Lake Powell below. Rockslides have made the descent impossible for vehicles, but hikers can scramble down to the lake and back in about one hour. The elevation change is 600 feet. The half-mile round-trip is strenuous. After a steep descent over boulders, look for steps of Uncle Ben's Dugway at the base of the notch. Below here the grade is gentler. Drill holes in the rock once held oak stakes against which logs, brush, and earth supported the outer wagon wheels. The inner wheels followed a narrow rut 4–6 inches deep. About two-thirds of the route down is now under water, although the most impressive road work can still be seen.

Calf Creek Recreation Area

This stunning canyon and park offers the most accessible glimpse of what the Escalante Canyon

The hike to Calf Creek Falls starts just off Highway 12 at the Calf Creek Campground.

country is all about. The trailhead to 126-foot **Calf Creek Falls** is here, and you should definitely make plans for the half-day hike, especially if you have no time for further exploration of this magical landscape. Otherwise, stop here to picnic in the shade of willows and cottonwoods. This is also the most convenient and attractive **campsite** for dozens of miles. The 13 campsites have water, fire pits, and picnic tables.

The Million-Dollar Road

Highway 12 between Escalante and Boulder was completed in 1935 by workers in the Civilian Conservation Corps. The cost was a budget-busting $1 million. Before then, mules carried supplies and mail across this wilderness of slickrock and narrow canyons. The section of Highway 12 between Calf Creek and Boulder is extraordinarily scenic—even jaded travelers used to the wonders of Utah will have to pull over and ogle the views from the **Hog's Back,** where the road crests a fin of rock above the canyons of the Escalante. Be here for sunset on a clear evening and you'll have a memory to carry for the rest of your life.

Boulder

Boulder is a tiny community in a lovely location at the base of Boulder Mountain, where the alpine air mixes with the desert breezes. The single best lodging choice in the Escalante region—the Boulder Mountain Lodge—is here, so plan accordingly. See the Boulder section for more information.

Anasazi State Park

Museum exhibits, an excavated village site, and a pueblo replica provide a look into the life of these ancient people. The Anasazi stayed here for 50–75 years some time between A.D. 1050 and 1200. They grew corn, beans, and squash in fields nearby. Village population peaked at about 200, with an estimated 40–50 dwellings. Why the Anasazi left or where they went isn't known for sure, but a fire swept through much of the village before the Anasazi abandoned it. Perhaps they burned the village on purpose, knowing they would move on. University of Utah students and

faculty excavated the village, known as the Coombs Site, in 1958 and 1959. You can view pottery, axe heads, arrow points, and other tools found at the site in the museum, along with more perishable items like sandals and basketry that came from more protected sites elsewhere. A diorama shows how the village might have appeared in its heyday. You can see video programs on the Anasazi and modern tribes upon request.

The self-guided tour of the ruins begins behind the museum, which is on Highway 12, 28 miles northeast of Escalante and 38 miles south of Torrey, 435/335-7308. You'll see a whole range of Anasazi building styles—a pit house, masonry walls, *jacal* walls (mud reinforced by sticks), and combinations of masonry and *jacal.* Replicas of habitation and storage rooms behind the museum show complete construction details. The park is open daily 8 A.M.–6 P.M. mid-May–mid-September, 9 A.M.–5 P.M. the rest of the year. Admission is $3 per person, or $6 per vehicle (whichever is the least). Books, videos, T-shirts, and postcards are sold.

Burr Trail Road

The Burr Trail Road, originally a cattle trail blazed by stockman John Atlantic Burr, extends from the town of Boulder on Highway 12 to the Notom-Bullfrog Road, which runs between Highway 24 near the eastern entrance to Capitol Reef National Park and Bullfrog Marina on Lake Powell, off Highway 276. Starting at Boulder, roughly the first third of this scenic 36-mile road is now paved. Pavement ends at the boundary of Capitol Reef National Park, where the route traverses the Circle Cliffs, as well as spectacular canyon areas such as Long Canyon and The Gulch. As the route meets the Waterpocket Fold, in Capitol Reef National Park, a breathtaking set of switchbacks rise some 800 feet in only one-half mile. These switchbacks are not considered suitable for RVs or vehicles towing trailers. The unpaved sections of the road are subject to changes caused by weather conditions. Visitors should inquire about road and weather conditions before setting out. Also inquire about hiking trails down into the Escalante canyons that depart from side roads to the Burr Trail.

The Burr Trail Road joins the Notom-Bullfrog Road just before exiting Capitol Reef park. For information on Notom-Bullfrog Road, see the Capitol Reef section.

SIGHTS ALONG U.S. 89

This tour proceeds from Kanab to the Utah-Arizona border. From Kanab to Page, Arizona, at the Colorado River's Glen Canyon Dam, is 80 miles. For information on Kanab, see the Southwestern Utah chapter.

Johnson Canyon Road

Eight miles east of Kanab, Johnson Canyon Road heads north along the western border of the monument before joining Skutumpah Road and Glendale Bench Road. This road system links up with several more remote backcountry roads in the monument and eventually leads to Cannonville along Highway 12. From U.S. 89, Johnson Canyon Road is paved for its initial miles. The road passes an abandoned movie set where the TV series *Gunsmoke* was sometimes filmed. These old sets are on BLM land and can usually be visited on foot. The road then climbs up through the Vermilion Cliffs and then the White Cliffs of the Grand Staircase. This portion of the route is quite scenic. The road then passes over Skutumpah Terrace, a rather featureless plateau covered with scrub. The northerly portions of this route near Highway 12 are described in the Sights Along Highway 12 section.

Pariah Townsite Road

This road has several names, including Paria Valley Road. It turns north off U.S. 89 at milepost 31. This five-mile-long dirt road is passable to cars when dry. It passes some towering and colorful canyons and mesas, among which the remains of a **1930s Western movie set** are slowly decaying. From the parking area, walking trails lead out to the abandoned bleached wood buildings, which make for great photo opportunities against the rugged backdrop. Farther along the road, as it approaches the Paria River, are the remains of the actual ghost town of Pareah, although there's not much left to see.

Paria Canyon and Vermilion Cliffs National Monument

The Paria Canyon—a set of magnificent slot canyons that drain from Utah down through northern Arizona to the Grand Canyon—is the focus of popular multiday canyoneering expeditions. The Paria Canyon and 293,000 acres of surrounding desert grasslands are now protected as the Vermilion Cliffs National Monument. Although the monument spreads south from the Utah-Arizona border, access to the monument's most famous sites is through back roads in Utah. In addition to the long Paria Canyon backpacking route, some shorter but strenuous day hikes explore this area; see the section Hikes in Paria Canyon/Vermilion Cliffs. For more information, contact the Kanab monument headquarters or stop at Paria Contact Station, near milepost 21 on U.S. 89.

Cottonwood Canyon Road

A few miles east of the ranger station, Cottonwood Canyon Road leads north. The unpaved road's lower portions, usually passable with cars in dry weather, pass through scenic landscapes as the road pushes north. The route climbs up across a barren plateau before dropping down onto the Paria River. Several good hikes lead off from roadside trailheads into steep side canyons. The route continues north along The Cockscomb, a long wrinkle of rock ridges that run north and south across the desert. At the northern end of this route are Grosvenor Arch, Kodachrome State Park, and Highway 12 (46 miles).

Smoky Mountain Road

At the little crossroads of **Big Water,** the GSENM is building a new visitors center to serve the needs of travelers to the monument and to Glen Canyon National Recreation Area (NRA), which is immediately adjacent to this area. The center is supposed to open in 2003. Joining Highway 89 at Big Water is Smoky Mountain Road. This long and rugged road links Big Water to Highway 12 at Escalante, 78 miles north. The southern portions of the route pass through Glen Canyon NRA, and side roads lead to remote beaches and flooded canyons. The original *Planet of the Apes* film was shot here, before this area was inundated by Lake Powell.

From Big Water, it's 19 miles to Page, Arizona, on U.S. 89.

HIKING

The monument preserves some of the best long-distance hiking trails in the American Southwest. Since the monument was established and the consequent increase in tourism, shorter day hikes have also been developed to serve travelers who want to sample the wonderful slot canyons and backcountry of this vast desert landscape without venturing too far afield.

Be sure to check at local visitors centers for road and trail conditions, and to get up-to-date maps. Many of the following hikes require extensive travel on backcountry roads, which can be impassable after rains and rough the rest of the time. In summer, these trails are hot and exposed: Always carry plenty of water and sunscreen and wear a hat.

Hiking the **Escalante River Canyon** is recognized worldwide as one of the great wilderness treks. Most people devote 4–6 days to exploring these slickrock canyons, which involve frequent scrambling (if not rock climbing), stream fording (if not swimming), and exhausting detours around rockfalls and logjams. Some day hikes are possible along the Escalante River drainage. Hikers without a week to spare can sample the landscape along the Dry Fork Coyote Gulch trail, which links two fascinating and beautifully constricted slot canyons.

Paria Canyon is another famed long-distance slickrock canyon hike that covers 37 miles between the border of Utah and the edge of the Colorado River's Marble Canyon. Several long day hikes leave from trailheads on the Paria Plateau, along the border with Arizona.

Other areas with developed hiking trails include the Skutumpah Road area and Cottonwood Canyon, in the center of the park. Otherwise, hiking in the monument is mostly on unmarked routes. Although the park is developing more day-hiking options, the rangers also encourage hardy adventurers to consider extended hikes across the rugged and primitive outback, beyond the busy canyon corridors. Call one of the visitors centers and ask for help from the rangers to plan a hiking adventure where there are no trails.

HIKES ALONG JOHNSON CANYON ROAD/ SKUTUMPAH ROAD

The northern portions of this road pass through the White Cliffs area of the Grand Staircase, and several steep and narrow canyons are trenched into these terraces. Rough hiking trails explore these slot canyons. The **Willis Creek Narrows** trailhead is nine miles south of Cannonville along Skutumpah Road. The relatively easy trail follows a small stream as it etches a deep and narrow gorge through the Navajo sandstone. From the parking area, where Skutumpah Road crosses Willis Wash, walk downstream along the wash. Follow the streambed, which quickly descends between slickrock walls. The canyon is at times no more than 6–10 feet across, while the walls rise up 200–300 feet. The trail follows the (usually dry) streambed through the canyon for nearly 2.5 miles. To return, backtrack up the canyon.

Approximately 1.5 miles farther south on Skutumpah Road, a narrow bridge vaults over **Bull Valley Gorge.** Like the Willis Creek Narrows, this is a steep and narrow cleft in the slickrock; however, scrambling along the canyon bottom is a greater challenge, part of the reward for which is viewing a wrecked automobile wedged between the canyon walls. From the bridge, walk upstream along a faint trail on the north side of the crevice until the walls are low enough to scramble down. From here, the canyon deepens quickly, and you'll have to negotiate several dry falls along the way (a rope will come in handy). When you reach the area below the bridge, look up to see a 1950s-model pickup truck trapped between the canyon walls. Three men died in this 1954 mishap; their bodies were recovered, but the pickup was left in place. The canyon continues another mile from this point; there is no loop trail out of the canyon, so turn back when you've seen enough.

SOUTH-CENTRAL UTAH

Twenty miles south of Cannonville, Skutumpah Road crosses **Lick Wash,** from which trails lead downstream into slot canyons to a remote *arroyo* (dry river bed) surrounded by rock-topped mesas. One of these lofty perches contains a preserve of now-rare native grasses. Although this area can be reached from a day hike, this is also a good place to base a multiday camping trip. The trail starts just below the road crossing on Lick Wash and follows the usually dry streambed as it plunges down into a narrow slot canyon. The canyon bottom is mostly level and easy to hike. After one mile, the canyon begins to widen, and after four miles Lick Wash joins Park Wash, a larger desert canyon.

Looming above this canyon junction are mesas topped with deep sandstone terraces that are part of the White Cliffs of the Grand Staircase. Rising to the east is **No Mans Mesa,** skirted on all sides by steep-sided cliffs. The 1,788 acres atop the mesa were grazed by goats for six months in the 1920s, but before or since then has never been grazed by herbivores. This pristine grassland is protected by the BLM as an Area of Critical Environmental Concern. Hardy hikers can scramble up a steep trail—used by the aforementioned goats—to visit this wilderness preserve. The ascent of No Mans Mesa is best considered an overnight trip from the Lick Wash trailhead.

HIKES ALONG COTTONWOOD CANYON ROAD

The northerly portions of this route pass by **Kodachrome Basin State Park,** with a fine selection of hiking trails through colorful rock formations. The short **Nature Trail** introduces the park's ecology. The **Panorama Trail** loops through a highly scenic valley with sand pipes and colorful rocks; the easy trail is three miles round-trip and takes about two hours. **Angel's Palace Trail** begins just east of the group campground and makes a three-quarter-mile loop with fine views; the elevation gain is about 300 feet. The **Grand Parade Trail** makes a 1.5-mile loop with good views of rock pinnacles; begin from the concession stand or group campground. **Eagles View Trail,** a historic cattle trail,

climbs nearly 1,000 feet up steep cliffs above the campground, then drops into Henrieville, two miles away; the highest overlook is a steep half-mile ascent from the campground. **Arch Trail** is a half-mile round-trip hike to a natural arch; access the trailhead by a signed dirt road or a two-mile (round-trip) trail; a brochure and numbered stops identify local plants.

Continue south on Cottonwood Canyon Road for 7.5 miles from the state park to the crossing of Round Valley Draw. From here, turn south on BLM Rd. 422 toward **Hackberry Canyon.** Hikers can travel the 22-mile length of this scenic canyon in three days or make day hikes from either end of the trail. The lower canyon meets Cottonwood Canyon at an elevation of 4,700 feet just above the mouth of the Paria River. Cottonwood Canyon Road provides access to both ends. A small spring-fed stream flows down the lower half of Hackberry. Many side canyons invite exploration. One of them, Sam Pollock Canyon, is on the west about 4.5 miles upstream from the junction of Hackberry and Cottonwood Canyons; follow it 1.75 miles up to **Sam Pollock Arch** (60 feet high and 70 feet wide). Available topographic maps include the metric 1:100,000 Smoky Mountain or the 7.5-minute Slickrock Bench and Calico Peak. Michael Kelsey's *Hiking and Exploring the Paria River* contains trail and trailhead information and a history of the Watson homestead, located a short way below Sam Pollock Canyon.

The confluence of the Paria, Hackberry, and Cottonwood Canyons provide the backdrop to an excellent, although strenuous, day hike. The **Box of the Paria River** involves some steep climbs up rocky slopes as it traverses a tongue of slickrock between the mouth of the Hackberry and Paria Canyons. The route then follows the Paria River through its "box" or cliff-sided canyon in The Cockscomb formation. The trail returns to the trailhead by following Cottonwood Canyon upstream to the trailhead. The round-trip hike is about seven miles long. Inquire at visitors centers for maps and about conditions.

Although not as well known as the lower canyon, the **upper Paria River Canyon** has some beautiful scenery and offers many side canyons to explore, too. The Paria lies west of both Hackberry and Cottonwood Canyons. Access to the upper end is from the Skutumpah or Cottonwood Canyon Road near Kodachrome Basin State Park (elev. about 5,900 feet). The usual lower entry is from near Pahreah ghost town (elev. 4,720 feet); turn north six miles from U.S. 89 between mileposts 30 and 31 and continue past the Pahreah movie set to road's end. (The clay road surface is very slippery when wet but is okay for cars when dry.) The upper canyon is about 25 miles long, and the hike takes 3–4 days (allowing some time to explore side canyons). You can find water at springs along the main canyon and in many side canyons (purify first); try not to use water from the river itself as it may contain chemical pollution. Topo maps are the metric 1:100,000 Kanab and Smoky Mountain or the 7.5-minute Cannonville, Bull Valley Gorge, Deer Range Point, and Calico Peak. Again, Michael Kelsey's *Hiking and Exploring the Paria River* is a good source of history and hiking information for this area.

HIKES ALONG THE ESCALANTE RIVER

The maze of canyons that drain the Escalante River presents exceptional hiking opportunities. You'll find everything from easy day hikes to challenging backpacking treks. The Escalante's canyon begins just downstream from the town of Escalante and ends at Lake Powell about 85 miles beyond. In all this distance, only one road (Highway 12) bridges the river. Many side canyons provide additional access to the Escalante, and most are as beautiful as the main gorge. The river system covers such a large area that you can find solitude even in spring, the busiest hiking season. The many eastern canyons remain virtually untouched.

> *The maze of canyons that drain the Escalante River presents exceptional hiking opportunities. You'll find everything from easy day hikes to challenging backpacking treks. The river system covers such a large area that you can find solitude even in spring, the busiest hiking season.*

The Escalante canyons preserve some of the quiet beauty once found in Glen Canyon, which is now lost under the waters of Lake Powell. Prehistoric Anasazi and Fremont cultures have left ruins, petroglyphs, pictographs, and artifacts in many locations. These archaeological resources are protected by federal law. *Please don't collect or disturb them.*

Before setting out, visit the rangers at the information center on the west edge of Escalante for the required free permit to backpack overnight in the GSENM, and to check on the latest trail and road conditions before setting out. Restrictions on group size may be in force on some of the more popular trails. You can also obtain topographic maps and literature that show trailheads, mileages, and other information that may be useful in planning trips. Some of the more popular trailheads have self-registration stations for permits.

The best times for a visit are early March–early June and mid-September–early November. Summertime trips are possible, too, but be prepared for higher temperatures and greater flash-flood danger in narrow canyons. Travel along the Escalante River involves frequent crossings, and there's always water in the main canyon, usually ankle- to knee-deep. Pools in the "Narrows" section between Scorpion Gulch and Stevens Canyon can be up to chest-deep in spots (which you can bypass), but that's the exception. All this wading can destroy leather boots, so it's best to wear canvas shoes or boots. High-topped boots, available at surplus stores, work well and prevent gravel from getting inside. Occasional springs, some tributaries, and the river itself provide drinking water. Always purify it first; the BLM warns of the unpleasant disease giardiasis, which is caused by an invisible protozoan. Don't forget insect repellent—mosquitos and deer flies seek out hikers in late spring and summer. Long-sleeved shirts and long pants also discourage biting insects and protect against the brush.

Escalante Canyon Trailheads

The many approaches to the area allow all sorts of trips. Besides the road access at Escalante and the Highway 12 bridge, hikers can reach the Escalante River through western side canyons from Hole-in-the-Rock Road or eastern side canyons from Burr Trail Road. The western-canyon trailheads on Hole-in-the-Rock Road can be more easily reached by car, thus facilitating vehicle shuttles. To reach eastern-canyon trailheads, with the exceptions of Deer Creek and the Gulch on Burr Trail Road, you'll need lots of time and, if the road is wet, a four-wheel-drive vehicle. Carry water for these more remote canyons; with the exception of Deer Creek, they're usually dry.

Town of Escalante to Highway 12 Bridge (15 miles)

This first section of canyon offers easy walking and stunning canyon scenery. Tributaries and sandstone caves invite exploration. You'll find good camping areas all along. Usually the river here is only ankle deep. Either enter Escalante River at the bridge next to the sawmill, or go one mile east of town on Highway 12 and turn north past the cemetery (visible from highway) and town dump. Almost immediately, the river knifes its way through the massive cliffs of the Escalante Monocline, leaving the broad valley of the upper river behind. Although there is no maintained trail along this stretch of the east-flowing river, it's relatively easy to pick your way along the river bank.

Death Hollow, which is far prettier than the name suggests, comes in to the Escalante from the north after 7.5 miles. Several good swimming holes carved in rock lie a short hike upstream from the Escalante; watch for poison ivy among the greenery. Continue farther up Death Hollow to see more pools, little waterfalls, and outstanding canyon scenery. You can bypass some pools, but some you'll need to swim—bring a little inflatable boat, air mattress, or waterproof bag to ferry packs.

Sand Creek, on the Escalante's north side 4.5 miles downstream from Death Hollow, is also worth exploring; deep pools begin a short way up from the mouth. After another one-half mile down the Escalante, a natural arch appears high on the canyon wall. Then the Escalante Natural Bridge comes into view about one-half mile farther, just two miles from the Highway 12 bridge. In fact, Escalante Natural Bridge makes a good day-hike destination upstream from the highway.

Highway 12 Bridge to Harris Wash (26.5 miles)

This is where many long-distance trekkers begin their exploration of the Escalante canyons. In this section, the Escalante Canyon offers a varied show: In places the walls close in to make constricted narrows, at other places they step back to form great valleys. Side canyons filled with lush greenery and sparkling streams contrast with dry washes of desert, yet all can be fun to explore. A good hike of 4–6 days begins at the highway bridge, goes down the Escalante to Harris Wash, then up Harris to a trailhead off Hole-in-the-Rock Road (37 miles total).

From the Highway 12 bridge parking area, a trail leads to the river. Canyon access goes through private property; cross the river at the posted signs to avoid barking dogs at the ranch just downstream. **Phipps Wash** comes in from the south (right side) after 1.5 miles and several more river crossings. Turn up its wide mouth one-half mile to see Maverick Bridge in a drainage to the right. To reach Phipps Arch, continue another three-quarters of a mile up the main wash, turn left into a box canyon, and scramble up the left side (see the 7.5-minute Calf Creek topo map).

Bowington (Boynton) Arch is an attraction of a north side canyon known locally as Deer Creek. Look for this small canyon on the left one mile beyond Phipps Wash; turn up it one mile past three deep pools and then turn left a short way into a tributary canyon. In 1878, gunfire resolved a quarrel between local ranchers John Boynton and Washington Phipps. Phipps was killed, but both their names live on.

Waters of **Boulder Creek** come rushing into the Escalante from the north in the next major side canyon, 5.75 miles below the Highway 12 bridge. The creek, along with its Dry Hollow and Deer Creek tributaries, provides good canyon walking; deep areas may require swimming or climbing up on the plateau. (You could also start down Deer Creek from Burr Trail Road where they meet, 6.5 miles southeast of Boulder at a primitive BLM campground; starting at the campground, follow Deer Creek 7.5 miles to Boulder Creek, then 3.5 miles down Boulder to the Escalante.) Deer and Boulder Creeks have water year-round.

High, sheer walls of Navajo sandstone constrict the Escalante River in a narrow channel below Boulder Creek, but the canyon widens again above **The Gulch** tributary, 14 miles below the highway bridge. Hikers can head up The Gulch on a day hike.

Alternately, descend The Gulch from Burr Trail Road to join the Escalante Canyon at this point (The Gulch trailhead is 10.8 miles southeast of Boulder). The hike from the road down to the Escalante is 12.5 miles, but there's one difficult spot: A 12-foot waterfall in a section of narrows about halfway down has to be bypassed. When Rudi Lambrechtse, author of *Hiking the Escalante*, tried friction climbing around the falls and the pool at their base, he fell 12 feet and broke his foot. That meant a painful three-day hobble out. Instead of taking the risk, Rudi recommends backtracking about 300 feet from the falls and friction climbing out from a small alcove in the west wall (look for a cairn on the ledge above). Climb up Brigham Tea Bench, walk south, then look for cairns leading back east to the narrows, and descend to the streambed (a rope helps to lower packs in a small chimney section).

Most springs along the Escalante are difficult to spot. One that's easy to find is in the first south bend after the Gulch; water comes straight out of the rock a few feet above the river. The Escalante Canyon becomes wider as the river lazily meanders along. Hikers can cut off some of the bends by walking in the open desert between canyon walls and riverside willow thickets. A bend cut off by the river itself loops to the north just before Horse Canyon, three miles below the Gulch. Along with its tributaries **Death Hollow** and **Wolverine Creek**, **Horse Canyon** drains the Circle Cliffs to the northeast. Floods in these mostly dry streambeds wash down pieces of black petrified wood. (Vehicles with good clearance can reach the upper sections of all three canyons from a loop road off Burr Trail Road.) Horse and Wolverine Creek Canyons offer good easy-to-moderate hiking, but if you really want a challenge, try Death Hollow (sometimes called "Little Death Hollow" to distinguish it from the larger one near Hell's Backbone Road). Starting from the Escalante River, go about two miles up Horse Canyon and turn right into Death Hollow; rugged scrambling over boulders takes you back into a long section of twisting narrows. Carry water for Upper Horse Canyon and its tributaries; Lower Horse Canyon usually has water.

About 3.5 miles down the Escalante from Horse Canyon, you enter Glen Canyon NRA and come to Sheffield Bend, a large, grassy field on the right. Only a chimney remains from Sam Sheffield's old homestead. Two grand amphitheaters lie beyond the clearing and up a stiff climb in loose sand. Over the next 5.5 river miles to Silver Falls Creek, you'll pass long bends, dry side canyons, and a huge slope of sand on the right canyon wall. Don't look for any silver waterfalls in **Silver Falls Creek**—the name comes from streaks of shiny desert varnish on the cliffs. You can approach Upper Silver Falls Creek by a rough road from Burr Trail Road, but a car shuttle between here and any of the trailheads on the west side of the Escalante River would take all day. Most hikers visit this drainage on a day hike from the river. Carry water with you.

When the Hole-in-the-Rock route proved so difficult, pioneers figured there had to be a better way to the San Juan Mission. Their new wagon road descended Harris Wash to the Escalante River, climbed part of Silver Falls Creek, crossed the Circle Cliffs, descended Muley Twist Canyon in the Waterpocket Fold, then followed Hall's Creek to Hall's Crossing on the Colorado River. Charles Hall operated a ferry there 1881–1884.

Old maps show a jeep road through Harris Wash and Silver Falls Creek Canyons, used before the National Park Service closed off the Glen Canyon NRA section. Harris Wash lies just one-half mile downstream and across the Escalante from Silver Falls Creek.

Harris Wash (10.25 miles one-way from trailhead to river)

Clear, shallow water glides down this gem of a canyon. High cliffs streaked with desert varnish are deeply undercut and support lush hanging gardens. Harris Wash provides a beautiful route to the Escalante River, but it can also be a destination in itself; tributaries and caves invite exploration along the way. The sand and gravel streambed makes for easy walking. Reach the trailhead from Highway 12 by turning south 10.8 miles on Hole-in-the-Rock Road, then left 6.3 miles on a dirt road (keep left at the fork near the end). Don't be dismayed by the drab appearance of upper Harris Wash. The canyon and creek appear a few miles downstream. The Harris Wash Trailhead now has a restriction of 12 persons per group.

Harris Wash to Lake Powell (42.75 miles)

The Escalante continues its spectacular show of wide and narrow reaches, side canyons to explore, and intriguing rock formations. A trip all the way from Harris Wash Trailhead to the Escalante, down the Escalante to near Lake Powell, then out to the Hurricane Wash Trailhead is 66.25 miles, taking 8–10 days. Many shorter hikes using other side canyons are possible, too.

Still in a broad canyon, the Escalante flows past **Fence Canyon** (on the west), 5.5 miles from Harris Wash. Fence Canyon has water and is a strenuous 3.5-mile cross-country route out to the end of Egypt Road. Get trail directions from a ranger and bring a topographic map. (Adventurous hikers could do a three-day, 20-mile loop via Fence Canyon, the Escalante River, and the northern arm of Twentyfive Mile Wash.) To reach the trailheads, take Hole-in-the-Rock Road 17.2 miles south of Highway 12, then turn left (east) 3.7 miles on the Egypt

Road for Twentyfive Mile Wash Trailhead or 9.1 miles for Egypt Trailhead.

Twentyfive Mile Wash, on the west side 11.5 miles below Harris Wash, is a good route for entering or leaving the Escalante River. The moderately difficult hike is 13 miles one-way from trailhead to river. Scenery transforms from an uninteresting dry wash in the upper part to a beautiful canyon with water and greenery in the lower reaches. To get to the trailhead, take Hole-in-the-Rock Road 17.2 miles south of Highway 12, then turn left 3.7 miles on Egypt Road.

Moody Creek enters the Escalante six meandering river miles below Twentyfive Mile Wash (or just 2.25 miles as the crow flies). A rough road off Burr Trail Road gives access to Moody Creek, Purple Hills, and other eroded features. The distance from trailhead to river is seven miles one-way (moderately strenuous), although most hikers find it more convenient to hike up from the Escalante. **Middle Moody Creek** enters Moody Creek three miles above the Escalante. Moody and Middle Moody Canyons feature colorful rock layers, petrified wood, a narrows, and solitude. Carry water because springs and water pockets cannot be counted on. Canyons on the east side of the Escalante tend to be much drier than those on the west side.

East Moody Canyon enters the Escalante 1.5 miles downstream from Moody Canyon, and it, too, makes a good side trip. There's often water about one-half mile upstream. Continuing down the Escalante, look on the left for a *rincon*, a meander cut off by the river. **Scorpion Gulch** enters through a narrow opening on the right, 6.5 miles below Moody Canyon. A strenuous eight-mile climb up Scorpion Gulch over rockfalls and around deep pools brings you to a trailhead on Early Weed Bench Road. Experience, directions from a ranger, and a topographic map are needed. A challenging four-day, 30-mile loop hike uses Fox Canyon, Twentyfive Mile Wash, the Escalante River, and Scorpion Gulch. Water is found only in lower Twentyfive Mile Wash, the river, and lower Scorpion Gulch. The Early Weed Bench turnoff is 24.2 miles south on Hole-in-the-Rock Road from Highway 12; head in 5.8 miles to Scorpion Gulch Trailhead.

In the next 12 miles below Scorpion Gulch, Escalante Canyon is alternately wide and narrow. Then the river plunges into the **Narrows,** a five-mile-long section choked with boulders; plan on spending a day picking a route through. Watch out for chest-deep water here! Remote and little-visited, **Stevens Canyon** enters from the east near the end of the Narrows. Stevens Arch stands guard 580 feet above the confluence; the opening measures 225 feet wide and 160 feet high. The upper and lower parts of Stevens Canyon usually have some water.

Coyote Gulch, on the right 1.5 miles below Stevens Canyon, marks the end of the Escalante for most hikers. In some seasons, Lake Powell comes within one mile of Coyote Gulch and occasionally floods the canyon mouth. Coyote can stay flooded for several weeks, depending on the release flow of Glen Canyon Dam and water volume coming in. The river and lake don't have a pretty meeting place—quicksand and dead trees are found here. Logjams make it difficult to travel in from the lake by boat.

Coyote Gulch has received more publicity than other areas of the Escalante, and you're more likely to meet other hikers here. Two arches, a natural bridge, graceful sculpturing of the streambed and canyon walls, deep undercuts, and a cascading creek make a visit well worthwhile. The best route in starts where Hole-in-the-Rock Road crosses Hurricane Wash, 34.7 miles south of Highway 12. It's 12.5 miles one-way from the trailhead to the river, and the hike is moderately strenuous. For the first mile, you follow the dry, sandy wash without even a hint of being in a canyon. Water doesn't appear for three more miles. You'll reach Coyote Gulch, which has water, 5.25 miles from the trailhead. Another way into Coyote Gulch begins at the Red Well Trailhead; it's 31.5 miles south on Hole-in-the-Rock Road, then 1.5 miles east (keep left at the fork). A start from Red Well adds three-quarters of a mile more to the hike than the Hurricane Wash route, but it is also less crowded.

Dry Fork of Coyote Gulch

Twenty-six miles south on the Hole-in-the-Rock Road is a series of narrow, scenic, and exciting-to-explore slot canyons reached by a moderate day

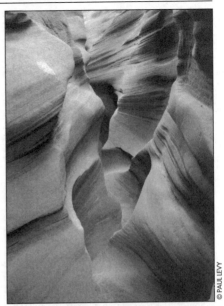

Peek-a-boo Canyon is a magical place to hike.

hike. The canyons feed into the Dry Fork of Coyote Gulch, reached from the Dry Fork trailhead. These three enchanting canyons are named **Peek-a-boo, Spooky,** and **Brimstone.** Exploring these slot canyons requires basic canyoneering or scrambling skills. From the trailhead parking lot, follow cairns down into the sandy bottom of Dry Fork Coyote Gulch. The slot canyons all enter the gulch from the north; watch for cairns and trails because the openings can be difficult to notice. The slots sometimes contain deep pools of water; chokestones and pour-offs can make access difficult. No loop trail links the three slot canyons; follow each until the canyon becomes to narrow to continue, then come back out. To make a full circuit of these canyons requires about 3.5 miles of hiking.

HIKES IN THE CALF CREEK RECREATION AREA

The hike to **Calf Creek Falls** is, for many people, the highlight of their first trip to the Escalante

© PAUL LEVY

SOUTH-CENTRAL UTAH

WALKING SOFTLY

Only great care and awareness can preserve the pristine canyons of the Escalante. You can help if you pack out all trash, avoid trampling on the fragile cryptobiotic soils (dark areas of symbiotic algae and fungus on the sand), travel in groups of 12 or fewer, don't disturb Native American artifacts, and protect wildlife by leaving your dogs at home. Most important, bury human waste well away from water sources, trails, and camping areas; unless there's a fire hazard, burn toilet paper to aid decomposition. Campfires in developed or designated campgrounds are allowed only in fire grates, fire pits, or fire pans. Wood collection in these areas is not permitted. The use of backpacker stoves is recommended by the National Parks Service and the Bureau of Land Management. Visitors are encouraged to maximize efforts to "leave no trace" of their passage in the area.

Leave No Trace, Inc. is a national organization dedicated to awareness, appreciation, and respect for our wildlands. The organization also promotes education of outdoor recreation that is environmentally responsible. More information about Leave No Trace is available at its website, www.lnt.org.

area. It's the dazzling enticement that brings people back for longer and more remote hiking trips. From the trailhead and park just off Highway 12, the trail winds between high cliffs of Navajo sandstone streaked with desert varnish, where you'll see beaver ponds, Native American ruins and pictographs, and the misty 126-foot-high **Lower Calf Creek Falls.** A brochure available at the trailhead next to the campground identifies many of the desert and riparian plant species along the way. Round-trip is 5.5 miles with only a slight gain in elevation; bring water and perhaps a lunch. Summer temperatures can soar, but the falls and the crystal-clear pool beneath stay cool. Sheer cliffs block travel farther upstream.

Calf Creek Campground, near the road, has 13 sites with drinking water early April–late October ($7). Reserve group sites through the Escalante visitors center.

HIKES IN PARIA CANYON/ VERMILION CLIFFS

The wild and twisting canyons of the Paria River and its tributaries offer a memorable experience for experienced hikers. Silt-laden waters have sculpted the colorful canyon walls, revealing 200 million years of geologic history. *Paria* means "muddy water" in the Paiute language. You enter the 2,000-foot-deep gorge of the Paria in southern Utah, then hike 37 miles downstream to Lee's Ferry in Arizona, where the Paria empties into the Colorado River. A handful of shorter but rugged day hikes lead to superb scenery and geologic curiosities.

Ancient petroglyphs and campsites show that Pueblo Indians traveled the Paria more than 700 years ago. They hunted mule deer and bighorn sheep while using the broad, lower end of the canyon to grow corn, beans, and squash. The Dominguez-Escalante Expedition stopped at the mouth of the Paria in 1776, and these were the first white men to see the river. John D. Lee and three companions traveled through the canyon in 1871 to bring a herd of cattle from the Pahreah settlement to Lee's Ferry. After Lee began a Colorado River ferry service in 1872, he and others farmed the lower Paria Canyon. Prospectors came here to search for gold, uranium, and other minerals, but much of the canyon remained unexplored. In the late 1960s, the BLM organized a small expedition whose research led to protection of the canyon as a primitive area. The Arizona Wilderness Act of 1984 designated Paria Canyon a wilderness, along with parts of the Paria Plateau and Vermilion Cliffs. In 2000, Vermilion Cliffs National Monument was created. For more information, check out the website at www.az.blm.gov/vermilion/vermilion.htm.

The **BLM Paria Canyon Ranger Station** is in Utah, 43 miles east of Kanab on U.S. 89 near milepost 21. It's on the south side of the highway, just east of the Paria River. Permits are required for hiking in the Paria Canyon and to visit other sites in Vermilion Cliffs National Monument.

Hiking Paria Canyon

Allow 4–6 days to hike Paria Canyon because

of the many river crossings and because you'll want to make side trips up some of the tributary canyons. The hike is considered moderately difficult. Hikers should have enough backpacking experience to be self-sufficient because help may be days away. Flash floods can race through the canyon, especially July–September. Rangers close the Paria if they think a danger exists. Because the upper end has the most narrow passages (between miles 4.2 and 9.0), rangers require that all hikers start here in order to have up-to-date weather information.

The actual trailhead is two miles south of the ranger station on a dirt road near a campground and old homestead site called White House Ruins. The exit trailhead is in Arizona at Lonely Dell Ranch of Lee's Ferry, 44 miles southwest of Page via U.S. 89 and 89A (or 98 miles southeast of Kanab on U.S. 89A).

You must register at a trailhead or the visitors center, or the Kanab BLM office at 318 North 100 East in Kanab, UT 84741, 435/644-2672; open Monday–Friday 8 A.M.–4:30 P.M. year-round. Permits to hike the canyon are $5 per day per person and per dog. The visitors center and the office both provide weather forecasts and brochures with map and hiking information. The visitors center always has the weather forecast posted at an outdoor information kiosk.

All visitors need to take special care to minimize their impact on this beautiful canyon. Check the BLM *Visitor Use Regulations* for the Paria before you go. Regulations include no campfires in the Paria and its tributaries, a pack-in/pack-out policy, and that latrines be made at least 100 feet away from river and campsite locations. Also, remember to take some plastic bags to carry out toilet paper; the stuff lasts years and years in this desert climate. You don't want to haunt future hikers with TP flowers!

The Paria ranger recommends a group size of six maximum; regulations specify a 10-person limit. No more than 20 people per day can enter the canyon for overnight trips. The best times to travel along the Paria are about mid-March–June and October–November. May, especially Memorial Day weekend, tends to be crowded. Winter hikers often complain of painfully cold feet. Wear shoes suitable for frequent wading; canvas shoes are better than heavy leather hiking boots. You can get good drinking water from springs along the way (see the BLM hiking brochure for locations); it's best not to use the river water because of possible chemical pollution from farms and ranches upstream. Normally the river's only ankle-deep, but in spring or after rainy spells, it can become waist-deep. During thunderstorms, levels can rise to more than 20 feet deep in the Paria Narrows, so heed weather warnings! Quicksand, which is most prevalent after flooding, is more a nuisance than a danger—usually it's just knee-deep. Many hikers carry a walking stick to probe the opaque waters for good crossing places.

Wrather Canyon Arch

One of Arizona's largest natural arches lies about one mile up this side canyon of the Paria. The massive structure has a 200-foot span. Turn right (southwest) at mile 20.6 on the Paria hike. (The mouth of Wrather Canyon and other points along the Paria are unsigned; follow your map.)

Shuttle Services

You'll need to make a 150-mile round-trip car shuttle for this hike or make arrangements for someone else to do it for you, using either your car (about $75) or theirs ($125–150). Contact the GSENM headquarters for a current list of authorized shuttle operators.

Buckskin Gulch and Wire Pass

Buckskin Pass is an amazing tributary of the Paria, with convoluted walls reaching hundreds of feet high. Yet the canyon narrows to as little as four feet in width. In places the walls block out so much light that it's like walking in a cave. Be *very* careful to avoid times of flash-flood danger. Hiking this 20-mile-long gulch can be strenuous, with rough terrain, deep pools of water, and log- and rock jams that may require the use of ropes. Conditions vary considerably from one year to the next.

Day hikers can get a taste of this incredible canyon country by driving to Wire Pass Trailhead, 8.5 bumpy miles down BLM Rd.

SOUTH-CENTRAL UTAH

700 (also called Rock House Valley Rd.), between mileposts 25 and 26, about 37 miles east of Kanab. From the trailhead, a relatively easy trail leads into **Wire Pass,** a narrow side canyon that joins Buckskin Gulch. The 3.5-mile in-and-out round-trip travels the length of Wire Pass to its confluence with Buckskin Gulch. From here, you can explore this exceptionally narrow canyon or follow Buckskin Gulch to its appointment with Paria Canyon (12.5 miles).

For the full experience of Buckskin Gulch, long-distance hikers can begin at Buckskin Gulch trailhead, 4.5 miles south of U.S. 89 off BLM Rd. 700. From here, it's 16.3 miles (one-way) to Paria Canyon. Continue down the Paria or turn upstream and hike six miles to exit at the White House Trailhead near the ranger station.

Coyote Buttes

You've probably seen photos of these dramatic rock formations: towering sand dunes frozen into rock. These much-photographed buttes are on the Paria Plateau, just south of Wire Pass. Access is strictly controlled, and you can only enter the area with advanced reservation and by permit. The number of people allowed into the area is also strictly limited; however, the permit process, fees, and restrictions are exactly the same as for Paria Canyon; see the Vermilion Cliffs monument website for information (www.az.blm .gov/vermilion/vermilion.htm).

The BLM has divided the area into Coyote North and Coyote South, with a limit of 10 people per day in each. The Wave—the most photographed of the buttes—is in the north, so this region is the most popular (and easiest to reach from Utah). Coyote North is reached from Wire Pass Trailhead; BLM staff members will give you a map and directions when you get your permit. After the trailhead, you're on your own because the wilderness lacks signs. Permits are more difficult to obtain in spring and autumn—the best times to visit—and on weekends. The fragile sandstone can break if climbed on, so it's important to stay on existing hiking routes and wear soft-soled footwear.

MOUNTAIN BIKING

Mountain bikes are allowed on all roads in the monument, but not on hiking trails. They are not allowed to travel cross country off roads, or to make their own route across slickrock; however, there are hundreds of miles of primitive road in the monument, with dozens of loop routes possible to cyclists on multiday camping trips. In addition to following the scenic **Burr Trail** from Boulder to Waterpocket Fold in Capitol Reef National Park, cyclists can loop off this route and follow the Circle Cliffs/Wolverine trail. This 45-mile loop traverses the headwaters of several massive canyons as they plunge to meet the Escalante River.

The **Hole-in-the-Rock Road** is mostly a one-way-in, one-way-out kind of road, but cyclists can follow side roads to hiking trailheads and big vistas over the Escalante canyons. Popular side roads are the 10-mile round-trip to the area known as Egypt, and the Fifty Mile Bench Road, a 27-mile loop trail from Hole-in-the-Rock Road that explores landscapes above Glen Canyon. The Left Hand Collet Road, a rough jeep trail that a mountain bike can bounce through easily enough, links Hole-in-the-Rock Road with the Smoky Mountain Road system, with links to both Escalante in the north and Big Water in the south.

Other popular routes in the **Big Water area** include the Nipple Butte loop and the steep loop around Smoky Butte and Smoky Hollow, with views down onto Lake Powell. **Cottonwood Canyon Road,** which runs between U.S. 89 and Cannonville, is another long-distance back road with access to a network of lesser traveled trails.

Request more information on mountain biking from the visitors centers. They have handouts and maps and can help cyclists plan backcountry bike adventures. This country is remote and primitive, and cyclists must take everything with them that they are likely to need. Also, there are no treated water sources in the monument, so cyclists need to transport all their drinking water or be prepared to purify it.

RAFTING

Most of the year, shallow water and rocks make boat travel impossible on the Escalante River, but for 2–3 weeks during spring runoff, river levels rise high enough, peaking between early April and late May. (In some years there may not be enough water in any season.) Keep in touch with the information center in Escalante to hit the river at its highest. Shallow draft and maneuverability are essential, so inflatable canoes or kayaks work best (also because they are easier to carry out at trip's end or if water levels drop too low for floating). Not recommended are rafts (too wide and bulky) and hard-shelled kayaks and canoes (they get banged up on the many rocks). The usual launch is the Highway 12 bridge; Coyote Gulch—a 13-mile hike—is a good spot to get out, as are the Crack in Wall route (a 2.75-mile hike on steep sand from the junction of Coyote and Escalante Canyons to Forty-Mile Ridge Trailhead; four-wheel drive needed; a rope is required to negotiate the vessel over the canyon rim) and Hole-in-the-Rock (a 600-foot ascent over boulders; rope suggested). You could also arrange for a friend to pick you up by boat from the Halls Crossing or Bullfrog Marina. River boaters need a free backcountry permit from either the BLM or the National Park Service.

FOUR-BY-FOUR AND OFF-ROAD EXPLORATION

Without a mountain bike or a pair of hiking boots, the best way to explore the backcountry of the GSENM is with a four-wheel-drive high-clearance vehicle; however, the scale of the monument, the primitive quality of many of the roads, and the extreme weather conditions common in the desert mean that you shouldn't head into the backcountry unless you are confident in your skills as a mechanic and driver. Choose roads that match your vehicle's capacity and your driving ability, and you should be okay. Some roads that appear on maps are slowly going back to nature: Rather than close some roads, park officials are letting the desert reclaim them. Other roads are being closed, so it's best to check on access and road conditions before setting out. Remember that many of the roads in the monument are *very* slow going. If you've got somewhere to be in a hurry, these corrugated, boulder-dodging roads may not get you there in time. Be sure to take plenty of water—not just for you to drink but also for your overheated radiator.

There are still some areas in the monument where non-street-legal vehicles, such as dirt bikes and all-terrain vehicles, are allowed. Check with rangers to verify.

Escalante

The outstanding scenery of the countryside surrounding the town of Escalante has been discovered, and the town is being dragged, kicking and screaming, into a new reality: as a major center for ecotourism. Escalante is a natural hub for exploration of the new GSENM. Even if you don't have the time or the inclination to explore the rugged canyon country that the monument protects, you'll discover incredible scenery just by traveling Highway 12 through the Escalante country.

At first glance, Escalante looks like a town that time has passed by. Only 818 people live here, in addition to the resident cows, horses, and chickens that you'll meet just one block off Main Street. Yet this little community is the biggest place for more than 60 miles around and a center for ranchers and travelers. Escalante (elev. 5,813 feet) has the neatly laid-out streets and trim little houses typical of Mormon settlements. The former Latter-day Saints' Tithing Office (behind the Griffin grocery store) dates from 1884. Pioneers had little cash then and paid their tithes in potatoes, fruit, and other produce. The building now has historic exhibits on the Daughters of Utah Pioneers; open by

To Loa
To Cathedral Valley (4WD)
To Hanksville

Bicknell
Chimney Rock Canyon
South Desert
Caineville
River

SUNGLOW CAMPGROUND
Chimney Rock
Fruita Schoolhouse
Fremont

PERRY EGAN FISH HATCHERY
Torrey
Teasdale
VISITOR CENTER
SCENIC DRIVE
Notom

Dixie National Forest

Boulder Mountain
SINGLETREE CAMPGROUND
Capitol

Aquarius
WILDCAT INFORMATION CENTER
Reef
Henry Mountains

Plateau
PLEASANT CREEK CAMPGROUND
Bowns Reservoir
National

OAK CREEK CAMPGROUND
Park
Waterpocket

SCENIC VIEW

BLUE SPRUCE CAMPGROUND
HELL'S BACKBONE RD.
12
Anasazi State Park

BARKER RESERVOIR CAMPGROUND
Box-Death Hollow Wilderness
Boulder

POSEY LAKE CAMPGROUND
Death Hollow
Sand Cr.
Deer Cr.
Boulder Cr.
The Gulch
Long Canyon
Horse Canyon
Wolverine Creek
BURR TRAIL
Muley Twist Canyon
Fold

Escalante Petrified Forest State Park
CALF CREEK RECREATION AREA
Little Death Hollow
Grand

Escalante
Silver Falls
BRIMHALL BRIDGE
To Bullfrog

Harris Wash
Escalante
Moody Creek
Middle Moody Canyon
East Moody Canyon
Circle
Gulch
Halls Creek

To Bryce Canyon National Park
DEVIL'S GARDEN
Twentyfive Mile Wash
Cliffs

Early Weed Bench
Scorpion Gulch

Kaiparowits
HOLE-IN-THE-ROCK RD.
Coyote Gulch
River
Stevens Canyon
Glen Canyon N.R.A.

Grand
Plateau
Straight Cliffs
STEVENS ARCH

Staircase-
Hurricane Wash
Fortymile Cr.
Fortymile Cr.

Escalante
DANCE HALL ROCK

VICINITY OF ESCALANTE
National
HOLE-IN-THE-ROCK

Monument
Willow Cr.
Lake Powell

0   15 mi
0   15 km

Glen Canyon National Recreation Area

© AVALON TRAVEL PUBLISHING, INC.

appointment (phone numbers of volunteers are listed on the door).

ACCOMMODATIONS

Under $50

The following are pretty basic, but perfectly acceptable: The **Moqui Motel,** 480 W. Main, 435/826-4210, has rooms and some kitchenettes and an RV park (no tents). The **Circle D Motel,** 475 W. Main, 435/826-4297, has a restaurant, and pets are welcome in some rooms. In addition to regular rooms, there's one two-bedroom unit ($87) and one four-bedroom ($110).

The following close in winter and are generally open March–October. The **Padre Motel,** 20 E. Main, 435/826-4276, 800/462-7923, or 800/733-8824, has regular motel rooms and five mini-suites with two bedrooms each. Bunkhouse-style cabins sleeping two are available at **Escalante Outfitters,** 310 W. Main, 435/826-4266.

$50–75

Right in town, **Escalante's Grand Staircase B&B,** 280 W. Main, 866/826-4890, has lovely and very private rooms. The pleasant and modern **Rainbow Country B&B,** 586 East 300 South, 435/826-4567 or 800/252-UTAH (800/252-8824), also offers custom tours. The B&B's four guest rooms share 2.5 baths; guests have the use of a hot tub, a pool table, and a TV lounge. The hosts offer several tour itineraries featuring your choice of hiking, back-road four-wheel-drive exploring, or even camping trips. You can also arrange personalized tours to suit your interests. The **Prospector Inn,** 380 W. Main, 435/826-GOLD (435/826-4653), is Escalante's newest motel; there's a restaurant and lounge on premises. Open year-round; children 12 and under stay free.

Campgrounds

In addition to the Escalante Petrified Forest State Park campground described in the Sights Along Highway 12 section, you can stay at **Broken Bow RV Camp,** 495 W. Main St., 435/826-4959 or 888/241-8785, which has cabins, sites for tents and RVs, plus showers and a launderette; closed in winter.

Calf Creek Recreation Area lies in a pretty canyon 15.5 miles east of Escalante on Highway 12; sites run $7 and are open early April–late October; you can reserve group sites through the BLM office. **Calf Creek Falls Trail** (5.5 miles round-trip) begins at the campground and follows the creek upstream to the 126-foot-high falls.

Campgrounds at **Posey Lake** (16 miles north) and **Blue Spruce** (19 miles north) sit atop the Aquarius Plateau in Dixie National Forest. Sites open around Memorial Day weekend and close in mid-September. Take the dirt Hell's Backbone Road from the east edge of town.

FOOD

The **Ponderosa Restaurant,** 45 North 400 West, 435/826-4658, offers Escalante's best food, in a large log lodge in the center of town. The menu focuses on steaks, chicken, burgers, and other American fare. Alcohol is served. The **Cowboy Blues Diner and Bakery,** 530 W. Main, 435/826-4251, serves Western-style food and bakery goods. The **Golden Loop Cafe,** 39 W. Main, 435/826-4433, has standard American fare. All are open daily for breakfast, lunch, and dinner. The **Trailhead Café,** at the corner of Main St. and 100 East, has good coffee and Internet access. **Escalante Outfitters,** 310 W. Main St, 435/826-4266, has a café, espresso coffee, pizza, and microbrewed beer.

INFORMATION AND SERVICES

The Escalante Interagency office, 755 W. Main, on the west edge of town, has an **information center** for visitors to Forest Service, BLM, and National Park Service areas around Escalante, P.O. Box 246, Escalante, UT 84726, 435/826-5499. This is also one of the best spots for information on the GSENM; open Monday–Friday (daily early March–late October) 8 A.M.–5 P.M.

Hikers or bikers headed for overnight trips in the monument system can obtain permits at the information center. Normally it's best to contact the information center first, but you can also communicate directly with the **Dixie National**

Forest office, P.O. Box 246, Escalante, UT 84726, 435/826-5400; the **Bureau of Land Management office,** P.O. Box 225, Escalante, UT 84726, 435/826-4291; or the **National Park Service office,** P.O. Box 511, Escalante, UT 84726, 435/826-4315.

Kazan-Ivan Memorial Clinic, on Center Street behind Bob Munson's Grocery, 435/826-4374, offers medical care on Mondays and Thursdays. The **Municipal Park** on the west edge of town has covered picnic tables, restrooms with water (except in winter), grills, and a small playground. **Escalante Outfitters,** 310 W. Main, 435/826-4266, probably has that camping item you forgot as well as topographic maps and books. For **guided tours** of the monument, contact **Escalante Outback Adventures,** 325 W. Main St, 435/826-4967 or 877/777-7988, www.escalante-utah.com.

HELL'S BACKBONE

This scenic 38-mile drive climbs high into the forests north of Escalante with excellent views of Death Hollow and Sand Creek Canyons and the distant Navajo, Fiftymile, and Henry Mountains.

Hell's Backbone Road reaches an elevation of 9,200 feet on the slopes of Roger Peak before descending to Hell's Backbone, 25 miles from town. Mule teams used this narrow ridge, with precipitous canyons on either side, as a route to Boulder until the 1930s. At that time, a bridge built by the Civilian Conservation Corps allowed the first vehicles to make the trip. You can still see the old mule path below the bridge. After 38 miles, the road ends at Highway 12; turn right 24 miles to return to Escalante or turn left three miles to Boulder. Cars can usually manage the gravel and dirt Hell's Backbone Road when it's dry. Snows and snowmelt, however, block the way until about late May. Check with the Interagency office in Escalante for current conditions. Trails and rough dirt roads lead deeper into the backcountry to more vistas and fishing lakes.

Posey Lake Campground (elev. 8,700 feet) offers sites amid aspen and ponderosa pines; open with drinking water from Memorial Day weekend to mid-September ($7). Rainbow and brook trout swim in the adjacent lake. A hiking trail (two miles round-trip) begins near space number 14 and climbs 400 feet to an old fire lookout tower, with good views of the lake and surrounding country. Posey Lake is 14 miles north of Escalante, then two miles west on a side road.

Blue Spruce Campground (elev. 7,860 feet) is another pretty spot, but it has only six sites. Anglers can try for pan-sized trout in a nearby stream. The campground, surrounded by blue spruce, aspen, and ponderosa pine, has drinking water from Memorial Day weekend to mid-September ($7); go north 19 miles from town, then turn left and drive one-half mile.

Boulder

About 150 people live in this farming community at the base of Boulder Mountain. Ranchers began drifting in during the late 1870s, although not with the idea of forming a town. By the mid-1890s, Boulder had established itself as a ranching and dairy center. Remote and hemmed in by canyons and mountains, Boulder remained one of the last communities in the country to rely on pack trains for transportation. Motor vehicles couldn't drive in until the 1930s. Today Boulder is worth a visit to see an excavated Anasazi village and the spectacular scenery along the way. Take paved Highway 12 either through the canyon and slickrock country from Escalante or over the Aquarius Plateau from Torrey (near Capitol Reef National Park). Burr Trail Road connects Boulder with Capitol Reef National Park's southern district via Waterpocket Fold and Circle Cliffs. A fourth way in is from Escalante on the dirt Hell's Backbone Road, which comes out three miles west of Boulder at Highway 12.

TOURS AND EXCURSIONS

Red Rock 'n Llamas, P.O. Box 1304, Boulder, UT 84716, 435/559-7325, offers fully outfitted hiking adventures in the Escalante Canyon area. Llamas will carry most of the gear, leaving you to explore in comfort. Most trips are four days and cost $500–650. Write for a schedule.

If llamas don't strike you as Western enough for your backcountry adventure, **Escalante Canyon Outfitters,** P.O. Box 1330, Boulder, UT 84716, 435/335-7311 or 888/326-4453, www.ecohike.com, offers full-service guided tours of the Escalante country with pack horses.

ACCOMMODATIONS

$50–75
Pole's Place (closed in winter), across the road from the state park, 435/335-7422 or 800/730-7422, has a well-maintained motel, café, and gift shop.

$75–100
You wouldn't expect to find one of Utah's nicest places to stay in tiny Boulder, but the **Boulder Mountain Lodge,** along Highway 12 right in town, 435/355-7460 or 800/556-3446, offers the kinds of facilities and setting that make this one of the few destination lodgings in the state. The lodge's buildings are grouped around the edge of a private, 15-acre pond that serves as an ad hoc wildlife refuge. You can sit on the deck or wander paths along the pond, watching and listening to the amazing variety of birds that make this spot their home. The guest rooms and suites are in a handsome and modern Western-style lodge facing the pond; rooms are nicely decorated with quality furniture and beddings, and there's a central Great Room with a fireplace and library.

Campgrounds

Hall's Store, next to Anasazi State Park, 435/335-7304, runs a small RV park ($13; self-contained; no tents). Otherwise, there are several Forest Service campgrounds on nearby Boulder Mountain (follow Highway 12 north from town).

Guest Ranches

Cowboy up at the **Boulder Mountain Ranch,** seven miles from Boulder on the Hell's Backbone Rd., P.O. Box 1373, Boulder, UT 84716, 435/355-7480, www.boulderutah.com/bmr. Guests have a choice of simple B&B accommodations in the lodge or free-standing cabins ($55–65), horseback riding, or multiday pack trips along the Great Western Trail. There are also two- to five-day riding and lodging packages based out of the ranch.

FOOD

The Boulder Mountain Lodge restaurant, **Hell's Backbone Grill,** 435/355-7460 or 800/556-3446, offers just about the only fine dining in all of southern Utah. You'll find fresh fish and seafood, adventurous game and meat preparations, and excellent desserts; open for three meals daily. For simpler fare, the **Burr Trail Cafe** (open Memorial Day weekend–autumn) is at the intersection of Highway 12 and Burr Trail Road, 435/335-7432.

INFORMATION AND SERVICES

Look for a **visitor information** booth in the center of town; usually it's in front of the Burr Trail Cafe. Open daily MayOctober about 9 A.M. 6 P.M. The two gas stations in Boulder sell groceries and snack food.

AROUND BOULDER

Boulder Mountain Scenic Drive

Highway 12 climbs high into forests of ponderosa pine, aspen, and fir on Boulder Mountain between the towns of Boulder and Torrey. The modern highway replaces what used to be a rough dirt road. Travel in winter is usually possible now, although heavy snows can close the road. Viewpoints along the drive offer sweeping panoramas of the Escalante Canyon country, Circle Cliffs, Waterpocket Fold, and the Henry Mountains. Hikers and anglers can explore the alpine country of Boulder Mountain and seek

out the 90 or so trout-filled lakes. The Dixie National Forest map (Escalante and Teasdale Ranger District offices) shows the back roads, trails, and lakes.

The U.S. Forest Service has three developed campgrounds about midway along this scenic drive: **Oak Creek** (18 miles from Boulder, elev. 8,800 feet), **Pleasant Creek** (19 miles from Boulder, elev. 8,700 feet), and **Singletree** (24 miles from Boulder, elev. 8,600 feet). The season with water lasts late May–mid-September; sites cost $8. Campgrounds may also be open in spring and autumn without water for $3. **Lower Bowns Reservoir** (elev. 7,400 feet) has primitive camping (no water or fee) and fishing for rainbow and some cutthroat trout; turn east five miles on a rough dirt road (not recommended for cars) just south of Pleasant Creek Campground.

Contact the **Teasdale Ranger District office,** near Torrey, 435/425-3702, for recreation information in the northern and eastern parts of Boulder Mountain; contact the **Escalante Ranger District office,** Escalante, 435/826-5499 or 435/826-5400, for the southern and western areas. **Wildcat Information Center,** near Pleasant Creek Campground, has forest information; open in the summer with irregular hours.

Capitol Reef National Park

Wonderfully sculptured rock layers in a rainbow of colors put on a fine show here. Although you'll find these same rocks throughout much of the Four Corners region, their artistic variety has no equal outside Capitol Reef National Park. About 70 million years ago, gigantic forces within the earth began to uplift, squeeze, and fold more than a dozen rock formations into the central feature of the park today—Waterpocket Fold, so named for the many small pools of water trapped by the tilted strata. Erosion has since carved spires, graceful curves, canyons, and arches. Waterpocket Fold extends 100 miles between Thousand Lake Mountain in the north and Lake Powell in the south. The most spectacular cliffs and rock formations of Waterpocket

Fold form Capitol Reef, located north of Pleasant Creek and curving northwest across the Fremont River toward Thousand Lake Mountain. The reef was named by explorers who found Waterpocket Fold a barrier to travel and likened it to a reef blocking passage on the ocean. The rounded sandstone hills reminded them of the Capitol Dome in Washington, D.C., hence the name Capitol Reef.

Roads and hiking trails in the park provide access to the colorful rock layers and to the plants and wildlife that live here. Remnants exist of the area's long human history—petroglyphs and storage bins of the prehistoric Fremont, a schoolhouse and other structures built by Mormon pioneers, and several small uranium

CAPITOL REEF NATIONAL PARK

Fishlake National Forest

To Richfield

72

Fremont

Loa   Lyman

Bicknell

Torrey

Teasdale

Dixie National Forest

Grover

Singletree

12

DETAIL 1

Old Wagon Trail   GOLDEN THRONE   THE TANKS

EGYPTIAN TEMPLE

Capitol Gorge   PIONEER REGISTER

Capitol Reef National Park

PLEASANT CREEK RD.

Pleasant Ck.

SOUTH DRAW (4-WHEEL DRIVE ONLY)

CATHEDRAL VALLEY   UPPER CATHEDRAL VALLEY OVERLOOK

UPPER SOUTH DESERT OVERLOOK

South Desert

LOWER SOUTH DESERT OVERLOOK

Middle Desert

Black Mtn. 6,038 ft

CAINVILLE WASH RD.

To Hanksville

Factory Butte 6,358 ft

Cainville   Fremont River

South Cainville Mesa

Waterpocket

SEE DETAIL 2

FRUITA

SCENIC DRIVE

Fold

SEE DETAIL 1

Pleasant Cr.

Capitol Reef National Park

CEDAR MESA

NOTOM-BULLFROG RD.

Stevens Mesa

Wildcat Mesa

Tarantula Mesa

Strike Valley   Waterpocket Fold   Muley Twist Canyon

DETAIL 2

CHIMNEY ROCK

Spring Canyon Route

Capitol Reef

NAVAJO KNOBS   THE CASTLE

PANORAMA POINT

SUNSET POINT   FRUITA SCHOOLHOUSE

VISITOR CENTER

GOOSENECKS OVERLOOK

FRUITA

PETROGLYPHS

HICKMAN BRIDGE

CAPITOL DOME

24

Cohab Cyn. Trail

Fremont Gorge Overlook Trail

Fremont River Trail

Frying Pan Trail

SCENIC DRIVE

Grand Wash Trail

Grand Wash Canyon

Fremont River

National Park

BURR TRAIL

BURR TRAIL SWITCHBACKS

THE POST

LOWER MULEY TWIST TRAILHEAD

Swap Mesa

Grand Staircase-Escalante National Monument

MULEY TANKS

HALLS CREEK OVERLOOK

Big Thomson Mesa

Glen Canyon National Recreation Area

To Bullfrog Marina and Lake Powell

0   5 mi
0   5 km

SOUTH-CENTRAL UTAH

© AVALON TRAVEL PUBLISHING, INC.

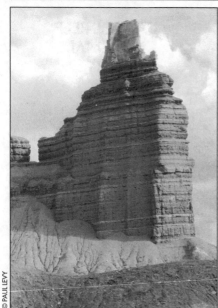

Chimney Rock is a landmark on the western edge of Capitol Reef National Park.

mines of the 20th century. Legends tell of Butch Cassidy and other outlaw members of the "Wild Bunch" who hid out in these remote canyons in the 1890s.

Even travelers short on time will enjoy a quick look at visitors center exhibits and a drive on Highway 24 through an impressive cross section of Capitol Reef cut by the Fremont River. You can see more of the park on the scenic drive, a narrow paved road that heads south from the visitors center. The drive passes beneath spectacular cliffs of the reef and enters scenic Grand Wash and Capitol Gorge Canyons; allow at least 90 minutes for the 21-mile round-trip (plus side trips). The fair-weather Notom-Bullfrog Road (paved as far as Notom) heads south along the other side of the reef for almost 80 miles with fine views of Waterpocket Fold. Burr Trail Road (dirt inside the park) in the south actually climbs over the fold in a steep set of switchbacks, connecting Notom Road with Boulder. Only drivers with high-clearance vehicles can explore Cathedral

Valley in the park's northern district. All of these roads provide access to viewpoints and hiking trails. A $5-per-vehicle park entrance fee is collected on the scenic drive.

Climate

Expect hot summer days (highs in the upper 80s and low 90s) and cool nights. Winter brings cool days (highs in the 40s) and night temperatures dropping into the low 20s and teens. Snow accents the colored rocks while rarely hindering traffic on the main highway. Winter travel on the back roads and trails may be halted by snow, but it soon melts when the sun comes out. Annual precipitation averages only seven inches, peaking in the late summer thunderstorm season.

Geology

Exposed rocks reveal windswept deserts, rivers, mud flats, and inland seas of long ago. Nearly all the layers date from the Mesozoic era (65–230 million years ago), when dinosaurs ruled the earth. Later uplift and twisting of the land, which continues to this day, built up the Colorado Plateau of southern Utah and the Rocky Mountains to the east. Immense forces squeezed the rocks until they bent up and over from east to west in the massive crease of Waterpocket Fold.

Flora and Fauna

Ponderosa pine and other cool-climate vegetation grow on the flanks of Thousand Lake Mountain (7,000–9,000 feet high) in the northwest corner of the park. Most of Waterpocket Fold, however, is at 5,000–7,000 feet, covered with sparse juniper and piñon pine that cling precariously in cracks and thin soils of the slickrock. The soil from each rock type generally determines what will grow. Mancos shale forms a poor clay soil supporting only saltbush, shadscale, and galleta grass. On Dakota sandstone mostly sage and rabbitbrush grow. Clays of the Morrison Formation repel nearly all plants, while its sandstone nurtures mostly juniper, piñon pine, and cliffrose; uranium prospectors discovered that *astragalus* and prince's plume commonly grow near ore deposits. Sands of the Summerville Formation nourish grasses and four-wing saltbush. The Fremont River and several creeks provide a lush habitat of cottonwood, tamarisk, willow, and other water-loving plants.

Streamside residents include beaver, muskrat, mink, tree lizard, Great Basin spadefoot toad, Rocky Mountain toad, and leopard frog. Spadefoot toads, fairy shrimp, and insects have adapted to the temporary water pockets by completing the aquatic phase of their short life cycles in a hurry. Near water or out in the drier country, you might see mule deer, coyote, gray fox, porcupine, spotted and striped skunks, badger, black-tailed jackrabbit, desert cottontail, yellow-bellied marmot, rock squirrel, Colorado chipmunk, Ord's kangaroo rat, canyon mouse, and five known species of bats. With luck, you may sight a relatively rare mountain lion or black bear.

While you can't miss seeing the many small lizards along the trails, snakes tend to be more secretive; those in the park include the striped whipsnake, Great Basin gopher snake, wandering garter snake, and the rarely seen desert faded pygmy rattlesnake. Some common birds are the sharp-shinned hawk, American kestrel, chukar, mourning dove, white-throated swift, black-chinned and broad-tailed hummingbirds, violet-green swallow, common raven, piñon and scrub jays, canyon and rock wrens, and rufous-sided towhee. Most wildlife, except birds, wait until evening to come out, and they disappear again the following morning.

Visitors Center

Start with a 10-minute slide show, which is shown on request, introducing Capitol Reef's natural wonders and history. A giant relief map gives you a bird's-eye view of the entire park. Rock samples and diagrams illustrate seven of the geologic formations in the park. Photos identify plants and birds found here. Prehistoric Fremont artifacts on display include petroglyph replicas, sheepskin moccasins, pottery, basketry, stone knives, spear and arrow points, and bone jewelry. Other historic exhibits outline exploration and early Mormon settlement.

Hikers can pick up a map of trails that are near the visitors center and of longer routes in the southern park areas; naturalists will want the checklists of plants, birds, mammals, and other wildlife; history buffs can learn more about the area's settlement and the founding of the park. Rangers offer nature walks, campfire programs, and other special events from Easter to mid-October; the bulletin board outside the visitors center lists what's on. Hours at the visitors center are daily 8 A.M.–7 P.M. June–September, daily 8 A.M.–4:30 P.M. the rest of the year. The visitors center is on Highway 24 at the turnoff for Fruita Campground and the scenic drive. For more information, contact Capitol Reef National Park, Torrey, UT 84775, 435/425-3791, www.nps.gov/care.

ALONG HIGHWAY 24

From the west, Highway 24 drops from the broad mountain valley near Torrey onto Sulphur Creek, with dramatic rock formations soaring into the horizon. A huge amphitheater of stone rings the basin, with formations such as Twin Rocks, Chimney Rock, and The Castle glowing in deep red and yellow tones. Ahead, the canyon narrows as the Fremont River slips between the cliffs to carve its chasm through Waterpocket Fold. Take in this incredible vista from **Panorama Point,** 2.5 miles west of the visitors center on the south side of the highway. Follow signs south for 0.15 mile to Panorama Point and views of Capitol Reef to the east and Boulder Mountain to the west. A sign explains how glacial meltwaters carried basalt boulders from Boulder Mountain to the reef 8,000–200,000 years ago.

Continue past Panorama Point one mile on a gravel road to the **Goosenecks of Sulphur Creek.** A short trail leads to the Goosenecks Overlook on the rim (elev. 6,400 feet) for dizzying views to the creek below. Canyon walls display shades of yellow, green, brown, and red. Another easy trail leads one-third mile to Sunset Point and panoramic views of the Capitol Reef cliffs and the distant Henry Mountains.

Remnants of the pioneer community of **Fruita** stretch along the narrow Fremont River Canyon. The **Fruita Schoolhouse** is just east of the visitors center on the north side of the highway. Early settlers completed this one-room log structure in 1896. Teachers struggled at times with rowdy students, but the kids learned their three R's in grades 1–8. LDS Church meetings, dances, town meetings, elections, and other community gatherings took place here. Lack of students caused the school's closing in 1941. Rangers are on duty some days in summer (ask at the visitors center). At other times, you can peer inside the windows and listen to a recording of a former teacher recalling what school life was like.

Farther down the canyon, 1.2 miles east of the visitors center on the north side of the highway, are several panels of Fremont **petroglyphs.** (Watch for the road signs.) Several human figures with headdresses and mountain sheep decorate the cliff. You can see more petroglyphs by walking to the left and right along the cliff face. Stay on the trail and *do not* climb the talus slope.

Behunin Cabin is 6.2 miles east of the visitors center on the south side of the highway. Elijah Cutlar Behunin used blocks of sandstone to build this cabin in about 1882. He moved on, though, when floods made life too difficult. Small openings allow a look inside the dirt-floored structure, but no furnishings remain.

Near the end of the narrow sandstone canyon, a small waterfall in the **Fremont River** attracts photographers and impromptu swimming parties. The river twists through a narrow human-made crack in the rock before making its final plunge into a pool below. A sign warns of hazardous footing above the falls, which are dangerous for children. Instead, take the sandy path from the parking area to where you can safely view the falls from below. Use extreme caution if you intend to cool off in the pool at the base of the waterfall because the undertow is strong and dangerous. Parking is 6.9 miles east of the visitors center on the north side of the highway.

ALONG THE SCENIC DRIVE

Turn south from Highway 24 at the visitors center to experience some of the reef's best scenery and to learn more about its geology. An illustrated pamphlet, available on the drive or in the visitors center, has keyed references to numbered stops along the 25-mile (round-trip) drive. Descriptions identify rock layers and explain how they were formed. Just a quick tour takes 90 minutes, but several hiking trails may tempt you to extend your stay. The scenic drive is paved, although side roads have gravel surfaces.

First you pass orchards and several of Fruita's buildings. A **blacksmith shop** (0.7 miles from the visitors center on the right) displays tools, harnesses, farm machinery, and Fruita's first tractor. The tractor didn't arrive until 1940—long after the rest of the country had modernized. In a recording, a rancher tells about living and working in Fruita.

The **Historic Gifford Homestead,** one mile south on the scenic drive, is typical of rural Utah farmhouses of the early 1900s. Cultural demonstrations and handmade sales items are available. A picnic area is just beyond; with fruit trees and grass, this makes a pretty spot for lunch. A short trail crosses orchards and the Fremont River to the Fruita Schoolhouse.

The scenic drive leaves the Fremont River valley and climbs up a desert slope, with the rock walls of the Waterpocket Fold rising to the east. Turn east into the **Grand Gulch,** a dry channel etched through the sandstone. A dirt road follows the twisting gulch one mile, with sheer rock walls rising along the sandy stream bed. At the road's end, an easy hiking trail follows the gulch 2.5 miles to its mouth along Highway 24.

Past the Slickrock Divide, the rock lining the reef deepens into a ruby red and forms itself into odd columns and spires that resemble statuary. Called the **Egyptian Temple,** this is one of the most striking and colorful areas along the scenic drive.

Turn right 8.3 miles from the visitors center, where the scenic drive curves east toward Capitol Gorge, onto **Pleasant Creek Road,** which continues south below the face of the reef. After three miles, the sometimes rough dirt road passes Sleeping Rainbow/Floral Ranch (closed to the public) and ends at Pleasant Creek. A rugged four-wheel-drive road continues on the other side but is much too rough for cars. Floral Ranch dates back to Capitol Reef's early years of settlement. In 1939 it became the Sleeping Rainbow

THE ORCHARDS OF CAPITOL REEF

Capitol Reef remained one of the last places in the West to be discovered by white settlers. First reports came in 1866 from a detachment of Mormon militia pursuing renegade Utes. In 1872, Professor Almon H. Thompson of the Powell Expedition led the first scientific exploration in the fold country and named several park features along the group's Pleasant Creek route. Mormons, expanding their network of settlements, arrived in the upper Fremont Valley in the late 1870s and spread downriver to Hanksville. Junction (renamed Fruita in 1902) and nearby Pleasant Creek (Sleeping Rainbow/Floral Ranch) were settled about 1880. Floods, isolation, and transport difficulties forced many families to move on, especially downstream from Capitol Reef. Irrigation and hard work paid off with prosperous fruit orchards and the sobriquet "the Eden of Wayne County." The aptly named Fruita averaged about 10 families who grew alfalfa, sorghum (for syrup), vegetables, and a wide variety of fruit. Getting the produce to market required long and difficult journeys by wagon. The region remained one of the most isolated in Utah until after World War II.

Although Fruita's citizens have departed, the National Park Service still maintains the old orchards. The orchards are lovely in late April, when the trees are in bloom beneath the towering canyon walls. Visitors are welcome to pick and carry away the cherries, apricots, peaches, pears, and apples during harvest seasons. Harvest times begin in late June or early July and end in October. You'll be charged about the same as in commercial pick-your-own orchards. You may also wander through any orchard and eat all you want on the spot before and during the designated picking season (no charge).

Guest Ranch, from the Indian name for Waterpocket Fold. Now the ranch belongs to the park, but the former owners still live here. Pleasant Creek's perennial waters begin high on Boulder Mountain to the west and cut a scenic canyon completely through Capitol Reef. Hikers can head downstream through the three-mile-long canyon and return, or continue another three miles cross-country to Notom Road.

The **Capitol Gorge** is the end of the scenic drive, 10.7 miles from the visitors center. Capitol Gorge is a dry canyon through Capitol Reef much like Grand Wash, although with a somewhat different character. Believe it or not, the narrow, twisting Capitol Gorge was the route of the main state highway through south-central Utah for 80 years! Mormon pioneers laboriously cleared a path so wagons could go through, a task they repeated every time flash floods rolled in a new set of boulders. Cars bounced their way down the canyon until 1962, when the present Highway 24 opened, but few traces of the old road remain today. Walking is easy along the gravel riverbed, but don't enter if storms threaten. An easy one-mile saunter down the

gorge will take day hikers past **petroglyphs** and a "register" rockface where pioneers carved their names. For other Capitol Gorge hikes, see following sections.

NORTH DISTRICT

Only the most adventurous travelers get into the remote canyons and desert country of the north. The few roads *cannot* be negotiated by ordinary cars. In good weather, high-clearance vehicles can enter the region from the east, north, and west. The roads lead through stately sandstone monoliths of Cathedral Valley, volcanic remnants, badlands country, many low mesas, and vast sand flats. Foot travel allows closer inspection of these features or lengthy excursions into the canyons of Polk, Deep, and Spring Creeks, which cut deeply into the flanks of Thousand Lake Mountain.

Mountain bikers enjoy these challenging roads as well, but they must stay on established roads. Much of the north district is good for horseback riding, too. **Cathedral Valley Campground's** five sites provide a place to stop for the night; rangers won't permit car camping elsewhere in the district. The **Upper Cathedral Valley Trail,** just below the campground, is an enjoyable one-mile walk offering excellent views of the Cathedrals. Hikers with a backcountry permit must camp at least one-half mile from the nearest road. You can purchase a small guide to this area at the visitors center.

SOUTH DISTRICT

Notom-Bullfrog Road

Capitol Reef is only a small part of Waterpocket Fold. The Notom-Bullfrog Road takes in nearly 80 miles of the fold's eastern side. This route crosses some of the younger geologic layers, such as those of the Morrison Formation that form colorful hills. In other places, eroded layers of the Waterpocket Fold jut up at 70-degree angles. The Henry Mountains to the east and the many canyons on both sides of the road add to the memorable panoramas. The road has been paved as far as Notom, and about 25 miles are paved on the southern end near Bullfrog. The rest of the road is good-condition dirt and gravel road. Most cars should have no trouble negotiating this road in good weather. Keep an eye on the weather before setting out, though; the dirt and gravel surface is usually okay for cars when dry but can be too slippery and gooey for *any* vehicle when wet. Sandy spots and washouts may present a problem for low-clearance vehicles; contact the visitors center to check current conditions. Have a full gas tank and carry extra water and food because no services are available between Highway 24 and Bullfrog Marina. Purchase a small guide to this area at the visitors center. Features and mileage along the drive from north to south include the following:

Mile 0.0: The turnoff from Highway 24 is 9.2 miles east of the visitors center and 30.2 miles west of Hanksville (another turnoff from Highway 24 is three miles east).

Mile 2.2: Pleasant Creek; the mouth of the canyon is 5–6 miles upstream, although it's only about three miles by heading cross-country from south of Notom. Hikers can follow the canyon

three miles upstream through Capitol Reef to Pleasant Creek Road (off the scenic drive).

Mile 4.1: Notom Ranch is to the west; once a small town, Notom is now a private ranch.

Mile 8.1: Burrow Wash; hikers can explore the narrow canyon upstream.

Mile 9.3: Cottonwood Wash; another canyon hike just upstream.

Mile 10.4: Five Mile Wash; yet another canyon hike.

Mile 13.3: Sheets Gulch; a scenic canyon lies upstream here, too.

Mile 14.1: Sandy Ranch Junction; high-clearance vehicles can turn east 16 miles to the Henry Mountains.

Mile 14.2: Oak Creek Access Road to the west; turn here for Oak Creek. The creek cuts a two-mile-long canyon through Capitol Reef that's a good day hike. Backpackers sometimes start upstream at Lower Bowns Reservoir (off Highway 12) and hike the 15 miles to Oak Creek Access Road. The clear waters of Oak Creek flow all year but must be treated for drinking.

Mile 14.4: Oak Creek crossing.

Mile 20.0: Entering Capitol Reef National Park; a small box has information sheets.

Mile 22.3: Cedar Mesa Campground to the west; the small five-site campground is surrounded by junipers and has fine views of Waterpocket Fold and the Henry Mountains. Sites have tables and grills; there's an outhouse but no drinking water; free. **Red Canyon Trail** begins here and heads west into a huge box canyon in Waterpocket Fold; four miles round-trip.

Mile 26.0: Bitter Creek Divide; streams to the north flow to the Fremont River; Halls Creek on the south side runs through Strike Valley to Lake Powell, 40 miles away.

Mile 34.1: Burr Trail Road Junction; turn west up the steep switchbacks to ascend Waterpocket Fold and continue to Boulder and Highway 12 (36 miles). Burr Trail is the only road that actually crosses the top of the fold, and it's one of the most scenic in the park. Driving conditions are similar to the Notom-Bullfrog Road—okay for cars when dry. Pavement begins at the park boundary and continues to Boulder. Although paved, the Burr Trail still needs to be driven slowly because of its curves and potholes. The section of road through Long Canyon has especially pretty scenery.

Mile 36.0: Surprise Canyon Trailhead; a hike into this narrow, usually shaded canyon takes 1–2 hours.

Mile 36.6: The Post; a small trading post here once served sheepherders and some cattlemen, but today this spot is just a reference point. Park here to hike to Headquarters Canyon. A trailhead for Lower Muley Twist Canyon via Halls Creek lies at the end of a half-mile-long road to the south.

Mile 37.5: Leaving Capitol Reef National Park; a small box has information sheets. Much of the road between here and Glen Canyon National Recreation Area has been paved.

Mile 45.5: Road junction; turn right (south) to continue to Bullfrog Marina (25 miles) or go straight (east) for Starr Springs Campground (23 miles) in the Henry Mountains.

Mile 46.4: The road to the right (west) goes to Halls Creek Overlook. This turnoff is poorly signed and easy to miss; look for it 0.9 mile south of the previous junction. Turn in and follow the road three miles, then turn right at a fork 0.4 mile to the viewpoint. The last 0.3 mile may be too rough for low-clearance cars. A picnic table is the only "facility" here. Far below in Grand Gulch, Halls Creek flows south to Lake Powell. Look across the valley for the double Brimhall Bridge in the red sandstone of Waterpocket Fold. A steep trail descends to Halls Creek (1.2 miles one-way), and it's possible to continue another 1.1 miles up Brimhall Canyon to the bridge. A register box at the overlook has information sheets on this route. Note, however, that the last part of the hike to the bridge requires difficult rock-scrambling and wading or swimming through pools! Hikers looking for another adventure might want to follow Halls Creek 10 miles downstream to the narrows. Here, convoluted walls as high as 700 feet narrow to little more than arms' length apart. This beautiful area of water-sculpted rock sometimes has deep pools that require swimming.

Mile 49.0: Colorful clay hills of deep reds, creams, and grays rise beside the road. This clay turns to goo when wet, providing all the traction of axle grease.

Mile 54.0: Beautiful panorama of countless mesas, mountains, and canyons. Lake Powell and Navajo Mountain can be seen to the south.

Mile 65.3: Junction with paved Highway 276; turn left (north) for Hanksville (59 miles) or right (south) to Bullfrog Marina (5.2 miles).

Mile 70.5: Bullfrog Marina (see Glen Canyon National Recreation Area).

Lower Muley Twist Canyon

"So winding that it would twist a mule pulling a wagon," said an early visitor. This canyon has some of the best hiking in the southern district of the park. In the 1880s, Mormon pioneers used the canyon as part of a wagon route between Escalante and new settlements in southeastern Utah, replacing the even more difficult Hole-in-the-Rock route. Unlike most canyons of Waterpocket Fold, Muley Twist runs lengthwise along the crest for about 18 miles before finally turning east and leaving the fold. Hikers starting from Burr Trail Road can easily follow the twisting bends down to Halls Creek, 12 miles away. Two trailheads and the Halls Creek route allow a variety of trips. You could start from Burr Trail Road near the top of the switchbacks (2.2 miles west of Notom-Bullfrog Road) and hike down the dry gravel streambed. After four miles, you have the options of returning the same way, taking the Cut Off route east 2.5 miles to the Post Trailhead (off Notom-Bullfrog Road), or continuing eight miles down Lower Muley Twist Canyon to its end at Halls Creek. Upon reaching Halls Creek, turn left (north) five miles up the creekbed or the old jeep road beside it to the Post. This section of creek lies in an open, dry valley. With a car shuttle, the Post would be the end of a good two-day, 17-mile hike, or you could loop back to Lower Muley Twist Canyon via the Cut Off route and hike back to Burr Trail Road for a 23.5-mile trip. It's a good idea to check the weather beforehand and avoid the canyon if storms threaten.

Cream-colored cliffs of Navajo sandstone lie atop the red Kayenta and Wingate Formations.

Impressively deep undercuts have been carved into the lower canyon. Spring and autumn offer the best conditions (summer temperatures can exceed 100°F). Elevations range from 5,640 feet at Burr Trail Road to 4,540 feet at the confluence with Halls Creek to 4,894 feet at the Post. An information sheet available at the visitors center and trailheads has a small map and route details. Topographic maps of Wagon Box Mesa, Mt. Pennell, and Hall Mesa, and the 1:100,000-scale Escalante and Hite Crossing maps are sold at the visitors center. You'll also find this hike described in Dave Hall's *Hiker's Guide to Utah* and in Michael Kelsey's *Canyon Hiking Guide to the Colorado Plateau* and *Utah Mountaineering Guide.* Carry all water for the trip because natural sources are often dry or polluted.

Upper Muley Twist Canyon

This part of the canyon has plenty of scenery. Large and small natural arches along the way add to its beauty. Upper Muley Twist Road turns north off Burr Trail Road about one mile west from the top of a set of switchbacks. Cars can usually go in one-half mile to a trailhead parking area, while high-clearance four-wheel-drive vehicles can head another 2.5 miles up a wash to the end of the primitive road. Look for natural arches on the left along this last section. **Strike Valley Overlook Trail** (0.75 mile round-trip) begins at the end of the road and leads to a magnificent panorama of Waterpocket Fold and beyond. Return to the canyon, where you can hike as far as 6.5 miles (one-way) to the head of Upper Muley Twist Canyon.

Two large arches lie a short hike upstream; Saddle Arch, the second one on the left, is 1.75 miles away. The **Rim Route** begins across from Saddle Arch, climbs the canyon wall, follows the rim (good views of Strike Valley and the Henry Mountains), and descends back into the canyon at a point just above the narrows, 4.75 miles from the end of the road. (The Rim Route is most easily followed in this direction.) Proceed upcanyon to see several more arches. A narrow section of canyon beginning about four miles

from the end of the road must be bypassed to continue; look for rock cairns showing the way around to the right. Continuing up the canyon past the Rim Route sign will take you to several small drainages marking the upper end of Muley Twist Canyon. Climb a high, tree-covered point on the west rim for great views; experienced hikers with a map can follow the rim back to Upper Muley Road (no trail or markers on this route). Bring all the water you'll need because there are no reliable sources in Upper Muley Twist Canyon.

HIKING

Fifteen day-hiking trails begin within a short drive of the visitors center. Of these, only Grand Wash, Capitol Gorge, Sunset Point, and Goosenecks are easy. The others involve moderately strenuous climbs and travel over irregular slickrock. Signs and rock cairns mark the way, but it's all too easy to wander off if you don't pay attention to the route.

Although most hiking trails can easily be done in a day, backpackers and mountain hikers might want to try longer trips in Chimney Rock/Spring Canyons in the north or Muley Twist Canyon and Halls Creek in the south. Obtain the required backcountry permit (free) from a ranger and camp at least one-half mile from the nearest maintained road or trail. (Cairned routes like Chimney Rock Canyon, Muley Twist Canyon, and Halls Creek don't count as trails but are backcountry routes.) Bring a stove for cooking because backcountry users may not build fires. Avoid camping or parking in washes at any time—torrents of mud and boulders can carry away everything!

HIKES ALONG HIGHWAY 24

Stop by the visitors center to pick up a map showing hiking trails and trail descriptions. These trailheads are along the main highway through the park and along the Fremont River. Note that the Grand Wash Trail cuts west through the reef to the scenic drive.

Chimney Rock Trail

The trailhead is three miles west of the visitors center on the north side of the highway. Towering 660 feet above the highway, Chimney Rock is a fluted spire of dark red rock (Moenkopi Formation) capped by a block of hard sandstone (Shinarump Member of the Chinle Formation). A 3.5-mile loop trail ascends 540 feet from the parking lot (elev. 6,100 feet) to a ridge overlooking Chimney Rock; allow 2.5 hours. Panoramic views take in the face of Capitol Reef. Petrified wood along the trail has been eroded from the Chinle Formation (the same rock layer found in Petrified Forest National Park in Arizona). It is illegal to take any of the petrified wood.

Spring Canyon Route

This moderately difficult hike begins at the top of the Chimney Rock Trail. The wonderfully eroded forms of Navajo sandstone present a continually changing exhibition. The riverbed is normally dry; allow about six hours for the 10-mile (one-way) trip from the Chimney Rock parking area to the Fremont River and Highway 24. (Some maps show all or part of this as "Chimney Rock Canyon.") Check with rangers for the weather forecast before setting off because flash floods can be dangerous, and the Fremont River (which you must wade across) can rise quite high. Normally, the river runs less than knee-deep to Highway 24 (3.7 miles east of the visitors center). With luck you'll have a car waiting for you. Summer hikers can beat the heat with a crack-of-dawn departure. Carry water because this section of canyon lacks a reliable source.

From the Chimney Rock parking area, hike Chimney Rock Trail to the top of the ridge and follow the signs for Chimney Rock Canyon. Enter the unnamed lead-in canyon and follow it downstream. A sign marks Chimney Rock Canyon, which is 2.5 miles from the start. Turn right 6.5 miles (downstream) to reach the Fremont River. A section of narrows requires some rock-scrambling (bring a cord to lower backpacks), or the area can be bypassed on a narrow trail to the left above the narrows. Farther down, a natural arch high on the left marks the halfway point.

Upper Chimney Rock Canyon could be explored on an overnight trip. A spring (purify before drinking) is located in an alcove on the right side about one mile up Chimney Rock Canyon from the lead-in canyon. Wildlife use this water source, so camp at least one-quarter mile away. Chimney Rock Canyon, the longest in the park, begins high on the slopes of Thousand Lake Mountain and descends nearly 15 miles southeast to join the Fremont River.

Sulphur Creek Route

This moderately difficult hike begins by following a wash across the highway from the Chimney Rock parking area, descending to Sulphur Creek, then heads down the narrow canyon to the visitors center. The trip is about five miles long (one-way) and takes 3–5 hours. Park rangers sometimes schedule guided hikes on this route. Warm weather is the best time because you'll be wading in the normally shallow creek. Three small waterfalls can be bypassed fairly easily; two falls are just below the goosenecks, and the third is about one-half mile before coming out at the visitors center. Carry water with you. The creek's name may be a mistake because there's no sulphur along it; perhaps outcrops of yellow limonite caused the confusion. You can make an all-day eight-mile hike in Sulphur Creek by starting where it crosses the highway between mileposts 72 and 73, five miles west of the visitors center.

Hickman Natural Bridge, Rim Overlook, and Navajo Knobs Trails

The trailhead is two miles east of the visitors center on the north side of the highway. The graceful Hickman Natural Bridge spans 133 feet across a small streambed. Numbered stops along the self-guided trail correspond to descriptions in a pamphlet available at the trailhead or visitors center. Starting from the parking area (elev. 5,320 feet), the trail follows the Fremont River's green banks a short distance before gaining 380 feet in the climb to the bridge. The last section of trail follows a dry wash shaded by cottonwood, juniper, and piñon pine trees. You'll pass under the bridge (eroded from the Kayenta Formation) at trail's end. Capitol Dome and other sculptured features of the Navajo sandstone surround the site. The two-mile round-trip hike takes about 90 minutes. Joseph Hickman served as principal of Wayne County High School and later in the state legislature during the 1920s; he and another local man, Ephraim Pectol, led efforts to promote Capitol Reef.

A splendid overlook 1,000 feet above Fruita beckons hikers up the **Rim Overlook Trail.** Take the Hickman Natural Bridge Trail one-quarter mile from the parking area, then turn right two miles at the signed fork. Allow 3.5 hours from the fork for this hike. Panoramic views take in the Fremont River valley below, the great cliffs of Capitol Reef above, the Henry Mountains to the southeast, and Boulder Mountain to the southwest.

Continue another 2.2 miles and more than 500 feet higher from the Rim Overlook to reach **Navajo Knobs.** Rock cairns lead the way over slickrock along the rim of Waterpocket Fold. A magnificent panorama at trail's end takes in much of southeastern Utah.

Cohab Canyon and Frying Pan Trails

Park at Hickman Natural Bridge Trailhead, then walk across the highway bridge. This trail climbs Capitol Reef for fine views in all directions and a close look at the swirling lines in the Navajo sandstone. After three-quarters of a mile and a 400-foot climb, you'll reach a trail fork: Keep right one mile to stay on Cohab Canyon Trail and descend to Fruita Campground or turn left onto Frying Pan Trail to Cassidy Arch (3.5 miles away) and Grand Wash (four miles away). The trail from Cassidy Arch to Grand Wash is steep. All of these interconnecting trails offer many hiking possibilities, especially if you can arrange a car shuttle. For example, you could start up Cohab Canyon Trail from Highway 24, cross over the reef on Frying Pan Trail, make a side trip to Cassidy Arch, descend Cassidy Arch Trail to Grand Wash, walk down Grand Wash to Highway 24, then walk (or car shuttle) 2.7 miles along the highway back to the start (10.5 miles total).

Cohab is a pretty little canyon in the Wingate sandstone overlooking the campground. Mormon polygamists supposedly used the canyon to escape federal marshals during the 1880s. Hiking the Frying Pan Trail involves an additional 600 feet of climbing from either Cohab Canyon or Cassidy Arch trail. Once atop Capitol Reef, the trail follows the gently rolling slickrock terrain.

Grand Wash

The trailhead is 4.7 miles east of the visitors center on the south side of the highway. One of only five canyons cutting completely through the reef, Grand Wash offers easy hiking and great scenery. There's no trail—just follow the dry gravel riverbed. Flash floods can occur during storms. Canyon walls of Navajo sandstone rise 800 feet above the floor and close in to as little as 20 feet in width. Cassidy Arch Trailhead (see Grand Wash Road under Hikes Along the Scenic Drive) is two miles away, and parking for Grand Wash from the scenic drive is one-quarter mile farther.

HIKES ALONG THE SCENIC DRIVE

These hikes begin from trailheads along the scenic drive that turns south from the visitors center. There is a $5 entrance fee to travel the scenic drive.

Fremont Gorge Overlook Trail

From the start at the Fruita blacksmith shop, the trail crosses Johnson Mesa and climbs steeply to the overlook about 1,000 feet above the Fremont River; round-trip distance is 4.5 miles.

Cohab Canyon Trail

The trailhead is across the road from the Fruita Campground, 1.3 miles from the visitors center. The trail follows steep switchbacks during the first one-quarter mile, then more gentle grades to the top, 400 feet higher and one mile from the campground. You can take a short trail to viewpoints or continue three-quarters of a mile down the other side of the ridge to Highway 24. (See description under Hikes Along Highway 24.) Another option is to turn right at the top on Frying Pan Trail to Cassidy Arch (3.5 miles one-way) and Grand Wash (four miles one-way).

Fremont River Trail

From the trailhead near the amphitheater at the Fruita Campground, 1.3 miles from the visitors center, the trail passes orchards along the Fremont River (elev. 5,350 feet), then begins the climb up sloping rock strata to a viewpoint on Miner's Mountain. Sweeping views take in Fruita, Boulder Mountain, and the reef. The round-trip distance of 2.5 miles takes about 90 minutes; the elevation gain is 770 feet.

Grand Wash Road

Turn left off the scenic drive 3.6 miles from the visitors center. This side trip follows the twisting Grand Wash for one mile. At road's end, you can continue on foot 2.25 miles (one-way) through the canyon to its end at the Fremont River (see Grand Wash under Hikes Along Highway 24).

Cassidy Arch Trail begins near the end of Grand Wash Road. Energetic hikers will enjoy good views of Grand Wash, the great domes of Navajo sandstone, and the arch itself. The 3.5-mile round-trip trail ascends the north wall of Grand Wash (Wingate and Kayenta Formations), then winds across slickrock of the Kayenta Formation to a vantage point close to the arch, also of Kayenta. Allow about three hours because the elevation gain is nearly 1,000 feet. The notorious outlaw Butch Cassidy may have traveled through Capitol Reef and seen this arch. Frying Pan Trail branches off Cassidy Arch Trail at the one-mile mark, then wends its way across three miles of slickrock to Cohab Canyon (see Cohab Canyon and Frying Pan Trails under Hikes Along Highway 24).

Old Wagon Trail

Wagon drivers once used this route as a shortcut between Grover and Capitol Gorge. Look for the trailhead 0.7 mile south of Slickrock Divide, between Grand Wash and Capitol Gorge. The old trail crosses a wash to the west, then ascends steadily through piñon and juniper woodland on Miners Mountain. After 1.5 miles, the trail leaves the wagon road and goes north one-half mile to a high knoll for the best views of the Capitol Reef area. The four-mile (round-trip) hike climbs 1,000 feet.

Capitol Gorge

Follow the well-maintained dirt road to the parking area in Capitol Gorge to begin these hikes. The first mile downstream is the most scenic: Fremont petroglyphs (in poor condition) appear on the left after 0.1 mile; narrows of Capitol Gorge close in at 0.3 mile; a "pioneer register" on the left at one-half mile consists of names and dates of early travelers and ranchers scratched in the canyon wall; and natural water tanks on the left at three-quarters of a mile are typical of those in Waterpocket Fold. Hikers can continue another three miles downstream to Notom Road.

The **Golden Throne Trail** also begins at the end of the scenic drive. Instead of heading down Capitol Gorge from the parking area, turn left up this trail for dramatic views of the reef and surrounding area. Golden Throne is a massive monolith of yellow-hued Navajo sandstone capped by a thin layer of red Carmel Formation. The four-mile round-trip trail climbs 1,100 feet in a steady grade to a viewpoint near the base of Golden Throne; allow four hours.

MOUNTAIN BIKING

Cyclists are restricted to existing roads, and because there are so few in the park, Capitol Reef doesn't have much of a reputation as a destination for mountain bikers. One exception is the challenging Cathedral Canyon Loop in the remote northern section of the park. The complete loop is more than 60 miles long and requires that cyclists be experienced and fit. Little water is available along the route, so this ride is best performed in spring or fall, when temperatures are lower. Contact the visitors center for more information on this and other routes.

ROCK CLIMBING

Rock climbing is allowed in the park and is especially popular in the relatively hard Wingate sandstone formations. Technical rock climbers should check with rangers to learn about restricted areas; registration is voluntary. Climbers must use "clean" techniques (no pitons or bolts) and keep at least 100 feet from rock-art panels and prehistoric structures. Because of the abundance of prehistoric rock art found there, the section of the rock wall north of Highway 24 between the Fruita Schoolhouse and the east end of the Kreuger Orchard (mile 81.4) is closed to climbing. Other areas closed to climbing are Hickman Natural Bridge and all other arches and bridges, Temple of the Moon, Temple of the Sun, and Chimney Rock.

CAMPGROUNDS

Fruita Campground stays open all year and has drinking water but no showers or hookups ($10); November–April you have to get water from the visitors center. The surrounding orchards and lush grass make this an attractive spot, situated one mile from the visitors center on the scenic drive. Sites often fill by early afternoon in the busy May–October season. One group camp-ground (by reservation only) and a picnic area are nearby. If you're just looking for a place to park for the night, check out the public land east of the park boundary off Highway 24. Areas on both sides of the highway (about nine miles east of the visitors center) may be used for primitive camping; no facilities or charge.

The five-site **Cedar Mesa Campground** is in the park's southern district just off Notom-Bull-frog Road (dirt); campers here enjoy fine views of Waterpocket Fold and the Henry Mountains. Open all year; no water or charge. From the visitors center, go east 9.2 miles on Highway 24, then turn right 22 miles on Notom-Bullfrog Road (avoid this road if wet). **Cathedral Valley Campground** serves the park's northern district; it has five sites (no water or charge) near the Hartnet Junction, about 30 miles north of Highway 24. Take either the Caineville Wash or Hartnet (has a river ford) roads; both are dirt and should be avoided if wet.

Torrey

Torrey (pop. 171) is an attractive little village, with a real Western feel. Only 11 miles west of the Capitol Reef National Park visitors center, it's a friendly and convenient place to stay, with several excellent lodgings and a good restaurant. Because Torrey is at the junction of Highways 12 and 24, it's a great hub for exploring the wild country of the Grand Staircase–Escalante National Monument area just to the south and Capitol Reef National Park to the east.

Other little towns lie along the Fremont River, which drains this steep-sided valley. Teasdale is a small community just four miles east, situated in a grove of piñon pines. Bicknell, a small farm and ranch town, is eight miles east of Torrey.

ACCOMMODATIONS

Under $50

The cabins at the center of town, at the **Torrey Trading Post,** 75 W. Main St., 435/425-3716, are just $35 per night. The **Capitol Reef Inn and Cafe,** 435/425-3271 (closed in winter), has standard motel rooms, a good café serving breakfast, lunch, and dinner, and a gift shop.

$50–75

The main business in Torrey is its old trading post and country store. Immediately behind it in a grove of trees is the **Chuck Wagon Lodge,** 435/425-3335 or 800/863-3288, with rooms in an older motel (less than $50) or in a brand-new and attractive lodgelike building. There's a pool, a hot tub, and some campsites; open March–November.

The **Wonderland Inn,** just east of town near the Hwy. 12 turnoff for Boulder, 435/425-3775 or 800/458-0216, has clean rooms and a restaurant serving breakfast, lunch, and dinner daily. The local **Super 8 Motel** is also just east of town on Hwy. 24, 435/425-3688.

In Teasdale, four miles west of Torrey, **Pine Shadows,** 125 South 200 West, 435/425-3939 or 800/708-1223, offers new pine bungalows in a piñon forest. Or you can stay in a historic pioneer-era home, also in nearby Teasdale. The **Cockscomb Inn B&B,** 97 S. State St., 435/425-3511 or 800/530-1038, has three guest rooms with queen beds, plus a garden cottage. All rooms have private bathrooms.

In Bicknell, the **Aquarius Motel,** 435/425-3835 or 800/833-5379, offers rooms, some with kitchens. There's also a café open daily for breakfast, lunch, and dinner.

$75–100

The **Days Inn,** at the junction of Hwy. 12 and Hwy. 24, 435/425-3111 or 888/425-3113, has a pool. Just east of Torrey, toward the park, is the **Best Western Capitol Reef Resort,** 435/425-3761 or 800/528-1234, which features luxury accommodations, a pool, and an attractive restaurant (open daily for breakfast, lunch, and dinner). There's also a brand-new **Holiday Inn Express,** east of town toward Capitol Reef, 435/425-3866 or 888/232-4082.

Over $100

The lovely **SkyRidge Bed and Breakfast** is one mile east of downtown, 435/425-3222. The modern inn has been decorated with high-quality Southwestern art and artifacts; all five guest rooms have private baths. SkyRidge sits on a bluff amid 75 acres; guests are invited to explore the land on foot or on bike.

The **Lodge at Red River Ranch,** between Bicknell and Torrey, 435/425-3322 or 800/20-LODGE (800/205-6343), is located beneath towering cliffs of red sandstone on the banks of the Fremont River. This wonderful wood-beamed lodge sits on a working ranch, but there's nothing rustic or unsophisticated about the accommodations here. The three-story structure is newly built, although in the same grand architectural style of old-fashioned mountain lodges. The great room has a massive stone fireplace, cozy chairs and couches, and a splendid Old West atmosphere. There are 15 guest rooms, most decorated according to a theme, and all have private baths. Guests are welcome to wander ranch paths, fish for trout, or tinker in the gardens and orchards. For information, write P.O. Box 69, Teasdale, UT 84773.

Campgrounds

For campers, **Thousand Lakes RV Park,** one mile west of town on Hwy. 24, 435/425-3500, has sites with showers, a laundry room, and a store; open April–October. Thousand Lakes also has a nightly Western-style cookout in an outdoor pavilion. **Wonderland Resort and RV Park,** one-half block south on Hwy. 12 from the Hwy. 24 junction, 800/458-0216, has both tenting and RV sites, phone and modem hookups, and laundry facilities. The U.S. Forest Service's **Sunglow Campground** is just east of Bicknell; sites are open mid-May–late October with water; elevation is 7,200 feet; the surrounding red cliffs really light up at sunset.

FOOD

Several of the motels in town offer American-style food, especially the café at the Capitol Reef Inn, although it's probably **Café Diablo,** 599 W. Main, 435/425-3070, that you'll remember long after you've left Utah. Its specialty is zesty Southwestern cuisine, with excellent dishes like chipotle ribs, shrimp with habañero peppers, and pumpkin seed trout. Because there aren't many restaurants this good in rural Utah, this place is worth taking a detour. Open for lunch and dinner; closed in winter.

INFORMATION

The **Teasdale Ranger Station** of the Dixie National Forest has information about hiking, horseback riding, and road conditions in the northern and eastern parts of Boulder Mountain and the Aquarius Plateau; books and forest maps are available. The office is two miles west of Torrey on Hwy. 24, then 1.5 miles south to Main and 138 East (P.O. Box 99, Teasdale, UT 84773), 435/425-3702; open Monday–Friday 8 A.M.–4:30 P.M.

Robber's Roost Bookstore, 185 W. Main St., 435/3265, is a good bookstore with a coffee shop. The bookstore regularly hosts Saturday-evening concerts and readings put on by the Entrada Institute, a local arts organization.

East of Capitol Reef National Park

HANKSVILLE

Ebenezer Hanks and other Mormon settlers founded this out-of-the-way community in 1882 along the Fremont River, then known as the Dirty Devil River. The isolation attracted polygamists like Hanks and other fugitives from the law. Butch Cassidy and his gang found refuge in the rugged canyon country of "Robbers' Roost" east of town.

Even by Utah standards, Hanksville is still pretty remote. The population is only about 400, but it has outlasted several other farm communities upstream. Today most people work at ranching, farming (hay, corn feed, and watermelons), mining, or tourism. Several houses and the old stone church on Center, one block south of the highway, survive from the 19th century.

Travelers exploring this scenic region find Hanksville a handy if desultory stopover; Capitol Reef National Park lies to the west, Lake Powell and the Henry Mountains to the south, the remote Maze District of Canyonlands National Park to the east, and Goblin Valley State Park to the north. The book *Hiking and Exploring Utah's Henry Mountains and Robbers Roost*, by Michael Kelsey, has a wealth of history and travel information about the Hanksville area.

Wolverton Mill

E. T. Wolverton built this ingenious mill during the 1920s at his gold-mining claims in the Henry Mountains. A 20-foot waterwheel, still perfectly balanced, powered ore-crushing machinery and a sawmill. Owners of claims at the mill's original site didn't like a steady stream of tourists coming through to see the mill, so it was moved to the BLM office at Hanksville. Drive south a half mile on 100 West to see the mill and some of its original interior mechanism.

Accommodations

$50–75: Drive by the **Desert Inn Motel,** 197 East 100 North, 435/542-3241, just to see ingenious "found-metal" dinosaur sculptures; if you want to stay the night, it offers clean, basic rooms. The newer **Whispering Sands Motel,** 68 East 100 North, 435/542-3238, has spacious rooms with cable TV and phones.

Campgrounds: In the center of town, **Redrock Campground,** 435/542-3235 or 800/894-3242 (reservations), offers sites for tents ($11) and RVs ($15 with hookups); amenities include showers and laundry. Open March 15–October 31.

Food

Hanksville's best food is at the south end of town. The **Slickrock Grill,** 435/542-3441, serves breakfast, lunch, and dinner and specializes in Dutch-oven cooking; closed December–January. **Blondie's Eatery,** 435/542-3255, and **Stan's Burger Shack,** 435/542-3441, are open daily with fast food.

Information and Services

The **post office** is at 118 East 100 North, 435/542-3422. The **Bureau of Land Management,** south a half mile on 100 West from Hwy. 24, P.O. Box 99, Hanksville, UT 84734, 435/542-3461, has regional travel literature, and the staff can tell you about road conditions, hiking, camping, and the buffalo herd in the Henry Mountains. A recreation map and USGS topo maps are available; open Monday–Friday 7:45 A.M.–noon and 12:45–4:30 P.M.

Caineville

Mormons founded this village on the Fremont River midway between the present-day Capitol Reef Visitors Center and Hanksville. **Sleepy Hollow Campground,** at milepost 95 on Hwy. 24, 435/456-9130, has a store, showers, and sites for tents and RVs. Facilities are shut down in winter, but primitive camping is permitted with reduced fees.

GOBLIN VALLEY STATE PARK

Thousands of spooky rock formations inhabit this valley. Little eyelike holes in the "goblins" make you wonder who's watching whom. All of the goblins have weathered out of the Entrada Formation, here a soft red sandstone and even softer siltstone. **Carmel Canyon Trail** (1.5-mile loop) begins at the northeast side of the parking lot at road's end, then leads into a strange landscape of goblins, spires, and balanced rocks. Just wander about at your whim; this is a great place for the imagination!

Curtis Bench Trail begins on the road between the parking lot and the campground and goes south to a viewpoint of the Henry Mountains; cairns mark the 1.5-mile (one-way) route. The state park provides a campground with showers on the drive in and a covered picnic area and an overlook at the end of the road. The park, P.O. Box 637, Green River, UT 84525, 435/564-8110 or 800/322-3770 (reservations), stays open all year; $5 per vehicle for day use or $14 per vehicle for camping. The turnoff from Highway 24 is at milepost 137, 21 miles north of Hanksville and 24 miles south of I-70; follow signs west five miles on a paved road, then south seven miles on a gravel road.

Temple Mountain Bike Trail traverses old mining roads, ridges, and wash bottoms about 12 miles north of the state park. Popular hikes near the state park include the Little Wild Horse and Bell Canyons Loop, Chute and Crack Canyons Loop, and Wild Horse Canyon. The park is also a good base for exploring the **San Rafael Swell** area to the northwest.

SOUTHERN SAN RAFAEL SWELL

The massive fold and uplift of the earth's crust called the San Rafael Swell is crossed by I-70 about 19 miles west of Green River. The east face and "flat irons" of the Swell, known as the San Rafael Reef, rise dramatically 2,100 feet above the desert. Several view areas allow stopping for a look at the colorful rock layers. San Rafael Swell is 80 miles long (north to south) and 30 miles wide (for a more complete discussion of the region's history and geology, see

Thousands of spooky rock formations inhabit Goblin Valley. Little eyelike holes in the "goblins" make you wonder who's watching whom.

The Castle Valley and North San Rafael Swell section in the Northeastern Utah chapter). For information, contact the BLM San Rafael Resource Area, 900 North and 700 East, Price, UT 84501, 435/637-4584.

Black Dragon Canyon

Don't worry about the dragon; he doesn't bite. This narrow canyon in the San Rafael Swell is just off I-70, 15 miles east of Green River. A quarter-mile walk up the streambed leads to a pair of pictograph panels of the dragon (he's actually red), human figures, a dog, and geometric designs. Continue farther upcanyon for more good scenery. To reach the trailhead, turn north on a dirt road from the I-70 westbound lane just past milepost 145; this isn't a regular exit and is not signed. If coming from the west, you'll have to turn around at the Hanksville Exit 147 and backtrack two miles. The dirt road crosses a wash (walk from here if it's filled with water), goes through a second gate, and crosses the streambed from Black Dragon Wash, 1.1 miles from I-70. Turn left 0.4 mile up the streambed (normally dry) to the canyon entrance. High-clearance vehicles can drive a short way up the canyon.

Hondoo Arch Loop

Dirt roads south of I-70 provide a scenic drive into some of the San Rafael's prettiest country. Either turn south and west 15 miles from I-70 Ranch Exit 129 or take the Goblin Valley State Park turnoff from Highway 24 and head west 20 miles to the beginning of the loop. The 29-mile loop drops into Reds Canyon with fine panoramas on the descent. Look for Hondoo Arch high in the cliffs across the Muddy River. Side roads off the loop go to Muddy River (beside Tomsich Butte), Hidden Splendor Mine, and other old mining areas. The Tomsich Butte area contains old cabins and uranium mines, which are dangerous to enter. Hikers can find many adventurous trips along the Muddy River, washes, and canyons of the area; check *Canyoneering the San Rafael*

Swell, by Steve Allen, for hiking details. The San Rafael Desert 1:100,000 topo map covers the loop area. Roads can become impassable after rain or snow; drivers of cars need to be especially careful in this remote area.

HENRY MOUNTAINS AND VICINITY

Great domes of intrusive igneous rock pushed into and deformed surrounding sedimentary layers about 70 million years ago. Erosion later uncovered the domes, revealing mountains towering 5,000 feet above the surrounding plateau. Mount Ellen's North Summit Ridge (elev. 11,522 feet) and Mount Pennell (elev. 11,320 feet) top the range. Scenic views and striking geologic features abound in and around the Henrys. Rock layers tilt dramatically in Waterpocket Fold to the west and in the Pink Cliffs on the south side of Mount Hillers. Sheer cliffs of the Horn, between Mount Ellen and Mount Pennell, attract rock climbers.

The arid land and rugged canyons surrounding the Henry Mountains so discouraged early explorers and potential settlers that the range wasn't even named or described until 1869, when members of the Powell River Expedition sighted it. Tales of a lost Spanish gold mine have long enticed prospectors, yet only modest amounts of the yellow metal have been found, mostly in the Bromide Basin. A brief gold boom here in the early 1890s gave rise to Eagle City mining camp along Crescent Creek. Other minerals occur in the area, too; a uranium mine is just south of the Henrys in Shootaring Canyon, near Ticaboo.

Vegetation ranges from sparse desert plants such as galleta grass and blackbrush on the lower slopes to piñon pine and juniper woodlands higher up, then to forests of ponderosa pine, aspen, Douglas fir, spruce, and bristlecone pine. Alpine plants and grasslands cover the highest summits. Buffalo, brought to the Henrys from Yellowstone National Park in 1941, form one of the few free-roaming herds in the United States. They winter in the southwestern part of the mountains, then move higher as the snow melts. Mule deer keep mostly to the higher elevations,

while pronghorn stay in the desert country to the east. Most of the bighorn sheep are found in the Little Rockies, a southeastern extension of the Henry Mountains. Mountain lions live near the Henrys, too, but they're more likely to see you than you are to see them!

Exploring the Henry Mountains

Roads with panoramic views cross the range between the high peaks at Bull Creek, Pennellen, and Stanton Passes. Most driving routes are best suited for high-clearance vehicles. The road through Bull Creek Pass (elev. 10,485 feet) is snow-free only early July–late October. Rains, which peak in August, occasionally make travel difficult in late summer. Roads tend to be at their best after grading in autumn, just before the deer-hunting season. Travel at the lower elevations is possible all year, though spring and autumn have the most pleasant temperatures. Check in first with the BLM office in Hanksville before exploring the backcountry. Staff members can advise you about water sources, road and trail conditions, and, in case of trouble, they will have an idea of where to look for you. Take precautions for desert travel, and have water, food, and extra clothing with you. The Henry Mountains remain a remote and little-traveled region.

Campgrounds

The only easily accessible campsites in the Henry Mountains are at **Starr Springs Campground,** off Hwy. 276 north of Ticaboo. The campground sits in an oak forest at the base of Mt. Hillers. Sites (elev. 6,300 feet) stay open all year and usually have water for a $7 fee early May–early October. **Panorama Knoll Trail** begins from the campground and makes a half-mile loop to an overlook. A good gravel road to Starr Springs Campground turns off Highway 276 near milepost 17 (23 miles north of Bullfrog and 43 miles south of Hanksville) and goes in four miles.

The handful of campgrounds along the Notom-Bullfrog Road route described in South District under Captiol Reef National Park operate May–October only; most have water. These campgrounds are upwards of 30 miles off the pavement on often-marginal roads. Check with the Hanksville BLM office for road conditions and details on campgrounds.

Hiking

Countless mountain and canyon hiking possibilities exist in the range; Michael Kelsey's book on the Henry Mountains has trip suggestions and practical advice. Most routes go cross-country or follow old mining roads. The **Mt. Ellen Summit Route** is a good day hike and probably attracts the greatest number of hikers. Easiest way is to follow the North Summit Ridge north from the road at Bull Creek Pass; there's an unsigned trail the first mile and on the final climb up Mount Ellen; elevation gain is 1,030 feet. Nearly all of this route lies above timberline with spectacular panoramas. Another popular approach begins from Dandelion Flat Picnic Area; a trail follows an old road that climbs the slopes part of the way, then it's cross-country; elevation gain is 3,400 feet. Either route is about four miles round-trip and takes half a day. Interestingly, Mount Ellen Peak shown on the maps isn't the true high point; the North Summit Ridge of Mount Ellen, just to the south, is 16 feet higher at 11,522 feet. You can also hike the South Summit Ridge south of Bull Creek Pass. See the 7.5-minute Mount Ellen and Dry Lakes Peak or the 15-minute Mt. Ellen topo maps.

Little Egypt

Eerie rock formations similar to those in Goblin Valley, but covering a smaller area, lie east of the Henrys. Kids will enjoy exploring the area, and it's a fine place for a picnic. Turn southwest 1.5 miles from Highway 95 between mileposts 20 and 21; when dry, the gravel road is usually okay for cars. No facilities or even a sign mark the site, so note mileage from Highway 95.

Dirty Devil Canyon Overlook

The muddy waters of the Dirty Devil River have carved a deep canyon southeast of Hanksville. Views from the overlook at Burr Point take in some impressive scenery. Desperadoes around the turn of the century hid out in the rugged canyonlands of "Robbers' Roost" across the river. In 1869, when one of Powell's expedition members was asked if the waters had trout, he replied with disgust that the smelly and muddy river was "a dirty devil." An unpaved road winds east for 11 miles from Highway 95 (between mileposts 15 and 16). Cars with good clearance should be okay in dry weather. Park near where the road makes a sharp right just before the edge, or follow the road south for other views. Walking along the rim also affords different perspectives.

Glen Canyon National Recreation Area

This vast recreation area covers 1.25 million acres, most of which spreads northeast into Utah. Lake Powell stands as the centerpiece, surrounded by beautiful canyon country. Just a handful of roads approach the lake, so you'll need to do some boating or hiking to explore this unique land of water and rock. The recreation area also includes a beautiful remnant of Glen Canyon in a 15-mile section of the Colorado River from Glen Canyon Dam to Lees Ferry. Admission to Glen Canyon National Recreation Area is $5 per vehicle or $3 per pedestrian or bicyclist for seven days. There is no charge for passing through Page on U.S. 89. For information on Glen Canyon National Recreation Area write: Superintendent, P.O.

Box 1507, Page, AZ 86040, 928/608-6404, www.nps.gpv/glca.

Note that *Arizona does not observe daylight savings time.* This means that late April–late October, the time in Page and surrounding areas will be an hour later than time in Utah.

LAKE POWELL

Conservationists deplored the loss of remote and beautiful Glen Canyon of the Colorado River beneath Lake Powell. Today, we have only words, pictures, and memories to remind us of its wonders. On the other hand, the 186-mile-long lake now provides easy access to an area most had not even known existed. Lake Powell is

GLEN CANYON NATIONAL RECREATION AREA

Fremont
Loa
Lyman
Fishlake National Forest
Capitol Reef National Park
Hanksville
Canyonlands National Park
CLEOPATRA'S CHAIR
HANS FLAT
PANORAMA POINT
Teasdale
U.S. FOREST SERVICE
Torrey
VISITOR CENTER
Capitol Reef
FRUITA
Caineville
Dirty Devil River
The Big Ridge
BAGPIPE BUTTE
Lookout Peak 11,124 ft
Dixie National Forest
LONESOME BEAVER
MCMILLAN SPRINGS
HOG SPRINGS REST AREA
Cataract Canyon
Colorado River
Dark Canyon Primitive Area
Manti-La Sal National Forest/ Dark Canyon Wilderness
CEDAR MESA
Box-Death Hollow Wilderness
Boulder
DEER CREEK
BURR TRAIL
Henry Mountains
Waterpocket Fold
DIRTY DEVIL
STARR SPRINGS
HITE
FARLEY CANYON
CALF CREEK
Escalante
Escalante River
WHITE CANYON
BLUE NOTCH CANYON
Lake Powell
Natural Bridges Nat'l Mon.
HOLE-IN-THE-ROCK RD
Straight Cliffs
DEVIL'S GARDEN
Glen Canyon National Recreation Area
SEE DETAIL 1
DEFIANCE HOUSE
Red Rock Plateau
Grand Gulch Primitive Area
Grand Staircase–Escalante National Monument
DANCE HALL ROCK
Glen Canyon
HOLE-IN-THE-ROCK
San Juan Arm
San Juan River
SMOKY MOUNTAIN RD
DANGLING ROPE MARINA
NAVAJO INDIAN RESERVATION
Rainbow Bridge Nat'l Mon.
UT AZ
Lake Powell
SEE DETAIL 2

DETAIL 1
BULLFROG NORTH
BULLFROG SOUTH
VISITOR CENTER
BULLFROG MARINA
STANTON CREEK
HALLS CROSSING MARINA
Glen Canyon National Recreation Area

DETAIL 2
LONE ROCK
Lake Powell
UT AZ
WAHWEAP MARINA
Antelope Island
CARL HAYDEN VISITOR CENTER
Paria Canyon-Vermilion Cliffs Wilderness
GLEN CANYON DAM
Page
LEES FERRY
PARK HEADQUARTERS
NAVAJO BRIDGE INTERPRETIVE CENTER
NAVAJO INDIAN RESERVATION

0   10 mi
0   10 km

© AVALON TRAVEL PUBLISHING, INC.

the second-largest human-made lake within the United States. Only Lake Mead, farther downstream, has a greater water-storage capacity. Lake Powell, however, has three times more shoreline—1,960 miles—and holds enough water to cover the state of Pennsylvania a foot deep! Bays and coves offer nearly limitless opportunities for exploration by boaters. Nearly all of the lake lies within Utah. Only the lower part—Glen Canyon Dam, Wahweap Resort and Marina, Antelope and Navajo Canyons, and the lower parts of Labyrinth, Face, and West Canyons—extends into Arizona. The elevation of the surface fluctuates 20–30 feet through the year and peaks in July. The Carl Hayden Visitors Center, perched beside the dam, offers tours of the dam, related exhibits, and an information desk for all the Glen Canyon National Recreation Area.

Climate

Summer, when temperatures rise into the 90s and 100s, is the busiest season for swimming, boating, and water-skiing. Visits during the rest of the year can be enjoyable, too, though activities shift more to sightseeing, fishing, and hiking. Spring and autumn are the best times to enjoy the backcountry. Winter temperatures drop to highs in the 40s and 50s, with freezing nights and the possibility of snow. Lake surface temperatures range from a comfortable 80°F in August to a chilly 45° in January. Chinook winds can blow day and night for periods February–May. Thunderstorms in late summer bring strong, gusting winds with widely scattered rain showers. Annual precipitation averages about seven inches.

Geology, Flora, and Fauna

The colorful rock layers that rise above the lake's surface tell a story of ancient deserts, oceans, and rivers. An uplift of the Colorado Plateau beginning about 60 million years ago started a cycle of erosion that has carved canyons and created delicately balanced rocks and graceful natural arches and bridges.

The desert comes right to the edge of the water because fluctuating lake levels prevent plant growth along the shore. Common plants of this high-desert country include prickly pear and hedgehog cacti, rabbitbrush, sand sagebrush, blackbrush, cliffrose, mariposa and sego lilies, globemallow, Indian paintbrush, evening primrose, penstemon, and Indian rice grass. Piñon pine and juniper trees grow on the high plateaus. Springs and permanent streams support sandbar willow, tamarisk, cattail, willow, and cottonwood. Look for hanging gardens of maidenhair fern, columbine, and other water-loving plants in small alcoves high on the sandstone walls.

Most animals here are secretive and nocturnal; you're more likely to see them in early morning or evening. Local mammals include pronghorn, mule deer, mountain lion, coyote, red and gray foxes, ringtail cat, spotted and striped skunks, bobcat, badger, river otter, beaver, prairie dog, Ord kangaroo rat, black-tailed jackrabbit, several species of squirrels and chipmunks, and many species of mice and bats. Some lizards you might see sunning on rocks are collared, side-blotched, desert horned, and chuckwalla. Snake species include common king snake, gopher, striped whipsnake, western rattlesnake, and western diamondback rattlesnake. Birds stopping by on their migrations include American avocet, Canada goose, and teal. Others, such as blue heron, snowy egret, and bald eagle, come for the winter. Birds you might spot any time of the year are American merganser, mallard, canyon wren, piñon jay, common raven, redtailed and Swainson's hawks, great horned and long-eared owls, peregrine and prairie falcons, and golden eagle.

Recreation

If you don't have your own craft, Wahweap and other marinas will rent a boat for fishing, skiing, or houseboating. Boat tours visit Rainbow Bridge (the world's largest natural bridge) and other destinations from Wahweap, Bullfrog, and Halls Crossing Marinas. Sailboats find the steadiest breezes in Wahweap, Padre, Halls, and Bullfrog Bays, where spring winds average 15–20 knots. Kayaks and canoes can be used in the more protected areas. All boaters need to be alert for approaching storms that can bring wind gusts up to 60 mph. Waves on open expanses of the lake are sometimes steeper than ocean waves and can exceed six feet from trough to crest.

Marinas and bookstores sell navigation maps of Lake Powell. You'll need an Arizona fishing license for the southern five miles of lake and a Utah license for the rest of Lake Powell. Obtain licenses and information from marinas on the water or sporting goods stores in Page. Anglers catch largemouth, smallmouth, and striped bass, northern and walleye pike, catfish, crappie, and carp. Smaller fish include bluegill, perch, and sunfish. Wahweap has a swimming beach (no lifeguards), and boaters can find their own remote spots. Scuba divers can swim underwater with the sizable bass. Hikers have a choice of easy day trips or long wilderness backpack treks. The canyons of the Escalante rate among America's premier hiking areas. Other good hiking spots within or adjacent to Glen Canyon NRA include Rainbow Bridge National Monument, Paria Canyon, Dark Canyon, and Grand Gulch. National Park Service staff at the Carl Hayden Visitors Center can suggest trips and supply trail descriptions. Several guidebooks to Lake Powell have detailed hiking, camping, and boating information. Most of the canyon country near Lake Powell remains wild and little explored—hiking possibilities are limitless! Be sure to carry plenty of water.

GLEN CANYON DAM

Construction workers labored 1956–1964 to build this giant concrete structure. It stands 710 feet high above bedrock, and its top measures 1,560 feet across. Thickness ranges from 300 feet at the base to just 25 feet at the top. As part of the Upper Colorado River Storage Project, the dam provides water storage (its main purpose), hydroelectricity, flood control, and recreation on Lake Powell. Eight giant turbine generators churn out a total of 1,150,000 kilowatts at 13,800 volts. Vertigo sufferers shouldn't look down when driving across Glen Canyon Bridge; cold, green waters of the Colorado River glide 700 feet below.

Carl Hayden Visitors Center

Photos, paintings, movies, and slide presentations in the visitors center show features of Glen Canyon National Recreation Area, including Lake Powell and construction of the dam. A giant relief map helps you visualize the rugged terrain surrounding the lake; look closely and you'll spot Rainbow Bridge. Guided tours inside the dam and generating room depart daily in summer every half hour 8:30 A.M.–3:30 P.M. You can begin a self-guided tour daily 8 A.M.– 5 P.M. (7 A.M.–6 P.M. in summer). A National Park Service staff operates an information desk where you can find out about boating, fishing, camping, and hiking in the immense Glen Canyon National Recreation Area, 928/608-6404 (general information) or 928/608-6200 (headquarters). The Glen Canyon Natural History Association, 928/645-3523, has books about the recreation area and its environs for sale next to the information desk. Souvenirs, snacks, and postcards can be purchased at a gift shop in the visitors center building. The visitors center is open daily 8 A.M.–7 P.M. mountain standard time in summer and 8 A.M.–5 P.M. the rest of the year. Tours, exhibits, and slide presentations are free. In summer, you can attend a campfire program several nights a week at nearby Wahweap Campground amphitheater.

RAINBOW BRIDGE NATIONAL MONUMENT

Rainbow Bridge forms a graceful span 290 feet high and 275 feet wide; the Capitol Building in Washington, D.C., would fit neatly underneath. The easiest way to Rainbow Bridge is by boat tour on Lake Powell from Wahweap, Bullfrog, or Halls Crossing Marina.

The more adventurous can hike to the bridge from the Cha Canyon Trailhead (just north across the Arizona-Utah border on the east side of Navajo Mountain) or from the Rainbow Lodge Ruins (just south of the Arizona-Utah border on the west side of Navajo Mountain). Rugged trails from each point wind through highly scenic canyons, meet in Bridge Canyon, then continue two miles to the bridge. The hike on either trail, or a loop with both (car shuttle needed), is 26–28 miles round-trip. Hikers must be experienced and self-sufficient; these trails cross wilderness. Because the trails are unmaintained and poorly marked, hikers should consult a Navajo Mountain (Utah) 15-minute topo map or the newer 7.5-minute Navajo Begay and Chaiyahi Flat maps.

No camping is allowed at Rainbow Bridge and no supplies are available. You may camp a half mile east of the bridge at Echo camp. The Dangling Rope Marina and National Park Service Ranger Station are 10 miles away, by water only. The best times to go are April–early June, September, and October. Winter cold and snow discourage visitors, and summer is hot and brings hazardous flash floods. The National Park Service offers *Hiking to Rainbow Bridge* trail notes; contact Glen Canyon NRA, P.O. Box 1507, Page, AZ 86040, 928/608-6404.

The National Park Service cannot issue hiking permits to Rainbow Bridge. Obtain the required tribal hiking permit ($6 one person, $10 group of 2–10, $20 group of 11 or more) and camping permit ($2 per person per night) from the Cameron visitors center (not always open) or Navajo Parks Department, P.O. Box 9000, Window Rock, AZ 86515, 928/871-6636. Both offices are open Monday–Friday about 8 A.M.–5 P.M.; the Cameron office is also open weekends April–September.

The only road access to the Navajo Mountain area is Indian Route 16 from Highway 98, between Page and Kayenta. To reach the east trailhead, drive north 32 miles on Indian Route 16 past Inscription House Trading Post to a road fork, and then turn right six miles to Navajo Mountain Trading Post. Continue on the main road 6.5 miles (go straight at the four-way junction) to an earthen dam. Drive straight across the dam, take the left fork after a half mile, and then go 1.6 miles to Cha Canyon Trailhead at the end of the road.

You can reach the west trailhead by driving north 32 miles on Indian Route 16 and turning left and driving about six miles at the road fork to the Rainbow Lodge Ruins. Always lock

vehicles and remove valuables at trailheads. Because Navajo Mountain is sacred to the Navajo, you need permission to climb from the Navajo Parks Department.

Boat Tours to Rainbow Bridge

By far the most popular way to visit Rainbow Bridge is to sign on with a boat tour and take a half- or whole day trip to see the national monument. Most tours leave from Wahweap Marina, off U.S. 89. In high season, there are six departures daily for Rainbow Bridge on a five-hour trip. There's at least one trip a day throughout the year. Cost is $87 adult, children $61. One day-long trip (includes lunch) departs daily April–October; $115 adult, childen $71. Minimum numbers required on all trips.

Once at Painted Arch, tour boats park at a floating dock, and you can walk to a viewing area beneath the arch, a distance of about half a mile.

Reservations are strongly suggested. Call the marina at 928/645-1070 for information, or register online at www.lakepowell.com.

MARINAS

The **National Park Service** provides public boat ramps, campgrounds, and ranger offices at most of the marinas. Rangers know current boating and back-road conditions, primitive camping areas, and good places to explore. **Lake Powell Resorts & Marinas,** P.O. Box 56909, Phoenix, AZ 85079, 800/528-6154 (602/278-8888 in greater Phoenix), fax 602/331-5258, www.lakepowell.com, operates marina services, boat rentals, boat tours, accommodations, RV parks, and restaurants; contact them for information and reservations (strongly recommended in summer). All the marinas stay open year-round; avoid crowds and peak prices by coming in autumn, winter, or spring. Private or chartered aircraft can fly to Page Airport, San Juan County Airport near Bullfrog, or an airstrip near Halls Crossing.

Wahweap

The name means "bitter water" in the Ute language. Wahweap Lodge and Marina, Lake

Powell's biggest, offers complete boaters' services and rentals, guided tours, deluxe accommodations, an RV park, and fine dining. Wahweap is seven miles northwest of Page, five miles beyond the visitors center. **Wahweap Lodge** is a very large complex of motel rooms, restaurants, and public areas. There are different kinds of rooms, starting at $165 (single or double) April–October, $105 (single or double) in winter; lake-view rooms cost about $10 more. Contact Lake Powell Resorts & Marinas for reservations at P.O. Box 56909, Phoenix, AZ 85079, 800/528-6154, www.lakepowell.com. Wahweap Lodge & Marina can also be reached at P.O. Box 1597, Page, AZ 86040, 928/645-2433. **Lake Powell Motel,** at Wahweap Junction (four miles northwest of Glen Canyon Dam on U.S. 89), has less-expensive rooms, starting at $85. Information and reservations are through Lake Powell Resorts.

Wahweap Campground is operated on a first-come, first-served basis by Lake Powell Resorts & Marinas; tent sites have drinking water but no showers or hookups. Campers may use the pay showers and laundry facilities at the RV park. The RV park, campground, and a picnic area are between Wahweap Lodge and Stateline. Primitive camping (no water or fee) is available at **Lone Rock** in Utah, six miles northwest of Wahweap off U.S. 89; cars need to be very careful not to stray into loose sand areas. Boaters may also camp along the lakeshore, but not within one mile of developed areas. A free picnic area and fish-cleaning station are just west of Wahweap Lodge. Public boat ramps are adjacent to the lodge and at Stateline, 1.3 miles northwest of the lodge and just into Utah. During summer (June–September), you can also obtain recreation information from the **Wahweap Ranger Station** near the picnic area; at other times see the staff at Carl Hayden Visitors Center.

The marina offers six **lake tours,** ranging from an hour-long paddle-wheel cruise around Wahweap Bay ($12) to trips to Rainbow Bridge, 50 miles away ($87–115). The marina also offers a full range of watercraft rentals, including houseboats. For information on tours, call 928/645-1070.

Antelope Point

The newest marina area on the lake, Antelope Point, is just north of Page and has complete boating facilities, plus a swimming beach.

Dangling Rope

This floating marina lies 42 miles uplake from Glen Canyon Dam. The only access is by boat. Services include a ranger station, store, minor boat repairs, gas dock, and sanitary pump-out station. A dangling rope left behind in a nearby canyon, perhaps by uranium prospectors, prompted the name. The dock for Rainbow Bridge is seven miles farther uplake in Bridge Canyon, a tributary of Forbidding Canyon.

San Juan

Boats can be hand-launched at **Clay Hills Crossing** at the upper end of the San Juan arm. An unpaved road branches 11 miles southwest from Highway 276 (road to Halls Crossing) to the lake; don't attempt the road after rains. River-runners on the San Juan often take out here; no facilities.

Halls Crossing

In 1880, Charles Hall built the ferry used by the Hole-in-the-Rock pioneers, who crossed the river to begin settlement in southeast Utah. The approach roads were so bad, however, that he moved the ferry 35 miles upstream to present-day Halls Crossing in the following year. Business continued to be slow, and Hall quit running the ferry in 1884.

Arriving at Halls Crossing by road, you'll first reach a small store offering rooms in trailer houses and an RV park. Coin-operated showers and laundry at the RV park are also open to the public. The separate National Park Service **campground,** just beyond and to the left, has sites with a good view of the lake, drinking water, and restrooms; $14. Continue a half mile on the main road to the boat ramp and **Halls Crossing Marina.** The marina has a larger store (groceries and fishing and boating supplies), tours to Rainbow Bridge, a boat rental office (fishing, ski, and houseboat), gas dock, slips, and storage. The **ranger station** is nearby,

CROSSING LAKE POWELL BY FERRY

The Halls Crossing/Bullfrog Ferry Service, a car ferry that crosses Lake Powell between the two marinas, offers a good way to get out onto the lake and get a sense for the size and drama of the region. (Taking the ferry isn't required, as Highway 95 crosses the lake farther north, at Hite.)

The crossing time from Halls Crossing to Bullfrog is 27 minutes (the crossing is only three miles, however). Fares for vehicles smaller than 19 feet 11 inches in length are $12, which includes the driver and all passengers. Bicycles are $3, and motorcycles are $5. Foot passengers are $3 adult.

During the high summer season, May 15–September 14, the ferries run on the hour daily beginning at 8 A.M. The final ferry from Halls Crossing departs at 6 P.M., and the final ferry from Bullfrog departs at 7 P.M. April 15–May 14, and September 15–October 31, the Halls Ferry begins operation at 8 A.M. and has sailings every two hours until 4 P.M. The Bullfrog ferry begins at 9 A.M. and has sailings every two hours until 5 P.M. The rest of the year, November 1–April 14, this same schedule continues, except the final sailings of the day are at 2 P.M. and 3 P.M., respectively.

For reservations and information regarding the ferries, lodging, tours, boating, and recreation at both Halls Crossing and Bullfrog Marina, contact Lake Powell Resorts & Marinas, 100 Lakeshore Dr., Page, AZ 86040, 800/528-6154, www.lakepowell.com.

nation 12 miles uplake; a sign marks the beginning of the trail to the ruins.

Bullfrog

Before the days of Lake Powell, Bullfrog Rapids gave boaters a fast and bumpy ride. Bullfrog Marina has the most extensive visitor facilities of Lake Powell's Utah marinas. If driving in on the highway, the **visitors center** is on the right, 435/684-2243; open daily 8 A.M.–5 P.M. The **clinic,** 435/684-2288, is here, too; open May 15–September 30. A large **campground** lies on the left; sites have drinking water and restrooms for $12. Continue on the main road to a junction; a service station, store, and marine service here offer repairs and supplies. Continue straight at the junction for a picnic area and the boat ramp; turn right at the service station for Defiance House Lodge and Restaurant, Trailer Village, Bullfrog Painted Hills RV Park, and Bullfrog Marina.

All-day **Rainbow Bridge tours** usually leave daily April 15–October 31 and stop on request to pick up passengers at Halls Crossing Marina. **Canyon Explorer tours** depart in the evening for two hours in nearby canyons during the same season. **Bullfrog Marina** has a store, snack bar, boat rentals (fishing, ski, and houseboat), gas dock, slips, and storage. Contact Lake Powell Resorts & Marinas for accommodation, boat rental, and tour reservations at P.O. Box 56909, Phoenix, AZ 85079, 800/528-6154, fax 602/331-5258, www.lakepowell.com. Bullfrog Resort & Marina can also be reached at P.O. Box 4055-Bullfrog, Lake Powell, UT 84533, 435/684-2233.

Defiance House Lodge, 435/684-3000 or 800/528-6154, offers luxury accommodations and the **Anasazi Restaurant** (open daily for breakfast, lunch, and dinner). Rooms begin at $120 (single or double) in summer (April–October) and $80 (single or double) in winter. The front desk at the lodge also handles **housekeeping units** (trailers) and an **RV park** and **tours** to Rainbow Bridge and local canyons. Showers, laundry, a convenience store, and a post office are at **Trailer Village.** The RV park has showers.

though rangers are usually out on patrol; look for their vehicle in the area if the office is closed. Contact Lake Powell Resorts & Marinas for accommodation, boat rental, and tour reservations at P.O. Box 56909, Phoenix, AZ 85079, 800/528-6154, fax 602/331-5258, www.lakepowell.com. The marina can also be reached at Highway 276, Lake Powell, UT 84533, 435/684-2261.

Stabilized Anasazi ruins at **Defiance House** in Forgotten Canyon make a good boating destito primitive camping areas with vehicle access elsewhere along Bullfrog Bay.

Hite

In 1883, Cass Hite came to Glen Canyon in search of gold. He found some at a place later named Hite City and set off a small gold rush. Cass and a few of his relatives operated a small store and post office, the only services for many miles. Travelers wishing to cross the Colorado River here had the difficult task of swimming their animals across. Arthur Chaffin, a later resident, put through the first road and opened a ferry service in 1946. The Chaffin Ferry served uranium prospectors and adventurous motorists until the lake backed up to the spot in 1964. A steel bridge now spans the Colorado River upstream from Hite Marina. Cass Hite's store and the ferry site are underwater about five miles downlake from Hite Marina.

The uppermost marina on Lake Powell, Hite lies 141 lake miles from Glen Canyon Dam. From here boats can continue uplake to the mouth of Dark Canyon in Cataract Canyon at low water or into Canyonlands National Park at high water. Hite tends to be quieter than the other marinas and is favored by some anglers and families. The turnoff for the marina is from Highway 95 between Blanding and Hanksville. On the way in, you'll find a small **store** with gas pumps, **housekeeping units** and a primitive **campground** (no drinking water; free). Primitive camping is also available nearby off Highway 95 at Dirty Devil, Farley Canyon, White Canyon, Blue Notch, and other locations. **Hite Marina,** at the end of the access road, has a small store, housekeeping units, gas dock, boat rentals (fishing, ski, and houseboat), slips, and storage. Hikers can make arrangements with the marina to be dropped off or picked up at Dark Canyon. A **ranger station** is occasionally open; look for the ranger's vehicle at other times. Contact Lake Powell Resorts & Marinas for accommodation and boat rental reservations at P.O. Box 56909, Phoenix, AZ 85079, 800/528-6154 fax 602/331-5258, www.lakepowell.com. Hite Marina can also be contacted at P.O. Box 501, Lake Powell, UT 84533, 435/684-2278.

Page, Arizona

Only sand and desert vegetation lay atop Manson Mesa in far northern Arizona, where Page now sits, until 1957. In that year the U.S. Bureau of Reclamation decided to build a giant reservoir in Glen Canyon on the Colorado River. Glen Canyon Dam became one of the largest construction projects ever undertaken: The 710-foot-high structure created a lake covering 250 square miles with a shoreline of nearly 2,000 miles. Workers hastily set up prefabricated metal buildings for barracks, dining hall, and offices. Trailers rolled in, one serving as a bank, another as a school. And thus was born the town of Page. The Bureau of Reclamation named it for John C. Page, who served as the bureau's commissioner 1937–1943.

The remote desert spot (elev. 4,300 ft.) gradually turned into a modern town with schools, businesses, and churches. Streets were named and grass and trees planted so that Page took on the appearance of an American suburb. Today, the town still looks new and clean. Though small (pop. 9,500), it's the largest community close to Lake Powell and offers travelers a variety of places to stay and eat.

Wedged between the Arizona Strip to the west, Glen Canyon National Recreation Area to the north, and the Navajo Reservation to the east and south, Page makes a useful base for visiting all of these areas. The town overlooks Lake Powell and Glen Canyon Dam; the large Wahweap Resort and Marina lies just six miles away.

SIGHTS AND HIKES
Powell Museum

This collection honors scientist and explorer John Wesley Powell. In 1869 Powell led the first expedition down the Green and Colorado River canyons, then ran the rivers a second time

1871–1872. It was he who named the most splendid section the Grand Canyon.

Old drawings and photographs illustrate Powell's life and voyages. Fossil and mineral displays interpret the thick geologic sections revealed by the canyons of the Colorado River system. Other exhibits contain pottery, baskets, weapons, and tools of Southwestern tribes, as well as memorabilia of early river runners, Page's pioneers, and Glen Canyon Dam. Related videos are shown on request. Regional books can be purchased. The staff offers travel info

and can book Lake Powell boat tours, all-day and half-day float trips, Corkscrew/Antelope Canyon tours, and scenic flights.

In summer (June–August), the museum is open Monday–Friday 8:30 A.M.–5:30 P.M.; spring and autumn hours are Monday–Friday 9 A.M.–5 P.M.; it's closed mid-December–mid-February. Admission is $1 adult, $.50 children kindergarten–8th grade. The museum is in downtown Page at the corner of 6 N. Lake Powell Blvd. and N. Navajo Dr., 928/645-9496 or 888/597-6873, www.powellmuseum.org.

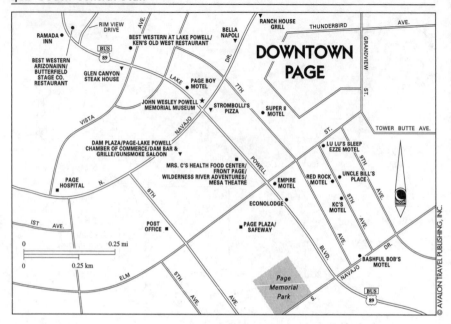

Navajo Village

The Navajo offer cultural programs about their beliefs and traditional skills at this living museum on the edge of town. A visit to the site to watch weavers, silversmiths, and artisans at work is $10 adult, $5 children 6–13, $25 family, while a mini tour of the village, which also includes an opportunity to watch native dancers, costs $25 adult, $19 children, $69 family. **An Evening with the Navajo** begins with a horse-drawn wagon ride to the re-created village, where you'll see demonstrations of cooking and craftsmanship plus two hours of presentation. Your hosts explain features of the sweat lodge and two types of hogans here. You'll enjoy a dinner of traditional foods, watch song and dance performances, and listen to stories around a fire. The four-hour evening presentations cost $50 adults and $35 children, $135 family. Contact the Page/Lake Powell Chamber of Commerce, 928/645-2741 or 888/261-7243, www.navajovillage.net.

The Best Dam View

An excellent panorama of Glen Canyon Dam and the Colorado River can be enjoyed just west of town. It's reached via Scenic View Road behind Denny's Restaurant off U.S. 89; turn west at the junction of U.S. 89 and N. Lake Powell Boulevard or west beside the Glen Canyon NRA headquarters building and turn at the sign for Scenic Overlook. A short trail leads down to the best viewpoint.

Rimview Trail

An eight-mile trail for walkers, joggers, and cyclists encircles Page with many views of the surrounding desert and Lake Powell. The unpaved route has some sandy and rocky sections that will challenge novice bike riders. If you find yourself more than 30 vertical feet below the mesa rim, you're off the trail. You can pick up a map from the chamber office. A popular starting point is at the short nature trail loop near Lake View School at North Navajo Drive and 20th Avenue in the northern part of town.

Corkscrew/Antelope Canyon

You'll see photos around town of the beautifully

convoluted red rock in this canyon, so narrow in places that you have to squeeze through. Sunshine reflects off the smooth Navajo sandstone to create extraordinary light and colors. Beams of light enter the canyons at midday, further entrancing visitors. Photographers don't wish to spoil the effect with a flash, so most bring a tripod to help capture the infinite shapes and patterns.

Antelope Canyon has a wider upper section known as Corkscrew and a narrower lower section. The shallow wash in between that you see from the highway gives no hint of the marvels up or downstream. Both can easily be reached from Page by driving south on Coppermine Road or east on Highway 98 to the junction at Big Lake Trading Post, then continuing east one mile on Highway 98 toward the power plant. Turn right into the parking area for the upper canyon, or stay on Highway 98 just 0.15 mile farther and then turn left half a mile at the sign on paved Antelope Point Road for the lower canyon. At either place you'll pay $6 for a tribal entry permit (good for both sections) plus shuttle or tour fees. The upper section has a shuttle charge of $20 adult, $12 children for the 3.5-mile drive to the trailhead and a one-hour visit; no walk-ins or private drive-ins are permitted. The lower canyon can be visited on self-guided hikes for $20 adult, $12 children plus the $6 entry fee. You can also take a guided excursion from Page.

The upper canyon ticket booth is usually open daily 8 A.M.–5 P.M. April–October; you can also obtain Rainbow Bridge hiking permits here. The lower canyon closes by 4 P.M. For information and off-season access, call Antelope Canyon Navajo Tribal Park at 928/698-2808; the office is four miles south of Page in Leche-e. Early April–late October, the canyon hours run on the Navajo Reservation's daylight saving time (when it's 4 P.M. in Page, it's 5 P.M. at Antelope). Late starts also run the risk of canyon access closing early if business is slow. In winter (November–March) you may need to telephone ahead to arrange a visit. Check the weather forecast before heading out, as slot canyons are deadly during a flash flood.

Local outfitters who offer Antelope Canyon shuttles (and feature other backcountry tours) include Antelope Canyon Tours, 928/645-9102, www.antelopecanyon.com, and Overland Canyon Tours, 928/608-4072, www.overlandcanyon.com.

Horseshoe Bend View

The Colorado River makes a sharp, 180-degree bend below this spectacular viewpoint. Look for the parking area just west of U.S. 89, 0.2 mile south of milepost 545; it's 2.5 miles south of Page's Gateway Plaza. A three-quarter-mile trail leads from the parking to the overlook. Photographers will find a wide-angle lens handy to take in the whole scene. Mornings have good light for pictures; afternoons can be dramatic if the sky is filled with clouds.

EVENTS

In March, fishermen test their skills in the **Bullfrog Open** bass tournament. **Indian Nights Pow Wow** in early June has amazing dances, drumming, and music.

On **July 4,** there's a parade followed by fireworks that light the sky over Glen Canyon Dam. **Mr. Burfel's Softball Tournament** plays in September. In October, **Air Affaire** takes off over Page with airplane acrobatics and parachutists.

Bullfrog's **Festival of Lights Parade** takes place on the Saturday after Thanksgiving. In December, the **Here Comes Santa Parade** marks the holiday season in Page. **Wahweap Festival of Lights Parade** on Lake Powell glides by on the first Saturday.

For more information on any Lake Powell event, ask at the marina where it's held. To learn about other events, contact Page/Lake Powell Chamber of Commerce, 928/645-2741.

RECREATION

Page High School features a year-round indoor **swimming pool** near the corner of S. Lake Powell Blvd. and Hwy. 98; 928/608-4100. Play **tennis** at the courts on S. Lake Powell Blvd. (Church Row). **Lake Powell National Golf Course,** 928/645-2023, offers an 18-hole championship golf course that wraps around the west side of the mesa; turn in on Clubhouse Dr. adjacent to the Courtyard by Marriott. **Glen Canyon Golf and Country Club,** 928/645-2715, has a 9-hole golf course west across U.S. 89 from the 18-hole course. **Twin Finn Diving Center** offers diving activities and classes and rents diving equipment and kayaks (both touring and sit-on-top) at 811 Vista Ave., 928/645-3114, www.twinfinn.com.

TOURS

You can obtain information and make reservations for many area tours through the Page/Lake Powell Chamber of Commerce (www.pagelakepowellchamber.org) or Powell Museum (www.powellmuseum.org).

Lake Powell Jeep Tours, 104 S. Lake Powell Blvd., 928/645-5501, www.jeeptour.com, offers regular and photographer's tours to Corkscrew Canyon in Antelope Wash year-round, weather permitting. **Roger Ekis' Antelope Canyon Tours,** 928/645-9102 or 435/675-9109, www.antelopecanyon.com, goes to both upper and lower Antelope Canyon except in winter. **Scenic Tours,** 928/645-5594, does 90-minute excursions to Corkscrew Canyon year-round, weather permitting. **J&C Outfitters,** 928/645-9557, www.atvtours.net takes visitors on guided ATV tours in the Page and Kaibab Plateau areas; beginners receive instruction.

Raft trips float down the Colorado River from just below Glen Canyon Dam to Lees Ferry, traveling over 15 miles of smooth-flowing water through the beautiful canyon of Navajo sandstone. Stop to inspect some fine petroglyphs; you're likely to see condors, blue herons, ducks, and other birds. Half-day trips leave once or twice daily March–October, weather permitting; the cost is $57 adults, $47 children 12 and under. All-day trips have more time on the water and include a lunch buffet; they run May 15–September 15 and cost $77 adults, $69 children 12 and under. Kayakers and canoeists can arrange for rafts to take them from Lees Ferry upstream to the dam. All Glen Canyon float trips depart from the Wilderness Outfitters Store, 50 S. Lake Powell Blvd., in the shopping center at the corner

of Elm St. and Lake Powell Blvd, 928/645-3279 or 800/528-6154.

ACCOMMODATIONS

Nearly all Page motels lie on or near Lake Powell Blvd./Hwy. 89L, a 3.25-mile loop that branches off the main highway. Page is a busy place in summer, however, and a call ahead is a good idea if you don't want to chase around town looking for vacancies. Expect to pay top dollar for views of the lake. The summer rates listed here drop in winter (November–March). The 8th Avenue places lie in Page's historic district, a quiet residential area two blocks off Lake Powell Boulevard. These apartments date back to 1958–1959, when they housed supervisors and foremen for the dam; today some of the buildings have been fixed up as pensions and motels.

Under $50

Uncle Bill's Place, 117 8th Ave., 928/645-1224, www.thedam.com/unclebill, features a quiet garden in back; you have a choice of rooms with shared bath and kitchen (under $50) or private suites (over $50). **KC's Motel,** 126 8th Ave., 928/645-2947 offers rooms with private bath. **Red Rock Motel,** 114 8th Ave., 928/645-0062, www.redrockmotel.com, has private baths and some kitchens (under $50), plus two-bedroom suites (over $50). **Bashful Bob's Motel,** around the corner at 750 S. Navajo Dr., 928/645-3919, www.page.az.net/bashfulbobsmotel, offers mostly two-bedroom apartments, all with kitchens;. **Navajo Trail Motel** has rooms at two downtown locations and on the southern outskirts; contact the office for all three places at 800 Bureau, 928/645-9508; the other motel units are at 630 Vista, behind Glen Canyon Steak House, and at 524 Haul Road.

$50–75

Lu Lu's Sleep EZZe Motel, 105 8th Ave., 928/608-0273 or 800/553-6211, has some of the most luxurious rooms on this street. **Page Boy Motel,** 150 N. Lake Powell Blvd., 928/645-2416, offers a swimming pool. **Econo Lodge** is at 121 S. Lake Powell Blvd., 928/645-2488 or 800/553-

2666. **Empire Motel,** 107 S. Lake Powell Blvd., 928/645-2406 or 800/551-9005, features a swimming pool. Farther south from downtown, **Motel 6,** 637 S. Lake Powell Blvd., 928/645-5888 or 800/4MOTEL6, has a pool.

$75–100

Best Western at Lake Powell, 208 N. Lake Powell Blvd., 928/645-5988 or 800/528-1234, has views, a pool, spa, and exercise room. The nearby **Best Western ArizonaInn,** 716 Rim View Dr. and N. Lake Powell Blvd. (across from Ramada Inn), 928/645-2466 or 800/826-2718, provides fine views, swimming pool, and adjacent restaurant. **Super 8 Motel** is at 75 S. 7th Ave., 928/645-2858 or 800/800-8000. **Comfort Inn,** 649 S. Lake Powell Blvd., 928/645-5858 or 800/228-5150, is south of downtown with a pool and spa. Next door, **Holiday Inn Express,** 751 S. Navajo Dr., 928/645-9000 or 800/HOLIDAY, offers two-bed rooms, pool, spa, and continental breakfast. **Lake Powell Day's Inn & Suites** lies on the south edge of town beside U.S. 89 with an outdoor pool and spa, 928/645-2800 or 877/525-3769.

Canyon Colors Bed & Breakfast, 225 S. Navajo Dr., 928/645-5979 or 800/536-2530, www.canyon-country.com/colors, has a pool, patio, and fireplaces. **Sunrise View Bed & Breakfast,** 1633 San Juan Court, 928/608-4763, www.canyon-country/sunrise, offers not only views but a shaded backyard and other extras.

$100–125

Ramada Inn, 287 N. Lake Powell Blvd., 928/645-8851 or 800/261-6702, features a swimming pool, restaurant, and great views over Lake Powell. **Courtyard by Marriott,** 600 Clubhouse Dr., 928/645-5000 or 800/321-2211, offers views, a restaurant, a pool, spa, exercise room, and adjacent 18-hole golf course.

Campgrounds

Page–Lake Powell Campground offers sites for tents and RVs with an indoor pool and spa, store, laundry, and showers; non-guests may use the showers or dump station for a small fee. The campground is 0.7 mile southeast of downtown

on Coppermine Road, 928/645-3374. Other campgrounds, an RV park, and motels are in the Wahweap area (see Wahweap under Glen Canyon National Recreation Area).

FOOD AND ENTERTAINMENT

Ranch House Grill, 819 N. Navajo Dr., 928/645-1420, is a handy place for breakfast and does American lunches too; open daily. **Dam Bar & Grill,** 644 N. Navajo Dr. in the Dam Plaza, 928/645-2161, serves up steak, barbecue, seafood, pasta, and sandwiches daily for dinner; it also has a sports bar. The adjacent **Gunsmoke Saloon,** 928/645-2161, features country bands and other music Wednesday–Saturday. **Family Tree Restaurant,** 287 N. Lake Powell Blvd., 928/645-8851, in the Ramada Inn offers a varied menu daily for breakfast, lunch, and dinner; in summer, you can choose a buffet for breakfast, lunch (usually just on Sunday), and dinner (seafood on Friday). **Butterfield Stage Co. Restaurant,** 704 Rim View Dr. next to Best Western ArizonaInn, 928/645-2467, serves American food daily for breakfast, lunch, and dinner; dinner choices include steak, prime rib, and seafood. **Pepper's Restaurant,** 600 Clubhouse Dr., 928/645-5000, at the Courtyard by Marriott offers American and continental cuisine with a Southwestern touch and is open daily for breakfast (also a buffet), lunch, and dinner. **Denny's** is open 24 hours and serves popular American fare for breakfast, lunch, and dinner at 669 Scenic View Dr. (turn west at the U.S. 89-N. Lake Powell Blvd. Junction), 928/645-3999.

For Chinese cuisine, try **Mandarin Gourmet Restaurant,** open daily for lunch and dinner in Gateway Plaza, 928/645-5516. **Bella Napoli,** 810 N. Navajo Dr., 928/645-2706, offers fine Italian cuisine daily for dinner in summer and Monday–Saturday for dinner the rest of the year; closed late December–mid-February. **Strombolli's Pizza,** 711 N. Navajo Dr., 928/645-2605, is open daily for lunch and dinner, except in winter; diners have a choice of indoor seating or the outdoor deck, a popular gathering spot for boaters in the summer.

You can buy **groceries** at Safeway (Page Plaza at corner of S. Lake Powell Blvd. and Elm St.), Bashas' (Gateway Plaza), or at Mrs. C's Health Food Center (32 S. Lake Powell Blvd.). Catch movies at **Mesa Theatre,** 42 S. Lake Powell Blvd., 928/645-9565.

OTHER PRACTICALITIES
Information and Services
The **Page/Lake Powell Chamber of Commerce,** 644 N. Navajo Dr. in the Dam Plaza (Box 727, Page, AZ 86040), 928/645-2741 or 888/261-7243, www.pagelakepowellchamber.org, offers information about area sights and services and books lake and river tours, Corkscrew/Antelope Canyon tours, and scenic flights. Open Monday–Saturday 8 A.M.–8 P.M. and Sunday 9 A.M.–6 P.M. May 16–October 16, then Monday–Friday 9 A.M.–5 P.M. the rest of the year.

The semicircular **Page Public Library** rises impressively from the mesa rim at 479 S. Lake Powell Blvd.; it has an Arizona/Native American collection, Internet computers, and fine views; it's open Monday–Thursday 10 A.M.–8 P.M. and Friday–Saturday 10 A.M.–5 P.M., 928/645-4270. **Front Page,** 48 S. Lake Powell Blvd., 928/645-5333, has regional titles, general reading, and office supplies.

The **post office** is located at 44 6th Ave., 928/645-2571. **Page Hospital** stands at the corner of 501 N. Navajo Dr. and Vista Ave., 928/645-2424.

Transportation
Wahweap Lodge, 928/645-2433, operates **Page Shuttle** frequently to Page and the airport. Most area motels also provide transportation for guests to and from the airport. **Avis** rents cars, 928/645-2024 or 800/331-1212.

Southeastern Utah

The Colorado River and its tributaries have carved extraordinary landscapes in southeastern Utah. Intricate mazes of canyons, delicate arches, and massive rock monoliths make this a region like no other. First-time visitors often need a while to appreciate this strange land before they're won over by the infinite colors and beauties of the sculptured rock. The thousands of canyons invite exploration—they offer solitude, ruins of prehistoric villages, wildlife, and dramatic records of geologic history.

THE LAND

About 300 million years ago, this land was at times a great Sahara-like desert and at others covered by water. Thick layers of sediment built up one on top of the other. During the last 50 million years, powerful forces within the earth slowly pushed the entire region a mile upward. The ancestral Colorado River and other streams appeared and began to carve the deep gorges seen today.

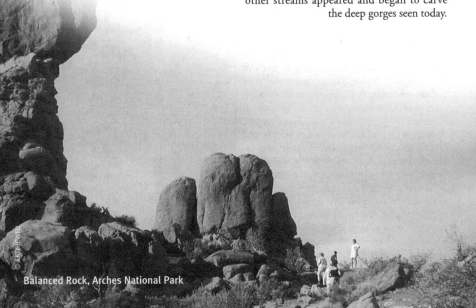

Balanced Rock, Arches National Park

Some of the younger rock layers of the uplifted Colorado Plateau have been eroded, yet the deposits that remain represent more than 150 million years. Ancient dunes, turned to stone, make up many of the sheer canyon cliffs, arches, and spires of the region. Delicate crossbedded lines of the former dunes add grace to these features. Forces within the restless plateau have also buckled and folded rock layers into great reefs as long as 100 miles. Weathering then carved them into rainbow-hued rock monuments. Volcanic pressures deep in the earth also shaped the land. Thick sediments above, however, prevented most of the molten rock from reaching the surface. Massive intrusions of magma bowed up overlying rock layers before cooling and solidifying. Erosion has since uncovered four of these dome-shaped ranges in southeastern Utah—the Henrys, the La Sals, the Abajos, and Navajo Mountain. Rain and snowmelt captured by these high peaks nourish the plants and wildlife of the region.

Climate

The high-desert country of southeastern Utah lies mostly between 3,500 and 6,500 feet in elevation. Annual precipitation ranges from an extremely dry three inches in some areas to about 10 inches over much of the land. Mountainous regions between 10,000 and 13,000 feet receive abundant rainfall in summer and heavy snows in winter. The rugged character of the canyon country causes many local variations in climate. Sunny skies prevail through all four seasons. Spring comes early to the canyon country with weather that's often windy and rapidly changing. Summer can make its presence known in April, though the real desert heat doesn't set in until late May or early June. Temperatures then soar into the 90s and 100s at midday, though the dry air makes the heat more bearable. Early morning is the choice time for travel in summer. A canyon seep surrounded by hanging gardens or a mountain meadow filled with wildflowers provides a refreshing contrast to the parched desert; other

SOUTHEASTERN UTAH

NEFERTITI

Green River

SEGO

Thompson

Westwater

Cisco

Green River State Park

CRYSTAL GEYSER

Arches National Park

FISHER TOWERS

HONDOO ARCH LOOP

San Rafael Swell

HONDOO ARCH

Moab

La Sal Mtns.

Mt. Waas 12,331 ft

Goblin Valley State Park

San Rafael Desert

Horseshoe Canyon

Dead Horse Point State Park

Manns Pk. 12,273 ft

Mt. Tomasaki 12,230 ft

Mt. Peale 12,721 ft

Canyonlands National Park

Canyonlands

Hanksville

Glen Canyon

National

CAMEO CLIFFS

La Sal

DIRTY DEVIL CANYON OVERLOOK

National

Cataract Canyon

Park

Mt. Ellen 11,522 ft

Recreation

NEWSPAPER ROCK HISTORICAL SITE

Mt. Pennell 11,320 ft

Area

Beef Basin

River

STARR SPRINGS CAMPGROUND

Monticello

Mt. Hillers 10,723 ft

HITE MARINA

Dark Canyon

Abajo Pk. 11,362 ft

Waterpocket Fold

Ticaboo

BURR TRAIL

Elk Ridge

The Causeway

Montezuma Canyon

Fry Canyon

Circle Cliffs

Colorado

The Bears Ears 9,058 ft

Blanding

Canyon

Natural Bridges National Monument

N.R.A.

Bullfrog Marina

Grand Gulch

Comb Ridge

HALLS CROSSING MARINA

Clay Hills

Hovenweep National Monument

COLORADO UTAH

Bluff

HOLE-IN-THE-ROCK

Montezuma Creek

Aneth

UTE INDIAN RES.

DANGLING ROPE MARINA

Mexican Hat

INDIAN

RAINBOW BRIDGE NATIONAL MONUMENT

NAVAJO

Monument Valley

FOUR CORNERS MONUMENT

RESERVATION

MONUMENT VALLEY VISITOR CENTER

To Kayenta, AZ

0   15 mi

0   15 km

SOUTHEASTERN UTAH HIGHLIGHTS

Spending the night at Sorrel River Ranch

Exploring Moab's brewpubs

The Fisher Towers

Mountain biking the Moab-area trails

Sego Canyon petroglyphs

Sunset at Delicate Arch

The view from Dead Point Horse State Park

Rafting the Colorado River's Cataract Canyon

Horseshoe Canyon's Great Gallery

Newspaper Rock

Hovenweep National Monument

Bluff, an oasis of hospitality and history in the southeastern Utah desert

---

ways to beat the heat include hiking in the mountains and river-rafting. Huge billowing thunderstorm clouds in late summer bring refreshing rains and coolness. Autumn begins after the rains and lasts into November or even December; days are bright and sunny with ideal temperatures, but nights become cold. Winter lasts only about two months at the lower elevations. Light snows on the canyon walls add new beauty to the rock layers. Nighttime temperatures commonly dip into the teens—too cold for most campers. Otherwise winter can be a fine time for travel. Heavy snows rarely occur below 8,000 feet.

Flash Floods

The bare rock and loose soils so common in the canyon country do little to hold back the flow of water. A summer thunderstorm or a rapid late-winter snowmelt can send torrents of mud and boulders rumbling down dry washes and canyons. Backcountry drivers, horseback riders, and hikers need to avoid hazardous locations when storms threaten or unseasonably warm winds blow on the winter snowpack. Logs and other debris wedged high on canyon walls give proof enough of past floods.

FLORA AND FAUNA

The region's elevation range—from 3,700 feet at Lake Powell to 12,721 feet atop the La Sal Mountains—provides a wide variety of habitats. Yet the dry conditions and thin or nonexistent soils limit both plant- and wildlife. Annuals simply wait for a wet year before quickly flowering and spreading their seeds. Piñon pines, junipers, and other plants often adapt by growing in rock cracks that concentrate moisture and nutrients. Small mammals such as mice, wood rats, rock squirrels, and chipmunks find food and shelter in these outposts of vegetation. Even meager soils permit growth of hardy shrubs like blackbrush, greasewood, sagebrush, rabbitbrush, and Mormon tea. Prickly pear and other types of cacti do well in the desert, too.

Perhaps the most unusual plant communities are the cryptobiotic crusts found on sandy soils. Mosses, lichens, fungi, algae, and diatoms live together in a gray-green to black layer up to several inches thick. Microclimates surrounding canyon seeps and springs provide a haven for hanging gardens of grasses, ferns, orchids, columbines, mosses, and other water-loving plants. River and stream banks have their own vegetation including river willows, cattails, tamarisks, and cottonwoods. Wildlife you might see in the semiarid desert are mule deer, desert bighorn sheep, pronghorns, coyotes, bobcats, foxes, skunks, porcupines, and many species of rodents. Ravens, eagles, hawks, owls, falcons, magpies, and smaller birds fly overhead. Watch out for the poisonous rattlesnakes and scorpions, though these shy creatures won't attack unless provoked.

At elevations between 7,000 and 8,500 feet, the desert gives way to forests of aspen, Gambel oak, ponderosa pine, and mountain mahogany. Conifers dominate up to the treeline, at about 12,000 feet. Alpine flowering plants, grasses, sedges, and mosses cling to the windy summits of the La Sal Mountains. Wildlife of the forests includes many of the desert dwellers, as well as elk, bear, mountain lion, marmot, and pika. A herd of bison roams freely in the Henry Mountains; the surrounding desert keeps them from going elsewhere.

HISTORY

Prehistoric Peoples

Nomadic bands of hunter-gatherers roamed the canyon country for at least 5,000 years. The climate was probably cooler and wetter when the first bands arrived; food plants and game animals would have been more abundant than today. Agriculture introduced from the south about 2,000 years ago brought about a slow transition to a settled village life. The Fremont culture emerged in the northern part of the region and the Anasazi in the southern part. Thousands of stone dwellings, ceremonial kivas, and towers built by the Anasazi still stand. Both groups also left behind intriguing rock art, either pecked in (petroglyphs) or painted (pictographs). The Anasazi and Fremont departed from this region about 800 years ago, perhaps because of drought, warfare, or disease. Some of the Anasazi moved south and joined the Pueblo tribes of present-day Arizona and New Mexico. The fate of the Fremont people remains a mystery.

After the mid-1200s and until white settlers arrived in the late 1800s, small bands of nomadic Ute and Paiute moved through southeastern Utah. The Navajo began to enter Utah in the early 1800s. None of the three Native American groups established firm control of the region north of the San Juan River. A remnant of the Ute and Paiute tribes now lives on the small White Mesa Reservation south of Blanding.

The Navajo

Relatives of the Athapascans of western Canada, the seminomadic Navajo wandered into New Mexico and Arizona between A.D. 1300 and 1500. This adaptable tribe learned agriculture, weaving, pottery, and other skills from their Pueblo neighbors, and they became expert horsemen and sheepherders with livestock obtained from the Spanish. Later, though, the old Navajo habits of raiding neighboring tribes and white settlements almost brought their downfall. In 1863–1864 the U.S. Army rounded up all the Navajo they could find and forced the survivors on "The Long Walk" from Fort Defiance in northeastern Arizona to a bleak camp in eastern New Mexico. This internment was a dismal failure, and the Navajo were released four years later.

In 1868 the federal government "awarded" land to the Navajo that has since grown to a giant reservation spreading from northeastern Arizona into adjacent Utah and New Mexico. The Navajo Nation, with 172,000 members, now ranks as the largest Native American tribe in the country. Their Utah land lies mostly south of Lake Powell and the San Juan River in the extreme southeastern corner of the state but includes some acreage north of the San Juan near Montezuma Creek. Oil, gas, and ranching are important sources of income. The Navajo own the spectacular Monument Valley Tribal Park on the Utah-Arizona border.

Religion is a vital part of Navajo culture. Most ceremonies involve healing and often take place late at night. If someone is sick, his or her family calls in a medicine man or woman who uses sandpaintings, chants, and dancing to effect a cure. The Navajo make beautiful silver jewelry and woven rugs. You'll see these in trading posts on and off the reservation. Colorful velveteen blouses and long flowing skirts like those worn by Navajo women are sometimes available for purchase; the Navajo women adopted the style during the tribe's 1860s New Mexico internment. It's what the U.S. Army wives were wearing!

Exploration and Settlement

Later explorers established the Old Spanish Trail through Utah to connect New Mexico with California. The route crossed the Colorado River near present-day Moab and was used 1829–1848, when the United States acquired the western territories. Fur trappers also traveled the canyons in search of beaver and other animals during the early 1800s; inscriptions carved into the sandstone record their passage. The U.S. Army's Macomb Expedition visited southeastern Utah in 1859 and made the first documented description of what's now Canyonlands National Park.

Major John Wesley Powell's pioneering river expeditions down the Green and Colorado in 1869 and 1871–1872 filled in many blank areas on the maps.

Hostile Native Americans discouraged early attempts by the Mormons to start settlements in southeastern Utah. The Elk Mountain Mission, founded in 1855 near present-day Moab, lasted only a few months before Utes killed three Mormons and sent the rest fleeing for their lives. Church members had better success during the 1870s in the Escalante area (1876) and Moab (1877).

For sheer effort and endurance, no group of pioneers is cited as much as the Hole-in-the-Rock Expedition of 1879–1880. Sixty families with 83 wagons and more than 1,000 head of livestock crossed some of the West's most rugged canyon country in an attempt to settle at Montezuma Creek on the San Juan River. They almost didn't make it: A journey expected to take six weeks turned into a six-*month* ordeal. The exhausted company arrived on the banks of the San Juan River on April 5, 1880. Too tired to continue just 20 easy miles to Montezuma Creek, they stayed and founded the town of Bluff. The Mormons established other towns in southeastern Utah, too, relying on ranching, farming, and mining for their livelihoods. None of the communities in the region ever reached a large size; Moab is the biggest. More and more people have come to realize that the scenery and wilderness qualities of this unique land are its most valuable resources.

Moab

By far the largest town in southeastern Utah, Moab (pop. 5,500) makes an excellent base for exploring Arches and Canyonland National Parks and the surrounding canyon country. Moab lies near the Colorado River in a green valley enclosed by high sandstone cliffs. The biblical Moab was a kingdom at the edge of Zion, and early settlers must have felt themselves at the edge of their world, too, being so isolated from Salt Lake City—the Mormon city of Zion. Moab's existence on the fringe of Mormon culture and the sizable gentile population gave the town a unique character.

In recent years, Moab has become nearly synonymous with mountain biking. The slickrock canyon country seems made for exploration by bike, and people come from all over the world to pedal the backcountry. River trips on the Colorado River are nearly as popular, and a host of other outdoor recreational diversions—from horseback riding to four-wheel jeep exploring to hot-air ballooning—combine to make Moab one of the most popular destinations in Utah.

Moab is also one of the most youthful and vibrant communities in the state; thousands of young people travel to Moab for the recreation, while hundreds of others work here as guides and outfitters. Call them recreationals, funpigs, gearheads, or even *yummies* (for Young Urban Macho Men Into Extreme Sports), but the fact is that tanned, fit, and Lycra-covered bodies are the norm here, and the town's brewpubs, bike shops, and cafés do a booming trade.

As Moab's popularity has grown, so have concerns that the town and the surrounding countryside are simply getting loved to death. The landscape has always been a staple in car ads (remember those Chevy pickups balanced on a red-rock pinnacle?); now the landscape sells the "Just Do It" lifestyle for MTV, Nike, and other merchandisers of youth culture. On a busy day, hundreds of mountain bikers form queues to negotiate the trickier sections of the famed Slick Rock Trail, and more than 20,000 people crowd into town on busy weekends to bike, hike, float, and party. As noted in an article in *Details* magazine, "Moab is pretty much the Fort Lauderdale of the intermountain West." Whether this old Mormon town and the delicate desert environment can endure such an onslaught of popularity is a question of increasing concern.

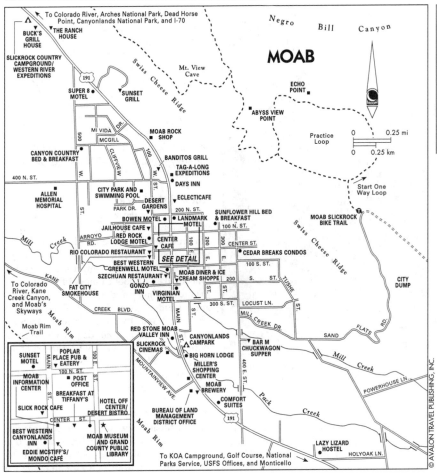

History

Prehistoric Fremont and Anasazi peoples once lived and farmed in the bottoms of the canyons around Moab. Their rock art, granaries, and dwellings can still be seen here. Nomadic Utes had replaced the earlier groups by the time the first white settlers arrived. The Old Spanish Trail, opened in 1829 between New Mexico and California, passed through Spanish Valley and crossed the Colorado River near present-day Moab.

Mormon missionaries tried to establish the Elk Mountain Mission here in 1855. They managed to plant some fields, build a stone fort, and convert some of the Utes before a series of attacks killed three missionaries and sent the others fleeing back to civilization. The valley reverted to the Native Americans and small numbers of explorers, outlaws, ranchers, and trappers for the next 20 years. Settlers with better success founded Moab in the 1870s. Troubles ceased after 1881, and the community became a quiet farming and ranching center.

Oil exploration in the 1920s caused some

Downtown Moab is a hybrid of early-20th-century storefronts and trendy new businesses.

© W. C. MCRAE

excitement, but nothing like that of the uranium boom that began in 1952. Moab's population tripled in just three years as eager prospectors swarmed into the canyons. One of these hopefuls, Charlie Steen, did hit it big. Experts had laughed at Charlie's efforts until he discovered the Mi Vida uranium bonanza about 30 miles south of town. An instant multimillionaire, he built a large mansion overlooking Moab and hosted lavish parties attended by Hollywood celebrities. Charlie Steen and most of the prospectors have moved on, but Moab has never been the same since.

SIGHTS

Dan O'Laurie Museum

This regional museum, 118 E. Center, 435/259-7985, tells the story of Moab's and Grand County's past, from prehistoric and Ute artifacts to the explorations of Spanish missionaries. Photos and tools show pioneer Moab life, much of which centered around ranching or mining; here, too, you'll find displays of rocks and minerals, as well as bones of huge dinosaurs that once tracked across this land. Ask for a *Moab Area Historic Walking Tour* leaflet to learn about historic buildings in town. Open in summer Monday–Saturday 1–8 P.M.; the rest of the year Monday–Thursday 3–7 P.M. and Saturday 1–7 P.M.; free.

Hole 'N the Rock

Albert Christensen worked 12 years to excavate his dream home within a sandstone monolith south of town. When he died in 1957, his wife Gladys worked another eight years to complete the project. The interior has notable touches like a 65-foot chimney drilled through the rock ceiling, paintings, taxidermy exhibits, and a lapidary room. The 5,000-square-foot, 14-room home 15 miles south of Moab on U.S. 191 is open for tours daily 8 A.M.–dusk in summer and daily 9 A.M.–5 P.M. the rest of the year; $2.50 adults, $1.50 ages 6–12. It also has a gift shop, 435/686-2250. A picnic area and snack bar are outside.

Moab's Skyway

One of Moab's new tourist attractions is this 12-minute tramway, which lifts you up 1,000 feet to the top of the red-rock rims that flank the city to the southwest. Once on top of the rims, you can relax with refreshments or hike along trails. An easy one-mile trail follows the rims; more adventurous hikers can use the skyway as a shortcut to Hidden Canyon (see Moab-Area Recreation). Bicycles are carried free on the skyway; from on top, you'll have nowhere to go but down on several biking trails. Tickets are $9 adults, $8 seniors, and $7 children 12 and under. Open daily 9 A.M.–late evening (lighted night rides are available in warm weather). The skyway is one mile west of Moab off Kane Creek Blvd. (turn west at the McDonald's), 435/259-7799.

ENTERTAINMENT AND RECREATION

Nightlife

A lot of Moab's nightlife focuses on Moab's two brewpubs, the rowdy and well-loved **Eddie McStiff's,** 57 S. Main in Western Plaza, 435/259-BEER (435/259-2337), and the newer and posher **Moab Brewery,** 686 S. Main St., 435/259-6333. For live music, try the **Outlaw Saloon,** 44 West 200 North, 435/259-2654, the **Club Río,** 100 W. Center St., 435/259-6666, or the **Sportsman's Lounge,** 1991 S. Hwy. 191, 435/259-9972.

For a selection of movies, head for **Slickrock Cinemas,** 580 Kane Creek Blvd., 435/259-4441.

Events

To find out about local happenings, contact the Moab Information Center, 435/259-8825. Major annual events include the **Moab Half Marathon** in late March (third Saturday). April brings the **Cannondale Cup Bicycle Race.**

Over Memorial Day weekend in May is the **Green River to Moab Friendship Cruise** on the Green and Colorado Rivers.

June kicks up dust at the fairgrounds with two rodeos: the professional **P.R.C.A. Rodeo** early in the month, and the **Canyonlands Rodeo,** with rodeo, parade, dance, horse racing, and 4-H gymkhana toward the end of the month.

August means it's time for the **Grand County Fair,** with agricultural displays, crafts, and arts judging. The **Moab Music Festival** keeps getting larger, with several weekends of music by jazz, bluegrass, and other groups, plus outdoor chamber music.

Shopping

Main Street, between 200 North and 200 South, has nearly a dozen galleries and gift shops with art and other gifts. **Hogan Trading Company,** 100 S. Main, 435/259-8118, has a great selection of Native American art; **Overlook Gallery,** 83 E. Center, features local artists and photographers.

Back of Beyond Books, 83 N. Main, 435/259-5154, features an excellent selection of regional books and maps. A good selection of books and maps is also sold at **Times Independent Maps,** 5 E. Center St., 435/259-7525.

Parks and Recreation

The **city park,** 181 West 400 North, 435/259-8226, has shaded picnic tables, a playground, and an outdoor swimming pool. **Lions Park** offers picnicking along the Colorado River two miles north of town. **Rotary Park,** on Mill Creek Drive, is family-oriented and has lots of activities for kids. **Moab Arts and Recreation,** 111 East 100 North, 435/259-6272, sponsors year-round activities for kids; you don't need to be a resident to take part.

Moab Golf Club, 2705 S. East Bench Rd., 435/259-6488, features an 18-hole course, a driving range, and a pro shop. Go south five miles on U.S. 191, turn left two miles on Spanish Trails Road, then right one-quarter mile on Murphy Lane.

ACCOMMODATIONS

Moab has been a tourist destination for generations and offers a wide variety of lodging choices, ranging from older motels to new upscale resorts. Luckily, lodgings are relatively inexpensive. The only time when Moab isn't busy is in the dead of winter, November–February. At all other times, be sure to make reservations well in advance.

If you're having trouble finding a room, **Moab/Canyonlands Central Reservations,** 435/259-5125, 800/748-4386, or 800/505-5343, www.moabutahlodging.com/reservations, can make bookings at 85 percent of Moab's accommodations, which include area bed-and-breakfasts, motels, condos, cabins, private houses, and luxury vacation homes. Summer rates are shown; those in winter typically drop 40 percent.

Under $50

The **Lazy Lizard Hostel,** 1213 S. U.S. 191, 435/259-6057, costs just $9 per night for simple dorm-style accommodations. You won't need a hostel card, and all guests share access to a hot tub, kitchen, barbecue, coin-operated laundry, and common room with cable TV. Camping ($6 per person), showers for nonguests ($2), and private rooms ($24 double occupancy) are offered, too. New log cabins here can sleep 2–4 ($30–45) people. The Lazy Lizard sits one mile south behind A-1 Storage; the turnoff is about 200 yards south of Moab Lanes.

For just a few more dollars, you can stay at the vintage **Hotel Off Center,** 96 E. Center, 435/259-4244 or 800/237-4685, which has basic rooms (bath down the hall) for $50 or bunks in a dorm ($12).

The small and simple **Silver Sage Inn,** 840 S. Main, 435/259-4420 or 888/774-6627, is the only standard motel with rooms for less than $50.

$50–75

The **Sunset Motel,** 41 West 100 North, 435/259-5191 or 800/421-5614, offers kitchenettes, a pool, and a hot tub, and pets are okay. The motel also offers a fully furnished apartment and a 12-sleeper with two bathrooms, four bedrooms, and a kitchen. The **Red Rock Lodge Motel,** 51 North 100 West, 435/259-5431, has rooms with refrigerators and coffeemakers; there's a hot tub and locked bicycle storage facilities. At the **Virginian Motel,** 70 East 200 South, 435/259-5951 or 800/261-2063, more than half the rooms have kitchenettes; pets are okay.

The **Red Stone Inn,** 535 S. Main St., 435/259-3500 or 800/772-1972, is a newer, one-story motel; most rooms have efficiency kitchens. Other amenities include a bicycle maintenance area, covered patio with gas barbecue grill, and guest laundry. Pets are okay in smoking rooms only with a $5-per-night fee. The **Days Inn,** 426 N. Main, 435/259-4468 or 800/329-7466, has a pool. The **Big Horn Lodge,** 550 S. Main, 435/259-6171 or 800/325-6171, has a pool and a restaurant.

$75–100

The local **Super 8 Motel,** 889 N. Main, 435/259-8868 or 800/800-8000, has a pool and a hot tub. The **Landmark Motel,** right in the center of Moab at 168 N. Main, 435/259-6147

or 800/441-6147, has a pool and a small water slide, a hot tub, a guest laundry room, and three family units. Right across the street, the **Bowen Motel,** 169 N. Main, 435/259-7132 or 800/874-5439, is a pleasant, homey motel with an outdoor pool and free continental breakfast.

The **Best Western Canyonlands Inn,** 16 S. Main, 435/259-2300 or 800/528-1234, is also in the heart of Moab, with suites, a pool, a fitness room and spa, a restaurant, and a bike storage area.

Canyon Country Bed & Breakfast, 590 North 500 West, 435/259-5262 or 800/350-5262, is a large Southwestern-style ranch home just north of downtown. The four guest rooms have both private and shared baths; guests share a hot tub and can rent kayaks and mountain bikes.

If you want seclusion and a wilderness setting, stay at the **Castle Valley Inn B&B,** in Castle Valley, 18 miles east of Moab, 435/259-7830 or 888/272-8181, www.castlevalleyinn.com. The inn adjoins a wildlife refuge in a stunning landscape of red-rock mesas and needle-pointed buttes. You can stay in one of the main house's five guest rooms or in one of the three bungalows with kitchens. For an additional fee and with advance notice, dinner is available for guests. Facilities include a hot tub. No children or pets are allowed; a two-night minimum is required on weekends. To reach Castle Valley Inn, follow Highway 128 east from Moab for 16 miles and turn south 2.3 miles toward Castle Valley. Open February 15–December 15.

The three two-bedroom cottages that compose **Desert Gardens,** 123–127 West 200 North, 435/259-5125 or 800/505-5343, each contain a full kitchen, bath, and living room. The cottages sit in a large shaded yard with access to a hot tub, barbecue, and nicely maintained gardens. Two-night minimum stay is required.

$100–125

The **Best Western Greenwell Motel,** 105 S. Main, 435/259-6151 or 800/528-1234, has a pool, an on-premises restaurant, and some kitchenettes. The **Ramada Inn,** 182 S. Main, 435/259-7141 or 888/989-1988, has nicely appointed rooms (some with balconies) and a pool, spa, and facilities for small meetings. South of downtown is the **Comfort Suites,** 800 S. Main, 435/259-5252 or 800/228-5150, an all-suites motel with large, nicely furnished rooms complete with microwaves and refrigerators. Facilities include an indoor pool, a spa, an exercise room, locked bike storage, and a guest laundry room.

One of the newest and most unique-looking accommodations in Moab is the **Gonzo Inn,** 100 West 200 South, 435/259-2515 or 800/791-4044. With a look somewhere between an adobe inn and a postmodern warehouse, the Gonzo doesn't try to appear anything but young and hip. Expect large rooms with Day-Glo colors, a pool, and a friendly welcome.

Located in an old residential area, the **Sunflower Hill Bed & Breakfast,** 185 North 300 East, 435/259-2974 or 800/662-2786, www.sunflowerhill.com, offers high-quality lodgings in one of Moab's original farmhouses and in a newly built garden cottage with patios and balconies. All 12 rooms have private baths, air conditioning, and queen-size beds; there are also two suites. Guests share access to an outdoor hot tub, bike storage, patios, and large gardens. Children are welcome from age 8; open year-round.

If you're looking for a bit more room or a longer-term stay, consider **Cedar Breaks Condos,** 10 South 400 East, 435/259-7830 or 888/272-8181, with six two-bedroom units with living rooms and full kitchens. Daily maid service is provided and breakfast food is stocked daily in the refrigerator.

Campgrounds

Up the Creek Campground, 555 S. Main St., 435/259-2213, is a friendly walk-in tent campground with showers and restrooms tucked into a residential neighborhood just a couple of blocks from Main Street. Sites at this privately run campground go for $10 per person. Spanish Trail RV Park, 2980 S. U.S. 191, 435/259-2411 or 800/787-2751, has showers, laundry, and restrooms and is open year-round. Sites range from $19 for tents to $24 for hookups. Canyonlands Campground, 555 S. Main St., 435/259-6848 or 800/522-6848, is open all year; it has showers, a

laundry room, a store, and a pool. Sites run $18–23. Slickrock Campground, one mile north of Moab at 1301½ N. U.S. 191, 435/259-7660 or 800/448-8873, remains open year-round; it has showers, a store, an outdoor café, a pool, and cabins with air conditioning and heat; $18 tents or RVs without hookups, $23 with basic hookup, and $30 for cabins. Moab Valley RV & Campark, two miles north of Moab at 1773 N. U.S. 191 (opposite the turnoff for Highway 128), 435/259-4469, is also open all year. It has showers; sites for tents or RVs start at $22. **Moab KOA,** four miles south of Moab at 3225 S. U.S. 191, 435/259-6682 or 800/562-0372, is open March–November; it has showers, a laundry room, a store, mini-golf, and a pool; $26 tents or RVs without hookups, $29 with hookups; Kamping Kabins go for $42.

The BLM now requires that all camping along the Colorado River (accessible by road above and below Moab), Kane Creek, and near the Moab Slickrock Bike Trail *must* be in developed designated sites (with toilets) or undeveloped designated sites (your own porta-potty required; no restrooms or fee). The following four camping areas are available along Highway 128 for a $10 fee. From the U.S. 191/Highway 128 junction, you'll find Jay Cee Park at 4.2 miles, Hal Canyon at 6.6 miles, Oak Grove at 6.9 miles, and Big Bend Recreation Site at 7.4 miles. Contact the Moab Information Center for locations of additional campgrounds. You'll also find campgrounds farther out at Arches and Canyonlands National Parks, Dead Horse Point State Park, La Sal Mountains, and Canyon Rims Recreation Area.

Guest Ranches

A short drive from Moab along the Colorado River's red-rock canyon is the region's premium luxury guest ranch, the **Sorrel River Ranch,** 17 miles northeast of Moab on Highway 128, 435/259-4642 or 877/359-2715, www.sorrelriver.com. The ranch sits on 240 acres in some of the most dramatic landscapes in the Moab area—just across the river from Arches National Park and beneath the soaring mesas of Castle Valley. Accommodations are in a series of beautifully furnished wooden lodges, all tastefully fitted with Old West–style furniture. All units have kitchenettes and a patio with porch swing or back deck overlooking the river (some rooms have both). Horseback rides are offered into the *arroyos* (dry river beds) behind the ranch; kayaks and bicycles can be rented. The ranch's restaurant, the River Grill Restaurant, has some of the best views in Utah and an adventurous menu that ranges from steaks to grilled duck breast.

FOOD

Moab has the best restaurants in all of southern Utah; no matter what else the recreational craze has produced, it has certainly improved the food. Several Moab-area restaurants are closed for annual vacation in February.

Breakfast and Light Meals

Start the day at **Breakfast at Tiffany's,** 90 E. Center, 435/259-2553, a happening coffee shop with fresh pastries and a deli. It's also open in the evenings for appetizers. For a traditional breakfast, try the excellent **Jailhouse Cafe,** 101 N. Main St., 435/259-3900. For what might be Utah's best bagels, stop by **Red Rock Bakery,** 74 S. Main, 435/259-5941. Another favorite is the **Mondo Café,** 59 S. Main St., in McStiff's Plaza, 435/259-5551; it serves freshly baked goods, espresso drinks, and sandwiches for lunch. The **Moab Diner & Ice Cream Shoppe,** 189 S. Main St., 435/259-4006, is a good place to know about—the breakfasts old-fashioned and abundant, a Southwestern green chili edge to the food, and the best ice cream in town; open for breakfast, lunch, and dinner. **EclectiCafe,** 352 N. Main, 435/259-6896, has a good selection of organic and vegetarian dishes, mostly with ethnic roots. Open for breakfast and lunch daily.

Casual Dining

Unless otherwise noted, each of the following establishments has a full liquor license. Entrées range $8–15.

A good spot for sandwiches or an afternoon smoothie is **Peace Tree Juice Cafe,** 20 S. Main, 435/259-8503. For light meals and snacks, try the **Poplar Place Pub & Eatery,** Main and 100 North, 435/259-6018, which serves pizza, pasta, and deli sandwiches in a pub atmosphere; open daily for lunch and dinner. The **Slick Rock Cafe,** 5 N. Main, 435/259-8004, is another versatile, if a bit touristy, restaurant. Open for breakfast, lunch, and dinner in a historic building downtown, the Slick Rock serves up-to-date food at reasonable prices, all with a spicy Southwestern or Caribbean kick.

Moab's best Mexican restaurant is **Bandito's Grill,** 467 N. Main, 435/259-3894, with a large selection of excellent house specialties and outdoor seating.

Only one restaurant in town serves Asian food: the **Szechuan Restaurant,** 105 S. Main, 435/259-8984. Fortunately, the food is good, spicy, and inexpensive. **Fat City Smokehouse,** 100 W. Center, 435/259-4302, specializes in Texas-style pit barbecue for lunch and dinner; open Monday–Saturday. Beer only.

For a Western night out, consider **Bar M Chuckwagon Supper,** on the banks of Mill Creek at 541 S. Mulberry Ln., just southeast of town, 435/259-2276. Tasty cowboy-style cooking is served up from chuck wagons, followed by live Western entertainment; open for dinner only (call to check on times) April–October Monday–Saturday; beer only. The meal plus entertainment costs $20 for everyone 11 years and older, $10 for younger children.

Brewpubs

After a hot day out on the trail, who can blame you for thinking about a cold brew and a good meal at a brewpub? Luckily, Moab has two excellent pubs to fill the bill. **Eddie McStiff's,** 57 S. Main in Western Plaza, 435/259-BEER (435/259-2337), was the first brewpub in Moab and is an extremely popular place to sip a cool one or eat a hearty meal of pasta, pizza, steaks, salads, chicken, and Mexican food. The pub is a convivial place to meet like-minded travelers; in good weather there's seating in a nice courtyard. You'll have to try hard not to have fun here; open daily for lunch and dinner.

There's more good beer and maybe better food at the **Moab Brewery,** 686 S. Main St., 435/259-

© W. C. MCRAE

In Moab, bicycles are welcome at the local brewpub.

6333, although this more recent restaurant has yet to attract the kind of scene you'll find at Eddie McStiff's. The atmosphere is light and airy, and the food is good—steaks, sandwiches, burgers, and a wide selection of salads. There's deck seating when weather permits.

Fine Dining

The **Ranch House** serves elegant meals in an 1896 pioneer house at 1266 N. U.S. 191 on the north edge of town, 435/259-5753; specialties are regional mountain West cuisine. Expect to pay $20–27 for entrées. Open daily for dinner; reservations recommended. The **Sunset Grill,** 900 N. U.S. 191, 435/259-7146, is in uranium king Charlie Steen's mansion high above Moab, with "million-dollar" sweeping views of the valley. Chefs offer steaks, fresh seafood, and a selection of modern pasta dishes ($17–28). Open Monday–Saturday for dinner.

Buck's Grill House, 1393 N. U.S. 191, 435/259-5201, is a steak house with a difference. The restaurant features a pleasant Western atmosphere, and the food seems familiar enough—steaks, prime rib, roast chicken, seafood, grilled pork loin—but the quality of

the preparation and the side dishes makes the difference. The butter spice rub on the cowboy steaks or prime rib is excellent. Entrées range $12–23.

The **River Grill** at Sorrel River Ranch, 17 miles northeast of Moab on Highway 128, has a lovely dining room that overlooks spires of red rock and the dramatic cliffs of the Colorado River. The scenery is hard to top, and the food is excellent, with a focus on prime beef and continental specialties (the chef is French-born). Fresh fish and seafood are flown in daily and form the basis for nightly specials.

Moab has two restaurants that feature the most up-to-the-moment cuisine. The **Center Cafe,** a long-time Moab favorite for its international menu and excellent service, has moved to 60 North 100 West, 435/259-4295. The menu is eclectic, with a wide selection of pasta dishes (including several vegetarian choices) and other inventive fare that feature continental influences and free-range and organic ingredients ($15–28). At its new location, the Center Café is now open for lunch and dinner Tuesday–Sunday. The new location also features a market for homemade breads, cheeses, and gourmet takeout.

The **Desert Bistro,** 92 Center St., 435/259-0756, features sophisticated cuisine in a spare but comfortable dining room. The focus of the seasonal menu is on local meats and game plus fresh fish and seafood cooked with Rocky Mountain regional aplomb ($17–25). Highly recommended.

OTHER PRACTICALITIES

Information

The **Moab Information Center,** Main and Center, 435/259-8825 or 800/635-MOAB (635-6622), is the place to start for nearly all local and area information. The National Park Service, the BLM, the U.S. Forest Service, the Grand County Travel Council, and the Canyonlands Natural History Association all are represented in this multiagency facility. Visitors needing help from any of these agencies should start at the information center rather than at the agency offices. Free literature is available, and a large selection of books and maps are sold. Especially useful is the free *Southeastern Utah Travel Guide,* which describes features of and opportunities for recreation in the Arches and Canyonlands National Parks. Included are comprehensive lists of tour operators, places to rent and purchase recreation equipment, and campgrounds. The office is open daily 8 A.M.–9 P.M. in summer (reduced hours the rest of the year). There are several Moab-related travel websites; probably the best is at www.discovermoab.com.

The **National Park Service office** in Moab, 2282 Southwest Resource Blvd., Moab, UT 84532 (three miles south of downtown), 435/259-7164, is headquarters for Canyonlands and Arches National Parks and Natural Bridges National Monument. Open Monday–Friday 8 A.M.–4:30 P.M. The **Manti–La Sal National Forest office** is also at 2282 Southwest Resource Blvd., 435/259-7155; open Monday–Friday 8 A.M.–noon and 12:30–4:30 P.M. The **BLM District office,** 82 E. Dogwood on the south side of town behind Comfort Suites, P.O. Box 970, Moab, UT 84532, 435/259-8193 (general information) is open open Monday–Friday 7:45 A.M.–4:30 P.M. Some land-use maps are sold; this is where you pick up your river-running permits.

Services

The **Grand County Public Library,** 25 South 100 East (next to the Dan O'Laurie Museum), 435/259-5421, is a good place for local history and general reading; open Monday–Thursday 1–9 P.M., Friday 1–5 P.M., and Saturday 10 A.M.–2 P.M. The library is for local residents, but others can use the services on a daily basis.

The **post office** is downtown at 50 East 100 North, 435/259-7427. **Allen Memorial Hospital** provides medical care at 719 West 400 North, 435/259-7191.

Transportation

There are currently no commercial flights between Moab and Salt Lake City. The only commercial flights to Moab are to and from Denver and Phoenix on Great Lakes Airlines, 800/554-5111, which is a regional partner of United Airlines. The Moab/Canyonlands Airfield is 16 miles north of Moab on Highway 191.

The only other public transport option to Moab is the ARK Shuttle run by Bighorn Express, 888/655-7433, www.bighornexpress.com, which makes one minibus run daily between Moab and Salt Lake City. Advance reservations are required. One-way fare is $50.

For rental cars, contact **Certified Ford,** 500 S. Main, 435/529-6107, or **Thrifty,** 400 N. Main, 435/259-7317, which has an office at the Moab airport. **Taxi** service includes shuttles for bicyclists and river-runners, 435/259-TAXI (435/259-8294).

SCENIC DRIVES AND EXCURSIONS

Each of the following routes is at least partly accessible to standard low-clearance highway vehicles. If you have a four-wheel-drive vehicle, you'll have the option of additional, off-road exploring.

Detailed travel information on these and other places is available in the books and separate maps by F. A. Barnes: *Canyon Country Off-*

Road Vehicle Trails: Island Area (north of Canyonlands National Park) and *Canyon Country Off-Road Vehicle Trails: Arches & La Sals Areas* (around Arches National Park). The BLM takes care of nearly all of this land; staff in the Moab offices may know current road and trail conditions.

Utah Scenic Byway 279

Highway 279 goes downstream through the Colorado River Canyon on the other side of the river from Moab. Pavement extends 16 miles past fine views, prehistoric rock art, arches, and hiking trails. A potash plant marks the end of the highway; a rough dirt road continues to Canyonlands National Park. From Moab, head north 3.5 miles on U.S. 191, then turn left on Highway 279. The highway enters the canyon at the Portal, 2.7 miles from the turnoff. Towering sandstone cliffs rise on the right, and the Colorado River drifts along just below on the left.

Stop at a signed pullout on the left 0.6 mile past the canyon entrance to see **Indian Ruins Viewpoint,** a small prehistoric Native American ruin tucked under a ledge across the river. The stone structure was probably used for food storage.

Groups of **petroglyphs** cover cliffs along the highway 5.2 miles from U.S. 191. These may not be signed; they are 0.7 mile beyond milepost 11. Look across the river to see The Fickle Finger of Fate among the sandstone fins of Behind the Rocks. A petroglyph of a bear is 0.2 mile farther down the highway. Archaeologists think that Fremont people and the later Utes did most of the artwork in this area.

A signed pullout on the right 6.2 miles from U.S. 191 points out **dinosaur tracks** and petroglyphs visible on rocks above. Sighting tubes help locate the features. It's possible to hike up the steep hillside for a closer look.

The aptly named **Jug Handle Arch,** with an opening 46 feet high and three feet wide, is close to the road on the right, 13.6 miles from U.S. 191. Ahead the canyon opens up. Underground pressures of salt and potash have folded the rock layers into an anticline.

At the **Moab Salt Plant,** mining operations inject water underground to dissolve the potash and other chemicals, then pump the solution to evaporation ponds. The ponds are dyed blue to hasten evaporation, which takes about a year. You can see these colorful solutions from Dead Horse Point and Anticline Overlook on the canyon rims.

High-clearance vehicles can continue on the unpaved road beyond the plant. The road passes through varied canyon country, with views overlooking the Colorado River. At a road junction in Canyonlands National Park (Island in the Sky District), you have a choice of turning left for the 100-mile White Rim Trail (four-wheel-drive only past Musselman Arch), continuing up the steep switchbacks of the Shafer Trail Road (four-wheel-drive recommended) to the paved park road, or returning the way you came.

Utah Scenic Byway 128

Highway 128 turns northeast from U.S. 191 just south of the Colorado River Bridge, two miles north of Moab. This exceptionally scenic canyon route follows the Colorado for 30 miles upstream before crossing at Dewey Bridge and turning north to I-70. The entire highway is paved. In 1986, a new bridge replaced the narrow Dewey suspension bridge that once caused white knuckles on drivers of large vehicles. The Lions Park picnic area at the turnoff from U.S. 191 is a pleasant stopping place. Big Bend Recreation Site is another good spot 7.5 miles up Highway 128.

A network of highly scenic jeep roads branches off Castle Valley and Onion Creek Roads into side canyons and the **La Sal Mountains Loop Road,** described in the book and separate map *Canyon Country Off-Road Vehicle Trails: Arches & La Sals Areas,* by F. A. Barnes. This paved scenic road goes through Castle Valley, climbs high into the La Sals, then loops back to Moab. Allow at least three hours to drive the 62-mile loop. The turnoff from Highway 128 is 15.5 miles up from U.S. 191.

A graded county road, **Onion Creek Road,** turns southeast off the highway 20 miles from U.S. 191 and heads up Onion Creek, crossing it many times. *Avoid this route if storms threaten.*

The unpleasant-smelling creek contains poisonous arsenic and selenium. Colorful rock formations of dark red sandstone line the creek, and you'll cross an upthrusted block of crystalline gypsum. After about eight miles, the road climbs steeply out of Onion Creek to upper Fisher Valley and a junction with Kokopelli's Trail, which follows a jeep road over this part of its route.

The Gothic spires of **Fisher Towers** soar as high as 900 feet above Professor Valley. The BLM has a picnic area nearby and a hiking trail that skirts the base of the three main towers; Titan, the tallest, is the third one.

In 1962, three climbers from Colorado made the first ascent of Titan Tower. The almost-vertical rock faces, overhanging bulges, and sections of rotten rock made for an exhausting 3.5 days of climbing (the party descended to the base for two of the nights). Their final descent from the summit took only six hours. See the November 1962 issue of *National Geographic* magazine for the story and photos. Supposedly, the name Fisher is not that of a pioneer, but a corruption of the geologic term *fissure* (a narrow crack). An unpaved road turns southeast off Highway 128 near milepost 21 (21 miles from U.S. 191) and continues two miles to the picnic area.

The modern two-lane concrete **Dewey Bridge** has replaced the picturesque wood-and-steel suspension bridge built in 1916. Here, the BLM has built the Dewey Bridge Recreation Site with a picnic area, trailhead, boat launch, and a small campground. Bicyclists and hikers can still use the old bridge; an interpretive sign explains its history. Drivers can continue on the highway to I-70 through rolling hills nearly devoid of vegetation.

Upstream from Dewey Bridge are the wild rapids of **Westwater Canyon.** The Colorado River cut this narrow gorge into dark metamorphic rock. You can raft or kayak down the river in one day or a more leisurely two days. Camping is limited to a single night. Unlike most desert rivers, this section of the Colorado also offers good river-running at low water levels in late summer and autumn. Westwater Canyon's inner gorge, where boaters face their greatest challenge, is only about 3.5 miles long; however, you can enjoy scenic sandstone canyons both upstream and downstream.

A bumpy four-wheel-drive route, the **Top-of-the-World Road,** climbs to an overlook with outstanding views of Fisher Towers, Fisher Valley, Onion Creek, and beyond. Turn right (east) on Entrada Bluffs Road (just before crossing Dewey Bridge). After 5.5 miles, keep straight on a dirt road when the main road curves left, then immediately turn right (south) and go uphill 100 yards through a gate (gateposts are railroad ties) and continue about 4.5 miles on the Top-of-the-World Road to the rim. Elevation here is 6,800 feet, nearly 3,000 feet higher than the Colorado River.

Kane Creek Scenic Drive

This road heads downstream along the Colorado River on the same side as Moab. The four miles through the Colorado River Canyon are paved, followed by six miles of good dirt road through Kane Springs Canyon. This route also leads to several hiking trails (see Moab-Area Recreation). People with high-clearance vehicles or mountain bikes can continue across a ford of Kane Springs Creek to Hurrah Pass and an extensive network of four-wheel-drive trails. The book and separate map *Canyon Country Off-Road Vehicle Trails: Canyon Rims & Needles Areas,* by F. A. Barnes, has detailed back-road information.

Moab-Area Recreation

Moab sits at the center of some of the most picturesque landscapes in North America. Even the most casual visitor will want to get outdoors and explore the river canyons, natural arches, and mesas. Mountain biking and river tours are the recreational activities that get the most attention in the Moab area, although hikers, climbers, and horseback riders will find plenty to do. If you're less physically adventurous, you can explore the landscape on scenic flights or on hot-air balloon trips, or follow old mining roads in four-wheel-drive vehicles to remote backcountry destinations.

Contact the Moab Information Center, 435/259-8825 or 800/635-6622, for full information about the area's recreational options; the center, at Main and Central in the center of town, has representatives of the National Park Service, the Bureau of Land Management (BLM), and the U.S. Forest Service on staff, and they can direct you to the adventure of your liking. The offices also have literature, books, and maps. BLM officials can also give locations of the developed and undeveloped designated campsites near the Moab Slickrock Bike Trail, Kane Creek, and along the Colorado River; you must use the designated sites in these areas.

Sports and Equipment Rentals

Rim Cyclery, 94 West 100 North, 435/259-5333, offers mountain bikes and cross-country skis, as well as mountain-bike tours. Mountain-bike rentals and tours are also available at **Moab Cyclery,** 391 S. Main, 435/259-7423; **Poison Spider Bicycles,** 497 N. Main, 435/259-7882; and **Western Spirit Cycling,** 38 South 100 West, 435/259-8969. Expect to pay about $45 per day to rent a mountain bike.

Canyon Voyages, 401 N. Main St., 435/259-6007, and **Tag-A-Long Expeditions,** 452 N. Main St., 435/259-8946, are two local rafting companies that rent rafts and kayaks for those who would rather organize their own river adventure. Canoe rental from **Red River Canoe Company,** 497 N. Main St., 435/259-7722,

costs $18–25 per person and includes necessary equipment and transportation.

You can rent jeeps and other four-wheel-drive vehicles at **Farabee 4X4 Adventures,** 83 S. Main, 435/259-7494, or **Slickrock Jeep Rentals,** 284 N. Main, 435/259-5678.

HIKING

To reach most of Moab's prime hiking trails requires a short drive to trailheads; these routes are all picturesque and are fully described as follows. For more options, pick up the brochure *Moab Area Hiking Trails* at the visitors center and turn to the chapters on Arches and Canyonlands National Parks.

Trails from Kane Creek Scenic Drive and U.S. 191 South

The high cliffs just southwest of town provide fine views of the Moab Valley, highlands of Arches National Park, and La Sal Mountains. The **Moab Rim Trail** turns off Kane Creek Boulevard 1.5 miles downriver from Moab. The total driving distance from the junction of Main Street and Kane Creek Boulevard is 2.6 miles; look for the trailhead on the left 0.1 mile after a cattle guard.

You can see the sky through Little Arch across the river from the trailhead. Four-wheel-drive vehicles can also ascend the Moab Rim Trail, although the rough terrain is considered difficult for them; the first 200 yards will give drivers a feel for the difficulty. The trail climbs northeast 1.5 miles along tilted rock strata of the Kayenta Formation to the top of the plateau. This hike is moderately difficult, with a gain of 940 feet and good views nearly all the way. Once on top, hikers can follow jeep roads southeast to Hidden Valley Trail and descend on a hiking trail to U.S. 191 south of Moab—a 5.5-mile trip one-way. Experienced hikers can also head south from the rim to **Behind the Rocks,** a fantastic maze of sandstone fins.

VICINITY OF MOAB

To Grand Junction, CO

Crescent Junction

To Green River

Cisco

Westwater Canyon

Big Triangle

River

Buckhorn Mesa

Salt Valley

Arches

Dolores

TOP OF THE WORLD RD.

DELICATE ARCH

River

Steamboat Mesa

Dome Plateau

Professor Valley

Sevenmile Mesa

Fisher Towers

MONITOR AND MERIMACK

National

Fisher Valley

Polar Mesa

Colorado

SORREL RIVER RANCH

CASTLE VALLEY INN B&B

Merimac Butte

Mill Canyon

Courthouse Wash

Moab Canyon

Park

Castle Valley

Castle Rock 6,656 ft

Castle Creek

Sevenmile Canyon

Big Bend

GEMINI TWINS ARCH

Arths Pasture

BOWTIE ARCH

Negro Bill Canyon

SAND FLATS RD. (KOKOPELLI TRAIL)

Creek

GEMINI BRIDGES

Moab

MORNING GLORY NATURAL BRIDGE

KOKOPELLI

Manti-La Sal

MOAB SLICKROCK

La Sal

Potash

Dead Horse Point State Park

Moab Rim

Mill Creek

LA SAL MOUNTAINS LOOP RD.

Manns Peak 12,270 ft

HIDDEN VALLEY

Pack Creek

National Forest

Mountains

Canyonlands

SHAFER TRAIL

POTASH RD.

KANE CREEK SCENIC DRIVE

Hunters Canyon

Behind the Rocks

National

Park

WHITE RIM RD.

Mount Peale 12,721 ft

0   5 mi

0   5 km

To Monticello

© AVALON TRAVEL PUBLISHING, INC.

You'll see not only a "hidden valley" from the **Hidden Valley Trail** but also panoramas of the Moab area and Behind the Rocks. The moderately difficult trail ascends 500 feet in a series of switchbacks to a broad shelf below the Moab Rim, then follows the shelf (hidden valley) to the northwest. It then crosses a low pass and follows a second shelf in the same direction. Near the end of the second shelf, the trail turns left to a divide, where you can see a portion of the remarkable fins of Behind the Rocks. This divide is one mile from the start and 680 feet higher in elevation. The trail continues one-third mile from the divide down to the end of the Moab Rim Trail, which is a jeep road

and hiking trail. Instead of turning left to the divide, you can make a short side trip (no trail) to the right for views of Moab.

To reach the Hidden Valley Trailhead, drive south three miles on U.S. 191 from Moab, turn right 0.4 mile on Angel Rock Road to its end (the turnoff is just south of milepost 122), then right 0.3 mile on Rimrock Lane.

A look at the topographic map will show that something strange is going on at the area called **Behind the Rocks.** Massive fins of Navajo sandstone 100–500 feet high, 50–200 feet thick, and up to one-half-mile long cover a large area. Narrow vertical cracks, sometimes only a few feet wide, separate the fins. Archaeological sites and several arches are in the area. No maintained trails exist here, and some routes require technical climbing skills. The maze offers endless exploration routes. If you get lost (which is very easy to do), remember that the fins are oriented east-west; the rim of the Colorado River Canyon is reached by going west, and Spanish Valley is reached by going east. Bring plenty of water, a topographic map (Moab 7.5-minute), and a compass. Access routes are Moab Rim and Hidden Valley Trails (from the north and east) and Pritchett Canyon (from the west and south). Although it is only a couple of miles from Moab, Behind the Rocks seems a world away. The BLM is studying a possible wilderness designation to protect the solitude and character of this strange country.

Hikers along **Hunters Canyon** enjoy seeing a rock arch and other rock formations in the canyon walls and the lush vegetation along the creek. Off-road vehicles have made tracks a short way up, then you'll be walking, mostly along the creekbed. Short sections of trail lead around thickets of tamarisk and other water-loving plants. Look for Hunters Arch on the right about one-half mile up. Most of the water in Hunters Canyon comes from a deep pool surrounded by hanging gardens of maidenhair fern. A dry fall and a small natural bridge lie above the pool. This pretty spot marks the hike's three-mile point and an elevation gain of 240 feet. At this point the hike becomes very brushy. To reach the trailhead from Moab, drive eight miles on Kane Creek Boulevard along the Colorado River and up Kane Creek Canyon. The road is asphalted where it fords Hunter Creek, but the asphalt is usually covered with dirt washed over it by the creek.

You can make a longer hike by going up Hunters Canyon and descending on Pritchett Canyon Road. The road crosses the normally dry creekbed just upstream from the deep pool. To bypass the dry fall above the pool, backtrack 300 feet down the canyon and rock-scramble up a short, steep slope—on your right heading upstream. At a junction just east of there, a jeep road along the north rim of Hunters Canyon meets Pritchett Canyon Road. Walk northeast one-half mile on Pritchett

Canyon Road to a spur trail on the left leading to Pritchett Arch. Then continue 4.5 miles on Pritchett Canyon Road to Kane Creek Boulevard. This country is more open and desert-like than Hunters Canyon. A 3.2-mile car shuttle or hike is needed to return to Hunters Canyon Trailhead.

Trails from Highway 279

The **Portal Overlook Trail** switchbacks up a slope, then follows a sloping sandstone ledge of the Kayenta Formation to an overlook. A panorama takes in the Colorado River, Moab Valley, Arches National Park, and La Sal Mountains. The hike is 1.5 miles (one-way), with an elevation gain of 980 feet. This trail is a twin of the Moab Rim Trail across the river. Begin from Jaycee Park Campground on the right, 3.8 miles from the turnoff at U.S. 191; mulberry trees shade the attractive spot. Expect to share this trail with many mountain bikers.

The 1.5-mile (one-way) **Corona Arch and Bowtie Arch Trail** leads across slickrock country to these impressive arches. You can't see them from the road, although a third arch—Pinto—is visible. The signed trailhead is on the right 10 miles from U.S. 191 (midway between mileposts 5 and 6); you'll see railroad tracks just beyond the trailhead. The trail climbs up from the parking area, crosses the tracks, and follows a bit of a jeep road and a small wash to an ancient gravel bar. Pinto (or Gold Bar) Arch stands to the left, although there's no trail to it. Follow cairns to Corona and Bowtie. Handrails and a ladder help in the few steep spots.

Despite being only a few hundred yards apart, each arch has a completely different character and history. Bowtie formed when a pothole in the cliffs above met a cave underneath. It used to be called Paul Bunyan's Potty before that name was appropriated for an arch in Canyonlands National Park. The hole is about 30 feet in diameter. Corona Arch, reminiscent of the larger Rainbow Bridge, eroded out of a sandstone fin. The graceful span is 140 feet long and 105 feet high. Both arches are composed of Navajo sandstone. If you have time for only one hike in the Moab area, this one is especially recommended.

SOUTHEASTERN UTAH

Trails off Highway 128

Negro Bill Canyon is one of the most popular hiking destinations in the Moab Area. The route follows a lively stream pooled by beavers and surrounded by abundant greenery and sheer canyon cliffs. The high point of the hike is Morning Glory Natural Bridge, the sixth-longest natural rock span in the country at 243 feet. The trailhead is on the right just after crossing a concrete bridge three miles from U.S. 191. A trail leads upcanyon, along the creek in some places, high on the banks in others.

To see Morning Glory Natural Bridge, head two miles up the main canyon to the second side canyon on the right, then follow a good side trail one-half mile up to the long, slender bridge. The spring and small pool underneath keep the air cool even in summer; ferns, columbines, and poison ivy grow here. The elevation gain is 330 feet. William "Nigger Bill" Granstaff was a mulatto who lived in the area 1877–1881. Modern sensibilities have changed his nickname to "Negro Bill."

Experienced hikers can continue up the main canyon about eight miles and rock-scramble (no trail) up the right side, then drop into Rill Creek, which leads to the North Fork of Mill Creek and into Moab. The total distance is about 16 miles one-way; you'll have to find your own way between canyons. The upper Negro Bill and Rill Canyons can also be reached from Sand Flats Road. The Moab and Castle Valley 15-minute and Moab 1:100,000 topographic maps cover the route. This would be a good overnight trip, although fast hikers have done it in a day. Expect to do some wading and rock-scrambling. Water from the creeks and springs is available in both canyon systems, but be sure to purify it first.

A car shuttle is necessary between the Negro Bill and Mill Creek trailheads. You can reach Mill Creek from the end of Powerhouse Lane on the east edge of Moab, but *don't park here.* Vehicle break-ins are a serious problem. Either have someone meet or drop you off here or park closer to town near houses. A hike up the North Fork offers very pretty scenery. A deep pool and waterfall lie three-quarters of a mile upstream;

follow Mill Creek upstream and take the left (north) fork. Negro Bill and Mill Creek Canyons are BLM wilderness study areas.

You can't miss the **Fisher Towers** as you drive Highway 128. These spires of dark red sandstone rise 900 feet above Professor Valley. You can hike around the base of these needle rocks on a trail accessed from the BLM picnic area. Titan, the third and highest rock tower, stands one mile from the picnic area; a viewpoint overlooks Onion Creek 1.1 miles farther along. Carry water for this moderately difficult hike.

Trails North of Moab, off U.S. 191

The short **Mill Creek Dinosaur Trail,** with numbered stops, identifies the bones of dinosaurs who lived here 150 million years ago. You'll see fossilized wood, too. Pick up the brochure from the Moab Information Center or at the trailhead. From Moab, go 14 miles north on U.S. 191 (or four miles north of the Dead Horse Point turnoff), and turn left two miles on a dirt road, keeping right at a fork 1.1 miles in.

You'll find many other points of interest nearby. A copper mill and tailings dating from the late 1800s lie across the canyon. Halfway Stage Station ruins, where travelers once stopped on the Thompson–Moab run, are a short distance down the other road fork. Jeepers and mountain bikers can do a 13- to 14-mile loop to Monitor and Merimac Buttes (an information sign just in from U.S. 191 has a map and details).

BIKING

Moab is the West's most noted mountain-bike destination. In addition to the famed and challenging slickrock trails (slickrock is the exposed sandstone that composes much of the land's surface here) that wind through astonishing desert landscapes, cyclists can pedal through alpine meadows in La Sal Mountains, while nearly abandoned four-wheel-drive tracks open up the backcountry to the adventurous. Be aware that the most famous trails, like the Slickrock Bike Trail, are not for beginning mountain bikers. You'll need to be fit, as well as expert in fat-tire technique to enjoy and, in some cases, make it all

MOUNTAIN-BIKE ETIQUETTE

When mountain biking in the Moab area, don't expect an instant wilderness experience. Because of the popularity of the routes, the fragile desert environment is under quite a bit of stress; be considerate of the thousands of other people who share the trails. By keeping these rules in mind, you'll help keep Moab from being loved to death.

• *Ride only on open roads and trails.* Much of the desert consists of extremely fragile plant and animal ecosystems, and riding recklessly through cryptobiotic soils can destroy desert life and lead to erosion. If you pioneer a trail, chances are someone else will follow the tracks, leading to ever more destruction.

• *Protect and conserve scarce water sources.* Don't wash, swim, walk, or bike through potholes, and camp well away from isolated streams and water holes. The addition of your insect repellent, body oils, suntan lotion, or lubrication from your bike can destroy the thronging life of a pothole. Camping right next to a remote stream can deprive shy desert wildlife of life-giving water access.

• *Leave all Native American sites and artifacts as you find them.* First, it's against the law to disturb antiquities; second, it's stupid. Enjoy looking at rock art, but don't touch the images—body oils hasten their deterioration. Don't even think about taking potsherds, arrowheads, or artifacts from where you find them. Leave them for others to enjoy or for archaeologists to decipher.

• *Dispose of human solid waste thoughtfully.* The desert can't easily absorb human fecal matter. Desert soils have few microorganisms to break down organic material, and, simply put, mummified turds can last for years. Be sure to bury human solid waste at least 6–12 inches deep in sand and at least 200 feet away from streams and water sources. Pack out toilet paper in resealable bags.

the way through these trails. Other trails are better matched to the skills of novices.

It's a good idea to read up on Moab-area trails before planning a trip here (heaps of books and pamphlets are available; see Suggested Reading in the Resources section). You can also hire an outfitter to teach you about the special skills needed to mountain bike in slickrock country, or join a guided tour. A good place to start is the Trails Illustrated *Bike Map #501* of the Moab area, which has mountain-bike routes color-coded according to difficulty. Or pick up a *Moab Area Mountain Bike Trails* map at the Moab Information Center.

Most people come to Moab to mountain bike mid-March–late May, and then again in fall, mid-September–October. Unless you are an early riser, summer is simply too hot for extended bike touring in these desert canyons. Be prepared for crowds, especially in mid-March, during spring break. In 1999, the Slickrock Trail alone attracted more than 150,000 riders.

If you've never biked on slickrock or in the desert, here are a few basic guidelines. Take care if venturing off a trail—it's a long way down some of the sheer cliff faces! A trail's steep slopes and sharp turns can be tricky, so a helmet is a must. Knee pads and riding gloves also protect from scrapes and bruises. Fat bald tires work best on the rock; partially deflated knobby tires do almost as well. Carry plenty of water—one gallon in summer, half a gallon in cooler months. Tiny plant associations, which live in fragile cryptobiotic soil, don't want you tearing through their homes; stay on the rock and avoid sand areas.

Dozens of trails thread the Moab area; some of the best and most noted are described as follows.

Slickrock Bike Trail

Undulating slickrock just east of Moab challenges even the best mountain bikers; this is not an area in which to learn mountain-bike skills. Originally, motorcyclists laid out this route, although now about 99 percent of riders rely on leg and lung power. The practice loop near the beginning allows first-time visitors a chance to get a feel for the slickrock. The "trail" consists only of painted white lines. Riders following it have less chance of getting lost or finding themselves in hazardous areas. Plan on about five hours to do the 9.6-mile main loop, and expect to do some walking.

Side trails lead to viewpoints overlooking Moab, the Colorado River, and arms of Negro Bill Canyon. Panoramas of the surrounding canyon country and La Sal Mountains add to the pleasure of biking.

To reach the trailhead from Main Street in Moab, turn east 0.4 mile on 300 South, turn right 0.1 mile on 400 East, turn left (east) 0.5 mile on Mill Creek Drive, then left 2.5 miles on Sand Flats Road.

The practice loop also makes an enjoyable 2.5-mile hike. Steep drop-offs into the tributaries of Negro Bill Canyon offer breathtaking views. It's best to walk off to the side of the white lines marking the route. You'll reach the practice loop one-quarter mile from the trailhead.

Kokopelli's Trail

Mountain bikers have linked together a series of back roads through the magical canyons of eastern Utah and western Colorado. You can start on Sand Flats Road in Moab and ride east to Castle Valley (21.1 miles), Fisher Valley (44.9 miles), Dewey Bridge (62.9 miles), Cisco Boat Landing (83.5 miles), Rabbit Valley (108 miles), and Loma (140 miles). Lots of optional routes and access points allow for many possibilities. Campsites along the trail have tables, grills, and outhouses. See the small book *The Utah-Colorado Mountain Bike Trail System, Route 1—Moab to Loma,* by Peggy Utesch, for detailed descriptions. An excellent brochure, *Kokopelli's Trail Map,* is available free at the Moab Information Center.

Gimini Bridges (Bull Canyon) Trail

This 14-mile trail passes through tremendous natural rock arches and the slickrock fins of the Wingate Formation, making this one of the most scenic of Moab-area trails; it's also one of the more moderate trails in terms of necessary skill and fitness. The trail begins 12.5 miles up Highway 313 (the access road to Dead Horse Point State Park), a total of 21 miles—all uphill—from Moab, so a shuttle or drop-off is a good idea.

Monitor and Merimack Trail

A good introduction to the varied terrains in the Moab area, the 13.2-mile Monitor and Merimack Trail also includes a trip to a dinosaur fossil bed. The trail climbs through open desert and up Tusher Canyon, then explores red sandstone towers and buttes across slickrock before dropping down Mill Canyon. At the base of the canyon, you can leave your bike and hike the Mill Canyon Dinosaur Trail before completing the loop to the parking area. Reach the trailhead by traveling 15 miles north of Moab on U.S. 191.

Guided Tours

Multiday tours vary in price depending on the difficulty of the trail and the degree of comfort involved. The charge for these trips is usually $125–150 per day, including food and shuttles. Be sure to inquire whether rates include bike rental.

Dreamrides Mountainbike Tours, 435/259-6419, www.dreamride.com, focuses on leading small, customized group tours. Most packages are three- or five-day tours at roughly $120 per day, accommodations extra. **Rim Tours,** 1233 S. U.S. 191, Moab, UT 84532, 435/259-5223 or 800/626-7335, www.rimtours.com, and **Kaibab Mountain Bike Tours,** operated out of Moab Cyclery at 391 S. Main, Moab, UT 84532, 435/259-7423 or 800/451-1133, www.kaibab-tours.com, lead several half-day (around $60–75), full-day ($75–120), and multiday trips on mountain bikes; some of their tours combine cycling with rafting and/or hiking.

Western Spirit Cycling, P.O. Box 411, Moab, UT 84532, 435/259-8969 or 800/845-BIKE (845-2453), www.westernspirit.com, offers 25 different bicycle tours in the western United States, with about one-third in Utah. Moab-area trips include the White Rim, the Maze, and the Kokopelli Trail.

Nichols Expeditions, 497 N. Main, 435/259-7882 or 800/635-1792, www.nicholsexpeditions.com, goes to all three districts of Canyonlands National Park and offers combination biking/kayaking trips that feature trips down the Colorado River.

Shuttle Services

Many mountain-bike trails are essentially one-way, and unless you want to cycle back the way you came, arrange a shuttle service to pick you up and return you to Moab or to your vehicle. Also, if you don't have a vehicle or a bike rack, use a shuttle service to get to more distant trailheads. **Roadrunner Shuttle,** 435/259-9402, and **Acme Bike Shuttle,** 435/260-2534, both operate shuttle services; the usual fare is $12 per person. Both companies will also shuttle hikers to trailheads or pick up rafters. Roadrunner also serves as a taxi service for groups.

RAFTING AND BOAT TOURS

Even a visitor with a tight schedule can get out and enjoy the canyon country on rafts and other watercraft. Outfitters offer both laid-back and exhilarating day trips, which usually require little advance planning. Longer, multiday trips include gentle canoe paddles along the placid Green River and thrilling expeditions down the Colorado River.

Reserve well in advance for most of the longer trips because the BLM and the National Park Service limit the number of trips through the backcountry, and space, especially in high season, is at a premium. Experienced rafters can also plan their own unguided trips, although you'll need a permit for all areas except for the day-long Fisher Towers float upstream from Moab.

The rafting season runs April–September, and jetboat tours run February–November. Contact the Moab Information Center and the National Park Service office for lists or brochures of tour operators; independent river-runners can also visit the center for Colorado River infomation, although you need to pick up permits from the BLM or National Parks offices. Most river-runners obtain their permits by applying in January and February for a March drawing; the Moab Information Center BLM Ranger can advise on this process and provide the latest information about available cancellations.

Moab-Area Outfitters

Moab is full of river-trip companies, and most offer day and multiday trips; in addition, many will combine raft trips with biking, horseback riding, hiking, or four-wheel-drive excursions. Call for brochures or check out the many websites

© TAG-A-LONG EXPEDITIONS

Take a day off from mountain biking to raft the Colorado River near Moab.

at www.discovermoab.com/tour.htm. Most of the following major outfitters offer trips to the major river destinations on the Colorado and Green Rivers as well as other rivers in Utah and the West. Inquire about special natural history or petroglyph tours, if these specialty trips interest you: **Western River Expeditions,** 801/942-6669 or 800/453-7450, www.westernriver.com; **Tag-A-Long Expeditions,** 452 N. Main, 435/259-8946 or 800/453-3292, www.tagalong.com; **Navtec Expeditions,** 321 N. Main (P.O. Box 1267, Moab, UT 84532), 435/259-7983 or 800/833-1278, www.navtec.com; **Canyon Voyages,** 435/259-6007 or 800/733-6007, www.canyonvoyages.com; **Adrift Adventures,** 378 N. Main, 435/259-8594 or 800/874-4483, www.adrift.net; **Moki-Mac,** 435/564-3361 or 800/284-7280, www.mokimac.com; **Sheri Griffith Expeditions,** 503/259-8229 or 800/332-2439, www.griffithexp.com.

Moab Rafting and Kayaking Destinations

For most of the following, full-day rates include lunch and beverages, while part-day trips include just lemonade and soft drinks. On overnight trips, you sleep in tents in backcountry campgrounds.

The **Colorado River** offers several exciting options. The most popular day-run near Moab starts upstream on the Colorado River near Fisher Towers and bounces through several moderate rapids on the way back to town. Full-day raft trips from Fisher Towers to near Moab generally cost $45–50 per person. Half-day trips run over much the same stretch of river (no lunch, though) and cost around $35 per adult.

For a more adventurous rafting day trip, the Colorado's rugged **Westwater Canyon** offers lots of white water and several Class III–IV rapids near the Utah-Colorado border. These long day trips are more expensive, typically $120–135 a day. The Westwater Canyon is also often offered as part of multiday adventure packages. The **Dolores River** joins the Colorado about two miles upstream from Dewey Bridge, near the Colorado border. The Dolores River offers exciting white

water in a narrow canyon during the spring runoff; the season is short, though, and the river is too low to run by mid-June. With plenty of Class III and IV rapids, this trip usually takes three days and costs around $500 per person.

The **Cataract Canyon** section of the Colorado River, which begins south of the river's confluence with the Green River and extends to the backwater of Lake Powell, usually requires four days of rafting to complete. This is the wildest white water in the Moab area, with big, boiling Class III and IV rapids. Costs range $550–750, depending on what kind of craft, the number of days, and whether you fly, hike, or drive out at the end of the trip.

The **Green River** also offers rafting (and canoeing) opportunities, although they are milder than the Colorado. Trips on the Green make good family outings. Most trips require five days, leaving from the town of Green River and taking out at Mineral Bottom, just above the Canyonlands National Park boundary. Highlights of the Green River include Labyrinth Canyon and Bowknot Bend. Costs are usually $500–600 for a five-day trip.

Rafting On Your Own

The Fisher Towers section of the Colorado is gentle enough for amateur rafters to negotiate on their own. Rent a raft or kayak from one of the rafting outfitters listed previously. A popular one-day raft trip with mild rapids begins from the Hittle Bottom Recreation Site, 23.5 miles up Highway 128 near Fisher Towers, and ends 14 river miles downstream at Take-Out Beach, 10.3 miles up Highway 128 from U.S. 191. You can rent rafts and the mandatory life jackets in Moab, and you won't need a permit on this section of river.

Experienced white-water rafters with permits can put in at the BLM's Westwater Ranger Station in Utah or at the Loma boat launch in Colorado. A start at Loma adds a day or two to the trip and the sights of Horsethief and Ruby Canyons. Normal take-out is at Cisco, although it's possible to continue 16 miles on slow-moving water through open country to Dewey Bridge.

Daily raft rentals begin at $85 or so; kayaks rent for $35.

Canoe Trips

Canoeists can also sample the calm waters of the Green River on multiday excursions with **Red River Canoe Company,** 800/753-8216, www.redrivercanoe.com. It runs scheduled trips to four sections of the river. Red River Canoe also offers trips to calmer stretches of the Colorado and Dolores Rivers. The company also conducts white-water canoe workshops on the Colorado's Professor Valley and combination canoe and mountain-bike trips. Cost ranges $110–140 per person per day.

Jetboat Tours

Guided jetboat excursions through Canyonlands National Park start at around $50 for a half-day trip. **Tex's Riverways,** 435/259-5101, www.texs-riverways.com, offers trips of various lengths on the Green and Colorado Rivers. **Tag-A-Long Expeditions,** 452 N. Main, 435/259-8946 or 800/453-3292, www.tagalong.com, and **Adrift Adventures,** 378 N. Main, 435/259-8594 or 800/874-4483, www.adrift.net, both offer half-day trips and full-day combination jetboat/jeep excursions.

Motorboat Tours

Canyonlands by Night tours leave at sunset in an open motorboat and go several miles upstream on the Colorado River; a guide points out canyon features. The sound and light show begins on the way back; music and historic narration accompany the play of lights on canyon walls. Cost is $26 adults, $16 ages 4–12; boats run April–mid-October. Dinner cruises are available. **Canyonlands by Day** trips go downriver into the Colorado River Canyon near Dead Horse Point. Of the two trips offered, one goes 60 miles downstream ($58 adults, $45 ages 4–12) and the other travels 30 miles ($38 adults, $28 ages 4–12). Tours operate March–October; reservations are a good idea because the boat fills up fast. Trips depart from the Spanish mission–style office just north of Moab, across the Colorado River, 435/259-5261, www.canyonlandsbynight.com.

FOUR-WHEEL TOURING

Road tours offer visitors a special opportunity to view unique canyonland arches and spires, indigenous rock art, and wildlife. An interpretive brochure at the Moab Information Center outlines the **Moab Area Rock Art Auto Tour,** which routes motorists to petroglyphs tucked away behind golf courses and ranches. You might also pick up a map of Moab-area four-wheel-drive trails: four rugged, 15- to 54-mile loop routes through the desert, which take from 2.5–4 hours to drive. Those who left their trusty four-by-four and off-road driving skills at home can take an off-road jeep tour through a private operator. Both **Tag-A-Long Expeditions,** 452 N. Main, Moab, UT 84532, 435/259-8946 or 800/453-3292, www.tagalong.com, and **Adrift Adventures,** 378 N. Main (P.O. Box 577, Moab, UT 84532), 435/259-8594 or 800/874-4483, www.adrift.net, have half-day (around $50) and full-day jeep tours (around $90) with combination jetboat or hiking options. Full-day tours include lunch.

Lin Ottinger's Tours, 600 N. Main, Moab, UT 84532, 435/259-7312, offers backcountry driving trips mid-April–mid-October. Lin has been poking around the canyons of this area since the uranium boom of the 1950s, and he knows the best places; frequent stops allow plenty of time to walk around for a look at Native American art and scenic and geologic features. Half-day trips are $65, full-day $80.

You can also rent four-by-fours from **Farabee 4X4 Adventures,** 401 N. Main, 435/259-7494 or 800/806-5337, or **Slick Rock Jeep Rental,** 284 N. Main, 435/259-5678.

AIR TOURS

You'll have a bird's-eye view of southeastern Utah's incredible landscape from Moab or Green River Airport with **Redtail Aviation,** P.O. Box 515, Moab, UT 84532, 435/259-7421 (Moab) or 800/842-9251. Flights include Arches National Park ($53) and Canyonlands National Park (Needles, Island in the Sky, and Maze Districts; $99). Longer tours are available, too. Rates are based on two or more persons. Flights operate all year. **Slickrock Air Guides,** 2231 S. U.S. 191, Moab, UT 84532, 435/259-6216 or 866/259-1626, www.slickrockairguides.com, offers a one-hour tour over the Canyonlands area for $99 per person, and $295 for 3.5 hours over Canyonlands, Natural Bridges, Lake Powell, and the Capitol Reef area with a stop for lunch at the Marble Canyon Lodge.

Green River and Vicinity

GREEN RIVER

The small town began in 1878 as a mail station on the long run between Salina in central Utah and the Colorado border. Today Green River is still the only sizable settlement (nearly 1,000 people) on this route, now I-70, with a number of quality places to stay. Travelers can stop for a rest or meal here, take a day trip on the river, or use the town as a base for exploring the scenic San Rafael Swell country nearby.

Green River is known for its melons. In summer, stop at roadside stands and partake of wondrous cantaloupe and watermelons. The blazing summer heat and ample irrigation water make such delicacies possible. **Melon Days** celebrates the harvest on the third weekend of September with a parade, city fair, music, canoe race, games, and free melons.

A pleasant **city park** offers shaded tables, playground, and tennis courts at the corner of Main and 100 East.

The town of Green River rests midway between two popular river-rafting areas. The Green River's Desolation and Gray Canyons are upstream, while Labyrinth and Stillwater Canyons lie downstream. Several river companies organize day and multiday trips through these areas.

John Wesley Powell River History Museum

Stop by this fine museum to learn about Powell's daring expeditions down the Green and Colorado Rivers in 1869 and 1871–1872. An excellent free multimedia presentation about both rivers uses narratives from Powell's trips; 21 minutes. Historic river boats on display include a replica of Powell's *Emma Dean.* Other exhibits show places to visit in the area.

The **Grand County Travel Council office,** in the museum, 435/564-3526, has local travel information (P.O. Box 335, Green River, UT 84525). A gift shop sells books, maps, Native American crafts, T-shirts, and other souvenirs.

The Powell Museum, on the east bank of the Green River, is at 885 E. Main (the I-70 business route through town), 435/564-3427/3428. Both the museum and the tourist office are open daily 9 A.M.–8 P.M. in summer and daily 9 A.M.–5 P.M. the rest of the year.

Floating Desolation and Gray Canyons

These canyons of the Green River cut through the Tavaputs Plateau, the vast and mostly untracked region between Roosevelt in the north and the town of Green River. Outfitters normally fly rafting parties into a remote airstrip at Sand Wash, south of Myton, and take 4–7 days to complete the 85-mile trip. Prices vary between outfitters. The river has a few Class III rapids, interspersed with flat water, making for a good family adventure. Expect to pay $800 for four days on the river, or up to $920 for a full week. Outfitters also offer day trips through the lower sections of the Gray Canyon, usually for around $50. Experienced kayakers or rafters can make the trip on their own; see the Green River Scenic Drive section for details.

For information on guided day or multiday Desolation and Gray Canyon trips, contact one of the following local companies: **Adventure River Expeditions,** 185 S. Broadway, 435/564-34545 or 800/564-3648, or **Moki-Mac River Expeditions,** 100 Silliman Ln., 435/564-3361. A number of Moab, Salt Lake City, and Grand Junction, Colorado, outfitters also offer multiday trips down Desolation Canyon; contact the

Green River tourist office or the BLM Price River Resource Area office, 600 Price River Dr., Price, UT 84501, 435/637-4591, for a complete list of licensed outfitters. You need both a permit and river-running experience to float the canyons on your own.

Canoeing Labyrinth and Stillwater Canyons

Labyrinth and Stillwater Canyons lie downstream from Green River, between the town of Green River and the river's confluence with the Colorado River in Canyonlands National Park. Primarily a canoeing or kayaking river, the Green at this point is calm and wide as it passes into increasingly deep, rust-colored canyons. This isn't a wilderness river, however, as regular power boats can also follow the river below town to the confluence with the Colorado River and head up the Colorado to Moab, 2–3 days and 186 river miles away. In fact, the town of Green River sponsors an annual **Friendship Cruise** on this route on Memorial Day weekend.

Some guided canoe trips leave from Mineral Canyon and paddle 52 miles to the river's confluence; the remainder of the trip through the Colorado's Cataract Canyon is on raft (around $1,000 for a six-day trip). You'll find both guided and self-guided canoe trips available between Green River State Park just south of town and the Mineral Canyon boat launch. Depending on how fast you paddle it will be a three- or four-day trip. Prices for a guided trip run between $400 and $525; canoe rentals are $15 to $20 a day, though the shuttle from Mineral Canyon back to Green River will cost you around $200 (for up to four people). For information on canoe trips on the Green River, contact **Moki-Mac,** 100 Silliman Ln., 435/564-3361; **Tex's Riverways,** P.O. Box 67, Moab, UT 84532, 435/259-5101; or **Red River Canoe Company,** 497 North Main St., Moab, UT 84532, 435/259-7722. Each company also offers shuttle and full rental service.

Accommodations

Green River has over a dozen well-kept older motels as well as new chain motels to choose from; unless noted, each of the following has a pool—a major consideration in this often sweltering desert valley.

Under $50: The **Bookcliff Lodge,** 395 E. Main, 435/564-3406, is part of a large motel and restaurant complex. Though it lacks a pool, the **Sleepy Hollow Motel,** 94 E. Main, 435/564-8189, is an attractive well-maintained brick motel.

$50–75: The **Super 8,** 1248 E. Main, 435/564-8888 or 800/888-8888, is out by I-70 Exit 162. The **Comfort Inn,** 1065 E. Main, 435/564-3300, operates a bit closer to town. The **Motel 6,** 946 E. Main, 435/564-3436 or 800/466-8356, is just two blocks from the river.

$75–100: The nicest place to stay in town is the **Best Western River Terrace Motel,** 880 E. Main, 435/564-3401 or 800/528-1234, with very large, nicely furnished rooms, some of which overlook the Green River.

Campgrounds: Four campgrounds, all with showers, offer sites for tents and RVs. **Shady Acres RV Park,** 360 E. Main, 435/564-8290, may be a bit too close to the noisy road for tent campers; open all year with store, showers, and laundry. **United Campground,** 910 E. Main, 435/564-8195 is set back a ways from the road; open all year with a pool, store, showers, and laundry. **Green River State Park,** 150 S. Green River Blvd., 435/564-3633 or 877/444-6777 (reservations), offers pleasant sites shaded by large cottonwoods and a boat ramp; open all year. **Green River KOA,** 550 S. Green River Blvd., 435/564-3651, has campsites and Kamping Kabins. Open April 1–October 15 with a pool, store, and laundry.

Food

Directly adjacent to the Best Western River Terrace Motel is a good restaurant, **The Tamarisk,** 435/564-8109, with riverfront views and open for three meals a day.

Other than motel restaurants and fast food, the one really notable place to eat in Green River is **Ray's Tavern,** 25 S. Broadway, 435/564-3511. Ray's doesn't look like much from the outside, but inside you'll find a friendly welcome, tables made from tree trunks, and some of the best steaks, chops, and burgers in this part of the state. Don't expect cuisine, but the food is good and the atmosphere is truly Western; beer drinkers will be glad for the selection of regional microbrews after a long day navigating the river or driving desert roads.

Services

The **post office** is on E. Main. **Green River Medical Center,** 250 E. Main, 435/564-3434, offers services Monday–Friday 9 A.M.–5 P.M.

VICINITY OF GREEN RIVER

Crystal Geyser

With some luck, you'll catch the spectacle of this cold-water geyser on the bank of the Green River. The gusher shoots as high as 60 feet but only three or four times daily, so you may have to spend a half day here in order to see it. Though the area offers no facilities, camping is possible nearby, so you might be able to see the geyser by moonlight. Staff at the Grand County Travel Council often know the latest eruption schedule. An eruption typically lasts seven minutes and discharges 4,350 cubic feet of salt water. Carbon dioxide and other gases power the gushing fountain. A 2,267-foot-deep petroleum test well drilled in 1935–1936 concentrated the geyser flow, but thick layers of old travertine deposits attest that mineral-laden springs have long been active at this site. Colorful newer travertine forms delicate terraces around the opening and down to the river. The orange and dark red of the minerals and algae make this a pretty spot, even if the geyser is only quietly gurgling.

Crystal Geyser is 10 miles south of town by road (boaters should look for the geyser deposits on the left about 4.5 river miles downstream from Green River). From downtown, drive east one mile on Main, turn left three miles on signed Frontage Road (near milepost 4), then turn right six miles on a narrow paved road just after going under a railroad overpass. The road goes under I-70, then is unpaved for the last 4.5 miles; keep right at a fork near some power lines. Some washes have to be crossed, so the drive isn't recommended after rains. When

the weather's fair, cars shouldn't have a problem. Buildings and antennas passed on the way belong to the Utah Launch Complex of White Sands Missile Range. From 1963 to 1979 several hundred Pershing and Athena rockets blasted off here for targets at White Sands, New Mexico, 400 miles away.

Green River Scenic Drive

Splendid cliffs of Gray Canyon enclose the Green River 10 miles north of town. An unpaved road winding 8.5 miles into the canyon allows drivers easy access to the scenery. Cars with good clearance can travel through the canyon in dry weather; when the clay road surface gets wet, don't attempt it in any vehicle.

From downtown Green River, head east on Main Street and turn north on Hastings Road (1200 East); it's the first paved road to the north past the bridge. After two miles the road follows the banks of the Green River a short way with views north to the castlelike cliffs of the Beckwith Plateau, through which the Green River has carved Gray Canyon. At 6.3 miles after turning off Main, make a right turn onto an unpaved road just before the paved road enters a ranch. The turn may have a small sign for Nefertiti. Follow the unpaved road 3.8 miles across a wash, then along the river to Swasey Beach and Rapids near the mouth of Gray Canyon. A primitive camping area under the cottonwoods is an inviting place to spend the night. The camping area has an outhouse; no drinking water or charge. A large sandy beach stretches along the shore just below the rapids.

The road becomes a bit rougher and narrows to a single lane in spots past Swasey Beach for the remaining 8.5 spectacular miles to Nefertiti. You'll see Price River Canyon entering Gray Canyon on the other side of the river two miles before Nefertiti. Look for petroglyphs near the end of the road. Hikers can explore many rugged side canyons or follow cattle trails a long distance upstream. Cowboys on horseback still work the range on the plateaus to the north much as they've always done. Cattle are driven on these trails to the high country in spring and brought back down in autumn.

Michael Kelsey's book *Canyon Hiking Guide to the Colorado Plateau* details hiking possibilities through Gray and Desolation Canyons and their side canyons.

Commercial **raft day trips** provide a more relaxed way of enjoying this extremely remote part of Utah. River-runners enjoy half a dozen lively rapids on the section of river from the boat launch just above Nefertiti Rapid to the takeout at Swasey Beach. You can also do it yourself. This makes a good day trip with rafts or kayaks; canoeists will find the white water very challenging. All boaters must wear life jackets and carry proper equipment (spare oar or paddle, extra life jacket, and bail bucket or pump). You will also need a portable toilet and, if planning a campfire, a firepan to contain the ashes. You won't need a permit, though the BLM has a register at the put-in.

SEGO CANYON AND GHOST TOWN

Prehistoric rock art and ruins of a coal-mining town lie within scenic canyons of the Book Cliffs just a short drive north from Thompson and I-70. In the early 1900s, a local rancher discovered thick seams of high-quality coal here. A mining camp, served by the Ballard and Thompson Railroad, sprang to life at the site. Residents named their little town after Utah's state flower, the sego lily, which grew profusely in the canyons. Population peaked at about 500; families lived in fine houses or in rustic dugouts, while the bachelors stayed in a two-story boardinghouse. Production continued through water shortages, fires, and management troubles until the early 1950s, when the railroads switched to diesel locomotives and no longer needed Sego's coal. The town folded and was sold for salvage. Plenty of good coal remains; if steam locomotives ever come back into style, perhaps Sego will, too!

Visitors to the town can see the company store's stone walls, the frame boardinghouse, dugout houses, railroad grades, and foundations of coal-handling structures. Cars with good

SEGO CANYON ROCK ART

If you approach Moab along I-70, consider a side trip to one of the premier rock-art galleries in Utah, just a short distance from the freeway junction with U.S. 191 to Moab. Sego Canyon is a showcase of prehistoric rock art—it preserves rock drawings and images that are thousands of years old. The Barrier Canyon Style drawings may be 8,000 years old; the more recent Fremont Style images were created in the last thousand years. Compared to these ancient pictures, the Ute etchings are relatively recent; experts speculate that they may have been drawn in the 1800s, when Ute villages still lined Sego Canyon. Interestingly, the newer petroglyphs and pictographs are more representational than the older ones. The ancient Barrier Canyon figures are typically horned ghostlike beings that look like aliens from early Hollywood sci-fi thrillers. The Fremont Style images depict stylized human figures made from geometric shapes; the crudest figures are the most recent. The Ute images are of buffaloes and hunters on horseback.

clearance can travel the road in dry weather; don't enter the canyons after recent rains or if storms threaten.

To reach Sego Canyon, take I-70 Thompson Exit 185 (25 miles east of Green River or five miles east of the U.S. 191 turnoff to Moab) and drive one mile north to Thompson. The small railroad community has a café and convenience store near I-70. Continue north across the tracks on a paved road, which becomes dirt after half a mile, into Thompson Canyon. At the first creek ford, 3.5 miles from town, look for petroglyphs and pictographs on cliffs to the left.

The ghost town lies one mile up Sego Canyon. Both the Sego and Thompson Canyon Roads lead deeper into the rugged Book Cliffs. Drivers with four-wheel drive and hikers can explore more of this land, seldom visited except in deer season.

M

SOUTHEASTERN UTAH

Arches National Park

A concentration of arches of marvelous variety has formed within the maze of sandstone fins at this park, one of the most popular in the United States. Balanced rocks and tall spires add to the splendor. Paved roads and short hiking trails provide easy access to some of the more than 1,500 arches in the park. If you're short on time, a drive to the Windows Section (23.5 miles round-trip) allows a look at some of the largest and most spectacular arches. To visit all the stops and hike a few short trails would take all day. The entrance fee of $10 per vehicle ($5 bicyclists) is good for seven days at Arches only. The park brochure available at the entrance station and visitors center has a map of major scenic features, drives, trails, and back roads.

Geology

An unusual combination of geologic forces created the arches. About 300 million years ago, evaporation of inland seas left behind a salt layer more than 3,000 feet thick in the Paradox Basin of this region. Sediments, including those that later became the arches, then covered the salt. Unequal pressures caused the salt to gradually flow upward in places, bending the overlying sediments as well. These upfolds, or anticlines, later collapsed when ground water dissolved the underlying salt. The faults and joints caused by the uplift and collapse opened the way for erosion to carve hundreds of freestanding fins. Alternate freezing and thawing action and exfoliation (flaking caused by expansion when water or frost penetrates the rock) continued to peel away more rock until holes formed in some of the fins. Rockfalls within the holes helped to enlarge the arches. Nearly all arches in the park eroded out of Entrada sandstone.

Eventually all the present arches will collapse, but we should have plenty of new ones by the time that happens! The fins' uniform strength and hard upper surfaces have proved ideal for arch formation. Not every hole in the rock is an arch. The opening must be at least three feet in one direction and light must be able to pass

through. Although the term "windows" often refers to openings in large walls of rock, windows and arches are really the same. Water seeping through the sandstone from above has created a second type of arch—the pothole arch. You may also come across a few natural bridges cut from the rock by perennial water runoff.

Flora and Fauna

Elevation at the park ranges from 3,960 feet along the Colorado River to 5,653 feet in the Windows area. Annual precipitation averages only 10–11 inches. Even so, plants and wildlife have found niches in this rugged high-desert country. Shrubs and grasslands cover most of the land not occupied by barren rock. Cottonwood trees grow along some of the washes while piñon pine and juniper form pygmy forests at the higher elevations. Specially adapted plant communities thrive in the dark cryptobiotic crusts on the soil. Hanging gardens surround springs and seeps. Tracks across the sands show the presence of shy or nocturnal wildlife. Animals include mule deer, coyote, gray fox, porcupine, bobcat, ringtail cat, kangaroo rat, antelope ground squirrel, collared lizard, and midget faded rattlesnake.

History

Prehistoric Anasazi and Fremont cultures hunted in the area and collected wild plant foods. The modern Utes hunted here, too. Chert, a hard rock from Salt Valley, provided material for toolmaking. Rock art and artifacts mark the former presence of these tribes. Most of the early settlers and cowboys of the region paid little attention to the scenery. However, in 1923 a prospector by the name of Alexander Ringhoffer interested officials of the Rio Grande Railroad in the scenic attractions at what he called Devils Garden (now known as Klondike Bluffs). The railroad men liked the area and contacted Stephen Mather, first director of the National Park Service. Mather started the political process that led to designation of two small areas as a

ARCHES
NATIONAL PARK

SOUTHEASTERN UTAH

Long Valley

Eagle Park

Salt

Valley

Klondike Bluffs

Yellow

Cat Flat

DARK ANGEL
DEVILS GARDEN
PRIVATE ARCH
DOUBLE O ARCH
LANDSCAPE ARCH
DEVILS GARDEN
MARCHING MEN
Salt
Valley
Wash
SKYLINE ARCH
BROKEN ARCH
SAND DUNE ARCH

ARCHES

NATIONAL

PARK

Fiery Furnace

Salt Wash

Winter Camp Ridge

DELICATE ARCH
WOLFE RANCH
DELICATE ARCH VIEWPOINT

PANORAMA POINT

Dry Mesa

Garden of Eden
COVE OF CAVES
BALANCED ROCK
NORTH/SOUTH WINDOW
Rock Pinnacles
Windows Section

Courthouse

The Great Wall

Wash

Petrified Dunes

Mat Martin Point

313

Sevenmile Canyon

191

SHEEP ROCK
COURTHOUSE TOWERS VIEWPOINT/ THE ORGAN
THREE GOSSIPS
Courthouse Towers
PARK AVENUE
VISITOR CENTER

128

Colorado River

Arths Pasture

MOON

0   2 mi

0   2 km

279

191

Moab

© AVALON TRAVEL PUBLISHING, INC.

national monument in 1929, but Ringhoffer's Devils Garden wasn't included until later. Early visitors had to endure travel over nonexistent or barely passable roads; see the August 1947 issue of *National Geographic* magazine for a well-written account of the monument as it once was. It grew in size over the years and became Arches National Park in 1971. The park now comprises 76,519 acres—it's small enough to be appreciated in one day, yet large enough to warrant extensive exploration.

Visitors Center

Located just past the entrance booth, the visitors center provides a good introduction to what to expect ahead. Exhibits identify the rock layers, describe the geologic and human history, and illustrate some of the wildlife and plants of the park. Staff members present a short slide program upon request and answer your questions. Look for the posted list of special activities; rangers host campfire programs and lead a wide variety of guided walks April–September. You'll also find checklists, pamphlets, books, maps, posters, postcards, and film here for purchase. See the ranger for advice and the free back-country permit required for overnight trips. The easy 0.2-mile **Desert Nature Trail** begins in front of the visitors center and identifies some of the native plants. Picnic areas lie outside the visitors center and at Balanced Rock and Devils Garden. The park is open all year; visitors cen-

---

EDWARD ABBEY: "RESIST MUCH, OBEY LITTLE"

Edward Abbey spent two summers in the late 1950s living in a trailer in Arches National Park. From this experience, he wrote *Desert Solitaire*, which, when it was published in 1968, introduced many readers to the beauties of Utah's slickrock country and the need to preserve it. In the introduction to this book, he gives a word of caution to slickrock pilgrims:

> *Do not jump into your automobile next June and rush out to the Canyon country hoping to see some of that which I have attempted to evoke in these pages. In the first place you can't see anything from a car; you've got to get out of the goddamned contraption and walk, better yet crawl, on hands and knees, over the sandstone and through the . . . cactus. When traces of blood begin to mark your trail you'll see something, maybe.*

This sense of letting the outdoors affect you—right down to the bone—pervades Abbey's writing. He advocated responding to assaults on the environment in an equally raw, gutsy way. Convinced that the only way to confront rampant development in the American West was by preserving its wilderness, he was a pioneer of radical environmentalism, a "desert anarchist." Long before Earth First!, Abbey's fictional characters blew up dams and created a holy environmentalist ruckus in *The Monkeywrench Gang*. Some of his ideas were radical, others reactionary, and he seemed deeply committed to raising a stir. Abbey's writing did a lot to change the way people think about the American West, its development, and staying true to values derived from the natural world.

Two recent biographies, *Edward Abbey: A Life,* by James M. Cahalan, and the less academic *Adventures with Ed,* by Abbey's good friend Jack Loeffler, help readers see the person behind the icon.

Cahalan, James M. *Edward Abbey: A Life.* Tucson: University of Arizona Press, 2001.

Loeffler, Jack. *Adventures with Ed: A Portrait of Abbey.* Albuquerque: University of New Mexico Press, 2002.

ter hours are daily 8 A.M.–4:30 P.M., with extended hours in summer. Arches National Park is five miles north of downtown Moab on U.S. 191, P.O. Box 907, Moab, UT 84532, 435/719-2299.

Devils Garden Campground

The park's campground is near the end of the 18-mile scenic drive, though in summer you must pre-register at the visitors center. The campground is open all year with water; $10. Try to arrive early during the busy Easter–October season; only groups can reserve spaces. Elevation here is 5,355 feet. During summer evenings, rangers at the Campfire Circle tell about the park's geology, history, wildlife, flora, and environment.

Hiking, Biking, and Climbing

Established trails lead to many fine arches and overlooks that can't be seen from the road. You're free to wander cross-country, too, but please stay on rock or in washes to avoid damaging the fragile cryptobiotic soils. Wear good walking shoes with rubber soles for travel across slickrock. The summer sun can be especially harsh on the unprepared hiker—don't forget water, hat, and sunscreen. The desert rule is to carry at least one gallon of water per person for an all-day hike. Take a map and compass for off-trail hiking. Be cautious on the slickrock; the soft sandstone can crumble easily. Also, remember that it's easier to go up a steep slickrock slope than to come back down! You can reach almost any spot in the park on a day hike, though you'll also find some good overnight possibilities. Areas for longer trips include Courthouse Wash in the southern part of the park and Salt Wash in the eastern part. All backpacking is done off-trail. A backcountry permit must be obtained from a ranger before camping in the backcountry. Hiking regulations include no fires, no pets, camping out of sight of any road (at least one mile away) or trail (at least a half mile away) and at least 300 feet from a recognizable archaeological site or nonflowing water source. Bicycles *must* stick to established roads in the park; cyclists have to contend with heavy traffic on the narrow paved roads and dusty, washboarded surfaces on

the dirt roads. Beware of the deep sand on the four-wheel-drive roads. Nearby, BLM and Canyonlands National Park areas offer much better mountain biking. Rock climbers don't need a permit, though they should first discuss their plans with a ranger. Most features named on USGS maps are *closed* to climbing.

SIGHTS AND HIKES ALONG THE PARK ROAD

A road guide to Arches National Park, available at the visitors center, has detailed descriptions that correspond to place-names along the main road. Be sure to stop only in parking lots and designated pullouts. Watch out for others who are sightseeing in this popular park. The following are major points of interest.

Moab Fault

The park road begins a long but well-graded climb from the visitors center up the cliffs to the northeast. A pullout on the right after 1.1 miles gives a good view of Moab Canyon and its geology. The rock layers on this side of the canyon have slipped down more than 2,600 feet in relation to the other side. Movement took place about six million years ago along the Moab Fault, which follows the canyon floor. Rock layers at the top of the far cliffs are nearly the same age as those at the *bottom* on this side! If you could stack the rocks of this side on top of rocks on the other side, you'd have a complete stratigraphic column of the Moab area—more than 150 million years' worth.

Park Avenue

South Park Avenue Overlook and Trailhead are on the left 2.1 miles from the visitors center. Great sandstone slabs form a "skyline" on each side of this dry wash. A trail goes north one mile down the wash to North Park Avenue Trailhead (1.3 miles ahead by road). Arrange to be picked up there or backtrack to your starting point. The large rock monoliths of Courthouse Towers rise north of Park Avenue. Only a few small arches exist now, though major arches may have formed in the past.

SOUTHEASTERN UTAH

Balanced Rock

This gravity-defying formation is on the right 8.5 miles from the visitors center. A boulder more than 55 feet high rests precariously atop a 73-foot pedestal. Chip Off the Old Block, a much smaller version of Balanced Rock, stood nearby until it collapsed in the winter of 1975–1976. For a closer look at Balanced Rock, take the 0.3-mile trail encircling it. There's a picnic area across the road. Author Edward Abbey lived in a trailer near Balanced Rock during a season as a park ranger in the 1950s; his journal became the basis for the classic *Desert Solitaire*.

Windows Section

Turn right 2.5 miles on a paved road past Balanced Rock. Short trails (one-quarter to one mile long one-way) lead from the road's end to some massive arches. Windows Trailhead is the start for North Window (an opening 51 feet high and 93 feet wide), South Window (66 feet high and 105 feet wide), and Turret Arch (64 feet high and 39 feet wide). Double Arch, a short walk from a second trailhead, is an unusual pair of arches; the larger opening—105 feet high and 163 feet wide—is best appreciated by walking inside. The smaller opening is 61 feet high and 60 feet wide. Together, the two arches frame a large opening overhead, but this isn't considered a true arch.

Garden of Eden Viewpoint, on the way back to the main road, has a good panorama of Salt Valley to the north. Under the valley, the massive body of salt and gypsum that's responsible for the arches comes close to the surface. Tiny Delicate Arch can be seen across the valley on a sandstone ridge. Early visitors to the Garden of Eden saw rock formations resembling Adam (with an apple) and Eve. Two other viewpoints of the Salt Valley area lie farther north on the main road.

Delicate Arch

Drive north 2.5 miles on the main road from the Windows junction and turn right 1.8 miles to the Wolfe Ranch, where a bit of pioneer history survives. John Wesley Wolfe came to this

© JUDY JEWELL

Hikers stop to contemplate Delicate Arch in the distance.

spot in 1888, hoping the desert climate would provide relief for health problems related to a Civil War injury. He found a good spring high in the rocks, grass for cattle, and water in Salt Wash to irrigate a garden. The ranch that he built provided a home for him and some of his family for more than 20 years, and cattlemen later used it as a line ranch. Then sheepherders brought in their animals, which so overgrazed the range that the grass has yet to recover. A trail guide available at the entrance tells about the Wolfe family and features of their ranch. The weather-beaten cabin built in 1906 still survives. A short trail leads to petroglyphs above Wolfe Ranch; figures of horses indicate that Utes did the artwork. Park staff can give directions to other rock-art sites; great care should be taken not to touch the fragile artwork.

Delicate Arch stands in a magnificent setting atop gracefully curving slickrock. Distant canyons and the La Sal Mountains lie beyond. The span is 45 feet high and 33 feet wide. A moderately strenuous hike to the arch begins at Wolfe Ranch and crosses the swinging bridge, climbs a slick-rock slope, follows a gully, then contours across steep slickrock to the main overlook. Round-trip distance is three miles with an elevation gain of 500 feet; carry water. This is one of the most scenic hikes in the park. Just before the end of the trail, walk up to a small arch for a framed view of the final destination. The classic photo of Delicate Arch is taken late in the afternoon when the sandstone glows with golden hues.

Another perspective on Delicate Arch can be obtained by driving 1.2 miles beyond Wolfe Ranch. Look for the small arch high above. A steep trail (a half-mile round-trip) climbs a hill for the best panorama.

Fiery Furnace

Return to the main road and continue three miles to the Fiery Furnace Viewpoint and Trail-head on the right. Closely packed sandstone fins form a maze of deep slots, with many arches and at least one natural bridge inside. The Fiery Furnace can be fun to explore (with the required free permit, obtainable at the visitors center), though route-finding is tricky. What look like obvious paths often lead to dead ends. Drop-offs and ridges make straight-line travel impossible. It's easy to get lost! Ranger-led hikes of about 90 minutes during the summer season provide the best way to see the wonders within. You'll need a reservation for this trip, obtainable in person only from the visitors center up to 48 hours in advance. The Fiery Furnace gets its name from sandstone fins that turn flaming red on occasions when thin cloud cover at the horizon reflects the warm light of sunrise or sunset. Actually, the shady recesses provide a cool respite from the hot summer sun.

Broken Arches

Trailhead is on the right 2.4 miles past the Fiery Furnace turnoff. A short trail leads to small Sand Dune Arch (opening is eight feet high and 30 feet wide) tucked within fins. A longer trail (one mile round-trip) crosses a field to Broken Arch, which you can also see from the road. The opening is 43 feet high and 59 feet wide. Up close, you'll see that the arch isn't really broken. These

arches can also be reached by trail from near comfort station 3 at Devils Garden Campground. Low-growing canyonlands biscuitroot, found only in areas of Entrada sandstone, colonizes sand dunes. Hikers can protect the habitat of the biscuitroot and other fragile plants by keeping to washes or rock surfaces.

Skyline Arch

Skyline Arch is on the right one mile past Sand Dune/Broken Arch Trailhead. In desert climates, erosion may proceed imperceptibly for centuries until a cataclysmic event happens. In 1940, a giant boulder fell from the opening of Skyline Arch, doubling the size of the arch in just seconds. The hole is now 45 feet high and 69 feet wide. A short trail leads to the base of the arch.

Devils Garden Trail

The trailhead, Devils Garden Picnic Area, and the campground all lie near the end of the main park road. Devils Garden offers fine scenery and more arches than any other section of the park. The trail leads past large sandstone fins to Landscape and six other named arches. Carry water if the weather is hot or if you might want to continue past the one-mile point at Landscape Arch. Adventurous hikers could spend days exploring the maze of canyons among the fins.

The first two arches lie off a short side trail to the right. Tunnel Arch has a relatively symmetrical opening 22 feet high and 27 feet wide. The nearby Pine Tree Arch is named for a piñon pine that once grew inside; the arch has an opening 48 feet high and 46 feet wide. Continue on the main trail to Landscape Arch, which has an incredible 306-foot span (six feet longer than a football field!). This is one of the longest unsupported rock spans in the world. The thin arch looks ready to collapse at any moment. A rockfall from the arch on September 1, 1991, worries some people who fear the end may be near. Height is 106 feet. Distance from the trailhead is two miles round-trip, an easy one-hour walk.

The trail narrows past Landscape Arch and continues a quarter mile to Wall Arch, in a long wall-like fin. The opening is 41 feet high and

68 feet wide. A short side trail branches off to the left beyond Wall to Partition Arch (26 feet high and 28 feet wide) and Navajo Arch (13 feet high and 41 feet wide). Partition was so named because a piece of rock divides the main opening from a smaller hole eight feet high and 8.5 feet wide. Navajo Arch is a rock-shelter type; perhaps prehistoric peoples camped here. The main trail continues northwest and ends at Double O Arch (four miles round-trip from the trailhead). Double O has a large oval-shaped opening (45 feet high and 71 feet wide) and a smaller hole (nine feet high and 21 feet wide) underneath. Dark Angel is a distinctive rock pinnacle a quarter mile northwest; cairns mark the way. Another primitive trail loops back to Landscape Arch via Fin Canyon. This route goes through a different area of Devils Garden but adds about one mile to your trip (three miles back to the trailhead instead of two). Pay careful attention to the trail markers to keep on the correct route.

Klondike Bluffs and Tower Arch

Relatively few visitors come to the spires, high bluffs, and fine arch in this northwestern section of the park. A fair-weather dirt road turns off the main drive 1.3 miles before Devils Garden

Trailhead, winds down into Salt Valley, and heads northwest. After 7.5 miles, turn left one mile on the road signed Klondike Bluffs to the Tower Arch Trailhead. These roads may be washboarded but are usually okay in dry weather for cars; don't drive on them if storms threaten. The trail to Tower Arch winds past the Marching Men and other rock formations; the distance is three miles round-trip. Alexander Ringhoffer, who discovered the arch in 1922, carved an inscription on the south column. The area can also be fun to explore off-trail (map and compass needed). Those with four-wheel-drive vehicles can drive close to the arch on a separate jeep road. Tower Arch has an opening 34 feet high by 92 feet wide. A tall monolith nearby gave the arch its name.

Four-Wheel-Drive Road

A rough road near Tower Arch in the Klondike Bluffs turns southeast past **Eye of the Whale Arch** in Herdina Park to Balanced Rock on the main park road, 10.8 miles away. The road isn't particularly difficult for four-wheel-drive enthusiasts, though normal backcountry precautions should be taken. A steep sand hill north of Eye of the Whale Arch is very difficult to climb for vehicles coming from Balanced Rock; it's better to drive from the Tower Arch area instead.

La Sal Mountains

The forests and lakes in Utah's second-highest mountain range provide a dramatic contrast to the barren slickrock and sands of the surrounding desert. Mount Peale (elev. 12,721 feet) crowns the range at a height nearly 9,000 feet above the Colorado River. Volcanic intrusions formed the La Sals about 30 million years ago, twisting and upturning surrounding rock layers at the same time. Streams and glaciers later carved knifelike ridges in the peaks and deep canyons in the foothills. The range comprises three distinct mountain groups in an area about 15 miles long from north to south and six miles wide. Major peaks in the northern part are Mount Waas (12,331 feet), Manns Peak (12,273 feet), and Mount Tomasaki (12,230

feet). The middle group contains Mount Mellenthin (12,646 feet), Mount Peale (12,721 feet), and Mount Tukuhnikivatz (12,483 feet). The Indian name of this last mountain is reputed to mean "land where the Sun shines longest." South Mountain (11,798 feet) dominates the southern group.

Wildlife you might see include black bear (one of the state's largest populations lives here), Rocky Mountain elk, mule deer, mountain lion, badger, ringtail cat, porcupine, pika, Merriam's turkey, and golden eagle. Native cutthroat and some brook and brown trout swim in streams at the middle to higher elevations. Reservoirs and Mill Creek contain rainbow trout. Early Spanish explorers, seeing the range

ISLANDS IN THE DESERT: ALPINE ECOSYSTEMS

Rising high above the desert are the La Sal, Henry, and Abajo Mountains. At elevations between 7,000 and 8,500 feet, the desert gives way to forests of aspen, Gambel oak, ponderosa pine, and mountain mahogany. Conifers dominate up to the treeline, at about 12,000 feet. Alpine flowering plants, grasses, sedges, and mosses cling to the windy summits of these mountains. Wildlife of the forests includes many of the desert dwellers, as well as elk, bear, mountain lion, marmot, and pika. A herd of bison roams freely in the Henry Mountains; the surrounding desert keeps them from going elsewhere. These high meadows, where temperatures rarely top 80°F, can be revivifying after broiling under the desert sun in the Colorado River canyon. Best of all, the high country are of the La Sals and the Abajos are less than an hour's drive from Moab, Arches, or Canyonlands park.

when it was covered with snow, named it La Sal ("salt"). Other names include Salt Mountains and Elk Mountains. Gold fever peaked here at the turn of the century with activity concentrated in Miners and Gold Basins. Old mines and ruins of former mining camps can still be found in these areas.

Hiking in the La Sals

Miners traveling through the mountains during the boom years built many of the trails in use today. The current network of about 18 trails totals around 65 miles. Trails cross the range from north to south and branch off to scenic lakes, basins, and canyons. Hiking conditions range from easy to difficult. Horseback riders can use the trails, too. Signs mark most trailheads and junctions, but backcountry users should still have topo maps and a compass. Nearly all the canyons and valleys have springs or streams (purify first). Climbers can choose from half a dozen peaks exceeding 12,000 feet. All summit routes require rock-scrambling and

route-finding skills. Hazards include loose rock, lightning, and altitude sickness. You can climb Mount Peale from the south off La Sal Pass Road from about three-quarters of a mile east of La Sal Pass; follow a jeep track here up a valley to either Mount Peale or Mount Tukuhnikivatz. Look for the most gradual slope; you'll find the best footing near the trees where roots have stabilized the dirt and rocks. The pass itself also makes a good starting point for Mount Tukuhnikivatz. See the 7.5-minute topo maps or the 1:100,000 La Sal map. Road conditions may be good enough for cars on the east side via Highway 46, but the west side from Pack Creek has much steeper and rougher conditions—don't try this road without a high-clearance vehicle! The Moab Information Center is the place to start your search for trail and climbing information.

Winter Sports

Cross-country skiers often head to Miners Basin, Beaver Basin, Geyser Pass, Gold Basin, La Sal Pass, and Dark Canyon. La Sal Mountains Loop Road (southern section) and 4.5 miles of Geyser Pass Road are plowed. Snowmobilers may also use the roads and trails in the mountains. Travelers here need proper experience, equipment, and knowledge of avalanche hazards and means of rescue. Always go with a companion. The Moab Information Center has information on groomed trails and marked routes for skiers and snowmobilers, or call 435/259-SNOW for information.

LA SAL MOUNTAINS LOOP ROAD

This paved road on the west side of the range provides a good introduction to the high country. Side roads and trails lead to lakes, alpine meadows, and old mining areas. Viewpoints overlook Castle Valley, Arches and Canyonlands National Parks, Moab Rim, and other scenic features. Vegetation along the drive runs the whole range from cottonwoods, sage, and rabbitbrush of the desert to forests of aspen, fir, and spruce. The 62-mile loop road can easily take a full day with stops for scenic overlooks, a picnic, and a bit of hiking or fishing. Because of the high elevations, the loop's season usually lasts May–October. Stock up on supplies in Moab—you won't find any stores or gas stations after leaving town. Before venturing off the Loop Road, check current backroad conditions with the U.S. Forest Service office in Moab, and ask for a road log of sights and side roads.

Dead Horse Point State Park

The land drops away in sheer cliffs from this lofty perch west of Moab. Nearly 5,000 square miles of rugged canyon country lie in the distance. Two thousand feet below, the Colorado River twists through a gooseneck on its long journey to the sea. The river and its tributaries have carved canyons that reveal a geologic layer cake of colorful rock formations. Even in a region of impressive views around nearly every corner, Dead Horse Point stands out for its exceptionally breathtaking panorama. You'll also see below you, along the Colorado River, the result of powerful underground forces: Salt, under pressure, has pushed up overlying rock layers into an anticline. This formation, the Shafer Dome, contains potash that is being processed by the Moab Salt Plant. You can see the mine buildings, processing plant, and evaporation ponds (tinted blue to hasten evaporation).

A narrow neck of land only 30 yards wide connects the point with the rest of the plateau. Cowboys once herded wild horses onto the point, then placed a fence across the neck to make a 40-acre corral. They chose the desirable animals from the herd and let the rest go. According to one tale, a group of horses left behind after such a roundup became confused by the geography of the point. They couldn't find their way off and circled repeatedly until they died of thirst within sight of the river below. You may hear other stories of how the point got its name.

Besides the awe-inspiring views, the park also offers a visitors center (with displays), campground, picnic area, group area, nature trail, and hiking trails. The point has become popular with hang gliders. If you are lucky in timing your visit, you may see one or more crafts gliding back and forth above or below the viewpoint. Dead Horse Point is easily reached by paved road, either as a destination itself or as a side trip on the way to the Island in the Sky District of Canyonlands National Park. From Moab, head northwest 10 miles on U.S. 191, then turn left 22 miles on Highway 313. The drive along Highway 313 climbs through a scenic canyon and tops out on a ridge with panoramas of distant mesas, buttes, mountains, and canyons. Several rest areas are along the road.

Visitors Center and Campground

Stop here for registration ($7 per vehicle for day use) and exhibits about the park. Staff will answer questions and provide checklists of local flora and fauna. A short slide presentation is given on request. In summer, rangers give talks at the amphitheater behind the visitors center. Books, maps, posters, postcards, film, T-shirts, charcoal, ice, and soft drinks can be purchased. Open daily 8 A.M.–6 P.M. in summer (May 16–September 15) and 9 A.M.–5 P.M. the rest of the year. Contact the park at P.O. Box 609, Moab, UT 84532, 435/259-2614 or 800/322-3770 (reservations). A short nature trail that begins outside introduces the high-desert country and its plants. Continue 1.5 miles on the main road to viewpoints and picnic areas on the point itself. Primitive trails connect the point with several other overlooks, the visitors center, and the campground. Ask for a map at the visitors center.

Kayenta Campground, just past the visitors center, offers sites with electric hookups but no showers; open with water approximately mid-March–late October; $11. The campground nearly always fills up during the main season. Either make reservations or try to arrive by early afternoon to ensure a space. Winter visitors may camp on the point; no hookups are available, but the restrooms have water.

Canyonlands National Park

The canyon country of southeastern Utah puts on its supreme performance in this vast park, which spreads across 527 square miles. The deeply entrenched Colorado and Green Rivers meet in its heart, then continue south as the mighty Colorado through tumultuous Cataract Canyon Rapids. These two rivers are administered as the park's River District. Additionally, they divide the main body of Canyonlands National Park into three other districts. Island in the Sky lies north between the rivers, the Maze is to the west, and Needles is to the east. In addition, a fifth district, the Horseshoe Canyon Unit with its trove of rock art, lies a dozen miles west of the park's main land block. Each district has its own distinct character. No bridges connect the three land districts in the main block, so most visitors have to leave the park to go from one region to another. The huge park can be seen in many ways and on many levels. Paved roads reach a few areas, four-wheel-drive roads go to more places, and hiking trails reach still more, yet much of the land shows no trace of human passage. To get the big picture, fly over this incredible complex of canyons (see Air Tours in the Moab-Area Recreation section). However, only a river trip or a hike lets you experience the solitude and detail of the land. The park can be visited in any season of the year, with spring and autumn the best choices. Summer temperatures can get into the 100s; carrying (and drinking) water becomes critical then; carry at least one gallon per person per day. Arm yourself with insect repellent from late spring to midsummer. Winter days tend to be bright and sunny, though nighttime temperatures can dip into the teens or subzeros. Visitors coming in winter should inquire about travel conditions, as snow and ice occasionally close roads and trails at the higher elevations.

Visiting the Park

There are five districts to the park, each affording great views, spectacular geology, a chance to see wildlife, and endless opportunities to explore. You won't find crowds or elaborate park facilities—most of Canyonlands remains a primitive backcountry park.

Island in the Sky District has paved roads on its top to impressive overlooks and to Upheaval Dome, a strange geologic feature. If you're short on time or don't want to make a rigorous backcountry trip, this district is the best choice. The "Island," actually a large mesa, is much like Dead Horse Point on a giant scale; a narrow neck of land connects the north side with the "mainland." Hikers and those with suitable vehicles can drop off the Island in the Sky and descend about 1,300 feet to the White Rim 4WD Road, which follows cliffs of the White Rim around most of the island.

Few visitors make it over to the **Maze District,** some of the wildest country in the United States. Only the rivers and a handful of four-wheel-drive roads and hiking trails provide access. Experienced hikers can explore the "maze" of canyons on unmarked routes. **Horseshoe Canyon Unit,** a detached section of Canyonlands National Park northwest of the Maze District, protects the Great Gallery, a group of pictographs left by a prehistoric culture.

Colorful rock spires prompted the name of the **Needles District.** Splendid canyons contain many arches, strange rock formations, and archaeological sites. Hikers enjoy day hikes and backpack treks on the network of trails and routes within the district. Drivers with four-wheel-drive vehicles have their own challenging roads through canyons and other highly scenic areas. Overlooks and short nature trails can be enjoyed from the paved scenic drive in the park. South of Moab, Highway 211 branches off U.S. 191, providing easy access to the Needles District.

The **River District** includes long stretches of the Green and the Colorado. River-running provides one of the best ways to experience the inner depths of the park. Boaters can obtain helpful literature and advice from park rangers. Groups planning their own trip through Cataract Canyon need a river-running permit. Flat-water permits are also required, and there's a fee.

CANYONLANDS
NATIONAL PARK

© AVALON TRAVEL PUBLISHING, INC.

Admission to the park is $10 per vehicle, or $5 per bicyclist or pedestrian. In addition, fees are charged for backcountry camping, four-wheel-drive exploration, and river-rafting. For information on the park, contact Canyonlands National Park, 2282 S. West Resource Blvd., Moab, UT 84532, 435/719-2313, www.nps.gov/cany.

Geology

Deep canyons of the Green and the Colorado have sliced through rocks representing 150 million years of deposition. The Paradox Formation, exposed in Cataract Canyon, contains salt and other minerals responsible for some of the folded and faulted rock layers in the region. Under the immense pressure of overlying rocks, the Paradox flows like plastic, forming domes where the rock layers are thinnest and causing cracks or faults as pressures rise and fall. Each of the overlying formations has a different color and texture; they're the products of ancient deserts, rivers, and seas that once covered this land. Views from any of the overlooks reveal that an immense quantity of rock has already been washed downriver toward California. Not so evident, however, is the 10,000 vertical feet of rock that geologists say once lay across the high mesas. The dry climate and sparse vegetation allow clear views of the remaining rock layers and the effects of erosion and deformation. You can read the geologic story at Canyonlands National Park in the 3,500 feet of strata that remain, from the bottom of Cataract Canyon to the upper reaches of Salt Creek in the Needles District.

Flora and Fauna

Extremes of flash flood and drought, hot summers, and cold winters discourage all but the most hardy and adaptable life. Desert grasses, small flowering plants, cacti, and shrubs like blackbrush and saltbush survive on the mostly thin soils and meager 8–9 inches of annual precipitation. Trees either grow in cracks that concentrate rainfall and nutrients or rely on springs or canyon streams for moisture. Piñon pine and juniper prefer the higher elevations of the park, while cottonwoods live in the canyon bottoms that have permanent subsurface water. Tamarisk, an exotic streamside plant, and willows often form dense thickets on sandbars along the Green and Colorado Rivers. The hanging gardens of lush vegetation that surround cliffside springs or seeps seem oblivious to the surrounding desert. Fragile desert ecology can easily be upset. Cattle, especially in the Needles District, once overgrazed the grasslands and trampled cryptobiotic crusts and other vegetation. Increased erosion and growth of undesirable exotic plants like cheatgrass have been the result. Scars left by roads and mines during the uranium frenzy of the 1950s can still be seen, most commonly in the Island in the Sky District.

Fewer than 10 species of fish evolved in the canyons of the Colorado and the Green. These fish developed streamlined bodies and strange features, such as humped backs, to cope with the muddy and varying river waters. Species include Colorado squawfish, humpback chub, bonytail chub, and humpback sucker; most of these live nowhere else. All have suffered greatly reduced populations and restricted ranges due to recent dam-building.

Of the approximately 65 mammal species living in the park, about one-third are rodents and another third are bats. You're most likely to see chipmunk, antelope ground squirrel, and rock squirrel, which are often active during the day. Most other animals wait until evening to come out and feed; in the morning, look for tracks of mule deer, bighorn sheep, coyote, gray fox, badger, porcupine, spotted skunk, beaver, black-tailed jackrabbit, wood rat, kangaroo rat, and many species of mice.

History

Prehistoric Anasazis once settled throughout this area, while the Fremont lived mostly west of the Green and Colorado Rivers. Both groups departed from the region in the middle to late 1200s. They left behind hundreds of archaeological sites with rock art, granaries, dwellings, and stone tools. Nomadic Utes later roamed through the canyons and drew rock art of their

POTHOLE ECOSYSTEMS

At Canyonlands it's easy to be in awe of the deep canyons and big desert rivers. But the little details of Canyonlands geology and ecology are pretty wonderful, too. Consider the potholes: shallow depressions dusted with wind-blown dirt. These holes, which range from less than an inch to several feet deep, fill after rainstorms and bring entire little ecosystems to life.

Pothole dwellers must be able to survive long periods of dryness, and then pack as much living as possible into the short wet periods. Some creatures, like the tadpole shrimp, live only for a couple of weeks. Others, like the spadefoot toad, hatch from drought-resistant eggs when water is present, quickly pass through the critical tadpole stage, then move onto dry land, returning to mate and lay eggs in potholes.

Though pothole dwellers are tough enough to survive in a dormant form during the long dry spells, most are very sensitive to sudden water chemistry changes, temperature changes, sediment input, being stepped on, and being splashed out onto dry land. Humans should never use pothole water for swimming, bathing, or drinking, as this can change the salinity or pH of a pool drastically. Organisms are unable to adapt to these human-generated changes, which occur suddenly, unlike slow, natural changes. While the desert pothole ecosystems may seem unimportant, they act as an indicator of the health of the larger ecosystems in which they occur.

own. The Navajo may have made trips into the park area from the south during the 1800s.

At least one mountain man, Denis Julien, visited the Colorado and Green Canyons in 1836, leaving his signatures but little else to tell of his travels. Julien may have been the first person to raft the rivers here. In 1859, Captain John Macomb and his party noted the beautiful rock sculptures in Needles on an overland trip, but they judged the country worthless. Major John Wesley Powell led the first scientific expedition by boat through the Green and lower Colorado River canyons in 1869, then repeated most of the journey 1871–1872. Cowboys brought in cattle during the 1870s. Some of their camps, corrals, and inscriptions still survive, though grazing no longer takes place in the park. The Powell Expedition and the later cowboys named many of the park's features. Uranium prospectors swarmed through the area with Geiger counters during the 1950s, staking thousands of claims and opening some mines. Most of the jeep roads in use today date from that time.

Serious interest in establishing a park didn't begin until the early 1960s. Stewart Udall, Secretary of the Interior under President John F. Kennedy, realized the area's potential as a na-

tional park while flying over the Colorado River to examine a possible dam site. The superintendent of Arches National Monument, Bates Wilson, also worked hard for creation of a new park here. Canyonlands National Park became a reality in 1964 and enlarged to its present size in 1971.

Visitors Centers and Information

Each of the land districts has a visitors center near the park entrance, but you may find it convenient to stop at the Moab Information Center, at the corner of Main and Center, 435/259-8825 or 800/635-MOAB. The offices have brochures, maps, and books, as well as someone to answer your questions.

Vehicle camping is allowed only in established campgrounds and designated backcountry campsites. Except for the main campgrounds at Willow Flat (Island in the Sky) and Squaw Flat (Needles), you'll need a backcountry permit for overnight stays. There is a $15 fee for a backpacking permit and a $30 fee for a vehicle site permit. Each of the three districts has a different policy for backcountry vehicle camping, so make sure that you understand the details. Backcountry permits will also be needed for any technical

ENDANGERED FISH OF THE COLORADO RIVER BASIN

Colorado squawfish *(Ptychocheilus lucius):* Native only to the Colorado and its tributaries, this species is the largest minnow in North America. It has been reported as weighing up to 100 pounds and measuring six feet long. Loss of habitat caused by dam construction has greatly curtailed its size and range. Fishers often confuse the smaller, more common roundtail chub *(Gila robusta)* with the Colorado squawfish; the chub is distinguished by a smaller mouth extending back only to the front of the eye.

Humpback chub *(Gila cypha):* Scientists first described this fish only in 1946 and know little about its life. This small fish usually weighs less than two pounds and measures less than 13 inches. Today the humpback chub hangs on the verge of extinction; it has retreated to a few small areas of the Colorado River, where the water still runs warm, muddy, and swift. The bonytail chub *(Gila robusta elegans)* has a similar size and shape, but without a hump; its numbers are also rapidly declining.

Humpback or razorback sucker *(Xyrauchen texanus):* This large sucker grows to weights of 10–16 pounds and lengths of about three feet. Its numbers have been slowly decreasing, especially above the Grand Canyon. They require warm, fast-flowing water to reproduce. Mating is a bizarre ritual in the spring: When the female has selected a suitable spawning site, two male fish press against the sides of her body. The female begins to shake her body until the eggs and spermatozoa are expelled simultaneously. One female can spawn three times, but she uses a different pair of males each time.

climbing and trips with stock; check with a ranger for details. Pets aren't allowed on trails and must always be leashed. No firewood collecting is permitted in the park; backpackers need stoves for cooking. Vehicle and boat campers can bring in firewood but must use grills or fire pans. The best maps for the park are a series of expensive topos printed on waterproof paper by Trails Illustrated; these have the latest trail and road information. A giant USGS topo map, Canyonlands National Park and Vicinity, has the same 1:62,500 scale at a lower cost, but without the updated information and fancy paper. Handouts from the ranger offices describe natural history, travel, and other aspects of the park.

Back-Road Travel

Canyonlands National Park offers hundreds of miles of exceptionally scenic jeep roads. Normally you must have a vehicle with both four-wheel drive and high clearance. Park regulations require all motorized vehicles to have proper registration and licensing for highway use (ATVs are prohibited); drivers must be licensed. It's essential for both motor vehicles and bicycles to stay on existing roads to prevent damage to the delicate desert vegetation. Carry tools, extra fuel, water, and food in case of breakdown in a remote area. Mountain bikers enjoy travel on many of the backcountry roads, too. Before making a trip, drivers and cyclists should talk with a ranger to register and to learn of current road conditions, which can change drastically from one day to the next. Also, the rangers will be more knowledgeable about where to seek help in case you become stuck. Primitive campgrounds are provided on most of the roads, but you'll need a backcountry permit from a ranger. Books on backcountry exploration include local author F. A. Barnes's *Canyon Country Off-Road Vehicle Trails: Island Area* and *Canyon Country Off-Road Vehicle Trails: Canyon Rims & Needles Areas* and Jack Bikers' *Canyon Country Off-Road Vehicle Trails: Maze Area* (see Suggested Reading for all titles).

RIVER DISTRICT

River-Running Above the Confluence

The Green and Colorado Rivers flow smoothly through their canyons above the confluence of the two rivers. Almost any shallow-draft boat can navigate these waters: canoes, kayaks, rafts, and power boats are commonly used. Any travel requires advance planning because of the remoteness of the canyons and the scarcity of river access points. No campgrounds, supplies, or other facilities exist past Moab on the Colorado River or the town of Green River on the Green. All river-runners must follow park regulations, which include the carrying of life jackets, use of a fire pan for fires, and packing out all garbage and solid human waste. The river flow on both the Colorado and the Green averages a gentle 2–4 mph (7–10 mph at high water). Boaters typically do 20 miles a day in canoes and 15 miles a day in rafts.

The Colorado has one modest rapid called the Slide, 1.5 miles above the confluence, where rocks constrict the river to one-third of its normal width; the rapid is roughest during high water levels in May and June. This is the only difficulty on the 64 river miles from Moab. Inexperienced canoeists and rafters may wish to portage around it. The most popular launch points on the Colorado are the Moab Dock (just upstream from the U.S. 191 bridge near town) and the Potash Dock (17 miles downriver on the Potash Road, Hwy. 279).

On the Green, boaters at low water need to watch for rocky areas at the mouth of Millard Canyon (33.5 miles above the confluence, where a rock bar extends across the river) and at the mouth of Horse Canyon (14.5 miles above the confluence, where a rock and gravel bar on the right leaves only a narrow channel on the left side). The trip from the town of Green River through Labyrinth and Stillwater Canyons is 120 miles. Launch places include Green River State Park (in Green River) and Mineral Canyon (52 miles above the confluence; reached on a fair-weather road from Highway 313).

No roads go to the confluence. Easiest return to civilization for nonmotorized craft is a pick-up by jetboat from Moab by Tex's Riverways or Tag-A-Long Tours (see Rafting and Boat Tours in the Moab-Area Recreation section). A far more difficult way out is hiking either of two trails just above the Cataract Canyon Rapids to four-wheel-drive roads on the rim. Park rangers require that boaters above the confluence obtain a backcountry permit either in person from the Moab office or by mail (two weeks in advance). River notes on boating the Green and Colorado are available on request from the Moab office, 435/259-3911. Bill and Buzz Belknap's *Canyonlands River Guide* has river logs and maps pointing out items of interest on the Green River below the town of Green River and all of the Colorado from the upper end of Westwater Canyon to Lake Powell. Don Baar's *A River Runner's Guide to Cataract Canyon* also has good coverage.

River-Running Through Cataract Canyon

The Colorado River enters Cataract Canyon at the confluence and picks up speed. The rapids begin four miles downstream and extend for the next 14 miles to Lake Powell. Especially in spring, the 26 or more rapids give a wild ride equal to the best in the Grand Canyon. The current zips along (up to 16 mph) and forms waves more than seven feet high! When the excitement dies down, boaters have a 34-mile trip across Lake Powell to Hite Marina; most people either carry a motor or arrange for a power boat to pick them up. Because of the real hazards of running the rapids, the National Park Service requires boaters to have proper equipment and a permit ($30). Many people go on a commercial trip in which everything has been taken care of (write the park for a list of boat companies). Private groups need to contact the Canyonlands River Unit far in advance for permit details at 2282 W. Resource Blvd., Moab, UT 84532, 435/259-3911.

ISLAND IN THE SKY DISTRICT

Panoramic views from the "Island" can be enjoyed from any point along the rim; you'll see much of the park and southeastern Utah. Short hiking trails lead to overlooks, Mesa Arch, Aztec Butte, Whale Rock, Upheaval Dome, and other features. Longer trails make steep, strenuous descents from the island to the White Rim 4WD Road below. Elevations on the island average about 6,000 feet. *Bring water for all hiking, camping, and travel on Island in the Sky.* No services are available, except at the visitors center in emergencies (bottled water is sold).

Visitors Center

Stop here for information about Island in the Sky and to see some exhibits; books and maps can be purchased. A $10 per-vehicle charge is made unless you have a receipt issued within the last seven days from the Needles District of Canyonlands. Obtain a backcountry permit ($15 for backpack camping, $30 for a vehicle campsite) if making an overnight hike or planning to stay at campgrounds along the White Rim 4WD Road (reservations by mail, phone, or in person are required for sites; $25 reservation fee). The visitors center is open daily 8 A.M.–4:30 P.M. with reservations made 12:30–4:30 P.M. Monday–Sat-

urday (may close noon–1 P.M. in winter), 435/259-4351. A bulletin board outside has park information. The visitors center is just before crossing "the neck" to Island in the Sky. From Moab, go northwest 10 miles on U.S. 191, turn left 15 miles on Highway 313 to the junction for Dead Horse Point State Park, then continue straight seven miles.

Shafer Canyon Overlook

Continue a half mile past the visitors center to this overlook on the left (just before crossing the neck). Shafer Trail Viewpoint, across the neck, provides another perspective a half mile farther. The neck is a narrow land bridge just wide enough for the road, and it's the only vehicle access to the 40-square-mile Island in the Sky. The overlooks have good views east down the canyon and the incredibly twisting **Shafer Trail Road.** Cattlemen Frank and John Schafer built the trail in the early 1900s to move stock to additional pastures (the "c" in their name was later dropped by mapmakers). Uranium prospectors upgraded the trail to a four-wheel-drive road during the 1950s so

Viewpoints from Island in the Sky showcase the confluence of the Green and Colorado Rivers.

© W. C. MCRAE

that they could reach their claims at the base of the cliffs. Today the Shafer Trail Road connects the mesa top with White Rim 4WD Road and Potash Road 1,200 feet and four miles below. High-clearance vehicles should be used on Shafer, preferably with four-wheel-drive if you plan to climb up. Road conditions can vary considerably, so contact a ranger before starting.

Neck Spring Trail

The trail begins near the Shafer Canyon Overlook. A brochure should be available at the trailhead. This moderately difficult hike follows a five-mile loop down Taylor Canyon to Neck and Cabin Springs, formerly used by ranchers, then climbs back to Island in the Sky Road at a second trailhead a half mile south of the start. Elevation change is 300 feet. Water at the springs supports maidenhair fern and other water-loving plants. Also watch for birds and wildlife attracted to this spot. Bring water with you, as the springs aren't suitable for drinking.

Lathrop Trail

This is the only marked hiking route going all the way from Island in the Sky to the Colorado River. The trailhead is on the left 1.3 miles past the neck. The first 2.5 miles cross Gray's Pasture to the rim, then the trail descends steeply, dropping 1,600 feet over the next 2.5 miles to White Rim 4WD Road. Part of this section follows an old mining road past several abandoned mines, all relics of the uranium boom; don't enter the shafts, as they're in danger of collapse and may contain poisonous gases. From the mining area, the route descends through a wash to White Rim 4WD Road, follows the road a short distance south, then goes down Lathrop Canyon Road to the Colorado River, another four miles with a descent of 500 feet. Total distance for the strenuous hike is nine miles one-way, with an elevation change of 2,100 feet. The trail has little shade and can be very hot.

Mesa Arch Trail

This easy trail leads to an arch on the rim. The trailhead is on the left 5.5 miles from the neck. On the way, the road crosses the grasslands and scattered juniper trees of Gray's Pasture. A trail brochure available at the start describes the ecology of the mesa. Hiking distance is only a half-mile round-trip with an 80-foot elevation change. The arch, eroded from Navajo sandstone, frames views of rock formations below and La Sal Mountains in the distance.

Murphy Point and Grand View Point

Go straight at the road junction just past the Mesa Arch Trailhead for these and other spectacular viewpoints. After 2.5 miles, a rough dirt road turns right 1.7 miles to Murphy Point. Hikers can take **Murphy Trail,** which begins off the road to the point, to White Rim 4WD Road. This strenuous route forks partway down; one branch follows Murphy Hogback (a ridge) to Murphy Campground on the four-wheel-drive road, and the other branch follows a wash to the road one mile south of the campground. A loop hike along both branches is nine miles round-trip with an elevation change of 1,100 feet.

Continue 2.5 miles on the main road past the Murphy Point turnoff to **Grand View Picnic Area,** a handy lunch stop. Two trails start here. **White Rim Overlook Trail** is an easy 1.5-mile hike (round-trip) east along a peninsula to an overlook of Monument Basin and beyond. **Gooseberry Trail** drops off the mesa and descends some extremely steep grades to the White Rim 4WD Road just north of Gooseberry Campground; the strenuous trip is 2.5 miles one-way with an elevation change of 1,400 feet.

Continue one mile on the main road past the picnic area to **Grand View Point,** perhaps the most spectacular panorama from Island in the Sky. Monument Basin lies directly below, and countless canyons, the Colorado River, the Needles, and mountain ranges are in the distance. **Grand View Trail** continues past the end of the road for other vistas from the point, which is the southernmost tip of Island in the Sky. The easy hike is 1.5 miles round-trip.

Green River Overlook and Willow Flat Campground

Return to the road junction, turn west a quarter mile, then turn south 1.5 miles on an unpaved road to the overlook. Soda Springs Basin and a section of the Green River (deeply entrenched in Stillwater Canyon) can be seen below. Small Willow Flat campground is passed on the way to the overlook; it's open all year (no water or charge). Rangers present campfire programs here spring through autumn. Sites often fill except in winter; a sign near the visitors center indicates when they're full.

Aztec Butte Trail

The trailhead is on the right one mile northwest of the road junction. Aztec Butte is one of the few areas at Island in the Sky with Native American ruins; shortage of water prevented permanent settlement. An easy trail climbs 200 feet in half a mile to the top of the butte for a good panorama of the Island.

Whale Rock

The trailhead is on the right 4.4 miles northwest of the road junction. An easy trail climbs this sandstone hump near the outer rim of Upheaval Dome. Distance is a half-mile round-trip with an ascent of 100 feet.

Upheaval Dome

Continue to the end of the road, 5.3 miles northwest of the road junction, for a look at this geological curiosity. There's also a small **picnic area** here. The easy **Crater View Trail** leads to overlooks on the rim of Upheaval Dome; the first viewpoint is a half-mile round-trip, the second a one-mile round-trip. A fantastically deformed pile of rock lies below within a crater about three miles across and 1,200 feet deep. For many years, Upheaval Dome has kept geologists busy trying to figure out its origin. They once assumed that salt of the Paradox Formation pushed the rock layers upward to form the dome. Now, however, there is strong evidence that a meteorite impact caused the structure. The surrounding ring depression (caused by collapse) and the convergence of rock layers upward toward the center correspond precisely to known impact structures. Shatter cones and microscopic analysis also indicate an impact origin. When the meteorite struck, sometime in the last 150 million years, it formed a crater up to

five miles across. Erosion removed some of the overlying rock, perhaps as much as a vertical mile. The underlying salt may have played a role in uplifting the central section.

Energetic hikers can reach Upheaval Dome from the parking area at the overlook or from White Rim 4WD Road below. **Syncline Loop Trail** makes a strenuous eight-mile circuit completely around Upheaval Dome; elevation change is 1,200 feet. The trail crosses Upheaval Dome Canyon about halfway around from the overlook; walk east 1.5 miles up the canyon to enter the crater itself. This is the only nontechnical route into the center of the dome. A hike around Upheaval Dome with a side trip to the crater totals 11 miles, best done as an overnight trip. Carry plenty of water for the entire trip; this dry country can be very hot in summer. The Green River is the only reliable source of water. From near Upheaval Campsite on White Rim 4WD Road, you can hike four miles on **Upheaval Trail** through Upheaval Canyon to a junction with the Syncline Loop Trail, then another 1.5 miles into the crater; elevation gain is about 600 feet.

Alcove Spring Trail

Another hiking possibility in the area, the Alcove Spring Trail leaves the road 1.5 miles before the Upheaval Dome parking area and connects with White Rim 4WD Road in Taylor Canyon. Total distance is 10 miles one-way (five miles on the trail in Trail Canyon and five miles on a jeep road in Taylor Canyon); elevation change is about 1,500 feet. Carry plenty of water—the strenuous trail is hot and dry.

White Rim 4WD Road

This driving adventure follows the White Rim below the sheer cliffs of Island in the Sky. Travel along the winding road presents a constantly changing panorama of rock, canyons, river, and sky. Keep an eye out for desert bighorn sheep. You'll see all three levels of Island in the Sky District, from the high plateaus to the White Rim to the rivers. Only four-wheel-drive vehicles with high clearance can make the trip. With the proper vehicle, driving is mostly easy but slow and winding; a few steep or rough sections have to be negotiated. The 100-mile trip takes 2–3 days. Allow an extra day to travel all the road spurs. Mountain bikers find this a great trip, too; most cyclists arrange an accompanying vehicle to carry water and camping gear. Primitive campgrounds along the way provide convenient stopping places. Obtain reservations and a backcountry permit for the White Rim campsites from the Island in the Sky visitors center; this can be done in person, by mail from the park headquarters in Moab, or by phone, 435/259-4351; open Monday–Saturday 12:30–4:30 P.M. Demand exceeds supply during the popular spring and autumn seasons, when you should make reservations as far in advance as possible. A $25 fee per reservation applies for White Rim trips. No services or developed water sources exist anywhere on the drive, so be sure to have plenty of fuel and water with some to spare. Access points are Shafer Trail Road (from near Island in the Sky) and Potash Road (Hwy. 279 from Moab) on the east and Mineral Bottom Road on the west. White Rim sandstone forms the distinctive plateau crossed on the drive. A close look at the rock reveals ripple marks and crossbeds laid down near an ancient coastline. The plateau's east side is about 800 feet above the Colorado River. On the west side, the plateau meets the bank of the Green River.

MAZE DISTRICT

Only adventurous and experienced travelers will want to visit this rugged land west of the Green and Colorado Rivers. Vehicle access wasn't even possible until 1957, when mineral-exploration roads first entered what later became Canyonlands National Park. Today, you'll need a high-clearance four-wheel-drive vehicle, a horse, or your own two feet to get around. The National Park Service plans to keep this district in its remote and primitive condition. An airplane flight, recommended if you can't come overland, provides the only easy way to see the scenic features here. However, the National Park Service is currently studying the future of such flights and they may be curtailed or discontinued. The names of erosional forms describe the landscape—Orange Cliffs, Golden Stairs, the Fins, Land of Standing Rocks, Lizard Rock, the Doll House, Chocolate Bars, the Maze, and Jasper Canyon. The many-fingered canyons of the Maze gave the district its name. Although not a true maze, these canyons give that impression.

Ranger Station and Information

Glen Canyon National Recreation Area borders the Maze District on the west with scenic canyons, cliffs, rock monuments, and overlooks of its own. The Hans Flat Ranger Station for the Maze District lies inside Glen Canyon NRA; the station is open daily 8 A.M.–4:30 P.M., 435/259-2652. (In winter the station may close, but a ranger is usually available.) *There are no developed sources of water in the Maze District.* Hikers can obtain water from springs in some canyons (check with a ranger to find which are flowing) or from the rivers; purify all water before drinking. The Maze District has nine camping areas (two at Maze Overlook, seven at Land of Standing Rocks) with a 15-person, three-vehicle limit. A backcountry permit is needed for these or for backpacking. Note that a backcountry permit in this district is *not* a reservation—you may have to share a site with someone else, especially in the popular spring months. Also, as in the rest of the park, only designated sites can be used for vehicle camping. You don't need a permit to camp in the Glen Canyon NRA or on BLM land. The Trails Illustrated topo map of the Maze District describes and shows the few roads and trails here; some routes and springs are marked on it, too. Agile hikers experienced in desert and canyon travel may want to take off on cross-country routes, which are either unmarked or lightly cairned. Extra care must be taken for preparation and travel in both Glen Canyon NRA and the Maze. Always talk with the rangers beforehand to find out current conditions. Be sure to leave an itinerary with someone reliable who can contact the rangers if you're overdue. Unless the rangers know where to look for you in case of breakdown or accident, a rescue could take weeks!

Dirt roads to the Hans Flat Ranger Station and Maze District branch off from Highway

24 (a half mile south of the Goblin Valley State Park turnoff) and Highway 95 (take Hite/Orange Cliffs Road between the Dirty Devil and Hite Bridges at Lake Powell). Easiest way in is the graded 46-mile road from Highway 24; it's fast, though sometimes badly corrugated. The Hite Road (also called Orange Cliffs Road) is longer, bumpier, and, for some drivers, tedious; it's 54 miles from the turnoff at Highway 95 to the Hans Flat Ranger Station via the Flint Trail. In winter or other times when the Flint Trail is closed, drivers must take Hite Road to reach the Maze Overlook, Land of Standing Rocks, and the Doll House areas. All roads to the Maze District cross Glen Canyon National Recreation Area. From Highway 24, two-wheel-drive vehicles with good clearance can travel to Hans Flat Ranger Station and other areas near, but not actually in, the Maze District. (All the mileages given here come from the author's vehicle—they're not always the same as signs.)

North Point

Hans Flat Ranger Station, and this peninsula that reaches out to the east and north, lie at an elevation of about 6,400 feet. Panoramas from North Point take in the vastness of Canyonlands, including all three districts. From **Millard Canyon Overlook,** just 0.9 mile past the ranger station, you can see arches, Cleopatra's Chair, and features as distant as the La Sals and Book Cliffs. For the best views, drive out to Panorama Point, about 10.5 miles one-way from the ranger station. A spur road goes left two miles to Cleopatra's Chair, a massive sandstone monolith and area landmark. The trailhead for **North Trail Canyon** begins just down North Point Road (or 2.4 miles from the ranger station). Two-wheel-drive vehicles can usually reach this spot, where hikers can follow the trail down seven miles (1,000-foot elevation change) through the Orange Cliffs, follow four-wheel-drive roads six miles to the Maze Overlook Trail, then one more mile into a canyon of the Maze. Because North Point belongs to the Glen Canyon NRA, you can camp on it without a permit.

Flint Trail

This narrow, rough, four-wheel-drive road connects the Hans Flat area with the Maze Overlook, Doll House, and other areas below. The road, driver, and vehicle should all be in good condition before driving it! Winter snow and mud close the road late December–March, as can rainstorms anytime. Check conditions first with a ranger. If you're starting from the top, stop at the signed overlook just before the descent to scout for vehicles headed up (the Flint Trail has very few places to pass). The top of the Flint Trail is 14 miles south of Hans Flat Ranger Station; at the bottom, 2.8 nervous miles later, you can turn left two miles to the Golden Stairs Trailhead or 12.7 miles to the Maze Overlook; keep straight 28 miles to the Doll House or 39 miles to Highway 95.

The Golden Stairs

Hikers can descend this steep two-mile (one-way) foot trail to the Land of Standing Rocks Road in a fraction of the time it takes for drivers to follow roads! The trail offers good views of Ernies Country and the Fins but lacks shade or water. The upper trailhead is east two miles from the road junction at the bottom of the Flint Trail.

Maze Overlook

Now you're actually in Canyonlands National Park and at the edge of the sinuous canyons of the Maze. You can stay at primitive camping areas (backcountry permit needed) and enjoy the views. **Maze Overlook Trail** drops one mile into the South Fork of Horse Canyon; a rope helps to lower packs in a difficult section. Once in the canyon you can walk around to the Harvest Scene, a group of prehistoric pictographs, or do a variety of day hikes or backpacks. These canyons have water in some places; check with the ranger when getting your permits. At least four routes connect with the four-wheel-drive road in Land of Standing Rocks (see the Trails Illustrated map). Hikers can also climb Petes Mesa from the canyons or head downstream to explore Horse Canyon (a dry fall blocks access to the Green River, however).

Land of Standing Rocks

Here, in the heart of the Maze District, strange-shaped rock spires stand guard over myriad canyons. Six camping areas offer scenic places to stay (permit needed). Hikers have a choice of many ridge and canyon routes from the four-wheel-drive road, a trail to a confluence overlook, and a trail that descends to the Colorado River near Cataract Canyon. The well-named Chocolate Bars can be reached by a hiking route from the Wall near the beginning of the Land of Standing Rocks. A good day hike makes a loop from Chimney Rock to the Harvest Scene pictographs; take the ridge route (toward Petes Mesa) one direction and the canyon fork northwest of Chimney Rock the other. Follow your topo map through the canyons and the cairns between the canyons and ridge. Other routes from Chimney Rock lead to lower Jasper Canyon (no river access) or into Shot and Water Canyons and on to the Green River. Tall, rounded rock spires near the end of the road reminded early visitors of dolls, hence the name Doll House. The Doll House makes a delightful place to explore in itself, or you can head out on routes and trails. **Spanish Bottom Trail** begins here, then drops steeply to Spanish Bottom beside the Colorado River in 1.2 miles (one-way); a thin trail leads downstream into Cataract Canyon and the first of a long series of rapids. **Surprise Valley Overlook Trail** branches off the Spanish Bottom Trail after about 300 feet and winds south past some dolls to a T-junction (turn right for views of Surprise Valley, Cataract Canyon, and beyond); the trail ends at some well-preserved granaries; 1.5 miles one-way. The **Colorado/Green River Overlook Trail** heads north five miles (one-way) from the Doll House to a viewpoint of the confluence. See the area's Trails Illustrated map for routes, trails, and roads.

Getting to the Land of Standing Rocks takes some careful driving, especially on a three-mile stretch above Teapot Canyon. The many washes and small canyon crossings here make for slow going. Short-wheelbase vehicles have the easiest time, as usual. The turnoff for Land of Standing Rocks Road is 6.6 miles from the junction at the bottom of the Flint Trail via a wash shortcut (add about three miles if driving via the four-way intersection). The lower end of the Golden Stairs foot trail is 7.8 miles in, the western end of Ernies Country route trailhead is 8.6 miles in, the Wall is 12.7 miles in, Chimney Rock is 15.7 miles in, and the Doll House is 19 miles in at the end of the road. If you drive from the south on the Hite/Orange Cliffs Road, stop at the self-registration stand at the four-way intersection, about 31 miles in from Highway 95; you can write your own permit for overnights in the park here. This may change, however, so check with a ranger for current information.

HORSESHOE CANYON UNIT

This canyon contains exceptional prehistoric rock art in a separate section of Canyonlands National Park. Ghostly life-size pictographs in the Great Gallery provide an intriguing look into the past. Archaeologists think that the images had religious importance, although the meaning of the figures remains unknown. The Barrier Canyon style of these drawings has been credited to an archaic Native American culture beginning at least 8,000 years ago and lasting until about A.D. 450. Horseshoe Canyon also contains rock art left by the subsequent Fremont and Anasazi. The relation between the earlier and later prehistoric groups hasn't been determined.

Great Gallery

Horseshoe Canyon lies northwest of the Maze District. Two moderately difficult trails and a very rough jeep road lead down the canyon walls. In dry weather, cars with good clearance can be driven to a trailhead on the west rim. To reach this trailhead from Highway 24, drive to a junction a half mile south of Goblin Valley State Park turnoff, then turn east 30 miles on a dirt road (keep left at the Hans Flat Ranger Station/Horseshoe Canyon turnoff 25 miles in). From the rim, the trail descends 800 feet in one mile on an old jeep road, now closed to vehicles. At the canyon bottom, turn right two miles upstream to the Great Gallery. The sandy canyon floor is mostly level; trees provide shade in some areas.

A four-wheel-drive road goes north 21 miles from Hans Flat Ranger Station and drops steeply into the canyon from the east side. The descent on this road is so rough that most people prefer to park on the rim and hike the last mile of road. A vehicle barricade prevents driving right up to the rock-art panel, but the 1.5-mile walk is easy. A branch off the jeep road goes to the start of **Deadman's Trail** (1.5 miles one-way), which is less used and more difficult.

Look for other rock art along the canyon walls on the way to the Great Gallery. Take care not to touch any of the drawings; they're very fragile as well as irreplaceable. (The oil from your hands will remove the paint.) Horseshoe Canyon also offers pleasant scenery and spring wildflowers. Carry plenty of water. Neither camping nor pets are allowed in the canyon, but you can stay on the rim. Contact the Hans Flat Ranger Station or the Moab office for road and trail conditions.

NEEDLES DISTRICT

The Needles District showcases some of the finest rock sculptures in Canyonlands National Park. Spires, arches, or monoliths appear in almost any direction you look. Prehistoric ruins and rock art exist in greater variety and quantity than elsewhere in the park. Year-round springs and streams bring greenery to the desert. A paved road, several four-wheel-drive roads, and many hiking trails offer a variety of ways to explore the Needles.

Needles Outpost

A general store just outside the park boundary offers a campground ($12 tent or RV without hookups), groceries, ice, gas, propane, snack bar, showers, jeep rentals and tours, and scenic flights. Call or write ahead, if possible, to arrange for jeep tours and scenic flights: P.O. Box 1107, Monticello, UT 84535, 435/979-4007. The season at Needles Outpost is mid-March–late October. Turnoff from Highway 211 is one mile before the Needles visitors center.

Visitors Center

Stop here to find out about hiking, back roads, and other aspects of travel in the Needles. The

© W. C. MCRAE

the slickrock desert of the Needles District

staff has backcountry permits (required for all overnight stays in the backcountry), maps, brochures, and books. Open daily 8 A.M.–5 P.M., 435/259-4711. A $10 per vehicle charge is made unless you have a receipt issued within the last seven days from Island in the Sky of Canyonlands. Outside of office hours, get information at the bulletin board. To reach the Needles District, go 40 miles south from Moab (or 14 miles north of Monticello), turn west on Highway 211, and continue 38 miles.

Scenic Drive

The main road continues 6.5 miles past the visitors center to Big Spring Canyon Overlook. On the way, you can stop at several nature trails, turn off on four-wheel-drive roads, or take short spur roads to trailheads and Squaw Flat Campground.

Roadside Ruin is on the left 0.4 mile past the visitors center. A one-third-mile loop trail goes near a well-preserved granary left by Anasazi. A trail guide available at the start tells about the Anasazi and the local plants.

Cave Spring Trail introduces the geology and ecology of the park and goes to an old cowboy line camp. Turn left 0.7 mile past the visitors center and follow signs about one mile to the trailhead. Pick up the brochure at the beginning. The 0.6-mile loop goes clockwise, crossing some slickrock; two ladders assist on the steep sections. Cowboys used the cave as a line camp from the late 1800s until establishment of the park in 1964; the line camp is just 50 yards in from the trailhead.

A road to **Squaw Flat Campground** and **Elephant Hill** turns left 2.7 miles past the ranger station. The campground, about a half mile in from the main road, has water and charges a $10 fee mid-March–September; it's open the rest of the year with no water or charge (water can be obtained year-round at the visitors center). Rangers present evening programs at the campfire circle on Loop A from spring through autumn. A **picnic area** is at the base of Elephant Hill, three miles past the campground turnoff and on the scenic drive. Hiking trails lead into wonderful rock forms and canyons from both the campground and picnic areas. Only experienced drivers in four-wheel-drive vehicles should continue past the picnic area up Elephant Hill.

Pothole Point Nature Trail is on the left of the main road 5 miles past the visitors center. Highlights of this 0.6-mile loop hike are the many potholes dissolved in the Cedar Mesa sandstone. A brochure illustrates the fairy shrimp, tadpole shrimp, horsehair worm, snail, and other adaptable creatures that spring to life when rains fill the potholes. You'll also enjoy fine views of distant buttes from the trail.

Slickrock Trail begins on the right 6.2 miles past the visitors center. The trail makes a loop of 2.4 miles round-trip and takes you north to an overlook of the confluence of Big Spring and Little Spring Canyons. Hiking is easy and offers good panoramas.

Big Spring Canyon Overlook, 6.5 miles past the visitors center, marks the end of the scenic drive but not the scenery. The **Confluence Overlook Trail** begins here and winds west to an overlook of the Green and Colorado Rivers (see Confluence Overlook Trail).

Hiking

The Needles District has about 55 miles of backcountry trails. Many interconnect to provide all sorts of day and overnight trips. Cairns mark the trails; signs point the way at junctions. You can normally find water in upper Elephant Canyon and canyons to the east in spring and early summer, though the remaining water often becomes stagnant by midsummer. Always ask the rangers about sources of water—don't depend on its availability. Treat water from all sources, including springs, before drinking. Chesler Park and other areas west of Elephant Canyon are very dry; bring all water. Mosquitoes, gnats, and deer flies can be very pesky from late spring to midsummer, especially in the wetter places—bring insect repellent. To plan your trip, obtain the small hiking map available from the visitors center, Trails Illustrated's Needles District map, or USGS topo maps.

Confluence Overlook Trail

This trail goes west 5.5 miles from Big Spring Canyon Overlook (at the end of the scenic drive) to a fine viewpoint overlooking the Green and Colorado Rivers 1,000 feet below. You might see rafts in the water or bighorn sheep on the cliffs. The trail crosses Big Spring and Elephant Canyons and follows a jeep road for a short distance. Higher points have good views of the Needles to the south. Except for a few short steep sections, this trail is level and fairly easy. A very early start is recommended in summer, as there's little shade. Carry water even if you don't plan to go all the way. This enchanting country has lured many a hiker beyond his or her original goal!

Hikes from Squaw Flat Trailhead

The main trailhead sits a short distance south of the campground and is reached by a separate signed road. You can also begin from a trailhead in the campground itself.

Peekaboo Trail winds southeast five miles (one-way) over rugged terrain, including some steep sections of slickrock (best avoided when wet, icy, or covered with snow). There's little shade; carry water. The trail follows Squaw

Canyon, climbs over a pass to Lost Canyon, then crosses more slickrock before descending to Peekaboo Campground on Salt Creek 4WD Road. Look for Anasazi ruins on the way and rock art at the campground. A rockslide took out Peekaboo Spring, shown on some maps. Options on this trail include a turnoff south through Squaw Canyon or Lost Canyon to make a loop of 8.75 miles or more.

Squaw Canyon Trail follows the canyon south for 3.75 miles one-way. Intermittent water can often be found until late spring. You can take a connecting trail (Peekaboo, Lost Canyon, and Big Spring Canyon) or cross a slickrock pass to Elephant Canyon.

Lost Canyon Trail, 3.25 miles long one-way, is reached via Peekaboo or Squaw Canyon Trail and makes a loop with them. Water supports abundant vegetation; you may need to wade. Most of the way is in the wash bottom, except for a section of slickrock to Squaw Canyon.

Big Spring Canyon Trail crosses an outcrop of slickrock from the trailhead, then follows the canyon bottom to the head of the canyon, 3.75 miles one-way. You can usually find intermittent water along the way except in summer. At canyon's end, a climb up steep slickrock (hazardous if covered by snow or ice) takes you to Squaw Canyon Trail and back to the trailhead for a good 7.5-mile loop. Another possibility is to turn southwest to the head of Squaw Canyon, then hike over a slickrock saddle to Elephant Canyon for a 10.5-mile loop.

Hikes from Elephant Hill Trailhead

Drive west three miles past the campground turnoff to the picnic area and trailhead at the base of Elephant Hill. Sounds of racing engines and burning rubber can often be heard from above as vehicles attempt the difficult four-wheel-drive road that begins just past the picnic area. All of the following destinations can also be reached by trails from the Squaw Flat Trailhead, though distances will be slightly greater.

Chesler Park is a favorite hiking destination. A lovely desert meadow contrasts with the red and white spires that gave the Needles District its name. An old cowboy line camp is on the west side of the rock island in the center of the park. Distance on **Chesler Park Trail** is about six miles round-trip. The trail winds through sand and slickrock before ascending a small pass through the Needles to Chesler Park. Once inside, **Chesler Park Loop Trail** (five miles) circles completely around the park. The loop includes the unusual half-mile **Joint Trail,** which follows the bottom of a very narrow crack. Camping in Chesler Park is restricted to certain areas; check with a ranger.

Druid Arch reminds many people of the massive stone slabs at Stonehenge, popularly associated with the druids, in southern England. The arch is an 11-mile round-trip (15 miles if you start at Squaw Flat Trailhead). Follow the Chesler Park Trail two miles to Elephant Canyon, turn up the canyon 3.5 miles, then make a quarter-mile climb to the arch. Upper Elephant Canyon has seasonal water, but the narrow canyon is closed to camping.

Lower Red Lake Canyon Trail provides access to Cataract Canyon of the Colorado River. This is a long, strenuous trip best suited for experienced hikers and completed in two days. Distance from the Elephant Hill Trailhead is 19 miles round-trip; you'll be walking on four-wheel-drive roads and trails. If you can drive Elephant Hill 4WD Road to the trail junction in Cyclone Canyon, the hike is only eight miles round-trip. The most difficult trail section is a steep talus slope that drops 700 feet in a half mile into the lower canyon. Total elevation change is 1,000 feet. The canyon has little shade and lacks any water source above the river. Summer heat can make the trip grueling; temperatures tend to be 5–10° hotter than on other Needles trails. The river level drops between midsummer and autumn, allowing hikers to go along the shore both downstream to see the rapids and upstream to the confluence. Undertows and strong currents make the river dangerous to cross.

Upper Salt Creek Trail

Several impressive arches and many inviting side canyons attract adventurous hikers to the extreme southeast corner of the park. The trail begins at the end of the 13.5-mile four-wheel-drive road up Salt Creek, then goes south 12 miles upcanyon to Cottonwood Canyon/Beef Basin Road near Cathedral Butte, just outside the park boundary. The trail is nearly level except for a steep climb at the end. Water can usually be found. Some wading and bushwhacking may be necessary. The famous "All-American Man" pictograph, shown on some topo maps (or ask a ranger), is in a cave a short way off to the east at about the midpoint of the trail; follow your map and unsigned paths to the cave but don't climb in—it's dangerous to both you and the ruins and pictograph inside. Many more archaeological sites can be discovered near the trail; they're all fragile and need great care when visited.

Four-Wheel-Drive Roads

A back-road tour allows you to see beautiful canyon scenery, arches, and Native American rock-art sites in the Needles District. Check with a ranger about special hazards before setting out. Also obtain a backcountry permit ($30 per vehicle) if you plan to use one of the campgrounds available along Salt Creek or in the area past Elephant Hill. Mountain bikers enjoy the challenge of going up Elephant Hill Road and the roads beyond. Colorado Overlook 4WD Road is good riding, too, but Salt Creek and the other eastern canyons have too much loose sand.

Salt Creek Canyon 4WD Road begins near Cave Spring Trail, crosses sage flats for the next 2.5 miles, then heads deep into this spectacular canyon. Round-trip distance, including a side trip to 150-foot-high Angel Arch, is 26 miles. Agile hikers can follow a steep slickrock route into the window of Angel Arch. You can also explore side canyons of Salt Creek or take the Upper Salt Creek Trail (the "All American Man" pictograph makes a good day-hike destination of 12 miles round-trip). **Horse Canyon 4WD Road** turns off to the left shortly before the mouth of Salt Canyon. Round-trip distance, including a side trip to Tower Ruin, is about 13 miles; other attractions include Paul Bunyan's Potty, Castle Arch, Fortress Arch, and side-canyon hiking. Salt and Horse Canyons can easily be driven in four-wheel-drive vehicles. Usually Salt Canyon is closed due to quicksand after flash floods in summer and shelf ice in winter.

Four-wheel-drive roads enter **Davis Canyon** and **Lavender Canyon** from Highway 211 east of the park boundary. Both canyons are accessed through Davis Canyon Road off Highway 211 and contain great scenery, arches, and Native American sites, and both are easily visited. Davis is about 20 miles round-trip and Lavender is about 26 miles round-trip. Try to allow plenty of time in either canyon, as there is much to see and many inviting side canyons to hike. You can camp on BLM land just outside the park boundaries—but not in the park itself.

Colorado Overlook 4WD Road begins beside the visitors center and follows Salt Creek to Lower Jump Overlook. Then it bounces across slickrock to a view of the Colorado River (upstream from the confluence). Driving is easy to moderate, though very rough the last 1.5 miles. Round-trip distance is 14 miles.

Elephant Hill 4WD Loop Road begins three miles past the Squaw Flat Campground turnoff. Only experienced drivers with stout vehicles should attempt the extremely rough and steep climb up Elephant Hill (coming up the back side of Elephant Hill is even rougher!). The loop is about 10 miles round-trip. Connecting roads go to the Confluence Overlook Trailhead (the viewpoint is one mile round-trip on foot), the Joint Trailhead (Chesler Park is two miles round-trip on foot), and several canyons. Some road sections on the loop are one-way. The parallel canyons in this area are grabens caused by faulting, where a layer of salt has shifted deep underground. In addition to Elephant Hill, a few other difficult spots must be negotiated. This area can also be reached by a long route south of the park using Cottonwood Canyon/Beef Basin Road from Highway 211, about 60 miles one-way. You'll enjoy spectacular vistas from the Abajo Highlands. Two *very* steep descents from Pappys Pasture into Bobbys Hole effectively make this section one-way; travel from Elephant Hill up Bobbys Hole is possible but much more difficult than going the other way and may require hours of roadbuilding. The Bobbys Hole route may be impassable at times—ask about conditions at the BLM office in Monticello or at the Needles visitors center.

SOUTHEASTERN UTAH

Utah's Southeastern Corner

BLM NEWSPAPER ROCK HISTORICAL MONUMENT

At Newspaper Rock a profusion of petroglyphs depicts human figures, animals, birds, and abstract designs. These represent 2,000 years of human history during which archaic tribes and Anasazi, Fremont, Paiute, Navajo, and Anglo travelers have passed through Indian Creek Canyon. The patterns on the smooth sandstone rock face stand out clearly, thanks to a coating of dark desert varnish. Newspaper Rock lies just 150 feet off Highway 211 on the way to the Needles District of Canyonlands National Park. A quarter-mile nature trail introduces you to the area's desert and riparian vegetation. Picnic areas lie along Indian Creek across the highway. The park is relatively undeveloped; no drinking water or charge. From U.S. 191 between Moab and Monticello, turn west 12 miles on Highway 211.

CANYON RIMS RECREATION AREA

Viewpoints atop the high mesa east of Canyonlands National Park offer magnificent panoramas of the surrounding area. The BLM has provided two fenced overlooks, two campgrounds, and good access roads. Other overlooks and scenic spots can be reached on jeep roads or by hiking. The 20-mile-long mesa, shown on maps as Hatch Point, features rock monoliths, canyons, slickrock, and rolling hills. You have a good chance of seeing the graceful antelope-like pronghorn that thrive in this high-desert country. The turnoff for Hatch Point of Canyon Rims is at milepost 93 on U.S. 191, 32 miles south of Moab and seven miles north of the Highway 211 junction for the Needles District. Canyon Rims Recreation Area has been greatly expanded recently to include surrounding BLM lands and the Beef Basin and Dark Canyon areas. Author

© W. C. MCRAE

Newspaper Rock preserves some of the richest and most fanciful prehistoric rock art in Utah.

UTAH'S SOUTHEASTERN CORNER

COLORADO

NM

Monticello

Blanding

Abajo Peak
11,360 ft

Abajo Mountains

Manti-La Sal

National

Forest

Newspaper Rock
State Historical
Monument

Edge of the Cedars
State Park

Hovenweep
National
Monument

CUTTHROAT CASTLE

HACKBERRY AND
HORSESHOE RUINS

HOLLY
RUINS

SQUARE TOWER
RUINS

HATCH
TRADING POST

CAJON
RUINS

Aneth

RESERVATION

Montezuma
Creek

FOUR CORNERS
MONUMENT

RECAPTURE
POCKET

FOURTEEN
WINDOW
RUIN

BUTLER WASH
RUINS

Comb Ridge

ST. CHRISTOPHER'S
EPISCOPAL MISSION

Bluff

SAND ISLAND
CAMPGROUND

BIG POCKET
OVERLOOK

Arch Canyon

ARCH CANYON
OVERLOOK

MULE CANYON
RUIN

VALLEY
OF THE
GODS

Mexican Hat

Canyonlands

National Park

Dark Canyon

Wilderness

Area

Natural
Bridges
National
Monument

Grand

Gulch

Primitive

Area

MULEY POINT
OVERLOOK

San Juan River

Goosenecks
State Park

INDIAN

MONUMENT VALLEY
VISITOR CENTER

Cataract Canyon

Fry Canyon

Glen Canyon

National

Recreation

Area

Monument

Valley

GOULDING
TRADING POST

Gouldings

To Kayenta, AZ

NAVAJO

ARIZONA

Hite

HITE CROSSING

Colorado River

Glen Canyon

Mt. Ellen
11,522 ft

Mt. Pennell
11,320 ft

Henry

Mountains

HALLS CROSSING
MARINA

BULLFROG BASIN
MARINA

National

Recreation

Area

Lake Powell

HOLE-IN-
THE-ROCK

RAINBOW BRIDGE
NATIONAL MONUMENT

To Hwy. 160

Capitol Reef National Park

Waterpocket Fold

BURR TRAIL

PARK

Grand
Staircase-
Escalante
National
Monument

10 mi

10 km

0

© AVALON TRAVEL PUBLISHING, INC.

and BLM volunteer Fran Barnes has written and published the large book *Canyon Country's Canyon Rims Recreation Area*, about exploring these areas. The book includes a 235-mile long "Canyon Rims Recreation Area Mountain Bike Challenge Route." For back-road travel in this area, you'll find Fran Barnes's book and separate map *Canyon Country Off-Road Vehicle Trails: Canyon Rims Recreation Area* very helpful. Cyclists will also find good info in Peggy and Bob Utesch's *Mountain Biking in Canyon Rims Recreation Area*. Also check out the website www.blm.gov/utah/moab/canyon_rims.html.

Needles Overlook

Follow the paved road 22 miles west to its end (turn left at the junction 15 miles in). The BLM has a picnic area and interpretive exhibits here. A fence protects visitors from the sheer cliffs that drop off more than 1,000 feet. You can see much of Canyonlands National Park and southeastern Utah. Look south for Six-Shooter Peaks and the high country of the Abajo Mountains; southwest for the Needles (thousands of spires reaching for the heavens); west for the confluence area of the Green and Colorado Rivers, the Maze District, the Orange Cliffs, and the Henry Mountains; northwest for the lazy bends of the Colorado River Canyon and the sheer-walled mesas of Island in the Sky and Dead Horse Point; north for the Book Cliffs; and northeast for the La Sal Mountains. The changing shadows and colors of the canyon country make for a continuous show throughout the day.

Anticline Overlook

Head west 15 miles on the paved road, then go straight (north) 17 miles on a good gravel road to the fenced overlook at road's end. Here you're standing 1,600 feet above the Colorado River. The sweeping panorama over the canyons, the river, and the twisted rocks of the Kane Creek Anticline is nearly as spectacular as that from Dead Horse Point, only 5.5 miles west as the crow flies. Salt and other minerals of the Paradox Formation pushed up overlying rocks into the dome visible below. Downcutting by the Colorado River has revealed the twisted rock layers.

The Moab Salt Mine across the river to the north uses a solution technique to bring up potash from the Paradox Formation several thousand feet underground. Pumps then transfer the solution to the blue-tinted evaporation ponds. Look carefully on the northeast horizon to see an arch in the Windows Section of Arches National Park, 16 miles away.

You can reach **Pyramid Butte Overlook** by a gravel road that turns west off the main drive two miles before Anticline Overlook; the road goes around a rock monolith to viewpoints on the other side (1.3 miles round-trip). Vehicles with four-wheel drive can go west out to **Canyonlands Overlook** (17 miles round-trip) on rough unmarked roads. The turnoff, which may not be signed, is about 0.3 mile south of the Hatch Point Campground turnoff.

Campgrounds

Each camping area has water (mid-April–mid-October), tables, grills, and outhouses and charges a $10 fee. **Windwhistle Campground,** backed by cliffs to the south, has fine views to the north and a nature trail; follow the main road from U.S. 191 for six miles and turn left. At **Hatch Point Campground,** in a piñon-juniper woodland, you can enjoy views to the north; water available April–mid-October. Go 24 miles in on the paved and gravel roads toward Anticline Overlook, then turn right one mile.

Trough Springs Trail

Hikers can follow this old livestock trail on the east side of Hatch Point. To reach the trailhead, turn east 0.6 mile on a dirt road five miles north of the Hatch Point Campground turnoff (or four miles south of Anticline Overlook). The trail begins from an abandoned well pad and follows the canyon to its mouth at Kane Creek Road. The first one-third mile follows a jeep road, then cairns mark the way. Carry water. The moderately difficult hike is five miles round-trip and has an elevation change of 1,200 feet.

Beef Basin

The rugged canyon country south of Canyonlands National Park's Needles District contains beautiful scenery, knock-out panoramas, and Anasazi pueblo ruins. You'll need a four-wheel-drive, high-clearance vehicle, maps, camping gear, and emergency supplies to explore this remote region. Drive in from the east via County Road 104, or from the south over the Abajo Highlands of the Manti–La Sal National Forest. Although these approach roads are graded, high-clearance vehicles are still recommended. Snow and mud close the roads in winter and spring, especially from the Abajo Highlands. The Beef Basin Road drops from the forests into a series of grassy parks. Spur roads branch out to other canyons and parks and make a loop in Beef Basin.

Many Anasazi pueblos stand out in the open in Middle and Ruin Parks; others lie tucked into canyon alcoves. One road runs northwest past Ruin Park, makes two *very* steep and rough descents into Bobbys Hole, then continues to Elephant Hill in Canyonlands National Park. Only hard-core jeepers should consider this route into Canyonlands National Park! The road may be impassable in the reverse (uphill) direction or totally impassable altogether; ask at the BLM office in Monticello or the Needles visitors center in the park.

Big Pocket Overlook

A rough jeep road branches north 2.5 miles from the Cottonwood Canyon/Beef Basin Road to spectacular panoramas of upper Salt and Lavender Canyons. Binoculars help to pick out natural arches and other details. The road, also good for hiking or mountain biking, makes a loop along the east side of this narrow peninsula. Although on BLM land, you'll be surrounded by some of the best views in the Needles District of Canyonlands National Park. A hiking trail into upper Salt Creek Canyon begins about one mile west of the Big Pocket Overlook turnoff.

Cameo Cliffs

Canyons, arches, and panoramas attract visitors to this little-known area east of U.S. 191. Author Fran Barnes called it Cameo Cliffs because the pink cliffs reminded him of an old-fashioned pink-and-white cameo locket. You're not likely to

see this unofficial name on maps, however. Barnes describes the area, divided by Highway 46 into Cameo Cliffs North and South, in a small guidebook and separate map, *Cameo Cliffs: Biking-Hiking-Four-Wheeling.*

MONTICELLO

The Mormon settlers who arrived in 1888 found the cool climate more suited to raising sheep and cattle than crops. Monticello (pronounced mon-tuh-SELL-o) lies at an elevation of 7,050 feet just east of the Abajo (uh-BAH-hoe) Mountains. The small town (pop. 1,900) is the seat of San Juan County (Utah's largest, at five million acres) and serves as a base for travelers to visit surrounding mountains and canyons, including the Needles District of Canyonlands National Park. Monticello is 54 miles south of Moab and 21 miles north of Blanding. Highway U.S. 491 (Central) goes east from downtown to the Colorado border (17 miles) and Mesa Verde National Park (89 miles).

The **Monticello Museum,** in the library building at the city park, 80 N. Main, has exhibits of Anasazi artifacts, pioneer memorabilia, historic documents, and mineral specimens; open Monday–Thursday 2–9 P.M., Friday 2–6 P.M., and Saturday 10 A.M.–2 P.M. June–August. The librarian next door at the county library can let you in outside official hours.

Entertainment and Events

Watch movies at **The Movies,** 696 E. Central, 435/587-2535. Annual events include **Monticello/Canyonlands Triathlon** in mid-March, **Pioneer Day** (parade, softball, games, and food) on July 24, **San Juan Golf Tourney and Mountain Cookout** in early August, and **San Juan County Fair** (rodeo, exhibits, and dance) on the third weekend in August.

Recreation

The **city park** has picnic areas and a playground at Main and Central. A covered **swimming pool** (open in summer, 801/587-2907), **tennis courts,** and **ball fields** are three blocks west of Main on Central. **Blue Mountain Meadows Public Golf**

Course, 549 S. Main (south edge of town), 435/587-2468, has nine holes, a pro shop, and snack bar.

Ranch Vacations and Trail Rides

Live the life of a cowboy on a working ranch run by third- and fourth-generation cowboys. **Dalton Gang Adventures** provides the horse, cattle, and range at $125 per person per day. This isn't your standard guest ranch—you'll be taken on as a working cowboy. Depending on the season, you'll be involved in trailing, moving pastures, and gathering and working cattle. Contact the ranch for a brochure that gives the activities of the different seasons: P.O. Box 8, Monticello, UT 84534, 435/587-2416.

Accommodations

$50–75: The unique offerings at **The Grist Mill Inn,** 64 South 300 East, 435/587-2597 or 800/645-3762, include bed-and-breakfast accommodations in a turn-of-the-20th-century flour mill, a granary, and a 1924 caboose. The inn is a showcase of sensitive architectural restoration. All rooms have private baths.

Navajo Trail National 9 Inn is a well maintained older motel at 248 N. Main, 435/587-2251 or 888/449-NINE. The **Days Inn,** 549 N. Main, 435/587-2458 or 800/329-7466, has an indoor pool and spa. **Triangle H Motel,** 164 E. Central, 435/587-2274 or 800/657-6622, has well-maintained rooms. **Best Western Wayside Inn,** 197 E. Central, 435/587-2261 or 800/633-9700, has a pool. The **Go West Inn Super 8,** 435/587-2489 or 877/2-GO-WEST, is on the north edge of town at 649 N. Main.

Campgrounds: With showers and laundry, **Mountain View RV Park,** 632 N. Main, 435/587-2974, is open May–October; tenters welcome. **Westerner Trailer Park,** 516 S. Main, near the golf course, 435/587-2762, welcomes both tents and RVs, has showers, and is closed in winter. **Monticello/Canyonlands KOA,** 435/587-2884, is on a ranch with buffalo, cows, horses, and other farm animals; go east five miles on Central/U.S. 491, then north a half mile. Open May–September, the KOA has Kamping Kabins, showers, store, and a pool.

The U.S. Forest Service has two campgrounds nearby on paved roads in the Abajos. **Dalton Springs** (elev. 8,400 feet) has water early June–early October. Go west 5.3 miles on 200 South. **Buckboard** (elev. 8,700 feet) has water mid-June–early October. Go west 6.5 miles on 200 South. Campgrounds may also be open off-season without water or fee.

Food

Wagon Wheel Pizza, 164A S. Main, 435/587-2766, spins out pizza, sandwiches, and salads daily for lunch and dinner. **MD Ranch Cookhouse,** 380 S. Main, 435/587-3299, dishes up cowboy food including steaks and buffalo in a Western atmosphere with genuine ranching artifacts; open daily for breakfast, lunch, and dinner (closed December–February). **Grandma's Kitchen,** 133 E. Central, 435/587-2870, features well prepared American fare for three meals a day. **Lamplight Restaurant,** 655 E. Central, 435/587-2170, is the best restaurant in the region, offering steaks, fish, prime rib, and a salad bar; open Tuesday–Saturday for dinner. **Los Tachos,** 280 E. Central, 435/587-2959, has Mexican and American food; open Monday–Saturday for lunch and dinner.

Information and Services

Visit the **San Juan County Multi-Agency visitors center,** on the side of the county courthouse, 117 S. Main (P.O. Box 490, Monticello, UT 84535), 435/587-3235 or 800/574-4386, for information about San Juan County towns and backcountry; staff and literature represent the San Juan County Travel Council, National Park Service, U.S. Forest Service, Bureau of Land Management, Canyonlands Natural History Association, and Utah Travel Council. Regional books and maps are sold. Open April–October Monday–Friday 8 A.M.–5 P.M. and Saturday and Sunday 10 A.M.–5 P.M., then Monday–Friday 9 A.M.–5 P.M. the rest of the year. The **Bureau of Land Management** San Juan Resource Area office, 435 N. Main (P.O. Box 7, Monticello, UT 84535), 435/587-1500, knows about Grand Gulch, Fish and Owl Canyons, Dark Canyon, Arch Canyon, and many other scenic hiking areas; they can also advise on back-road travel in San Juan County. Open Monday–Friday 7:45 A.M.–4:30 P.M. The **Manti–La Sal National Forest office,** 496 E. Central (P.O. Box 820, Monticello, UT 84535), 435/587-2041, has information about roads, camping, and hiking in the Abajos and surrounding high country; its Monticello district includes the upper reaches of Dark Canyon. Open Monday–Friday 8 A.M.– noon and 12:30–4:30 P.M. The **public library** at 80 N. Main in the city park, 435/587-2281, has general reading and an extensive collection of southeastern Utah history; open Monday–Thursday 2–9 P.M., Friday 2–6 P.M., and Saturday 10 A.M.–2 P.M.

Four Corners School of Outdoor Education offers programs on the wildlife, geology, and archaeology of the Southwest. Write for a brochure at P.O. Box 1029, Monticello, UT 84535, 435/587-2156.

The **post office** is at 197 S. Main, 435/587-2294. **San Juan Hospital** provides medical care at 364 West 100 North, 435/587-2116.

VICINITY OF MONTICELLO

Abajo Peak

The rounded Abajos (or Blues, as they're sometimes called) actually rise higher than they seem to. Early Spanish explorers climbed the La Sals to the northeast and named these mountains Abajo (below). Intrusive volcanic rocks created the range in much the same way as they formed the Henry and La Sal Mountains. Abajo Peak tops the range at 11,362 feet. You can easily reach the summit by road (high-clearance vehicles work best); head west 0.9 mile on 200 South from U.S. 191, then turn left 13 miles on South Creek Road (pavement ends one mile in at Loyd's Lake). You'll likely see deer and raptors, as well as summer wildflowers, on the drive up. Panoramas on a clear day at the top take in the Four Corners region, including mountain ranges in Colorado, Shiprock in New Mexico, the Chuska Mountains in Arizona, Monument Valley, Cedar Mesa, the Henry Mountains, the Needles District of Canyonlands National Park, the La Sal Mountains, and the forests and meadows of the Abajos.

Other peaks and canyons of the Abajos have good hiking trails; see the foresters in Monticello and the Manti–La Sal Forest map and the more detailed Trails Illustrated topo map for the back roads and trails of the area. The metric 1:100,000 Blanding topo map covers nearly all the range.

You can enjoy several scenic drives in the Abajos. Cars with good clearance can often do these trips in dry weather; ask at the U.S. Forest Service office in Monticello. The range can be crossed to Blanding by heading west on 200 South, turning southwest on Forest Route 079 up North Canyon, then descending along Johnson Creek (about 37 miles total one-way). A longer drive continues west from the junction of Forest Routes 079 and 095 to Elk Ridge and through the Bears Ears to Highway 95 near Natural Bridges National Monument. The drive has great views of rugged canyons and forested hills. You'll cross a knife-edge ridge on the Causeway at about the middle of Forest Route 095; at the west end, turn south around the upper drainages of Dark Canyon to the Bears Ears on Forest Route 088 or turn north to Beef Basin and Big Pocket Overlook Roads (see Canyon Rims Recreation Area). Winter visitors come to the mountains for cross-country skiing and snowmobiling, though no trails or ski areas exist (Blue Mountain Ski Area has closed). The road from Monticello to Dalton Springs is plowed for winter access. A good scenic loop saves about 16 miles from the highway route between Monticello and Canyonlands National Park; take Forest Route 105 about nine miles to Forest Route 174, perhaps stopping to enjoy a beautiful scenic overlook of Canyonlands from a high point before descending to Route 174, which brings you, in another six miles, to Highway 211 near Newspaper Rock.

BLANDING

The largest town in San Juan County, Blanding (pop. 3,520) is also a handy travelers' stop. The state park on the northwest edge of town provides an excellent introduction to the Anasazi, who left behind many ruins in the Four Corners area. Pioneers began work on an irrigation system in 1897 to bring water from the Abajo Mountains to the rich soil of White Mesa. The first families arrived at the town site, then known as Sidon, in 1905. Many of the Mormon farmers who followed had been driven from Mexico by political and religious intolerance or had lost their farms to floods at nearby Bluff. Residents apparently liked changing the name of their community. Originally known as Sidon, the town became Grayson, then Blanding. The story goes that in 1915 townsfolk jumped at the offer of a free library by Thomas W. Bicknell on the condition that they name their town after him. The town of Thurber in central Utah also wanted the library, so it was divided between the two communities; Thurber became Bicknell and Grayson became Blanding, the maiden name of Mrs. Bicknell.

Edge of the Cedars State Park

Prehistoric Anasazi built at least six groups of pueblo structures between A.D. 700 and 1220 just outside present-day Blanding. The state museum features an excellent array of pottery, baskets, sandals, jewelry, and stone tools. The pottery collection on the second floor stands out for its rich variety of styles and decorative designs. Other displays illustrate Anasazi life and how archaeologists have learned about these ancient peoples through studies of stratigraphy, dendrochronology, and village layouts. The Special Exhibits room has changing shows related to the region and inhabitants. An observation tower in the museum provides panoramic views of the ruins outside and of mountains in four states; signs identify the features.

A short trail behind the museum leads past six clusters of ruins, each of which contains both rectangular rooms on the surface and circular depressions of underground kivas and pit houses. Only Complex 4 has been excavated and partly restored to give an idea of the village's appearance when the Anasazi lived here. You may enter the kiva by descending a ladder through the restored roof; the walls and interior features are original. The other five ruin groups haven't been restored and require some imagination. A large pit near Complex 4 is all that remains of a great

kiva, a structure rarely seen this far north. Edge of the Cedars likely served as an important community center in its day.

The museum also has exhibits and artifacts of the people who followed the Anasazi—the Utes and Navajo and the early Anglo pioneers. You may enter a Navajo hogan outside. Videos and slide presentations, shown on request in the auditorium, illustrate Anasazi, Navajo, and pioneer cultures. There's often an art or photo exhibition in the auditorium as well as in the art gallery. **Archaeology Week**, held in spring, has demonstrations and talks. A gift shop sells books on the region's Native Americans and pioneer history. Picnic tables outside provide a spot for having lunch. Edge of the Cedars, 435/678-2238, is open daily 9 A.M.–6 P.M. May 16–September 15, then daily 9 A.M.–5 P.M. the rest of the year; closed Thanksgiving Day, Christmas Day, New Year's Day, Civil Rights Day, and Presidents Day; $2 adults, $1 ages 6–16, or $5 per vehicle. Head north on Main from downtown and follow signs one mile.

The Dinosaur Museum

This museum, 754 South 200 West, 435/678-3454, showcases the prehistoric plant and animal life of this corner of Utah. Exhibits include life-size models of dinosaurs as well as fossils and skeletons. Don't miss the History Hall of Hollywood Dinosaurs, which recounts the evolution of film's depictions of the thunder lizard. Open Monday–Saturday 9 A.M.–5 P.M. April 15–October 15; adults $2, children and seniors $1.

Events and Shopping

A three-day **Fourth of July Celebration** has fireworks, a parade, horse events, "meller-dramas," and a mudbog competition. Navajo and Utes produce handpainted ceramics at **Cedar Mesa Pottery,** Main and 300 South, 435/678-2241. You can step into the adjacent factory on weekdays to watch the craftspeople at work. **Blue Mountain Trading Post,** one mile south of town, has a large selection of high-quality Native American art and crafts; the adaptable Navajo produce much of the work—even the kachina dolls (borrowed from Hopi traditions).

Recreation

Blanding Pool and a **tennis court** are at 50 West and 200 South, 435/678-2157. **Reservoir Park** (picnic area and playground) and the nine-hole **Blanding Golf Course** are three miles north on 300 West; the small reservoir has trout fishing. **Recapture Reservoir** offers boating and trout fishing three miles northeast of town; head northeast 1.3 miles on U.S. 191, turn left (north) on a paved road between mileposts 53 and 54 (just before the highway enters a road cut), then go 1.7 miles to the lake's southern shore; this road is the old highway and makes a good boat ramp where submerged. For access to the north and west sides of the reservoir, follow U.S. 191 across the dam, continue a half mile, then turn west onto a gravel road. Anglers can also turn in at either end of the dam to fish from the shore. No facilities are at the reservoir, though people sometimes camp (the west end is best).

Tours

Flights by **Scenic Aviation** fly over spectacular canyon country. Destinations include Canyonlands National Park, Lake Powell, and Monument Valley. Half-hour flights start at $50. Call 435/678-3222 for more information; the airport is three miles south of town.

Accommodations

Under $50: The **Cliff Palace Motel** offers basic accommodation at 132 S. Main, 435/678-2264 or 800/553-8093. The **Sunset Inn,** 88 W. Center, 435/678-3323, is a good deal with all queen beds, remote-control cable TVs, and a hot tub; pets allowed.

$50–75: The hospitality is gracious and the facilities are top-notch at **The Grayson Country Inn B&B,** 118 East 300 South (turn east one block at Cedar Mesa Pottery), 435/678-2388 or 800/365-0868. It features rooms in a 1908 Victorian home, plus an additional cottage with three bedrooms for a family or group. All rooms have private baths. **Rogers House B&B,** 412 S. Main, 435/678-2493 or 800/355-3932, is a renovated 1915 home with private baths, whirlpool tubs, and queen-size beds.

The **Four Corners Inn,** 131 E. Center, 435/678-3257 or 800/574-3150, has a restaurant, free continental breakfast, and children under 12 stay free. The **Comfort Inn,** at 711 S. U.S. 191, 435/678-3271 or 800/622-3250, has suites, guest laundry, indoor pool, hot tub, and exercise room. A new **Super 8,** 755 S. Main, 435/678-3880 or 800/800-8000, is on the south edge of town. The **Best Western Gateway Inn,** 88 E. Center, 435/678-2278 or 888/921-2279, has a pool and restaurant.

Campgrounds: At the south edge of town, **KamPark** has a store and showers on S. U.S. 191, 435/678-2770; both tents and are RVs welcome. **Devil's Canyon Campground** (elev. 7,100 feet) in the Manti–La Sal National Forest has sites with water early May–late October (no water or fee off-season). A quarter-mile nature trail begins at the far end of the campground loop. Go north eight miles on U.S. 191, then west 1.3 miles on a paved road (turnoff is between mileposts 60 and 61). **Nizhoni Campground** (elev. 7,760 feet), also in the Manti–La Sal National Forest, has sites with water early June–late September. Turn north 14 miles on 100 East in Blanding (last part is a gravel road). You can also reach Nizhoni on back ways from Monticello via the Abajo Peaks or from Natural Bridges National Monument via the Bears Ears, Elk Ridge, and the Causeway.

Food

Elk Ridge Restaurant, 120 E. Center, 435/678-3390, offers a varied American menu with a few Mexican items; open daily except Sunday for breakfast, lunch, and dinner. The best place for a full meal is the **Old Tymer Restaurant,** 733 S. Main, 435/678-2122, with sandwiches, steak, prime rib, and chicken; open for three meals a day.

Information and Services

The staff at the state park knows about Blanding and can tell you of other Anasazi ruins in the area. The **public library** is at Main and 300 South, 435/678-2335; open Monday–Saturday.

White Mesa Institute, 639 West 100 South (50-1), Blanding, UT 84511, sponsored by the College of Eastern Utah, offers educational programs for youth and adults on the archaeology, modern tribes, pioneer history, wildlife, and geology of the Southwest.

The **post office** is at the corner of Main and 100 North, 435/678-2627. The **Blanding Clinic** provides medical services at 930 North 400 West, 435/678-2254. Contact the county hospital in Monticello at 435/678-2830.

HOVENWEEP NATIONAL MONUMENT

The Anasazi built many impressive masonry buildings during the early to mid-1200s, near the end of their 1,300-year stay in the area. A drought beginning in A.D. 1274 and lasting 25 years probably hastened their migration from this area. Several centuries of intensive farming, hunting, and woodcutting had already taken their toll on the land. Archaeologists believe the inhabitants retreated south in the late 1200s to sites in northwestern New Mexico and northeastern Arizona. The Ute word Hovenweep means "deserted valley," an appropriate name for the lonely high-desert country left behind. The Anasazi at Hovenweep had much in common with the Mesa Verde culture, though the Dakota sandstone here doesn't form large alcoves suitable for cliff-dweller villages. Ruins at Hovenweep remain essentially unexcavated, awaiting some future archaeologist's trowel.

The Anasazi farmers had a keen interest in the seasons because of their need to know the best time for planting crops. Astronomical stations (alignments of walls, doorways, and tiny openings) allowed the sun priests to determine the equinoxes and solstices with an accuracy of one or two days. This precision also may have been necessary for a complex ceremonial calendar. Astronomical stations at Hovenweep have been discovered at Hovenweep Castle and Unit-Type House of Square Tower Ruins and at Cajon Ruins.

Admission to the monument is $6 per vehicle, or $3 per person.

Visitors Center

Hovenweep National Monument protects six

Hovenweep National Monument

© W. C. MCRAE

groups of villages left behind by the Anasazi. The sites lie near the Colorado border southeast of Blanding. Square Tower Ruins Unit, where the visitors center is, has the greatest number of ruins and the most varied architecture. In fact, you can find all of the Hovenweep architectural styles here. The visitors center, 970/749-0510, has a few exhibits on the Anasazi and photos of local wildlife. A ranger will answer your questions, provide brochures and handouts about various aspects of the monument, and give directions for visiting the other ruin groups. Related books can be purchased. Hours at the visitors center are 8 A.M.–4:30 P.M. year-round; the ruins stay open all the time. There's also a small campground at the monument, $10 a site, no reservations. Mesa Verde National Park administers Hovenweep from Mesa Verde National Park, CO 81330, 970/529-4465. Nearest places for groceries and fuel are Aneth (20 miles south in Utah; has a telephone), Hatch Trading Post (16 miles west in Utah; groceries only), and Ismay Trading Post (14 miles southeast in Colorado). Gnats can be very pesky in May and June; be sure to bring insect repellent.

One approach from U.S. 191 between Blanding and Bluff is to head east nine miles on Highway 262, continue straight six miles on a small paved road to Hatch Trading Post, then follow signs 16 miles. A good way in from Bluff is to go east 21 miles on the paved road to Montezuma Creek and Aneth, then follow signs north 20 miles. A scenic 58-mile route through Montezuma Canyon begins five miles south of Monticello and follows unpaved roads to Hatch and on to Hovenweep; you can stop at the BLM's Three Turkey Ruin on the way. From Colorado, take a partly paved road west and north 41 miles from U.S. 491 (the turnoff is four miles south of Cortez).

Square Tower Ruins

This extensive group of Anasazi towers and dwellings lines the rim and slopes of Little Ruin Canyon, a short walk from the visitors center. Obtain a trail guide booklet from the ranger station; the booklet's map shows the several loop trails. You can take easy walks of less than a half mile on the rim or combine all the trails for a loop of about two miles with only one up-and-down section in the canyon. The booklet has good descriptions of Anasazi life and architecture and of the plants growing along the trail. You'll see towers (D-shaped, square, oval, and round), cliff dwellings, surface dwellings, storehouses, kivas, and rock art. Take care not to disturb the fragile ruins. Keep an eye out for the prairie rattlesnake (a subspecies of the western rattlesnake), which is active at night in summer and during the day in spring and autumn. Please stay on the trail—don't climb ruin walls or walk on rubble mounds.

Other Ruins

These are good to visit if you'd like to spend more time in the area. You'll need a map and directions from a ranger to find them, as they aren't signed. One group, the Goodman Point, near Cortez, Colorado, has relatively little to see except unexcavated mounds.

Holly Ruins group is noted for its Great House, Holly Tower, and Tilted Tower. Most of Tilted Tower fell away after the boulder on which it sat shifted. Great piles of rubble mark the sites of structures built on loose ground. Look for remnants of farming terraces in the canyon below the Great House. A hiking trail connects the campground at Square Tower Ruins with Holly Ruins; the route follows canyon bottoms and is about eight miles round-trip. Ask a ranger for a map and directions. Hikers could also continue to Horseshoe Ruins (one mile farther) and Hackberry Ruins (one-third mile beyond Horseshoe). All of these lie just across the Colorado border and about six miles (one-way) by road from the visitors center.

Horseshoe Ruins and **Hackberry Ruins** are best reached by an easy trail (one mile round-trip) off the road to Holly Ruins. Horseshoe House, built in a horseshoe shape similar to Sun Temple at Mesa Verde, has exceptionally good masonry work. Archaeologists haven't determined the purpose of the structure. An alcove in the canyon below contains a spring and small shelter. A round tower nearby on the rim has a strategic view. Hackberry House has only one room still intact. Rubble piles and wall remnants abound in the area. The spring under an alcove here still has a good flow and supports lush growths of hackberry and cottonwood trees along with smaller plants.

Cutthroat Castle Ruins were remote even in Anasazi times. The ruins lie along an intermittent stream rather than at the head of a canyon like most other Hovenweep sites. Cutthroat Castle is a large multistory structure with both straight and curved walls. Three round towers stand nearby. Look for wall fragments and the circular depressions of kivas. High-clearance vehicles can go close to the ruins, about 11.5 miles (one-way) from the visitors center. Visitors with cars can drive to a trailhead and then walk to the ruins (1.5 miles round-trip on foot).

Cajon Ruins are at the head of a little canyon on Cajon Mesa in the Navajo Reservation in Utah, about nine miles southwest of the visitors center. The site has a commanding view across the San Juan Valley as far as Monument Valley. Buildings include a large multiroom structure, a round tower, and a tall square tower. An alcove just below has a spring and some rooms. Look for pictographs, petroglyphs, and grooves in rock (used for tool grinding). Farming terraces were located on the canyon's south side.

BLUFF

The 1880 Hole-in-the-Rock Expedition arrived here after an epic journey by wagon train from Escalante. Too tired to go any farther, they chose this section of the San Juan River Canyon in which to plant their fields and build new homes. They hoped that their presence here would secure the region for Mormon settlement and lead to conversion of the Native Americans. The settlers tried repeatedly to farm the fertile canyon soils, only to have the river wash their fields away. Most residents gave up and moved to more promising areas, but many of those who stayed prospered with large cattle herds.

In the past few years, Bluff has become a rather unlikely mecca for recreationalists and escapees from urban congestion. A growing number of outfitters make it easy to get out and enjoy the remarkable scenery hereabouts.

Today Bluff is a sleepy community of about 300 inhabitants, nestled in a very striking physical location. Take the signed Bluff City Historic Loop to see pioneer houses along the back streets. Many visitors also drive to the cemetery atop a small hill to read inscriptions and enjoy views of the valley (turn in beside Turquoise RV Park, turn left just past the Decker Pioneer House, and follow the paved road to the top). Native Americans from the Navajo Reservation across the river occasionally have dance performances, horse races, rodeos, and other get-togethers in Bluff.

In the past few years, Bluff has become a rather unlikely mecca for recreationalists and escapees from urban congestion. The quality of lodging is better than almost any other town of this size in the state, and a growing number of outfitters make it easy to get out and enjoy the remarkable scenery hereabouts.

Floating the San Juan River

From the high San Juan Mountains in southern Colorado, this intriguing river winds its way into New Mexico, enters Utah near Four Corners, and twists through spectacular canyons before ending at Lake Powell. Sand waves spring up during flooding, usually in May and June. The waves can pop up out of flat water to heights of three feet and occasionally as much as seven or eight feet! Swift currents on the sandy bottom cause these harmless waves, which can migrate up or downstream before disappearing.

Below the town of Bluff, the muddy river picks up speed and dives deep within its canyon walls. Most boaters put in at Sand Island Campground near Bluff and take out at the town of Mexican Hat, 30 river miles downstream. This trip combines ancient Native American ruins, rock art, and a trip through Monument Upwarp and the Upper Canyon, with fast water for thrills (Class III rapids) and weirdly buckled geology to ponder. Longer trips continue on through the famous Goosenecks, the "entrenched meanders" carved thousands of feet below the desert surface, and through more Class III rapids on the way to Clay Hills Crossing or Paiute Farms (not always accessible) on Lake Powell. Allow at least four days for the full trip, though more time will allow exploration of side canyons and visits to Anasazi sites. Rafts, kayaks, and canoes can be used. The season now usually lasts all year, because of the Navajo Reservoir upstream.

Many commercial river-running companies offer San Juan trips. If you go on your own, you should have river-running experience or be with someone who has. Private groups need to obtain permits from the BLM San Juan Resource Area office well in advance: P.O. Box 7, Monticello, UT 84535, 435/587-2141. The book *San Juan Canyons, A River Runner's Guide,* by Don Baars and Gene Stevenson, has a river log with detailed maps, practical advice, and background.

Some people also like to run the river between Montezuma Creek and Sand Island, a leisurely trip of 20 river miles. The solitude often makes up for the lack of scenery. It's easy to get a river permit for this section because no use limits or fees apply.

If you're looking for a multiday trip on the San Juan, contact some of the larger Moab-based outfitters, who often offer a San Juan trip when interest allows. Or contact local **Wild Rivers Expeditions,** P.O. Box 118, Bluff, UT 84512, 435/672-2244 or 800/422-7654 out of state, www.riversandruins.com, which offers both day and multiday trips out of Bluff; trips run daily in summer and only a day's notice is usually needed to join a float. Day excursions to Mexican Hat cost $94 (motors may be used if water level is low). The office is on the main highway through town.

Accommodations

$50–75: Attractive **Desert Rose Inn,** 701 W. Main St., 735/672-2303 or 888/475-7673, www.desertroseinn.com, is one of the nicest lodgings in all of southern Utah. The large, lodge-like log structure has two-story wraparound porches and rooms furnished with pine furniture, quilts, and Southwestern art. At the edge of the property are a number of handsome one-bedroom log cabins. Definitely a class act.

The other great place to stay is **Recapture Lodge,** 220 E. Main St., P.O. Box 309, Bluff, UT 84512, 435/672-2281. For many years the heart and soul of Bluff, the lodge is operated by long-time outfitters and the lodge has an easy nonchalance that is immediately welcoming. Besides rooms and kitchenettes, Recapture Lodge has a swimming pool, hot tub, launderette, tours, and llama pack trips. Groups can reserve rooms in the 1898 Decker Pioneer House. The owners know of Native American ruins and scenic places in the backcountry. They offer free slide shows in the evenings during the season and can suggest places to go. Or you can take one of their organized full-day naturalist tours to Monument Valley, Comb Ridge, Recapture Pocket, and other locations. Guided camping trips can also be arranged in the canyon country of southeastern

Utah. They also can provide a shuttle service for rafting trips. **Kokopelli Inn Motel,** 435/672-2322 or 800/541-8854, just next door, is a pleasant place to stay, though it pales in comparison to Bluff's unique lodges.

Campgrounds: Near the center of Bluff, **Cadillac Ranch R.V. Park,** 435/672-2262 or 800/538-6195, has RV hookups and tenting sites. **Cottonwood R.V. Park,** on the west end of Bluff, 435/672-2287, has both tent and RV sites. **Sand Island Recreation Area** is a primitive camping area along the San Juan River three miles south of town; large cottonwood trees shade this pretty spot. No drinking water or charge; tenters need to watch for thorns in the grass. River runners often put in at the campground. You can see a panel of pictographs along the cliff one-third mile downstream from the camping area along a gravel road.

Other Practicalities

Cow Canyon Trading Post, 435/672-2208, is a café that serves homemade dinners in an old trading post on the northeast edge of town; open Thursday–Monday April–October. The trading post is open all year with Native American crafts. **Twin Rocks Trading Post,** also on the Bluff City Historic Loop, 435/672-2341, has a café and a selection of high-quality Native American crafts, much of it produced locally by the Navajo. The **post office** is on the main highway. A small **library/travel information center,** open irregular hours, sits on the Historic Loop behind the post office.

VICINITY OF BLUFF

The canyon country of Cedar Mesa, Comb Ridge, and other nearby areas has beautiful scenery, Anasazi ruins, and abundant wildlife. Recapture Pocket has unusual rock formations (it's *west* of Recapture Creek—not east, as some maps show). Local information should be obtained for backcountry trips.

St. Christopher's Episcopal Mission

Father Harold Lieber came to the Bluff area in 1943 and established this mission for the Navajo.

Relying on donations and volunteer help, he built a school, chapel, and other buildings. Visitors are welcome to the pleasant tree-shaded grounds; go east two miles on the paved road from the northeast edge of Bluff.

San Juan Footbridge and 14-Window Ruin

An easy walk of about two miles round-trip crosses a suspension bridge over the San Juan River and follows roads to this Anasazi cliff dwelling. From Bluff, drive east two miles on the paved road to St. Christopher's Episcopal Mission, continue straight 1.3 miles, and turn right a half mile on a dirt road (it may not be signed; keep right at a fork 0.1 mile in) to the footbridge. Walk across the bridge, follow dirt roads winding southeast about a half mile to a road running beneath the cliffs, turn right (west) a half mile, and look for the ruins in an alcove on the left. You can scramble up for a closer look, but don't enter the rooms—the ruins can easily be damaged. The walk passes farm lands on the Navajo Reservation; please resist the temptation to take shortcuts across the fields.

WEST OF BLANDING TO NATURAL BRIDGES NATIONAL MONUMENT

Utah 95 turns west from U.S. 191 four miles south of Blanding and crosses Comb Ridge, Cedar Mesa, and many canyons. Follow Highway 95 to Natural Bridges National Monument or continue on to Hite Marina, where a highway bridge crosses Lake Powell. Highway 261 turns south along Cedar Mesa before twisting down the hairpin curves of the Moki Dugway north of Mexican Hat (this section of the road is not paved).

Utah 276 turns off for Halls Crossing Marina and the car ferry across Lake Powell to Bullfrog Marina. At the junction of Highways 276 and 95, a large sign lists the departure times for the ferry service. Note that the times on the sign may be different than the times listed in the widely circulated flyer found in every tourist office. Confirm the departure times before making the 42-mile journey to Halls Crossing. For more information, see the sidebar "Crossing Lake Powell by Ferry" in the South-Central Utah chapter.

Fill up with gas before venturing out on Highway 95; you won't find any gas stations on the highway until Hanksville, which is 122 miles away. Hite and the other Lake Powell marinas do have gas and supplies, however.

Cedar Mesa and its canyons have an exceptionally large number of prehistoric Anasazi sites. Several groups of ruins lie just off the highway. Hikers will discover many more. If you would like to explore the Cedar Mesa area, drop in at the **Kane Gulch Ranger Station,** four miles south on Highway 261 from Highway 95. The BLM staff issues the permits required to explore the Cedar Mesa backcountry at $8 per person for overnight stays in Grand Gulch, Fish Creek Canyon, and Owl Creek Canyon. The number of people permitted to camp at a given time is limited, so call ahead; 435/587-1532. BLM people will also tell you about archaeological sites and their values, current hiking conditions, and locations of water. Day hikers will pay a $2 fee to hike certain sections of the monument. Check out www.blm.gov/utah/monticello for current information.

Butler Wash Ruins

Well-preserved pueblo ruins left by the Anasazi lie tucked under an overhang across the wash 11 miles west on Highway 95 (between mileposts 111 and 112) from U.S. 191. At the trailhead on the north side of the highway, follow cairns a half mile through juniper and piñon pine woodlands and across slickrock to the overlook.

Comb Ridge

Geologic forces have squeezed up the earth's crust in a long ridge running 80 miles south from the Abajo Peaks into Arizona. Sheer cliff faces plunge 800 feet into Comb Wash on the west side. Engineering the highway down these cliffs took considerable effort. A parking area near the top of the grade offers expansive panoramas across Comb Wash. The overlook is between mileposts 108 and 109, 2.5 miles west of Butler Wash Ruins. Scenic **jeep roads** between Highway 95 and U.S. 163 follow the west side of Comb Ridge through Comb Wash and the east side of Comb Ridge through Butler Wash. Another jeep road traces the route of the 1880 Mormon Hole-in-the-Rock Expedition between Highway 261 on Cedar Mesa and Comb Wash (a high-clearance vehicle is needed to go down, a four-wheel drive to go up).

In 1923, the West's last shoot-out between Native Americans and settlers took place in the Comb Ridge area. Conflicts between Utes and ranchers had simmered for 57 years, with whites taking the Utes' land and the Utes taking the settlers' livestock. A group of renegade Utes under Chief Posey fled to this rugged area, knowing that the Blanding posse would have great difficulty finding the few trails that existed then. The posse, however, caught up with the Utes, killing one of them. The disheartened Utes then surrendered. Old Chief Posey, who had been shot earlier in Blanding, evaded capture only to die of his wounds about a week later, alone in a cave. The event drew national attention to the plight of the tribe, which was later given the White Mesa Indian Reservation 12 miles south of Blanding.

Arch Canyon

This tributary canyon of Comb Wash has spectacular scenery and many Native American ruins. Much of the canyon can be seen on a day hike, but 2–3 days are needed to explore the upper reaches. The main streambeds usually have water (purify before drinking). To reach the trailhead, turn north 2.5 miles on a dirt road in Comb Wash (between mileposts 107 and 108 of Highway 95), go past a house and water tank, then park in a grove of cottonwood trees before a stream ford. This is also a good place to camp. The mouth of Arch Canyon lies just to the northwest (it's easy to miss!). Sign in at the register here. Look for a Native American ruin just up Arch Canyon on the right. More ruins lie tucked under alcoves farther upcanyon.

From the trailhead (elev. 5,200 feet), the canyon extends about 13 miles upstream into Elk Ridge and has several tributary canyons worth exploring. The first one is 2.5 miles up on the right; it goes 1.5 miles to a ruin and a spring. A second canyon on the right, six miles up the main canyon, also has a ruin and springs 1.5 miles up. Texas Canyon appears on the left 7.5 miles up (elev. 5,600 feet) in a grove of ponderosa pines; look across Arch Canyon from this junction to see a large arch. Texas Canyon goes back about five miles and has one fork. Continuing up Arch Canyon, you'll see a second arch on the right, then Butts Canyon on the right nine miles from the trailhead. From this point, Arch and Butts Canyons both extend about four miles to their heads (elev. 7,500 feet). Spring and autumn are the best times for hiking, though the upper reaches can be fine in summer, too. In late spring and early summer, arm yourself with long pants and insect repellent against the deer flies. Most of the route follows the canyon bottoms; sometimes off-road vehicles travel the lower few miles. See the 7.5-minute topos, the 1:100,000 Blanding map, or Trails Illustrated's Grand Gulch Plateau map. The BLM offices at Kane Gulch or Monticello can advise on hiking.

Arch Canyon Overlook

A road and short trail to the rim of Arch Canyon provide a beautiful view into the depths. Turn north four miles on Texas Flat Road (County 263) from Highway 95 between mileposts 102 and 103, park just before the road begins a steep climb, and walk east on an old jeep road about a quarter mile to the rim. This is a fine place for a picnic, although it has no facilities or guardrails. Texas Flat Road is dirt but okay when dry for cars with good clearance. Trucks can continue up the steep hill to other viewpoints of Arch and Texas Canyons.

Mule Canyon Ruin

Archaeologists have excavated and stabilized this Anasazi village on the gentle slope of Mule Canyon's South Fork. A stone kiva, circular tower, and 12-room structure can be seen, all originally connected by tunnels. Cave Towers, two miles to the southeast, would have been visible from the top of the tower here. Signs describe the ruin and periods of Anasazi development. Turn north 0.3 mile on a paved road from Highway 95 between mileposts 101 and 102. Hikers can explore other

Native American ruins in North and South Forks of Mule Canyon; check with the Kane Gulch Ranger Station for advice and directions. You might see pieces of pottery and other artifacts in this area. Please leave *every* piece in place so that future visitors can enjoy the discovery, too. Federal laws also prohibit removal of artifacts.

NATURAL BRIDGES NATIONAL MONUMENT

Streams in White Canyon and its tributaries cut deep canyons, then formed three impressive bridges. Silt-laden floodwaters sculpted the bridges by gouging tunnels between closely spaced loops in the meandering canyons. You can distinguish a natural bridge from an arch because the bridge spans a streambed and was initially carved out of the rock by flowing water. In the monument, these bridges illustrate three different stages of development, from the massive, newly formed Kachina Bridge to the middle-aged Sipapu Bridge, to the delicate and fragile span of Owachomo. All three natural bridges will continue to widen and eventually collapse under their own weight. A nine-mile scenic drive has overlooks of the picturesque bridges, Anasazi ruins, and the twisting canyons. You can follow short trails down from the rim to the base of each bridge or hike through all three bridges on an 8.6-mile trail loop. Paved highways allow easy access to the monument: From Blanding, drive 42 miles west on Highway 95; from Hite Marina, drive 50 miles southeast on Highway 95; from Halls Crossing Marina, drive 59 miles northeast on Highway 276; from Mexican Hat, drive 44 miles north via Highway 261 (there's a three-mile section of steep unpaved switchbacks). The National Park Service has a visitors center and a small campground.

History

Ruins, artifacts, and rock art indicate a long Native American occupation by tribes ranging from archaic groups to the Anasazi. Many fine cliff dwellings built by the Anasazi still stand. In 1883, prospector Cass Hite passed on tales of the huge stone bridges that he had discovered on a trip up White Canyon. Adventurous travelers, in-

cluding a 1904 *National Geographic* magazine expedition, visited this isolated region to marvel at the bridges. The public's desire for their protection led President Theodore Roosevelt to proclaim the area a national monument in 1908. Federal administrators then changed the original bridge names from Edwin, Augusta, and Caroline to the Hopi names used today. Although the Hopi never lived here, the Anasazi of White Canyon very likely have descendants in the modern Hopi villages in Arizona.

Visitors Center

From the signed junction on Highway 95, drive in 4.5 miles on Highway 275 to the visitors center (elev. 6,505 feet). Monument Valley Overlook, two miles in, has a panorama south across a vast expanse of piñon pine and juniper trees to Monument Valley and distant mountains. A slide show in the visitors center illustrates how geologic forces and erosion created the canyons and natural bridges. Exhibits introduce the tribes that once lived here, as well as the area's geology, wildlife, and plants. Outside in front, labels identify common plants of the monument. Rangers will answer your questions about the monument and surrounding area. If asked, staff will provide details on locations of ruins and rock-art sites. You can purchase regional books, topo and geologic maps, postcards, slides, and film. Checklists of birds, other wildlife, and plants are available, too. Hours at the visitors center are daily 8 A.M.–5 P.M. March–April and the month of October, 8 A.M.–6 P.M. May–September, and 9 A.M.–4:30 P.M. the rest of the year; closed holidays October–April. Admission is $6 per vehicle, or $3 per person or bicyclist. Bridge View Drive is always open during daylight hours except after heavy snowstorms. A winter visit can be very enjoyable; ice or mud often closes the steep Sipapu and Kachina Trails, but the short trail to Owachomo Bridge usually stays open. Pets aren't allowed on the trails or in the backcountry at any time. Address is P.O. Box 1, Natural Bridges, Lake Powell, UT 84533, 435/692-1234. The nearest accommodations and café are at Fry Canyon, 26 miles northwest of the visitors center on Highway 95; the closest gas is 40 miles east near Blanding or 50 west miles at Hite.

Photovoltaic Array

A large solar electric-power station sits across the road from the visitors center. This demonstration system, the largest in the world when constructed in 1980, has a quarter-million solar cells spread over nearly an acre and produces up to 100 kilowatts. Batteries, located elsewhere, store a two-day supply of power. The monument lies far from the nearest power lines, so the solar cells provide an alternative to continuous running of diesel-powered generators.

Natural Bridges Campground

Drive 0.3 mile past the visitors center and turn right into the campground, set in a forest of piñon pine and juniper. Sites stay open all year; $10. Obtain water from a faucet in front of the visitors center. Rangers give talks several evenings each week during the summer season. The campground is often full, but there is a designated overflow area near the intersection of Highway 95 and Highway 261. RVs or trailers more than 21 feet long will also have to use this parking area.

Bridge View Drive

The nine-mile drive begins its one-way loop just past the campground. You can stop for lunch at a picnic area. Allow about 90 minutes for a quick trip around. To make all the stops and do a bit of leisurely hiking will take most of a day. The crossbedded sandstone of the bridges and canyons is the 265-million-year-old Cedar Mesa Formation.

Sipapu Bridge viewpoint is two miles from the visitors center. The Hopi name refers to the gateway from which their ancestors entered this world from another world below. Sipapu Bridge has reached its mature or middle-aged stage of development. The bridge is the largest in the monument and has a span of 268 feet and a height of 220 feet. Many people think Sipapu the most magnificent of the bridges. Another view and a trail to the base of Sipapu are 0.8 mile farther. The viewpoint is about halfway down on an easy

trail; allow a half hour. A steeper and rougher trail branches off the viewpoint trail and winds down to the bottom of White Canyon, probably the best place to fully appreciate the bridge's size. Total round-trip distance is 1.2 miles with an elevation change of 600 feet.

Horse Collar Ruin, built by the Anasazi, looks as though it has been abandoned only a few decades, not 800 years. At 3.1 miles from the visitors center, a short trail leads to an overlook. The name comes from the shape of the doorway openings in two storage rooms. Hikers walking in the canyon between Sipapu and Kachina Bridges can scramble up a steep rock slope to the site. Like all ancient ruins, these are very fragile and must not be touched or entered. Only with such care will future generations of visitors be able to admire the well-preserved structures. Other groups of Anasazi dwellings can be seen in or near the monument too; ask a ranger for directions.

Kachina Bridge viewpoint and trailhead are 5.1 miles from the visitors center. The massive bridge has a span of 204 feet and a height of 210 feet. A trail, 1.5 miles round-trip, leads to the canyon bottom next to the bridge; elevation change is 650 feet. Look for pictographs near the base of the trail. Some of the figures resemble Hopi kachinas (spirits) and inspired the bridge's name. Armstrong Canyon joins White Canyon just downstream from the bridge; floods in each canyon abraded opposite sides of the rock fin that later became Kachina Bridge.

Owachomo Bridge viewpoint and trailhead are 7.1 miles from the visitors center. An easy walk leads to Owachomo's base—a half-mile round-trip with an elevation change of 180 feet. Graceful Owachomo spans 180 feet and is 106 feet high. Erosive forces have worn the venerable bridge to a thickness of only nine feet. Unlike the other two bridges, Owachomo spans a smaller tributary stream instead of a major canyon. Two streams played a role in the bridge's formation. Floods coming down the larger Armstrong Canyon surged against a sandstone fin on one side while floods in a small side canyon wore away the rock on the other side. Eventually a hole formed, and waters flowing down the side canyon took the shorter route through the bridge. The name Owachomo means "flat-rock mound" in the Hopi language; a large rock outcrop nearby inspired the name. Before construction of the present road, a trail winding down the opposite side of Armstrong Canyon provided the only access for monument visitors. The trail, little used now, connects with Highway 95.

Hiking

A canyon hike through all three bridges can be the highlight of a visit to the monument. Unmaintained trails make an 8.6-mile loop in White and Armstrong Canyons and cross a wooded plateau. The trip is easier if you start from Sipapu and come out the relatively gentle grades at Owachomo. Most people take 5–6 hours for this moderately difficult hike. You can save 2.5 miles by arranging a car shuttle between Sipapu and Owachomo Trailheads. Another option is to go in or out on the Kachina Bridge Trail midway, cutting the hiking distance about in half. On nearing Owachomo Bridge from below, a small sign points out the trail, which bypasses a deep pool. The canyons remain in their wild state; you'll need some hiking experience, water, proper footwear, compass, and map (the handout available at the visitors center is adequate). The USGS 7.5-minute topo maps also cover this area. When hiking in the canyons, keep an eye out for natural arches and Native American writings. Please don't step on midget faded rattlesnakes or other living entities (such as the fragile cryptobiotic soil). Be aware of flash-flood dangers, especially if you see big clouds billowing in the sky in an upstream direction. You don't need a hiking permit, though it's a good idea to talk beforehand with a ranger to find out current conditions. Overnight camping within the monument is permitted only in the campground. Backpackers, however, can go up or down the canyons and camp outside the monument boundaries. Just be careful to choose high ground in case a flood comes rumbling through! Note that vehicles can't be parked overnight on the loop drive.

VICINITY OF NATURAL BRIDGES NATIONAL MONUMENT

Fry Canyon Lodge

The store here originally served uranium mining camps during the 1950s. Today this venerable café and motel, 435/259-5334, www.frycanyon.com, offer the only services on Highway 95 between Blanding and Hite Marina. Rooms cost $75–90. In winter, the café may be closed, but accommodations are usually still available. Two Anasazi ruins can be viewed nearby; a road goes to an overlook of one ruin and a short trail goes to the other. Ask for directions. Fry Canyon is 19 miles northwest of the Natural Bridges National Monument turnoff and 24 miles southeast of the Hite Marina turnoff.

Dark Canyon

This magnificent canyon system lies about 15 air miles north of Natural Bridges National Monument. Dark Canyon, with its many tributaries, begins in the high country of Elk Ridge and extends west to Lake Powell in lower Cataract Canyon. Steep cliffs and the isolated location have protected the relatively pristine environment. The upper canyons tend to be wide with open areas and groves of Douglas fir and ponderosa pine. Creeks dry up after spring snowmelt, leaving only widely scattered springs as water sources for most of the year. Farther downstream, the canyon walls close in and the desert trees of piñon pine, juniper, and cottonwood take over. At its lower end, Dark Canyon has a year-round stream and deep plunge pools; cliffs tower more than 1,400 feet above the canyon floor. Springs and running water attract wildlife, including bighorn sheep, black bear, deer, mountain lion, coyote, bobcat, ringtail cat, raccoon, fox, and spotted skunk.

Experienced hikers enjoy the solitude, wildlife, Anasazi ruins, and varied canyon scenery. Although it's possible to visit Dark Canyon on a day hike, it takes several days to get a feel for this area. To explore the entire canyon and its major tributaries would take weeks! Hiking through the canyons is mostly easy, though strenuous scrambles are needed to bypass a few pour-offs and other obstacles. Elevations of Dark Canyon range from 8,200 feet at its upper end to 3,700 feet at Lake Powell. Hikers must be extra cautious and self-sufficient, because outside help can be days away. Check with people at the BLM or U.S. Forest Service offices before a trip. Horses can do the trails in the upper (National Forest) section but not in the constricted lower canyon. Maps available are the 7.5-minute topos, the 1:100,000 Hite Crossing and Blanding maps, and Trails Illustrated's map of the Abajos and Dark Canyon. Or look for the *Dark Canyon Trail Guide,* published by Canyonlands Natural History Association.

The upper half of the canyon system lies within Dark Canyon Wilderness, administered by the Manti–La Sal National Forest, P.O. Box 820, Monticello, UT 84535, 435/587-2041. The Monticello office has information sheets on the 10 access trails to Dark Canyon and can advise on road conditions to the trailheads. Loop hikes can be made in the tributary canyons. Woodenshoe Canyon is used by more than 50 percent of visitors to the area. Snow and mud usually block roads, all of which are unpaved, until mid-May or early June. When the roads are closed, hikers sometimes drive to Bears Ears Pass and hike to their trailhead. Spring through autumn are good hiking seasons in the higher country, though snowmelt sometimes causes spring flooding.

The lower half of Dark Canyon, currently designated a primitive area, lies mostly within BLM land; the area is a candidate for wilderness status. Trail notes describing hiking conditions, water sources, trailheads, and wilderness etiquette are available from the BLM offices at Kane Gulch Ranger Station (trailhead for Grand Gulch) or Monticello (435 N. Main, Monticello, UT 84535, 435/587-1500). Obtain a $2 day trip, $8 overnight permit from the BLM before visiting its lands.

The **Sundance Trail** is the most popular entry to lower Dark Canyon. The start of the trail can be reached on dirt roads that branch off Highway 95 southeast of the Hite Marina turnoff; this approach can be used year-round in dry weather. Cairns mark the trail, which drops 1,200 feet in less than one mile on a steep talus slope. Boaters can reach the lower end of Dark Canyon in Glen Canyon National Recreation Area by going 14 miles up Lake Powell from Hite Marina. The lower canyon can be hiked year-round, with spring and autumn the best choices.

Grand Gulch Primitive Area

Within this twisting canyon system lies some of the most captivating scenery and largest concentrations of Anasazi ruins in all of southeastern Utah. The main canyon begins only about six miles southeast of Natural Bridges National Monument. From an elevation of 6,400 feet, Grand Gulch cuts deeply into Cedar Mesa on a tortuous path southwest to the San Juan River, dropping 2,700 feet in about 53 miles. Sheer cliffs, alcoves, pinnacles, Anasazi cliff dwellings, rock-art sites, arches, and a few natural bridges line Grand Gulch and its many tributaries. Canyon depths reach 600 feet. Nearly all of Grand Gulch has been cut out of Cedar Mesa sandstone. The lower 1.5 miles of canyon also reveal exposures of the older Cutler Formation (Halgaito Shale Member) and the Honaker Trail Formation. Wildlife to look for include mule deer, mountain lion, black bear, coyote, bobcat, fox, ringtail cat, spotted skunk, cottontail, white-tailed antelope squirrel, white-throated wood rat, Ord kangaroo rat, piñon mouse, Great Basin gopher snake, Hopi rattlesnake, and midget faded rattlesnake. Some birds in the area are red-tailed hawk, great horned owl, peregrine falcon, mourning dove, titmouse, rock wren, and piñon jay. Vegetation includes piñon pine, juniper, cottonwood, Gambel oak, singleleaf ash, willow, sagebrush, blackbrush, rabbitbrush, prickly pear cactus, and flowering annuals.

The Anasazi left behind hundreds of dwellings and thousands of pictographs and petroglyphs. They lived in Grand Gulch A.D. 200–400 (Basketmaker II), 650–725 (late Basketmaker III), and 1060–1270 (Pueblo II–III); droughts may have caused all three departures. Mormon pioneers of the Hole-in-the-Rock Expedition named the canyon in 1880, but the exhausted group was in no mood to enjoy the scenery.

Kane Gulch and Bullet Canyon provide access to the upper end of Grand Gulch from the east side. A popular loop hike using these canyons is 23 miles long (3–4 days); arrange a 7.5-mile car shuttle or hitch. Ask at the ranger station if a shuttle service is available. Collins Canyon, reached from Collins Spring Trailhead, leads into lower Grand Gulch from the west side. Hiking distance between Kane Gulch and Collins Spring Trailheads is 38 miles one-way (5–7 days). A car shuttle of about 29 miles (including eight miles of dirt road) is needed. River runners can travel up the mouth from the San Juan River. The San Juan is 53 miles from Kane Gulch Trailhead and 19 miles from Collins Spring Trailhead. The lower third of Grand Gulch (below Collins Canyon) lacks the abundant Anasazi sites found in the middle and upper reaches and has few water sources.

The book *Wind in the Rock,* by Ann Zwinger, presents a personal account of the wonders of travel in Grand Gulch and nearby canyons. Spring and autumn are the choice times for hiking; it is also possible in summer, though you'll want to sit out the midday heat. Winter snow makes some of the slickrock sections hazardous. Be sure to visit the BLM's Kane Gulch Ranger Station or Monticello office for a permit and information. You must have a day-use ($2) or overnight camping permit ($8) to enter the area. The BLM map of Grand Gulch Primitive Area shows the topography, mileages for each section of canyon, and major points of interest; it's good for both planning a trip and using while hiking. Other maps include the 7.5-minute, 1:100,000 metric, and Trails Illustrated's Grand Gulch Plateau topos. Springs provide water in most parts of Grand Gulch but aren't always reliable, especially in summer; the BLM staff can give you an idea of what to expect. "Innocent vandalism" caused by visitors touching and climbing on the ruins and middens has caused serious damage. BLM staff will offer advice and literature on how to safely visit the ancient sites. Pot hunting has been another problem; report any suspicious behavior to the BLM. Grand Gulch receives heavy use, so respecting the ruins and camping without leaving any traces are extra important.

Kane Gulch Ranger Station

The BLM provides permits, archaeological information, current hiking conditions, literature, and sales of maps and books at this bare-bones facility. (Try to get maps in advance as rangers are sometimes out on patrol.) The station is at Kane Gulch Trailhead, four miles south on Highway 261 from Highway 95; open daily, dependably 8 A.M.–noon early March–late November. No telephone, water, or trash collection is available. Normally this is the best place for firsthand information. You can also visit the BLM office at 435 N. Main in Monticello (P.O. Box 7, Monticello, UT 84535), 435/587-1500. Open year-round Monday–Friday 7:45 A.M.–4:30 P.M. Everyone visiting the Cedar Mesa backcountry should drop in for the required permit and to get the latest information. Permits run $5 per person for overnight camping and are limited to 12 persons. Note that groups of eight or more people with pack animals need to obtain permits at least three weeks beforehand from the ranger station or office. Help protect fragile desert soils by keeping all vehicles—including mountain bikes—on established roads. Campfires are not permitted in the canyons.

Fish Creek and Owl Creek Loop Hike

Varied canyon scenery, year-round pools, Anasazi ruins, and a magnificent natural arch make this an excellent hike. Fish Creek and its tributary Owl Creek lie east of Grand Gulch on the other side of Highway 261. A 1.5-mile trail atop Cedar Mesa connects upper arms of the two creeks to make a 15.5-mile loop. From the trailhead (elev. 6,160 feet), the path descends 1,400 feet to the junction of the two creeks. Opinions differ as to which direction to begin the loop, but either way is fine. Owl Creek might be the better choice for a day hike because it's closer to the trailhead and has the added attractions of easily accessible ruins just a half mile away and Nevill's Arch 3.5 miles farther (one-way). Contact the Kane Gulch or Monticello BLM offices for trail notes and current trail and water conditions. Permits cost $2 for day trips, $8 for overnight trips. Maps are essential for navigation, because it's easy to get off the route in some places. The BLM trail notes have a topo map. Camping places are easy to locate; just avoid washes. You can always find at least intermittent water in the upper parts of both creeks.

The canyons have been carved in Cedar Mesa sandstone, which forms many overhangs where the Anasazi built cliff dwellings. Unfortunately, nearly all ruins sit high in the cliffs and can be hard to spot from the canyon bottoms (canyon depths average 500 feet). Binoculars come in handy for seeing the ruins, some of which are marked on the topo maps. Climbing equipment may not be used to reach the ruins.

The turnoff for the trailhead is between mileposts 27 and 28 of Highway 261, one mile south of Kane Gulch Ranger Station. Head east 5.2 miles on San Juan County 253, passable by cars when dry, to a parking area at the site of an old drill hole. A sign points the way north 1.5 miles to Fish Creek and southeast a quarter mile to Owl Creek. Cairns show the way into the canyons, then you just follow the creekbeds. The route into Fish Creek goes north 1.5 miles across the mesa from the trailhead (watch closely for cairns—it's easy to miss the trail where it climbs out of a wash), makes a steep descent into an arm of Fish Creek, and follows Fish Creek downstream to the confluence with Owl Creek; total distance from the trailhead to this point is nine miles one-way. Turn right 2.5 miles up Owl Creek, normally dry in this section, to Nevill's Arch. It's possible to rock-scramble up the slope to the window of the arch, where you'll enjoy fine views of the canyons and beyond. Owl Creek has water and becomes prettier and prettier as you head upstream. On the four miles from the arch to the trailhead, you'll need to circumvent three pour-offs—the first and second by going around to the right, the third by going to the left (look for the cairned routes). The first and second pour-offs have small waterfalls and idyllic pools. Above the third pour-off, you'll pass a well-preserved group of Anasazi ruins on the left. From here there's only a short but steep scramble to the rim, then a quarter mile across slickrock back to the trailhead.

Slickhorn Canyon

Adventurous hikers enjoy the Native American ruins and impressive scenery in this rugged canyon south of Grand Gulch. Canyon depths along Slickhorn's 12-mile length range from about 300 feet in the northern reaches to 800 feet near the confluence with the San Juan River. Boulders, talus slopes, and pour-offs in the streambed hamper travel and discourage casual visitors. Allow about four days to explore Slickhorn Canyon and some of its tributaries. A more ambitious trip is to go down Slickhorn to the San Juan River, hike downstream along a high, narrow ledge to the mouth of Grand Gulch, then travel up to one of the Grand Gulch trailheads in a week or more of hiking. The BLM offices at Kane Gulch and Monticello have information sheets, trailhead information, and a map; overnight permits are $8. The BLM's Grand Gulch hiking map covers this area. Several trailheads can be reached by turning west on an unpaved road from Highway 261 opposite the signed Cigarette Springs Road, 9.4 miles south of the Kane Gulch Ranger Station.

John's Canyon

This varied canyon lies southeast of Grand Gulch and Slickhorn Canyons. A fingerlike network of deep narrow canyons in the upper drainages contrasts with a broad alluvial bottom downstream that's up to a mile wide. The main canyon is about 13 miles long and empties into the San Juan River. Canyon depths average about 1,000 feet. Experienced hikers will find the going relatively easy, as there are only a few boulder falls and small pour-offs in the upper canyons. High pour-offs in the lower canyon, however, effectively block access to the San Juan River. A map and information sheet available from the BLM offices have trailhead and spring information and a brief description of hiking in the canyon. Cliffs and overhangs on the rim in the north restrict access to only a few points; the BLM map shows one entry point, reached by a short dirt road off Highway 261. In the south, a jeep road branches off Highway 316 (the road to Goosenecks State Park), follows the rim of the San Juan River west, and then turns up into middle John's Canyon.

MEXICAN HAT

Spectacular geology surrounds this tiny community perched on the north bank of the San

Juan River. Folded layers of red and gray rock stand out dramatically. Alhambra Rock, a jagged remnant of a volcano, marks the southern approach to Mexican Hat. Another rock, which looks just like an upside-down sombrero, gave Mexican Hat its name; you'll see this formation two miles north of town. The land has never proved good for much except its scenery; farmers and ranchers thought it next to worthless. Stories of gold in the San Juan River brought a frenzy of prospecting 1892–1893, but the mining proved mostly a bust. Oil, first struck by drillers in 1908, has brought mostly modest profits. The uranium mill across the river at Halchita gave a boost to the economy from 1956 until it closed in 1965. Mexican Hat now serves as a modest trade and tourism center. Monument Valley, Valley of the Gods Scenic Drive, Goosenecks State Park, and Grand Gulch Primitive Area lie only short drives away. The shore near town can be a busy place in summer as river runners on the San Juan put in, take out, or just stop for ice and beer.

Accommodations

$50–75: The **San Juan Inn & Trading Post,** at a dramatic location above the river just west of town, 435/683-2220 or 800/447-2022, offers rooms, Native American trade goods, and a restaurant, the **Olde Bridge Bar and Grill,** 435/683-2220, serving American, Mexican, and Navajo food daily for breakfast, lunch, and dinner. **Canyonlands Motel,** 435/683-2230, offers recently remodeled rooms; closed in winter. **Mexican Hat Lodge,** 435/683-2222, offers rooms, a pool, and a restaurant (American food daily for lunch and dinner). **Burch's Motel,** 435/683-2221, has motel rooms and a café with American, Mexican, and Navajo food (open daily for breakfast, lunch, and dinner), Native American crafts, groceries, and car shuttles.

Campgrounds: In addition to rooms, **Burch's Motel,** above, has tent camping for $12, and RV sites for $18 with hookups. **Valle's Trading Post and RV Park,** 435/683-2226, open all year, has tent and RV sites with hookups for $12. The trading post offers crafts, groceries, showers, vehicle storage, and car shuttles. **Burch's Cattle Co.** offers horseback riding, 435/683-2221.

VICINITY OF MEXICAN HAT
Valley of the Gods

Great sandstone monoliths, delicate spires, and long rock fins rise from the broad valley. This strange red-rock landscape resembles better-known Monument Valley but on a smaller scale. A 17-mile dirt road winds through the spectacular scenery. Cars can usually travel the road at low speeds if the weather is dry (washes are crossed). Allow 1–1.5 hours for the drive. The east end of the road connects with U.S. 163 at milepost 29 (7.5 miles northeast of Mexican Hat or 15 miles southwest of Bluff); the west end connects with Highway 261 just below the Moki Dugway switchbacks (four miles north of Mexican Hat on U.S. 163, then 6.6 miles northwest on Highway 261).

Goosenecks State Park

The San Juan River winds through a series of incredibly tight bends 1,000 feet below. So closely spaced are the bends that the river takes six miles to cover an air distance of only 1.5 miles! The bends and exposed rock layers form exquisitely graceful curves. Geologists know the site as a classic example of entrenched meanders, caused by gradual uplift of a formerly level plain. Signs at the overlook explain the geologic history and identify the rock formations. Goosenecks State Park is an undeveloped area with a few tables and vault toilets the only facilities. Camping is available; no water or charge. From the junction of U.S. 163 and Highway 261, four miles north of Mexican Hat, go one mile northwest on Highway 261, then turn left three miles on Highway 316 to its end.

Muley Point Overlook

One of the great views in the Southwest lies just a short drive from Goosenecks State Park and more than 1,000 feet higher. Although the view of the Goosenecks below is less dramatic than at the state park, the 6,200-foot elevation provides a magnificent panorama across the Navajo Indian Reservation to Monument Valley and countless canyons and mountains. To get here, travel northwest nine miles on Highway 261 from the Goosenecks turnoff. At the top of the Moki

Dugway switchbacks (an 1,100-foot climb on gravel roads with sharp curves and 5–10 percent grades), turn left (southwest) 5.3 miles on gravel County Road 241 (the turnoff may not be signed) and follow it toward the point. This road is not suitable for wet-weather travel.

MONUMENT VALLEY

Towering buttes, jagged pinnacles, and rippled sand dunes make this an otherworldly landscape. Changing colors and shifting shadows during the day add to the enchantment. Most of the natural monuments are remnants of sandstone eroded by wind and water. Agathla Peak and some lesser summits are roots of ancient volcanoes, whose dark rock contrasts with the pale yellow sandstone of the other formations. The valley lies at an elevation of 5,564 feet in the Upper Sonoran Life Zone; annual rainfall averages about 8.5 inches.

In 1863–1864, when Kit Carson was ravaging Canyon de Chelly in Arizona to round up the Navajo, Chief Hoskinini led his people to the safety and freedom of Monument Valley. Merrick Butte and Mitchell Mesa commemorate two miners who discovered rich silver deposits on their first trip to the valley in 1880. On their second trip both were killed, reportedly shot by Paiutes. Hollywood movies made the splendor of Monument Valley known to the outside world. *Stagecoach,* filmed here in 1938 and directed by John Ford, became the first in a series of Westerns that has continued to the present. John Wayne and many other movie greats rode across these sands.

The Navajo have preserved the valley as a tribal park with a scenic drive, visitors center, and campground. From Mexican Hat, drive 22 miles southwest on U.S. 163 and turn left 3.5 miles to the visitors center. From Kayenta, go 24 miles north on U.S. 163 and turn right 3.5 miles. At the junction of U.S. 163 is a village-worth of outdoor market stalls, where you can stop to buy Navajo art and crafts.

Visitors Center

An information desk, exhibits, and a crafts shop are open daily 8 A.M.–7 P.M. May–September,

then daily 8 A.M.–5 P.M. the rest of the year; 435/727-3287. Visitors pay a $5 fee ($2 ages 60 and over, free for six and under), collected on the entrance road. Be prepared to run a gauntlet of Navajo entrepreneurs who will meet you at your car to offer you jeep or horseback tours of the monument for varying amounts of money.

Monument Valley Drive

A 17-mile, self-guided scenic drive begins at the visitors center and loops through the heart of the valley. Overlooks provide sweeping views from different vantage points. The dirt road is normally okay for cautiously driven cars. Avoid stopping and becoming stuck in the loose sand that sometimes blows across the road. Allow 90 minutes for the drive; open 8 A.M.–7 P.M. in summer and 8 A.M.–5 P.M. the rest of the year. No hiking or driving is allowed off the signed route. Water and restrooms are available only at the visitors center.

Valley Tours

Take one of several guided tours leaving daily year-round from the visitors center to visit sites such as a hogan, a cliff dwelling, and petroglyphs in areas beyond the self-guided drive. The trips last 2.5–3 hours and cost $20–32 per person. Guided horseback rides from near the visitors center cost around $20 for an hour; longer day and overnight trips can be arranged too. If you'd like to hike in Monument Valley, you must hire a guide; hiking tours of two hours to a day or more can be arranged at the visitors center.

Campgrounds

Sites at **Mitten View Campground** near the visitors center cost $14; coin-operated hot showers are available. The season is mid-March–mid-October. Tenters should be prepared for winds in this exposed location. Goulding's Lodge has the nearest motel, restaurant, and store. Motels are also found at Kayenta in Arizona and Mexican Hat and Bluff in Utah.

Goulding's Lodge and Trading Post

This is by far the nicest place to stay in the Monument Valley area, though it's not cheap. Harry Goulding and his wife Mike opened this dramatically located trading post in 1924. It's tucked under the rimrocks two miles west of the U.S. 163 Monument Valley turnoff, just north of the Arizona-Utah border.

Goulding's Museum, in the old trading post building, displays prehistoric and modern artifacts, movie photos, and memorabilia of the Goulding family. Open daily, but may close in winter; admission by donation. Modern motel rooms, most with incredible views of Monument Valley, start at $160 in summer, less off season; guests can use a small indoor pool; meals are available in the dining room. A gift shop sells souvenirs, books, and high-quality Native American crafts. The nearby store has groceries and gas pumps. Monument Valley tours operate year-round; $32 half day, $70 full day, with a six-person minimum (children under 12 go at half price). Horseback riding is also available. The lodge stays open all year. For accommodation and tour info, write P.O. Box 360001, Monument Valley, UT 84536, 435/727-3231 or 800/874-0902.

Monument Valley Campground, 435/727-3235, offers tent and RV sites a short drive west; rates are $14 tents, $22 RVs with hookups. Open April–October. The Seventh-Day Adventist Church runs a hospital and mission nearby.

FOUR CORNERS MONUMENT

A concrete slab marks the point where Utah, Colorado, New Mexico, and Arizona meet. It's the only spot in the United States where you can put your finger on four states at once. Over 2,000 people a day are said to stop at the marker in the summer season. Average stay?—7–10 minutes. On the other hand, five national parks and 18 national monuments are within a radius of 150 miles from this point! Native Americans, mostly Navajo with perhaps some Ute and Pueblo, set up dozens of craft and refreshment booths in summer. Navajo Parks and Recreation collects a $2 per vehicle ($1 motorcycle) fee during the tourist season.

KAYENTA

The "Gateway to Monument Valley" is a town of 5,200 in a bleak, windswept valley (elev. 5,660 feet) in Arizona. Its name is loosely derived from the Navajo word Teehindeeh, meaning "bog hole," as there were once shallow lakes here. Kayenta, a handy stop for travelers, has several good motels and restaurants.

Shopping and Tours

Look for **Native American crafts** at the motels, Lee's Trading Co. (in the Kayenta shopping center), and Burch's Indian Room (near Wetherill Inn). **Tours** in four-wheel-drive vehicles to Monument Valley and surrounding country can be arranged from both motels; costs start at about $50 half day or $80 full day, with a minimum of 4–6 persons.

Accommodations

$75–100: One mile north of U.S. 160, **Best Western Wetherill Inn** is in the center of town on U.S. 163, 520/697-3231. Its name honors John Wetherill, an early trader and rancher of the region who discovered Betatakin, Mesa Verde, and other major Anasazi sites. The new adobe-style **Hampton Inn,** on U.S. 160, 520/697-3170 or 800/426-7866, has a pool and very nicely furnished rooms.

$100–125: The **Holiday Inn,** on U.S. 160 at the turnoff for Kayenta, 520/697-3221 or 800/HOLIDAY, has expansive rooms, a restaurant, and pool.

Food

The **Holiday Inn**'s restaurant, 520/697-3221, has good Navajo tacos and standard American fare; open daily for breakfast, lunch, and dinner. The **Blue Coffee Pot,** 520/697-3396, is nearby on the other side of the highway; open daily for breakfast, lunch, and dinner. **Golden Sands Cafe,** near the Wetherill Inn, 520/697-3684, offers American food daily for breakfast, lunch, and dinner.

Resources

Suggested Reading

Description and Travel

Angus, Mark. *Salt Lake City Underfoot.* Salt Lake City: Signature Books, 1996. Walkers' Guide to Salt Lake City history and neighborhoods.

Bannan, Jan Gumprecht. *Utah State Parks: A Complete Recreational Guide.* Seattle: Mountaineers Books, 1995. A guide to all of Utah's state parks, complete with maps, hiking routes, campground evaluations, and other recreational information.

Barnes, F. A. *Canyon Country Off-Road Vehicle Trails.* Moab: Arch Hunter Books. A series of backcountry driving guides to the canyon areas of southern and eastern Utah. This series originally had over 25 slim volumes, but only seven are currently in print (many are still available locally in Utah bookstores). Current volumes cover Arches and La Sal areas, the Maze, Needles, Island and Canyon Rims areas in Canyonlands National Park (three books), and a volume dedicated to the Moab area.

Barnes, F. A., and M. M. Barnes. *Cameo Cliffs: Biking-Hiking-Four-Wheeling.* Moab: Arch Country Books, 1992. Canyons, arches, and panoramas attract visitors to this little-known area east of U.S. 191. Author Fran Barnes named the area Cameo Cliffs because the pink cliffs reminded him of an old-fashioned pink-and-white cameo locket. (You're not likely to see this unofficial name on maps, however.) Barnes describes the area, divided by Highway 46 into Cameo Cliffs North and South, in this small guidebook and separate map of the same name.

Barnes, F. A., and M. M. Barnes. *Canyon Country's Canyon Rims Recreation Area.* Moab: Arch Hunter Books, 1992. Comprehensive, large-format guide to this vast area south and east of

Canyonlands National Park—or, as the author's subtitle explains, "The rest of Canyonlands National Park. Park-quality land that was left out of Canyonlands National Park." You'll find good background information on geology, flora, fauna, archaeology, and history. Practical advice will help you prepare for this remote region and enjoy the viewpoints, scenic drives, hiking, and mountain biking. Well-illustrated with black-and-white photos, but you'll need the separate *Off-Road Vehicle Trail Map: Canyon Rims Recreation Area* to follow the road and trail descriptions.

Benchmark Maps. *Utah Road & Recreation Atlas.* Medford, OR: Benchmark Maps, 2002. Shaded relief maps emphasize landforms, and recreational information is abundant. Use it to locate campgrounds, back roads, and major trailheads, though there's not enough detail to rely on it for hiking.

Bezy, John. *Bryce Canyon: The Story Behind the Scenery.* Las Vegas: KC Publications, Inc., 1988. Large color photos illustrate Bryce's creation, wonderful erosion forms, winter scenery, history, wildlife, and flora.

Bickers, Jack. *The Labyrinth Rims: 60 Accesses to Green River Overlooks.* 4-WD Trailguide Publications, 1989. Maps and descriptions lead you to more than 60 overlooks in this deep, meandering canyon between the town of Green River and the confluence of the Green and Colorado Rivers.

Carr, Stephen L. *The Historical Guide to Utah Ghost Towns.* Salt Lake City: Western Epics, 1987. Excellent book about Utah's fading ghosts. The historic photos, well-written text, good directions, and maps will add to the pleasure of back-road travel. Check for this at a library, as it's hard to find.

Casey, Robert L. *A Journey to the High South-west*. Old Saybrook, CT: Globe Pequot Press, 2000. Introduction, history, and travel in southern Utah and adjacent Arizona, New Mexico, and Colorado.

Cunningham, Bill and Polly Burke. *Wild Utah*. Helena, MT: Falcon Publishing Company, 1998. Utah contains more than a million acres of legally protected wilderness. This book provides the information needed to get off the beaten track and into 45 different roadless areas. The authors' comprehensive descriptions thoroughly discuss the land, ecosystems and habitats, and opportunities for exploration and recreation.

Eardley, A. J., and James W. Schaack. *Zion: The Story Behind the Scenery*. Las Vegas: KC Publications, 1992. Large color photos illustrate descriptions of Zion's rock layers, canyons, prehistoric peoples, settlers, and ecology.

Hagood, Allen. *Dinosaur: The Story Behind the Scenery*. Las Vegas: KC Publications, 1990. Introduction to the dinosaurs, fossil excavation, geology, and canyons of Dinosaur National Monument in northeastern Utah; has 65 color photos.

Huegel, Tony. *Utah Byways: 65 Backcountry Drives for the Whole Family, including Moab, Canyonlands, Arches, Capitol Reef, San Rafael Swell and Glen Canyon*. Wilderness Press, 2000. If you're looking for off-highway adventure, then this is your guide. The book includes detailed directions, human and natural history, outstanding photography, full-page maps for each of the 65 routes, and an extensive how-to chapter for beginners.

Kerig, Bill. *Underground Utah: Guide to Real Fun*. Boulder, CO: Mountain Sports Press, 2001. If you thought Utah was entirely staid and conservative, check out this engaging book.

McClenahan, Owen. *Utah's Scenic San Rafael*. Self-published (P.O. Box 892, Castle Dale, UT 84513), 1986. The author, a local "desert rat," takes you on driving tours through the scenic San Rafael region of east-central Utah. About half the trips can be done by car; the others need high clearance or four-wheel drive.

Porter, Eliot. *The Place No One Knew: Glen Canyon on the Colorado*. San Francisco: Sierra Club Books, 2000. Beautiful color photos show a world now lost to the waters of Lake Powell. Thoughtful quotations from many individuals accompany the illustrations.

Powell, Allan Kent. *The Utah Guide*. Golden, CO: Fulcrum Publications, 1995. Comprehensive and well-written guide to the state, with strong historical bent.

Roylance, Ward J. *Utah: A Guide to the State*. Utah: A Guide to the State Foundation, 1982. An updated version of the book published by the W.P.A. Writers Program in 1941. Much of the original material and format have been preserved. The comprehensive introduction to Utah's people and history is followed by 11 tours of the state.

Rutter, Michael J. *Fun with the Family in Utah: Hundreds of Ideas for Day Trips with the Kids*. Old Saybrook, CT: Globe Pequot Press, 2000. Comprehensive guide to events, recreation, history, and activities with the family in mind.

Sierra Club. *Desert Southwest: the Sierra Club Guides to the National Parks*. New York: Random House, 1996. Beautiful color photos illustrate the wildlife and scenic beauties of Utah's five national parks. The other parks described are Mesa Verde in Colorado, Grand Canyon and Petrified Forest in Arizona, Carlsbad Caverns in New Mexico, and Guadalupe Mountains and Big Bend in Texas. The text tells of the history, geology, wildlife, and flora. Maps and trail descriptions show hiking possibilities.

Stegner, Wallace, ed. *This Is Dinosaur: Echo Park Country and Its Magic Rivers.* Niwot, CO: Roberts Rinehart, Inc., 1985. Essays on this rugged land—its geology, dinosaurs, wildlife, Native Americans, explorers, river-running, and visiting Dinosaur National Monument.

Utah Division of Wildlife Resources. *Lakes of the High Uintas.* Utah Division of Wildlife Resources (1596 W. North Temple, Salt Lake City, UT 84116), 1981–1985. Anglers headed for the Uintas will find this series of 10 booklets of detailed lake descriptions very useful. Also has practical advice on camping, hiking, and horse travel.

Utah Writers' Program of the Work Projects Administration. *Utah: A Guide to the State.* Hastings House, 1941. This classic guidebook to Utah still makes good reading. A lengthy introduction followed by detailed descriptions of towns and natural features provide rich historical background. The book offers a look at Utah before the postwar industrialization. Although it is out of print, libraries usually have a copy, and some used bookstores carry it. Much of the material has been incorporated in the 1982 guide of the same name by Ward J. Roylance.

Wharton, Gayen and Tom. *Foghorn Outdoors Utah Camping.* Emeryville, CA: Avalon Travel Publishing, 2001. The best guide to public and private campgrounds across the state. A great resource if you're planning on doing any backcountry exploration.

Wharton, Tom. *Utah! A Family Travel Guide.* Salt Lake City: Wasatch Publishers, Inc., 1999. How to enjoy Utah's great outdoors with the kids. Also suggests museums, parks, and ski areas that the younger set will like. The well-illustrated guide contains many clever bits of wisdom.

Zwinger, Ann. *Wind in the Rock: the Canyonlands of Southeastern Utah.* Tucson: University of Arizona Press, 1986. Well-written accounts of hiking in the Grand Gulch and nearby canyons. The author tells of the area's history, archaeology, wildlife, and plants.

Hiking, Bicycling, Skiing, and Climbing

Adkison, Ron. *Best Easy Day Hikes Grand Staircase–Escalante and the Glen Canyon Region.* Helena, MT: Falcon Publishing Company, 1998. Features 19 hikes in south-central Utah Canyon Country, including the Grand Staircase–Escalante National Monument; also includes Paria Canyon.

Adkison, Ron. *Hiking Grand Staircase–Escalante and the Glen Canyon Region.* Helena, MT: Falcon Publishing Company, 1998. The vast Escalante/Glen Canyon area of southern Utah is nearly roadless, and hiking is about the only way you'll have a chance to visit these beautiful and austere canyons. This guide includes detailed information on 59 hikes, including Paria Canyon and Grand Gulch, in addition to the Grand Staircase–Escalante National Monument.

Allen, Steve. *Canyoneering the San Rafael Swell.* Salt Lake City: University of Utah Press, 1992. Eight chapters each cover a different area of this exceptional, though little-known, canyon country. Trail and route descriptions cover adventures from easy rambles to challenging hikes. The author provides some climbing notes, too. Detailed road logs help you get there, whether by mountain bike, car, or truck.

Barnes, F. A. *Canyon Country Hiking and Natural History.* Salt Lake City: Wasatch Publishers, Inc., 1977. Introduction to the delights of hiking amongst the canyons and mountains in southeastern Utah.

Barnes, F. A. *Canyon Country Slickrock Hiking and Biking.* Moab: Canyon Country Publications, 1990. "An illustrated guide to a completely different kind of hiking and mountain biking in the canyon country of southeastern Utah." A good introduction, areas to explore, personal anecdotes, and many black-and-white photos make this book fun to read and use.

Barnes, F. A. *Hiking the Historic Route of the 1859 Macomb Expedition.* Moab: Canyon Country Publications, 1989. Captain John Macomb led the first expedition to explore and write about what's now Canyonlands National Park. Adventurous hikers can retrace part of Macomb's route, thanks to the descriptions, maps, and photos in this little guide.

Barnes, F. A., and Tom Kuehne. *Canyon Country Mountain Biking.* Moab: Canyon Country Publications, 1988. Authors tell how to get the most out of biking the canyon country of southeastern Utah. Trail descriptions take you through Arches and Canyonlands National Parks, the La Sal Mountains, and Canyon Rims Recreation Area.

Bomka, Gregg. *Mountain Biking Utah.* Helena, MT: Falcon Publishing Company, 1999. Detailed route descriptions of over 100 rides, from the Salt Lake City area through Moab and Brian Head. Easy-to-use maps and elevation profiles included.

Brereton, Thomas, and James Dunaway. *Exploring the Backcountry of Zion National Park: Off Trail Routes.* Fredonia, AZ: Zion Natural History Association, 1988. Leave the crowds behind and discover Zion's backcountry.

Brinkerhoff, Brian. *Best Easy Day Hikes Salt Lake City.* Helena, MT: Falcon Publishing Company, 1999. More than 20 short hikes in the Wasatch Front canyons near Salt Lake City.

Campbell, Todd. *Above and Beyond Slickrock.* Salt Lake City: Wasatch Publishers, Inc.,

1999. Exploring the slickrock country of southeastern Utah.

Crowell, David. *Mountain Biking Moab.* Helena, MT: Falcon Publishing Company, 1997. A handy guide to the many trails around Moab, from the most popular to the little explored, in a handy size: small enough to take on the bike with you.

Davis, Mel, and John Veranth. *High Uinta Trails: A Hiking & Backpacking Guide to the High Uintas Wilderness.* Salt Lake City: Wasatch Publishers, Inc., 1999. Guide to hiking, backpacking, camping, and fishing in the High Uintas wilderness of northeastern Utah.

Green, Stewart M. *Rock Climbing Utah.* Helena, MT: Falcon Publishing Company, 1998. Amazingly comprehensive guide to climbing routes throughout the state. Route maps are superimposed over photographs to make sure climbers find the right route. Topo maps also included, as well as info on camping and travel.

Grubbs, Bruce. *Hiking Great Basin National Park.* Helena, MT: Falcon Publishing Company, 1998. A guide to 21 high-country hikes in this little visited national park on the Utah-Nevada border.

Hall, David. *Hiking Utah.* Helena, MT: Falcon Publishing Company, 1996. Good selection of 60 trips within Utah. The day and overnight hikes range from easy to difficult. An introduction will help you get started hiking.

Jensen, Michael. *Skiers Guide to Utah.* Gulf Publishing Company, 1995. A guide to downhill-skiing areas throughout the state.

Kals, W. S. *Land Navigation Handbook.* San Francisco: Sierra Club Books, 1983. This handy pocket guide will enable you to confidently explore Utah's extensive backcountry. Not only explains how to use map and compass but also other navigation methods such as altimeter and using the sun and stars.

Keilty, Maureen. *Best Hikes in Utah with Children.* Seattle: The Mountaineers, 2000. This guide describes 75 child-tested trails in all parts of Utah including hikes of easy, moderate, and difficult challenges, plus a few hikes that offer wheelchair access. Maps and photographs let readers know what to expect of hikes.

Kelsey, Michael R. *Canyon Hiking Guide to the Colorado Plateau.* Provo: Kelsey Publishing, 1999. One of the best guides to hiking in southeastern Utah's canyon country. Geologic cross sections show the formations you'll be walking through. The book has descriptions and maps for 64 trips in Utah, 38 hikes in adjacent Arizona, 13 in Colorado, and 2 in New Mexico. The author is ahead of his time in using just the metric system, but the book is otherwise easy to follow.

Kelsey, Michael R. *Hiking and Exploring Utah's Henry Mountains and Robbers Roost.* Provo: Kelsey Publishing, 1990. You'll find adventure and scenic beauty in this little-known region of high mountains and rugged canyons. Descriptions and maps cover 37 destinations. The book provides an excellent background of the region's history, mining, geology, and wildlife. Fascinating stories relate the escapades of Butch Cassidy. Uses metric system.

Kelsey, Michael R. *Hiking and Exploring Utah's San Rafael Swell.* Provo: Kelsey Publishing, 1990. Motorists driving across I-70 in east-central Utah get just a glimpse at the massive rock fold called the San Rafael Swell. This book presents the area's fascinating history and shows the way to hidden canyons with 30 hikes. Good maps and geologic cross sections. Uses metric system.

Kelsey, Michael R. *Hiking, Biking and Exploring Canyonlands National Park and Vicinity.* Provo:

Kelsey Publishing, 1992. The author's newest guide emphasizes hiking and local history. He used his mountain bike and hiking boots to explore the backcountry, rather than a four-wheel-drive vehicle. Uses metric system.

Kelsey, Michael R. *River Guide to Canyonlands National Park.* Provo: Kelsey Publishing, 1991. How to do a trip on the Green and Colorado Rivers and the many hikes and things to see along the way. Lots of local lore, too. Begins at the town of Green River on the Green and Moab on the Colorado; coverage ends at the confluence area (there's not much on Cataract Canyon). Uses metric system.

Lambrechtse, Rudi. *Hiking the Escalante.* Salt Lake City: Wasatch Publishers, Inc., 1999. "A wilderness guide to an exciting land of buttes, arches, alcoves, amphitheaters, and deep canyons." Introduction to history, geology, and natural history of the Escalante region in southern Utah. Contains descriptions and trailhead info for 42 hiking destinations. The hikes vary from easy outings suitable for children to a highly challenging four-day backpack trek.

Probst, Jeffrey. *High Uintas Backcountry.* Outland Publishing, 1996. The number one selling guide to the Uinta highcountry, with nearly 100 hiking trails from easy to long-distance, and information on the area's 600 lakes.

Ringholz, Raye Carleson. *Park City Trails.* Salt Lake City: Wasatch Publishers, Inc., 1999. Hikes and cross-country ski tours in the mountains and canyons surrounding this old mining town. Includes a walking tour of Park City.

Schneider, Bill. *Best Easy Day Hikes Canyonlands and Arches.* Helena, MT: Falcon Publishing Company, 1997. Twenty-one hikes in this popular vacation area, geared to travelers who are short on time or aren't able to explore the canyons on more difficult trails.

Schneider, Bill. *Exploring Canyonlands and Arches National Parks.* Helena, MT: Falcon Publishing Company, 1997. A hiking guide to these two Moab-area parks. Includes 63 easy and more difficult hikes.

Trails Illustrated. *Moab Bike Routes.* Evergreen, CO: Trails Illustrated, 1995. Handy plasticized topo map with Moab-area routes. Trails Illustrated also produces trail guides to the various national forests in Utah.

Utesch, Peggy. *The Utah-Colorado Mountain Bike Trail System, Route I—Moab to Loma: Kokopelli's Trail.* Moab: Canyon Country Publications, 1990. Learn about desert bicycling, then take off with the detailed descriptions in this well-illustrated guide. The 130-mile trail twists over spectacular terrain between Moab, Utah, and Loma, Colorado.

Utesch, Peggy, and Bob Utesch. *Mountain Biking in Canyon Rims Recreation Area.* Moab: Canyon Country Publications, 1992. An illustrated mountain-bikers' guide to exploring this vast and beautiful area south and east of Canyonlands National Park. You'll need the separate map *Canyon Country Off-Road Vehicle Trail Map: Canyon Rims Recreation Area* by F. A. Barnes.

Waterman, Laura, and Guy Waterman. *Backwoods Ethics: Environmental Issues for Hikers and Campers.* Woodstock, VT: Countryman Press, 1993. Thoughtful commentaries on how hikers can visit the wilderness with the least impact. Case histories dramatize the need to protect the environment.

Boating and River-Running

Abbey, Edward. *Down the River.* New York: E. P. Dutton, 1991. Abbey's love for the wilderness comes through in thoughtful descriptions of travels along rivers through deserts of the West.

Evans, Laura, and Buzz Belknap. *Dinosaur River Guide.* Evergreen, CO: Westwater Books, 1973. Topo maps show the canyons and points of interest along the Green and Yampa Rivers in Dinosaur National Monument of northeastern Utah and adjacent Colorado. Includes Lodore, Whirlpool, and Split Mountain Canyons of the Green River. Notes and photos provide historical background.

Goldwater, Barry M. *Delightful Journey: Down the Green & Colorado Rivers.* Tempe, AZ: Arizona Historical Foundation, 1970. Fewer than 100 people had run the entire Grand Canyon in 1940, when Goldwater joined a 47-day, 1,463-mile expedition from Green River, Wyoming, to Lake Mead in Arizona.

Nichols, Gary. *River Runners' Guide to Utah and Adjacent Areas.* Salt Lake City: University of Utah Press, 1986. A comprehensive guidebook to running Utah's many rivers—the little-known ones as well as the popular Green and Colorado. Maps, photos, safety info, and difficulty ratings let you know the excitement and hazards of what you're getting into.

Tejada-Flores, Lito. *Wildwater: the Sierra Club Guide to Kayaking and Whitewater Boating.* San Francisco: Sierra Club Books, 1982. Comprehensive introduction to river-running: choosing boats and equipment, river techniques, safety, practical advice on trip planning, overview of river possibilities in the United States, and history of white-water boating.

Zwinger, Ann. *Run, River, Run: a Naturalist's Journey Down One of the Great Rivers of the American West.* Tucson: University of Arizona Press, 1984. An excellent description of the author's experiences along the Green River from its source in the Wind River Range of Wyoming to the Colorado River in southeastern Utah. The author weaves geology, Native American ruins, plants, wildlife, and her personal feelings into the text and drawings.

Memoirs

Abbey, Edward. *Desert Solitaire.* Ballantine Books, 1991. A meditation on the Red Rock Canyon Country of Utah. Abbey brings his fiery prose to the service of the American outback, while excoriating the commercialization of the West.

Stegner, Wallace. *Mormon Country.* University of Nebraska Press, 1982. Stegner tells the story of the early Mormon experience in this highly readable near-epic.

Williams, Terry Tempest. *Refuge: An Unnatural History of Family and Place.* Vintage Books, 1992. A memoir of a family devastated by cancer (caused by federal government atomic testing), overlain with a natural history of birdlife along the Great Salt Lake. Haunting, deeply spiritual, and beautifully written.

History and Current Events

Alexander, Thomas G., Richard Sadler, and Susan A. Whetstone. *Utah, the Right Place: The Official Centennial History.* Gibbs Smith Publisher, 1996. A good overview of the state's history, with an understandable focus on the Mormon experience. Lots of good photos and illustrations.

Bennet, Cynthia Larsen. *Roadside History of Utah.* Missoula, MT: Mountain Press Publishing Co., 1999. A very readable account of the state's history organized by driving tours. Full of great stories, yarns, and amazing human stories.

Colbert, Edwin H. *The Great Dinosaur Hunters and Their Discoveries.* Mineola, NY: Dover Publications, 1984. Discovery of the "terrible lizards" in England during the 1820s and the worldwide fossil searches that followed. Includes early digging in what's now Dinosaur National Monument. Many photos and drawings illustrate the lively text.

Dellenbaugh, Frederick S. *A Canyon Voyage: The Narrative of the Second Powell Expedition.* Tucson: University of Arizona Press, 1984. Well-written account of John Wesley Powell's second expedition down the Green and Colorado Rivers, 1871–1872. The members took the first Grand Canyon photographs and obtained much valuable scientific knowledge.

Goodman, Doug, and Daniel McCool. *Contested Landscape: The Politics of Wilderness in Utah and the West.* Salt Lake City: University of Utah Press, 1999. A collection of essays that frame the contentious political debate over land-use policy in Utah.

Krakauer, Jon. *Under the Banner of Heaven: A Story of Violent Faith.* New York: Doubleday Books, 2003. The story of two fundamentalist, polygamous brothers who killed their sister-in-law and nephew upon receiving what they considered to be a message from God.

McCormick, John S., and Rod Decker. *The Gathering Place: An Illustrated History of Salt Lake City.* Salt Lake City: Signature Books, 2000. Fascinating guide to history of the City of Zion, with excellent photos.

Miller, David E. *Hole-in-the-Rock.* Salt Lake City: University of Utah Press, 1959. Detailed account of pioneers struggling to build a 200-mile wagon road to the remote southeastern corner of Utah in 1879–1880. A group of about 250 men, women, and children in 80 wagons navigated some of the West's most rugged country to become the first white settlers in San Juan County.

Peterson, Charles S. *Utah, a Bicentennial History.* New York: W.W. Norton & Co., 1977. Good popular history of Utah's exploration, Mormon settlements, economic changes, and politics up to modern times.

Powell, John Wesley. *The Exploration of the Colorado River and its Canyons.* Mineola, NY:

Dover Publications, reprinted 1997 (first published in 1895). Powell's 1869 and 1871–1872 expeditions down the Green and Colorado Rivers. His was the first group to navigate through the Grand Canyon. A description of the 1879 Uinta Expedition is included.

Archaeology

Lister, Robert, and Florence Lister. *Those Who Came Before.* Southwest Parks and Monuments, 1983. A well-illustrated guide to the history, artifacts, and ruins of prehistoric Southwest Native Americans. The author also describes parks and monuments containing archaeological sites.

Slifer, Dennis. *Guide to Rock Art of the Utah Region: Sites with Public Access.* Albuquerque: University of New Mexico Press, 2000. The most complete guide to rock-art sites, with descriptions of over 50 sites in the Four Corners region. Complete with maps and directions, and with an overview of rock-art styles and traditions.

Utah Native Americans of Today

Dedera, Don. *Navajo Rugs: How to Find, Evaluate, Buy and Care for Them.* Cody, WY: Northland Press, 1996. Dedera gives the history of Navajo weaving, illustrates how it's done, shows regional styles, and offers practical advice on purchasing.

Gilpin, Laura. *The Enduring Navajo.* Austin: University of Texas Press, 1994. Excellent book about the Navajo—their homes, land, ceremonies, crafts, tribal government, and trading posts.

Locke, Raymond F. *The Book of the Navajo.* Holloway House Publishing, 1992. Navajo legends, art, and history from early to modern times.

Zolbrod, Paul G. *Diné bahané: The Navajo Creation Story.* Albuquerque: University of New Mexico Press, 1988. Deities, people, and animals come to life in this translation of Navajo mythology.

Natural Sciences

Baars, Donald L. *The Colorado Plateau: A Geologic History.* Albuquerque: University of New Mexico Press, 1994. Written for the layperson, this book takes you on a tour of the Four Corners area geology from the ancient twisted rocks at the bottom of the Grand Canyon to the fiery volcanism and icy glaciations of the Pleistocene epoch.

Craighead, John J. (and others). *A Field Guide to Rocky Mountain Wildflowers.* Boston: Houghton Mifflin Co., 1998. Handy guide takes in Utah's high country. A plant key and detailed descriptions make identification easy. Illustrated with line drawings and color photos.

Chronic, Halka. *Roadside Geology of Utah.* Missoula, MT: Mountain Press Publishing Company, 1990. This layperson's guide tells the story of the state's fascinating geology as seen by following major roadways.

Dodge, Natt N. *100 Roadside Wildflowers of Southwest Uplands in Natural Color.* Southwest Parks and Monuments Association, 1989. Introduction with a brief description and color photo for those flowers usually found in southern Utah above 4,500 feet.

Fagan, Damian. *Canyon Country Wildflowers.* Helena, MT: Falcon Publishing Company, 1998. A comprehensive field guide to the diverse flora of the Four Corners area.

Fleischner, Thomas Lowe. *Singing Stone: A Natural History of the Escalante Canyons.* Salt Lake City: University of Utah Press, 1999. A former Outward Bound instructor who has guided many city people through the Escalante Canyons, Fleischner knows the area well and lends first-hand vitality to his information on the area's plants, animals, ecology, geology and pre-history.

Halfpenny, James, and Elizabeth Biesiot. *A Field Guide: Mammal Tracking in Western America*. Boulder, CO: Johnson Books, 1988. No need to guess what animal passed by. This well-illustrated guide shows how to read trails of large and small wildlife. More determined detectives can study the scatology chapter.

Hamilton, Wayne L. *The Sculpturing of Zion: Guide to the Geology of Zion*. Springdale, UT: Zion Natural History Association, 1984. Outstanding book explaining geologic forces and history. Clear graphs, drawings, and beautiful color photography illustrate the nontechnical text.

Kappele, William A. *Rockhounding Utah*. Helena, MT: Falcon Publishing Company, 1996. Informative and comprehensive guide to 86 rock-collecting sites. Each description includes concise information on the material to be found there, the tools to bring, the best season to visit, and what vehicle to drive.

MacMahon, James A. *Deserts*. New York: Alfred A. Knopf, The Audubon Society Nature Guides, 1985. Comprehensive naturalist's guide to the Great Basin, Colorado Plateau, and other arid regions of the West. Many color photos help identify the birds, mammals, fish, insects, reptiles, amphibians, and flora.

McIvor, D. E. *Birding Utah*. Helena, MT: Falcon Publishing Company, 1998. A guide to 100 areas of bird-watching interest throughout the state, plus black-and-white photos of common species, checklists, plus a good compendium on the state's eco-regions and vegetation communities.

Olin, George, and Dale Thompson. *Mammals of the Southwest Deserts*. Tucson, AZ: Southwest Parks and Monuments Association, 1982. Well illustrated with black-and-white and color drawings.

Stokes, William L. *Geology of Utah*. Salt Lake City: Utah Museum of Natural History Occasional Paper, No. 6, 1989. A comprehensive overview of Utah's geologic history, rock layers, fossils, and landscapes.

Sweet, Muriel. *Common Edible and Useful Plants of the West*. Happy Camp, CA: Naturegraph Publishers, 1976. Nontechnical descriptions of plants and trees that have food, medicinal, and other uses. Most of these were first discovered by Native Americans and used later by pioneer settlers.

Welsh, Stanley L., and Bill Ratcliffe. *Flowers of the Canyon Country*. Moab: Canyonlands Natural History Association, 1995. Beautiful color photography makes this book a pleasure to use while traveling in southern Utah. Each flower has a photo and nontechnical description.

Internet Resources

Although a virtual visit to Utah cannot replace the real thing, you'll find an enormous amount of helpful information on the World Wide Web. Thousands of websites interlink to cover everything from ghost towns to the latest community news.

Travel
www.utah.com
The Utah Travel Council is a one-stop shop for all sorts of information on Utah. It takes you around the state to sights, activities, events, maps, and offers links to local tourist offices. The accommodations listings are the most up-to-date source for current prices and options.

www.yahoo.com
The well-organized Yahoo site will take you almost anywhere in Utah. Select Regional, U.S. States, then Utah.

http://utah.citysearch.com
City Search sites are great for finding a community's news, arts, entertainment, and Internet links.

www.state.ut.us
The official State of Utah website has travel information, agencies, programs, and what the legislature is up to.

www.visitsaltlake.com
Find the scoop on all aspects of visiting Salt Lake City, including accommodations (sometimes with special deals), events, and activities ranging from genealogical research to bird-watching. It's also a good place to find special deals on ski passes.

www.skiutah.com
If you're thinking snow, glide over to Ski Utah, where you'll also find summer activities at the ski resorts.

www.ghosttowns.com/states/ut/ut.html
Histories and photos of Utah's loneliest towns.

The Great Outdoors
www.nps.gov
The National Park Service offers pages for all their areas at this site, where a click-on map will take you to Utah's parks. You can also enter this address followed by a slash and the first two letters of the first two words of the place (first four letters if there's just a one-word name); for example, www.nps.gov/brca takes you to Bryce Canyon National Park and www.nps.gov/zion leads to Zion National Park.

www.gorp.com/gorp/location/ut/ut.htm
The Great Outdoor Recreation Pages offer lots of hiking and other outdoor information, including specifics on national forests and wilderness areas.

http://parks.state.ut.us
The Utah State Parks site offers details on the large park system.

www.desertusa.com
Desert USA's Utah section discusses places to visit and what plants and animals you might meet there.

www.americansouthwest.net/utah
Utah Guide provides an overview of national parks, national recreation areas, and some state parks.

Education
www.utah.edu
The University of Utah in Salt Lake City offers museums, sporting events, and cultural activities.

www.byu.edu
Cultural life in Provo revolves around Brigham

Young University. The website has a list of events.

www.lds.org

Learn about the Mormon religion at the Church of Jesus Christ of Latter-day Saints' site.

News and Sports
www.sltrib.com

The *Salt Lake Tribune* is the state's newspaper of record.

www.desnews.com

Salt Lake's other major newspaper, the *Deseret Morning News*, has good regional and LDS coverage.

www.slweekly.com

Salt Lake City's alternative weekly newspaper has online event listings and in-depth articles on city issues.

Index

Dinosaurs

Index

Hiking

Index

Scenic Drives

Acknowledgments

Many thanks go to the hundreds of people who assisted in making *Moon Handbooks Utah* complete and accurate. We are especially indebted to people of the National Park Service, U.S. Forest Service, Bureau of Land Management, and Utah State Parks, whose high standards help make Utah such a wonderful place to visit. I'd also like to thank Ken Kraus of the Utah Travel Council for his advice and help, and give special thanks to Stuart and Janet, and Jeff and Kim for the Utah-sized hospitality.

—Bill McRae

Special thanks to Jason Mathis of the Salt Lake Convention and Visitors Bureau for all his help. Thanks also to Barbara Dunlea of Alta Lodge, Laura Schaffer of Snowbird, and Brenda of Alta Ski Area for making the skiing extra-fun, even for this blue-run skier. Mayor Bill Levitt of Alta told the best stories, and Christa Graff at Deer Valley, Krista Rowles of Park City Mountain Resort, Katie Eldridge at The Canyons, Dave Field at Snowbird, Connie Marshall at Alta, and Jay Burke at Solitude gave me the chance to really explore these areas.

—Judy Jewell

U.S.~Metric Conversion

1 inch	=	2.54 centimeters (cm)
1 foot	=	.304 meters (m)
1 yard	=	0.914 meters
1 mile	=	1.6093 kilometers (km)
1 km	=	.6214 miles
1 fathom	=	1.8288 m
1 chain	=	20.1168 m
1 furlong	=	201.168 m
1 acre	=	.4047 hectares
1 sq km	=	100 hectares
1 sq mile	=	2.59 square km
1 ounce	=	28.35 grams
1 pound	=	.4536 kilograms
1 short ton	=	.90718 metric ton
1 short ton	=	2000 pounds
1 long ton	=	1.016 metric tons
1 long ton	=	2240 pounds
1 metric ton	=	1000 kilograms
1 quart	=	.94635 liters
1 US gallon	=	3.7854 liters
1 Imperial gallon	=	4.5459 liters
1 nautical mile	=	1.852 km

To compute Celsius temperatures, subtract 32 from Fahrenheit and divide by 1.8. To go the other way, multiply Celsius by 1.8 and add 32.

Fahrenheit   Celsius

230°   110°
220°
210°   100° Water Boils
200°
190°   90°
180°   80°
170°
160°   70°
150°
140°   60°
130°
120°   50°
110°
100°   40°
90°
80°   30°
70°   20°
60°
50°   10°
40°
30°   0°   Water Freezes
20°
10°   -10°
0°
-10°   -20°
-20°   -30°
-30°
-40°   -40°

12
24
11 23   13 1
10 22   14 2
9 21   15 3
8 20   16 4
  19 18 17 5
   7   6

Keeping Current

Although we strive to produce the most up-to-date guidebook humanly possible, change is unavoidable. Between the time this book goes to print and the moment you read it, a handful of the businesses noted in these pages will undoubtedly change prices, move, or even close their doors forever. Other worthy attractions will open for the first time. If you have a favorite gem you'd like to see included in the next edition, or see anything that needs updating, clarification, or correction, please drop us a line. Send your comments via email to atpfeedback@avalonpub.com, or use the address below.

Moon Handbooks Utah
Avalon Travel Publishing
1400 65th Street, Suite 250
Emeryville, CA 94608, USA
www.moon.com

Editor: Kathryn Ettinger
Series Manager: Kevin McLain
Copy Editor: Deana Shields
Graphics Coordinator: Justin Marler
Production Coordinator: Jacob Goolkasian
Cover Designer: Kari Gim
Interior Designers: Amber Pirker, Alvaro
    Villanueva, Kelly Pendragon
Map Editor: Olivia Solís
Cartographers: Mike Morgenfeld, Naomi Alder
    Dancis, Suzanne Service, Kat Kalamaras,
    Olivia Solís, Tim Lohnes
Proofreader: Jenica Szymanski
Indexer: Greg Jewett

ISBN: 1-56691-599-6
ISSN: 1531-5568

Printing History
1st Edition—1988
7th Edition—April 2004
5 4 3 2 1

Text © 2004 by W. C. McRae and Judy Jewell.
Maps © 2004 by Avalon Travel Publishing, Inc.
All rights reserved.

Avalon Travel Publishing is a division of Avalon Publishing Group, Inc.

Some photos and illustrations are used by permission and are the property of the original copyright owners.

Front cover photo: © John Elk III
Table of contents photos: © Bill Weir, © Judy Jewell, © W. C. McRae, © Paul Levy, © Tag-A-Long Expeditions

Printed in USA by Malloy